Study Guide
and
Solutions Manual

Marvin L. Hackert
University of Texas at Austin

Roger K. Sandwick
SUNY Plattsburgh

Chemistry and Life

*An Introduction to General, Organic,
and Biological Chemistry*

Fifth Edition

John W. Hill   Stuart J. Baum   Dorothy M. Feigl

PRENTICE HALL Upper Saddle River, NJ 07458

Editor: *Ben Roberts*
Associate Editor: *Mary Hornby*
Production Editor: *James Buckley*
Production Coordinator: *Ben D. Smith*
Special Projects Manager: *Barbara A. Murray*
Supplement Cover Manager: *Paul Gourhan*

© 1997 by **PRENTICE-HALL, INC.**
Simon & Schuster/A Viacom Company
Upper Saddle River, NJ 07458

Printed in the United States of America

10 9 8 7 6 5 4 3 2 1

ISBN 0-13-574666-3

Prentice-Hall International (UK) Limited, *London*
Prentice-Hall of Australia Pty. Limited, *Sydney*
Prentice-Hall Canada, Inc., *Toronto*
Prentice-Hall Hispanoamericana, S.A., *Mexico*
Prentice-Hall of India Private Limited, *New Delhi*
Prentice-Hall of Japan, Inc., *Tokyo*
Simon & Schuster Asia Pte. Ltd., *Singapore*
Editora Prentice-Hall do Brasil, Ltda., *Rio de Janeiro*

Contents

PART I - *Chapter Summaries and Self Tests*

Foreword

This Study Guide and Solutions Manual is a learning tool written to supplement the text, *Chemistry and Life*, by John Hill, Stuart Baum, and Dorothy Feigl. However, all of the Study Guide material can prove useful to any student in a course covering General, Organic and Biological Chemistry with an allied health science perspective.

Part I, the Study Guide portion of this manual, is designed to supplement the textbook. It can serve as a set of "lecture notes," chapter summaries, a tutorial to help with difficult subject areas, and as a source of practice problems with answers to help check your mastery of the material. Each unit begins with a list of KEY WORDS and a CHAPTER SUMMARY. This course covers topics normally presented to chemistry or biochemistry majors over a full three-year sequence with separate courses in General, Organic, and Biochemistry. Even though your course will not go into as much depth, you will be exposed to much of the same terminology and the language used in those courses. Mastering the language of chemistry and biochemistry is an essential first step toward understanding the concepts of chemistry. (*I often have students who feel that they should receive credit for a foreign language for taking this course.*) Each of the KEY WORDS listed at the beginning of a unit is highlighted in bold italics when it is first used in the CHAPTER SUMMARY. This should help you identify and understand the meaning of these terms. The CHAPTER SUMMARY is a section-by-section outline of the textbook. It can serve as the basis for your lecture notes and as a quick review of the material presented in the chapter. Also included are most of the important structures that you might be asked to know or be familiar with during this course. In the DISCUSSION section that follows, difficult concepts are explained in more detail and study hints are presented. Each unit ends with a SELF-TEST. Only after you think that you have mastered the material, should you take the SELF-TEST. It will provide a final check on your understanding of the chapter's material. If you are still having difficulty, seek assistance from your instructor or teaching assistant.

Part II, the Solutions Manual portion of this manual, presents the worked out solutions to all end of chapter problems from the text. You should try to solve these problems on your own before looking to the solutions provided herein. If your answer differs from the one given here, review your work, using the step by step procedures provided.

We, the authors, can provide you with a good text and Study Guide/Solutions Manual to help you master the material in this course. However, your success in this course will depend mostly on *you* and what *you* do with these materials. Here are a few good study suggestions.

* Review your syllabus to obtain an overview of the material and what topic will be covered before each lecture.

* Read the CHAPTER SUMMARY in this Study Guide and also read your text material *before* the lecture so you will be prepared to receive information and insight from your instructor. Remember, learning is an incremental process; *"We can only learn that which we almost already know."* Real learning also requires repetitive exposure to the material.

* Before each class review your lecture notes taken since the start of that unit. This will help you gradually build your accumulated knowledge of the subject. Keep up and try not to cram just before exams.

* Look over the KEY WORDS at the beginning of each chapter and then review them at the end of a unit to make sure that you understand their meaning.

* Finally, this Guide and the text provide a wealth of practice problems. Work through these exercises, do not simply look at them. Only by doing the problems will you be able to measure your own level of understanding of the material.

　　　　　We hope that you will find the new text and this Study Guide and Solutions Manual to be helpful. We invite your suggestions and comments so that we might improve this Guide for the aid of future students. Please send your comments on the Study Guide by email to M.Hackert @mail.utexas.edu. and on the end of Chapter Solutions to Sandwirk@splava.cc.plattsburgh.edu.

Marvin L. Hackert
Professor of Chemistry and Biochemistry
The University of Texas at Austin

Roger K. Sandwick
Department of Chemistry
State University of New York at Plattsburg,

* * *Acknowledgments* * *

I would like to thank John Hill, Stuart Baum and Dorothy Feigl for the privilege of putting together this study guide for their text, *Chemistry and Life*. I would also like to thank Brian for his assistance with the typing of the earlier drafts of this work and my wife Bretna for her proofreading and patience while this work was completed. Finally, I am grateful to Mary Hornby of Prentice Hall for her assistance and to all the students who have used this Study Guide.

M.L.H.

I would like to thank Kellee Bruce for proofing the answers to these problems and to thank my wife and family for their support.

R.K.S.

CHAPTER 1: MATTER AND MEASUREMENT

KEY WORDS

milli	*force*	*potential energy*	*liter*	*chemistry*	*elements*
kilo	*matter*	*kinetic energy*	*heat*	*calorie*	*compounds*
centi	*mass*	*work*	*temperature*	*joule*	*physical property*
deci	*weight*	*meter*	*Fahrenheit*	*density*	*chemical property*
micro	*energy*	*kilogram*	*Celsius*	*hypothesis*	*specific gravity*
mega	*liquid*	*gaseous*	*Kelvin*	*gravity*	*specific heat*
nano	*solid*	*molecules*	*composition*	*formula*	*homogeneous*
atoms	*mixtures*	*chemical symbol*	*solution*	*SI units*	*heterogeneous*

SUMMARY

1.1 Science and the Human Condition
   A. Modern chemistry has roots in the alchemy of the Middle Ages, but was born in the 17th century with an emphasis on experimentation.
   B. Modern drugs for medicine, fertilizers for crops, nutritional supplements, plastics, and synthetic fibers are all the products of modern chemistry.

1.2 Problems in Paradise
   A. Such modern problems as toxic wastes, pollution, and carcinogens are also products of chemistry.
   B. The answers to these problems will also have to come from chemistry and will require an educated, informed society to ensure that chemistry is used for the human good.

1.3 The Way Science Works - Sometimes
   A. Science is cumulative. The "body of knowledge" is constantly growing and changing.
   B. It is not the "body of facts" that characterizes science but the organization of those facts according to concepts that can be tested by experimentation.
   C. The scientific method involves making observations, gathering data, organizing that data, forming a *hypothesis*, and subjecting that hypothesis to experimental verification.

1.4 What Is Chemistry? Some Fundamental Concepts
   A. *Chemistry* - A study of the composition, structure and properties of matter and the changes that occur in matter.
      1. *Atoms* are the smallest units we associate with the chemical behavior of matter.
      2. *Molecules* are composed of bonded, groups of atoms.
   B. *Matter* occupies space and has mass.
      1. *Mass* measures a quantity of matter that is independent of its relative position.
      2. *Weight* measures a force such as the gravitational force of attraction between an object and the earth. Weight varies with gravity; mass does not.
      3. *Composition* refers to the types of atoms present and their relative proportions.
   C. Properties
      1. *Physical properties* can be observed without reference to other substances. A physical change occurs without a change in composition of the substance (melting, grinding).
      2. *Chemical properties* describe how one substance reacts with another substance. Chemical changes are associated with changes in chemical properties (combustion, color, density).
   D. States of Matter: *solid*, *liquid*, or *gaseous* states

1.5 Elements, Compounds and Mixtures
    A. A *substance* (elements or compounds) has a defined or fixed composition.
        1. *Elements* are pure fundamental substances represented by a *chemical symbol*, e.g. iron = Fe.
        2. *Compounds* are pure substances made up of two or more elements that are chemically combined
            in a fixed ratio and represented by a *chemical formula*, e.g. glucose = $C_6H_{12}O_6$.
    B. The composition of a *mixture* is variable.
        1. A *homogeneous mixture* has the same composition and properties throughout the *solution*.
        2. A *heterogeneous mixture* varies in composition and or properties (sand/water mixture).

1.6 Energy and Energy Conversions
    A. *Energy* - the capacity for doing work.
        1. *Potential energy* of an object is that which is stored by virtue of its position or composition.
        2. *Kinetic energy* is the energy of motion (K.E. $= \frac{1}{2}\, mv^2$).
        3. Energy is often classified in other ways depending on some characteristic of the energy
            considered, such as radiant, solar, thermal (*heat*), electrical, chemical, or nuclear energy.
        4. Chemical energy changes are associated with changes in the electronic arrangements of atoms.
    B. *Work* - Force acting through a distance.

1.7 Electric Forces
    A. *Force* - push or pull that sets objects in motion.
    B. *Gravity* is the force of attraction between two masses which determines the weight of the object.
    C. Electrical forces involving charged particles are important in chemistry. Like electrical charges repel
        one another. Unlike charges attract one another.

1.8 Measurement: The Modern Metric System (SI units)
    A. Length   - *meter* (m);   1 m   = 1.09 yd   = 39.37 in.
    B. Mass   - *kilogram* (kg);   1 kg   = 1000 g   = 2.20 lb
    C. Volume - *liter* (L);   1 L   = 1.06 qt
    D. The decimal nature of the metric system.
        1. *giga-* (G)   x 1,000,000,000.
        2. *mega-* (M)   x   1,000,000.
        3. *kilo-* (k)   x   1,000.
        4. *deci-* (d)   x   0.1
        5. *centi-* (c)   x   0.01
        6. *milli-* (m)   x   0.001
        7. *micro-* (μ)   x   0.000001
        8. *nano-* (n)   x   0.000000001

1.9 Measuring Energy: Temperature and Heat
    A. *Temperature* is an intensive, physical property that tells us the direction of heat (energy) flow when
        two bodies are brought in contact. There are three commonly used "Temperature scales."
        1. *Celsius* (°C)   °C   = (°F − 32) x (5/9)
        2. *Kelvin* (K)   K   = °C + 273
        3. *Fahrenheit* (°F) °F   = (9/5) x (°C) + 32
    B. Reference temperatures

	°C	K	°F
1. Freezing point of water	0	273	32
2. Boiling point of water	100	373	212
3. Absolute zero	−273	0	−460

C. Heat Energy - *joule* (J) or *calorie* (cal). A calorie is the amount of heat energy required to increase the temperature of 1 gram of water from 14.5 °C to 15.5 °C.
  1. 1 cal = 4.184 J;   1 Calorie (food measure) = 1000 cal or 1 kcal
  2. A typical cookie has about 50-100 Cal (50-100 kcal) of heat energy. Fast walking for one hour burns about 350 Cal (350 kcal), i.e. one hour of exercise burns off abut 3 cookies.
D. The *specific heat* of a substance is the amount of heat required to increase the temperature of 1 g of that substance by 1.0 °C.
  1. The specific heat of water is very high, about 1.0 cal/(g·°C), while that of iron is 0.108 cal/(g·°C).
  2. The general formula for specific heat problems is:
     Heat absorbed or released = (mass) x (specific heat) x ΔT

1.10 Density (density = mass / volume)
  A. *Density* is mass per unit of volume (g/mL or g/cm³).
     Densities of common substances in (g/mL) (Note - density varies with temperature.):

air	ethanol	ice (0°C)	**water**	sugar	aluminum	iron	mercury	gold
0.0012	0.79	0.92	**1.0**	1.6	2.7	7.2	13.6	19.3

  B. *Specific gravity* is a ratio of density of the substance to the density of water. Specific gravity has no units.
  1. Specific gravity can be measured with a hydrometer.
  2. The specific gravity of mercury is 13.6.

DISCUSSION

Much of the first chapter in the text is intended to place chemistry in both an historical and a contemporary perspective--to give you a feeling for chemistry as it affects society. If, after reading the chapter, you recognize chemistry as something more than just a course required for your particular academic program, then you have indeed understood what we were trying to say. In addition to this overview, Chapter 1 also introduces several concepts important to our further study of chemistry. These include the international system of measurement; the meaning of terms such as matter, force, and energy; different temperature scales; density and specific gravity. The problems at the end of the chapter are meant to check your understanding of this material. The following questions offer another opportunity for you to test yourself on Chapter 1.

Note: Many of these problems are more than tests of your memory. A number of them require preliminary calculations before an answer can be selected. You are expected to know the metric prefixes and units of measure, but you may also need to refer back to the metric conversion factors presented in Section 1.8.

SELF-TEST

1. Which of the following represents an hypothesis?
     a. Mary read her textbook assignment and Sally did not.
     b. Mary did her homework and Sally did not.
     c. Mary attended class and took good notes, Sally did not.
     d. Mary got an A in the course and Sally did not.
     e. Students who read their assignments, do their homework, and attend lectures earn higher grades than those students who do not do those things.
2. Which of the following represents a physical change?
     a. burning this study guide   b. tearing a page from this book

3. Identify the element(s) among the following.
    a. Aluminum   b. milk   c. NaCl   d. Pb   e. mercury
4. Identify the compound(s) among the following.
    a. Aluminum   b. milk   c. NaCl   d. Pb   e. mercury
5. Identify the mixture(s) among the following.
    a. Aluminum   b. milk   c. NaCl   d. Pb   e. mercury
6. Which of the following abbreviations stands for a unit of length?
    a. mL   b. mg   c. mm   d. cc
7. The prefix nano is equivalent to:
    a. 10^{-2} b. 10^3 c. 10^{-3} d. 10^6 e. 10^{-6} f. 10^{-9}
8. Which of the following units of measure is equivalent to a cc?
    a. mL   b. cm   c. mm   d. mg   e. gr
9. How long is 0.2 cm?
    a. 0.02 mm   b. 2 mm   c. 20 mm   d. 200 mm   e. 0.002 mm
10. How many millimeters are there in 10 cm?
    a. 1   b. 10   c. 100   d. 1000   e. 10,000
11. How many cubic centimeters are there in a deciliter?
    a. 0.01   b. 0.1   c. 1   d. 10   e. 100
12. An object that weighs 10 μg also weighs:
    a. 0.001 mg   b. 0.01 mg   c. 0.1 mg   d. 1 mg   e. 100 mg   f. 10^{-6} g
13. If a container holds 5 mL, it will hold:
    a. 5000 L   b. 0.05 L   c. 50 cm^3 d. 0.5 cc   e. 0.005 L
14. Approximately how wide in cm is a coin that is 2.0 inches in diameter?
    a. 2   b. 4   c. 5   d. 6   e. 7   f. 8
15. Lorraine is 150 cm tall and weighs 82 kg. She is:
    a. skinny   b. just about perfect   c. a bit chubby   d. obese
16. If 10 mL of A has a mass of 8 g, then the density of A is:
    a. 0.5 g/mL   b. 1 g/mL   c. 1.2 g/mL   d. 4 g/mL   e. 0.8 g/mL
17. If a container that can hold 5 g of water is filled with 10 g of another liquid, what is the density of the other liquid?
    a. 0.5 g/mL   b. 2 g/mL   c. 10 g/mL   d. 0.5   e. 2   f. 10
18. What is the specific gravity of a compound if 5 mL of it weighs 15 g?
    a. 0.3   b. 0.3 g/mL   c. 3   d. 3 g/mL   e. 6   f. 12
19. If a bottle will hold 10 g of water or 30 g of bromine, the specific gravity of bromine is:
    a. 0.33   b. 3 g/mL   c. 3   d. 30 g/mL   e. 30
20. If a liter of a substance weighs 1250 g, its specific gravity is:
    a. 1250   b. 1.2 g/cc   c. 0.80   d. 2 g/mL   e. 1.25   f. 0.08
21. If the density of a substance is 8 g/mL, what volume would 40 g of the substance occupy?
    a. 0.32 mL   b. 0.5 mL   c. 2 mL   d. 5 mL   e. 20 mL
22. Will a bar of soap (volume of 250 cc; mass of 300 g) float on water?
    a. yes   b. no
23. The boiling point of water is:
    a. 100 °C   b. 212 °F   c. 373 K   d. all of these   e. none of these
24. On the absolute temperature scale, temperatures are reported in:
    a. °Celsius   b. °Centigrade   c. °Fahrenheit   d. Kelvin
25. A temperature of 98.6 °F is the same as:
    a. 0 °C   b. 32 °C   c. 37 °C   d. 100 °C   e. 212 °C
26. A temperature of -40 °C is equivalent to:
    a. -7 °F   b. -40 °F   c. -57 °F   d. -81 °F   e. -113 °F

27. A temperature of 273 °C is equal to:

 a. Zero K   b. 100 K   c. 273 K   d. 546 K   e. -273 K

28. A temperature of 77 °F is equal to how many degrees Celsius?

 a. 25   b. 61   c. 81   d. 171   e. 196

29. One food Calorie equals:

 a. 1000 cal   b. 1000 kcal   c. 1 cal   d. 0.001 kcal

30. A cola that contains 150 Calories also contains:

 a. 0.150 cal   b. 0.150 kcal   c. 1500 cal   d. 1.5 kcal   e. 150 kcal

31. We wish to heat 40 g of water from 15 °C to 25 °C. The amount of heat energy required is:

 a. 4 cal   b. 40 cal   c. 100 cal   d. 400 cal   e. 1000 cal

32. If 40 cal of energy are added to 10 g of water originally at 50 °C, the final temperature of the water will be:

 a. 4 °C   b. 10 °C   c. 46 °C   d. 54 °C   e. 60 °C   f. 90 °C

33. How many cal are released as 50g of water cools from 100 °C to room temperature (25 °C)?

 a. 50   b. 750   c. 1250   d. 3750   e. 7500

34. Which has the greatest potential energy?

 a. a small rock moving at high speed at sea level
 b. a large rock moving at slow speed at sea level
 c. a large rock balanced at the edge of a mountain top
 d. a small rock balanced on a ledge halfway down the same mountain
 e. none of the choices is clearly the best

35. This form of matter is characterized by its tendency to maintain its volume but not its shape.

 a. gas   b. liquid   c. solid

36. High compressibility is a property associated with:

 a. gases   b. liquids   c. solids

37. If two charged particles attract one another:

 a. one particle must be negatively charged
 b. both particles must be negatively charged
 c. both particles must be positively charged

38. T F The boiling point of water is 100 °F at 1 atm pressure

39. T F Chemistry is the study of matter and the changes it undergoes.

40. T F Chemistry is not concerned with changes in energy.

41. T F The United States is a leader among nations using the metric system.

42. T F Manufactured chemical products have greatly affected our life-style.

43. T F The ultimate source of nearly all energy on Earth is the sun.

44. T F If measured on the Moon, your mass would be different from your mass measured on the Earth, although your weight would be the same.

ANSWERS:

1. e	10. c	19. c	28. a	37. a
2. b	11. e	20. e	29. a	38. F
3. a,d,e	12. b	21. d	30. e	39. T
4. c	13. e	22. b	31. d	40. F
5. b	14. c	23. d	32. d	41. F
6. c	15. d	24. d	33. d	42. T
7. f	16. e	25. c	34. c	43. T
8. a	17. b	26. b	35. b	44. F
9. b	18. c	27. d	36. a	

Special Topic A: Unit Conversions

KEY WORDS

factor-label method   *dimensional analysis*   *conversion factor*   *density*
specific heat   *one equation / one unknown*   *unit-conversion method*

SUMMARY

It is often necessary to convert a measurement from one kind of unit into another type of unit.

A.1 Conversions Within a System

    A. Quantities can be expressed in a variety of different units (6 ft, 2 yd, 72 in). *Conversion factors* are "unit value ratios" that permit the conversion from one type of unit to another.

1 Ton = 2000 lb	1 mile = 1760 yd	1 gal = 4 qt	1 Cup = 8 fl. oz
1 lb = 16 oz	1 yd = 3 ft	1 qt = 2 pints	½ fl. oz. = 1 T
	1 ft = 12 inches	1 pint = 2 Cups	1 T = 3 tsp

    B. In the metric system, conversion factors for a given type of unit are all multiples of ten.

1 Kg = 1000 g	1 Km = 1000 m	1 L = 1000 mL
1 g = 1000 mg	1 m = 100 cm	1 mL = 1000 mL

    C. It is important to keep track of the units to ensure that the conversion factors are being applied correctly.

       1. 5 g = ? kg;   5 g x $\dfrac{1 \text{ kg}}{1000 \text{ g}}$ = 0.005 kg

       2. 3.5 kg = ? g: 3.5 kg x $\dfrac{1000 \text{ g}}{1 \text{ kg}}$ = 3500 g

A.2 Conversions Between Systems

    A. Conversion to a different system of units may seem like working in a foreign language until you become familiar with the new units. Remember, all conversion factors must express an identity relationship; mass to mass, length to length, volume to volume, etc.

1 Kg = 2.2 lb	1 mile = 1.61 Km	1 L = 1.06 qt
1 lb = 454 g	1 m = 39.37 in	1 qt = 0.946 L
1 oz = 28.4 g	1 in = 2.54 cm	

    B. Some problems require several conversion factors. These can be carried out one step at a time or "chained" together using the *unit conversion method* (also called the *factor-label method* or *dimensional analysis*) as shown in this example.

       A man runs the 100 m dash in 10.0 s. What is his speed in miles per hour?
         (Note: 1 m = 39.37 in., 12 in. = 1 ft, 5280 ft = 1 mile ; 60 s = 1 min, 60 min = 1 hr)

$$\dfrac{100 \text{ m}}{10 \text{ s}} \text{ x } \dfrac{39.37 \text{ in.}}{1 \text{ m}} \text{ x } \dfrac{1 \text{ ft}}{12 \text{ in.}} \text{ x } \dfrac{1 \text{ mile}}{5280 \text{ ft}} \text{ x } \dfrac{60 \text{ s}}{1 \text{ min}} \text{ x } \dfrac{60 \text{ min}}{1 \text{ hr}} = 22 \dfrac{\text{mile}}{\text{hr}}$$

Given   x   (meters to miles)   x   (s to hr)   = New Value

A.3 Density Problems

A. Many terms used in chemistry involve ratios of several quantities, thus the units of such quantities also involve ratios of other units.
    1. **Density** = g/mL
    2. **Specific Heat** = cal/(g · °C)

B. **One equation - one unknown**: When working with equations of several parameters, you can solve for the value of any one of the variables provided you know the values of all of the others simply by rearranging the equation to solve for the missing parameter.

Density = mass/volume;   Mass = density x volume;   Volume = mass/density

    1. Calculate density, given mass of 225 g and a volume of 30 mL.

$$\text{density} = \frac{225 \text{ g}}{30 \text{ mL}} = 7.5 \text{ g/mL}$$

    2. Calculate mass, given density of 7.5 g/mL and volume of 30 mL..

$$\text{mass} = (7.5 \text{ g/1 mL}) \times 30 \text{ mL} = 225 \text{ g}$$

DISCUSSION

You will find that the effort you invest in becoming familiar with dimensional analysis will help you a great deal later in the course. The problems that follow are relatively simple but illustrate the basic principle of dimensional analysis using factors with which you are more familiar. Keep in mind that the basic idea is to set up an equation such that the value given in one set of units multiplied by appropriate conversion factors will yield the desired value in the new set of units.

Original Value x Conversion Factors = New Value Sought
(old units)   (desired units)

In the case of the sprinter described in A.2.B above, his speed was given in m/sec, but we wanted to know his speed in mi/hr. This required two sets of conversion factors, one to convert meters to miles and another to convert seconds to hours. Note that the latter conversion appears awkward (reciprocal) because the second units appeared in the denominator of the given. However, if you set up the conversion factors so that the appropriate units cancel, you will find that this will take care of itself.

        (m/s)   x   (meters to miles)   x   (1/s to 1/hr)   =   (miles/hr)

or   (m/s)   x   (miles / m)   x   (sec / hr)   =   (miles/hr)

This set of problems provides practice in converting among British, SI, metric, and apothecary units. You may need to refer back to Chapter 1 for needed conversion factors.

SELF-TEST

1. Brian is 6'2" tall. How tall is he is meters? (1 inch = 2.54 cm)
    a. 74   b. 6.20   c. 1.45   d. 1.88   e. 2.10
2. Bretna is 1.80 m tall. How tall is she in feet and inches?

      a. 5′3″   b. 6′2″   c. 5′9″   d. 5′5″   e. 5′11″

3. How wide in inches is 35-mm film?
      a. 0.35 in.   b. 0.71 in.   c. 1.4 in.   d. 7.1 in.   e. 14 in.

4. We may define a premature baby as one who weighs less than 5 lb at birth. What is the corresponding birth weight in the metric system?
      a. 11 kg   b. 2.3 kg   c. 5.0 kg   d. 0.2 kg   e. 50 kg

5. Chris is 1.94 meters tall and weighs 70 kg. Chris would be described as _____.
      a. slim   b. average   c. heavy   d. grossly overweight

6. If a prescription calls for 400 mg of Edrisal and each Edrisal tablet contains 0.40 grams, how many tablets should be taken?
      a. 1   b. 2   c. 3   d. 4   e. 5

7. You are to administer 0.20 g of a medication by injection. The container label reads 50 mg/mL. How many cubic centimeters should you administer?
      a. 40 cm^3 b. 50 cm^3 c. 2 cm^3 d. 4.0 cm^3 e. 20 cm^3

8. Seven grams of aspirin is enough to fatally poison a small child. If aspirin tablets contain 5 grains per tablet, how many tablets would there be in a fatal dose? (There are 15 grains per gram.)
      a. 35   b. 21   c. 7   d. 75   e. 1125

9. How fast in km/hr is the 65 mph speed limit?
      a. 34   b. 550   c. 27.5   d. 68   e. 105

10. How many liters will a 15.0 gal gas tank in a Ford pickup hold?
      a. 15.0 L   b. 56.6 L   c. 60.0 L   d. 45.3 L   e. 63.6L

11. What is the volume of 1 pound (28.4 g / oz) of gold (density = 19.3 g/mL)?
      a. 18.6 mL   b. 1.3 mL   c. 454 mL   d. 3.5 mL   e. 23.5 mL

12. Gas in Europe was for sale at one place for $3.89/gal and across the street for $1.00/L. Which is the better deal?
      a. $3.98 / gal   b. $1.00 / L   c. both are equal in price

13. A square plot of land one mile on each edge is 640 acres. Given that there are 5280 ft / mile, approximately how many feet on each edge is needed for a square, one acre home site?
      a. 50 ft   b. 100 ft   c. 150 ft   d. 200 ft   e. 400 ft

14. If on average a child is born in the U.S. every 10 sec, how many births would occur in the U.S. each year? (365 days / year)
      a. 365,000   b. 3.2 million   c. 5.23 billion   d. 211 million   e. 43 million

15. How tall are you in meters?

16. How much do you weigh in kg?

ANSWERS

1. d	3. c	5. a	7. d	9. e	11. e	13. d	15. _____
2. e	4. b	6. a	8. b	10. b	12. b	14. b	16. _____

CHAPTER 2: ATOMS

KEY WORDS

atom	*atomic theory*	*electrons*	*orbitals*	*cons. of mass*
mass number	*quantized*	*protons*	*ground state*	*definite proportions*
element	*chemical property*	*neutrons*	*excited state*	*multiple proportions*
compound	*isotopes*	*nucleus*	*atomic number*	*atomic weight*
molecule	*radioactivity*	*periodic table*	*period*	*energy levels*
law	*cathode rays*	*VSEPR*	*group*	*electron configuration*

SUMMARY

The prevailing view of matter held by early Greek philosophers in the 5th century B.C. was that of endless divisibility. This was the view supported by Aristotle. Democritus, a student of Leucippus, believed there must be a limit to the divisibility of matter and called his ultimate particles "atomos" meaning "indivisible." We now define an *atom* as the smallest, characteristic particle of an element. The Greeks believed that there were only four elements: earth, air, fire, and water.

The scientific and political revolution in France led to the acceptance of experimental data as the basis for accepting or rejecting scientific theories. Boyle (1661) proposed that pure substances capable of being broken down into simpler substances were compounds, not elements. Lavoisier (1782) helped establish chemistry as a quantitative science and used systematic names for elements. He proposed that matter is neither created nor destroyed during a chemical change - *law of conservation of mass*. Proust (1799) concluded from compositional analyses that elements combine in definite proportions to form compounds - *law of definite proportions*.

2.1 Dalton's Atomic Theory (1803)
   A. Dalton extended the ideas of Lavoisier and Proust with the *law of multiple proportions*.
   B. Dalton proposed his atomic theory to explain the "laws" of chemistry. A *chemical law* is a statement that summarizes data obtained from experiments. A *theory* is a model that consistently explains observations.
      1. All matter is made up of small, indestructible and indivisible atoms.
      2. All *atoms* of a given element are identical, but different elements have different atoms.
      3. *Compounds* are formed by combining atoms.
      4. A chemical reaction involves a change in the way atoms combine to form *molecules* but does not involve a change in the atoms themselves.
   C. Dalton was later shown to be wrong on the first two assumptions, atoms are divisible and some elements have *isotopes*, but Dalton's atomic theory served to explain a large body of experimental data. An important consequence of his theory was the emphasis on relative atomic masses.

2.2 The Nuclear Atom
   A. The electrical nature of the atom was discovered in the 19th century.
      1. Crookes (1875) - vacuum *cathode ray* tube.
      2. Thomson (1897) - cathode rays were deflected in an electric field and thus must be charged particles. These negatively charged particles were called *electrons* and were found to be the same for all gases used to produce them.
      3. Goldstein (1886) - used an apparatus similar to the Crookes tube to study the positive atomic particles. The positively charged particles were found to be more massive than electrons and

also varied with the type of gas used in the experiment. The lightest positive particle obtained was derived from hydrogen and was called a *proton*.

4. The French physicist Becquerel discovered that some atoms fall apart. Polish-born chemist, Marie Curie, named this *radioactivity.*

5. Milligan (1909) - measured the charge on an electron.

> **Electrons**, (−) negative charge, 9.1×10^{-28} g;
> **Protons** , (+) positive charge, 1.7×10^{-24} g

B. Rutherford directed a beam of alpha particles at a thin sheet of gold foil and to his amazement observed that some of the alpha particles were deflected sharply, and some even bounced back toward the source. In 1911 Rutherford formulated his nuclear theory of the atom, which postulated that all of the positive charge and virtually all of the mass of an atom were concentrated in a tiny nucleus surrounded by the negatively charged electrons. Rutherford (1914) proposed that protons constitute the positively charged matter of all atoms, not just those of hydrogen.

C. Chadwick (1932) discovered an uncharged nuclear particle called a *neutron*, which has about the same mass as a proton. In chemistry, all atoms can be thought of as having a small positively charged *nucleus* containing protons and neutrons, which is surrounded by negatively charged electrons. An oversimplified but useful chemical view of the atomic nucleus is that it consists of protons, neutrons, and the force that holds them together.

1. proton   (p)   -   1.007276 amu -   charge 1+
2. neutron   (n)   -   1.008665 amu -   charge 0
3. electron   (e-)   -   0.000549 amu -   charge 1−

Note: The mass of the neutron is slightly greater than the mass of a proton plus an electron, corresponding to the binding energy required ($\Delta E = \Delta mc^2$).

D. The *atomic number* of an element is determined by its number of protons. An element is a substance in which all atoms have the same atomic number. Atoms with the same number of protons (and atomic number) but a different number of neutrons are called *isotopes*. All isotopes of a given element have very similar chemical properties.

2.3 Nuclear Arithmetic

A. All isotopes can be represented by a nuclear symbol;

> A = mass number = protons (p) + neutrons (n) ;   6p + 6n   or   A = 12
>
> $^{A}_{Z}X$ where ($^{12}_{6}C$)   X = chemical symbol ; C for Z = 6
>
>   Z = atomic number = number of protons (p) ;   6p or Z = 6

B. Atomic weights (or atomic masses) listed in the periodic table are the isotopically weighted average value for that element.

2.4 The Bohr Model of the Atom

A. The light emitted by atoms excited by a flame is not a continuous spectrum but contains instead only a few discrete lines. Light of different energies has different colors ($E_{red} < E_{blue}$).

B. Niels Bohr (1913) postulated that the discrete spectra arose because the energy of an electron in an atom was *quantized* and could take on only certain discrete values of energy.

C. The Bohr model of the atom was based on the known laws of planetary motion.

1. Electrons orbit the nucleus in a manner analogous to planets orbiting the sun.
2. Different *energy levels* correspond to different orbits with the lowest orbit (*ground state*) being the closest, and the higher energy orbits (*excited states*) being more distant from the nucleus.
3. The maximum number of electrons in any given energy level was represented by the formula $2n^2$.

D. Bohr diagrams (Mg Z = 12)

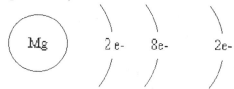

2.5 Electron Configurations
   A. de Broglie (1925) postulated that electrons were particles with wave-like properties.
   B. Quantum mechanics is a highly mathematical discipline that treats electrons as waves and gives
      their locations in terms of probabilities.
      1. Schrodinger (1929) used wave equations to describe the modern picture of the atom.
      2. Electrons were no longer described as being in definite planetary orbits but instead, according to
         a high degree of probability, were confined to three-dimensional charge clouds referred to as
         orbitals.
      3. The letters "s, p, d and f" are used to refer to different types of orbitals:

Orbital		Number of Orbitals	Number of Electrons
s	spherical	1	2
p	perpendicular	3	6
d	diffuse	5	10
f	fundamental	7	14

   C. Energy levels and orbitals
      1. Each orbital can be occupied by 1 "lone" electron or by 2 "paired" electrons.
      2. Each energy level "n" contains n^2 orbitals that can contain up to $2n^2$ electrons.
      3.

Energy Level	Orbital	(number)	Electrons	(subtotal)
1	1s	1	2	(2)
2	2s	1	2	
	2p	3	6	(8)
3	3s	1	2	
	3p	3	6	
	3d	5	10	(18)
4	4s	1	2	
	4p	3	6	
	4d	5	10	
	4f	7	14	(32)

   D. The *electron configuration* of an atom is determined by "filling" the lower energy levels first.
      The general order for filling orbitals is:

$1s^2$ $2s^22p^6$ $3s^23p^6$ $4s^23d^{10}4p^6$ $5s^24d^{10}5p^6$
1   2   3   4   5
(-------------------------------period-------------------------------)

Examples
N (Z = 7) $1s^2$ $2s^22p^3$
Cl (Z = 17) $1s^2$ $2s^22p^6$ $3s^23p^5$
Ba (Z = 56) $1s^2$ $2s^22p^6$ $3s^23p^6$ $4s^23d^{10}4p^6$ $5s^24d^{10}5p^66s^2$

2.6 The Periodic Table
    A. By the mid-1800s there were several known elements but no successful way had been determined to classify the elements.
    B. Mendeleev's *periodic table* (1869) grouped elements together with properties and is the basis for the modern periodic table.
       1. *Period* - *horizontal row* in the table.
       2. *Group* - *vertical column* in the table; members of the same group have similar chemical properties due to similar outer electron configurations. Some of these groups of elements are given family names.

Group IA	-	alkali metals	- ns^1
Group IIA	-	alkaline earths	- ns^2
Group VIIA	-	halogens	- ns^2np^5
Group VIIIA	-	noble gases	- ns^2np^6

    C. The *chemical properties* of an element are defined by its number of electrons (or electron structure) and by its number of protons, not by its atomic mass. All atoms of the same element have the same number of protons, which defines the element's atomic number. Elements in the modern periodic table are arranged in order of increasing atomic number (not atomic mass) and are grouped according to their electronic structure.
    D. *Periodic properties* and trends in the periodic table. Most elements are metals (lower left). Non-metals are in the upper right of the periodic table. Metallic character, size and ionization energy vary as shown.

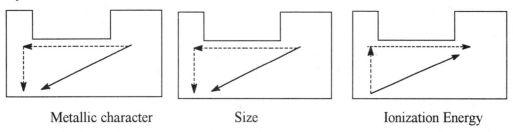

          Metallic character   Size   Ionization Energy

2.7 Which Model to Use?
    A. Use the simplest model that fits the task at hand.
       1. Dalton's billiard ball model of the atom is useful in describing the behavior of gases.
       2. Bohr's planetary model helps one understand the sizes of atoms and energy levels. The Valence Shell Electron Pair Repulsion (*VSEPR*) model is an extension of the Bohr theory which we will use to explain the shape of molecules.
       3. Schrodinger's quantum mechanical model can be used to better understand the principles of chemical bonds, magnetic properties, and spectral properties.

DISCUSSION

    A number of terms are introduced in Chapter 2. These terms are basic to the language of chemistry. As in any language, it is important to learn the vocabulary or it will be difficult to understand the material. Before you proceed, review the KEY WORDS. A number of individuals also were introduced in this chapter. It will be our habit to associate developments in chemistry with the people who were responsible for them. The emphasis that individual instructors place on such biographical information will vary greatly. However, the contributions of a number of individuals mentioned in this chapter are so fundamental to the development of chemistry as a science that many of their names will become familiar to students of chemistry. At the end of the SELF-TEST, you will have an opportunity to match the most prominent individuals mentioned with the fundamental concepts they helped to develop.

It is important that you be able to write down the electron configurations of the Group A type elements. You should be able to do this by looking at the position of the element in the periodic table and remembering a few simple steps.

1. The atomic number gives you the number of electrons in the neutral atom. Add electrons for any negative charge on anions and subtract electrons for the positive charge on cations.

2. Use the order-of-filling given below to write the electron configuration.

$$1s^2 \quad 2s^22p^6 \quad 3s^23p^6 \quad 4s^23d^{10}4p^6 \quad 5s^24d^{10}5p^6 \quad 6s^24f^{14}5d^{10}6p^6$$

Note: You do not have to memorize this general order-of-filling since this information correlates directly with the buildup of the periodic table. The figure given below relates the subshell configuration to the positions of various groups in the periodic chart. Once you master this relationship, it will be much easier to write down electron configurations. Note the position of zinc (Zn) in the table below. Zinc would have a ground state electronic configuration of $1s^2 \ 2s^22p^6 \ 3s^23p^6 \ 4s^23d^{10}$. The sum of the exponents in the electron configuration describing the neutral atom must equal the atomic number (30 for Zn). Finally, it is often useful to represent all filled inner shell electrons by the symbol of the corresponding noble gas. Thus a short-hand way of expressing the electron configuration for Zn would be: $Zn = [Ar] \ 4s^23d^{10}$.

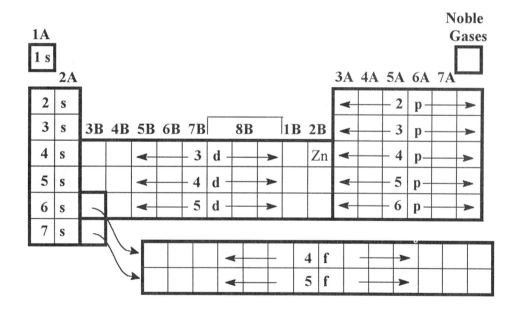

Electron configurations and the periodic table.

Being able to write an electron configuration may seem like an interesting exercise but may be of little practical importance to you at this time. However, you will find that this information is of great value to you later on in predicting preferred ion forms of the elements and in writing molecular formulas.

Example 1. What ion form would you predict for the element fluorine?

$$F: 1s^2 \quad 2s^2 2p^5 \qquad\qquad F^-: 1s^2 \quad 2s^2 2p^6$$

Fluorine will want to gain 1 electron to form a stable 1⁻ anion, which yields the noble gas electron configuration of Ne.

Example 2. What ion form would you predict for the element magnesium?

$$Mg: 1s^2 \quad 2s^2 2p^6 \quad 3s^2 \qquad\qquad Mg^{2+}: 1s^2 \quad 2s^2 2p^6$$

Magnesium will lose 2 electrons to form a stable 2+ cation with the same electron configuration as the noble gas Ne.

These examples show how knowledge of the periodic table and electron configurations can help you predict the common ion form of an element. This information also helps you to predict that the correct molecular formula for magnesium fluoride would be MgF_2 (one magnesium ion for every two fluoride ions).

Numerical problems are few in this chapter. Only the law of definite proportions lends itself to arithmetic manipulation. Remember that a molecule is a fixed combination of at least two atoms. For example, all molecules of water (H_2O) incorporate exactly two hydrogen atoms and one oxygen atom, and all molecules of carbon dioxide (CO_2) have two atoms of oxygen for each carbon atom. After reviewing the examples in the chapter, try the following problems.

Problems

The analysis of the compound magnesium chloride shows it to consist of 25% magnesium and 75% chlorine by weight.
1. How many grams of magnesium are present in 10 g of magnesium chloride?
2. How many pounds of magnesium are present in a 100-lb sample of the compound?
3. A sample of the compound weighed 20 g. How many grams of magnesium and how many grams of chlorine are present in this sample?
4. How large a sample of the compound is required to have 5 g of magnesium?
5. How many grams of chlorine will combine completely with 100 g of magnesium to produce the compound?
6. An analysis shows that a sample of magnesium chloride contains 1.5 g of magnesium and 6 g of chlorine. Is this consistent with the law of definite proportions?

SELF-TEST (Refer to a periodic table.)

1. Which term, as used by scientists, best fits this definition: a statement that summarizes the data obtained from observations?
       a. law   b. model   c. theory
2. Which term best describes Einstein's thoughts on relativity?
       a. law   b. model   c. theory
3. Which of the following facts does not fit Dalton's atomic theory?
       a. All atoms of oxygen are different from all atoms of nitrogen.
       b. Atoms are not destroyed in chemical reactions.
       c. Combinations of atoms rearrange during a chemical reaction.
       d. All oxygen atoms have the same number of protons but may have different atomic masses.

4. Which of the following postulates of Dalton's atomic theory conflicts with the existence of radioactivity?
    a. All matter is made up of small, indestructible and indivisible atoms.
    b. All atoms of a given element are identical, but different elements have different atoms.
    c. Compounds are formed by combining atoms.
    d. A chemical reaction involves a change in the way atoms combine to form molecules but does not involve a change in the atoms themselves.

5. According to the law of definite proportions, if a sample of compound A contains 10 g of sulfur and 5 g of oxygen, then another sample of A that contains 50 g of sulfur must contain:
    a. 100 g of oxygen   b. 50 g of oxygen   c. 25 g of oxygen

6. If 100 g of sulfur dioxide contains 50% sulfur by weight, then 0.5 g of sulfur dioxide will contain what percentage of sulfur by weight?
    a. 0.5%   b. 25%   c. 50%   d. 75%

7. You have 10 g of element A and 10 g of element B. Compound X is known to consist of 40% A and 60% B. According to the law of definite proportions, if you mix all of your A and B together to form compound X:
    a. You will get 20 g of X.
    b. After all possible X has formed, some A will be left unreacted.
    c. After all possible X has formed, some B will be left unreacted.
    d. The compound X that forms will consist of 50% A and 50% B.

8. What is the maximum amount (g) of X that could be produced in question #7?
    a. 10.0   b. 20.0   c. 15.0   d. 16.7   e. 12.5

9. Which of the following illustrates the law of multiple proportions?
    a.   A sample of a compound contains 3 g of carbon and 4 g of oxygen; a second sample
            of the same compound contains 6 g of carbon and 8 g of oxygen.
    b.   A sample of one compound contains 6 g of carbon and 8 g of oxygen; a sample
            of another compound contains 6 g of carbon and 2 g of hydrogen.
    c.   A sample of one compound contains 6 g of carbon and 8 g of oxygen; a sample
            of another compound contains 6 g of carbon and 16 g of oxygen.

10. The anode and a cation are:
    a. positively charged   b. negatively charged   c. neutral

11. When an evacuated Crookes' tube is discharged,
    a. negative electrons jump from cathode to anode.
    b. negative electrons jump from anode to cathode.
    c. positive electrons jump from anode to cathode.

12. Rutherford's gold foil experiment offered evidence in support of the theory that:
    a. an atom has a very compact nucleus.
    b. the atoms of an element can have different masses.
    c. gold is a radioactive element.

13. According to the Bohr model, how many electrons are there in the highest energy level of a ground state chlorine atom?
    a. 1   b. 2   c. 3   d. 6   e. 7   f. 8   g. 13   h. 18

14. In the Bohr model of the sodium atom, the lowest energy level contains how many electrons?
    a. 1   b. 2   c. 3   d. 4   e. 5   f. 6   g. 7   h. 8

15. Which element should be chemically similar to sulfur, S ?
    a. Na   b. O   c. C   d. Ar

16. Which element would you expect to be chemically similar to Sr?
    a. Co   b. Ba   c. K

17. Which is the proper electron configuration for Si?
    a. $1s^2\ 2s^22p^6\ 3s^23p^4$ b. $1s^2\ 2s^22p^6\ 3s^2\ 4s^2$
    c. $1s^2\ 2s^22p^6\ 3s^2$ d. $1s^2\ 2s^22p^6\ 3s^23p^2$

18. Predict the major ion form for aluminum.
    a. Al^{2+} b. Al^{2-} c. Al^{3+} d. Al^{3-} e. Al^{4+}

19. Which is the proper electron configuration for Cl^- ?
    a. $1s^2\ 2s^22p^6\ 3s^23p^5$ b. $1s^2\ 2s^22p^6\ 3s^2\ 4s^24p^6$
    c. $1s^2\ 2s^22p^6\ 3s^2$ d. $1s^2\ 2s^22p^6\ 3s^23p^6$

20. How many electrons and neutrons are in a neutral atom of ^{123}Sb?
    a. 38, 85   b. 50, 23   c. 51, 72   d. 51, 21   e. 50, 73

21. A particle contains 16 protons, 18 electrons, and 17 neutrons.
    A. The atomic mass number is: 16   17   18   33   34   51
    B. The symbol for the element is: Si   P   S   Cu   Zn   Ga
    C. The particle has a charge of: 0   1+   2+   1-   2-   3-
    D. If an electron were removed, which of the above answers would have to be changed:
            a   b   c
    E. If a neutron were added to the original particle, which of the answers would have to be
       changed: a   b   c
    F. If a proton were added to the original particle, which of the answers would have to be
       changed: a   b   c

22. Given:

	Atom A	Atom B	Atom C	Atom D	Atom E	Atom F
No. of electrons	13	6	8	16	8	7
No. of neutrons	14	7	7	16	6	8
No. of protons	14	5	7	16	8	7

    a. Which atoms have the same atomic mass?   A   B   C   D   E   F
    b. For which atom(s) is the atomic number 5?   A   B   C   D   E   F
    c. Which atom(s) is(are) neutral?   A   B   C   D   E   F
    d. Which is(are) nitrogen?   A   B   C   D   E   F

23. Refer to the diagram to answer the following questions:

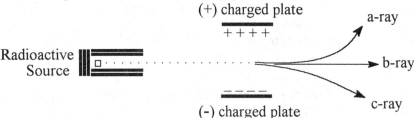

    A. The a-ray
       a. could be a stream of electrons
       b. could be a stream of protons
       c. could be a stream of neutrons
    B. The b-ray
       a. could be a stream of γ-rays
       b. could be a stream of neutrons
       c. could be a stream of protons
    C. The c-ray
       a. could be a stream of protons
       b. could be a stream of electrons
       c. could be a stream of neutrons

Matching: (A name may be associated with more than one concept.)

Name of Person	Concept
a. Becquerel	___ 24. proponent of the atomic structure of matter among the ancient Greeks
b. Bohr	___ 25. proposed the modern atomic theory
c. Chadwick	___ 26. law of conservation of mass
d. Curie	___ 27. discovered radioactivity
e. Dalton	___ 28. law of definite proportions
f. Democritus	___ 29. law of multiple proportions
g. Lavoisier	___ 30. made quantitative measurements the standard of chemical
h. Mendeleev	experimentation
i. Proust	___ 31. periodic table of the elements
j. Thomson	___ 32. the nuclear atom
k. Rutherford	___ 33. the atom as a miniature solar system
l. Milligan	___ 34. measured the charge on an electron
	___ 35. discovered the electron
	___ 36. discovered the neutron
	___ 37. explained the line spectra of the elements
	___ 38. discovered new radioactive elements

ANSWERS

Problems

1. 2.5 g
2. 25 lb
3. 5 g of magnesium and 15 g of chlorine
4. 20 g of magnesium chloride
5. 300 g of chlorine
6. No

Self-Test

1. a	11. a	21. A) 33	23. A) a	30. g
2. c	12. a	B) S	B) a,b	31. h
3. d	13. e	C) -2	C) a	32. k
4. a	14. b	D) c	24. f	33. b
5. c	15. b	E) a	25. e	34. l
6. c	16. b	F) a, b, c	26. g	35. j
7. b	17. d	22. a) C, E	27. a	36. c
8. d	18. c	b) B	28. i	37. b
9. c	19. d	c) D, E	29. e	38. d
10. a	20. c	d) C, F		

CHAPTER 3: NUCLEAR PROCESSES

KEY WORDS

X-ray	*nucleus*	*fission*	*beta decay*	*curies*	*Geiger counter*
radioactivity	*proton*	*isotopes*	*gamma decay*	*roentgen*	*scintillation*
chemical rxns.	*neutron*	*fusion*	*half-life*	*rad*	*medical imaging*
nuclear rxns.	*electron*	*alpha decay*	*transmutation*	*rem*	*LD$_{50}$/30 days*
chain rxn.	*penetrating power*	*critical mass*	*CAT, PET, MRI*	*plasma*	*ultrasonograph*

SUMMARY

3.1 Discovery of Radioactivity
    A. Roentgen (1895) - discovery of *X rays*.
    B. Henri Becquerel - discovery of *radioactivity*
    C. Marie and Pierre Curie - studies on radioactivity, discovery of radium.

3.2 Types of Radioactivity
    A. Chemical reactions involve changes in the outer electrons of an atom, while nuclear reactions involve changes within the nucleus of an atom. Some nuclei are unstable and undergo spontaneous reactions called radioactive decay.
    B. Rutherford classified 3 types of radioactivity.

1. *Alpha decay*	α particles	4	amu	2+
2. *Beta decay*	β particles	1/1837	amu	1-
3. *Gamma decay*	γ rays	0	amu	0

    C. Examples of the major types of radioactivity:
      1. **Alpha (α)** decay is characterized by the giving off of particles consisting of 2 protons + 2 neutrons.

$$^{226}_{88}\text{Ra} \rightarrow {}^{222}_{86}\text{Rn} + {}^{4}_{2}\text{He}$$

      2. **Beta (β)** decay is characterized by the emission of a *nuclear electron* as a neutron is converted to a proton.

$$^{14}_{6}\text{C} \rightarrow {}^{14}_{7}\text{N} + {}^{0}_{1-}\text{e}$$

      3. **Gamma (γ)** decay is characterized by the emission of high energy photons ("*nuclear X-rays*") and occurs when an excited nucleus drops to a lower energy state, emitting the energy difference as "light."

3.3 Penetrating Power of Radiation
    A. The intensity of all point radiation sources decreases with the square of the distance from the source, i.e. the intensity is only 1/4 strength at twice the distance. However, the penetrating power of different types of radiation varies widely. This is due in part to their masses but also to their charges. A charged particle will undergo more interactions with matter and will lose energy faster than an uncharged particle:

        penetrating power : $\alpha < \beta < \gamma$.

B. External α-particles are stopped easily, but internal α-emitters are very dangerous due to the large number internal ions that will be produced even over the short distances that α-particles can travel in flesh.

3.4 Radiation Measurement

A. Curie, R, rad, rem

1. *Curies* (Ci) - 1 Ci = 3.7×10^{10} disintegrations per second (~ activity of 1 g Ra).
2. *Roentgen* (R) - a measure of exposure to ionizing radiation; 1R = amount of gamma or X rays required to produce ions carrying 2.1 billion units of electrical charge in 1 cc of dry air at 0 °C and 1 atm.
3. Radiation absorbed dose (*rad*) - 1 rad = 100 ergs (2.4×10^{-6} cal) of radiant energy absorbed per gram of tissue; 500 rads would be lethal to most people; average yearly dose absorbed from medical and dental X rays is about 1 rad. Our exposure to cosmic rays and natural radioisotopes amounts to about 100-600 millirads/yr.
4. Roentgen equivalent in man (*rem*) - a measure of the biological damage produced by a particular dose of radiation. A radiation worker should not be exposed to more than 5 rem/year.

B. Radiation Detectors

1. *Geiger counter* - radiation ionizes gas, causing current signal.
2. *Scintillation* counter - radiation produces a photon, which is amplified by a photomultiplier and counted as an electronic signal.
3. Film badge - radiation "blackens" film.

3.5 Half-Life

A. Radioactivity is dependent on the *isotope* involved but generally independent of any outside influences such as temperature or pressure.
B. *Radioactivity* is a random process but for large populations has a predictable half-life characteristic of that isotope. The *half-life* is that period of time during which one-half of the radioactive atoms undergo decay. The half-life of radioisotopes varies from less than a second to millions of years.
C. The fraction of the original radioactive sample remaining after "n" half-lives is given by $(1/2)^n$ or 1/2, 1/4, 1/8, 1/16, and so forth.

3.6 Radioisotopic dating

A. The half-lives of some isotopes can be used to estimate the age of rocks and archeological artifacts.

1. Rocks: Uranium-238 decays with a half-life of 4.5 billion years, eventually decaying to lead-206. The ratio of Pb-206 to U-238 remaining can therefore be used to date very old rocks back to the origin of earth.
2. Artifacts: Carbon-14 is formed in the upper atmosphere and decays to Nitrogen-14 with a half-life of 5730 years. The amount of C-14 remaining can be used to estimate the age of organic objects as old as 50,000 years. C-14 dating has been useful to detect forgeries of ancient artifacts.
3. Tritium: Hydrogen-3 has a half-life of 12.3 years is useful in dating materials less than 100 years old.

3.7 Artificial Transmutation and Induced Radioactivity

A. Nuclear changes can also be brought about by the bombardment of stable nuclei with subatomic particles.

$$^{9}_{4}\text{Be} + \;^{4}_{2}\text{He} \;\rightarrow\; ^{12}_{6}\text{C} + \;^{1}_{0}\text{n}$$

B. *Transmutations* have led to the discovery of fundamental particles such as the neutron.

C. A common application of artificial transmutations is to produce unstable, radioactive isotopes by the bombardment of other isotopes with subatomic particles.

$$^{27}Al \quad + \quad \alpha \text{ particle} \quad \rightarrow \quad ^{30}P \quad + \quad \text{a neutron}$$

D. Many isotopes used in medicine undergo decay by electron capture (E.C.).

$$^{125}I \quad + \quad e\text{-} \quad \rightarrow \quad ^{125}Te \quad + \quad X\text{-rays}$$

3.8 Fission and Fusion

A. Albert Einstein (1905) derived a relationship between matter and energy as part of his theory of relativity.

$$E = mc^2 \quad \text{where} \quad E \quad = \quad \text{energy}$$
$$m \quad = \quad \text{mass}$$
$$c \quad = \quad \text{speed of light}$$

B. Nuclear energy changes are many orders of magnitude greater than chemical energy changes. One g of matter is the energy equivalent of burning approximately 21 billion kilocalories, or 9×10^{13} J.

C. Nuclear *fission* refers to the process of splitting heavy atomic nuclei into major fragments. Enormous amounts of energy are released during this process.

D. Neutron bombardment of uranium-235 produces Xe-143, Sr-90 plus three free neutrons which can be used to split other U-235 atoms to create a *chain reaction*. The *critical mass* is the minimum amount of fissionable material needed to sustain a chain reaction.

E. Binding energy is the energy that the nucleus no longer has; it represents the energy given up when the nucleus formed. It is related to the mass defect (isotopic mass − mass number) by $E = mc^2$. The most stable nuclei are in the vicinity of iron (Z = 26), implying that large amounts of energy are also available from combining very light nuclei to produce heavier nuclei, that is nuclear *fusion*. Hydrogen is the most abundant element in the universe. In stars like our sun, very high temperatures permit light nuclei to fuse as hydrogen forms helium, for example. Temperatures of 50,000,000 °C must be maintained to promote fusion reactions. Hydrogen bombs utilize a small fission bomb to create the high temperatures needed for the fusion process. In fusion reactors, magnetic fields are used to control the *plasma* of nuclei and free electrons.

F. Many radioactive daughter isotopes may be produced as nuclear fallout from nuclear fission reactions. Several of these daughter isotopes are dangerous when they are incorporated into the food chain. Strontium-90 can substitute for calcium and is incorporated into the bone matter; Cesium-137 mimics potassium; Iodine-131 is concentrated in the thyroid.

3.9 Nuclear Medicine

A. Radiation and Living Things

1. Cells that are constantly and rapidly being replaced are more susceptible to radiation damage than are other cells that are replaced less frequently.

2. The $LD_{50}/30$ days for whole body exposure in man is about 400 rems. *$LD_{50}/30$* is the lethal dose required to kill 50% of the populations within 30 days.

3. Acute radiation syndrome is characterized by a short latent period followed by nausea, vomiting, a drop in white blood cell count, fever, diarrhea, hair loss, and death.

B. Nuclear Tools in Medical Diagnosis

1. Iodine-131 - size, shape and activity of the thyroid gland

2. Cobalt-58 - vitamin B_{12} uptake

3. Iron-59 - formation and lifetime of RBCs

4. Gadolinium-153 - bone mineralization, osteoporosis

5. Technetium-99m - good γ-source for imaging of brain, lungs, cardiovascular system

6. Cobalt-60 is a powerful gamma emitter used in radiation therapy to destroy localized malignancies.
7. See Table 3.4 for other examples.
C. The radiation used in cancer treatment can cause radiation sickness, nausea and vomiting, and can lead to birth defects and to some forms of leukemia.

3.10 Medical Imaging
A. Modern computer aided medical imaging methods provide a means of looking at internal organs without resorting to surgery.
B. There are many such techniques, each utilizing a different energy source.
1. *CAT* scan - Computer aided tomography of X-ray and γ scans
2. *PET* - Positron emission tomography
3. *Ultrasonography* - Echo analysis of high frequency sound waves
4. *MRI* - non-ionizing, non-radioactive, low-energy nuclear magnetic resonance imaging

3.11 Other Applications
A. Radioactive isotopes can substitute chemically for their non-radioactive counterparts but have the advantage of being easily detected.
B. The radioisotopes of ^{14}C and ^{3}H have helped unravel complex metabolic pathways.
C. Radioisotopes and Animals and Vegetables
1. Irradiation of foodstuffs for preservation.
2. Purposeful mutations of plants by irradiation has led to improved strains of many crops.

3.12 The Nuclear Age Revisited
A. The Atomic Bomb
1. Much of the early work on nuclear fission was carried out by German scientists.
2. During WW II the United States initiated the Manhattan Project to study atomic energy.
   a. August 6, 1945, a uranium bomb was dropped on Hiroshima.
   b. August 9, 1945, a plutonium bomb was dropped on Nagasaki. Pu-239 is fissionable and can be made from the more abundant isotope U-238. August 14, 1945, Japan surrendered.
B. More lives have been saved through nuclear medicine than lost by nuclear bombs, which have not been used in warfare since 1945.
C. Nuclear power continues to represent a plentiful source of energy.
1. Nuclear power plants use the same fission reactions as nuclear bombs. However, boron and cadmium control rods absorb neutrons to control the reactions. The heat released generates steam which is used to produce electricity without air pollution. The United States has about 100 nuclear power plants.
2. The advantages are no soot, ash, sulfur oxides, etc.
3. The disadvantages are high construction costs, limited and expensive fuel, radioactive waste products, waste heat that causes thermal pollution, radiation leakage and accidents, and the possibility of a major accident like Three Mile Island (1979) and Chernobyl (1986).

DISCUSSION

Many new words were introduced in this chapter. Review those listed under the KEY WORDS section to test your recall of the correct meaning of each term. Two types of quantitative material were introduced: balancing of nuclear equations and problems dealing with half-lives. The key to balancing nuclear equations is to remember that the sum of atomic numbers (Z) and of atomic mass numbers (A) must be equal on each side of the equation. The proper chemical symbol can then be deduced from the correct atomic number once it has been determined. It is also helpful to memorize the characteristics of α and β (β^- or e^-) decay with respect to the effect that they have on the atomic and mass numbers (Z and A) for the newly produced daughter nucleus.

Decay type		Particle	Parent		Daughter
alpha	α	^4_2He	$^A_Z X$	$\longrightarrow$	$^{(A-4)}_{(Z-2)} X$
beta	β	$^0_{1-}e$	$^A_Z X$	$\longrightarrow$	$^{(A)}_{(Z+1)} X$

Problems

Balance the following equations by supplying the missing component.

1. $^{14}_7N \quad + \quad ? \quad \rightarrow \quad ^{18}_9F$

2. $^{90}_{38}Sr \quad \rightarrow \quad ? \quad + \quad ^0_{1-}e$

3. $^{238}_{92}U \quad \rightarrow \quad ^4_2He \quad + \quad ?$

4. $^{60}_{27}Co \quad \rightarrow \quad ? \quad + \quad \beta^-$

5. $^{56}_{26}Fe \quad + \quad ^2_1H \quad \rightarrow \quad ^{54}_{25}Mn \quad + \quad ?$

6. $^{239}_{94}Pu \quad + \quad ^1_0n \quad \rightarrow \quad ? \quad + \quad ^0_{1-}e$

7. $? \quad + \quad ^1_1H \quad \rightarrow \quad ^4_2He \quad + \quad ^4_2He$

8. $^3_1H \quad + \quad ^2_1H \quad \rightarrow \quad ^4_2He \quad + \quad ?$

9. $^{241}_{95}Am \quad + \quad ? \quad \rightarrow \quad ^{243}_{97}Bk \quad + \quad 2\, ^1_0n$

10. $^{235}_{92}U \quad + \quad ^1_0n \quad \rightarrow \quad ^{103}_{42}Mo \quad + \quad ? \quad + \quad 2\, ^1_0n$

11. $? \quad + \quad ^1_0n \quad \rightarrow \quad ^{141}_{56}Ba \quad + \quad ^{91}_{36}Kr \quad + \quad 3\, ^1_0n$

12. Write an equation for the alpha decay of thorium-228.
13. Protactinium-234 has a half-life of one minute. After 5 minutes, how many micrograms of this isotope remain in a sample that originally contained 80 μg?

14. If the half-life of polonium-218 is 3 minutes and a sample originally contains 64 mg of this isotope, how much of the isotope remains after 9 minutes?
15. Radioactive ^{154}Tm has a half-life of 5 seconds. After 20 seconds, how many milligrams of this isotope remain in a sample that originally contained 160 mg?
16. Radioactive nitrogen-13 has a half-life of 10 minutes. After an hour, how much of this isotope would remain in a sample that originally contained 96 mg?

SELF-TEST (Refer to a periodic table.)

1. Isotopes of the same element have the same:
    a. number of neutrons   b. atomic number   c. atomic weight
2. Which form of nuclear radiation most closely resembles X-rays?
    a. alpha rays   b. beta rays   c. gamma rays
3. Which is the least penetrating radiation?
    a. alpha rays   b. beta rays   c. gamma rays
4. Which is the most penetrating radiation?
    a. alpha rays   b. beta rays   c. gamma rays
5. In general, which type of radiation is most useful when diagnostic scanning of an internal organ is desired?
    a. alpha rays   b. beta rays   c. gamma rays   d. cosmic rays
6. Which of the radiation-detecting devices signals when the radiation ionizes gas molecules and causes an electric current to flow?
    a. Geiger counter   b. scintillation counter   c. film badge
7. Which type of radiation is not a stream of charged particles?
    a. alpha rays   b. beta rays   c. gamma rays   d. cosmic rays
8. Which is considered an ionizing radiation?
    a. α rays   b. β rays   c. γ rays   d. cosmic rays   e. all of these
9. Which type of radiation can be stopped by a sheet of paper?
    a. alpha rays   b. beta rays   c. gamma rays
10. If the intensity of radiation is 32 units at a distance of 1 m from the source, then the intensity at 4 m from the source is:
    a. 8 unit   b. 2 units   c. 4 units   d. 20 units   c. 16 units
11. Which describes the activity of the radioactive source?
    a. curie   b. roentgen   c. rad   d. rem   e. $LD_{50}/30$ days
12. Which is used to measure the dose of radiation absorbed by tissue?
    a. curie   b. roentgen   c. rad
13. A minimum lethal whole body dose of radiation for most human beings would be in the range:
    a. 5-10 rads   b. 50-100 rads   c. 500-1000 rads   d. 5000-10,000 rads
14. You are exposed to ionizing radiation:
    a. because of atmospheric testing of nuclear weapons
    b. when your teeth are X-rayed by a dentist
    c. simply because you live on the earth
    d. for all of these reasons
    e. in none of these instances
15. Which hydrogen isotope contains two neutrons?
    a. protium (^1H)   b. deuterium (^2H)   c. tritium (^3H)
16. Which is an isotope of ^{16}O?
    a. ^{16}C b. ^{18}O c. ^{16}N d. ^{16}O

17. For which of the following would Sr be an improper chemical symbol?

     a. $^{90}_{38}X$ b. $^{88}_{38}X$ c. $^{90}_{39}X$

18. If ^{173}Yb emits a β particle, the product is an isotope of: Cl Ar Sc Ti V Mn Mo Tc Ru Lu Rh Pd

19. Which isotope is particularly useful for both diagnostic and therapeutic work with the thyroid gland?

     a. cobalt-60   b. iodine-131   c. technetium-99m

20. The isotope with ideal properties for a large number of diagnostic scanning uses, including the brain, is:

     a. I-131   b. Tc-99m   c. U-235   d. U-238   e. Co-60

21. Which process does this equation illustrate: $^2H + {}^2H \rightarrow {}^4He$?

     a. fission   b. fusion   c. radioactivity

22. Which of the following properties makes technetium-99m a good isotope for diagnostic scanning procedures?

     a. It does not emit alpha or beta rays.

     b. It emits extremely high-energy gamma rays.

     c. It has a very long half-life.

     d. All of these reasons.

23. Which of the following nuclear events would not be described as an example of transmutation?

     a. emission of an alpha particle

     b. emission of a beta particle

     c. emission of a neutron

24. Which medical imaging technique involves the use of ionizing radiation?

     x. PET   b. MRI   c. ultrasonography

25. What isotope is produced if a single neutron is ejected when ^{242}Cm is bombarded by an α-particle?

     a. ^{242}Am b. ^{246}Cf c. ^{246}Cm d. ^{245}Cf e. ^{243}Bk

ANSWERS

Problems

1. ^4_2He 4. $^{60}_{28}Ni$ 7. ^7_3Li 10. $^{131}_{50}Sn$ 13. 2.5 μg

2. $^{90}_{39}Y$ 5. ^4_2He 8. ^1_0n 11. $^{234}_{92}U$ 14. 8 mg

3. $^{234}_{90}Po$ 6. $^{240}_{95}Am$ 9. ^4_2He 12. $^{228}_{90}Th \rightarrow {}^4_2He + {}^{224}_{88}Ra$ 15. 10 mg

                                                                    16. 1.5 mg

Self-Test

1. b	7. c	13. c	19. b	25. d
2. c	8. e	14. d	20. b	
3. a	9. a	15. c	21. b	
4. c	10. b	16. b	22. a	
5. c	11. a	17. c	23. c	
6. a	12. c	18. Lu	24. a	

CHAPTER 4: CHEMICAL BONDS

KEY WORDS

cations	*electron configuration*	*ionic bond*	*linear*	*bonding pairs*
anions	*electron dot symbols*	*covalent bond*	*bent*	*nonbonding pairs*
metals	*molecular formula*	*polar covalent*	*trigonal*	*polar*
nonmetals	*structural formula*	*electronegativity*	*pyramidal*	*nonpolar*
valence	*polyatomic ions*	*octet rule*	*tetrahedral*	*stoichiometry*
salt	*double bond*	*triple bond*	*Lewis symbol*	

SUMMARY

There are over 100 elements but "*billions and billions*" of possible compounds. This chapter introduces the concept of chemical bonding, the forces that enable atoms to join together to form compounds.

4.1 The Art of Deduction: Stable Electron Configurations
   A. Noble gasses are typically stable, undergoing few reactions.
   B. Atoms can gain or lose electrons to form ions.
      1. *Cations* - positively charged ions
      2. *Anions* - negatively charged ions
   C. The more stable ions have an electron configuration with a filled outer electron level (like the noble gases). Na looses an electron to become Na+ with 10 electrons arranged similarly to Ne.

4.2 Lewis (Electron Dot) Formulas
   A. *Electron dot symbols* (Lewis symbols) are a useful way to represent atoms or ions. The nucleus and the inner levels (core) are represented by the chemical symbol; the outer or *valence* electrons are represented by dots.

   Atoms: sodium Na · , chlorine :C̈l · ; Ions: sodium ion Na$^+$, chloride ion [:C̈l:]$^-$

   B. Electron dot formulas are more convenient to use than energy level diagrams. For the Group A elements, the number of valence electrons is equal to the group number. The valence electrons are represented by dots.
   C. Electron dot formulas for the first 18 elements. Note: It is useful to represent the first four electrons as lone dots (unpaired electrons) on each side of the symbol before pairing any of the dots.

1A	2A	3A	4A	5A	6A	7A	Noble Gases
H·							He:
Li·	·Be·	·B·	·C̈·	:N̈·	:Ö·	:F̈·	:N̈e:
Na·	·Mg·	·A̤l·	·S̤i·	:P̈·	:S̈·	:C̈l·	:Är:

27

4.3 Sodium Reacts With Chlorine: The Facts

A. Sodium is a very soft, reactive metal normally stored under oil.

B. Chlorine is a greenish-yellow, reactive gas that is used as a disinfectant for swimming pools.

C. When sodium metal is added to chlorine gas, a violent reaction takes place and produces a white, stable, water-soluble solid known as sodium chloride (table salt).

4.4 The Sodium-Chlorine Reaction: Theory

A. Sodium reacts with chlorine by giving up an electron to chlorine.

$$Na \cdot \ + \ :\ddot{Cl} \cdot \ \longrightarrow \ Na^+ \ + \ [:\ddot{Cl}:]^-$$

B. The ion products of this reaction are stable because both ions have stable, noble-gas type electron configurations. The ions have opposite charges, so sodium chloride forms a crystalline solid stabilized by ionic bonds, $Na^+ Cl^-$.

4.5 Ionic Bonds: Some General Considerations

A. *Metals* (Na, K, etc.) are located on the left side of the periodic table, while *nonmetals* (N, O, Cl, etc.) are located on the right side of the periodic table. Metals tend to form cations by giving up electrons to nonmetals which then form anions. The resulting *salt* that is produced is held together by *ionic bonds*.

B. The number of electrons given up or taken on can usually be predicted from the group number of the element, being equal to the group number for metals and equal to eight minus the group number for nonmetals.

Na	Mg	Al	Si	P	S	Cl
+1	+2	+3	(+4,-4)	(+5,-3)	-2	-1

4.6 Names of Simple Ions and Ionic Compounds

A. Cations - add "ion" to the name of the parent element: Na^+, sodium ion.

B. Anions - change the ending to "-ide" and add "ion": Cl^-, chloride ion.

C. Some elements have more than one stable ion form. In those cases, Roman numerals are used to indicate the charge of the ion: Fe^{2+}, iron(II) ion; Fe^{3+}, iron(III) ion.

D. The least common multiple is used to determine the correct *stoichiometry*, or numbers of cations and anions needed for the correct formula for an *ionic* compound.

E. Examples

Name	Formula
sodium chloride	NaCl
magnesium chloride	$MgCl_2$
iron(II) bromide	$FeBr_2$
iron(III) fluoride	FeF_3
aluminum oxide	Al_2O_3

4.7 Covalent Bonds: Shared Electron Pairs

A. Many compounds are composed of elements that are unable to transfer electrons completely between them to form stable ionic bonds. These elements achieve stable electronic configurations by sharing pairs of electrons.

B. A bond formed by sharing a pair of electrons is called a *covalent bond*. Many covalently bonded atoms, except hydrogen, seek an arrangement that surrounds them with eight electrons (*octet rule*) with filled outer shell s and p orbitals. It is important to distinguish shared or bonded pairs of electrons from unshared or lone pairs of electrons which do not contribute to bonding. For convenience a shared pair of electrons is often represented as a dash and lone pairs are omitted entirely. Cl_2 has 1 shared or bonding pair (single bond), the rest are nonbonding pairs of electrons. N_2 has 3 bonding pairs of electrons, a triple bond.

$$:\ddot{C}l\cdot \;\; + \;\; \cdot\ddot{C}l: \;\; \longrightarrow \;\; \boxed{:\ddot{C}l:\ddot{C}l:} \;\; \text{or} \;\; :\ddot{C}l-\ddot{C}l: \;\; \text{or} \;\; Cl_2$$

$$\cdot\ddot{N}\cdot \;\; + \;\; \cdot\ddot{N}\cdot \;\; \longrightarrow \;\; \boxed{:N:::N:} \;\; \text{or} \;\; :N\equiv N: \;\; \text{or} \;\; N_2$$

4.8 Multiple Covalent Bonds

A. Some atoms are able to share two pairs (*double bond*) or three pairs (*triple bond*) of electrons to achieve the stable octet.

B. Examples: Double bond - sharing 2 pairs of electrons   Triple bond - sharing 3 pairs of electrons

$$:\ddot{O}::C::\ddot{O}: \;\; \text{or} \;\; O=C=O \qquad\qquad :N:::N: \;\; \text{or} \;\; :N\equiv N:$$
$$\text{or } N_2$$

4.9 Unequal Sharing: Polar Covalent Bonds

A. In many compounds the electron pair is unequally shared between the two bonded atoms. This type of bonding is referred to as a *polar covalent* bond.

B. The element in a polar covalent bond that more often has the electrons is said to carry a "partial" negative charge and to be more "*electronegative*" than the other element. For example, fluorine is more electronegative than hydrogen. Thus, HF has a polar bond   ($^{\delta+}H—F^{\delta-}$)

4.10 Polyatomic Molecules: Water, Ammonia, and Methane

A. Water: A Bent Molecule

1. The *molecular formula* for water is H_2O.

2. The *electron dot formula* for water is:

$$H:\ddot{O}: \; = \; H-O \atop \backslash_H$$

3. Water is shown as a *bent* molecule, rather than a linear molecule, because we know that water has a permanent dipole.

net dipole
$$\delta^+ \longrightarrow \delta^- \atop H-O \backslash_{} \atop \backslash H \delta^+$$
, not
$$\delta^+ \longrightarrow \delta^- \longleftarrow \delta^+ \atop H-O-H$$
dipoles cancel

B. Ammonia: A *Pyramidal* Molecule

1. The molecular formula for ammonia is NH_3.

2. The electron dot formula for ammonia is:

$$H:\ddot{N}:H \atop \ddot{H}$$
or
$$\overset{..}{N} \atop H\diagup \diagdown H \atop H$$
pyramidal shap

C. Methane: A *Tetrahedral* Molecule
   1. The molecular formula for methane is CH_4.
   2. The electron dot formula for methane is:

   tetrahedral shape

4.11 Names for Covalent Compounds
   A. Common Names - H_2O (water), CH_4 (methane), NH_3 (ammonia).
   B. Prefixes - mono (1), di (2), tri (3), tetra (4), penta (5), hexa (6), hepta (7), octa (8), etc.
      NO_2 = nitrogen **di**oxide; N_2O_4 = **di**nitrogen **tetra**oxide; CCl_4 = carbon **tetra**chloride

4.12 Polyatomic Ions
   A. A number of polyatomic ions are so common that they have been given names and are usually treated as one entity.
   B.

Name	Formula	Name	Formula
Ammonium ion	NH_4^+	Nitrate ion	NO_3^-
Carbonate ion	CO_3^{2-}	Phosphate ion	PO_4^{3-}
Bicarbonate ion	HCO_3^-	Phosphite ion	PO_3^{3-}
Hydroxide ion	OH^-	Sulfate ion	SO_4^{2-}
Cyanide	CN^-	Nitrite	NO_2^-

4.13 Electronegativity
   A. *Electronegativity* refers to the tendency of an atom to attract electrons to itself.
   B. Nonmetals (upper right in the periodic table) are more electronegative than metals (lower left). Fluorine is the most electronegative element and metals like cesium are the least electronegative.

Electronegativities (EN)	Li	Be	B	C	N	O	F
	1.0	1.5	2.0	2.6	3.1	3.5	4.0

   C. The difference in electronegativities is a measure of bond polarity. $EN_{Na} = 0.9$, $EN_{Cl} = 3.2$)
      1. NaCl, an ionic compound; $\Delta EN = 2.3$
      2. N_2, a covalent, nonpolar compound; $\Delta EN = 0.0$
   D. Bonds with DEN > 2 are considered ionic; Bonds with DEN < 0.4 are nonpolar, covalent.

4.14 Rules for Writing Lewis Formulas
   A. Different atoms form different numbers of bonds. The number of covalent bonds an atom can form is called its *valence*.
   B. Hydrogen   H   monovalent ;   Oxygen   O   divalent
      Nitrogen   N   trivalent   ;   Carbon   C   tetravalent
   C. Steps in writing an electron dot formula.
      1. Calculate the total number of valence electrons.
      2. Write the skeletal structure.
      3. Apply the "octet-rule" - place 8 electrons around all outer atoms and 2 electrons around H atoms.
      4. Any valence electrons that remain are assigned to the central atom.
      5. If the central atom has fewer than 8 electrons, a multiple bond is likely. Move non-bonding electron pairs to form double and/or triple bonds as needed. (See Discussion.)

4.15 Exceptions to the Octet Rule
   A. Most compounds of C, N, O, and F always obey the octet rule.
   B. There are many exceptions to the octet rule.
      1. Free radicals - atoms and molecules with an unpaired electron. NO, NO_2
      2. Boron and beryllium compounds. BF_3, $BeBr_2$
      3. Compounds involving elements in the 3rd period and beyond. PCl_5, SF_6

DISCUSSION

Chapter 4 marks a turning point in our study of chemistry. If, instead of chemistry, English literature were our area of study, we would just be at the point of having learned to read. You can't appreciate fine literature (or even not-so-fine literature) unless you understand that those little squiggles on paper are letters of the alphabet, that letters of the alphabet are symbols representing sounds we make to communicate with one another, and that the right combinations of letters make words that have meaning. In the first three chapters we learned to use chemical symbols to represent bits of matter. In Chapter 4, we've finally begun to read and write the "words" of chemistry--the formulas for compounds. In Chapter 5 we'll be composing "sentences," i.e., equations, and eventually we'll be able to read and understand some of the most complex "literature" of chemistry, including the chemical version of the story of life.

Right now, it's necessary that you become comfortable dealing with the structures of compounds. The fact that sodium chloride is an ionic compound is of great importance to its role in living systems. The fact that water is a polar covalent molecule is just as important. You must understand what ionic, covalent, and polar mean in order to understand what makes these structural features important.

First, how do you know whether a compound is ionic or covalent? A fairly reliable rule states that ionic compounds are formed when a Group 1A or 2A element combines with a Group 6A or 7A element. (When using this rule, consider hydrogen as a Group 7A element.) Group 3A and 5A elements sometimes form ionic compounds and sometimes do not. Group 4A elements tend to form covalent bonds. Since we're interested in general trends, we tend to use clear-cut cases in our examples. Ionic compounds are formed when the positive and negative ions form compounds. We emphasize recognizing ionic compounds because they are less common, and if the compound isn't ionic, then it's covalent or polar covalent.

Let's assume that you are able to recognize which combinations of elements will not form ionic compounds. You are therefore dealing with covalent bonding. Putting together covalent molecules is much like working jigsaw puzzles. You move pieces around until everything fits. Once again, you may start with electron dot structures for the elements involved or with a valence bond parts list. If you use electron dot symbols, here are some rules of thumb to follow:

   a. Any single (unpaired) electron should be paired with a single electron on another atom.
   b. The objective is to give each atom an octet of electrons (except hydrogen, which is satisfied with a duet).
   c. This is a hint more than a rule: Elements that can form only one bond (hydrogen and the Group 7A elements) should be fitted into the structure last.

Here are three examples to supplement those given in the chapter.

Example 1. Write the electron dot and valence bond structures for H_2S.

Step 1: Write down the Lewis structures of the parts $\cdot \ddot{S} :$ $H \cdot$ $H \cdot$

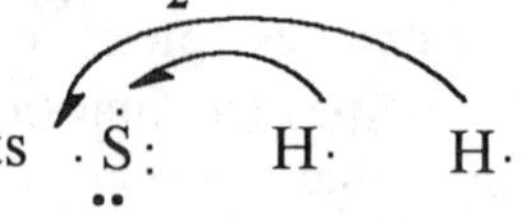

Step 2: Note that a single electron on S and a single electron on H can
join to form a single, covalent bond.
$$H : \ddot{\underset{\cdot\cdot}{S}} :$$
with H above

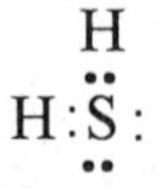

Note, in the valence bond structure of this molecule, the shared
pair of electrons are replaced with a line (dash) between the ato

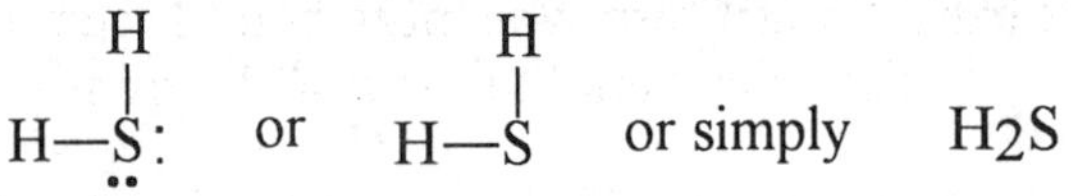

$$H—\underset{\cdot\cdot}{\overset{H}{S}} : \quad \text{or} \quad H—\overset{H}{S} \quad \text{or simply} \quad H_2S$$

Voila !!!   (unshared electrons not shown)

Example 2. Construct the CH_4S molecule.

Step 1: $\cdot \dot{C} \cdot$ $H \cdot$ $H \cdot$ $H \cdot$ $H \cdot$ $\cdot \ddot{S} \cdot$

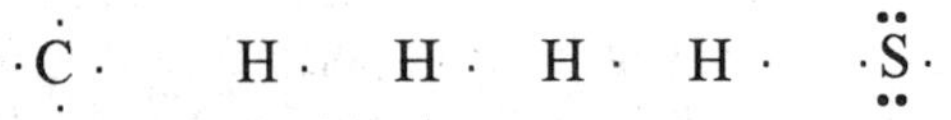

Step 2: Combine C and S

$\cdot \dot{C} \cdot \ddot{S} \cdot$

4 bonds still
needed

$\cdot \dot{C} \cdot \ddot{S} \cdot$

$H \cdot$ $H \cdot$ $H \cdot$ $H \cdot$

4 hydrogens also
need bonds

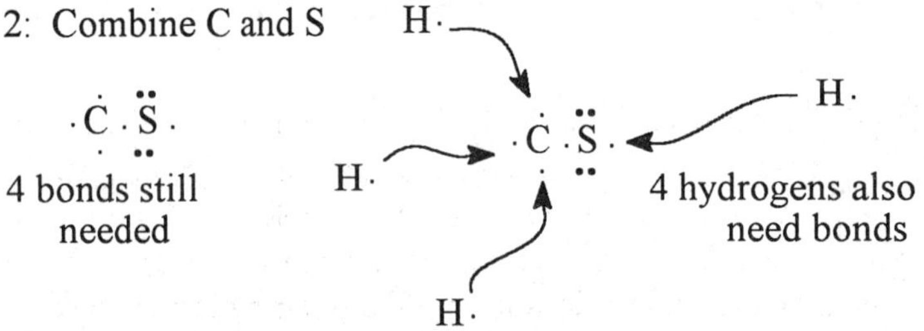

Step 3: Add hydrogens

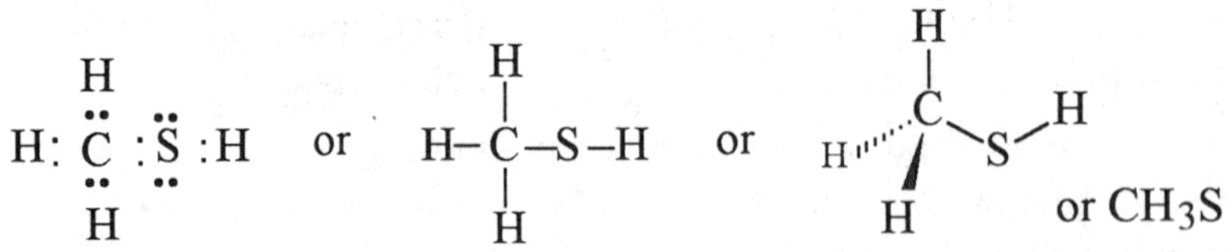

$$H : \underset{\cdot\cdot}{\overset{\cdot\cdot}{C}} : \underset{\cdot\cdot}{\overset{\cdot\cdot}{S}} : H \quad \text{or} \quad H—\underset{H}{\overset{H}{C}}—S—H \quad \text{or} \quad \text{(3D structure)} \quad \text{or } CH_3S$$

(with H's on C and H on S)

Example 3. Construct the N_2H_2 molecule.

Step 1: $\cdot \overset{\cdot\cdot}{\underset{\cdot}{N}} \cdot$ $\cdot \overset{\cdot\cdot}{\underset{\cdot}{N}} \cdot$ H·   H·

Step 2:   pair the 2 N

$\cdot \overset{\cdot\cdot}{\underset{\cdot}{N}} : \overset{\cdot\cdot}{\underset{\cdot}{N}} \cdot$ H·   H·

4 bonds still   only 2 hydrogens
needed   that need bond

Step 3: give one hydrogen to each N

H : $\overset{\cdot\cdot}{N}$: $\overset{\cdot\cdot}{N}$: H

Step 4: each N must form one more bond (octet rule),
so they share another pair of electrons

H : $\overset{\cdot\cdot}{N}$ :: $\overset{\cdot\cdot}{N}$: H   or   H—N=N—H

Polarity is the last of the general concepts dealing with chemical bonding that was introduced in this chapter. One speaks of polar bonds or polarity only for covalently bonded molecules, and even then, not for all covalently bonded molecules. A covalent bond is polar only if it forms between elements of unequal electronegativity. A molecule is polar only if it contains polar dipoles that do not cancel one another out.

The bond in Br—Br is not polar because the bonding atoms are of identical electronegativity; the bond in Br—F is polar because the two elements are of different electronegativities. Water is a polar molecule, but carbon dioxide is not, despite the fact that both molecules have bonds joining atoms of very different electronegativity. Water is "bent," but carbon dioxide is "linear." The two sets of unequally shared electrons (represented by the arrows) in water yield a polar molecule, in carbon dioxide they cancel each other out so even though carbon dioxide has polar bonds it is a nonpolar molecule.

net dipole $\delta^+ \longrightarrow \delta^-$ $H—O$ $H \delta^+$ vs. $\delta^- \longleftarrow \delta^+ \longrightarrow \delta^-$ $O=C=O$ dipoles cancel

We end our discussion with the importance of molecular shapes because the shape of a molecule helps determine whether the molecule is polar or nonpolar, and that influences its solubility and interaction properties. You will learn how to predict shapes of molecules in the next unit (Special Topic B).

Many of the problems at the end of the chapter are like grade school spelling drills or vocabulary tests. They simply ask you to practice over and over drawing ions or putting together molecules or naming compounds. This practice should establish firmly the rules governing chemical structure in your mind. In case it hasn't, here is some additional help.

Problems

1. You should be able to draw electron dot symbols for any element in the A groups (IA, IIA, etc.). To do this write the symbol for the element and surround it with dots representing the valence (outermost) electrons. The number of valence electrons is given by the group number. For practice, draw electron dot structures for atoms of these elements:

    a. nitrogen   d. calcium   g. potassium   i. sulfur
    b. carbon   e. silicon   h. fluorine   j. aluminum
    c. argon   f. hydrogen

2. Electron dot structures for ions are drawn either by adding electron dots to complete the octet or by removing electron dots to empty the outermost level. Electrons are added to elements with 5 or more valence electrons; they are subtracted from elements with 3 or fewer valence electrons. For the following elements, how many electron dots would you add to or remove from the electron dot symbols of the atoms to form the ions?

    a. magnesium   c. oxygen   e. potassium   g. sulfur
    b. chlorine   d. calcium   f. fluorine   h. aluminum

3. The charge is written to the upper right of the electron dot symbol for an ion. The charge is equal to the number of electrons added to or removed from the neutral atom to form the ion. The charge is positive if electrons are removed and negative if electrons are added. Write the proper ionic form for the stable ions that are formed from the eight elements listed in problem 2.

4. Compounds are formed from the following sets of elements. Indicate whether the compound would be ionic or covalent. (Note that you're not being asked to draw the compounds, just to evaluate their tendency to form ionic or covalent bonds.)

    a. Ba and O   e. Na and H   h. F and Ca
    b. C and S   f. C and H   i. Li and O
    c. N and O   g. Ca and Cl   j. Rb and F
    d. Br and Cl

5. Write structural formulas (electron dot and valence bond) for the following compounds:
    a. PCl_3 b. SiH_4 c. CO_2 d. H_2CO e. HNCS

SELF-TEST (Refer to the periodic table.)

1. The charge on an ion formed from sulfur would be:
    a. S^+ b. S^{2+} c. S^{3+} d. S^- e. S^{2-} f. S^{3-}

2. The aluminum ion is:
    a. Al^+ b. Al^{2+} c. Al^{3+} d. Al^{4+} e. Al^{2-} f. Al^{4-}

3. The ion formed from iodine is:
    a. I^+ b. I^{2+} c. I^{6+} d. I^{7+} e. I^- f. I^{7-}

4. The name of the ion CN^- is:
    a. acetate   b. ammonium   c. carbonate   d. cyanide   e. nitrate

5. How many protons are there in the Mg^{2+} ion?
    a. 2   b. 6   c. 10   d. 12   e. 20   f. 40

6. The electron dot symbol for lithium is:
    a. Li·   b. ·Li·   c. ·Li·   d. ·Li·   e. ·Li·   f. :Li: g. :Li: h. :Li:

7. The electron dot symbol for a carbon atom is:
    a. $C\cdot$ b. $\cdot C\cdot$ c. $\cdot\,\overset{\cdot}{C}\cdot$ d. $\cdot\overset{\cdot}{C}\cdot$ e. $:C\cdot$ f. $:\overset{\cdot}{C}\cdot$ g. $:\overset{\cdot\cdot}{C}\cdot$ h. $:\overset{\cdot\cdot}{\underset{\cdot\cdot}{C}}:$

8. Which is the best formula for magnesium oxide?
    a. MgO b. MgO_2 c. Mg_2O d. Mg_2O_2

9. Which is the correct formula for a compound of boron and sulfur?
    a. BS b. BS_2 c. B_2S d. BS_3 e. B_3S f. B_2S_3

10. Which is the correct formula for a compound of aluminum and oxygen?
    a. AlO b. Al_3O c. AlO_3 d. Al_2O_3

11. Ferrous chloride is:
    a. $FeCl$ b. $FeCl_2$ c. $FeCl_3$ d. Fe_2Cl e. Fe_3Cl f. Fe_2Cl_3

12. Copper(I) sulfide is:
    a. CuS b. Cu_2S c. CuS_2 d. Cu_2S_2 e. $Cu(SO_4)_2$

13. Calcium sulfate is the name of:
    a. $CaSO_4$ b. Ca_2SO_4 c. $Ca(SN)_2$ d. Ca_2NO_3 e. $Ca(SO_3)_2$

14. Which is the correct formula for aluminum sulfate?
    a. $AlSO_4$ b. Al_2SO_4 c. $Al_2(SO_4)_3$ d. Al_2SO_3 e. $Al(SO_3)_2$

15. Name this compound: $Ca(NO_2)_2$
    a. calcium nitrite   b. copper nitrate   c. calcium nitrate   d. nitrous calcite

16. What is the correct formula for dinitrogen tetraoxide?
    a. NO_2 b. N_2O c. NO d. N_2O_3 e. N_2O_4

17. Which is the most electronegative element among the following?
    a. O   b. S   c. Se   d. Te

18. Which element is most electronegative?
    a. C   b. N   c. O   d. F

19. Which is the most likely structure for a compound incorporating Be and F?
    a. Be^+F^- b. $Be^{2+}F^{2-}$ c. $Be^{2+}2F^-$ d. $2\,Be^+F^{2-}$ e. $Be^{2+}F^-$

20. Which would be expected to have ionic bonding?
    a. CO_2 b. NCl_3 c. $SiCl_4$ d. $NaBr$

21. The compound formed from these elements would <u>not</u> be ionic:
    a. calcium and fluorine   b. sodium and sulfur
    c. nitrogen and oxygen   d. lithium and bromine

22. Which is the best description of the bonding in ClBr?
    a. Cl—Br   b. $\underset{\delta^+}{Cl}$—$\underset{\delta^-}{Br}$ c. $\underset{\delta^-}{Cl}$—$\underset{\delta^+}{Br}$ d. Cl^+Br^- e. Cl^-Br^+

23. Which compound contains a polar covalent bond?
    a. NaF b. HF c. F_2

24. Which of the following bonds would be most polar?
    a. C—C   b. C—N   c. C—O   d. C—F   e. C—H

25. Which of the following would have the most polar bond?
    a. F—Cl   b. Cl—Cl   c. I—Br   d. F—I

26. The valence bond formula of hydrogen sulfide is:
    a. H_2S b. H—S—H   c. $2H^+S^{2-}$

27. Based on bonding rules, which is <u>not</u> a reasonable formula?
    a. N_2 b. O_2 c. F_2 d. Ne_2

28. Which molecule is polar?
    a. Cl — Be — Cl   b. $\underset{F}{\overset{F\quad F}{\diagdown\!\!B\!\!\diagup}}$ c. $\overset{\diagup F}{\underset{\diagdown F}{O}}$ d. F — F

29. The CF_4 molecule is:
      a. linear   b. bent   c. tetrahedral   d. pyramidal

30. The NH_3 molecule is :
      a. linear   b. bent   c. tetrahedral   d. pyramidal

31. A triple bond involves the sharing of a total of how many electrons?
      a. 1   b. 2   c. 3   d. 4   e. 5   f. 6   g. 7   h. 8

32. The correct electron dot formula for carbon dioxide is:
      a. :C̈:Ö:C̈:   b. :Ö:Ö:C̈:   c. :Ö::C::Ö: d. :Ö:C:Ö:

33. Which is the most reasonable valence bond formula for C_2F_2?
      a. F—C—C—F b. C—F—F—C   c. F=C—C=F d. F=C=C=F e. F—C≡C—F

34. The correct electron dot formula for HNO is:
      a. H:N::Ö: b. :H:N::Ö: c. H:Ö:N: d. :H:Ö:N:

35. A reasonable structure for C_2H_3OCl is:

           H   H   H O   H   O   Cl

a. H—C=O—C—Cl   b. H—C—C—Cl c. H—C—Cl—C—H d. H—C≡C—O—H

                                            H   H

ANSWERS

Problems

1. a. :N̈·   b. ·C̈·   c. :Ar̈:   d. Ca: e. ·S̈i·   f. H·   g. K·   h. :F̈:   i. ·S̈:   j. ·Al·

2.   a. remove two   c. add two   e. remove one   g. add two
        b. add one   d. remove two f. add one   h. remove three

3.   a. Mg^{2+} c. O^{2-} e. K^+ g. S^{2-}
        b. Cl^- d. Ca^{2+} f. F^- h. Al^{3+}

4. Ionic: a, e, g, h, i, j   Covalent: b, c, d, f

5. a. :C̈l:P̈:C̈l: b.   H:S̈i:H   c. :Ö::C::Ö: d. H:C::Ö: e. H:N̈::C::S̈:
     :C̈l: H   H

                                 H
Cl—P—Cl   H—Si—H   O=C=O   H—C=O   H—N=C=S
   Cl   H   H

Self-Test

1.	e	6.	a	11.	b	16.	e	21.	c	26.	b	31.	f
2.	c	7.	d	12.	b	17.	a	22.	c	27.	d	32.	c
3.	e	8.	a	13.	a	18.	d	23.	b	28.	c	33.	e
4.	d	9.	f	14.	c	19.	c	24	d	29.	c	34.	a
5.	d	10.	d	15.	a	20.	d	25.	d	30.	d	35.	b

Special Topic B: Molecular Shapes and Properties

KEY WORDS

VSEPR	*linear*	*triangular*	*trigonal*	*tetrahedral*
pyramidal	*bent*	*lone pairs*	*bonded pairs*	

B1. Molecular Shapes

    A. The molecular formula of a compound provides information about its composition.

    B. The structural formula indicates the bonding arrangement of its atoms.

                Molecular Formula   ***Structural Formula***

$$H_2O \quad | \quad C_2H_6 \quad || \quad H-O_{\backslash H} \quad | \quad H-\overset{\overset{\displaystyle H}{|}}{C}-\overset{\overset{\displaystyle H}{|}}{\underset{\underset{\displaystyle H}{|}}{C}}-H$$

    C. Valence Shell Electron Pair Repulsion (***VSEPR***) theory is often used to predict the arrangement of atoms about a central atom. The theory postulates that groups of electrons surrounding a central atom will repel one another and arrange to move as far apart as possible.

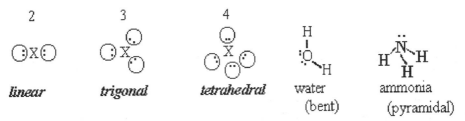

        linear   *trigonal*   *tetrahedral*   water   ammonia
                                                      (bent)   (pyramidal)

       Water is surrounded by four pairs of electrons (2 ***bonded pairs*** + 2 ***lone pairs***). These four pairs of electrons will point toward the corners of a tetrahedron, but the water molecule will be ***bent*** shaped since only two hydrogens occupy two of the four positions. Similarly ammonia (NH_3) has four pairs of electrons (three bonded pairs and one lone pair) tetrahedrally surrounding the central N, but its shape is referred to as ***pyramidal***. Shape describes the placement of atoms, not electron pairs.

    D. If a molecule consists of a central atom surrounded by 2, 3, or 4 other atoms or combination of atoms and lone pairs, it is possible to predict its shape from the VSEPR rules (above).

    E. Some examples

#Bonded Atoms	# Lone Pairs	Example	Shape (See below)
2	0	CO_2	linear
3	0	BF_3	trigonal
4	0	CH_4	tetrahedral
3	1	NH_3	pyramidal
2	2	H_2O	bent ($\sim 109°$)
2	1	O_3	bent ($120°$)

$$O=C=O \qquad \overset{\displaystyle F}{\underset{\displaystyle F}{B}}-F \qquad \overset{\displaystyle H}{\underset{\underset{\displaystyle H}{}}{C}}\cdots H \qquad H-\overset{\displaystyle N}{\underset{\underset{\displaystyle H}{}}{}}\cdots H \qquad H-O_{\backslash H} \qquad O=O_{\backslash O}$$

B2. Polar and Nonpolar Molecules
  A. Polar bonds may or may not result in a polar molecule, depending on its shape.
  B. Linear molecules with polar bonds are nonpolar: O=C=O

$$O=S_{\diagdown O}$$

  Bent molecules with polar bonds are polar.

SELF-TEST (Refer to the periodic table.)

1. The molecule H_2 is _____ in shape.
         a. linear   b. bent   c. tetrahedral   d. trigonal   e. pyramidal
2. The molecule H_2S is _____ in shape.
         a. linear   b. bent   c. tetrahedral   d. trigonal   e. pyramidal
3. The molecule CO_2 (two double bonds) is _____ in shape.
         a. linear   b. bent   c. tetrahedral   d. trigonal   e. pyramidal
4. The molecule NH_3 is _____ in shape.
         a. linear   b. bent   c. tetrahedral   d. trigonal   e. pyramidal
5. The molecule SO_2 is _____ in shape.
         a. linear   b. bent   c. tetrahedral   d. trigonal   e. pyramidal
6. The nitrate ion (NO_3^-) is _____ in shape.
         a. linear   b. bent   c. tetrahedral   d. trigonal   e. pyramidal
7. The CF_4 molecule is _____ in shape:
         a. linear   b. bent   c. tetrahedral   d. trigonal   e. pyramidal
8. H_2S is a _____ molecule.
         a. polar   b. nonpolar
9. CO_2 (two double bonds) is a _____ molecule.
         a. polar   b. nonpolar
10. NH_3 is a _____molecule.
         a. polar   b. nonpolar
11. CF_4 is a _____ molecule:
         a. polar   b. nonpolar
12. Fluorine (F_2) is a _____ molecule.
         a. polar   b. nonpolar

ANSWERS

| 1. a | 3. a | 5. b | 7. c | 9. b | 11. b |
| 2. b | 4. e | 6. d | 8. a | 10. a | 12. b |

CHAPTER 5:   CHEMICAL REACTIONS

KEY WORDS

reactions	*balanced equation*	*activated complex*	*exothermic*	*law of combining*
equations	*coefficients*	*energy of activation*	*endothermic*	*volumes*
reactants	*Avogadro's number*	*reversible reaction*	*reaction rate*	*orientations*
products	*formula weight*	*reaction mechanism*	*LeChatelier's*	*enzymes*
catalyst	*mole*	*dynamic equilibrium*	*principle*	*rate law*
molar mass	*stoichiometric*	*collisions*	*atomic weight*	*element*
Avogradro's				
hypothesis				

SUMMARY

5.1 Balancing Chemical Equations

    A. A chemical *equation* is shorthand notation for describing chemical *reactions* as the *reactants* A (shown on the left) are converted to *products* P (shown on the right).   A → P.

    B. Chemical equations involve electronic rearrangements as chemical bonds are broken and formed. The nuclei of all atoms remain unchanged during chemical reactions.

    C. Because atoms are conserved in chemical reactions, the same number of each kind of atom must appear on each side of a *balanced* chemical *equation*. **Hint**: If an element occurs in just one compound on each side of the equation, try balancing that element first (i.e. H). Balance all elements last (i.e. O_2).

$$2 H_2 + O_2 \rightarrow 2 H_2O$$

5.2 Volume Relationships in Chemical Equations

    A. In 1809, Gay-Lussac determined the "*Law of Combining Volumes*" that the volumes of gaseous reactants and products were always in a small whole number ratio.

        2 vol. hydrogen + 1 vol. oxygen   →   2 vol. water
        3 vol. hydrogen + 1 vol. nitrogen   →   2 vol. ammonia

    B. *Avogadro* explained the law of combining volumes on the basis of a *hypothesis* that equal volumes of all gases (at the same temperature and pressure) contain the same number of molecules.   The reactions above can be re-expressed as a chemical equation in which chemical formulas represent the substances involved and *stoichiometric coefficients* reflect the combining volumes.

$$2 H_2 + (1) O_2 \rightarrow 2 H_2O$$
$$3 H_2 + (1) N_2 \rightarrow 2 NH_3$$

5.3 Avogadro's Number: **6.02×10^{23}**

    A. Chemists cannot weigh individual atoms. Dalton proposed a table of relative atomic weights based on hydrogen being assigned a relative mass of 1. Thus, carbon is 12, oxygen is 16, and so forth.

    B. The *atomic weight* of any element, expressed in grams, contains 6.02×10^{23} atoms. The number 6.02×10^{23} is called *Avogadro's number*. *(Avogadro's number is so big that a computer that can count to 10 million in 1 sec would still need 2 billion years to count up to 6.02×10^{23}!!!)*

5.4 Molecular Weights and Formula Weights

    A. Each *element* has a characteristic *atomic weight*.

    B. The *formula weight* of a substance is the sum of the atomic weights of all the atoms in the formula.

    C. The *molecular weight* is the sum of the weights of all the atoms represented in a molecular formula.

5.5 Chemical Arithmetic and the Mole

Chapter 5 - Chemical Reactions

    A. Chemists count atoms and molecules by the *mole*, not by the dozen. A *mole* of a substance (atoms, molecules, ions) contains 6.02×10^{23} units of that substance.

    B. A *molar mass* of a substance equals the mass of one mole of that substance. The molar mass is numerically equal to the formula weight, but expressed as g/mol.

    C. The mole/mass relationships can be used as conversion factors between gram amounts and mole amounts (1 mol C = 12 g C or 12g C/ mol C).

5.6 Mole and Mass Relationships in Chemical Equations

    A. Atoms react in small whole number ratios. In the laboratory we cannot count numbers of atoms or molecules, instead we measure out an amount (grams) of a substance.

    B. The *stoichiometric coefficients* of a chemical equation directly express the atom (or mole) ratios of reactants and products.

    C. Combining formula weight information with these stoichiometric coefficients means that a chemical equation also indirectly expresses the mass ratios of reactants and products.

    D. The mole method illustrates the steps in going from mole ratios to mass ratios.

        1. Balance the equation.

        2. Determine the molar masses (molecular weights) of interest.

        3. Convert from grams to number of moles of reactant using the molar mass.

        4. Use the stoichiometric coefficients of the balanced chemical equation to convert from the mole amount of the given substance (reactant) to the mole amount of the substance of interest (product).

        5. Finally, use the molar mass of the substance of interest to convert from moles to grams of the desired substance.

$$\text{consider} \quad a\,A \rightarrow b\,B$$

$$\mathbf{g\ of\ A} \quad \times \quad \left[\frac{1\ \text{mole A}}{\text{g A}}\right] \quad \times \quad \left\{\frac{b\ \text{moles B}}{a\ \text{moles A}}\right\} \quad \times \quad \left[\frac{\text{g B}}{1\ \text{mole B}}\right] \quad (\rightarrow \mathbf{g\ B})$$

5.7 Structure, Stability, and Spontaneity

    A. Energy changes also take place during chemical reactions. *Exothermic* reactions result in the release of heat; *endothermic* reactions require energy to be supplied to convert reactants to products.

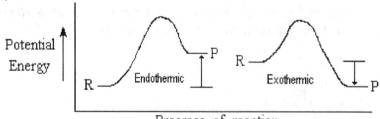

    B. In exothermic reactions, the electronic arrangement of the products represents a more stable (lower potential energy) arrangement than the original arrangement in the reactants. Therefore, exothermic reactions are energetically favorable, or "down hill."

    C. The conversion of reactants to products always proceeds through an intermediate activated complex. Because a reaction is energetically favorable does not mean that it is instantaneous. It may or may not proceed rapidly, depending on the *energy of activation* needed to form the activated complex. The energy of activation is the energy needed to get to the "top of the energy hill" (See 5.11).

5.8 Reversible Reactions
- A. Many reactions involve the interconversion of reactants and products, that is, the products can react to reform the original reactants. Such reactions are said to be *reversible* reactions.
- B. Opposing reactions are common in nature. Respiring cells "burn" glucose to CO_2 and H_2O with the release of energy (exothermic) while other cells can carry out the endothermic process of photosynthesis, using the energy of sunlight to convert CO_2 and H_2O into glucose.
- C. For reversible reactions, the energy barrier may be approached from either side.

5.9 Reaction Rates: Collisions, Orientation, and Energy
- A. The *reaction rate* refers to how rapidly product is produced per given unit of time, $\Delta[P]$/sec.
- B. In order for reactant molecules to produce a product, the reactant species must come together via molecular *collisions* with the proper *orientation* and with sufficient *energy* to overcome the *energy of activation* barriers.
- C. "Proper orientation" simply means that the reactive surfaces on the reactant molecules must approach one another with proper juxtaposition to permit required bonding rearrangements to take place.

5.10 Reaction Rates: The Effect of Temperature
- A. Increasing the temperature of a reaction by 10 ^{O}C often doubles the rate of the reaction.   Changes in temperature affect rates of chemical reactions in two ways:
    1. At higher temperatures, the molecules move more rapidly, so they collide more frequently. This is a minor effect.
    2. More importantly, a small increase in temperature, which might bring about only a 2% increase in average molecular velocity, can cause a doubling of the number of molecules with energy above the threshold needed to overcome the *energy of activation* for the reaction.
- B. It is noteworthy that chemical reactions in our bodies take place at essentially constant temperature, 37 ^{O}C, yet occur very rapidly due to the presence of enzymes, which are biocatalysts. The activity of these enzymes can be "killed" by temperatures that are either too high or too low.

5.11 Reaction Rates: Catalysis
- A. A *catalyst* is a substance that increases the rate of a chemical reaction without itself being changed.
- B. Most catalysts act by providing an alternate pathway, or different *reaction mechanism*, for the reaction to occur, one that has a lower activation energy requirement.

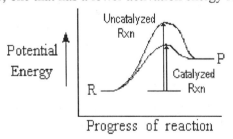

- C. Biological catalysts, called *enzymes*, mediate nearly all reactions that take place in living systems.

5.12 Reaction Rates: The Effect of Concentration
- A. The concentration of reactants affects the *rate* of chemical reactions by increasing the number of collisions that will occur.
- B. The dependence of reaction rate on the concentration of reactants must be determined experimentally and is expressed as a *rate law*.

C. Information about rates of chemical reactions can be used to postulate a *mechanism* for the chemical reaction, i.e., a step-by-step description of the chemical changes that occur in the overall process.

5.13 Equilibrium in Chemical Reactions
   A. A condition of *dynamic equilibrium* is established for a reversible reaction when the rate of the forward reaction equals the rate of the reverse reaction.
   B. Equilibrium is established for reversible reactions in isolated systems.
   C. When a system at equilibrium is subjected to a "stress" (such as the addition of reactants or products, or a change in temperature or pressure), the system rearranges in such a way as to minimize that stress. This is referred to as *Le Chatelier's principle* (1884).

DISCUSSION

The subject of this chapter is the chemical equation and the information it contains. You probably never realized how much information is contained in a chemical equation. Much of the chapter is devoted to a discussion of the concepts and terminology needed to extract every last bit of data from an equation. Therefore, one of the first things you should do is make sure you understand the terms listed under the KEY WORDS section.

Molar mass, Formula weight, Mole, and Avogadro's number are interrelated terms. The formula weight of a compound expressed in grams (the gram formula weight) is a mole of the compound; a mole of the compound contains Avogadro's number of the compound units, which is equal to 6.02×10^{23} units.

1 gram formula weight = 1 mole = Avogadro's number = 6.02×10^{23} units

You can treat this relationship as a multiple conversion factor. If you calculate the formula weight of a compound and remember the above relationships, then you can interconvert units expressed in grams to moles or to molecules and vice versa.

Example. Interconversions involving methane, CH_4.

Formula weight: atomic weight of C = 12;   1 x 12 = 12
                    atomic weight of H = 1;   4 x 1   = _4_
                                          formula weight = 16

Once we have the gram formula weight or molar mass, we also know that there are:
   16 g of CH_4/1 mole of CH_4; Avogadro's number of CH_4 molecules
                    or 6.02×10^{23} CH_4 molecules/16 g of CH_4
   How many moles are in 4 g of CH_4? 4 g x [1 mole] = 0.25 mole
                                             16 g
   How many grams are in 4 moles of CH_4? 4 moles x [16 g] = 64 g
                                                      1 mole
   How many molecules are in 4 g of CH_4? 4 g x [6.02×10^{23} molecules] = 1.5×10^{23} molecules
                                                   16 g
   How many molec. are in 4 moles of CH_4? 4 mol x [6.02×10^{23} molec] = 24×10^{23} molecules
                                                      1 mole

Let's suppose you are now totally at ease with moles and formula weights and such. That brings us to equations. **The first thing you should check in an equation is whether or not it is balanced.** (We'll supply the correct reactants and products.) If the equation isn't balanced, the quantitative information derived from it may be incorrect. As we indicated in the chapter, you won't be balancing extremely complex equations, but you should be able to handle those shown at the end of the chapter. Once you have a balanced equation, the coefficients in that equation give you the following information directly:

a. The combining ratio of molecules (or other formula units like ion pairs)
b. The combining volume ratios of gaseous reactants and products, assuming temperature and pressure are maintained constant
c. The combining ratio of moles of molecules (or other formula units)

The coefficients **do not** give you directly the combining weight ratios. Thus, from the equation:

$$CH_4 + 2\,O_2 \rightarrow CO_2 + 2\,H_2O \quad \text{(all gases)} \quad \text{you know:}$$

a. 1 molecule of methane (CH_4) reacts with 2 molecules of oxygen (O_2) to give 1 molecule of carbon dioxide (CO_2) and 2 molecules of water (H_2O).
b. 1 volume of methane gas reacts with 2 volumes of oxygen gas to produce 1 volume of carbon dioxide gas and 2 volumes of water vapor.
c. 1 mole of methane reacts with 2 moles of oxygen to give 1 mole of carbon dioxide and 2 moles of water.

The equation does **not** say that 1 gram of methane reacts with 2 grams of oxygen to produce 1 gram of carbon dioxide and 2 grams of water. If you want to find how many grams of oxygen react with 1 gram of methane, you must first convert grams to moles and only then use the equation to determine the combining ratio. After using the equation, you'll have the answer in moles and must convert to grams.

The examples in the chapter demonstrate the use of equations to obtain information about combining ratios. Review those examples, then the problems at the end of the chapter. For more practice, try problems 5 and 6 below.

Problems

1. Calculate the formula weights. We're using relatively complicated formulas just to make sure you understand when a subscript applies to a particular atom in the formula and when it applies to a polyatomic ionic group of atoms. You'll require a periodic table or a list of atomic weights.
   a. $(NH_4)_2SO_4$ c. $Be(NO_3)_2$ e. $Al_2(C_2O_4)_3$ g. $SrSO_4$
   b. $Ca(NO_3)_2$ d. $(NH_4)_2C_2O_4$ f. $Ca(C_2H_3O_2)_2$

2. The following questions refer to the compound $C_5H_8O_2$.
   a. How many moles of $C_5H_8O_2$ are in 100 g? in 200 g? in 25 g? in 3.687 g?
   b. How many grams of $C_5H_8O_2$ are in 1 mole? in 8 moles? in 0.8 mole? in 0.01 mole?
   c. How many molecules of $C_5H_8O_2$ are in 1 mole of the compound? in 0.5 mole? in 3 moles? in 100 g? in 50 g? in 300 g?
   d. How many carbon atoms are in one $C_5H_8O_2$ molecule? in one mole of $C_5H_8O_2$? in 100 g of $C_5H_8O_2$?
   e. How many hydrogen atoms are in one $C_5H_8O_2$ molecule? in one mole of $C_5H_8O_2$? in 100 g of $C_5H_8O_2$?

3. For additional practice interconverting these units, answer these questions for the compound $PbCrO_4$. A calculator would be useful because these numbers will not be as easy.
   a. How many moles of $PbCrO_4$ are in 100 g? in 200 g? in 25 g? in 3.687 g?
   b. How many grams of $PbCrO_4$ are in 1 mole? in 8 moles? in 0.8 mole? in 0.01 mole?
   c. How many molecules of $PbCrO_4$ are in 1 mole of the compound? in 0.5 mole? in 3 moles? in 100 g? in 50 g? in 300 g?
   d. How many oxygen atoms are in one $PbCrO_4$ molecular unit? in one mole of $PbCrO_4$? in 100 g of $PbCrO_4$?

4. Here are some additional equations to balance.

    a. Zn $+$ KOH $\rightarrow$ K_2ZnO_2 $+$ H_2

    b. HF $+$ Si $\rightarrow$ SiF_4 $+$ H_2

    c. B_2O_3 $+$ H_2O $\rightarrow$ $H_6B_4O_9$

    d. $SiCl_4$ $+$ H_2O $\rightarrow$ SiO_2 $+$ HCl

    e. SnO_2 $+$ C $\rightarrow$ Sn $+$ CO

    f. Fe_2O_3 $+$ C $\rightarrow$ FeO $+$ CO_2

    g. Fe_3O_4 $+$ C $\rightarrow$ Fe $+$ CO

    h. $Fe(OH)_3$ $+$ H_2S $\rightarrow$ Fe_2S_3 $+$ H_2O

    i. Ca_3P_2 $+$ H_2O $\rightarrow$ PH_3 $+$ $Ca(OH)_2$

    j. Bi_2O_3 $+$ C $\rightarrow$ Bi $+$ CO

5. Refer to the equation: $CS_2 + 2\ CaO \rightarrow CO_2 + 2\ CaS$.

    a. How many moles of CO_2 are obtained from the reaction of 2 moles of CS_2?
        from the reaction of 2 moles of CaO?

    b. How many moles of CaO are consumed if 0.3 mole of CS_2 react?
        if 0.3 mole of CaS are produced?

    c. How many grams of CaS are obtained if 152 g of CS_2 are consumed in the reaction?
        if 7.6 g of CS_2 are consumed?
        if 22 g of CO_2 are produced?
        if 44 g of CO_2 are produced?

    d. How many grams of CaO are required to react completely with 38g of CS_2?
        with 152 g of CS_2?   to produce 36 g of CaS?

6. Refer to the equation: $C_3H_8 + 5\ O_2 \rightarrow 3\ CO_2 + 4\ H_2O + 500$ kcal
        (All compounds are gases; temperature and pressure are held constant.)

    a. If 5 L of C_3H_8 react, what volume of CO_2 will be produced?
        what volume of O_2 will react?

    b. Answer the same questions for the reaction of 5 mL of C_3H_8.
        for the reaction of 5 m^3 of C_3H_8.

    c. If 22 g of C_3H_8 are burned, how many grams of CO_2 are produced?
        How many grams of O_2 are consumed? How many kilocalories of heat are produced?

    The last question in problem 6 brings energy into the discussion of chemical reactions. That question implies correctly that you treat energy like any other product or reactant, using the balanced equation to establish the ratio of energy produced (or consumed) to moles of chemical species involved. And in case you're wondering about this point, note that you are not able to supply the energy portion of an equation. The amount of energy required for the balanced equation would simply have to be given in a problem such as that in 6 above.

    Terms and concepts associated with the energy changes accompanying chemical reactions were reviewed at the end of the chapter. Your understanding of this terminology, plus the concepts of equilibria, Le Chatelier's principle, and other material treated in this chapter are reviewed in the **SELF-TEST** below.

SELF-TEST

1. How many moles are there in 120 g of glucose ($C_6H_{12}O_6$)?

    a. 1.0   b. 0.5   c. 0.67   d. 1.2   e. 1.5

2. How much does Avogadro's number of sulfur atoms weigh?

    a. 16 amu   b. 32 amu   c. 16 g   d. 32 g   e. 6.02×10^{23} g

3. How many atoms are there in 2 moles of helium?
      a. 2×10^{23} b. 6.02×10^{23} c. 12.04×10^{23} d. 6.02×10^{46}

4. One-half mole of CO_2 weighs:
      a. 8 g   b. 12 g   c. 22 g   d. 32 g   e. 48 g   f. 64 g

5. Avogadro's number of hydrogen molecules (H_2) weighs:
      a. 1 g   b. 2 g   c. 3 g   d. 4 g   e. 6.02×10^{23} g

6. How many molecules of water are in 9 g of H_2O?
      a. 23×10^{23} b. 6×10^{23} c. 2×10^{23} d. 3×10^{23} e. 18×10^{23}

7. How many hydrogen atoms are present in 0.5 mole of H_2O?
      a. Avogadro's number   b. 0.5 x Avogadro's number   c. 2 x Avogadro's number

8. What is the molar mass of CO_2?
      a. 22   b. 16   c. 12   d. 44   e. 60

9. Avogadro's number is not:
      a. the number of atoms in one mole of He
      b. the number of molecules in one mole of H_2
      c. the number of atoms in one mole of Br_2

10. If one mole of A weighs 40 g and one mole of B weighs 20 g, then:
      a. T F each A atom weighs twice as much as each B atom
      b. T F 40 g of A contains twice as many atoms as 20 g of B
      c. T F 1 mole of A weighs as much as two moles of B

11. Consider the following reaction diagram. Identify the letter corresponding to the activation energy for the reverse reaction $(P \rightarrow R)$.

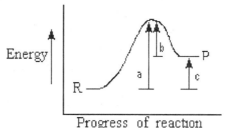

      a. a   b. b   c. c

12. Is the reaction depicted $(R \rightarrow P)$ in Question 11 exothermic or endothermic?
      a. exothermic   b. endothermic

13. According to this energy diagram:

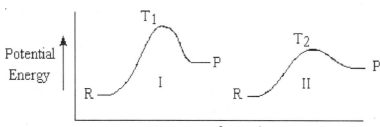

      a. Reaction $(R \rightarrow P)$ is : endothermic or exothermic?
      b. For which reaction was a catalyst used? reaction I or reaction II?
      c. For reaction I, the activation energy is the difference between: T_1 and R, T_1 and P, R and P?
      d. The net energy change for the reaction $(R \rightarrow P)$ is the difference in energy between:
            R and T_2 T_2 and P   R and P?
      e. For the reverse reaction $(P \rightarrow R)$, the net energy change for the reaction results in energy
            being _?_ by the system: (absorbed   released   unused)

45

14. An increase in reaction rate is not expected to accompany an increase in:
    a. concentration of reactants   b. temperature   c. activation energy

15. In general, which reaction would be expected to have the higher activation energy?
    a. strongly exothermic reaction   b. strongly endothermic reaction

16. An increase in temperature generally results in an increase in the rate of a reaction. Which of the following does <u>not</u> account, at least in part, for this phenomenon?
    a. reacting particles collide more frequently.
    b. collisions of faster moving particles supply the activation energy for the reaction.
    c. at higher temperature reactions change from endothermic to exothermic.

17. The decomposition of potassium chlorate, $KClO_3$, produces oxygen and potassium chloride. What is the coefficient for oxygen in a properly balanced equation?

$$KClO_3 \rightarrow KCl + O_2$$

    a. 1   b. 2   c. 3   d. 4   e. 6

18. How many moles of oxygen can be produced from the decomposition of one mole of $KClO_3$?
    a. 1   b. 1.5   c. 2   d. 0.5   e. 3

19. How many grams of oxygen can be produced from the decomposition of 100 g of $KClO_3$?
    a. 39   b. 28   c. 53   d. 84   e. 93

20. What is the <u>sum</u> of the coefficients in a properly balanced equation describing the combustion of propane gas to produce carbon dioxide and water.

$$C_3H_8 + O_2 \rightarrow CO_2 + H_2O$$

    a. 6   b. 8   c. 4   d. 13   e. 15

21. How many moles of oxygen are required to react with 3 moles of propane?
    a. 4   b. 12   c. 5   d. 15   e. 18

22. How many grams of CO_2 are produced from the complete combustion of 100 g of propane?
    a. 100   b. 300   c. 88   d. 132   e. 200

23. A catalyst:
    a. increases the activation energy and increases the rate of a reaction.
    b. decreases the activation energy and decreases the rate of the reaction.
    c. increases the activation energy and decreases the rate of the reaction.
    d. decreases the activation energy and increases the rate of the reaction.

24. Refer to this reaction in which all compounds are gases:

$$2 A + 3 B \rightarrow 3 X + Y + heat$$

    The reaction is originally at equilibrium. Predict the direction of the shift in equilibrium for:

Stress	Shift		
a. addition of compound A	right	left	no change
b. removal of compound X	right	left	no change
c. an increase in pressure	right	left	no change
d. an increase in temperature	right	left	no change
e. addition of a catalyst	right	left	no change

25. Ammonia is produced by the reaction of nitrogen and hydrogen. The production of ammonia would be favored by _____ pressure.

$$N_2 + 3 H_2 \rightarrow 2 NH_3$$

    a. high   b. low   c. neither high nor low

ANSWERS

Problems

1.   a. 132   b. 164   c. 133   d. 124   e. 318   f. 158   g. 184

2.   The formula weight of $C_5H_8O_2 = 100$
      a. 1 mole;   2 moles;   0.25 mole;   0.03687 mole
      b. 100 g;   800 g;   80 g;   1 g
      c. 6.02×10^{23}; 3.01×10^{23}; 18.06×10^{23}; 6.02×10^{23}; 3.01×10^{23}; 18.06×10^{23}
      d. 5;   5 moles or 30×10^{23};   5 moles or 30×10^{23}
      e. 8;   8 moles or 48×10^{23};   8 moles or 48×10^{23}

3.   The formula weight of $PbCrO_4 = 323$
      a. 0.31 moles; 0.62 moles; 0.077 mole; 0.0114 mole
      b. 323 g;   2584 g;   258 g;   3.23 g
      c. 6.02×10^{23}; 3.01×10^{23}; 18.06×10^{23}; 1.86×10^{23}; 0.93×10^{23}; 5.6×10^{23}
      d. 4;   4 mole or 2.4×10^{24};   0.309 moles or 1.86×10^{23}

4.   a. Zn $+$ $2 KOH$ $\rightarrow$ K_2ZnO_2 $+$ H_2
      b. $4 HF$ $+$ Si $\rightarrow$ SiF_4 $+$ $2 H_2$
      c. $2 B_2O_3$ $+$ $3 H_2O$ $\rightarrow$ $H_6B_4O_9$
      d. $SiCl_4$ $+$ $2 H_2O$ $\rightarrow$ SiO_2 $+$ $4 HCl$
      e. SnO_2 $+$ $2 C$ $\rightarrow$ Sn $+$ $2 CO$
      f. Fe_2O_3 $+$ CO $\rightarrow$ $2 FeO$ $+$ CO_2
      g. Fe_3O_4 $+$ $4 C$ $\rightarrow$ $3 Fe$ $+$ $4 CO$
      h. $2 Fe(OH)_3$ $+$ $3 H_2S$ $\rightarrow$ Fe_2S_3 $+$ $6 H_2O$
      i. Ca_3P_2 $+$ $6 H_2O$ $\rightarrow$ $2 PH_3$ $+$ $3 Ca(OH)_2$
      j. Bi_2O_3 $+$ $3 C$ $\rightarrow$ $2 Bi$ $+$ $3 CO$

5.   a. 2 moles of CO_2;   1 mole of CO_2
      b. 0.6 mole of CaO;   0.3 mole of CaO
      c. 288 g of CaS;   14.4 g of CaS;   72 g of CaS;   144 g of CaS
      d. 56 g of CaO;   224 g of CaO;   28 g of CaO

6.   a. 15 L of CO_2;   25 L of O_2
      b. for 5 mL of C_3H_8: 15 mL of CO_2;   25 mL of O_2
          for 5 m^3 of C_3H_8: 15 m^3 of CO_2;   25 m^3 of O_2
      c. 66 g of CO_2;   80 g of O_2;   250 kcal

Self-test

1. c	10. T, F, T	14. c	23. d
2. d	11. b	15. b	24. a. right
3. c	12. b	16. c	b. right
4. c	13. a. endothermic	17. c	c. right
5. b	b. reaction II	18. b	d. left
6. d	c. T_1 and R	19. a	e. no change
7. a	d. R and P	20. d	25. a
8. d	e. released	21. d	
9. c		22. b	

CHAPTER 6: OXIDATION AND REDUCTION

KEY WORDS

oxide

oxidation

oxidation number

redox

reduced

reduction

reducing agent

oxidizing agent

antiseptics

disinfectants

bleaching

photosynthesis

SUMMARY

Chemical reactions can be classified in many ways, in this chapter we study oxidation-reduction reactions. Reduced forms of matter (methane) are high in energy, while oxidized forms of matter (CO_2) are low in energy.

6.1 Oxygen: Abundant and Essential

    A. Oxygen is the most abundant element on this planet.

        1. Air   --   21% oxygen (free)

        2. Water   --   89% oxygen (combined)

        3. Earth's crust   --   45% oxygen (combined)

        4. People   --   60% oxygen (combined)

    B. Oxygen is a gas at room temperature. The normal boiling point of O_2 is -183°C.

    C. Fuels such as natural gas, gasoline, coal, and the foods we eat all need oxygen for combustion to release their stored chemical energy.

6.2 Chemical Properties of Oxygen: Oxidation

    A. Materials react with oxygen to form *oxides* by the process called *oxidation.*

    B. The substances that combine with oxygen are said to be oxidized.

        1. $4 Fe + 3 O_2 \rightarrow 2 Fe_2O_3$ iron III oxide (rust)

        2. $CH_4 + 2 O_2 \rightarrow 2 H_2O + CO_2$ carbon dioxide

6.3 Hydrogen: A Reactive Lightweight Element

    A. Hydrogen represents only 0.9% of the mass of the Earth's crust but 15.1% of the atoms. Hydrogen is the most abundant element (90% of all atoms) in the universe. Free or uncombed hydrogen is very rarely found on Earth, but combined hydrogen is found in water, natural gas, petroleum products, and in all foodstuffs.

    B. Preparation and properties of hydrogen

        1. $Zn + HCl \rightarrow ZnCl_2 + H_2 \uparrow$

           (active metal)   (acid)   (gas)

        2. Hydrogen is a colorless and odorless gas. It is very light but highly flammable.

        3. Absorbed H_2 on metal surfaces, such as Pt or Ni, is unusually reactive and used in surface catalysis.

    C. Chemical Properties of Hydrogen: Reduction

        1. Hydrogen likes to combine with oxygen to form water. It will react with many metal oxides to remove the oxygen and form the free metal.

           $CuO + H_2 \rightarrow Cu + H_2O$

        2. The substance that reacts with hydrogen is said to be *reduced*, and this process is called *reduction*.

6.4 Oxidation and Reduction: Some Definitions.

A. *Oxidation*: Three Definitions

1. Addition of oxygen: $2\ Ba\ +\ O_2\ \rightarrow\ 2\ BaO$

2. Loss of hydrogen: $CH_3CH_2OH\ +\ X\ \rightarrow\ CH_3COH\ +\ XH_2$

3. Loss of electrons: $Fe^{2+}\ \rightarrow\ Fe^{3+}\ +\ e^-$

B. *Oxidation* can also be characterized by an increase in *oxidation state* or *oxidation number*. Oxidation numbers are a form of bookkeeping to help us understand the changes that take place in "formal charge" during oxidation-reduction (*redox*) reactions. Rules for assigning oxidation numbers:

class	oxidation number	Example
1. Free elements	0	$Al^{(0)}$
2. Metal compounds		
Group 1A elements	+1	$Na^{(+1)}Cl$
Group 2A elements	+2	$Ba^{(+2)}Cl_2$
3. Hydrogen		
In most compounds	+1	$H^{(+1)}_2O,\ CH^{(+1)}_4$
Metal hydrides	-1	$NaH^{(-1)}$
4. Oxygen		
In most compounds	-2	$H^{(+1)}_2O^{(-2)}$
In peroxides	-1	$H^{(+1)}_2O^{(-1)}_2$
5. Uncharged compounds		
Sum of oxidation numbers = 0		$C^{(-4)}H^{(+1)}_4$
6. Polyatomic ions		
Sum of oxidation numbers = charge		$H_3PO_4 : O(-2),\ H(+1),\ P(+5)$

C. *Reduction*: Three Definitions

1. Loss of oxygen $CuO\ +\ H_2\ \rightarrow\ Cu\ +\ H_2O$

2. Addition of hydrogen $N_2\ +\ 3\ H_2\ \rightarrow\ 2\ NH_3$

3. Addition of electrons (Decrease in oxidation number).

$Fe^{3+}\ +\ e^-\ \rightarrow\ Fe^{2+}$

6.5 Oxidizing and Reducing Agents

A. The substance being reduced is the *oxidizing agent*. Oxygen is the most common oxidizing agent and is used to "burn" all sorts of fuels and foodstuffs.

$C_6H_{12}O_6 + 6\ O_2\ \rightarrow\ 6\ CO_2 + 6\ H_2O$

glucose   (Oxygen is being reduced and is the oxidizing agent.)

B. In a redox reaction, the substance being oxidized is called the *reducing agent*.

$CuO\ +\ H_2\ \rightarrow\ Cu\ +\ H_2O$

(Hydrogen is being oxidized and is the reducing agent.)

6.6 Some Common Oxidizing Agents

A. The dichromate ion ($Cr_2O_7^{2-}$) is another common laboratory oxidizing agent as Cr goes from Cr^{+6} to Cr^{+3}.

$Cr_2O_7^{2-}\ +\ 3\ C_2H_5OH\ +\ 8\ H^+\ \rightarrow\ 2\ Cr^{3+}\ +\ 3\ C_2H_4O\ +\ 7\ H_2O$

B. Hydrogen peroxide is a syrupy, colorless liquid usually used as a 3% or 30% aqueous solution. It forms water when used as an oxidizing agent.

$PbS\ +\ 4\ H_2O_2\ \rightarrow\ PbSO_4\ +\ 4\ H_2O$

C. Potassium permanganate ($KMnO_4$) is a black solid that forms deep purple solutions. The permanganate ion (Mn^{+7}) is a common laboratory oxidizing agent as it is reduced to Mn^{+2}.

$$MnO_4^- + 5\,Fe^{2+} + 8\,H^+ \rightarrow Mn^{2+} + 5\,Fe^{3+} + 4\,H_2O$$
(purple)   (colorless)

D. The halogens are common oxidizing agents.

$$Cl_2 + Mg \rightarrow Mg^{2+} + 2\,Cl^-$$

E. Oxidation and Antiseptics
   1. Many common *antiseptics* are mild oxidizing agents: 3% H_2O_2, 0.01% $KMnO_4$, $KClO_3$, $NaOCl$, solutions of iodine.
   2. Common *disinfectants* include bleaching powder [$Ca(OCl)_2$], chlorine (Cl_2), and ozone (O_3). Ozone is used in many European cities to treat drinking water in place of chlorine.

F. Oxidation: Bleaching and Stain Removal
   1. Common *bleaching* agents act by removing mobile or high energy electrons whose absorption properties account for the unwanted colors.
      a. Laundry bleaches (Clorox)- 5.25% $NaOCl$ (sodium hypochlorite)
      b. Bleaching powder - $Ca(OCl)_2$
      c. Hydrogen peroxide - bleaches hair by oxidizing the melanin pigments to colorless compounds.
   2. Stain removal can involve solubilization or conversion to colorless materials by either oxidizing or reducing agents.
      a. Hydrogen peroxide - blood stains from cotton
      b. Oxalic acid - rust spots removed through complex formation
      c. Cornstarch - used as an absorbent
      d. Acetone - used as a solvent

6.7 Some Reducing Agents of Interest
   A. Hydrogen gas and elemental carbon are used as reducing agents.

$$2\,Fe_2O_3 + 3\,C \rightarrow 4\,Fe + 3\,CO_2$$

   B. Hydrogen gas serves as a reducing agent.

$$WO_3 + 3\,H_2 \rightarrow W + 3\,H_2O$$

   C. Hydrogen peroxide can also serve as a reducing agent as O(-1) is oxidized to free oxygen.

$$2\,MnO_4^- + 5\,H_2O_2 + 6\,H^+ \rightarrow 2\,Mn^{2+} + 5\,O_2 + 8\,H_2O$$

   D. Organic hydroquinones are used to "fix" silver in photographic film by reducing Ag^+ ions that have been exposed to light to free Ag metal.

6.8 Oxidation, Reduction and Living Things
   A. Reduced compounds represent a form of stored potential energy. The driving force to produce reduced compounds is ultimately derived from the sun in the processes of *photosynthesis*.

$$6\,CO_2 + 6\,H_2O + energy \rightarrow 6\,O_2 + C_6H_{12}O_6$$

   Plants and the animals that feed on plants use these materials to make other reduced compounds such as the carbohydrates, fats, and proteins that constitute our major food materials.
   B. We produce energy to meet our metabolic and body needs by releasing the energy stored in these reduced compounds as we combust them back to CO_2 and water.

Carbohydrates	$+ O_2$	$\rightarrow$	CO_2	$+ H_2O$	$+$ energy
Fats	$+ O_2$	$\rightarrow$	CO_2	$+ H_2O$	$+$ energy
Proteins	$+ O_2$	$\rightarrow$	CO_2	$+ H_2O + $ urea	$+$ energy

DISCUSSION

It is impossible to overemphasize the importance of oxidation-reduction processes. Think of it this way. You are powered by the energy of sunlight, only you can't simply unfold solar panels as artificial satellites do and convert sunlight to stored electrical energy to be tapped as necessary. You are a chemical factory and not an artificial satellite, solar-powered or otherwise. So somehow you have to tap that solar energy in a chemical way. This is precisely the role of oxidation-reduction reactions in life processes--they plug you into the sun. The later chapters of the text will detail the sequence of reactions that accomplishes this objective. Right now we are concerned with familiarizing ourselves with the general features of oxidation-reduction reactions.

We've spent much time in this chapter developing your ability to recognize when a compound is oxidized or reduced. In addition to the three definitions used in the text, we have included the concept of *oxidation number*. On first encounter, oxidation numbers may seem to be mysterious and magical. They were conjured up by chemists to make it easier to deal with oxidation-reduction reactions. It is the mystery of oxidation numbers that we have tried to dispel. They simply represent a means of assessing oxidation or reduction. You should be able to look at an equation and recognize when oxidation (and reduction) has occurred. (Always remember that one process is impossible without the other.) If you can do that without referring to oxidation numbers--fine. But we think you'll find, just as chemists already have, that occasionally a consideration of oxidation numbers makes the evaluation process a little easier.

In Problems 1 and 2 below we're offering additional practice in determining oxidation states and in evaluating the components of oxidation- reduction equations. These problems supplement those at the end of the chapter.

Problems

1. Determine the oxidation states of the <u>underlined</u> atoms.

a. $\underline{O}_3$
b. $\underline{N}_2$
c. $\underline{N}H_3$
d. $\underline{Cr}O_3$
e. $\underline{Cr}_2O_7^{2-}$
f. $Na\underline{O}Cl$
g. $H\underline{Cl}O_4$
h. $H\underline{Cl}O_2$
i. $K\underline{I}O_3$
j. $H_5\underline{I}O_6$
k. $H_3\underline{P}O_4$
l. $H_4\underline{P}_2O_7$
m. $Ca\underline{HP}O_4$
n. $H\underline{S}_2O_7^-$
o. $\underline{N}_2O_3$
p. $\underline{N}_2O_4$
q. $\underline{N}_2O_5$
r. $\underline{N}O_2^-$
s. $\underline{C}_2H_6$
t. $\underline{C}H_2O_2$
u. $\underline{C}_2H_4O_2$
v. $\underline{C}H_4O$
w. $\underline{C}O_2$
x. $\underline{C}_3H_6O_3$
y. $\underline{C}_3H_4O_5$
z. $\underline{C}_{12}H_{22}O_{11}$

2. Identify the element being oxidized, the element being reduced, the oxidizing agent and the reducing agent for each equation.

a. $4\,Na \quad + \quad CO_2 \quad\quad\quad\quad \rightarrow \quad\quad 2\,Na_2O \quad + \quad C$
b. $C_2H_4 \quad + \quad 3\,O_2 \quad\quad\quad\quad \rightarrow \quad\quad 2\,CO_2 \quad + \quad 2\,H_2O$
c. $2\,Ag^+ \quad + \quad Cu \quad\quad\quad\quad \rightarrow \quad\quad 2\,Ag \quad + \quad Cu^{2+}$
d. $5\,CO \quad + \quad I_2O_5 \quad\quad\quad\quad \rightarrow \quad\quad I_2 \quad + \quad 5\,CO_2$
e. $3\,SO_2 \quad + \quad 2\,CrO_3 \quad + \quad 3\,H_2O \quad \rightarrow \quad\quad Cr_2O_3 \quad + \quad 3\,H_2SO_4$

SELF-TEST

1. The most common element in the universe is:
    a. O_2 b. H_2 c. N_2 d. He   e. C
2. On Earth we do <u>not</u> find a large abundance of oxygen in the form of:
    a. O_2 b. H_2O c. H_2O_2 d. SiO_2
3. A substance is oxidized if it:
    a. gains oxygen atoms   b. gains hydrogen atoms
    c. gains electrons   d. all of these   e. none of these
4. In the reaction, $C_2H_4 + H_2O \rightarrow C_2H_6O$, carbon is:
    a. oxidized   b. reduced   c. neither oxidized nor reduced
5. Hydrogen is no longer used in lighter-than-air ships because:
    a. it is more dense than helium
    b. it is a strong oxidizing agent
    c. under certain conditions it reacts explosively to form water
    d. it is too difficult to obtain from petroleum products
6. Platinum is a useful catalyst in reactions involving hydrogen because:
    a. the hydrogen absorbed on the catalyst's surface is more reactive than molecular hydrogen
    b. the activation energy of the reaction using platinum is lower
    c. both of the above statements are correct
    d. neither of the above statements is correct
7. Two common oxidizing agents change color when they are reduced. They are   (select two):
    a. H_2 b. $KMnO_4$ c. $Na_2Cr_2O_7$ d. O_2 e. NaOCl
8. Which compound can be an oxidizing agent or a reducing agent?
    a. H_2O_2 b. $KMnO_4$ c. H_2
9. Hydrogen peroxide used as an oxidizing agent is reduced to:
    a. O_2 b. H_2O c. H_2O_2 d. H_2
10. Disinfectants, antiseptics and bleaches are frequently:
    a. oxidizing agents   b. reducing agents
11. In photosynthesis, carbon dioxide is _____ to a sugar.
    a. oxidized   b. reduced
12. Which is <u>not</u> a reason that ozone is preferred over chlorine as a disinfectant for water?
    a. Ozone is less expensive than chlorine.
    b. Chlorine has been shown to form toxic byproducts.
    c. Ozone is more effective against some viruses.
    d. Chlorine imparts a distinctive taste to water.
13. In general, animals, including humans, are:
    a. oxidizing agents   b. reducing agents
14. The oxidation number of Cl in $HClO_3$ is:
    +1   +2   +3   +5   +7   +8   -1   -2   -3   -4   -6   -7   -8
15. The oxidation number of Sn in SnO_3^{2-} is:
    +1   +2   +3   +4   +5   +6   +7   8   -1   -2   -3   -6   -7   -8
16. The oxidation number of P in $H_2PO_4^-$ is:
    +1   +2   +3   +4   +5   +6   +7   +8   -1   -2   -3   -4   -5   -8
17. In the equation: $FeO + C \rightarrow Fe + CO$
    a. FeO is an(a):   oxidizing agent   reducing agent
    b. C is: oxidized   reduced

18. According to the equation: SO_2 + HNO_3 + H_2O → H_2SO_4 + NO
    a. sulfur is being: oxidized   reduced
    b. HNO_3 is the: oxidizing agent   reducing agent
19. In the reaction : $N_2 + 2\,H_2O$ → NH_4^+ + NO_2^- , nitrogen is:
    a. oxidized   b. reduced   c. both   d. neither
20. Consider: $3\,C_2H_4 + 2\,MnO_4^- + 4\,H_2O$ → $3\,C_2H_6O_2 + 2\,MnO_2 + 2\,OH^-$.
    a. What is the oxidation number of C in C_2H_4?
       +1 +2 +3 +4 +5 -1 -2 -3 -4 -5 0
    b. What is the oxidation number of C in $C_2H_6O_2$?
       +1 +2 +3 +4 +5 -1 -2 -3 -4 -5 0
    c. Is carbon being oxidized or reduced?
21. Balance each of the following redox reactions and underline the oxidizing agents.
    a. KCl + MnO_2 + H_2SO_4 → K_2SO_4 + $MnSO_4$ + Cl_2 + H_2O
    b. $KMnO_2$ + $FeSO_4$ + H_2SO_4 → K_2SO_4 + $MnSO_4$ + $Fe_2(SO_4)_3$ + H_2O
    c. Cu + HNO_3 → $Cu(NO_3)_2$ + NO + H_2O
22. Butane lighters rely on the ready combustion of butane (C_4H_{10}) to form carbon dioxide and water.
    a. Write a balanced reaction for the combustion of butane with oxygen.
    b. How many moles of carbon dioxide are produced from 6 moles of butane?
    c. How many grams of oxygen are required to completely combust 100 g of butane?
    d. If 200 g of butane are reacted with 200 g of oxygen, which reactant will be present in excess?

ANSWERS

Problems

1. a. 0   b. 0   c. -3   d. +6   e. +6   f. +1   g. +7   h. +3   i. +5   j. +7   k. +5   l. +5   m. +5
    n. +6   o. +3   p. +4   q. +5   r. +3   s. -3   t. +2   u. 0   v. -2   w. +4   x. 0   y. +2   z. 0
2. a. Na is oxidized and C is reduced. Na is the reducing agent and CO_2 is the oxidizing agent.
    b. C is being oxidized and O is being reduced.
        C_2H_4 is the reducing agent and O_2 is the oxidizing agent.
    c. Cu is being oxidized and Ag+ is reduced. Cu is the reducing agent and Ag+ is the oxidizing agent.
    d. C is being oxidized and I is being reduced.
        CO is the reducing agent and I_2O_5 is the oxidizing agent.
    e. S is being oxidized, Cr is being reduced. SO_2 is a reducing agent and CrO_3 is an oxidizing agent.

Self-Test

l. b	5. c	9. b	13. a	17. a. oxidizing agent	19. c	
2. c	6. c	10. a	14. +5	b. oxidized	20. a. -2	
3. a	7. b, c	11. b	15. +4	18. a. oxidized	b. -1	
4. c	8. a	12. a	16. +5	b. oxidizing agent	c. oxidized	

21.   a. $2\,KCl$ + $\underline{MnO_2}$ + $2\,H_2SO_4$ → K_2SO_4 + $MnSO_4$ + Cl_2 + $2\,H_2O$
       b. $2\,K\underline{Mn}O_2$ + $10\,FeSO_4$ + $8\,H_2SO_4$ → K_2SO_4 + $2\,MnSO_4$ + $5\,Fe_2(SO_4)_3$ + $8\,H_2O$
       c. $3\,Cu$ + $8\,H\underline{N}O_3$ → $3\,Cu(NO_3)_2$ + $2\,NO$ + $4\,H_2O$
22.   a. $2\,C_4H_{10} + 13\,O_2$ → $8\,CO_2$ + $10\,H_2O$
       b. 24 m CO_2 c. 1.72m C_4H_{10} = 11.2m or 359g O_2 d. C_4H_{10}

CHAPTER 7: GASES

KEY WORDS

matter	*kinetic theory*	*Henry's law*	*Gay-Lussac's law*
solid	*Boyle's law*	*diffusion*	*ideal gas law*
Charles' law	*Dalton's law*	*STP*	*gaseous*
partial pressure	*vapor pressure*	*molar volume*	*hemoglobin*
liquid	*pressure*	*temperature*	*barometer*
	Avogadro's Law	*absolute temperature*	*relative humidity*

SUMMARY

The Earth's atmosphere is composed of gases weighing about 5.2×10^{15} metric tons (14.7 lb/in^2). It is estimated that 99% of the Earth's atmosphere lies within 30km of the Earth's surface.

7.1 Air: A Mixture of Gases
A. *Matter* can exist in the *solid*, *liquid*, or *gaseous* state. The theory of gases will help us to understand all three states of matter.
B. Dry air: 78% N_2, 21% O_2, 1% Ar. Humid air can be up to 4% water vapor.

7.2 The Kinetic Molecular Theory
A. Experimentally, gases have low densities, are readily compressed, fill their containers, and expand on heating.
B. *Kinetic* Molecular *Theory* of gases
   1. All matter is composed of tiny, discrete particles called molecules.
   2. Molecules are in rapid, constant, random motions.
   3. Distances between particles are large compared to the diameter of the particles.
   4. Forces between gaseous particles are small.
   5. Gaseous particles undergo elastic collisions with themselves and with their containers.
   6. The average kinetic energy of a gas is proportional to its absolute *temperature*.
C. These collisions are responsible for the "*pressure*" of gases.
D. *Temperature* is just a reflection of the average kinetic energy of the gas particles.

7.3 Atmospheric Pressure
A. **Pressure** is *Force per unit of area* (P = F/A). The pressure of the atmosphere can be measured by how high a column of liquid it will support. Such a device is called a *barometer*. The mercury barometer was invented by Torricelli in 1643.
B. Units of pressure
   1. Common: 1 atm = 760 mm Hg = 760 Torr = 29.92 in Hg = 14.7 psi (lb/in.^{2})
   2. SI: The SI unit for pressure is the pascal (1Pa = 1N/m^2) 1 atm = 101.3kPa

7.4 Boyle's Law: Pressure-Volume Relationship
A. Boyle (1662) determined that for a given mass of gas at constant temperature, the volume varies inversely with the pressure.
   Boyle's Law: PV = k; P α 1/V; V α 1/P   (where k is a constant)
B. Boyle's law can be explained by kinetic-molecular theory, since the number of collisions against the container walls (pressure) will go down as the distance between the walls (volume) increases.
C. Artificial respirators, such as the "iron lung," are based on Boyle's law. As the bellows move out the pressure surrounding the chest is reduced, allowing air to flow into the patient's lungs.

7.5 Charles' Law: Temperature-Volume Relationship

    A. Charles (1787) observed that the volume of a gas at constant pressure varies directly with its absolute or Kelvin temperature.

        Charles' Law : $V \propto T$; $V = kT$; $V/T = k$ (T expressed in Kelvin, k is a constant)

    B. A plot of V vs. T (volume vs. Temperature) gives a straight line. By extrapolating this line, it would appear that the volume of a gas would become zero at -273.15 $^{\circ}$C. In 1848 Kelvin assigned this temperature the zero point on an ***absolute temperature*** scale or Kelvin scale.

    C. Charles' law can also be explained by kinetic-molecular theory. Since the average kinetic energy increases with increasing temperature, the particles move further per unit of time and therefore can maintain the same pressure in a larger volume at the higher temperature.

    D. Gay-Lussac's Law: Pressure-Temperature Relationship

        1. Joseph Gay-Lussac conducted experiments similar to those of Charles to determine that the pressure of a gas at constant volume varies directly with its absolute temperature.

          Gay-Lussac's Law : $P \propto T$; $P = kT$; $P/T = k$ (T expressed in Kelvin, k is a constant)

        2. Gay-Lussac's law can be explained by kinetic-molecular theory by the same reasoning used for Charles' law.

7.6 Avogadro's Law: The Molar Volume of a Gas

    A. ***Avogadro's Law*** - at a fixed temperature and pressure the volume of a gas is directly proportional to the number of molecules or moles of a gas present.

        $V \propto n$; $V = kn$ (k is a constant)

    B. Standard temperature and pressure (***STP***) conditions are defined as 0° C and 1 atmosphere (atm).

    C. The volume of 1 mole of most gases at STP is 22.4 L. This quantity is known as the ***molar volume*** of a gas.

7.7 The Combined Gas Laws

    A. Boyle's and Charles' laws can be combined to express the pressure, volume, and temperature relationship of an ideal gas.

    B. Combined Gas Law. $PV \propto T$ or $P_1V_1/T_1 = P_2V_2/T_2$

7.8 The Ideal Gas Law (PV = nRT)

    A. Avogadro's hypothesis that equal volumes of gases at the same temperature and pressure contain equal numbers of molecules allows us to relate P, V, T and moles (n).

        $PV/T \propto n$ or $PV \propto nT$ or $PV/_{nT} = $ constant $ = R$ (Ideal Gas Constant)

    B. The ideal gas law can be expressed in equation form as follows:

        Ideal Gas Law: $PV = nRT$ (R = universal gas constant = 0.0821 L-atm/mol-K)

7.9 Henry's Law: Pressure-Solubility Relationship

    A. Henry (1801) reported that the solubility of a gas in a liquid at a given temperature is directly proportional to the pressure of the gas at the surface of the liquid, ***Henry's Law***.

    B. Henry's law has important applications to the manufacture of carbonated beverages, to deep-sea diving (Diver's Bends), and to several areas of therapy.

7.10 Dalton's Law of Partial Pressures

    A. Dalton (1803) discovered that the total pressure of a mixture of gases is equal to the sum of the ***partial pressures*** exerted by the separate gases. This finding is known as Dalton's law.

        Dalton's Law of Partial Pressures: $P_{total} = P_1 + P_2 + \cdots$

    B. The ***vapor pressure*** of a liquid refers to the partial pressure of the gas phase above the liquid phase.

C. The vapor pressure of water varies with temperature. Cold air holds less water vapor than warm air.

T($^{\circ}$C):	0	20	30	40	60	80	100
v.p. in Torr:	5	18	32	55	149	355	760

D. **Relative humidity** compares the actual amount of water vapor in the air to the maximum amount the air could hold if it were saturated at that temperature. For example, if the water pressure in air is 9mm Hg, it is at 50% relative humidity (relative to the maximum value), since the vapor pressure of water at 20 $^{\circ}$C is 18mm Hg.

7.11 Partial Pressures and Respiration

A. **Diffusion** refers to the process whereby a substance "flows" from a region of higher concentration to regions of lower concentration.

B. Inspired air is rich in O_2 and poor in CO_2, while metabolizing cells are rich in CO_2 and poor in O_2. Diffusion facilitates the transfer of needed O_2 from the lungs to the cells and the removal of waste CO_2 from the cells out via the lungs.

C. Our bodies need more oxygen than can be dissolved in blood plasma alone. Most of the oxygen in the bloodstream combines with a protein molecule called **hemoglobin**, which picks up O_2 at the lungs and releases it at the respiring cells. Hemoglobin also helps with CO_2 transport but most CO_2 is transported as the bicarbonate ion (HCO_3^-). Carbon monoxide poisoning is due in part to tight CO binding to hemoglobin so the hemoglobin is no longer available for O_2 transport.

DISCUSSION

As always, we assume that you've worked through the problems at the end of the chapter in the text. You should, therefore, have a pretty good idea of how well you understand the gas laws of Boyle, Charles, and Gay-Lussac.

The following diagrams present the briefest summary of these laws:

V ↑ P ↓	V ↑ T ↑	P ↑ T ↑
Boyle's Law	Charles' Law	Gay-Lussac's Law

The diagrams should call to mind which of the variables vary directly and which vary inversely. Thus, volume and pressure move in opposite directions. Volume and temperature move together, as do pressure and temperature. Also remember that any units of volume and pressure can be used in these gas laws, as long as you are consistent, but temperature variations must be calculated using the absolute (Kelvin) scale. Beyond these few reminders, the best way for you learn these gas laws is to work more practice problems to sharpen your skills.

Problems

1. A gas with a pressure of 500 mm Hg at 0 $^{\circ}$C occupies a volume of 500 mL.
   a. If the temperature is changed to 273 $^{\circ}$C while the pressure is held constant, what will the new volume be?
   b. If the volume of the original gas was compressed to 100 mL and the temperature was maintained constant, what would the pressure be?
   c. What would the volume be at STP?

2. If a gas occupies 2 L at 27 °C and 1 atm:
   a. What would the volume be if the temperature remained constant but the pressure decreased to 0.25 atm?
   b. What would the volume be if the pressure remained constant but the temperature decreased to -123 °C?
   c. What would the volume be at STP?

3. A balloon was filled with gas to a volume of 60 L at a temperature of 30 °C and a pressure of 750 torr.
   a. What will the volume of the balloon be if it drifts to a point where the temperature is still 30 °C but the pressure is only 250 torr?
   b. What will the volume of the balloon be if the pressure remains constant but the temperature drops to -71 °C?
   c. What would the volume be at STP?

4. A rigid container is filled with gas at 86 °F and 20 psi and then sealed. What will the pressure inside the container be if it is heated to 212 °F?

5. What is the pressure of 0.25 mol of He that occupies a volume of 4.0 L at 300 K?

Use the **SELF-TEST** to check your understanding of the remaining material in Chapter 7. Remember that some of the **SELF-TEST** questions do require calculations like the problems above; that is, they are asking for more than simple recall of factual material. You may need to refer to a periodic table for atomic weights.

SELF-TEST

1. One atmosphere is approximately equal to _____ Pascals.
      a. 1.0   b. 100   c. 10,000   d. 100,000   e. 1000

2. Which gas has the highest partial pressure in the atmosphere?
      a. CO_2 b. H_2O c. O_2 d. N_2

3. If a pressure is reported as 1 torr, it is also:
      a. 760 mm Hg   b. 760 atm   c. 1 mm Hg   d. 1 atm

4. The conditions expressed in the abbreviation STP do not include:
      a. 0 °C   b. 273 K   c. 760 mm Hg   d. 1 atm   e. 1 torr

5. Expressed in inches of mercury, one standard atmosphere is 29.92″ of Hg. What is the atmospheric pressure in mm Hg when the weatherman reports that the "barometer is holding steady at 27.8″ Hg?"
      a. 740   b. 706   c. 930   d. 785   e. 721

6. According to the kinetic molecular theory, if you increase the temperature of a gas without changing the volume of the gas, the particles of the gas will:
      a. strike the container walls more often   b. strike the walls with less force
      c. lose kinetic energy   d. increase in size

7. Boyle's law would be explained by the kinetic molecular theory in the following way:
   a. If the volume of a gas sample decreases, the particles move faster and strike the walls of the container more often, and this is measured as an increase in pressure.
   b. If the volume of a gas is decreased, the distance between the walls of the container decreases and the particles strike the walls more often, resulting in an increase in pressure.
   c. Both of the above explanations are incorrect because a decrease in volume results in decrease in the pressure of a gas.

8. An increase in the pressure of a gas at constant temperature corresponds to:
    a. an increase in the concentration of the gas
    b. a decrease in the concentration of the gas
    c. an increase in the size of the particles of the gas

9. In applying each of the following gas laws, which variable is held constant?
    a. Boyle's law   (pressure, temperature, or volume)
    b. Gay-Lussac's law   (pressure, temperature, or volume)
    c. Charles' law   (pressure, temperature, or volume)

10. Henry's law can be used to explain the
    a. operation of an iron lung
    b. bends experienced by deep sea divers
    c. process of respiration

11. If a gas occupies 2 L at 3 atm, how many liters will it occupy at 6 atm if the temperature isn't changed?
    a. 1   b. 2   c. 4   d. 8   e. 16   f. 32

12. If a gas occupies 2 L at 273 $^{\circ}$C, what is the volume at 0 $^{\circ}$C if the pressure does not change?
    a. 1/273   b. 0.5   c. 1   d. 2   e. 4   f. 273

13. If a mixture of gases has a total pressure of 200 mm Hg and the partial pressure of nitrogen in the mixture is 60 mm Hg, then the percent of nitrogen in the mixture is:
    a. 60%   b. 50%   c. 200%   d. 15%   e. 30%

14. If the concentration of water vapor in the air is 1% and the total atmospheric pressure equals 1 atm, then the partial pressure of water vapor is:
    a. 0.1 atm   b. 1 mm Hg   c. 7.6 mm Hg   d. 100 atm   e. 760 mm Hg

15. If a sample of gas at STP contains 10% helium, what is the partial pressure of helium in the sample?
    a. 0.1 atm   b. 0.1 mm Hg   c. 10 atm   d. 10 mm Hg   e. 7.6 atm

16. If the relative humidity is 50% on a day when the temperature is 30 $^{\circ}$C, the partial pressure of water vapor in the air is:
    a. 16 mm Hg   b. 30 mm Hg   c. 50 mm Hg   d. 32 mm Hg   e. 64 mm Hg

17. The molar volume of argon gas (atomic number 18) is:
    a. 4 g/L   b. 4 moles   c. 4 L   d. 6.02 x 10^{23} e. 22.4 L

18. A flask contains Avogadro's number of hydrogen atoms at STP. The volume of the flask is how many liters?
    a. 1   b. 11.2   c. 20   d. 22.4   e. 6.02 x 10^{23}

19. If a container holds 0.5 mole of N_2 gas at STP, the container holds how much N_2?
    a. 6.02 x 10^{23} molec.   b. 0.5 x 10^{23} molec.   c. 7 g   d. 14 g   e. 28 g

20. If a container holds 2 g of helium at STP, how big is the container?
    a. 0.5 L   b. 11.2 L   c. 20 L   d. 22.4 L   e. 44.8 L

21. The approximate density of CO_2 gas at STP is:
    a. 1 g/mL   b. 2 g/mL   c. 2 g/L   d. 44 g/ml   e. 44 g/L   f. 22.4 g/L

22. What is the approximate mass of 2 L of butane or C_4H_{10} gas at STP?
    a. 10 g   b. 20 g   c. 22.4   d. 58 g   e. 5 g

23. How many moles of Ne occupy 2.0 L at STP?
    a. 20   b. 11.2   c. 0.05   d. 0.09   e. 1.0

24. What is the approximate temperature of 1.0 mol of an ideal gas that occupies 22.4 L at 0.50 atm pressure?
    a. 0 $^{\circ}$C   b. 273 K   c. 100 $^{\circ}$C   d. 200 $^{\circ}$C   e. 273 $^{\circ}$C

25. Nitrogen is collected over water at 30 $^{\circ}$C. If the total pressure within the collection vessel is 1 atm, the partial pressure of nitrogen is:
    a. 0.68 atm   b. 32 torr   c. 728 torr   d. 760 mm Hg   e. 792 mm Hg

26. Consider an autoclave where we want a steam temperature of 160 $^{\circ}C$. For the fixed volume of the autoclave, steam is at 100 $^{\circ}C$ when the pressure is 1 atm. What pressure is required for steam at this higher temperature?

    a. 1.60 atm   b. 1.16 atm   c. 1.10 atm   d. 5.40 atm   e. 792 mm Hg

27. Consider an automobile tire that is initially at 32 psi (2.17 atm) at a temperature of 25 $^{\circ}C$. What is the pressure in the tire after 100 miles of driving if the tire temperature is now 50 $^{\circ}C$? (Assume the volume remains constant.)

    a. 4.34 atm   b. 64 psi   c. 3.06 atm   d. 28.9 psi   e. 34.7 psi

28. The bends result from which dissolved gas being released as a deep sea diver ascends?

    a. H_2O b. O_2 c. N_2 d. CO_2 e. He

29. The mechanism by which we inspire air depends on our ability to____?____ the size of our chest cavity.

    a. increase   b. decrease

30. In respiratory therapy, the highest humidity is imparted to a gas mixture to be administered through the:

    a. mouth   b. nose   c. trachea

31. The formation of oxyhemoglobin is favored by _____ P_{O_2}.

    a. high   b. low

32. If the partial pressure of a gas in the alveoli is 104 torr and the gas tension of venous blood is 40 torr:

    a. the net diffusion of the gas will be from alveoli to blood

    b. the net diffusion of the gas will be from blood to alveoli

    c. nothing happens because gas tension and partial pressure have nothing to do with one another

33. Where would you expect the P_{CO_2} to be highest?

    a. in the alveoli immediately after inspiration of fresh air

    b. in the venous blood

    c. in the arterial blood

    d. in a cell that is metabolically active

ANSWERS

Problems

1. a. 1.00 L;   b. 2500 mm Hg;   c. 329 mL
2. a. 8 L;   b. 1 L;   c. 1.82 L
3. a. 180 L;   b. 40 L;   c. 53 L
4. 24.6 psi
5. 1.5 atm

Self-Test

1. d	8. a	13. e	20. b	27. e
2. d	9. temperature	14. c	21. c	28. c
3. c	volume	15. a	22. e	29. a
4. e	pressure	16. a	23. d	30. c
5. b	10. b	17. e	24. e	31. a
6. a	11. a	18. b	25. c	32. a
7. b	12. c	19. d	26. b	33. d

CHAPTER 8: LIQUIDS AND SOLIDS

KEY WORDS

interionic forces	*dispersion*	*condensation*	*unit cell*
dipole forces	*liquids*	*equilibrium*	*metallic*
hydrogen bonds	*viscosity*	*boiling point*	*ionic solids*
H donor	*surface tension*	*distillation*	*molar heat*
H acceptor	*vaporization*	*solids*	*heat of fusion*
intermolecular forces	*London forces*	*crystal lattice*	*molecular solids*
melting point	*specific heat*	*density*	*ion pairs*
sublimation	*covalent network*	*crystalline*	

CHAPTER SUMMARY

8.1 Sticky Molecules: Intermolecular Forces
  A. *Intermolecular forces* determine the physical properties of fluids and solids. Strong intermolecular forces favor solids and would require higher temperatures to separate the molecules. Gaseous molecules tend to have weak *intermolecular forces* allowing the distances between gas particles to be very large. The particles in liquids and solids are held closer together because the intermolecular forces between their particles are much larger.
    1. Types of intermolecular forces: *interionic > hydrogen bonds > dipole > dispersion*
    2. Strength of intermolecular forces: *solid > liquid > gas*
  B. The physical state of a substance depends on its molecular weight and the type of forces operating between particles.
    1. All ionic substances are solids at room temperature.
    2. Most metals are solids at room temperature.
    3. Molecular substances exist as solids, liquids, or gases at room temperature. For a series of related molecules with the same type of intermolecular forces, the heavier molecules in the series will be solids and the lighter molecules in the series will be gases.

	F_2	Cl_2	Br_2	I_2
Molecular weight:	38	71	160	254
Physical state:	gas	gas	liquid	solid

8.2 Ionic Bonds as "Intermolecular Forces"
  A. *Interionic forces* are the strongest of the intermolecular forces. Most ionic compounds are solids at room temperature. There are no "molecules" in ionic solids, just a lattice of "*ion pairs*."
  B. The strength of the "*ionic bonds*" increases with increasing charge on the ion and decreases as the distance between charges increases. Thus, ionic forces decrease and *dispersion* forces become more important for very large, singly charged ions such as Ag^+, I^-.

8.3 Dipole Forces
  A. Unsymmetrical molecules containing polar bonds are dipoles with centers of partially negative and positive charges.
  B. Polar molecules attract one another as the positive end of one molecule interacts with the negative end of another molecule. Dipole forces are weaker than ionic bonds.

N_2 (b.pt. = -196 °C) ; $^{\delta+}C{=}O^{\delta-}$ (b.pt. = -192 °C) both with M.Wt. 28.0.

8.4 Hydrogen Bonds
   A. Compounds containing H attached to small, electronegative elements such as N, O, or F exhibit
      stronger attractive forces than would be expected on the basis of dipolar forces alone. These forces
      are called hydrogen bonds. Note the anomalously high boiling point of water.

	H_2O	:	H_2S	H_2Se	H_2Te
M.Wt.	18	:	34	84	130
b. pt.	100 °C	:	-60 °C	-41°C	-2 °C

   B. A *hydrogen bond* is not a covalent bond but is rather an interaction of the partially positive
      hydrogen of the *donor* molecule with the lone pair of nonbonded electrons of a N, O, or F of the
      acceptor molecule. Hydrogen bonds are usually represented by a dashed line.

   C. Hydrogen bonds are primarily limited to those molecules containing N, O, or F, and are very
      important in stabilizing the structures of important biomacromolecules such as proteins, nucleic
      acids, and polysaccharides.

8.5 Dispersion Forces
   A. Nonpolar compounds also have attractive intermolecular forces due to momentary induced dipoles
      that arise from the motions of electrons about the nuclei of all compounds.
   B. These transient attractive forces, called *dispersion* or *London forces*, are fairly weak but are
      present in all molecules and increase as the size and number of electrons of the molecule increase.

	F_2	Cl_2	Br_2	I_2
Molecular weight:	38	71	160	254
Physical state:	gas	gas	liquid	solid

8.6 The Liquid State
   A. Molecules of a liquid are in constant motion but close together, thus they can be compressed only
      slightly and diffuse much more slowly than gases.
   B. Properties of Liquids
      1. *Viscosity* - resistance to flow; viscosity is less for small, symmetrical molecules and also
         decreases with increasing temperature.
      2. *Surface tension* - surface molecules of liquids with strong intermolecular forces tend to form
         "beads" to minimize the surface area.

8.7 From Liquid to Gas: Vaporization
   A. Terms
      1. *Vaporization* - the conversion of a liquid to vapor; heat is required to vaporize a liquid to vapor.
      2. *Evaporation* - the conversion of a liquid to a vapor upon exposure to air.
      3. *Condensation* - the conversion of vapor to liquid; heat is released during condensation.
      4. *Equilibrium* - a dynamic state of a system in which opposing processes are occurring at the same
         rate.
      5. *Boiling point* - the temperature at which the vapor pressure of a liquid equals atmospheric
         pressure.
      6. *Normal boiling point* - the temperature at which a liquid boils under standard pressure (1 atm).
      7. *Distillation* - the separation of volatile components by boiling off and then condensing the vapor.

8. *Molar heat of vaporization* - the quantity of heat required to vaporize 1 mole of a liquid at constant pressure; for water this quantity is 540 cal/g or 9.7 kcal/mole.

B. A liquid placed in a closed container will evaporate until it reaches its vapor pressure at that temperature. No further net evaporation then takes place because the rate of vaporization equals the rate of condensation. The system is in *dynamic equilibrium*.

8.8 The Solid State

A. Molecules of a solid are also close together but vibrate in fixed positions.

B. Particles in *crystalline* solids are arranged in regular patterns. The *unit cell* is the small, repeating segment of a *crystal lattice*; simple cubic, body-centered cubic, and face-centered cubic are three common unit cell types found in crystalline solids.

C. Classes of solids

1. *Ionic solids* - high melting points, hard; NaCl
2. *Molecular solids* - low melting points; paraffin
3. *Covalent network* - atoms linked by covalent bonds in three dimensions, forming one gigantic "molecule"; diamond
4. *Metallic solids* - malleable, good conductors, in metallic bonding a sea of electrons surround the metal ions; copper

8.9 From Solid to Liquid: Melting (Fusion)

A. As the temperature is increased, most solids attain sufficient energy to overcome the forces that hold them in the solid lattice and melt to form a liquid. The temperature at which this takes place is called the *melting point*.

B. The molar *heat of fusion* is the heat energy input required to convert 1 mole of a solid to liquid at its normal melting point. This quantity is generally less than the molar heat of vaporization because the difference in intermolecular forces between solid and liquid is less than between liquid and gas. The heat of fusion for water is 80 cal/g or 1.44 kcal/mole.

C. A few volatile solids pass directly from the solid state to the vapor state (CO_2, or "dry ice"). This process is called *sublimation*.

8.10 Water: A Most Unusual Liquid

A. Physical state - Most substances of low molecular weight (~18) are gases at room temperature. Water is a liquid because of its strong intermolecular forces.

B. *Density* - The density of ice at 4 $^{\circ}$C is 0.917 g/cm^3, less than the 1.00 g/cm^3 of water at 4 $^{\circ}$C. Thus ice floats and northern lakes do not freeze solid. This same property of ice expansion can cause car radiators and living cells to rupture upon freezing. "Flash-freezing" avoids this growth of large ice crystals.

C. *Specific Heat* -Water has a high specific heat, 1.0 cal/(g-$^{\circ}$C) and thus resists rapid changes in temperature. The water in our bodies and the oceans of the Earth act as thermostats to moderate temperature variations.

D. Heat of vaporization - Water has a very high heat of vaporization. Thus, large amounts of body heat can be dissipated by small amounts of perspiration.

E. Polar solvent - Water is a polar molecule capable of dissolving polar and ionic substances. A typical cell is nearly 65% water. Water is the "solvent of life."

DISCUSSION

Many new terms were introduced in Chapter 8. A knowledge of these is essential to an understanding of the concepts introduced in the chapter. Take time now to review the list of terms in the KEY WORDS section. Each key word is identified in the SUMMARY. Numerical problems in this chapter deal with energy changes associated with changes of state and changes of temperature. Energy must be supplied to a system to convert a solid to a liquid, to convert a liquid to a gas, or to raise the temperature of a gas or a liquid or a solid. The reverse changes (liquid to solid, gas to liquid, or decreases in temperature) occur if energy is removed from the system.

The system gains or loses energy in definite stages. You can raise the temperature of a solid by supplying it with energy only until it reaches the melting point. Then any energy you add will be used up in converting solid to liquid. While this change is occurring, the temperature stays the same (at the melting point). As soon as the solid is completely converted to a liquid, additional energy will be used to increase the temperature of the liquid. Eventually the boiling point of the liquid is reached. Then the temperature remains constant while additional energy is used to convert liquid to gas. When this conversion is complete, the temperature of the gas can be raised by supplying more energy.

To calculate the energy needed for each of these changes, you need the proper heat constant:

Change Effected	Constant Used
Increase or decrease temperature of solid	Specific heat of solid
Conversion of solid to liquid or vice versa	Heat of fusion
Increase or decrease in temperature of liquid	Specific heat of liquid
Conversion of liquid to gas or vice versa	Heat of vaporization
Increase or decrease in temperature of gas	Specific heat of gas

A change that starts with a solid and ends with a gas should simply be treated as a multistep calculation (see Example 8.6 in the text). Problems at the end of the chapter offer practice in dealing with these energy changes. A few more are offered below for additional practice. Since the energy changes involving water are so important to life on this planet, all of the additional problems deal with this substance. The pertinent constants are:

specific heat of ice	=	0.50 cal/g/$^\circ$C
specific heat of water	=	1.0 cal/g/$^\circ$C
specific heat of steam	=	~0.5 cal/g/$^\circ$C
heat of fusion of water	=	80 cal/g
heat of vaporization of water	=	540 cal/g

Chapter 8 - Liquids and Solids

Problems

1. 200 g of water at 20 °C was heated to 40 °C. How much energy was required?
2. A sample of water weighing 80 g cooled from 100 °C to 25 °C. How much heat was released to the surroundings?
3. How many calories are required to convert 15 g of water to steam at 100 °C?
4. How many calories are required to convert 15 mL of water, originally at 20 °C, to steam at 100 °C?
5. Approximately how much heat is removed from the body in one day by the evaporation of 500 mL of perspiration?
6. How many calories are required to convert 1 mole of ice to water at 0 °C?
7. If 1 g of steam at 120 °C is condensed, cooled and converted to ice at -20 °C, how much energy is released to the surroundings?
8. The types of bonding in column B are responsible for maintaining the lattice structure of the materials in column A. Choose from column B the type of bonding that plays the most significant role for each item in column A.

Column A	Column B
a. ___ Fe	1. ionic bonding
b. ___ H_2	2. dipole interactions
c. ___ CO_2	3. hydrogen bonding
d. ___ HCN	4. dispersion forces
e. ___ NH_3	5. metallic bonding
f. ___ KCl	

SELF-TEST

1. Predict which of these compounds would be a gas at STP.
   a. Au   b. $CH_3 — CH_2 —CH_3$ c. Mg   d. NaCl   e. I_2
2. Which of the following intermolecular forces are weakest?
   a. ion-ion   b. dipole-dipole   c. hydrogen bonding   d. London / dispersion
3. Dipole-dipole interactions are _____ hydrogen bonds.
   a. stronger than   b. weaker than   c. equal in strength to
4. In general, which is the strongest type of intermolecular bonding?
   a. ionic bonding   b. dipole interactions   c. hydrogen bonding
5. At room temperature ionic compounds exist as:
   a. solids   b. liquids   c. gases
6. For which compound would you expect the interionic forces to be strongest?
   a. LiF   b. BeO   c. BN
7. For which compound would the dispersion forces be greatest?
   a. Cl_2 b. Br_2 c. I_2
8. Which type of force would not be operating in a solid sample of HCl?
   a. dipolar forces   b. interionic forces   c. dispersion forces
9. Which represents the best arrangement for a pair of dipoles?

   a. (+   -) (+   -)   b. (+   -) (-   +)   c. (+   -)   d. (+   -)
                                                      (-   +)   (+   -)

10. For which compound is hydrogen bonding a significant attractive force?
    a. F—N=O   b. Cl—N=O   c. H—N=O   d. H—C≡C—H

11. Which of the following correctly illustrates hydrogen bonding?

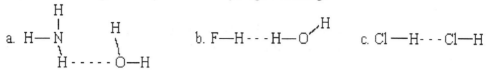

    a. $H-N$ ... with H and $\dot{O}-H$ b. $F-H---H-O$ with H c. $Cl-H---Cl-H$

12. Which compound would you expect to have the highest melting point?
    a. C_3H_8 b. C_8H_{18} c. $C_{18}H_{38}$

13. Which compound would you expect to have the strongest hydrogen bonding in the liquid state?
    a. CH_3-O-CH_3 b. CH_3-OH c. CH_3-CH_3 d. $CH_3-CO-CH_3$ (acetone)

14. If compound A has a lower vapor pressure than compound B at a given temperature, which compound would be expected to have the lower boiling point?
    a. A   b. B   c. The boiling point would be the same at 760 mm Hg.

15. Which noble gas would have the highest boiling point?
    a. He   b. Ne   c. Ar   d. Kr   e. Xe

16. The atmospheric pressure is 670 Torr. Water will boil at:
    a. less than 100 °C   b. exactly 100 °C   c. more than 100 °C

17. The vapor pressures of liquids X, Y, and Z at 75 °C are 300, 644 and 1126 Torr, respectively. Which of these, if any, has a normal boiling point below 75 °C?
    a. X   b. Y   c. Z   d. all of these   e. none of these   f. X and Y

18. All of the following are gases at room temperature. Which one will liquefy most easily when pressurized at a fixed temperature?
    a. O_2 b. NH_3 c. SiH_4 d. F_2 e. H_2

19. Which of the following processes is endothermic?
    a. cooling   b. condensation   c. solidification   d. melting

20. The boiling points of water, ethanol, diethylether, and chloroform are 100 °C, 78.5 °C, 28 °C, and 119 °C. Which liquid would you predict to have the lowest vapor pressure at room temperature?
    a. water   b. ethanol   c. diethylether   d. chloroform

21. If a liquid and its vapor are at equilibrium in a closed container and the temperature is increased, which rate increases?
    a. rate of vaporization   b. rate of condensation   c. both   d. neither

22. In general, which is expected to be larger for a given substance?
    a. molar heat fusion   b. molar heat vaporization   c. specific heat

23. Which would be expected to have the highest heat of vaporization?
    a. CH_4 b. H_2O c. LiF

24. When is the viscosity of a lubricating oil highest?
    a. at room temperature   b. at 150 °C   c. at -15 °C

25. If you start with 1 g of ice at 0 °C and add 120 calories of heat energy, the temperature of the water will be:
    a. 0 °C   b. 10 °C   c. 20 °C   d. 30 °C   e. 40 °C   f. 80 °C   g. 100 °C

26. The molar heat capacity of some molecule (X, liq.) is 10 cal/K-mol, its heat of vaporization is 5000 cal/mol, and its normal boiling point is 75 °C. How many calories are required to convert one mole of X at 60 °C to one mole of X vapor at 75 °C at 1 atm pressure?
    a. 5150   b. 4850   c. 150   d. 5650   e. 4750

27. Refer to the following specific heats:
    For x = 0.1 cal/g-°C   For y = 0.4 cal/g-°C   For z = 0.8 cal/g-°C
    a. Which material has the highest heat capacity?   x   y   z
    b. If all are supplied with the same amount of heat, which will reach the highest temperature?
         x   y   z

28. Which property of water is regarded as unusual?
    a. physical state at room temperature
    b. the relative density of solid and liquid
    c. heat of vaporization
    d. specific heat
    e. all of these
    f. none of these

ANSWERS

Problems

1. 4 kcal	2. 6.0 kcal	3. 8.1 kcal	4. 9.3 kcal;
5. 270 kcal	6. 1.44 kcal	7. 0.74 kcal	

8. a. 5   b. 4   c. 4   d. 2   e. 3   f. 1

Self-Test

1. b	8. b	15. e	22. b
2. d	9. c	16. a	23. c
3. b	10. c	17. c	24. c
4. a	11. a	18. b	25. e
5. a	12. c	19. d	26. a
6. c	13. b	20. d	27. z, x
7. c	14. b	21. c	28. e

CHAPTER 9:   SOLUTIONS

KEY WORDS

solution
homogeneous
solute
solvent
hydration
hydrate
aqueous
miscible
soluble
osmolality
reverse osmosis

insoluble
dilute
concentrated
concentration
saturated
supersaturated
anhydrous
efflorescent
hygroscopic
osmotic pressure
unsaturated

deliquescent
dynamic
  equilibrium
molarity
colligative
osmosis
semipermeable
  membrane
isotonic
boiling pt. elevation

hypotonic
plasmolysis
hemolysis
hypertonic
crenation
colloid
Tyndall effect
emulsion
dialysis
 freezing pt. depression

SUMMARY

9.1 Solutions: Definitions and Types
   A. *Solution* - a *homogeneous* mixture of two or more substances
   B. *Solute* - the substance being dissolved, minor component
   C. *Solvent* - the substance doing the dissolving, major component
   D. *Aqueous Solution* - solution in which the solvent is water

9.2 Qualitative Aspects of Solubility
   A. Miscible vs. Insoluble
      1. Substances are *miscible* when they can be mixed in all proportions.
      2. Substances are said to be *insoluble* when their solubility is very low, near zero.
   B. Dilute vs. Concentrated
      1. *Dilute* solutions contain relatively little solute.
      2. *Concentrated* solutions contain a great deal of solute.

9.3   Solubility of Ionic Compounds
   A. The dissolution of salts requires energy for the breakdown of the crystal lattice and separation of solvent molecules, while energy is released by the solvation of ions. Substances are most *soluble* when the energy released exceeds the energy absorbed.
   B. *Hydration* is the process in which water molecules surround the solute. The unique structure of water, being a polar molecule with hydrogen bonding capabilities, enables water to dissolve many ionic compounds. Most compounds of Na^+, K^+, NH_4^+ and NO_3^- are soluble while most compounds of PO_4^{3-} and CO_3^- salts are not.   (See Table 9.2 in the text.)

9.4 Solubility of Covalent Compounds
   A. "Like Dissolves Like" - Nonpolar substances such as fats and oils are normally readily soluble in nonpolar solvents such as carbon tetrachloride or benzene.
   B. The solubility of polar substances in a polar solvent such as water depends on its size and ability to form hydrogen bonds with water. For polar organic (carbon-based) compounds, the solubility decreases appreciably when the ratio of C to O plus N exceeds 4:1.
   C. Other terms:
      1. *Hydration* - interaction of water with a solute.

67

2. *Hydrate* - crystalline compound with bound water.
3. *Anhydrous* - "dry" compound; hydrate minus water.
4. *Efflorescent* - compounds that become anhydrous upon standing in air.
5. *Hygroscopic* - compounds that form hydrates upon standing in air.
6. *Deliquescent* - compounds that are so hygroscopic that they dissolve in accumulated water upon standing in air.

9.5 Dynamic Equilibrium
    A. A solution that contains all of the solute that it can at a given temperature is said to be *saturated*; less than this the solution is *unsaturated*. At the saturation point there must be some solid in *dynamic equilibrium* with the solution so the rate of dissolution is just equal to the rate of precipitation.
    B. A *supersaturated* solution is a nonequilibrium, metastable solution that contains solute in excess of what it would contain if it were at equilibrium.

9.6 Solutions of Gases in Water
    A. Aqueous solutions of gases are fairly common, i.e., blood, "soda pop," ammonia cleansers, etc.
    B. Unlike most solids, the solubility of a gas decreases with increasing temperature but increases with increasing pressure.

9.7 Molarity
    A. *Dilute* and *concentrated* are relative terms. Chemists need more quantitative ways to describe solutions. The *concentration* of a solution expresses a ratio of the amount of *solute per amount of solution*. The amount of solute can be expressed in units of grams, mL or moles.
    B. *Molarity* (M) = moles of solute per liter of solution   M = [# moles / V (L)];   # moles = M x V(L)

9.8 Percent Concentration
    A. % by volume   (v/v)%   = $\dfrac{\text{vol. of solute}}{\text{vol. of solution}}$ x 100

    B. % by mass   (w/w)%   = $\dfrac{\text{g of solute}}{\text{g of solution}}$ x 100

    C. mass/volume percent   mg %   = $\dfrac{\text{mg solute}}{100 \text{ mL (or dL) solution}}$ x 100

    D. Parts per billion   (ppb)   = $\dfrac{\text{mg of solute}}{\text{kg of solution}}$
       (1 cent/ $10 million)
    E. Ratio Concentrations
        1. Many liquids (drugs, insecticides, etc.) are purchased in concentrated form and must be diluted before use.
        2. Dilution formula: $C_s \times V_s = C_d \times V_d$; C_s = concentration of stock solution; C_d = concentration of dilute solution.

9.9 Colligative Properties of Solutions
    A. *Colligative properties* are properties such as *boiling point elevation, freezing point depression,* and *osmotic pressure* that depend more on the number rather than type of particles in solution.
    B. Solutions have lower vapor pressures than the pure solvent. Consequently the boiling points of solutions are elevated (0.51 °C/molal for water).
    C. The freezing point of a solution is depressed (-1.86 °C/molal for water).
    D. *Osmolality* = osmol/L where an osmol is a mole of solute particles.

9.10 Solutions and Cell Membranes: Osmosis
- A. The molecular sieve theory of *osmosis* holds that a *semipermeable membrane* has pores large enough to permit the passage of solvent water molecules but too small to permit passage of larger molecules.
- B. During osmosis solvent will continue to flow through the semipermeable membrane from the dilute region to the more concentrated region until the *osmotic pressure* builds up on the concentrated side to halt the flow of solvent.
- C. Solutions like 0.89% sodium chloride (0.16M) or 5.5% glucose (0.31M) are said to be *isotonic* since they exert the same osmotic pressure as cellular fluids. When a cell is placed in a solution with a lower osmotic pressure (*hypotonic*), it may rupture (*plasmolysis* or *hemolysis*), and when it is placed in a solution of higher osmotic pressure (*hypertonic*), it may shrivel (*crenation*).
- D. *Reverse osmosis* can take place by using high pressure (> osmotic pressure) to force solvent through a semipermeable membrane and out of solution. This process can be used to produce drinking water from sea water.

9.11 Colloids
- A. *Colloids* are large particles that form *colloidal dispersions*, which are in between true, homogeneous solutions (sugar water) and heterogeneous suspensions (sand in water).
- B. Colloids do not settle out on standing nor can they be separated by filtering through filter paper. However, colloids can be observed by the scattering of a beam of light as it passes through a colloidal dispersion, a process known as the *Tyndall effect* (after John Tyndall, 1869).
- C. The most important colloids in biological systems are *emulsions* in which either liquids or solids are dispersed in water. Substances such as soap and bile salts that stabilize emulsions are called emulsifying agents.

9.12 Dialysis
- A. *Dialysis* refers to the process whereby small molecules and ions pass through a semipermeable membrane (dialyzing membrane) from areas of higher concentration to areas of lower concentration.
- B. The kidneys are an example of a complex dialyzing system responsible for the removal of high concentrations of toxic waste products from the blood.

DISCUSSION

Aqueous solutions are very important in chemistry and biology. The material in this chapter can be divided into three main areas. Sections 1-6 deal with the concept of solubility and the many qualitative terms that are used to describe solutions. Sections 7-9 treat the quantitative aspects of solutions. Finally, sections 10-14 cover the biological importance of colloids, membranes and the processes of osmosis and dialysis.

The terms soluble/insoluble and miscible/immiscible have similar meanings and are just a few of the many qualitative terms used to describe solutions. To say something is soluble simply means that a significant amount of the solute dissolves in the solvent, whereas miscible implies that solute and solvent can be mixed in all proportions. If one wishes to be somewhat more precise in describing the amount of solute dissolved in a particular solvent, the terms unsaturated, saturated and supersaturated can be employed. Except for saturated, these terms, too, are quite imprecise. An unsaturated solution can be further described as being dilute or concentrated, depending on how close the solution is to saturation.

If a more precise description of a solution is required, a quantitative measure of concentration must be used. The concentration of a solution always expresses a ratio of the amount of solute per a given amount of solvent or solution present. There are many terms used to express concentration, depending on the units used to express the amount of solute and solvent or solution present. The amount of solute is usually expressed in either grams or volume. Some of the most common definitions for concentration used in this text are:

$$\text{molarity (M)} = \frac{\text{moles of solute}}{\text{liter of solution}} \quad \text{where moles of solute} = \frac{\text{g of solute}}{\text{GFW of solute}}$$

$$\text{volume (v/v) \%} = \frac{\text{vol. of solute}}{\text{vol. of solution}} \times 100$$

$$\text{weight (w/w) \%} = \frac{\text{g of solute}}{\text{g of solution}} \times 100$$

Two important differences between molarity and percent concentrations should be noted. First, molarity expresses the amount of solute in moles. Therefore, the formula of the solute must be known and its formula weight used in calculating molarity. On the other hand, when using percent concentrations the nature of the solute can be ignored since it is only the gram or volume amount of solute that is needed for the calculation. A second difference between molarity and percent concentrations lies in the size of the solution sample referred to. A 1.0 molar solution refers to 1 mole per liter whereas a 1 percent solution contains 1 g per 100 g or 1 mL per 100 mL of solution. The following example illustrates the relationship of these two forms of expressing concentration.

$$1 \text{ M NaOH} = \frac{1 \text{ mol NaOH}}{1 \text{ L solution}} = \frac{40 \text{ g NaOH}}{1000 \text{ mL soln.}} = \frac{4 \text{ g NaOH}}{100 \text{ mL soln.}} \sim \frac{4 \text{ g NaOH}}{100 \text{ g soln.}}$$

$$\Uparrow \qquad\qquad\qquad\qquad\qquad\qquad\qquad\qquad \Downarrow$$

$$\text{Molarity} = 1 \qquad\qquad\qquad\qquad\qquad\qquad (\text{w/w})\% = 4$$

Note that all of the above refer to the amount of solution in the denominator. It is also possible to express concentration in terms of the amount of solvent in the denominator. In fact, most chemical handbooks express saturation limits in terms of "grams of solute"/100 g solvent.

The last part of this chapter deals with colloids, osmosis and dialysis. The subtleties that distinguish osmosis from dialysis often present difficulties. In both osmosis and dialysis there is the tendency for the concentrations on either side of the semipermeable membrane to equalize. In dialysis this involves the flow of small molecules or ions as they diffuse from a region of higher solute concentration through the membrane to a region of lower solute concentration. In osmosis, it is the flow of solvent that is involved. There is a net flow of solvent (water) from a region of higher solvent concentration (lower solute concentration and lower osmotic pressure) to a region of lower solvent concentration (higher solute concentration and higher osmotic pressure). Thus, the net flow of water is from a solution of low osmotic pressure to a solution of high osmotic pressure. These points are summarized in the following diagram:

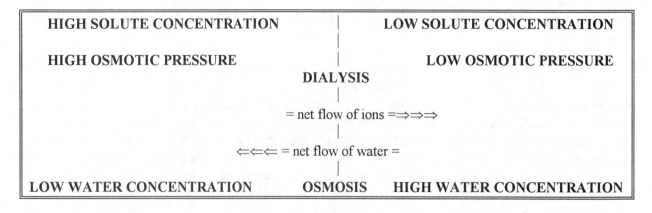

The quantitative treatment of solutions is best learned by working problems. Remember that concentration by itself does not say anything about the amount of solute but always expresses a ratio of the amount of solute to a given amount of solvent or solution. The two most common types of quantitative problems dealing with concentrations are:
1. calculate the concentration given the amounts of solute and solution.
2. calculate the amount of solute needed for a given volume and concentration of the solution.

The problems at the end of Chapter 9 in the text will help improve your understanding of this material.

Problems

1. Calculate the molarity of the solution that results if the stated amount of solute is dissolved in 1 L of solution.
    a. 29.2 g NaCl   d. 4.0 g NaOH
    b. 49 g H_2SO_4 e. 80 g of $CaBr_2$
    c. 74.5 g $(NH_4)_3PO_4$

2. Calculate the molarity (Volumes given are of the solution).
    a. 5.85 g NaCl in 2 L   d. 0.4 g of NaOH in 50 mL
    b. 4.9 g of H_2SO_4 in 50 mL   e. 40 g of $CaBr_2$ in 0.4 L
    c. 74.5 g of $(NH_4)_3PO_4$ in 10 L

3. How many moles of solute are present in each of the following?
    a. 1 L of 2 M NaCl   d. 50 mL of 5 M NaOH
    b. 10 mL of 0.1 M H_2SO_4 e. 5 mL of 0.64 M $CaBr_2$
    c. 10 L of 0.01 M $(NH_4)_3PO_4$

4. How many grams of solute are present in 1 L of each of the following solutions?
    a. 2 M NaCl   d. 5 M NaOH
    b. 0.1 M H_2SO_4 e. 0.64 M $CaBr_2$
    c. 0.01 M $(NH_4)_3PO_4$

5. How many grams of solute are there in each of the following?
    a. 50 mL of 2 M NaCl   d. 2 L of 5 M NaOH
    b. 2 mL of 0.1 M H_2SO_4 e. 5 mL of 0.64 M $CaBr_2$
    c. 10 L of 0.01 M $(NH_4)_3PO_4$

6. How many grams of solute are present in 100 g of each of the following solutions?
    a. 10% NaCl   d. 40% NaOH
    b. 0.5% H_2SO_4 e. 2% $CaBr_2$
    c. 12% $(NH_4)_3PO_4$

7. How many grams of solute are present in each of the following solutions?
    a. 40 g of 10 % NaCl   d. 1 kg of 40% NaOH
    b. 10 mL of 0.5% H_2SO_4 e. 1 L of 2% $CaBr_2$
    c. 10 g of 12% $(NH_4)_3PO_4$

8. What are the molarity, the approximate weight percent, and the mg % concentrations of a solution in which 0.4 g of NaOH is dissolved in 100 mL of solution?

You can check your understanding of the rest of the material covered by going through the **SELF-TEST**.

SELF-TEST

1. If a teaspoon of salt is added to a liter of water, water is the:
    a. solute   b. solvent   c. solution
2. The process of water molecules being attracted to and surrounding solute ions/particles is called:
    a. hydrogenation   b. solventation   c. salutation   d. hydrolysis   e. solvation
3. If a small amount of sugar is dissolved in a large amount of water, sugar is the:
    a. solute   b. solvent   c. solution
4. A mixture is homogeneous if:
    a. the components of the mixture are so intimately mixed that all samples of the mixture have the same composition.
    b. the mixture has a lower osmotic pressure than physiological saline
    c. the mixture will absorb water from the air
5. If the energy required to break the crystal lattice is greater than the energy of solvation,
    a. the solid dissolves in the solvent   b. the solid is insoluble in the solvent
6. Generally, if a seed crystal is added to a supersaturated solution,
    a. the crystal dissolves
    b. the crystal causes all of the solute to precipitate from solution
    c. solute precipitates until an unsaturated solution forms
    d. some solute precipitates and equilibrium is established with the saturated solution
7. An increase in temperature <u>usually</u> results in _____ of a solid solute.
    a. an increase in solubility   b. a decrease in solubility
    c. an increase in density   d. an increase in boiling point
8. Oil and water are:
    a. miscible   b. immiscible
9. Salts incorporating all but one of the following ions are usually soluble. Which ion is the exception?
    a. NO_3^- b. CO_3^{2-} c. Na^+ d. NH_4^+
10. Which of the following compounds would you expect to be soluble in water?
    a. $CaCO_3$ b. $PbSO_4$ c. HgS d. $(NH_4)_3PO_4$
11. Salts incorporating all but one of the following ions are usually insoluble. Which ion is the exception?
    a. CO_3^- b. PO_4^{3-} c. NO_3^- d. $S^=$
12. Which term is used to describe a compound that loses water on standing in dry air?
    a. efflorescent   b. deliquescent   c. hygroscopic
13 Which is least likely to dissolve in water?
    a. ionic compound   b. polar compound   c. nonpolar compound
14. The compound $Na_2CO_3 \cdot 7\ H_2O$ is a(an):
    a. hydroxide   b. hydrate   c. anhydrous compound
15. Which is generally <u>not</u> true? An increase in temperature increases:
    a. the rate of a reaction
    b. the solubility of a salt in water
    c. the solubility of a gas in water

16. Which compound would not be expected to dissolve in water?
    a. $CH_2CH_2CH_3$ b. $CH_3CH_2CH_2$ c. $CH_3CH_2CH_3$ d. $CH_2CH_2CHCH_2CH_2$
        OH NH_2 OH OH OH

17. The solubility of sodium chloride in water is 36% at 20 °C. At the same temperature, therefore, a solution of 30 g NaCl in 1 liter of water would be classified as:
    a. dilute   b. concentrated   c. saturated   d. supersaturated

18. If a 36% solution of NaCl is saturated, then if 4 g of NaCl is used to prepare 10 mL of a solution at the same temperature, the resulting solution would be:
    a. dilute   b. concentrated   c. saturated

19. If a solution is saturated when its concentration is 5%, then at the same temperature 200 g of the solution would be supersaturated if it contained _____ grams of solute.
    a. 2.5   b. 5   c. 10   d. 12

20. If the concentration of sodium hydroxide is 10%, then the amount of NaOH in 200 mL of solution is:
    a. 2 g   b. 5 g   c. 20 g   d. 50 g   e. 100 g   f. 200 g

21. In 400 mL of a 0.25 M solution of NaOH there are how many grams of NaOH?
    a. 2   b. 5   c. 10   d. 40   e. 4   f. 500

22. How many millimoles of HCl are there in 100 mL of 0.01 M HCl solution?
    a. 10   b. 1   c. 10^{-1} d. 10^{-2} e. 10^{-4} f. 10^{-5}

23. What is the formula weight of a compound if 20 g of the compound in 500 mL of solution gives a 0.5 M solution?
    a.10   b. 20   c. 40   d. 50   e. 60   f. 80

24. What is the formula weight of a compound if 20 g of the compound in 300 mL of solution gives a 0.2 M solution?
    a.200   b. 600   c. 167   d. 333   e. 667   f. 100

25. How many grams of $(NH_4)_2SO_4$ are needed to prepare 100 mL of a 2.5M solution?
    a. 13.2   b. 26   c. 132   d. 33   e. 66   f. 100

26. You have only 30 g of $CaBr_2$ and want to prepare a 0.20M solution. How many liters of the solution can you prepare with your 30 g of $CaBr_2$.
    a. 1.0 L   b. 0.75 L   c. 0.50 L   d. 0.44 L   e. 0.20 L

27. A solution containing 100 mg of solute in 1 L of solution has concentration of:
    a. 1 mg%   b. 10 mg%   c. 100 mg%   d. 1000 mg%

28. Which equality is correct?
    a. 1 ppm = 1000 ppb   b. 1000 ppm = 1 ppb

29. A solution that has been diluted 1:3 is less concentrated than the solution that has been diluted:
    a. 1:2   b. 1:30   c. 1:3000

30. Compared with pure water, a solution containing one mole of sugar per kg of water:
    a. melts at and boils at a higher temperature
    b. melts at and boils at a lower temperature
    c. melts higher and boils lower
    d. melts lower and boils higher

31. The freezing point in °C of a solution that contains 2 moles of sugar per kg of water is:
    a. -2   b. 2   c. 80   d. -80   e. -3.72   f. 1.02   g. -1.02

32. Which solution has the higher osmotic pressure?
    a. 0.1 M NaCl   b. 0.5 M NaCl

33. Which aqueous solution has the highest boiling point?
    a. 0.7M NaCl   b. 0.6M $CaCl_2$ c. 0.4M $Al_2(SO_4)_3$ d. 0.8M NH_4NO_3

34. Which of the following aqueous solutions has the lowest freezing point?
    a. 1.0M NaCl   b. 1.2M NH_4NO_3 c. 1.0M $CaCl_2$ d. 0.8M $AlCl_3$

35. A solution contains particles of three sizes (., o, O). If two of these types of particles pass through a dialyzing membrane, the two must be:
    a. . and o   b. . and O   c. o and O
36. In both dialysis and osmosis which particles do not pass through the membrane?
    a. water   b. small molecules   c. colloids
37. The net flow of water through a semipermeable membrane as equilibrium is approached is:
    a. from a solution of higher osmotic pressure to one of lower osmotic pressure
    b. from a solution of lower osmotic pressure to one of higher osmotic pressure
38. If two solutions with concentrations of 0.1 M sugar and 0.5 M sugar respectively are separated by a semipermeable membrane, during osmosis there is a net flow of:
    a. sugar molecules from the 0.1 M solution to the 0.5 M solution
    b. sugar molecules from the 0.5 M solution to the 0.1 M solution
    c. water molecules from the 0.1 M solution to the 0.5 M solution
    d. water molecules from the 0.5 M solution to the 0.1 M solution
39. Red blood cells undergo hemolysis if placed in a solution that has a _____ osmotic pressure than the solution inside the blood cells.
    a. higher   b. lower
40. Crenation of cells occurs when the cells are placed in a(an) _____ solution.
    a. hypotonic   b. isotonic   c. hypertonic   d. physiological saline
41. Which is not true of a colloidal dispersion?
    a. Particles may have a diameter of 10 nm.
    b. The dispersion exhibits the Tyndall effect.
    c. The dispersion does not settle out on standing.
    d. The dispersed particles can be filtered by slowly passing the dispersion through filter paper.
    e. All of the above are true of a colloidal dispersion.
42. Which type of mixture cannot exist as a colloidal dispersion?
    a. solid in solid   b. liquid in liquid   c. gas in gas
43. An emulsifying agent is used to:
    a. bring about precipitation of solute from a true solution
    b. stabilize a colloidal dispersion
    c. filter the particles of a suspension
44. In the Tyndall effect, one observes:
    a. the precipitation of solute triggered by addition of a seed crystal
    b. particles slowly settling out of a suspension
    c. a beam of scattered light
45. Blood sugar levels are about 100 mg glucose ($C_6H_{12}O_6$) / 100 mL blood or 0.10%. If a person has 6.0 L of blood, how many grams of glucose does this represent? _____ How many oz of glucose? _____
46. Associate the items on the right with the best term on the left.
    ___ colligative property   a. oil and vinegar dressing
    ___ Tyndall effect   b. de-icing roadways
    ___ osmotic presssure   c. ice cream
    ___ dialysis   d. kidney machine
    ___ colloid   e. light house
    ___ immiscible   f. cell membranes
    ___ emulsifying agent   g. detergent

ANSWERS

Problems

1. a. 0.5 M	b. 0.5 M	c. 0.5 M	d. 0.1 M	e. 0.4 M
2. a. 0.05 M	b. 1 M	c. 0.05 M	d. 0.2 M	e. 0.5 M
3. a. 2 mol	b. 0.001 mol	c. 0.1 mol	d. 0.25 mol	e. 0.0032 mol
4. a. 117 g	b. 9.8 g	c. 1.49 g	d. 200 g	e. 128 g
5. a. 5.85 g	b. 0.0196 g	c. 14.9 g	d. 400 g	e. 0.64 g
6. a. 10 g	b. 0.5 g	c. 12 g	d. 40 g	e. 2 g
7. a. 4 g	b. ~0.05 g	c. 1.2 g	d. 400 g	e. ~20 g

8. 0.1 M, 0.4%, 400 mg%

Self-Test

1. b	10. d	19. d	28. a	37. b
2. e	11. c	20. c	29. a	38. c
3. a	12. a	21. e	30. d	39. b
4. a	13. c	22. b	31. e	40. c
5. b	14. b	23. f	32. b	41. d
6. d	15. c	24. d	33. c	42. c
7. a	16. c	25. d	34. d	43. b
8. b	17. a	26. b	35. a	44. c
9. b	18. c	27. b	36. c	45. 6, 0.21
				46. b,e,f,d,c,a,g

CHAPTER 10: ACIDS AND BASES I

KEY WORDS

acid	*weak acids*	*hydroxide ion*	*antacids*
Arrhenius	*ortho acids*	*salt*	*Brønsted-Lowry*
hydronium ion	*meta acid*	*neutralization*	*conjugate acid*
strong acids	*base*	*acid rain*	*conjugate base*
proton donor	*proton acceptor*	*anhydride*	*alkalosis*
carboxylic acid	*amines*		

SUMMARY

10.1 Acids and Bases: Definitions and Properties.
   A. Characteristic properties of *acids*.
      1. Taste sour
      2. Stinging sensation
      3. Turn blue litmus red
      4. React with active metals to produce H_2 gas
      5. React with alkalis or bases to produce water and a salt
   B. Characteristic properties of *bases*.
      1. Taste bitter
      2. Feel slippery
      3. Turn litmus from red to blue
      4. React with acids to produce water and salt
   C. *Arrhenius* (1887) proposed that acid properties are actually the properties of hydrogen ions (H^+) and defined acids as compounds that yield hydrogen ions in aqueous solutions. Arrhenius defined bases as compounds that yield *hydroxide ions* (OH^-) in aqueous solutions. *Neutralization* refers to the reaction of an acid and a base to form water ($H^+ + OH^- \rightarrow H_2O$).
   D. The hydronium ion (H_3O^+) is used to represent the hydrated proton [$H(H_2O)_4^+$ would be better but more cumbersome].
   E. *Brønsted-Lowry* defined an acid as a *proton donor* and a base as a *proton acceptor*. Thus all acids exist as *conjugate acid/conjugate base* (or c.a./c.b.) pairs.
      1. c.a. = c.b. + H^+
      2. The conjugate base of a strong conjugate acid (HCl) will be a weak base (Cl^-). Similarly, the c.b. of a weak c.a. (HPO_4^{2-}) will be a strong base (PO_4^{3-}).
      3. $H_2PO_4^- + OH^- \rightarrow HPO_4^{2-} + H_2O$
             c.a.   c.b.   c.b.   c.a.
             stronger pair   weaker pair
   F. Some common acids
      1. Monoprotic: HCl, HNO_3, CH_3COOH (acetic acid)
      2. Diprotic: H_2SO_4, H_2CO_3
      3. Triprotic: H_3PO_4, $C_3H_4OH(COOH)_3$ (citric acid)

10.2 Strong and Weak Acids
   A. *Strong acids* are those that ionize completely, or nearly so, in aqueous solutions.
      $$HCl + H_2O \rightarrow H_3O^+ + Cl^-$$

B. *Weak acids* ionize only slightly in aqueous solutions. (A 1.0 M acetic acid solution is only 0.42% dissociated.)

$$CH_3COOH + H_2O \rightleftharpoons CH_3COO^- + H_3O^+$$

C. Formulas of inorganic acids traditionally have the hydrogen first (HCl, HNO_3, H_2SO_4) whereas for organic acids the hydrogen is traditionally written last as part of the carboxylic acid ($-COOH$) group. However, you should keep in mind that structurally the hydrogen is bonded to the oxygen in both HNO_3 (as NO_2OH) and $HCOOH$.

10.3 Names of Some Common Acids

A. Naming acid / Naming anion   Examples

1. hydro___ic acid	___ide	HCl	hydrochloric acid	Cl^-	chloride
2. hypo___ous acid	hypo___ite	$HClO$	hypochlorous acid	ClO^-	hypochlorite
3. ___ous acid	___ite	$HClO_2$	chlorous acid	ClO_2^-	chlorite
4. ___ic acid	___ate	$HClO_3$	chloric acid	ClO_3^-	chlorate
5. per___ic acid	per___ate	$HClO_4$	perchloric acid	ClO_4^-	perchlorate

B. *Strong acids* give up their protons readily.
1. HCl - hydrochloric acid
2. HBr - hydrobromic acid
3. HI - hydroiodic acid
4. HNO_3 - nitric acid
5. H_2SO_4 - sulfuric acid

C. *Weak acids* do not give up their protons readily.
1. H_3PO_4 - phosphoric acid (moderately strong)
2. HF - hydrofluoric acid
3. CH_3COOH - acetic acid
4. H_2CO_3 - carbonic acid
5. NH_4^+ - ammonium ion
6. HCN - hydrogen cyanide or hydrocyanic acid
7. H_3BO_3 - boric acid

D. *Ortho and meta acids* - any acid with 3 or more replaceable hydrogens can have water (H_2O) removed to form the meta acid.
1. H_3PO_4 - phosphoric acid (ortho form) - PO_4^{3-} phosphate ion
2. $(HPO_3)_3$ - meta phosphoric acid

10.4 Some Common Bases

A. Arrhenius defined bases as compounds that yield *hydroxide ions* (OH^-) in aqueous solutions.

B. Some compounds produce OH^- ions by reacting with water.

$$HOH + :NH_3 \rightarrow NH_4^+ + OH^-$$
$$H_2O + CO_3^{2-} \rightarrow HCO_3^- + OH^-$$

C. Organic amines are related to ammonia and are common weak bases in living cells.

D. Common bases
1. Strong bases: $NaOH$ (lye), KOH, $Ca(OH)_2$ (lime)
2. Weak bases: NH_3, CH_3COO^- ion, CN^- ion, etc.

10.5 Acidic and Basic Anhydrides

A. Nonmetal oxides are acid *anhydrides*.

$$SO_3 + H_2O \rightarrow H_2SO_4$$

B. Metal oxides are basic anhydrides

$$CaO + H_2O \rightarrow Ba(OH)_2$$

10.6 Neutralization Reactions

A. An acid reacts with an equivalent amount of base in a ***neutralization*** reaction to produce water and a *salt*.

$$HCl\ (aq) + NaOH\ (aq) \rightarrow H_2O + NaCl\ (aq)$$

B. Net ionic equation for neutralization

$$H_3O^+ + Cl^- + Na^+ + OH^- \rightarrow 2\,H_2O + Na^+ + Cl^-$$
$$\text{or} \quad H_3O^+ + OH^- \rightarrow 2\,H_2O$$

10.7 Reactions of Acids with Carbonates and Bicarbonates

A. Carbonates (CO_3^{2-}) and bicarbonates (HCO_3^-) are salts of the weak and unstable carbonic acid (H_2CO_3).

1. $H_2CO_3 + OH^- \rightarrow HCO_3^- + H_2O$
2. $H_2CO_3 + 2\,OH^- \rightarrow CO_3^{2-} + 2\,H_2O$

B. Carbonic acid is not very stable.

$$H_2CO_3\ (aq) \rightarrow H_2O + CO_2\ (g)$$

C. *Acid rain* and marble statues

1. Sulfur-containing coal produces SO_2.
2. SO_2 reacts with O_2 to produce SO_3.
3. SO_3 combines with water to form H_2SO_4 (acid rain).
4. Limestone and marble contain $CaCO_3$.

$$CaCO_3 + H_2SO_4\ (aq) \rightarrow Ca^{2+}(aq) + CO_2\ (g) + H_2O + SO_4^{2-}(aq)$$

10.8 Antacids: A Basic Remedy

A. The stomach secretes HCl to aid in digestion of food. Over indulgence and stress can lead to hyperacidity and ulcers. Ulcers are holes in the mucosal lining of the stomach caused by excess acidity or certain bacteria.

B. *Antacids*

1. Alka-Seltzer - sodium bicarbonate + citric acid + aspirin
2. Tums - flavored calcium carbonate
3. Phillips "Milk of Magnesia" - suspension of magnesium hydroxide
4. Maalox - combination of aluminum and magnesium hydroxides
5. Rolaids - aluminum sodium dihydroxy carbonate

C. All antacids are bases, and overuse can make the blood too alkaline, *alkalosis.*

10.9 Acids, Bases, and Human Health

A. Strong acids and bases are corrosive poisons that can cause chemical "burns."

B. Most acids and bases produced in this country are used by industry, but some can be found around the house.

1. H_2SO_4 - automobile batteries, some drain cleaners
2. HCl (muriatic acid) - toilet bowl cleaner
3. NaOH (lye) - drain and oven cleaner

DISCUSSION

We will begin by reviewing the definitions of acids. Acids were defined in the chapter in three ways: as compounds that yield hydrogen ions; as compounds that yield hydronium ions in aqueous solutions; and as compounds that act as proton donors. It is now generally accepted that a hydrogen ion does not exist in solution as an independent unit. Thus the second and third definitions are attempts to be a bit more accurate in describing the action of an acid.

A hydrogen ion and a proton are identical species. The Bohr picture of a hydrogen atom is:

A hydrogen ion is the hydrogen atom minus its outer shell electron. For hydrogen, with only one electron, that means that the ion is simply the hydrogen nucleus. The hydrogen nucleus contains a single proton. Therefore, $H^+ = p$. The preferred term for this species is proton, but the symbol most commonly used is H^+. The proton or hydrogen ion does not exist as an independent species in solution. In aqueous solutions, protons from acids are transported by water molecules. This is where the hydronium ion comes in. It's like transferring food from your plate to your mouth. It's the food that's transferred, but a fork carries it from one place to another. In reactions involving acids in aqueous solutions, the proton is being transferred, but a water molecule carries the proton from one place to another.

The many reactions discussed in this chapter can be classified under just a few headings. First, there are what we could call "the defining equations." These are the equations that say "this compound is an acid," or "this compound is a base." Since acids and bases were defined in a number of ways in the chapter, the defining equation can be written in a number of ways.

Equation for an Arrhenius acid:	$HCl \rightarrow H^+ + Cl^-$
Equation for a Brønsted-Lowry acid:	$HCl + H_2O \rightarrow H_3O^+ + Cl^-$

Both equations indicate that HCl is an acid, but the second one emphasizes that the proton is transferred and not simply released. The extent to which this reaction proceeds to the right determines whether the acid is called strong or weak. Table 10.1 in the text lists several important strong and weak acids and is worth committing to memory.

Equations for an Arrhenius base:	$NaOH \rightarrow Na^+ + OH^-$
Equations for a Brønsted-Lowry base:	$OH^- + H_3O^+ \rightarrow H_2O + H_2O$
	$NH_3 + H_2O \rightarrow NH_4^+ + OH^-$

Notice that the equation for ammonia qualified under both definitions: it shows the release of hydroxide ion (Arrhenius) and it also shows ammonia picking up a proton (Brønsted-Lowry). For sodium hydroxide, we use two different equations. To satisfy the Arrhenius definition, we simply show sodium hydroxide dissociating to produce the hydroxide ion in solution. To satisfy the Brønsted-Lowry definition, we concentrate on the hydroxide ion from sodium hydroxide and show it picking up a proton.

The remaining reactions can be categorized into three groups.

1. Neutralization: Acid plus base yields salt plus water.
$$HCl \quad + \ NaOH \qquad \rightarrow \qquad NaCl \ + \ H_2O$$
2. Reaction of active metal with acid yields salt plus hydrogen gas.
$$Mg \quad + \ H_2SO_4 \qquad \rightarrow \qquad MgSO_4 \qquad + \ H_2$$
3. Reaction of carbonate (or bicarbonate) with acid yields salt plus carbon dioxide plus water.
$$2\,HCl \ + \ Na_2CO_3 \qquad \rightarrow \qquad 2\,NaCl \ + \ CO_2 \ + \ H_2O$$
$$HCl \quad + \ NaHCO_3 \qquad \rightarrow \qquad NaCl \ + \ CO_2 \ + \ H_2O$$
We note again that the very important reaction of carbonic acid:
$$H_2CO_3 \ \rightarrow \ CO_2 \ + \ H_2O$$
is not a general reaction of acids or even a general reaction of weak acids. It is a chemical property peculiar to carbonic acid. The equation indicates the special instability of carbonic acid. If this compound is produced in a reaction, e.g.,

$$HCl \ + \ NaHCO_3 \ \rightarrow \ NaCl \ + \ H_2CO_3$$
$$\Downarrow \ \ \text{it (immediately) decomposes.}$$
$$H_2O \ + \ CO_2$$

Notice that when another weak acid, such as acetic acid, is produced in a reaction:
$$HCl \ + \ CH_3COONa \ \rightarrow \ NaCl \ + \ CH_3COOH$$

the acid does not decompose. We call your attention to this property of carbonic acid because the equilibrium between carbon dioxide, carbonic acid and bicarbonate ion play an extremely important role in controlling the acidity of the blood. This subject will be discussed in Chapter 11.

SELF-TEST

1. According to the theory of Arrhenius, the properties of acids are the properties of:
   a. H^+ b. OH^- c. H_2O d. NH_3
2. According to the theory of Arrhenius, the properties of bases are the properties of:
   a. H^+ b. OH^- c. H_2O d. NH_3
3. According to the Brønsted-Lowry theory, an acid is
   a. a proton donor   b. a proton acceptor
   c. an hydronium ion donor   d. an hydronium ion acceptor
4. According to the Brønsted-Lowry theory, a base is
   a. a proton donor   b. a proton acceptor
   c. an hydronium ion donor   d. an hydronium ion acceptor
5. If litmus paper changes color from blue to red when placed in an aqueous solution, the solution is:
   a. acidic   b. basic   c. neutral
6. Which is a monoprotic acid?
   a. H_2CO_3 b. H_2SO_4 c. CH_3COOH d. H_3PO_4
7. Which is the weakest acid?
   a. HCl b. HNO_3 c. H_2SO_4 d. H_2CO_3
8. Which is a strong acid?
   a. H_2CO_3 b. CH_3COOH c. H_3PO_4 d. HNO_3 e. HCN
9. According to the equation $C_6H_5OH \ + \ H_2O \ \rightleftharpoons \ C_6H_5O^- \ + \ H_3O^+$, the compound C_6H_5OH is a:
   a. strong acid   b. strong base   c. weak acid   d. weak base

10. According to the equation shown in question 9, which set constitutes a conjugate acid-base pair?
    a. C_6H_5OH and H_2O b. C_6H_5OH and $C_6H_5O^-$ c. C_6H_5OH and H_3O^+

11. According to the equation $C_6H_5OH + OH^- \rightarrow C_6H_5O^- + H_2O$, the compound C_6H_5OH is the:
    a. acid   b. base   c. salt   d. buffer

12. The conjugate partner of a strong acid is a:
    a. strong acid   b. weak acid   c. strong base   d. weak base

13. According to the Brønsted-Lowry theory, a weak acid:
    a. holds on to its protons relatively tightly
    b. has a very weak hold on its protons

14. The formula for phosphoric acid is:
    a. H_2PO_3 b. H_3PO_3 c. H_2PO_4 d. H_3PO_4

15. The name of the acid HBr is:
    a. hydrobromic acid   b. bromic acid   c. bromous acid   d. bromate acid

16. If ClO_3^- is the chlorate ion, then $HClO_3$ is:
    a. hydrochloric acid   b. chloric acid   c. chlorous acid   d. chlorate acid

17. If ClO_2^- is the chlorite ion, then chlorous acid would be:
    a. H_2ClO_3 b. $HClO_3$ c. $HClO_2$ d. H_3ClO_4

18. Identify the correct formula for sodium hypochlorite.
    a. Na_2ClO_3 b. $NaClO_3$ c. $NaClO_2$ d. $NaClO$

19. Identify the correct formula for potassium perchlorate.
    a. K_2ClO_3 b. $KClO_3$ c. $KClO_4$ d. $KClO$

20. Identify the correct formula for sodium chlorate.
    a. Na_2ClO_3 b. $NaClO_3$ c. $NaClO_2$ d. $NaClO$

21. Which oxide when added to water would produce an acidic solution?
    a. K_2O b. BaO c. SO_2 d. MgO e. Na_2O

22. The metaborate ion is BO_2^-. Orthoboric acid is:
    a. BO_2^{3-} b. BO_3^{3-} c. HBO_2 d. H_3BO_3

23. Which is regarded as a strong base in aqueous solution?
    a. KOH b. $Mg(OH)_2$ c. NH_3

24. Which base exists primarily in un-ionized form in aqueous solution?
    a. KOH b. $Mg(OH)_2$ c. NH_3

25. Which is not highly ionized in aqueous solution?
    a. $NaOH$ b. $Ca(OH)_2$ c. H_2SO_4 d. CH_3COOH e. $(NH_4)_3PO_4$

26. Muriatic acid is:
    a. H_3PO_4 b. H_2SO_4 c. H_2CO_3 d. HCl

27. Which set of reactants does not produce a gas when mixed?
    a. $NaHCO_3$ and HCl
    b. $NaOH$ and HCl
    c. Mg and HCl
    d. All of the reactions yield a gaseous product.

28. Which is not a product of the reaction: $Na_2CO_3 + HNO_3 \rightarrow$?
    a. H_2 b. Na^+ c. CO_2 d. H_2O e. NO_3^-

29. The equation, $H_2CO_3 \rightarrow CO_2 + H_2O$, indicates that carbonic acid is:
    a. a weak acid   b. a strong acid   c. an unstable acid

30. Lye is the common name for:
    a. $NaOH$ b. NH_3 c. HCl d. H_2CO_3

31. Which equation describes a neutralization reaction?
    a. $Cu + 2 Ag^+ \rightarrow 2 Ag + Cu^{2+}$
    b. $2 HNO_3 + Zn \rightarrow Zn(NO_3)_2 + H_2$
    c. $CH_3COOH + NaOH \rightarrow CH_3COONa + H_2O$
    d. All of the equations are for neutralization reactions.

32. The net ionic equation that describes a neutralization reaction is:
    a. $H^+ + OH^- \rightarrow H_2O$
    b. $HCO_3^- + H^+ \rightarrow H_2CO_3$
    c. $H_2CO_3 \rightarrow CO_2 + H_2O$
    d. $M + 2 H^+ \rightarrow M_2^+ + H_2$

33. Which of the following has the highest concentration of H+ ion in aqueous solution?
    a. 0.30 M H_2CO_3 b. 0.20 M HCl   c. 0.50 M HCOOH   d. 1.0 M NH_3

34. The conjugate acid of HPO_4^{-2} is:
    a. H_3PO_4 b. $H_2PO_4^-$ c. HPO_3^{-2} d. H_2PO_4 e. HPO_3^{-2}

35. The conjugate base of HPO_4^{-2} is:
    a. H_3PO_4 b. $H_2PO_4^-$ c. HPO_3^{-2} d. H_2PO_4 e. PO_4^{-3}

36. Which process is described by the equation:
    $$H_2SO_4 (aq) + CaCO_3 (s) \rightarrow CaSO_4(aq) + H_2O + CO_2(g)$$
    a. erosion of limestone by acidic pollutants
    b. neutralization of stomach acid by an antacid
    c. the oxidation of an active metal by an acid

37. Which is not found in antacid preparations?
    a. $CaCO_3$ b. $Mg(OH)_2$ c. NaOH   d. $NaHCO_3$

38. Hydrochloric acid is found:
    a. in the stomach   b. in toilet bowl cleaners   c. in both a and b

39. Which is the bicarbonate ion?
    a. H_2CO_3 b. $H_2CO_4^-$ c. HCO_3^{-2} d. HCO_3^- e. CO_3^{-2}

40. Which solution does not cause severe chemical burns on contact with skin?
    a. concentrated sulfuric acid
    b. concentrated hydrochloric acid
    c. concentrated sodium hydroxide solution
    d. concentrated sodium chloride solution
    e. All cause severe chemical burns.

ANSWERS

1. a	9. c	17. c	25. d	33. b
2. b	10. b	18. d	26. d	34. b
3. a	11. a	19. c	27. b	35. e
4. b	12. d	20. b	28. a	36. a
5. a	13. a	21. c	29. c	37. c
6. c	14. d	22. d	30. a	38. c
7. d	15. a	23. a	31. c	39. d
8. d	16. b	24. c	32. a	40. d

CHAPTER 11:   ACIDS AND BASES   II

KEY WORDS

equivalent weight	*titration*	*ion product*	*acidosis*
equivalence point	*end point*	*hydrolysis*	*alkalosis*
normality (N)	*pH, pOH*	*buffer*	*indicators*
neutralization	*standard*	*dilution*	

SUMMARY

11.1 Concentrations of Acids and Bases
  A. *Dilution* problems (Recall: Concentration x Volume = Amount of Solute)
    1. It is frequently necessary to prepare dilute solutions from more concentrated stock solutions.
    2. V_c x M_c = V_d x M_d that is, **amount** in concentrated solution = **amount** in diluted solution.
  B. Equivalents and normality
    1. Not all acids and bases are *equivalent* in the number of protons donated or accepted. H_2SO_4 donates 2 protons per molecule while HCl can only donate 1. H_2SO_4 is said to have 2 equivalents per mole.

Common Acid or Base	Equivalents per mole (*n*)
HCl, HNO_3, NaOH, NH_3	1
H_2SO_4, H_2CO_3, $Ca(OH)_2$, $Mg(OH)_2$	2
H_3PO_4	3

    2. *Equivalent weight* = Formula weight/*n*
    3. *Normality (N)*
        N = equivalents/L of solution;   N = *n* x Molarity

11.2 Acid-Base Titrations
  A. For acid-base reactions, the *equivalence point* occurs when the same number of equivalents of acid and base have been added so that *neutralization* has occurred.
  B. *Titration* is a process for determining the amount of an unknown substance by adding an equivalent amount of a reactive substance of known concentration. Titrations can be used with many types of systems providing there is some *indicator* that produces a detectable change (*end point*) to signal that the *equivalence point* has been reached. Phenolphthalein is a common indicator that is colorless in its conjugate acid form (acidic solutions) but turns pink in its conjugate base form (basic solutions).
  C. Typical steps in titrating an unknown acid with a standard base:
    1. A carefully measured aliquot of the acid sample is placed in a flask.
    2. A few drops of an indicator dye are added to the acid sample.
    3. A *standard* base solution is then added slowly from a burette until the dye changes color. This is the end point of the titration and should also represent the equivalence point.
    4. Calculations: At the equivalence point - # equivalents of acid = # equivalents of base,

      or N_a x V_a = N_b x V_b , so that $N_a = N_b$ x $\dfrac{V_b}{V_a}$

11.3 The pH Scale
  A. Water can act as both an acid and a base.
    1. H_2O + H_2O $\rightleftharpoons$ H_3O^+ + OH^-
         55.5 M   .0000001 M   .0000001 M

2. Pure water at 25°C is a neutral solution having

$$[H_3O^+] = [OH^-] = 0.0000001 \text{ M} = 1.0 \times 10^{-7} \text{ M}$$

B. *Ion product* of water, K_w

1. $K_w = [H_3O^+] \times [OH^-] = 1.0 \times 10^{-14}$

2. This equation, defining the ion product of water, applies to any aqueous solution at 25°C. Thus a solution 0.1 M in H_3O^+ must also be 10^{-13} M in OH^-.

C. The pH scale

1. *pH* = -log $[H_3O^+]$;   *pOH* = -log $[OH^-]$

2. pH + pOH = 14

3. **pH < 7 acidic; pH = 7 neutral; pH > 7 basic**

4.

$[H_3O^+]$	$[OH^-]$	pH	pOH	solution
10^{-7}	10^{-7}	7	7	neutral
10^{-4}	10^{-10}	4	10	acidic
10^{-9}	10^{-5}	9	5	basic
1.0	10^{-14}	0	14	acidic

5. Students of chemistry should be familiar with pH and be able to fill in a table like the one above when given any one of the first four values. When the $[H_3O^+]$ is not a simple power of ten, it is necessary to use a "log table" or a calculator with a "log" function to determine the pH (e.g. if $[H_3O^+] = 6.3 \times 10^{-8} = 10^{0.8} \times 10^{-8} = 10^{-7.2}$, thus pH = 7.2).

$[H_3O^+] =$	6.3×10^{-7}	6.3×10^{-8}	6.3×10^{-9}
pH =	6.2	7.2	8.2

(Note that a change of one pH unit always implies a ten fold change in [H+] concentration.)

D. Measuring pH

1. Many organic indicator dyes are different colors in their conjugate acid and conjugate base forms and can be used to estimate ±1 pH unit.

2. pH meters measure $[H_3O^+]$ concentration electronically to about 0.01 pH units.

11.4 Salts in Water: Acidic, Basic, or Neutral?

A. Many salts dissolve in water to produce acidic or basic solutions as the weak conjugate acid (c.a.) or conjugate base (cab.) reacts with water (*hydrolysis*) to produce new H_3O^+ or OH^- ions.

1. Ammonium chloride in solution (acidic)

$$NH_4^+ + H_2O \rightleftharpoons H_3O^+ + NH_3$$

2. Sodium cyanide in solution (basic)

$$CN^- + H_2O \rightleftharpoons HCN + OH^-$$

B. Rules

1. Salt of a strong acid   + strong base → neutral salt solution
   HCl   NaOH   (NaCl)

2. Salt of a strong acid   + weak base → acidic salt solution
   HCl NH_3 (NH_4Cl)

3. Salt of a weak acid   + strong base → basic salt solution
   HCN   NaOH   (NaCN)

4. Salt of a weak acid   + weak base → ? (depends on their relative strengths)

11.5 Buffers: Control of pH

A. A *buffer* solution is one that resists changes in pH upon addition of acid or base.

B. Chemically, a buffer is a solution of a weak conjugate acid-conjugate base pair. The conjugate acid (c.a.) neutralizes incoming base, and the conjugate base (c.b.) neutralizes incoming acid.

11.6 Buffers in Blood
   A. Blood plasma pH is ~ 7.4. If it falls below 6.8 *(acidosis)* or rises above 7.8 *(alkalosis)*, it can lead to death.
   B. Our bodies are acid factories. The stomach produces HCl, our muscles produce lactic acid, and respiration produces H_2CO_3. To maintain blood pH, buffers are needed. Three of the most important are:
   1. Bicarbonate/carbonic acid system

$$HCO_3^- + H^+ \quad \Leftrightarrow \quad H_2CO_3 \quad \Leftrightarrow \quad H_2O + CO_2$$
   (kidneys)   (lungs)

   The ratio of HCO_3^-/H_2CO_3 must be maintained at about 20:1 for this system to buffer at pH 7.4. This ratio is maintained in part because excess HCO_3^- can be removed by the kidneys and excess CO_2 removed via the lungs.
   2. $HPO_4^{2-}/H_2PO_4^-$ (monohydrogen phosphate/dihydrogen phosphate)
   3. The c.b. $(-COO^-)$ and c.a. $(-NH_3^+)$ pairs of protein molecules

11.7 Acidosis and Alkalosis
   A. *Acidosis*: blood pH < 7.35
      1. Prolonged, strenuous exercise
      2. Starvation, diabetes mellitus
   B. *Alkalosis*: blood pH > 7.45

DISCUSSION

   The use of equivalents and normality may seem to introduce unnecessary confusion now that you are just getting comfortable with molarity. However, equivalents are a more convenient unit for expressing the relative amounts of reacting substances. You will find that expressing concentrations in terms of equivalents/L, or normality, will make acid-base titration calculations easier to handle. We offer below a comparison of calculations of moles and molarity and equivalents and normality. Sulfuric acid is used as the example, and we propose to calculate the concentration of a solution containing 9.8 g of H_2SO_4 in a total of 2 L of solution.

Moles and Molarity	Equivalents and Normality
Formula Wt. = 98	Equivalent Wt. = (Formula Wt./2) = 49
Gram Form. Wt. (GFW) = 98 g/mole	Gram Equiv. Wt. (GEW) = 49 g/equiv.
Number of moles: weight/GFW	Number of equivalents: weight/GEW
Example: $\dfrac{9.8\ g}{98\ g/mole}$ = 0.1 mol	Example: $\dfrac{9.8\ g}{49\ g/equivalent}$ = 0.2 equiv.
Molarity: $\dfrac{\text{moles of solute}}{\text{liters of solution}}$	**Normality**: $\dfrac{\text{equivalents of solute}}{\text{liters of solution}}$
Example: $\dfrac{0.1\ mole}{2\ L}$ = **0.05 M**	Example: $\dfrac{0.2\ equivalent}{2\ L}$ = **0.1 N**
M x 2 = N for H_2SO_4 (since there are 2 equiv. / mol)	

We could have calculated the molarity and then used the relationship of $N = 2 \times M$ to determine the normality. The 2 in that relationship and the 2 in the denominator of the calculation of equivalent weight above are both derived from the fact that sulfuric acid is a diprotic acid, i.e., it supplies two protons.

The other major concept involving calculations that was introduced in this chapter is the pH scale. We could introduce more mathematics by asking you to work with more difficult logarithms in dealing with pH, such as examples 11.9 and 11.10 of the text, but what we really want you to do is to become comfortable with the concept of pH. For that reason, we'll stick to calculations involving simple powers of ten (i.e., 0.001 or 10^{-3}) so you can clearly see the pattern for conversion from concentration units to pH or pOH units. You should be able to interconvert among pH, $[H^+]$, pOH and $[OH^-]$ by using the definition of pH (or pOH) and the ion product constant of water. Thus, if you know $[H^+]$ equals 10^{-6} M, then you also know that the pH is 6, the pOH is 8 (because pH + pOH = 14), and $[OH^-]$ equals 10^{-8} M.

Similarly: If $[OH^-] = 10^{-3}$ M, then pOH = 3, pH = 11, $[H^+] = 10^{-11}$ M.
 If pH = 9, then $[H^+] = 10^{-9}$ M, pOH = 5, $[OH^-] = 10^{-5}$ M.
 If pOH = 1, then $[OH^-] = 10^{-1}$ M, pH = 13, $[H^+] = 10^{-13}$ M.

Although pOH is as easy to calculate as pH, the latter value is almost always quoted. Therefore, you will find it most useful to gear your thinking to the pH scale. Remember that low pH means that there are lots of protons available and high pH means that there are few protons available. Low pH means acidic, high pH means basic. The variations in pH, pOH, $[H^+]$, and $[OH^-]$ can be summarized as follows.

	Acidic	Neutral	Basic	
pH	1	7	13	
$[H^+]$	10^{-1}	10^{-7}	10^{-13}	
$[OH^-]$	10^{-13}	10^{-7}		10^{-1}
pOH	13	7	1	

Problems   The following problems supplement those at the end of the chapter.

1. Oxalic acid ($H_2C_2O_4$) is a diprotic acid.
    a. Calculate the formula weight and the equivalent weight of oxalic acid.
    b. Calculate the number of equivalents in 9.0 g of oxalic acid; in 450g; in 18.0 g.
    c. Calculate the normality of the following aqueous solutions of oxalic acid: 9.0 g in 1 L of
        solution;   450 g in 5 L; 18 g in 500 mL.
    d. What are the molarities of the solutions in part c?
2. In many instances, particularly when the common mineral acids like H_2SO_4, H_3PO_4, HNO_3, etc., are
    involved, solutions of the acids are prepared by diluting the concentrated acids. Review Examples 11.1
    and 11.2 in the chapter, then try the following.
        a. Concentrated H_2SO_4 is 36 N. What volume of this acid should be used in preparing 500 mL of
            12 N H_2SO_4?   2 L of 3.6 N H_2SO_4? 100 mL of 9 M H_2SO_4?
        b. What concentration of solution results when concentrated H_2SO_4 is diluted as indicated? 10 mL
            diluted to 100 mL; 0.5 L diluted to 2.5 L; 100 mL diluted to 0.2 L?
3. Determine the unknown concentration from the given titration data.
        a. If 20 mL of 0.5 N HCl were required to titrate 50 mL of NaOH, what is the normality of the
            NaOH?

b. If 15 mL of 0.4 N H_2SO_4 were required to titrate 45 mL of NaOH, what is the normality of the NaOH?

c. If 30 mL of 0.4 M H_2SO_4 were required to titrate 60 mL of NaOH, what is the molarity of the NaOH?

d. If 100 mL of 0.1 N H_2SO_4 were required to titrate 200 mL of $Ba(OH)_2$, what is the concentration of the barium hydroxide solution in normality?   in molarity?

4. Fill in the blanks in the table.

	pH	pOH	$[H^+]$	$[OH^-]$	acidic or basic?
a.	2	___	___	___	_____
b.	___	7.6	___	___	_____
c.	___	___	10^{-10} M	___	_____
d.	___	___	___	0.01 M	_____

SELF-TEST

1. If 4 equivalents of a substance are dissolved in 200 mL of solution, the concentration is:
    a. 1.25 N   b. 2 N   c. 4 N   d. 8 N   e. 20 N

2. If 2 g of an acid in 0.5 L of solution gives a 0.1 N solution, what is the equivalent weight of the acid?
    a. 1   b. 2   c. 4   d. 10   e. 20   f. 40   g. 100   h. 200   i. 400

3. If a sample contains 1 milliequivalent of H_2SO_4, how many grams of H_2SO_4 does it contain?
    a. 0.0049   b. 0.0098   c. 0.0196   d. 0.049   e. 0.098   f. 0.196   g. 49   h. 98   i. 196

4. Twenty milliequivalents of a compound per liter of solution gives a solution with a concentration of:
    a. 20 N   b. 2 N   c. 0.2 N   d. 0.02 N   e. 0.002 N

5. If 72 g of H_3X in 1 L of solution gives a 3 N solution, then the equivalent weight of H_3X is:
    a. 3   b. 6   c. 8   d. 12   e. 16   f. 24   g. 48   h. 72

6. When used with sulfuric, hydrochloric or nitric acids, the term dilute refers to a concentration of:
    a. 1 M   b. 1 N   c. 6 M   d. 6 N   e. 12 M   f. 36 N

7. How many mL of a stock 6.0 N HCl solution are required to prepare 50.0 mL of a 0.10 N HCl solution?
    a. 0.833   b. 6.0   c. 8.33   d. 1.2   e. 1.6   f. 2.4

8. How many mL of a stock 8.0 N KCN solution are required to prepare 10.0 mL of a 0.010 N KCN solution?
    a. 0.10   b. 0.125   c. 0.40   d. 0.08   e. 0.0125   f. 0.008

9. A standard base is:
    a. sodium hydroxide
    b. a solution of base of known concentration
    c. a basic solution with pH 7

10. A solution is considered strongly acidic if its pH is:
    a. 4   b. 6   c. 7   d. 8   e. 13   f. 0

11. What is the pH of a 0.0001 M solution of HCl?
    a. 10^4 b. 10^{-4} c. 10^{10} d. 10^{-10} e. 4   f. -4   g. 10

12. What is the pH of a 0.001 M solution of NaOH?
    a. 10^3 b. -11   c. 10^{11} d. 10^{-11} e. 3   f. -3   g. 11

13. What is the [OH⁻] concentration in a solution with pH 4?
     a. 10 M   b. 4 M   c. 10^{-10} M   d. 10^{-4} M

14. A solution is classified as a basic solution if:
     a. $[OH^-] = 10^{-8}$ M   b. $[H^+] = 10^{-4}$ M   c. pH = 7   d. pH = 9

15. Which of the following is a typical indicator?
     a. a mixture of a weak acid and its salt   b. litmus   c. a burette

16. Consider these solutions:
     (1) 0.001 M NaOH   (2) a solution with pH 9   (3) a solution with pOH 6   (4) 10^{-5} M HCl .
     If the solutions are arranged left to right in the order of increasing acidity, the order is:
     a. 1 2 3 4
     b. 4 3 2 1
     c. 1 4 3 2
     d. 4 3 1 2
     e. 2 1 3 4

17. In a titration an indicator is used to:
     a. buffer the solution
     b. make the end point of the titration visible
     c. neutralize the acid or base present

18. Which of the following salts, when dissolved, results in a solution with a pH greater than 7?
     a. NH_4Cl b. $(NH_4)_2SO_4$ c. KBr   d. KCN   e. KNO_3

19. Which of the following salts, when dissolved, results in a solution with a pH less than 7?
     a. NH_4Cl b. Na_2SO_4 c. KCl   d. K_3PO_4 e. NaCN

20. If the pH of a solution of a salt is 6, the salt must be one that was formed from:
     a. a strong acid and a strong base
     b. a strong acid and a weak base
     c. a weak acid and a strong base
     d. a weak acid and a weak base

21. The pH of a solution of a salt obtained from the titration of acetic acid with potassium hydroxide is :
     a. somewhat acidic   b. somewhat basic   c. neutral

22. An aqueous solution of NH_4NO_3 is slightly acidic because of the following equilibrium:
     a. $H_2O \rightarrow H^+ + OH^-$
     b. $NO_3^- + H_2O \rightleftharpoons HNO_3 + OH^-$
     c. $NH_4^+ + H_2O \rightleftharpoons NH_3 + H_3O^+$

23. A student titrated 15.0 mL of an unknown acid solution with 25.0 mL of a 0.100 M KOH solution. What is the normality of the unknown acid?
     a. 0.115   b. 0.150   c. 0.230   d. 0.167   e. 0.126

24. A student titrated 20.0 mL of an unknown acid solution with 32.4 mL of a 0.115 M KOH solution. What is the normality of the unknown acid?
     a. 0.153   b. 0.084   c. 0.224   d. 0.347   e. 0.186

25. A buffer is:
     a. used to establish the end point of a titration
     b. used to maintain the pH of a solution
     c. a combination of a strong acid and a strong base

26. If a solution is buffered at pH 6, then addition of a small amount of base will result in a pH of approximately:
     a. 4   b. 6   c. 8

27. Addition of a small amount of <u>acid</u> to a solution buffered with $HPO_4^{-2}/H_2PO_4^-$ results in the following shift in equilibrium:

    a. $H^+ + HPO_4^{2-} \rightarrow H_2PO_4^-$ b. $H_2PO_4^- + H^+ \rightarrow H_3PO_4$

    c. $H_2PO_4 \rightarrow H^+ + HPO_4^{2-}$

28. Which of these buffers does not play a major role in stabilizing the pH of the blood?

    a. CH_3COOH/CH_3COO^- b. H_2CO_3/HCO_3^- c. $H_2PO_4^-/HPO_4^{2-}$

29. A titration experiment revealed that a H_3PO_4 solution was 0.12 N. What is the molarity of this acid solution?

    a. 0.12 M   b. 0.24 M   c. 0.04 M   d. 0.36 M   e. 0.06 M

30. What is the pH of a solution whose pOH = 4.7?

    a. 4.7   b. 7.0   c. 9.3   d. 11.7   e. 9.7

31. What is the $[OH^-]$ of a 0.00167 M HCl solution?

    a. 0.00167   b. 6.0×10^{-12} c. 3.0×10^{-7} d. 6.0×10^{-11} e. 6.0×10^{-10}

32. What is the pH of a 0.00167 M HCl solution?

    a. 1.67   b. 1.12   c. 3.0   d. 0.60   e. 2.78

33. What is the pH of a 0.04 M KOH solution?

    a. 1.40   b. 9.6   c. 3.9   d. 12.6   e. 10.4

34. What is the $[H^+]$ of a solution at pH 3.5?

    a. 0.00167   b. 8.84×10^{-3} c. 5.3×10^{-5} d. 3.16×10^{-4} e. 6.0×10^{-4}

35. A condition called acidosis is diagnosed when the blood pH:

    a. falls below 7.35

    b. rises above 7.45

    c. is anywhere outside the range 7.35-7.45

ANSWERS

Problems

1.   a. formula weight = 90; equivalent weight = 45
    b. 0.2; 10; 0.4
    c. 0.2 N; 2 N; 0.8 N
    d. 0.1 M; 1 M; 0.4 M

2.   a. 167 mL;   0.2 L;   50 mL
    b. 3.6 N or 1.8 M;   7.2 N or 3.6 M;   18 N or 9 M

3.   a. 0.2 N;   b. 0.13 N: c. 0.4 M;   d. 0.05 N, 0.025 M

4. **pH Table**

	pH	pOH	$[H^+]$	$[OH^-]$	acidic or basic
a.	2	12	10^{-2} M	10^{-12} M	acidic
b.	6.4	7.6	4×10^{-7} M	2.5×10^{-8} M	acidic
c.	10	4	10^{-10} M	10^{-4} M	basic
d.	12	2	10^{-12} M	0.01 M	basic

Self-Test

1. e	6. d	11. e	16. a	21. b	26. b	31. b
2. f	7. a	12. g	17. b	22. c	27. a	32. e
3. d	8. e	13. c	18. d	23. d	28. a	33. d
4. d	9. b	14. d	19. a	24. e	29. c	34. d
5. f	10. f	15. b	20. b	25. b	30. c	35. a

Special Topic C: Equilibrium Calculations

KEY WORDS
reversible reaction   *equilibrium constant* K_{eq}, K_a, K_b, K_w *Henderson-Hasselbalch*

SUMMARY

C.1 Equilibrium Constant Expressions
    A. Consider a general *reversible reaction*: $aA + bB \Leftrightarrow cC + dD$

$$K_{eq} = \frac{[C]^c\,[D]^d}{[A]^a\,[B]^b}$$ where [ ] = molar concentration at equilibrium

    B. The *equilibrium constant* for a reaction is a constant at the given temperature.

C.2 Ionization of Weak Acids; K_a
    A. Consider the dissociation of a general weak acid HA.
        $HA + H_2O \Leftrightarrow H_3O^+ + A^-$

$$K_{eq} = \frac{[H_3O^+]\,[A^-]}{[HA]\,[H_2O]}$$

    B. The $[H_2O]$ in dilute solutions is always ~ 55.5 M. Define K_a as

$$K_a = K_{eq} \times [H_2O] = \frac{[H_3O^+]\,[A^-]}{[HA]}$$

    C. The larger the value of K_a, the stronger the acid.
    D. Calculate $[H^+]$ from K_a for a 1 M solution of HA.

	HA	$\Leftrightarrow$	H^+	+	A^-
initial [ ]	1.0		0		0
equilibrium [ ]	1-x		x		x

$$K_a = \frac{[H^+]\,[A^-]}{[HA]} = \frac{(x)(x)}{(1.0 - x)} \sim \frac{(x)^2}{1.0}$$ since for weak acids $x <<< 1.0$

$$x = \sqrt{K_a};$$ The $[H^+]$ concentration of a 1.0 M weak acid solution is
equal to the square root of its K_a.

C.3 Equilibria Involving Weak Bases; K_b
    A. Consider the equilibrium expression for a general conjugate base.
        $A^- + H_2O \Leftrightarrow HA + OH^-$

        therefore, $$K_{eq} = \frac{[HA]\,[OH^-]}{[A^-][H_2O]}$$

    B. Define K_b as

$$K_b = K_{eq} \times [H_2O] = \frac{[HA]\,[OH^-]}{[A^-]}$$

C. The larger the value of K_b, the stronger the base.   **Note: $K_a \times K_b = K_w = [H^+][OH^-] \sim 10^{-14}$**

Note: Defining   **$pK_a = -\log K_a$** and **$pK_b = -\log K_b$**, then   **$pK_a + pK_b = 14$**

These relationships are illustrated in the following Table.

Ionization Constants for Some Weak Acids in Water at 25 °C						
Name	**c.a.**	**c.b.**	**K_a**	**K_b**	**pK_a**	**pK_b**
Phosphoric acid	H_3PO_4	$H_2PO_4^-$	7.5×10^{-3}	1.3×10^{-12}	2.1	11.9
Hydrofluoric acid	HF	F^-	6.6×10^{-4}	1.5×10^{-11}	3.2	10.8
Acetic Acid	CH_3COOH	CH_3COO^-	1.8×10^{-5}	5.6×10^{-10}	4.7	9.3
Carbonic acid	H_2CO_3	HCO_3^-	4.2×10^{-7}	2.4×10^{-8}	6.4	7.6
Dihydrogen Phos.	$H_2PO_4^-$	HPO_4^{-2}	6.2×10^{-8}	1.6×10^{-7}	7.2	6.8
Hydrocyanic acid	HCN	CN^-	6.2×10^{-10}	1.6×10^{-5}	9.2	4.8
Ammonia	NH_4^+	NH_3	5.6×10^{-10}	1.8×10^{-5}	9.3	4.7
Monohydrogen Phos.	HPO_4^{-2}	PO_4^{-3}	3.6×10^{-13}	2.8×10^{-2}	12.4	1.6

C.4 Calculations Involving Buffers

A. Buffer solutions resist changes in pH upon addition of either acid or base. Buffer solutions are made by using a mixture of a weak acid and its conjugate base. The buffer effect of the buffer solution works best when the $[H^+]$ is approximately equal to the K_a value of the conjugate acid, or pH ~ pK_a of the acid.

B. From the expression for K_a, we note that the $[H^+] = K_a$ when the $[c.b] = [c.a.]$.

$$K_a = [H]^+ \times \frac{[A^-]}{[HA]}$$

C. Henderson-Hasselbalch Equation

1. From K_a: $[H^+] = K_a \times \frac{[HA]}{[A^-]}$

2. Taking the negative of the log of both sides:

$$-\log [H^+] = -\log K_a + \log \frac{[A^-]}{[HA]}$$

or **$pH = pK_a + \log \dfrac{[A^-]}{[HA]}$**   (The **Henderson-Hasselbalch** Equation)

D. The *Henderson-Hasselbalch* equation states that the pH of a c.b./c.a. pair will be numerically equal to the pK_a of that c.b./c.a. pair when $[c.b.] = [c.a.]$. Thus the pH optimum of a buffer is equal to the pK_a of the c.a. in the buffer.

$[c.b.]/[c.a.] =$	0.1	1.0	10.0
pH =	$pK_a - 1.0$	pK_a	$pK_a + 1.0$

Titration Curve of Weak Acid

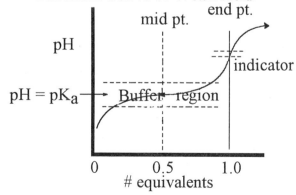

91

DISCUSSION

The treatment of dynamic equilibrium was handled qualitatively in Chapters 10 and 11. We can use Le Chatelier's principle to qualitatively predict the shifts in equilibrium distributions when a stress is placed on the system. In order to treat dynamic equilibria in a quantitative manner, it is necessary to be able to write equilibrium constant expressions for any given balanced, reversible chemical reaction. We will first demonstrate how to write equilibrium expressions with a few simple rules and then we will look at the subject of equilibrium calculations. The latter requires us to understand the meanings of various types of equilibrium expressions and to be able to solve simple algebraic problems with them.

The formula for the equilibrium constant (K_{eq}) of a generalized balanced chemical equation
$$aA + bB \Leftrightarrow cC + dD \quad \text{is given by the } \textbf{Law of Mass Action } \text{as:}$$

$$K_{eq} = \frac{[C]^c [D]^d}{[A]^a [B]^b} \quad \text{where [ ] refers to the molar concentration at equilibrium of that species.}$$

Expressed in words, the equilibrium constant is defined as the product of the equilibrium concentrations of all products of the reaction divided by the product of the equilibrium concentrations of all reactants, each raised to the power corresponding to its stoichiometric coefficient in the balanced chemical equation.

The value of K_{eq} is a constant for a given reaction at the given temperature. The numerical value of the equilibrium constant reveals a lot about the tendency for the reaction to form products as written.

$K_{eq} > 10^4$ - reaction tends to go to completion as written
$K_{eq} > 1$ - reaction favors the formation of products
$K_{eq} = 1$ - reaction favors the formation of neither products nor reactants
$K_{eq} < 1$ - reaction favors the retention of the reactants
$K_{eq} < 10^{-4}$ - forward reaction tends not to occur to any large extent

For equilibria in aqueous solution, the concentration of water is not included in the expression even though it may be involved in the reaction,   i.e.,
$$HCN + H_2O \Leftrightarrow H_3O^+ + CN^-$$
is treated as
$$HCN \Leftrightarrow H^+ + CN^-$$

The $[H_2O]$ is not included because for most aqueous solutions the concentration of water is essentially constant at 55.5 M. The same argument applies to equilibria involving solids. A solid is not really part of the solution and its concentration in the solid is a constant, so solids are also left out of equilibrium constant expressions.

The following examples illustrate these rules.

Gases:
$$N_2 + 3H_2 \Leftrightarrow 2NH_3 \qquad\qquad H_2 + Cl_2 \Leftrightarrow 2HCl$$

$$K = \frac{[NH_3]^2}{[N_2][H_2]^3} \qquad\qquad\qquad K = \frac{[HCl]^2}{[H_2][Cl_2]}$$

Solutions:

$$Ag^+ + 2 NH_3 \Leftrightarrow Ag(NH_3)^{2+} \qquad\qquad HCN \Leftrightarrow H^+ + CN^-$$

$$K = \frac{[Ag(NH_3)^{2+}]}{[Ag^+][NH_3]^2} \qquad\qquad K = \frac{[H^+][CN^-]}{[HCN]}$$

Solids:

$$BaSO_4 \Leftrightarrow Ba^{2+} + SO_4^{2-} \qquad\qquad Ag^+ + Cl^- \Leftrightarrow AgCl$$

$$K = [Ba^{2+}][SO_4^{2-}] \qquad\qquad K = \frac{[1]}{[Ag^+][Cl^-]}$$

The constants for different types of equilibrium processes are given special names:

K_a = acid dissociation or ionization constant
K_b = base ionization constant
K_{sp} = solubility product constant

      We will study the solubility product constant later. The remainder of this special topic deals with equilibrium calculations involving solutions of weak acids, weak bases, or both (buffers).

      Equilibrium calculations involving weak acids or weak bases are generally of two types: calculate K_a or K_b given the concentrations, or calculate $[H^+]$ or $[OH^-]$ given the initial concentration and K_a. Buffers are solutions of both a weak acid and its conjugate base. The conjugate base is frequently supplied as the salt of the weak acid. Thus buffer calculations illustrate the common ion effect. Buffer problems can be expressed in terms of the resulting $[H^+]$ or pH. Frequently, buffer problems refer to the pH of the solution and not its $[H^+]$. The Henderson-Hasselbalch equation is a logarithmic rearrangement of the acid ionization constant expression to state explicitly how the pH of a buffer system varies with the ratio of [c.b.]/[c.a.].

Henderson-Hasselbalch Equation	$pH = pK_a + \log \dfrac{[c.b.]}{[c.a.]}$

Note that when the [c.b.] = [c.a.], then $pH = pK_a$, which is the same as saying $[H^+] = K_a$. Both of these kinds of buffer calculations are illustrated in the text and in Examples 3 and 4 below.

Examples

1. Calculate K_a or K_b given the concentrations of each species.

     Consider the reaction: $HCN \Leftrightarrow H^+ + CN^-$
     Calculate the K_a for hydrocyanic acid given that the equilibrium concentrations are:

     $[H^+] = [CN^-] = 7.9 \times 10^{-6}$ M; $[HCN] = 0.10$ M

a. Write the correct equilibrium expression:

$$K_a = \frac{[H^+][CN^-]}{[HCN]}$$

b. Insert the appropriate concentrations and solve for K_a:

$$K_a = \frac{(7.9 \times 10^{-6})(7.9 \times 10^{-6})}{(0.10)} = 6.2 \times 10^{-10}$$

2. Calculate the $[H^+]$ or $[OH^-]$ given the value of K_a and the initial total concentration of the weak acid or base. This type of problem can be considerably more difficult to work than problems like the one in Example 1, unless we can assume that the acid or base is so weak that the equilibrium concentration of the un-ionized acid or base is not significantly different from the initial total concentration of the acid or base. Again, consider the reaction of hydrocyanic acid, but now we want to calculate the $[H^+]$ of a 1.0 M HCN solution.

a. Write out the reaction and express both the initial and equilibrium concentrations.

	HCN	⇔	H⁺	+	CN⁻
initial [ ]	1.0		0		0
at equilibrium [ ]	1.0 - x		x		x

b. Write the equilibrium constant expression as given in 1.a above.
c. Insert the given data and solve for $[H^+] = x$.

$$K_a = 6.2 \times 10^{-10} = \frac{(x)(x)}{(1.0 - x)} \sim \frac{(x)(x)}{(1.0)} \sim \frac{(x)^2}{(1.0)}$$

or $x^2 = 6.2 \times 10^{-10}$ or $x = 2.5 \times 10^{-5} = [H^+]$

Note: You can always check to determine if the assumption was correct. Is $1.0 - x \sim 1.0$? $1.000000 - .000025 = .999975 \sim 1.0$. Yes, the assumption was justified in this instance. (It is also possible to solve such equations without making such assumptions by using the quadratic equation, but you will not be required to do this in this text.)

3. Calculate the $[H^+]$ of a solution that is 0.1 M in HCN and 0.1 M in KCN.
   a. Write out the ionization constant expression.

$$K_a = \frac{[H^+][CN^-]}{[HCN]}$$

b. Insert the appropriate concentrations where

$[H^+]$ = x
$[CN^-]$ = concentration of the soluble salt, $[KCN]$ = 0.1 M
$[HCN]$ = concentration of the initial acid, $[HCN]$ = 0.1 M

$$K_a = \frac{(x)(0.1)}{(0.1)} \quad \text{or} \quad K_a = x = [H^+] = 6.2 \times 10^{-10}$$

Note: The hydrogen ion concentration will always be numerically equal to the value of K_a when the buffer consists of equal amounts of a conjugate acid and its conjugate base.

4. Calculate the pH of a solution that is 0.1 M in HCN and 0.01 M in KCN. The pK_a of hydrocyanic acid is 9.2.

   a.
   $$pH = pK_a + \log \frac{[CN^-]}{[HCN]}$$

   b. $pK_a = 9.2$; $[CN^-] = 0.01$ M; $[HCN] = 0.1$ M

   c. $pH = 9.2 + \log \frac{(0.01)}{(0.1)} = 9.2 + \log(0.1) = 9.2 - 1.0 = 8.2$

   Your understanding of this material can be reviewed by working the questions at the end of the special topic in the text. The **SELF-TEST** will give you additional practice on equilibrium calculations.

SELF-TEST

1. Write the equilibrium constant expression for each of the following reactions.
   a. $N_2 + O_2 \Leftrightarrow 2 NO$ (all gases)
   b. $2 P(s) + 3 Cl_2(g) \Leftrightarrow 2 PCl_3(g)$
   c. $H_3PO_4 \Leftrightarrow H^+ + H_2PO_4^-$
2. The K_a for hydrofluoric acid is 6.6×10^{-4} and that for hydrocyanic acid is 6.2×10^{-10}. Which is the weaker acid?
   a. hydrofluoric acid   b. hydrocyanic acid
3. Calculate the $[H^+]$ of a 0.0001 M solution of HCN ($K_a = 6.2 \times 10^{-10}$).
   a. 2.0×10^{-5} b. 2.0×10^{-7} c. 2.5×10^{-7} d. 2.5×10^{-6} e. 2.5×10^{-8}
4. Determine the K_a for an acid HX if the $[H^+]$ of a 0.200 M solution of HX is 0.00003 M.
   a. 9.0×10^{-10} b. 3.0×10^{-9} c. 3.0×10^{-7} d. 2.5×10^{-7} e. 4.5×10^{-9}
5. Determine the K_a for an acid HX if the pH of a 0.100 M solution of HX is 4.5.
   a. 1.0×10^{-8} b. 9.0×10^{-10} c. 3.0×10^{-7} d. 2.5×10^{-8} e. 4.5×10^{-9}
6. What is the $[H^+]$ of a solution that is 0.40 M in HF and 0.20 M in NaF? ($K_a = 6.6 \times 10^{-4}$).
   a. 2.5×10^{-7} b. 1.3×10^{-3} c. 6.0×10^{-8} d. 2.5×10^{-7} e. 2.5×10^{-7}
7. What is the pH of a solution that is 0.20 M in HF and 0.10 M in NaF? ($pK_a = 3.2$).
   a. 3.2   b. 3.0   c. 3.5   d. 2.2   e. 2.9

   (Problems 8 - 15 refer to acetic acid; $K_a = 1.8 \times 10^{-5}$; $pK_a = 4.7$)

8. The $[H^+]$ of a 1.0 M acetic acid solution is:
   a. 1.0 M   b. 0.3 M   c. 0.0042 M   d. 1.8×10^{-5} M
9. The hydrogen ion concentration of a 0.30 M acetic acid solution is:
   a. 0.10 M   b. 0.023 M   c. 1.8×10^{-6} M   d. 0.0023 M
10. The $[H^+]$ of a 0.20 M acetic acid solution that is also 0.20 M in sodium acetate is:
    a. 0.10 M   b. 1.8×10^{-5} M   c. 1.8×10^{-6} M   d. 0.0013 M
11. The hydrogen ion concentration of a 0.30 M acetic acid solution that is also 0.60 M in potassium acetate is:
    a. 1.8×10^{-5} M   b. 0.10 M   c. 9×10^{-6} d. 3.6×10^{-5}
12. The pH of a solution that is 0.30 M in acetic acid that is also 0.20 M in sodium acetate is:
    a. 0.2   b. 4.7   c. 4.9   d. 5.0   e. 4.5

13. The pH of a 0.10 M acetic acid solution that is also 1.0 M in sodium acetate is:

    a. 4.7   b. 5.7   c. 3.7   d. 1.0

14. The pH of a 1.0 M acetic acid solution that is also 0.01 M in sodium acetate is:

    a. 2.7   b. 3.7   c. 4.7   d. 5.7   e. 6.7   f. 1.0

15. What ratio of acetate/acetic acid is needed to prepare a buffer at pH 5.7?

    a. 100:1   b. 10:1   c. 1:1   d. 1:10   e. 1:100

ANSWERS

1. a. $K = \dfrac{[NO]^2}{[N_2][O_2]}$ b. $K = \dfrac{[PCl_3]^2}{[Cl_2]^3}$ c. $K = \dfrac{[H^+][H_2PO_4^-]}{[H_3PO_4]}$

2. b	6. b	11. c
3. c	7. e	12. e
4. e	8. c	13. b
5. a	9. d	14. a
	10. b	15. b

CHAPTER 12: ELECTROLYTES

KEY WORDS

electricity	*metal*	*ionization*	*battery*	*electrolysis*
anode	*conductor*	*electrolyte*	*electroplating*	*precipitation*
cathode	*nonmetal*	*nonelectrolyte*	*activity series*	*solubility product*
anion	*nonconductor*	*volt*	*corrosion*	*fuel cell*
cation	*dissociation*	*edema*	*hypertension*	*colligative property*

SUMMARY

12.1 Early Electrochemistry
  A. In 1752 Benjamin Franklin demonstrated that lightning was a form of electricity.
  B. In 1800, Volta invented a battery that produced electric current. Soon many chemists were using this process of *electrolysis* to split compounds.
  C. Terms
    1. *Electricity*   -   flow of electrons
    2. *Electrolysis*   -   splitting of compounds by means of electricity
    3. *Anode*   -   positively charged electrode; site of oxidation
    4. *Cathode*   -   negatively charged electrode; site of reduction
    5. *Anions*   -   negative ions attracted to the anode
    6. *Cations*   -   positive ions attracted to the cathode

12.2 Electrical Conductivity
  A. Most metals are good conductors of electricity because they have mobile electrons in conduction bands that permit outer electrons to flow while the nucleus and inner electrons remain fixed.
  B. Most *nonmetals* are *nonconductors* in their solid state, but may conduct electricity as melts or in solutions.
  C. Electrolytes are salts that form ions in solution that can carry an electric current.
    1. Strong *electrolytes* - good *conductors* in aqueous solution; (strong acids and bases, soluble salts)
    2. Weak electrolytes - conduct electricity but do so poorly; (weak acids and bases, slightly soluble salts)
    3. *Nonelectrolytes - nonconductors*; (substances that do not produce any ions in solution)
  D. Most molecular compounds (glucose) are nonelectrolytes or weak electrolytes.

12.3 The Theory of Electrolytes: Ionization and Dissociation
  A. Arrhenius (1887) and modern theory of electrolytes
    1. *Electrolytes* form ions in solution by *dissociation* or *ionization*.
    2. The algebraic sum of all positive and negative charges is zero, so the electrolyte solution as a whole is neutral.
    3. Each particle (ion or undissociated molecule) in solution makes the same contribution to colligative property effects (boiling point elevation, osmotic pressure, etc.).
    4. Weak electrolytes produce few ions in solution.
    5. *Nonelectrolytes* exist as molecular rather than ion forms in solution.
  B. Boiling-point elevation, freezing-point depression, and osmotic pressure are colligative properties that depend on the number (not kind) of particles in a given amount of solvent. Since electrolytes break into ions in solution, on a mole-for-mole basis electrolytes give rise to larger effects than do nonelectrolytes.

C. Freezing-point depression of 1 kg of water is $-1.86\,^{\circ}C$ per mole of dissolved particles. Boiling point elevation of 1 kg of water is $+0.52\,^{\circ}C$ per mole of dissolved particles.

D. An ionic solid dissociates in water while a polar molecule interacts with water causing it to ionize.

12.4 Electrolysis: Chemical Change Caused by Electricity

A. *Electrolysis* is the process of using electricity to bring about chemical change. It is used for the preparation of many metals, *electroplating*, and in the medical removal of hair and warts.

B. Electrolysis of molten NaCl
   1. Anode   - oxidation: $2\,Cl \rightarrow Cl_2 + 2\,e^-$
   2. Cathode - reduction: $2\,e^- + 2\,Na^+ \rightarrow 2\,Na$

12.5 Electrochemical Cells: Batteries

A. Electricity can cause chemical change and chemical change can produce electricity.
   1. When a reactive metal is placed in contact with the ions of a less reactive metal (see the activity series below), it will give up its electrons (oxidation) while it reduces the less reactive metal ion. The *volt* is a measure of electrical potential.
   2. The redox half-reactions can be placed in separate compartments so the electrons exchanged must flow through an external circuit. This flow of electrons is an electric current produced by the electrochemical cell. A *battery* is technically a series of such cells.

B. Some batteries use irreversible reactions and when the reactions are used up the battery is "dead." Other batteries, like your car battery, can be "recharged" by connecting the battery to an external electric energy source and forcing the electrons to flow in the opposite direction.

C. Note: Ionic processes in and around cells also give rise to electrical potentials.
   1. ECG (electrocardiograph) - monitors the electrical changes associated with the beating of the heart.
   2. EEG (electroencephalograph) - monitors electrical activity of the brain.

D. Fuel Cells
   1. A *fuel cell* is a device in which chemical reactions are used to produce electricity directly.
   2. Spacecraft use fuel cells based on the reaction of hydrogen with oxygen to produce water.
   $$2\,H_2 + O_2 \rightarrow 2\,H_2O$$

12.6 The Activity Series

A. Some very reactive metals react with water to produce hydrogen; others react with steam or acids, and some do not react with water or acids to produce hydrogen (see Table 12.2).

Most Active:	Li, Na, K, Rb, Cs, Ca	- react with water, producing hydrogen
$\downarrow$	Mg, Al, Zn, Cr, Fe	- react with steam, producing hydrogen
$\downarrow$	Ni, Sn, Pb	- react with acids, producing hydrogen
Least Active:	Cu, Ag, Hg, Pt, Au	- do not react with acids to form hydrogen

B. It is possible to arrange these metals according to their relative activity in an "*activity series*" with reactive metals like K at the top and unreactive metals like Au at the bottom.
   1. The position of a metal in such a table reflects its tendency to give up electrons.
   2. A metal can transfer electrons to the ions of any metal below it.
   $$Fe + Cu^{2+} \rightarrow Fe^{2+} + Cu \qquad \text{(Copper metal is deposited on the iron)}$$

C. *Corrosion* is the chemical attack of a metal by substances in the environment.
   1. The rusting of iron is an electrochemical process requiring iron, water, O_2 and an electrolyte to complete the circuit.
   $$2\,Fe + O_2 + 2\,H_2O \rightarrow 2\,Fe(OH)_2$$
   $$4\,Fe(OH)_2 + O_2 + 2\,H_2O \rightarrow 4\,Fe(OH)_3$$

2. Silver tarnish is Ag_2S formed when silver is oxidized to Ag^+ which reacts with H_2S in the air.

$$2\,Ag^+ + H_2S \rightarrow Ag_2S + 2\,H^+$$

Aluminum, being more reactive than silver, can be used to reduce the silver tarnish back to free silver metal.

12.7 Precipitation: The Solubility Product Relationship; K_{sp}

A. A salt will start precipitating from solution when its solubility has been exceeded.

1. $BaSO_4(s) \rightleftharpoons Ba^{2+}(aq) + SO_4^{2-}(aq)$

    0. 00001 M   0.00001 M   at 18°C

$$K_{sp} = [Ba^{2+}]\,[SO_4^{2-}] = 1 \times 10^{-10} \text{ at 18°C or solubility product constant, } K_{sp} = 1 \times 10^{-10}$$

NOTE: K_{sp} is a special type of K_{eq}. The concentration of a solid is a constant and not included in equilibrium constant expressions (refer to Special Topic C).

2. It is important to remember that $BaSO_4$ will precipitate whenever the product of the two ions reaches 1×10^{-10}, not when both ion concentrations reach 10^{-5} M.

B. Solubility products differ greatly in magnitude. In the list below silver acetate is the most soluble and mercury sulfide is the least soluble, but all of these are relatively insoluble materials.

Compound	Formula	K_{sp}
silver acetate	$AgC_2H_3O_2$	2.0×10^{-3}
calcium carbonate	$CaCO_3$	4.8×10^{-9}
silver chloride	$AgCl$	1.2×10^{-10}
silver chromate	Ag_2CrO_4	2.4×10^{-12}
mercury sulfide	HgS	3.0×10^{-53}

C. Many very insoluble precipitates can be made to go into solution by adding substances that tie up or remove one of the precipitating ions.

Zinc sulfide: $K_{sp} = 1.1 \times 10^{-21}$; $ZnS \rightleftharpoons Zn^{2+} + S^{2-}$

ZnS will dissolve in acid solutions because the equilibrium can be shifted to the right by the removal of sulfide.

$$S^{2-} + 2\,H_3O^+ \rightarrow H_2S\,(g) + 2\,H_2O$$

D. Our teeth and bones are largely calcium phosphate salts. The K_{sp} for calcium phosphate is 4×10^{-27}. However, the concentrations of Ca^{2+} and PO_4^{3-} ions in the body are also quite low. Osteoporosis, brittle bone disease caused by loss of calcium, is common in adults who consume fewer dairy products or who absorb calcium from foods less efficiently. Teeth can dissolve under acidic conditions that reduce the phosphate ion concentration, such as:

1. Chronic acidosis
2. Loss of salivary glands
3. Bulimia - binge eating followed by induced vomiting
4. Plaque

12.8 The Salts of Life: Minerals

A. A variety of inorganic compounds are necessary for proper growth and repair of body tissues.

B. Salt intake in our diets is a potential concern. NaCl is essential to life, but high salt levels increase water retention that cause swelling (*edema*) and high blood pressure (*hypertension*).

C. A partial listing of elements (other than H, C, N, and O) essential for living systems.

Ca - bones, teeth, blood clotting, milk

P - bones, teeth, ATP, nucleic acids, membranes

K - intracellular cation, muscle contraction

S - amino acids methionine and cysteine

Na - extracellular cation, osmotic pressure

Cl - anion, HCl in gastric juice

Mg - enzyme cofactor, nerve impulses

Fe - hemoglobin for O_2 transport, cytochromes

F - teeth enamel, bones

I - thyroxin in thyroid (goiter)

Co - vitamin B12

Zn, Mn, Mo, Cn, Cr, Se, V, As - enzyme cofactors

DISCUSSION

Much of the terminology of this chapter (see question 1 at the end of the chapter) was introduced originally in Chapter 2. The phenomena of freezing-point depression, boiling-point elevation and osmotic pressure were originally discussed in Chapter 9 and oxidation/reduction in Chapter 6. Thus, this chapter ties together many ideas that may have seemed unrelated. Some review of relevant material in the earlier chapters may prove helpful to understanding the material in the present chapter. For anyone new to the subject, electrolytes seem to cause more confusion when they are weak than when they are strong. The confusing culprit is usually the solubility product relationship, a concept introduced with weak electrolytes.

If, while covering the material on solubility products, you find that you were distracted by the arithmetic involved in multiplying powers of 10, read through Appendix II in the text. The mathematical manipulation of exponential numbers is quite straightforward. If it's causing problems, you probably just need to refresh your memory on the rules of exponential arithmetic.

It is also possible that your first encounter with the formula for solubility products has left you unnecessarily confused. We'll attempt to clarify the concept by using examples.

The product of the ion concentrations of barium sulfate ($BaSO_4$) is written: $[Ba^{2+}] [SO_4^{2-}]$

The product of the ion concentrations of barium phosphate ($Ba_3(PO_4)_2$) is: $[Ba^{2+}]^3 [PO_4^{3-}]^2$

The exponents introduced in the second product are a reflection of the structure of the compound. Each unit of barium sulfate, $BaSO_4$, produces one barium ion (Ba^{2+}) and one sulfate ion (SO_4^{2-}) in solution. Each unit of barium phosphate, $Ba_3(PO_4)_2$, produces three barium ions and two phosphate ions (PO_4^{3-}) in solution. The solubility product is defined in such a way that this difference between the two compounds is taken into account. The simplest way to state this is to say that the exponents in the solubility product formula are equal to the subscripts, which indicate the combining ratio of the ions in the compound formula.

For a given salt (at a given temperature, although we are ignoring temperature for the moment) the product of the ion concentrations cannot exceed the value of the solubility product constant. Such constants are determined experimentally and are listed in chemical handbooks and Table 12.3. The symbol for solubility product constant is K_{sp}. Frequently, you would not calculate a solubility product constant or K_{sp}, since its value has to be determined experimentally or supplied to you. What we have been doing in this chapter is calculating the product of ion concentrations for various solutions. We then compare this calculated value with the known K_{sp} for a given salt. If the calculated value exceeds the K_{sp}, we conclude that precipitation of the salt occurs. If the calculated value is equal to or smaller than the K_{sp}, no precipitation occurs, and in the latter case, more of the salt can be dissolved in the solution.

Evaluating when one exponential number exceeds or is less than another can sometimes present difficulty. In problems involving K_{sp}, we routinely compare numbers with negative exponents. Remember that the value of a number with a large negative exponent is smaller than the value of a number with a small negative exponent.

$$10^{-12} \qquad \text{is smaller than} \qquad 10^{-6}$$
$$1.7 \times 10^{-21} \qquad \text{is larger than} \qquad 1.2 \times 10^{-22}$$
$$9.7 \times 10^{-9} \qquad \text{is smaller than} \quad 2.5 \times 10^{-5}$$

Finally, let's take a quick look at what may be one last source of confusion. The solubility product relationship has been defined in such a way that it incorporates exponents for those salts whose formulas indicate a combining ratio involving more than one cation or anion, e.g., $Ca_3(PO_4)_2$.

For calcium phosphate, the solubility product is:

$$K_{sp} \;=\; [Ca^{2+}]_3 \cdot [PO_4^{3-}]_2$$

If the concentration of calcium ion in a solution is 0.01 M and the concentration of phosphate ion is adjusted to 0.0001 M, the product of the ion concentrations for calcium phosphate is:

$$(0.01)^3 \, (0.0001)^2 \;=\; (0.000001)\,(0.00000001) \;=\; 0.00000000000001$$

But most scientists would immediately convert those concentrations to exponential form:

$$0.01 = 10^{-2} \quad \text{and} \quad 0.0001 = 10^{-4}. \text{ The product of the ion concentrations may then be}$$

written:

$$(10^{-2})^3 \cdot (10^{-4})^2 = (10^{-6}) \times (10^{-8}) = 10^{-14}$$

If you don't use exponential numbers regularly, you may find the appearance of exponents within exponents confusing. Scientists would simply argue that it is easier to raise 10^{-2} to the third power (multiply the exponents to get 10^{-6}). If you raise 0.01 to the third power by long-hand multiplication, you would have to do something like this:

$$
\begin{array}{r}
.01 \\
\times\, .01 \\
\hline
.0001 \\
\times\, .01 \\
\hline
.000001
\end{array}
$$

.01 $\Big\}$ -- total of 4 decimal places

.0001   4 decimal places

total of 6 decimal places --

6 decimal places .000001

You get the same answer (0.000001 = 10^{-6}), but it probably took longer.

Example: K_{sp} **problems.** The K_{sp} for calcium phosphate is 4×10^{-27} (at 37 $^{\circ}$C). Will calcium phosphate precipitate at 37 $^{\circ}$C from a solution in which calcium ion concentration is 0.01 M and phosphate ion concentration is 0.0001 M?

Steps:

1. What is the formula for calcium phosphate? $Ca_3(PO_4)_2$
2. What is the solubility product formula for $Ca_3(PO_4)_2$? $[Ca^{2+}]^3 \cdot [PO_4^{3-}]^2$
3. What is the product for the given ion concentrations?
$$(0.01)^3(0.0001)^2 \quad \text{or} \quad (10^{-2})^3(10^{-4})^2 \;=\; (10^{-6})(10^{-8}) \;=\; 10^{-14}$$
4. Does this exceed the K_{sp} for calcium phosphate?

Yes, 10^{-14} is larger than 4×10^{-27},

Calcium phosphate will precipitate from this solution.

Sometimes, instead of just stating the ion concentrations as we did above, these concentrations are given indirectly. In these instances, the concentration of the soluble salt that was dissolved to produce the ion in solution is given. We would say 0.01 mole of calcium chloride (which yields 0.01 mole of calcium ion) and 0.0001 mole of sodium phosphate (which yields 0.0001 mole of phosphate ion) were dissolved in 1 L of solution. The results would be the same as given in the example. This discussion supplements the material in Section 12.8 in the text. We are not so much interested in your becoming expert at working solubility product problems as we are in your understanding the chemical explanations of such processes as bone growth and tooth decay. The following problems are presented for those of you who want to double-check your understanding of the solubility product relationship.

Problems

1. Write the solubility product formulas for the following compounds. Note: These problems do not involve arithmetic evaluations, just which ions are involved and what are the proper exponents.
   a. Na_2SO_4 b. $BaCO_3$ c. Ag_2S.   d. $Ba(OH)_2$ e. AlF_3 f. $Mg_3(PO_4)_2$ g. $MgNH_4PO_4$
   h. copper(I) hydroxide   i. copper(II) hydroxide   j. iron(III) phosphate
   k. iron(II) carbonate   l. calcium phosphate   m. calcium hydrogen phosphate
2. The K_{sp} of barium carbonate ($BaCO_3$) is 5.1×10^{-9}. Will precipitation of this salt occur from a solution in which both the barium ion and carbonate ion concentrations were originally 0.001 M?
3. The K_{sp} of aluminum sulfide (Al_2S_3) is 2×10^{-7}. Will precipitation occur if the concentration of aluminum ion is 0.1 M and sulfide ion is 0.01 M?
4. A solution is prepared by dissolving 0.1 mole of sodium nitrate ($NaNO_3$) and 0.01 mole of barium chloride ($BaCl_2$) in one liter of the solution. If the K_{sp} of barium nitrate, $Ba(NO_3)_2$, is 4.5×10^{-3}, will this salt precipitate from solution?

SELF-TEST

1. Carbontetrachloride (CCl_4) is a:
   a. strong electrolyte   b. weak electrolyte   c. nonelectrolyte
2. Identify the missing product in the following reaction.
   $$Mg(s) + H_2O \rightarrow Mg(OH)_2 + ?$$
   a. Mg   b. O_2 c. H_2 d. $Mg(OH)_2$ e. MgO
3. Which is not a strong electrolyte?
   a. NaCl   b. $NaHCO_3$ c. HCl   d. NaOH   e. NH_3
4. Identify the most reactive metal in the following list.
   a. Cu   b. Na   c. Fe   d. Mg   e. Li
5. Identify the least reactive metal in the following list.
   a. Cu   b. Na   c. Fe   d. Mg   e. Li
6. Which of the following metals will not react with acid to release hydrogen?
   a. Ca   b. Zn   c. Fe   d. Ni   e. Ag
7. Which will cause the electric light of the conductivity apparatus to glow only weakly?
   a. sodium acetate   b. acetic acid   c. sodium hydroxide
8. Which will not conduct an electric current efficiently?
   a. ionic solid   b. metallic solid   c. ionic melt   d. solution of ions
9. Which conducts a current most efficiently in solution?
   a. strong acid   b. weak base   c. insoluble salt   d. sugar
10. If one mole of each of the following salts were dissolved in 0.50 L of water, which of the solutions would show the greatest freezing point depression?
    a. NaCl   b. NH_4NO_3 c. $MgCl_2$ d. K_3PO_4

11. Estimate the freezing point of a 6.0 M NaCl solution.
    a. - 6 °C   b. - 3 °C   c. - 11 °C   d. - 8 °C   e. - 15 °C

12. Estimate the boiling point of a 6.0 M NaCl solution.
    a. 106 °C   b. 103 °C   c. 111 °C   d. 108 °C   e. 115 °C

13. Which is <u>not</u> true of nonelectrolytes?
    a. Nonelectrolytes fail to yield ions in solution.
    b. When dissolved, nonelectrolytes have no effect on freezing point, boiling point or osmotic pressure of the solution.
    c. Nonelectrolytes do not conduct an electric current in solution.

14. The osmotic pressure of a solution is greatest if it contains
    a. one mole of particles whose formula weight is 50
    b. one mole of particles whose formula weight is 400
    c. two moles of particles whose formula weight is 20
    d. All of these solutions would have the same osmotic pressure.

15. A solution of hydrogen chloride in water conducts electricity because, in water, hydrogen chloride undergoes a process called:
    a. dissociation   b. ionization   c. melt formation

16. Soluble salts conduct electricity in solution because they undergo a process called:
    a. dissociation   b. ionization   c. melt formation

17. When sodium sulfide dissolves in water, it yields two sodium ions and one sulfide ion. Therefore, a solution of sodium sulfide:
    a. is not electrically neutral as a whole
    b. is electrically neutral as a whole but still conducts an electric current
    c. is electrically neutral as a whole and does not conduct an electric current

18. In electrolysis, oxidation occurs at the:
    a. anode   b. cathode

19. In the reaction, $MgCl_2 \rightarrow Mg + Cl_2$, which element is formed at the anode?
    a. Mg b. Cl_2 c. $MgCl_2$

20. In electroplating, the metal is plated:
    a. on the anode   b. on the cathode
    c. on neither the anode or cathode   d. on both the anode and cathode

21. Electrical batteries generate a current by taking advantage of:
    a. a difference in the tendency of chemical species to give up electrons
    b. the ability of a solution to build up an excess of positive charge
    c. the ability of a solution to build up an excess of negative charge

22. A car battery is often a lead-acid storage battery that uses lead (Pb) and lead oxide (PbO_2) that form lead sulfate ($PbSO_4$). Which is the cathode in a lead-acid storage battery?
    a. Pb b. PbO_2 c. $PbSO_4$

23. The efficiency of converting fossil fuels to heat to generate electricity is about __?__ %.
    a. 10%   b. 20%   c. 35%   d. 60%   e. 90%

24. The efficiency of an electrochemical cell to generate electricity is about __?__ %.
    a. 20%   b. 30%   c. 40%   d. 60%   e. 90%

25. The electrical activity of the <u>brain</u> is measured by:
    a. an electrolysis apparatus   b. a battery
    c. an electrocardiograph   d. an electroencephalograph

26. A salt will precipitate from solution if the product of the ion concentrations for the salt:
    a. exceeds the solubility product constant for the salt
    b. is less than the solubility product constant for the salt
    c. is equal to the solubility product constant for the salt

27 If the solubility product constant for a salt is 3×10^{-9}, precipitation of the salt will occur if the product of the ion concentrations in the solution is:

    a. 9.4×10^{-10} b. 2.0×10^{-9} c. 4.6×10^{-8}

28. The concentration of calcium ion in a solution is 10^{-2} M. The concentration of fluoride ion in the solution is 10^{-1} M. What is the ion product for CaF_2 in this solution?

    a. 10^{-1} b. 10^{-2} c. 10^{-3} d. 10^{-4} e. 10^{-5} f. 10^{-6} g. 10^{-7}

29. The solubility product constant for CaF_2 is 2.7×10^{-11}. Will calcium fluoride precipitate from the solution described in question 28?

    a. yes   b. no

30. If bone formation occurs as calcium phosphate precipitates from solution, removal of phosphate ion from the solution will result in:

    a. more rapid bone formation   b. decrease in the rate of bone formation

    c. no change in the precipitation of calcium phosphate

31. The formation of dental caries is favored by:

    a. a decrease in the pH at the surface of the tooth

    b. an increase in the pH at the surface of the tooth

    c. an increase in the phosphate ion concentration at the surface of the tooth

32. Iodide salts are important to the:

    a. oxygen transport system of the body   b. the functioning of the thyroid gland

    c. proper development of bone and teeth

33. The ions of which element are incorporated in the hemoglobin molecule?

    a. iron   b. iodine   c. calcium   d. phosphorus   e. sodium

34. Classify each of the following as a strong (s), weak (w), or nonelectrolyte (n).

    a. $NaNO_3$ b. CH_3COOH c. $(NH_4)_2SO_4$ d. glucose   e. NH_3

ANSWERS

Problems

1. a. $[Na^+]^2[SO_4^{2-}$ b. $[Ba^{2+}][CO_3^{2-}]$ c. $[Ag+]^2[S^{2-}]$ d. $[Ba^{2+}][OH^-]^2$
    e. $[Al^{3+}][F^-]^3$ f. $[Mg^{2+}]^3[PO_4^{3-}]^2$ g. $[Mg^{2+}][NH_4^+][PO_4^{3-}]$
    h. CuOH, $[Cu^+][OH^-]$ i. $Cu(OH)_2$, $[Cu^{2+}][OH^-]^2$ j. $FePO_4$, $[Fe^{3+}][PO_4^{3-}]$
    k. $FeCO_3$, $[Fe^{2+}][CO_3^{2-}]$ l. $Ca_3(PO_4)_2$, $[Ca^{2+}]^3[PO_4^{3-}]^2$ m. $CaHPO_4$, $[Ca^{2+}][HPO_4^{2-}]$

2. Ion product = $(10^{-3})(10^{-3}) = 10^{-6}$ The ion product is greater than the solubility product constant; the salt will precipitate.

3. Ion product = $(10^{-1})^2(10^{-2})^3 = 10^{-8}$ The ion product is smaller than the solubility product constant; the salt will not precipitate.

4. Ion product = $(10^{-2})(10^{-1})^2 = 10^{-4}$ The ion product is smaller than the solubility product constant; the salt will not precipitate.

Self-Test

1. c	6. e	11. c	16. a	21. a	26. a	31. a
2. c	7. b	12. a	17. b	22. b	27. c	32. b
3. e	8. a	13. b	18. a	23. c	28. d	33. a
4. e	9. a	14. c	19. b	24. e	29. a	34. s, w, s, n, w
5. a	10. d	15. b	20. b	25. d	30. b	

Special Topic D: Inorganic Chemistry

KEY WORDS

noble gas	*allotropes*	*nonmetals*	*acid rain*
alkali	*photochemical smog*	*acidic oxide*	*halogen*
alkaline earth	*metals*	*ozone*	*synergistic*
organic	*basic oxide*	*London smog*	*transition element*
inorganic	*greenhouse effect*	*metalloid*	*hard water*

SUMMARY

Organic chemistry is based on the compounds of carbon.
Inorganic chemistry is the chemistry of all the other elements.

D.1 Group 8A: The Noble Gases (ns^2np^6)

    A. This relatively new group of elements is exceptionally resistant to chemical reactions and exists in nature as monatomic gases.

    B. The *noble gases* are unreactive due to their filled outer valence electronic structures (ls^2 or ns^2np^6).

    C. Members of the *noble gas* family are:

        1. Helium (He) - formed by alpha decay of heavy radioactive elements; nonflammable; good lifting power; also used in breathing mixtures for deep-sea divers.

        2. Neon (Ne) - used in lighted signs for advertising.

        3. Argon (Ar) - most abundant noble gas in the atmosphere; used in light bulbs.

        4. Kryton (Kr) and Xenon (Xe) - rare and expensive; several compounds of xenon and kryton have been prepared; XeF_4.

        5. Radon (Rn) - radioactive.

D.2 Group 1A: The *Alkali* Metals (ns^1)

    A. Group 1A elements of lithium (Li), sodium (Na), potassium (K), rubidium (Rb), cesium (Cs), and francium (Fr) are the alkali family. The alkalis are soft *metals* with low melting points. They are highly reactive and form basic hydroxides.

    B. Lithium salts are used in the treatment of manic-depressive psychoses. Sodium is found in common table salt (NaCl). Sodium and potassium ions help maintain osmotic pressure and the electrical potential of cells.

D.3 Group 2A: The *Alkaline Earth* Elements (ns^2)

    A. The alkaline earth elements are beryllium (Be), magnesium (Mg), calcium (Ca), strontium (Sr), barium (Ba), and radium (Ra). These *metals* are fairly reactive, form 2+ ions, and have *basic oxides* and hydroxides.

    B. Be - very poisonous; forms covalent rather than ionic bonds
        Mg - chlorophyll (photosynthesis), enzymes, nerves
        Ca - bones and teeth; $CaCO_3$ in limestone; *hard water*

D.4 Group 3A: Boron and Aluminum (ns^2np^1)

    A. Group 3A consists of a *metalloid* boron (B) and metals aluminum (Al), gallium (Ga), indium (In), and thallium (Tl).

    B. Aluminum

        1. Aluminum is light and strong, often used in place of steel.

        2. Aluminum is more reactive than iron and "rusts" more readily, but Al_2O_3 forms a hard, protective surface layer on aluminum while iron oxide is porous and flaky.

        3. Al is the most abundant metal in the Earth's crust. It occurs primarily as bauxite ($Al_2O_3 \cdot xH_2O$). Pure aluminum can be obtained by the Hall process, the electrolysis of melted aluminum oxide. This requires a lot of electricity; it is far cheaper to recycle Al. Hall discovered this procedure in 1886 while a college student.

D.5 Group 4A: Some Compounds of Carbon (ns^2np^2)

    A. Group 4A consists of carbon (C), silicon (Si), germanium (Ge), tin (Sn) and lead (Pb).

    B. Carbon forms millions of different compounds with hydrogen, nitrogen and oxygen. The study of hydrocarbons and their derivatives is called organic chemistry.

    C. Inorganic carbon

        1. Carbon exists in multiple *allotropic* forms: graphite, diamond, and the recently discovered Fullerenes or "Buckyballs" (Nobel Prize, 1996). *Allotropes* are modifications of an element that can exist in more than one form in the same physical state.

        2. When burned, carbon compounds form CO and/or CO_2. CO is an invisible, odorless, tasteless but deadly gas. It combines with hemoglobin in the blood and prevents oxygen transport.

        3. CO_2 is the product of complete combustion and respiration. It is not poisonous, but CO_2 levels in the atmosphere are increasing and contribute to the "*greenhouse effect*," which could cause a global warming trend.

        4. Many minerals such as limestone are composed of a carbonate salt (Limestone = $CaCO_3$).

D.6 Group 5A: Some Nitrogen Compounds (ns^2np^3)

    A. Group 5A consists of nitrogen (N), phosphorous (P), arsenic (As), antimony (Sb), and bismuth (Bi).

    B. Nitrogen makes up 78% of the atmosphere, but must first be "fixed" before it is a useful source of nitrogen for living systems.

        1. Some nitrogen is fixed by lightning

$$N_2 + O_2 \;\rightarrow\; 2\,NO \;\; (\text{and in subsequent steps to}) \;\rightarrow\; NO_2 \;\rightarrow\; HNO_3$$

        2. Fritz Haber, a German, discovered how to fix nitrogen industrially on the eve of World War I.

$$3\,H_2 + N_2 \;\rightarrow\; 2\,NH_3$$

This NH_3 was used to make ammonium nitrate, an explosive. However, today the Haber process is used to make nitrogen fertilizer to increase food production.

C. Air Pollution
1. Automobiles also fix nitrogen, leading to the production of NO and NO_2. Sunlight can decompose NO_2 leading to ozone production. The *photochemical smog* in cities such as Los Angeles consists of unburned hydrocarbons and nitrogen oxides from automobiles and usually occurs in dry sunny climates.

automobile engine:
$$N_2 + O_2 \rightarrow 2\,NO$$
$$2\,NO + O_2 \rightarrow 2\,NO_2$$
warm air:
$$NO_2 + sunlight \rightarrow NO + O$$
$$O + O_2 \rightarrow O_3 \ (ozone)$$

2. NO_2 is an irritant to the eyes and respiratory system. *Ozone* (O_3) is a toxic pollutant.
3. These nitrogen oxides also contribute to *acid rain*, but most of the NO and NO_2 in the atmosphere is produced by natural processes.

D.7 Group 6A: Compounds of Oxygen and Sulfur (ns^2np^4)

A. Group 6A consists of *nonmetals* oxygen (O), sulfur (S), selenium (Se), tellurium (Te), and polonium (Po).
B. Oxygen is very common. It is found as free O_2 in the atmosphere and in combined forms in the earth's crust, water, carbohydrates, proteins, etc. Ozone (O_3) is an allotropic form of oxygen. Oxygen reacts with many elements to form oxides.
1. The oxides of metals are generally basic, oxides of nonmetals are *acid oxides*.
2. Ozone near the surface of the earth is a toxic and harmful pollutant.
C. Sulfur occurs in nature in both combined and elemental forms. Sulfur compounds are also important components of proteins and drugs. Elemental sulfur occurs as S_8, a ring of eight S atoms.
1. Sulfur reacts with many metals and hydrogen to form sulfides (S^{2-}). H_2S is a toxic gas with the characteristic odor of rotten eggs.
2. Sulfur can also have oxidation numbers of +4 as in SO_2 or +6 as in SO_3.
D. *Industrial (London) smog* is a mixture of smoke, fog, soot, sulfur oxides and sulfuric acid.
E. *Acid rain* is caused when sulfur oxides combine with moisture to produce the corresponding acids. Burning sulfur containing coal releases large amounts of sulfur oxides into the air. Sulfur dioxide and particulate matter have a combined *synergistic* effect, that is, the combined effect is greater than the sum of the parts taken separately. Acid rain can corrode metals, decompose buildings and statues, and make lakes so acidic that all life is destroyed.

D.8 Group 8A: The Halogens (ns^2np^5.)

A. All *halogens* ("salt formers") have seven valence shell electrons. They exist as diatomic molecules and usually form −1 anions. This family of elements react with metals to form salts; NaCl, NaF, KF, etc.
B. The members of this family are:
1. Fluorine (F_2) - a gas; small amounts of fluoride are incorporated in tooth enamel to prevent cavities; most fluoride salts are poisons; NaF is a common rat poison; HF is an acid used to etch glass.
2. Chlorine (Cl_2) - a gas; Cl^- is the major anion in living cells; Cl_2 is used in water treatments to kill bacteria; NaOCl is a common bleaching ingredient; HCl is used for digestion in the stomach.
3. Bromine (Br_2) - a liquid; AgBr is used in photographic film; HBr is a strong acid.
4. Iodine (I_2) - a solid; iodized salt is used to prevent goiter; needed for proper thyroid function.

D.9 The B Groups: Some Typical Transition Elements
   A. All B Group elements are metals. There are 10 *transition elements* in each of the 4th through 6th periods of the periodic table, which correspond to filling the 3rd through 5th d orbitals, respectively. Most transition metals exhibit more than one oxidation state, and many form colored compounds $(MnO_4^-$; deep purple color).
   B. A number of transition metals are essential to life: Fe, Cu, Zn, Co, Mn, V, Cr, Mo. Iron is found in hemoglobin and the cytochromes; cobalt is a component of vitamin B_{12}; and many of the others are cofactors for enzymes.

DISCUSSION

There are no major new chemical concepts introduced in this Special Topic. We have paused in our theoretical development of the subject to undertake a brief, descriptive survey of several families of elements. We had previously been looking below the surface of matter--developing a picture of its atomic and molecular structure--evaluating phenomena like evaporation or precipitation with models such as the kinetic molecular theory. Now we are looking at various elements as we might actually encounter them in our environment. We are making the point that structural theories were developed, for the most part, to account for observed properties of compounds. For example, the observed chemical inertness of the noble gases led to the development of the octet rule. The unifying theme of this chapter is that chemistry is not merely a classroom subject, but a collection of observable phenomena. Your understanding of the theory of chemistry enhances your appreciation of what you observe around you.

Several groups of compounds were identified by family names in this chapter. The periodic table shown below identifies the most common groups by their names.

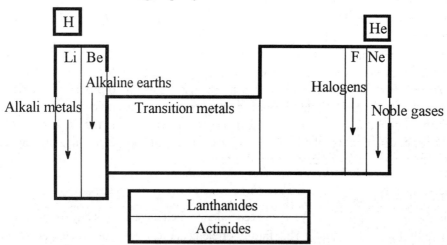

The questions at the end of the chapter in the text will lead you through a detailed review of the descriptive material in the chapter. After you've covered those questions, try the **SELF-TEST**.

SELF-TEST

1. Potassium is considered to be a(an):
   a. alkali metal   b. alkaline earth metal   c. transition metal   d. noble gas   e. halogen
2. Which is a halogen?
   a. I   b. Ca   c. Cs   d. C   e. Co

3. Which is a transition element?
    a. Ca   b. Co   c. Cs   d. Cl   e. Ar
4. Which is an alkaline earth metal?
    a. C   b. Cs   c. Ca   d. Cl   e. Co
5. Which element is characterized by its extreme nonreactivity?
    a. Al   b. Ne   c. Na   d. F_2
6. One of the noble gases is formed in the alpha decay of radioactive elements. Which one?
    a. He   b. Ne   c. Ar   d. Kr   e. Xe   f. Rn
7. The compounds of which element are generally excluded from studies of inorganic chemistry?
    a. B   b. C   c. K   d. Ar   e. U
8. The noble gases have been employed for a number of purposes. Which of the following does <u>not</u> apply to one or more of the noble gases?
    a. used to provide the lift for lighter-than-air ships
    b. used to dilute oxygen in breathing mixtures
    c. used to provide unreactive atmospheres for various purposes
    d. used to absorb sunlight in the upper atmosphere
9. Which hydrohalic acid is involved in the digestive process?
    a. HF   b. HCl   c. HBr   d. HI   e. H_2SO_4
10. A mixture of nitrogen oxides, unburned hydrocarbons, and higher than normal levels of ozone are the characteristics of:
    a. Industrial smog
    b. photosynthesis
    c. photochemical smog
11. The term "inert gas" is no longer used for the noble gases because:
    a. helium can cause the bends
    b. the noble gases have formed some compounds such as XeF_4
    c. the noble gas radon-226 is radioactive
    d. neon signs glow
12. Chlorine and fluorine (or their compounds) are added to drinking water in some areas. Which of the following is <u>not</u> an objective of this water treatment?
    a. the destruction of bacteria
    b. strengthening of tooth enamel
    c. reduction of the incidence of goiter
13. Which family of elements forms oxides that are classified as acidic?
    a. alkali metals   b. alkaline earth metals   c. nonmetals
14. Which condition is associated with Industrial rather than photochemical smog?
    a. sunny, dry weather
    b. combustion of high sulfur coal
    c. operation of automobiles
15. Which of these compounds is one of the primary pollutants associated with Industrial-type smog?
    a. NO   b. O_3 c. SO_2 d. N_2
16. The greenhouse effect results from an increase in the concentration of one of the following substances in the atmosphere. Which one?
    a. CO_2 b. NO_2 c. O_3 d. SO_2 e. particulates
17. Because of the greenhouse effect, the temperature of the Earth is expected to:
    a. increase   b. decrease

18. In which location is ozone considered beneficial to life on Earth?
    a. in the upper atmosphere
    b. at ground level
    c. Ozone is extremely toxic and is never considered beneficial to life.
19. Which pollutant does <u>not</u> contribute significantly to the formation of acid rain?
    a. SO_3 b. NO_2 c. CO
20. Which is a combination that exhibits a harmful, synergistic effect?
    a. sulfur dioxide and particulate matter as pollutants
    b. oxygen and nitrogen as a breathing mixture
    c. ozone and aerosol propellants in the upper atmosphere
21. Nitrogen fixation is accomplished by:
    a. some bacteria   b. lightning   c. automobile engines
    d. the Haber process   e. all of these   f. none of these
22. Nitrates are used as:
    a. fertilizers   b. explosives   c. both a and b   d. neither a nor b
23. Which is not an allotropic form of carbon?
    a. Fullerenes   b. carbon dioxide   c. diamond   d. graphite
    e. all of the above are allotropic forms of carbon
24. Partial but incomplete combustion of carbon yields:
    a. CO   b. CO_2 c. CH_4
25. Of the following toxic gases, which is colorless, odorless and tasteless?
    a. NO_2 b. H_2S c. NH_3 d. CO
26. Which pollutant could be responsible for the observed lowering of the Earth's average temperature?
    a. O_3 b. CO_2 c. particulates
27. Which is an allotrope of oxygen?
    a. S   b. O_3 c. CO   d. CO_2 e. SO   f. O
28. Alkali metal ions:
    a. contribute to the osmotic pressure of fluids in living systems
    b. maintain electrical potentials in cells
    c. both a and b
29. The presence of certain ions in water causes the water to be classified as hard. Which ion is <u>not</u> included in this group?
    a. Mg^{2+} b. Fe^{2+} c. Fe^{3+} d. K^+ e. Ca^{2+}
30. Which alkaline earth metal ion is found in chlorophyll?
    a. Be   b. Mg   c. Ca   d. Sr   e. Ba   f. Ra
31. In transition elements:
    a. the outer electron shell is a perfect octet
    b. inner electron shells are not completely filled
    c. both of the above are true
32. Which transition metal is not recognized as necessary for good health?
    a. Fe   b. Co   c. Mn   d. Hg
33. Identify the family with the characteristic, outer shell electronic structure ns^2.
    a. alkali metal   b. alkaline earth   c. transition metal   d. halogen   e. noble gas
34. Identify the family with the characteristic, outer shell electronic structure ns^2np^5.
    a. alkali metal   b. alkaline earth   c. transition metal   d. halogen   e. noble gas
35. Identify the family with the characteristic, outer shell electronic structure ns^2np^6.
    a. alkali metal   b. alkaline earth   c. transition metal   d. halogen   e. noble gas
36. Identify the chemical family for the element zinc.

    a. alkali metal   b. alkaline earth   c. transition metal   d. halogen   e. noble gas

37. Identify the chemical family for the element iodine.

    a. alkali metal   b. alkaline earth   c. transition metal   d. halogen   e. noble gas

38. Identify the chemical family for the element argon.

    a. alkali metal   b. alkaline earth   c. transition metal   d. halogen   e. noble gas

39. Identify the chemical family for the element samarium.

    a. alkali metal   b. alkaline earth   c. transition metal   d. lanthanide   e. noble gas

40. Identify the chemical family for the element silver.

    a. alkali metal   b. alkaline earth   c. transition metal   d. halogen   e. noble gas

ANSWERS

1. a	9. b	17. a	25. d	33. b
2. a	10. c	18. a	26. c	34. d
3. b	11. b	19. c	27. b	35. e
4. c	12. c	20. a	28. c	36. c
5. b	13. c	21. e	29. d	37. d
6. a	14. b	22. c	30. b	38. e
7. b	15. c	23. b	31. b	39. d
8. d	16. a	24. a	32. d	40. c

CHAPTER 13: HYDROCARBONS

KEY WORDS

IUPAC	*methyl*	*combustion*	*hydrogenation*	*polymer*
organic	*ethyl*	*substitution*	*halogenation*	*plastics*
inorganic	*propyl*	*alkene*	*hydration*	*polyethylenes*
saturated	*isopropyl*	*unsaturated*	*polymerization*	*polyesters*
alkane	*butyl*	*cis-trans*	*alkynes*	*polyamides*
isomers	*s-butyl*	*addition*	*aromatic*	*plasticizers*
alkyl	*t-butyl*	*halides*	*chloroform*	*homologous*
ortho-	*meta-*	*para-*	*carcinogen*	*CFCs, HFCs*
freons	*refrigerants*	*perhalo*	*polyvinylchlorides*	*resonance*

SUMMARY

13.1 *Organic* versus *Inorganic*

A. Compounds obtained from plants and animals were called **organic** because they were isolated from organized (living) systems. Today, thousands of organic compounds have been synthesized in the laboratory and organic chemistry is defined simply as the study of carbon compounds.

B. Comparison of physical and chemical properties:
   1. Most organic compounds tend to be insoluble in water, have low melting and boiling points, are flammable, have low densities, and utilize covalent bonds.
   2. Many **inorganic** compounds, such as NaCl, are soluble in water, have high melting and boiling points, are not flammable, have high densities, and utilize ionic bonds.

13.2 Alkanes: Saturated Hydrocarbons

A. A hydrocarbon is a molecule composed of only C and H. In a **saturated** hydrocarbon, or **alkane**, each carbon is bonded to four other atoms; there are no double or triple bonds.

B. Alkanes form a **homologous** series with the formula C_nH_{2n+2}.
   1. Methane CH_4
   2. Ethane C_2H_6 or CH_3CH_3
   3. Propane C_3H_8 or $CH_3CH_2CH_3$

C. Alkanes with 4 or more carbons have isomers. *Isomers* are different compounds with the same molecular formula. C_4H_{10} = $CH_3-CH_2-CH_2-CH_3$ and $CH_3-\underset{\underset{CH_3}{|}}{C}H-CH_3$
   butane   isobutane

D. Naming Alkanes - All alkanes have the "-ane" ending with a standard "**root**" used to indicate the number of carbon atoms. These "**roots**" are as follows:

meth - 1	eth - 2	prop - 3	but - 4	pent - 5
hex - 6	hept - 7	oct - 8	non - 9	dec - 10

13.3 Condensed Structural Formulas

A. **Structural formulas** show the bonding of all atoms explicitly by using bondlines as shown here for ethane and pentane.

ethane
```
        H H
        | |
    H-C-C-H
        | |
        H H
```

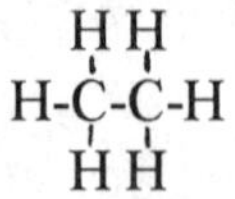

pentane
```
        H H H H H
        | | | | |
    H-C-C-C-C-C-H
        | | | | |
        H H H H H
```

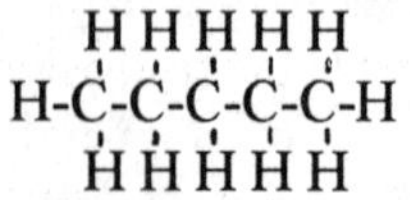

B. **Condensed structural formulas** are more convenient and easier to write because all (or almost all) bond lines are omitted. Hydrogens and other groups are written next to the carbon atom to which they are attached.

ethane CH_3CH_3 pentane $CH_3CH_2CH_2CH_2CH_3$

13.4 Alkyl Groups

A. An *alkyl* group results when a hydrogen atom is removed from an alkane ($CH_4 \rightarrow CH_3-$) .

B. Alkyl groups and are named by replacing the "-ane" ending with "-yl."

methyl	CH_3-	*ethyl*	CH_3-CH_2-	*propyl*	$CH_3-CH_2-CH_2-$
isopropyl	$CH_3-CH-CH_3$	*butyl*	$CH_3-CH_2-CH_2-CH_2-$		

s-butyl $CH_3-CH-CH_2-CH_3$

isobutyl $CH_3-CH-CH_2-$ *t-butyl* $CH_3-\overset{CH_3}{\underset{CH_3}{C}}-$
            CH_3

13.5 The Universal Language: **IUPAC Nomenclature**

A. The International Union of Pure and Applied Chemistry (*IUPAC*) has established formal rules for naming compounds.

> *Substituents --- Root --- Ending*

B. IUPAC rules for alkanes
1. Branched carbon chain molecules are named as substituents of the "parent" compound (the longest continuous carbon chain in the molecule).
2. All names end in "-ane" for saturated hydrocarbons with "roots" as given in 13.2.D.
3. Hydrocarbon substituents or *alkyl* groups and are named by replacing the "-ane" with "-yl."
4. The lowest possible arabic numerals are used to indicate the positions of substituents attached to the parent chain.
5. If the same alkyl group appears more than once, the numbers of all the carbons to which it is attached are expressed.
6. The additional prefixes di-, tri-, and tetra- are used if 2, 3, or 4 substituents of the same type are attached to the parent chain.
7. Common non-alkyl substituents are:

nitro = $-NO_2$, hydroxy = $-OH$,   fluoro = $-F$, chloro = $-Cl$,   bromo = $-Br$
8. Substituents should be listed in alphabetical order.

$CH_3-CH-CH_2-CH-CH_2-CH_3$
     Cl CH_3 2-chloro-4-methylhexane

13.6 Physical Properties of Alkanes

A. 1-4 C (gases) ; 5-16 C (liquids) ; > 17 C (solids)

B. All alkanes are insoluble in and less dense than water.

13.7 Physiological Properties of Alkanes

A. Methane - physiologically inert

B. 2-6 C alkanes - anesthetics

C. Liquid alkanes - dermatitis from contact with skin; chemical pneumonia

D. Heavier alkanes - emollients (skin softeners); petroleum jelly

13.8 Chemical Properties of Alkanes: Little Affinity

A. Alkanes are not reactive toward strong acids, strong bases, or most oxidizing or reducing agents.

B. Paraffin ("little affinity") wax is a mixture of solid alkanes.

C. Reactions:

    1. Combustion: $CH_4 + 2 O_2 \rightarrow CO_2 + 2 H_2O + heat$

            Note: Combustion with insufficient oxygen can produce toxic carbon monoxide, CO.

                     $2 CH_4 + 3 O_2 \rightarrow 2 CO + 4 H_2O + heat$

    2. Substitution: $H_3C\text{-}H + Cl\text{-}Cl \rightarrow H_3C\text{-}Cl + H\text{-}Cl$

       or simply $CH_4 + Cl_2 \rightarrow CH_3Cl + HCl$

13.9 Halogenated Hydrocarbons

A. Halogenated hydrocarbons, or *alkyl halides*, are compounds in which one or more hydrogens have been replaced by halogen atoms (F, Cl, Br, or I).

    1. Common names: Alkyl group followed by the appropriate halide; ethyl bromide = $CH_3\text{-}CH_2\text{-}Br$.

    2. IUPAC names treat the halogen as a substituent on the parent compound;   bromoethane.

B. Halogenated hydrocarbons rarely occur in nature, but synthetic alkyl halides have a multitude of uses from pesticides to *plastics* in our modern society.

C. Polyhalogenated Hydrocarbons: It is also possible to replace all hydrogens by halogens to form *perhalo* compounds, CF_3CF_3.

    1. Methane Series

         Methyl chloride (CH_3Cl) -refrigerant

         Methylene chloride (CH_2Cl_2) -solvent

         Chloroform $(CHCl_3)$ -early anesthetic; solvent; *carcinogen* (cancer producer)

         Carbon tetrachloride (CCl_4) -dry cleaning solvent; possible carcinogen (at high

            temperatures, CCl_4 can react with water to form the deadly gas phosgene ($COCl_2$).

    2. Ethane Series - Isomers

         Ethyl chloride (CH_3CH_2Cl)--only one form

         Dichloroethane - two isomers: $ClCH_2CH_2Cl$ Cl_2CHCH_3

                            1,2-dichloroethane   1,1-dichloroethane

         Trichloroethane - two isomers: CCl_3CH_3 $CHCl_2CH_2Cl$

                            1,1,1-trichloroethane   1,1,2-trichloroethane

D. **Chlorofluorocarbons** (*CFCs*) are frequently used as *refrigerants* (*freons*) and in aerosol cans.

    1. CF_2Cl_2 (a freon) and related compounds are very stable, but can be broken down by UV radiation to produce halide radicals (Cl·) which in turn break down the ozone layer.

    2. CFCs have been banned in the US for use in aerosols but are still used extensively as refrigerants.

    3. Fluorinated hydrocarbons (HFCs) break down in the lower atmosphere instead of the stratosphere and are being used as replacements for CFCs.

13.10 Cycloalkanes

A. It is possible to form ring or cyclic structures with compounds of 3 or more carbons. These cycloalkanes have properties similar to their noncyclic counterparts.

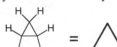

       cyclopropane   cyclobutane   cyclopentane   cyclohexane

B. Cyclopropane (C_3H_6) is an anesthetic.

13.11 Alkenes: Structure and Nomenclature
  A. *Alkenes* are *unsaturated* hydrocarbons characterized by a carbon- carbon double bond, $C=C$.
    The double bond atoms are planar, and there is no free rotation about the double bond.
  B. Nomenclature
    1. All names end in "-ene" with "root"s as given in 13.2.D.
    2. The parent compound is the longest chain of atoms that contains the double bond.
    3. The position of the double bond is indicated by the first carbon involved in the double bond.
    4. Substituents are identified as discussed for alkanes above (13.4 and 13.5).
      CH_3-C=C-CH-CH_3
        H H Br   4-bromo-2-pentene   Note: The double bond gets the lowest number.
  C. Common alkenes
    1. Ethene; CH_2=CH_2 (also called ethylene). Over 25 billion pounds of ethene are produced in the
      U.S. It is used in the production of plastics (polyethylene) and antifreeze (ethylene glycol).
    2. Propene; CH_3CH=CH_2 (also called propylene) is used extensively for plastics and isopropyl
      alcohol.
  D. The double bond of alkenes, like the ring structures of cycloalkanes, imposes geometric restrictions
    that can be lead to geometric or *Cis-Trans* isomers (See also Chapter 18). The requirements for
    cis-trans isomers are:
    1. Restricted rotation within the molecule (double bonds or ring formation)
    2. Two nonidentical groups on each of the doubly bonded carbons

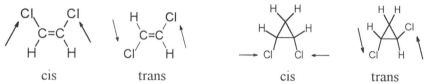

            cis   trans   cis   trans

13.12 Alkenes and Living Things
  A. The physiological properties of alkenes are similar to those of alkanes.
  B. 1. Ethylene - anesthetic; ripening of fruit
    2. Butadiene, CH_2=CH-CH=CH_2 - found in coffee
    3. Carotene - Vitamin A and vision
13.13 Chemical Properties of Alkenes
  A. *Combustion*: $C_2H_4 + 3 O_2 \rightarrow 2 CO_2 + 2 H_2O +$ heat
  B. *Addition* reactions:
    1. *Hydrogenation* CH_2=$CH_2 + H_2 \rightarrow CH_3$-$CH_3$
    2. *Halogenation* CH_2=$CH_2 + Br_2 \rightarrow$ Br-CH_2-CH_2-Br
      (brown-red)   (colorless)
    3. *Hydration* CH_2=$CH_2 +$ H-OH $\rightarrow CH_3$-CH_2-OH   (alcohol)
    4. *Polymerization*   n $C=C$ + n $C=C \rightarrow$ -(-C-C-C-C-)n-

13.14 Polymerization
  A. *Polymer* comes from the Greek term for "many parts." The building blocks of polymers are called
    monomers ("one part").
  B. There are two general types of polymerization reactions:
    1. Addition polymerization - uses an addition reaction in such a way that the polymeric product
      contains all the atoms of the starting monomeric units. Alkenes react by addition reactions and
      are common starting materials for most addition polymers. Some addition polymers are
      polyethylenes, polypropylene, polystyrene, "teflon," and the "PVCs" (see Table 13.11)

    2. Condensation polymerization - uses a condensation reaction that results in the formation of a nonpolymeric "by-product." The "by-product" is often water which is produced when ester and amide linkages are formed. Condensation polymers include *polyamides* (nylon), *polyesters* (Dacron), and **polyurethanes** (foam rubber). Natural materials such as proteins, cellulose and starch are condensation polymers.

    3. Synthetic polymers represent over half of the compounds produced by the chemical industry.

C. *Plasticizers:* Hard and brittle polymers can be made more flexible by the addition of small molecule internal lubricants called *plasticizers*.

    1. *Polyvinyl chloride* (PVC) is normally hard and brittle but can be used for garden hoses, auto seat covers, etc. by the addition of plasticizers.

    2. Plasticizers are usually lost by evaporation and with age the plastic becomes brittle and breaks.

13.15 Alkynes

A. *Alkynes* are unsaturated hydrocarbons characterized by a carbon-carbon triple bond, $-C\equiv C-$.

B. The rules for naming alkynes are similar to those for naming alkenes, except that the "-yne" ending is used.

C. The physical and chemical properties of alkynes are also very similar to those of the corresponding alkenes.

D. Ethyne; $HC\equiv CH$ (acetylene) is the most common alkyne. It is used in oxyacetylene torches and as the starting material for vinyl and acrylic plastics.

13.16 Benzene

A. *Benzene* was first isolated in 1825 by Michael Faraday who determined it had the empirical formula of CH_2. Later it was determined to have the molecular formula C_6H_6.

B. In 1865, Kekule proposed a cyclic structure for benzene. However, it has been determined that all of the bonds in benzene are identical and that there are no real double bonds in benzene. Benzene doesn't react by addition reactions, but rather by *substitution* reactions like alkanes. The structure of benzene can not be described by a single "Lewis" structure and is said to have *resonance* forms. Resonance compounds *are not* oscillating between their resonance forms, there is really just one hybrid form. However, you will see benzene represented by each of the structures shown below:

13.17 Aromatic Hydrocarbons: Structure and Nomenclature

A. Compounds containing the benzene ring-type structure are called *aromatic* compounds. Many have pleasant aromas; others stink.

B. Many aromatic compounds go by their common names.

toluene

    o-xylene   napthalene

    The *ortho-* (o-), *meta-* (m-), and *para-* (p-) prefixes refer to the (1,2-), (1,3-), and (1,4-) disubstituted benzenes, respectively.

C. Aromatic substituents are also possible: phenyl   benzyl

D. Benzpyrene is a polycyclic aromatic carcinogen found in coal tar and charcoal-broiled steaks.

Benzpyrene

13.18 Uses of Benzene and Benzene Derivatives

   A. All aromatic hydrocarbons are insoluble in water. Benzene, toluene, and the xylenes are common organic solvents. Aromatic compounds react by substitution (not addition) on the benzene ring.

   B. Nitrobenzene is used to manufacture aniline which in turn is used to make many dyes and drugs.

   C. The aromatic ring of benzene is also present in the amino acids (Phe, Tyr, and Trp) and vitamin related cofactors riboflavin, Vit. K, and folic acid.

   D. Physiological properties

      1. Most aromatic hydrocarbons present toxic hazards. Prolonged exposure to benzene may cause leukemia.

      2. Toluene is somewhat less toxic than benzene.

DISCUSSION

   Much of Chapter 13 has been devoted to the subject of nomenclature. In many ways, nomenclature is a game like Monopoly or poker or baseball. There are rules to be learned and, in the beginning, it sometimes seems that you'll never remember all of them. However, by the time you finish working through the questions at the end of the chapter, you should have a pretty good grasp of the rules. We strongly recommend that you do take the time to work these problems. You'll find that an investment of time now will be paid back in understanding of later chapters. The basic rules for naming hydrocarbons provide a foundation for naming all other families of organic compounds. The following summary restates briefly the more important rules for naming hydrocarbons.

IUPAC Nomenclature involves three parts.

Substituents --- Root --- Ending				
Roots - length of the longest C chain.				
meth - 1	eth - 2	prop - 3	but - 4	pent - 5
hex - 6	hept - 7	oct - 8	non - 9	dec - 10

Ending - identifies the functional class. (Note: The last four will be covered in future chapters.)

alkane	alkene	alkyne	alcohol	aldehyde	ketone	carboxylic acid
"-ane"	"-ene"	"-yne"	"-ol"	"-al"	"-one"	"-oic"

Substituents: Alkyl groups: replace the "-ane" ending with "-yl."

methyl CH_3- *ethyl* CH_3-CH_2- *propyl* $CH_3-CH_2-CH_2-$

isopropyl $CH_3-CH-CH_3$ *butyl* $CH_3-CH_2-CH_2-CH_2-$

s-butyl $CH_3-CH-CH_2-CH_3$

isobutyl $CH_3-CH-CH_2-$ *t-butyl* $CH_3-\overset{CH_3}{\underset{CH_3}{C}}-$
                CH_3

Non-alkyl: nitro = $-NO_2$, hydroxy = $-OH$, fluoro = $-F$, chloro = $-Cl$, bromo = $-Br$

Halocarbons Nomenclature: The halogens are named as substituents of a parent hydrocarbon molecule.
    Examples: chloromethane, 1-bromo-2-methylpropane, fluoroethene, 1,3,5-trichlorobenzene
Common Names: Alkyl halide--Compounds are named as derivatives of the halides.
    Examples: methyl chloride, isobutyl bromide, vinyl fluoride, cyclopentyl iodide

---

Addition polymers are made by reacting alkenes. Condensation polymerization involves chemistry we will encounter in our study of alcohols, amines and carboxylic acids. Polyester formation differs from simple esterification only in the number of functional groups per molecule which react. In simple esterification, an alcohol with one hydroxyl group reacts with an acid with one carboxyl group:

$$R\text{-}\overset{\overset{O}{\|}}{C}\text{-OH} \ + \ HO\text{-}R' \ \rightarrow \ R\text{-}\overset{\overset{O}{\|}}{C}\text{-O-}R' \ + \ H_2O \qquad \textbf{esterification}$$

In **polymerization**, the only difference is that each molecule must have at least 2 functional groups. In polyester formation, for example, one molecule may have 2 hydroxyl groups and the other 2 carboxyl groups or every molecule may have one hydroxyl and one carboxyl group:

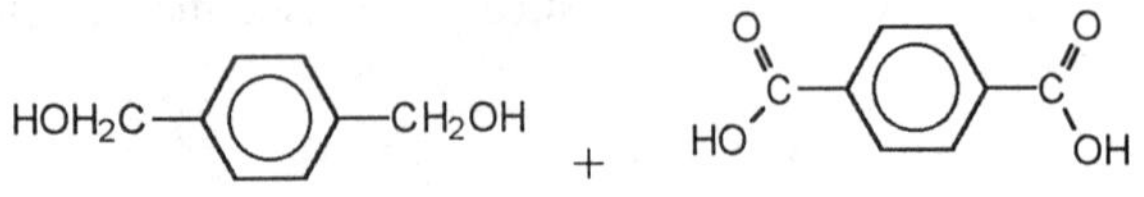

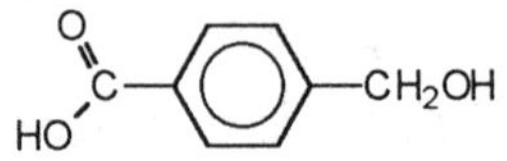

The reaction of both functional groups on each on each molecule ties hundreds or thousands of these monomers together to form the polymer.

Problems:

1. Draw and name the nine isomeric alkanes containing a total of seven carbon atoms.
2. a. Draw and name the thirteen isomeric alkanes (not including geometric isomers) containing a total of six carbon atoms.
   b. Which of the compounds in part (a) can exist as cis/trans isomers.
3. Draw and name the seven isomeric alkynes containing a total of six carbon atoms.
4. Draw and name the eight compounds containing a benzene ring and 3 additional saturated carbon atoms.
5. Draw and name each of the six compounds containing a total of five saturated carbon atoms and incorporating a ring.

The rest of the chapter material is reviewed in the **SELF-TEST**.

SELF-TEST

1. The simplest hydrocarbon is:
     a. CH_2 b. C_2H_4 c. C_2H_6 d. CH_3 e. CH_4
2. The one element necessarily present in every organic compound is:
     a. hydrogen   b. oxygen   c. carbon   d. nitrogen   e. sulfur
3. A series of carbon compounds in which each member differs by $-CH_2-$ from the preceding member of the series is known as a(n):
     a. aromatic series   b. homologous series   c. hydrocarbon series   d. paraffin series
4. Compounds containing only carbon and hydrogen are known as:
     a. methane   b. hydrocarbons   c. carbohydrates   d. isomers   e. aromatic

5. Which term would be associated with the term paraffins.
    a. alkanes   b. alkenes   c. alkynes   d. alcohols

6. Compounds comprised of the same number and kinds of atoms but different in their atomic arrangement are known as:
    a. isotopes   b. isomers   c. homologs   d. allotropes

7. In ethylene the two carbons are joined by a(n):
    a. ionic bond   b. single bond   c. double bond   d. triple bond

8. Restricted rotation about double bonds results in:
    a. geometric isomerism   b. fused ring compounds   c. aromatic compounds

9. Which compound does not contain a double bond?
    a. acetylene   b. butene   c. cyclohexene   d. propylene

10. In the name cyclohexane, the prefix "cyclo" means that:
    a. the carbon atoms are joined in a ring
    b. the compound is explosive
    c. the compound is a derivative of benzene
    d. each carbon is attached to every other carbon atom
    e. the carbons have a valence of three

11. Which is an unsaturated hydrocarbon?

    a. $H-\overset{\overset{\displaystyle H}{|}}{\underset{\underset{\displaystyle Cl}{|}}{C}}-\overset{\overset{\displaystyle H}{|}}{\underset{\underset{\displaystyle Cl}{|}}{C}}-H$ b. $H_3C-\overset{\overset{\displaystyle H}{|}}{C}=O$ c. $H-\overset{\overset{\displaystyle H}{|}}{C}=\overset{\overset{\displaystyle H}{|}}{C}-H$ d. $H-\overset{\overset{\displaystyle H}{|}}{\underset{\underset{\displaystyle H}{|}}{C}}-\overset{\overset{\displaystyle H}{|}}{\underset{\underset{\displaystyle H}{|}}{C}}-O-H$

12. Benzene and its derivatives are commonly known as:
    a. alkenes   b. aromatics   c. cycloparaffins   d. alkanes

13. Which is not an acceptable structure for benzene?
    a.   b.   c.

14. How many compounds having the formula C_3H_8 are possible?
    a. 1   b. 2   c. 3   d. 4   e. 5   f. 6

15. Which is a paraffin?

    a. $CH_2=CHCH_2CH_2CH_2CH_3$ b.
    c. $CH_3CH_2CH_2CH_2CH_2\ CH_2CH_2CH_2CH_3$ d. $HC\equiv CCH_2CH_2CH_2CH_3$

16. In each part of this question, a group of structures (a through d) is presented. All except one of the structures in each group represent the same compound. Pick out the one structure that is actually a different compound. For simplicity we are drawing only the carbon skeletons.

  A.   a. C-Ċ-C-Ċ-C   b. C-C-C-Ċ-C-C   c. C-C-Ċ-C-Ċ-C   d. Ċ-C-Ċ-C-C

  B.   a. C=C-C-C-C   b. C=Ċ-C-Ċ   c. C-C-C-Ċ=C   d. C-Ċ-C-Ċ

  C.   a. C-C-Ċ-Ċ=C   b. C=Ċ-Ċ-C-C   c. C=Ċ-Ċ-Ċ   d. C-Ċ-C-Ċ=C

17. Which is the correct name for $CH_3\text{-}\overset{|}{\underset{|}{C}}\text{-}CH_3$?
    CH_3
    a. butyl   b. isobutyl   c. sec-butyl   d. t-butyl

18. Which alkene exists as a pair of cis/trans isomers?
    a. $CH_3CH_2CH_2C=CHCH_3$ b. $CH_3C=CCH_3$ c. $CH_3CH\text{-}CHCHCH_3$ d. $CH_3C=CHCH_2CH_3$
    CH_3 H_3C CH_2CH_3 H_3C CH_3 CH_3

19. Which is <u>not</u> a reasonable structure for a dimethylbenzene?
    a.   b.   c.   d.

20. The IUPAC name for $CH_3CH_2CH_2CH_2CHCH_3$ is:
    $CH_2CH_2CH_3$
    a. 2-propylhexane   b. 5-methylheptane   c. 4-methyloctane   d. 5-methyloctane

21. The IUPAC name for $CH_3CH_2C=CH_2$ is:
    $H_2C\text{-}CH_3$
    a. 2-ethyl-1-butene   b. 2-ethyl-2-butene
    c. 3-ethyl-3-butene   d. 3-methyl-3-pentene

22. Propylene is:

    a.   b.   c.   d. $CH_2=CH\text{-}CH_3$ e. $HC\equiv C\text{-}CH_3$

23. Which compound is a cycloalkane?

    a. $CH_3CH_2CH_2CH_2CH_3$ b. $CH_2=CH_2$ c. $HC\equiv CCH_2CH_3$ d.   e.

24. Acetylene is a(n):
    a. alkane   b. alkene   c. alkyne   d. aromatic compound   e. paraffin

25. Which is <u>not</u> a gas?
    a. methane   b. ethene   c. acetylene   d. octane

26. If hexane and water are mixed, the result is:
    a. a clear solution of hexane dissolved in water
    b. a layer of hexane sitting on top of a layer of water
    c. a layer of water sitting on top of a layer of hexane

27. If just two positions on a benzene ring are substituted, how many isomers are possible?
    a. 1   b. 2   c. 3   d. 4   e. 5   f. 6   g. depends on the substituents

28. Two adjacent substituents on a benzene ring are said to be:
    a. ortho to one another   b. meta to one another
    c. para to one another   d. 1,1-disubstituted

29. Addition reactions are characteristic of:
    a. alkanes   b. alkenes   c. aromatic compounds

30. Substitution reactions are characteristic of:
    a. alkanes   b. alkenes   c. alkynes   d. aromatics

31. The reaction of bromine, Br_2, with benzene results in bromobenzene plus _____.
    a. benzobrome   b. H_2 c. Br·   d. Hbr

32. The raw material from which most hydrocarbons are obtained is:
    a. gasoline   b. petroleum   c. animal fats   d. vegetable oils

33. Methane gas can cause death through:
    a. chemical pneumonia   b. carcinogenesis   c. asphyxiation

34. Which act as emollients?
    a. gaseous alkanes
    b. low boiling liquid alkanes
    c. high boiling liquid alkanes

35. Which hydrocarbon is used as an effective anesthetic?
    a. methane   b. benzene   c. cyclopropane

36. Hydrogenation of vegetable oils produces:
    a. butter   b. saturated fats   c. unsaturated fats

37. A common fused-ring aromatic compound is:
    a. benzene   b. naphthalene   c. toluene

38. In each case, select the property that is typical of organic rather than inorganic compounds.
    A.   a. melt below 200 $^{\circ}$C   b. melt above 200 $^{\circ}$C
    B.   a. water soluble   b. water insoluble
    C.   a. ionic bonding   b. covalent bonding
    D.   a. specific gravity less than 1   b. specific gravity greater than 1
    E.   a. flammable   b. nonflammable

39. Which is not an appropriate name for CH_2=CH-Cl?
    a. chloroethylene   b. chloroethene
    c. methylene chloride   d. vinyl chloride

40. Which compound represents chloroform?

    a. F-$\overset{\text{F}}{\underset{\text{Cl}}{\text{C}}}$-F   b. H-$\overset{\text{Cl}}{\underset{\text{Cl}}{\text{C}}}$-Cl   c. F-$\overset{\text{Cl}}{\underset{\text{Cl}}{\text{C}}}$-Cl   d. H-$\overset{\text{H}}{\underset{\text{H}}{\text{C}}}$-$\overset{\text{H}}{\underset{\text{F}}{\text{C}}}$-F

41. The IUPAC name is:
$$CH_3CH_2\overset{\text{CH}_3}{\underset{\text{Br}}{\text{C}}}\text{--}\underset{\text{Cl}}{\text{CH}}CH_3$$
    a. 3-bromo-4-chloro-3-methylpropane
    b. 2-chloro-3-bromo-3-hexane
    c. 3-bromo-2-chloro-3-methylpentane
    d. 3-bromo-4-chloro-3-methylpentane

42. Perchlorobenzene is:
    a.   b.   c.   d.

43. Which is not an alkyl halide?
    a. CH_3CH_2Cl b. $CH_3CH_2CH_2Br$ c.   d.

$$CH_3-\overset{\text{CH}_3}{\underset{\text{CH}_3}{\text{C}}}-Cl$$

44. For which compound is the symbol Ar-Br <u>not</u> appropriate?

  a.   b.   c.   d.

 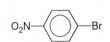 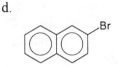

45. Which is <u>not</u> an aliphatic compound?

  a. $CH_3CH_2CH_2Br$ b. Cl-CH=CH-Cl   c.   d. CHF_3 e.

46. Which is <u>not</u> a reason for discontinuing the use of carbon tetrachloride in fire extinguishers?
  a. The compound is flammable.
  b. Exposure to the compound itself can cause severe liver damage.
  c. The compound can react with water to form the extremely toxic gas phosgene.
  d. All of the above are valid reasons for discontinuing use of CCl_4 in fire extinguishers.

47. Which compound enjoyed widespread use as an anesthetic at one time?
  a. CH_3Cl b. CH_2Cl_2 c. $CHCl_3$ d. CCl_4

48. The most important use for vinyl chloride is:
  a. as a dry cleaning solvent
  b. as the starting material for the synthesis of vinyl plastics
  c. as a pesticide
  d. as an anesthetic
  e. as a plasticizer

49. If water and chloroform are mixed,
  a. the two miscible liquids form a clear solution
  b. a water layer floats on top of a chloroform layer
  c. a chloroform layer floats on top of a water layer

50. Which compound would propyl chloride most closely resemble in boiling point?
  a. ethane (C_2H_6)   b. pentane (C_5H_{12})   c. heptane (C_7H_{16})

51. The small-molecule starting materials from which macromolecules can be constructed are called:
  a. monomers   b. polymers   c. segmers

52. Which compound would not serve as a monomer in <u>addition</u> polymerization?
  a. CH_2=CH-COOH   b. CH_2=CHCH$_2$OH   c. HO-CH$_2$-COOH

53. The polymer formed from CH_2=C-CH$_3$ is:
         |
         Cl

    CH_2Cl Cl   Cl CH_2Cl
     | | | |
 a. -[-CH$_2$=C-]$_n$-   b. -[-CH$_2$=C-CH$_2$-]$_n$-   c. -[-CH$_2$-C-]$_n$-   d. -[-CH$_2$-CH-]$_n$-
                     |
                     CH_3

54. If the monomer is CH_3-CH=CH-Cl, the polymer is:
     Cl   Cl   Cl CH_3
     | | | |
 a. [- CH$_3$CH=CH-]$_n$ b. [-CH$_3$CH$_2$-CH-]$_n$ c. [-CH$_3$CH=CH-]$_n$ d. [-CH-CH-]$_n$
                             |
                             Cl

55. Plasticizers are:
  a. polymers which show elastic properties
  b. polymers which soften on heating
  c. molecules which confer pliability on otherwise brittle polymers

ANSWERS:

Problems: Nomenclature and Isomerism - Only the carbon skeleton of structural formulas is given.
(c & t = cis and trans isomers)

1. C-C-C-C-C-C-C   heptane

  C-C-C-C-C-C   2-methylhexane
   |
   C

  C-C-C-C-C-C   3-methylhexane
     |
     C

   C
   |
  C-C-C-C-C   2,2-dimethylpentane
   |
   C

   C C
   | |
  C-C-C-C-C   2,3-dimethylpentane

   C   C
   | |
  C-C-C-C-C   2,4-dimethylpentane

    C
    |
  C-C-C-C-C   3,3-dimethylpentane
    |
    C

  C-C-C-C-C   3-ethylpentane
    |
    C-C

   C C
   | |
  C-C-C-C   2,2,3-trimethylbutane
   |
   C

2. C=C-C-C-C-C   1-hexene

  C-C=C-C-C-C   2-hexene (c & t)

  C-C-C=C-C-C   3-hexene (c & t)

    C
    |
  C=C-C-C-C   2-methyl-1-pentene

     C
     |
  C=C-C-C-C   3-methyl-1-pentene

      C
      |
  C=C-C-C-C   4-methyl-1-pentene

    C
    |
  C-C=C-C-C   2-methyl-2-pentene

  C-C=C-C-C   3-methyl-2-pentene
     |
     C   (c & t)

      C
      |
  C-C=C-C-C   4-methyl-2-pentene
          (c & t)

    C C
    | |
  C=C-C-C   2,3-dimethyl-1-butene

     C
     |
  C=C-C-C   3,3-dimethyl-1-butene
     |
     C

    C-C
    |
  C=C-C-C   2-ethyl-1-butene

    C C
    | |
  C-C=C-C   2,3-dimethyl-2-butene

3. C≡C-C-C-C-C   1-hexyne;   C-C≡C-C-C-C   2-hexyne;   C-C-C≡C-C-C   3-hexyne

    C
    |
 C≡C-C-C-C   3-methyl-1-pentyne;

     C
     |
 C-C≡C-C-C   4-methyl-2-pentyne;

      C
      |
 C≡C-C-C-C   4-methyl-1-pentyne

    C
    |
 C≡C-C-C   3,3-dimethyl-1-butyne
    |
    C

4. 1,2,3-trimethylbenzene 1,2,4-trimethylbenzene 1,3,5-trimethylbenzene

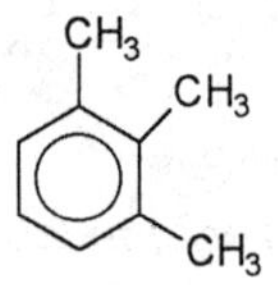

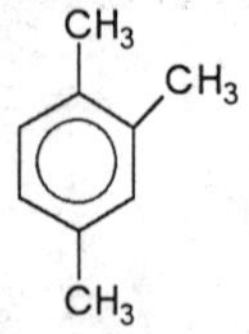

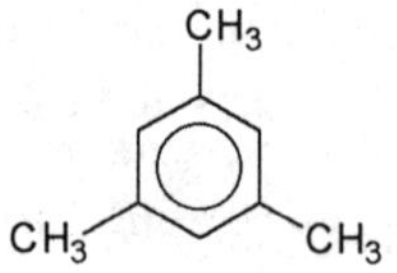

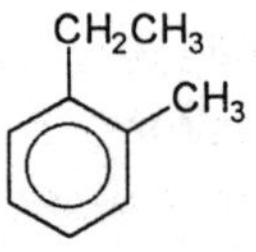

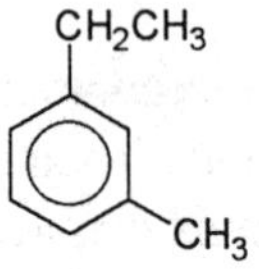

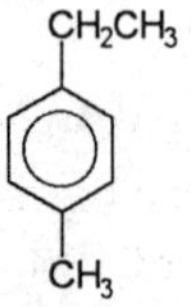

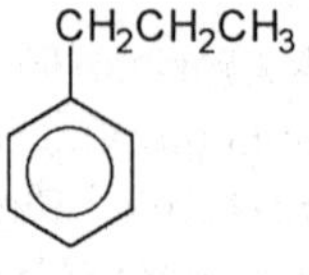

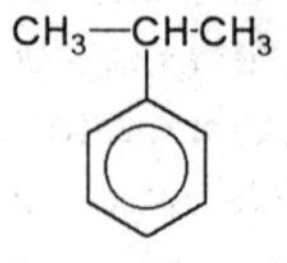

(1,2-) (1,3-) (1,4-)

o-, m-, and p-ethylmethylbenzene n-propyl- and isopropyl benzene

5.

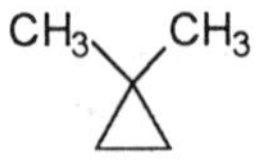

1,1-dimethylcyclopropane 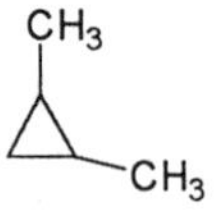 1,2-dimethylcyclopropane (cis & trans)

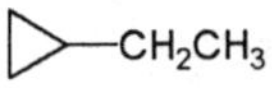

ethylcyclopropane 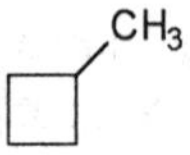 methylcyclobutane 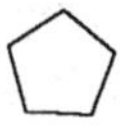 cyclopentane

Self-Test

1. e	12. b	21. a	32. b	39. c	50. b
2. c	13. c	22. d	33. c	40. b	51. a
3. b	14. a	23. d	34. c	41. c	52. c
4. b	15. c	24. c	35. c	42. c	53. c
5. a	16. A. b	25. d	36. b	43. d	54. d
6. a	B. d	26. b	37. b	44. a	55. c
7. c	C. d	27. c	38. A. a	45. e	
8. a	17. d	28. a	B. b	46. a	
9. a	18. a	29. b	C. b	47. c	
10. a	19. a	30. a, d	D. a	48. b	
11. c	20. c	31. d	E. a	49. b	

Special Topic E: Petroleum

KEY WORDS

gasoline   kerosene   100 octane   tetraethyllead   paraffins
cracking   engine knock   petroleum   distillation   petrochemicals

SUMMARY

E.1 Natural Gas and Gasoline

    A. *Petroleum* is a complex mixture of hydrocarbons produced by the decomposition of animal and vegetable matter entrapped in the earth's crust. One barrel of crude oil equals 42 gallons. It consists largely of a mixture of alkanes consisting of 1 to 40 carbons that are in turn used to produce most *petrochemicals*. Crude oil is the liquid and natural gas is the gaseous parts of petroleum. These are separated by fractional *distillation* into various groups by size:

# C s	Fraction
1-4	Natural gas (80% CH_4, 10% C_2H_6)
5-12	*Gasoline*
12-16	*Kerosene*
15-18	Heating oil
17-up	Lubricating oil
20-up	*Paraffins*, etc.

    B. Fractions containing 12 or more carbons can be converted into more valuable gasoline by a process called *cracking*, which involves heating in the absence of air. The unsaturated hydrocarbons are the starting materials for making plastics and detergents.

E.2 The Octane Rating of Gasoline

    A. The "octane-rating" was established in 1927 when it was observed that isooctane was best at minimizing "*engine knock*." It was assigned an octane rating of "*100 octane*." Heptane, a straight, 7-carbon alkane caused a very bad "knock" and was assigned "0 octane." A gasoline rated "90 octane" performed the same as a mixture of 90% isooctane and 10% heptane.

    B. *Tetraethyllead* is an "octane booster." When added at as little as 1 part per 1000 parts of gasoline, it can increase the octane reading from 55 to 90 or more. However, lead is toxic and tetraethyllead is being replaced by other "octane boosters" such as methyl t-butyl ether, methanol, ethanol, and t-butyl alcohol.

SELF-TEST

1. The process in which large hydrocarbon molecules are heated in the absence of air and converted to smaller and more highly branched structures is called:
    a. combustion   b. cracking   c. hydration   d. hydrogenation
2. Tetraethyllead is a(n):
    a. gasoline additive   b. anesthetic   c. emollient
3. Hydrocarbons having from 5-12 carbons are called _____.
    a. gasolines   b. heating oil   c. paraffins   d. kerosenes
4. Hydrocarbons having from 12-16 carbons are called _____.
    a. gasolines   b. heating oil   c. paraffins   d. kerosenes
5. Hydrocarbons having from 15-18 carbons are called _____.
    a. gasolines   b. heating oil   c. paraffins   d. kerosenes

ANSWERS:

1. b   2. a   3. a   4. d   5. b

CHAPTER 14: ALCOHOLS, PHENOLS & ETHERS

KEY WORDS

functional group	*primary*	*Markovnikov's rule*	*carbolic acid*	*glycols*
alcohol	*secondary*	*fermentation*	*ethers*	*glycerol*
ethanol	*tertiary*	*phenol*	*peroxides*	*absolute*
hydroxyl	*diol*	*triol*	*azeotrope*	*alcohol*
denatured	*proof spirit*	*aldehyde*	*ketone*	*aryl*

SUMMARY

14.1 The Functional Group

   A. A *functional group* is a group of atoms that confers characteristic chemical and physical properties on a family of organic compounds. Alcohols, phenols and ethers are related to water with one or both of its hydrogens replaced by an organic group. *Alcohols* have a *hydroxyl* (-OH) group attached to an aliphatic carbon, while *phenols* have an *aryl* group.

   B.
Alcohol	*Phenol*	*Ether*
R-OH	Ar-OH	-C-O-C-

   CH_3CH_2OH (phenol) $CH_3CH_2-O-CH_2-CH_3$

   (ethanol)   (diethyl ether)

14.2 Classification and Nomenclature of Alcohols

   A. Alcohols include molecules as diverse as ethanol (beverage alcohol), cholesterol, glucose, and vitamin A.

   B. Common names
      1. Alkyl group + alcohol;   ethyl alcohol
      2. Alcohols are subdivided based on the number of C atoms attached to the carbon bearing the -OH group [primary (0 or 1), secondary (2) and tertiary (3)].

   $-CH_2-OH$ -C-CH-C-   -C-C-C-
                  OH   OH

   primary (1^O)   *secondary (2^O)*   *tertiary (3°)*

   C. IUPAC system - identify the longest continuous C chain for the corresponding alkane that still contains the hydroxyl group, drop the "-e" and add "-ol." Identify the position of the hydroxyl group by the number of the carbon to which it is bonded. For "*diols*" and "*triols*," retain the "-e" of the parent alkane.

   OH   OH OH OH
   $CH_3-CH-CH_2-CH_3$ $CH_2-CH-CH_2$
   2-butanol   1,2,3-propanetriol (glycerol)

14.3 Physical Properties of Alcohols

   A. Alcohols can use the -OH group to form hydrogen bonds, thus they have higher boiling points than the corresponding hydrocarbons. Most common alcohols are liquids at room temperature.

   $CH_3-CH_2—\ddot{O}:----H—\ddot{O}$
                   | CH_2-CH_3
                   H

B. The lower molecular weight alcohols are completely miscible with water, but the solubility decreases dramatically when the C/O ratio exceeds 4:1.

14.4 Preparation of Alcohols

A. Most alcohols are made by the hydration of the corresponding alkenes in the presence of acid.

1. $CH_2=CH_2$ + HOH ——$H+$——→ CH_3-CH_2-OH

2. *Markovnikov's Rule* - "the rich get richer." When there is a difference, the hydrogen goes on the carbon atom of the double bond that already has more hydrogens bonded to it.

$$CH_3-CH=CH_2 + H-OH \rightarrow CH_3-CH-CH_3$$
$$\uparrow \qquad \uparrow \qquad\qquad OH \uparrow$$

B. Methanol (wood alcohol) is produced commercially from: CO + $2 H_2$ $\xrightarrow[ZnO, Cr_2O_3]{200 \text{ atm, } 350\,^{o}C}$ CH_3OH

C. *Ethanol* is produced by *fermentation*.

$$\underset{\text{starch}}{(C_6H_{10}O_5)_x} \longrightarrow \underset{\text{glucose}}{C_6H_{12}O_6} \longrightarrow \underset{\text{ethanol}}{2\ C_2H_5OH} + 2\ CO_2$$

1. Source of sugar: grain, corn, molasses.
2. Grind and cook the grain to produce mash.
3. The enzyme diastase is added to convert the starch to maltose.
4. Yeast is added to convert the maltose to glucose and finally to ethanol (up to 18%).
5. This is filtered and distilled to produce more concentrated liquors. The *proof spirit* value is twice the percent alcohol by volume, e.g. 50% alcohol in gin = 100 "proof."

14.5 Physiological Properties of Alcohols

A. Most alcohols are fairly poisonous, but ethanol and glycerol are less so than the others.

B. Methanol is a common industrial solvent. It is oxidized in the body to formaldehyde.

$$CH_3OH \xrightarrow{\text{liver enzymes}} \overset{H}{\underset{H}{\diagdown}}C=O \text{ (formaldehyde)}$$

C. Ethanol is also toxic, but much less so than methanol. It too is oxidized in the liver, but to acetaldehyde, which can in turn be converted to harmless acetate and finally to CO_2.

Ethanol   acetaldehyde   acetate   carbon dioxide

$$CH_3CH_2-OH \longrightarrow H_3C-\overset{O}{\overset{\|}{C}}-H \longrightarrow CH_3COO^- \longrightarrow CO_2$$

In laboratory tests, acetaldehyde is 27x less toxic to rats than is formaldehyde. However, prolonged intake of excessive amounts of ethanol can lead to fatty liver, followed by deterioration of the liver and other complications. Alcohol is a depressant of the central nervous system. A blood alcohol concentration of 0.1% is legal evidence of intoxication.

D. Water forms a constant boiling *azeotrope* containing 95% ethanol and 5% water. Absolute alcohol is 100% ethanol (200 proof). *Denatured* alcohol is ethanol with an additive which makes it unfit to drink.

E. A 70% isopropyl alcohol solution is common "rubbing alcohol."

F. Ethanol and methanol can be blended with gasoline to make "gasohol" to increase the octane rating of unleaded gasolines.

14.6 Chemical Properties of Alcohols
A. Dehydration of alcohols
1. Alkene formation

$$CH_3-CH_2-OH \xrightarrow[180°C]{conc. H_2SO_4} \underset{H \quad H}{\overset{H \quad H}{C=C}} + H_2O$$

2. Ether formation

$$CH_3CH_2-OH + H-O-CH_2CH_3 \longrightarrow CH_3CH_2-O-CH_2CH_3 + H_2O$$

B. Oxidation of alcohols
1. Primary alcohols are oxidized to *aldehydes* (then carboxylic acids).

$$R-CH_2-OH \longrightarrow R-\overset{O}{\overset{\|}{C}}-H \longrightarrow R-\overset{O}{\overset{\|}{C}}-OH$$

2. Secondary alcohols are oxidized to the corresponding *ketone*.

$$\underset{OH}{R-CH-CH_3} \xrightarrow[H^+]{K_2Cr_2O_7} \underset{O}{R-\overset{\|}{C}-CH_3}$$

3. Tertiary alcohols are resistant to such mild oxidation.

14.7 Multifunctional Alcohols: Glycols and Glycerol
A. *Glycols*: Dihydric alcohols
1. Ethylene glycol or ethanediol - Main ingredient in permanent antifreeze; oxidized in the body to oxalic acid, $HO-CH_2CH_2-OH$, kidney stones are crystals (ppt.) of calcium oxalate.
2. Propylene glycol - Solvent for drugs; nontoxic since it is oxidized to pyruvic acid, which can enter our body's metabolism.
B. *Glycerol* (or glycerin) is a trihydric alcohol (1,2,3-propanetriol). It is nontoxic and a product of the breakdown of fats (triglycerides). Glycerol reacts with nitric acid to form glycerol trinitrate (nitroglycerin), an oily explosive liquid used to make dynamite and is also a drug used to relieve chest pain. Glycerol is also used as a lubricant, in hand lotions, and in the production of plastics and synthetic fibers.

14.8 Phenols
A. *Phenols* are compounds with a hydroxyl group attached directly to an aromatic ring or *aryl* group:

       or simply Ar-OH.

1. Compared with hydrocarbons, phenols have relatively high boiling points (most are solids at room temperature) because of intermolecular hydrogen bonding.
2. By definition phenols have at least 6 carbon atoms, which is the borderline of water-solubility for compounds containing one oxygen. Phenols, in contrast to alcohols, are weakly acidic and thus most phenols are soluble in basic solutions.

B. Phenol (*carbolic* acid) was introduced by Joseph Lister in 1867 as the first widely used antiseptic.
C. Hexachlorophene (a chlorinated diphenol) was once widely used in germicidal cleaning solutions (pHisohex) and deodorant soaps but was found to cause neurological disease.
D. Bakelite is a condensation polymer of formaldehyde and phenol.

E. Nomenclature—Simple compounds are named as derivatives of phenol, but many of the most interesting phenols are referred to by their common names.

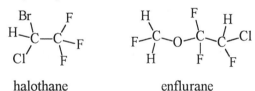

| phenol | o-nitrophenol | m-cresol | catechol | hydroquinone |

Other phenol compounds include picric acid, cresol, vanillin, resorcinol and BHT.

14.9 Ethers

A. **Ether** compounds can be considered to be derivatives of water in which both hydrogens have been replaced by alkyl or aryl groups. (e.g., R-O-R, R-O-Ar, Ar-O-Ar)

B. Ethers are named by naming the groups attached to the "-O-" and adding "ether."

CH_3-O-CH_3 = dimethyl ether; CH_3CH_2-O-CH_2CH_3 = diethyl ether.

C. Physical properties

1. Ethers have a boiling point comparable to hydrocarbons of similar molecular weight because ether molecules cannot hydrogen bond with one another in pure form (no H bond donors).

2. Ethers are more soluble in water than corresponding hydrocarbons because ethers can interact with water molecules as acceptors in hydrogen bonding.

D. Chemically ethers are quite inert, more like alkanes, and often are used as an organic extraction medium. They are also very flammable and upon standing in air can form explosive **peroxides**.

$$-\overset{|}{\underset{H}{C}}-O-\overset{|}{\underset{|}{C}}- \quad + \quad O_2 \quad \rightarrow \quad -\overset{|}{\underset{\underset{O\text{-}OH}{|}}{C}}-O-\overset{|}{\underset{|}{C}}-$$

E. Anesthesia - An anesthetic acts to block pain. Many anesthetics are fat soluble and appear to work by dissolving in the fat-like membranes of nerve cells to depress conductivity of neurons.

1. Diethyl ether is a well-known anesthetic that acts as a central nervous system depressant.

2. Nitrous oxide (laughing gas, N_2O) was introduced in 1772.

3. Chloroform ($CHCl_3$) was used in 1847.

4. Fluorine-containing compounds (halothane, enflurane).

| halothane | enflurane |

DISCUSSION

Chapter 14 introduces the carbon-oxygen single bond (-C-O-) into our study of organic chemistry. Alcohols, phenols, and ethers all share this bonding pattern, yet have distinct physical and chemical properties. You should be able to classify compounds into each of these three categories on the basis of their chemical formulas. The physical properties can be correlated with the fact that alcohols and phenols can serve as donors in hydrogen bond formation while ethers cannot do so. The nomenclature in this chapter is complicated by the fact that many of these compounds are referred to by their common names. You should memorize the formulas of methanol, ethanol, glycerol and phenol since you will use them frequently in subsequent chapters. The chemistry of alcohols was treated in more detail than the reactions of phenols and ethers. In particular, take time to review the oxidation behavior of the various types of alcohols before attempting the **SELF-TEST**.

SELF-TEST

1. Which is an alcohol?

   a. C_2H_5OH b. $CH_3\text{-}\overset{O}{\overset{\|}{C}}\text{-}CH_3$ c. $CH_3\text{-}O\text{-}CH_3$ d. C_6H_6

2. Which compound is an ether?

   a. $\underset{CH_2\text{-}CH\text{-}CH_2}{\overset{OH \quad OH \quad OH}{}}$ b. CH_3CH_2OH c. $CH_3\text{-}O\text{-}C_3H_7$ d. $CH_3\text{-}\overset{O}{\overset{\|}{C}}\text{-}CH_3$

3. A combination of atoms that confers chemical and physical properties on a compound is called a(n);

   a. ether   b. functional group   c. hydrogen bond

4. The presence of a hydroxyl group attached directly to a benzene ring makes the compound a(n):

   a. alcohol   b. ether   c. phenol   d. base   e. explosive

5. This compound is a(n);

   a. alcohol   b. aldehyde   c. benzene   d. ether   e. phenol

6. Which compound is a phenol?

   a. CH_3CH_2OH b. $CH_3\text{-}O\text{-}CH_3$ c. $\underset{CH_2\text{-}CH_2}{\overset{OH \quad OH}{}}$ d. $CH_3\text{-}\overset{}{\underset{O}{C}}\text{-}H$ e.

7. For which compound is R-O-Ar an appropriate abbreviation?

   a.   b. CH_3OH c. $CH_3\text{-}O\text{-}CH_3$ d.   e.

8. Which compound is a trihydric alcohol?

   a. rubbing alcohol   b. propylene glycol   c. glycerol

9. Which is/are primary alcohols?

   a. CH_3OCH_3 b. $\underset{CH_3}{\overset{}{CH_3CH\text{-}CH_2OH}}$ c. $\underset{OH}{\overset{}{CH_3CH_2CHCH_3}}$ d. $\underset{CH_3}{\overset{OH}{CH_3CCH_3}}$

10. Which is/are secondary alcohols?

    a. $CH_3CH_2CH_2CH_2OH$ b. $\underset{CH3}{\overset{}{CH_3CH_2CH_2CHOH}}$ c. $\underset{H}{\overset{CH_3}{CH_3C\text{-}OH}}$ d. $CH_3\text{-}O\text{-}CH_2CH_3$ e. $\overset{OH}{CH_2OH}$

11. Which compound is a tertiary alcohol?

    a.   b.   c.   d.

12. The compound $CH_3CH_2\underset{CH_3}{\overset{}{CH}}\text{-}OH$ is <u>not</u> properly called:

    a. 2-butanal   b. isobutyl alcohol   c. sec-butyl alcohol   d. 2-butanol

13. The correct name of $CH_3\text{-}O\text{-}CH_2CH_3$ is:

    a. diethyl ether   b. ethyl ether   c. methyl ethyl ether   d. ethyl methyl oxide

14. Wood alcohol is the same as:

    a. methanol   b. 2-propanol   c. glycerin   d. grain alcohol   e. rubbing alcohol

15. Phenol is:

a.   b.   c. $CH_3CH_2CH_2$-OH   d. $CH_3CH_2CH_2CH_2CH_2OH$

16. The formula of anesthetic "ether" is:

a. CH_3OCH_3 b. C_2H_5OH c. $CH_3CH_2\overset{\overset{O}{\|}}{C}CH_2CH_3$ d. C_2H_5-O-C_2H_5

17. Which compound would have the highest boiling point?

a. CH_3CH_3-O-CH_2CH_3 b. $CH_3OCH_2CH_2OH$ c. $CH_3\underset{OH}{CH}-\underset{OH}{CH_2}$ d. $CH_3CH_2CH_2CH_2OH$

18. Which compound would be expected to have the lowest boiling point?

a. $CH_3CH_2CH_2OH$ b. CH_3-O-CH_2CH_3 c. HO-CH_2CH_2-OH

19. The alcohol present in alcoholic beverages is:

a. methyl alcohol   b. isopropanol   c. ethyl alcohol   d. denatured alcohol

20. Alcohols boil at appreciably higher temperatures than hydrocarbons of similar formula weight because:

a. they have a higher molecular weight   b. alcohols are strongly acidic

c. alcohols are ionic compounds   d. alcohols are soluble in water

e. the molecules of the alcohol are associated through hydrogen bonding

21. Which alcohol is least soluble in water?

a. CH_3OH b. C_3H_7OH c. $C_6H_{13}OH$ d. $C_{10}H_{21}OH$

22. Which compound would be most soluble in water?

a. CH_2=$CHCH_2CH_3$ b. $CH_3CH_2OCH_2CH_3$ c. $CH_3CH_2\underset{OH}{CH}-CH_2OH$

23. Which compound is not miscible with water?

a. CH_3CH_2OH b. $\underset{OH\ \ OH}{CH_2-CH_2}$ c.

24. Which compound not miscible with water would be soluble in dilute base?

a. $CH_3CH_2CH_2CH_2CH_2CH_3$ b.   c.

25. Fermentation of carbohydrates leads to the formation of:

a. methyl alcohol   b. ethyl alcohol   c. glucose   d. 1-propanol

26. Which solution could not be obtained directly from the fermentation reaction?

a. 10% ethyl alcohol in water

b. 30% ethyl alcohol in water

c. 10 proof ethyl alcohol

d. 20 proof ethyl alcohol

27. Dehydration of alcohols does not produce:

a. ethers   b. alkenes   c. aldehydes

28. Which term describes the reaction: CH_2=CH_2 + H_2O $\xrightarrow{\ H+\ }$ $\underset{OH\ \ H}{CH_2-CH_2}$?

a. combustion b. dehydration c. hydration   d. oxidation

29. Markovnikov's rule indicates that:

a. when alcohols are dehydrated, they yield alkenes in preference to ethers.

b. primary and secondary alcohols are readily oxidized, but tertiary alcohols are not.

c. when water adds to alkenes, the hydrogen of water adds to the double-bonded carbon with the most hydrogens.

30. Which product would be expected from the hydration of 1-butene?

131

a. $CH_3CH_2CH_2CH_2OH$ b. $CH_3CH-CH_2CH_3$ c. $CH_3CH_2CH_2-O-CH_3$ d. $CH_3\overset{OH}{\underset{CH_3}{C}}-CH_3$
                                OH

31. Which compound is <u>not</u> readily oxidized?

a. $CH_3\underset{CH_3}{CH}-CH_2OH$ b. $CH_3CH_2\underset{OH}{CH}-CH_3$ c. $CH_3\overset{OH}{\underset{CH_3}{C}}-CH_3$ d. $CH_3CH_2\underset{H}{C}=O$

32. What is the product of the reaction: $CH_3\overset{OH}{CH}-CH_3$ $\xrightarrow{K_2Cr_2O_7,\ H+}$?

a. CH_3COOH b. $CH_3CH_2CH_2OH$ c. $CH_3CH_2\underset{H}{C}=O$ d. CH_3CH_2COOH e. $CH_3\overset{}{\underset{O}{C}}-CH_3$

33. In chemical reactivity, ethers resemble:
      a. alcohols   b. alkanes   c. phenols

34. Air oxidation of ethers results in the formation of:
      a. aldehydes   b. carboxylic acids   c. ketones   d. peroxides

35. Denatured alcohol refers to:
      a. any alcohol not produced by fermentation
      b. grain alcohol that is highly taxed
      c. ethyl alcohol that has been treated with something to make it unfit to drink

36. The toxicity of wood alcohol results from its oxidation by liver enzymes to:
      a. carbon dioxide   b. formaldehyde   c. grain alcohol   d. methanol

37. Which is quite toxic when ingested by humans?
      a. ethylene glycol   b. propylene glycol   c. glycerol

38. Which compound is widely used as a general anesthetic?
      a. dimethyl ether   b. diethyl ether   c. bis(chloromethyl)ether (BCME)

39. What is the product when this compound undergoes oxidation?

a. (cyclohexane-COOH)   b. (benzene-OH)   c. (benzene)   d. (cyclohexanone =O)   e. cyclohexene

40. Select the response that gives the proper order for increasing solubility in water.
      a. butanol < hexane < diethyl ether
      b. diethyl ether < butanol < hexane
      c. hexane < butanol < diethyl ether
      d. diethyl ether < hexane < butanol
      e. hexane < diethyl ether < butanol

ANSWERS:

1.	a	9.	b	17.	c	25.	b	33. b
2.	c	10.	b and c	18.	b	26.	b	34. d
3.	b	11.	d	19.	c	27.	c	35. c
4.	c	12.	a and b	20.	e	28.	c	36. b
5.	d	13.	c	21.	d	29.	c	37. a
6.	e	14.	a	22.	c	30.	b	38. b
7.	d	15.	b	23.	c	31.	c	39. d
8.	c	16.	d	24.	b	32.	e	40. e

CHAPTER 15: ALDEHYDES AND KETONES

KEY WORDS

carbonyl	*ketal*	*acetal*	*acetone*	*aldehyde*
hemiacetal	*imine*	*tautomerism*	*ketone*	*hemiketal*
enol	*aldol condensation*	*Tollens'*	*hydrate*	*formaldehyde*
hydrogen bond				

SUMMARY

15.1 The Carbonyl Group: A Carbon-Oxygen Double Bond
   A. The *carbonyl* double bond is polar and tends to undergo addition reactions.
   B. Aldehydes and Ketones - *Ketones* have two carbons attached to the carbonyl carbon, *aldehydes* have at least one hydrogen attached to the carbonyl carbon.

aldehyde   ketone

15.2 How to Name the Common Aldehydes
   A. Common names are frequently used for many aldehydes.
      1. *Formaldehyde* ($H_2C=O$) is a gas. Formalin, a 40% solution of formaldehyde, is a familiar biological preservative. Others in this series are:
         2C - acetaldehyde   4C - butyraldehyde
         3C - propionaldehyde   5C - valeraldehyde
      2. The positions of substituents are indicated by a Greek letter (α, β, γ) where α corresponds to the C adjacent to the carbonyl group.
   B. The IUPAC rules for naming aldehydes are derived from the corresponding alkanes, dropping the "-e" and adding "-al." Note: No number is needed since the aldehyde carbonyl group is always on the end.

$$CH_3\text{-}CH\text{-}CH_2\text{-}C \overset{\overset{O}{\|}}{} $$
         Cl   H

   β-Chlorobutyraldehyde (Common name)
   3-chlorobutanal   (IUPAC name)

15.3 Naming the Common Ketones
   A. Common names
      The simplest ketone has 3 carbons and is called *acetone*. Others are named like ethers using the alkyl groups in alphabetical order and the word ketone.

   $$\underset{\text{acetone}}{H_3C \overset{\overset{O}{\|}}{\underset{}{C}} CH_3}$$ $$\underset{\text{ethyl methyl ketone}}{CH_3\text{-}\overset{\overset{O}{\|}}{C}\text{-}CH_2\text{-}CH_3}$$

   B. The IUPAC rules for ketones use the longest continuous C chain containing the carbonyl group as the parent, the "-e" ending is dropped and "-one" added. The positions of the carbonyl group and of substituents are given by numbers.

   $$CH_3\text{-}\overset{\overset{O}{\|}}{C}\text{-}CH_2\text{-}CH_2\text{-}CH_2\text{-}F \quad = \quad \text{5-fluoro-2-pentanone}$$

15.4 Physical Properties of Aldehydes and Ketones
   A. The physical properties of these compounds are greatly influenced by the marked polarity of the carbon-oxygen double bond, increasing the boiling point of aldehydes and ketones over the corresponding ethers.

$$\overset{\delta+}{\underset{/}{\overset{\backslash}{C}}}=\overset{\delta-}{O}$$

   B. Pure aldehydes and ketones can not "*hydrogen bond*" because they are not hydrogen donors. However, they can participate as hydrogen bond acceptors and thus behave like alcohols in their water solubility.

15.5 Preparation of Aldehydes and Ketones
   A. Aldehydes are made by oxidizing 1° alcohols.
   B. Ketones can be made by oxidizing 2° alcohols.

$$R\text{-}CH_2\text{-}OH \xrightarrow{[O]} R\text{-}\overset{O}{\overset{\|}{C}}\text{-}H \;\;;\;\; R\text{-}\overset{OH}{\overset{|}{CH}}\text{-}R' \xrightarrow{K_2CrO_7,\ H_2SO_4} R\text{-}\overset{O}{\overset{\|}{C}}\text{-}R'$$

15.6 Chemical Properties of Aldehydes and Ketones
   A. Oxidation: Aldehydes are readily oxidized to carboxylic acids while ketones resist mild oxidation.
       1. *Tollens'* reagent is a very gentle oxidant that is used to test for the presence of aldehydes. When Tollens' reagent oxidizes an aldehyde, silver ion is reduced to free silver forming an easily recognizable mirror on the surface of the tube.

$$R\text{-}CHO + 2Ag(NH_3)_2^+ + 2OH^- \rightarrow R\text{-}COO^-NH_4^+ + 2\ Ag^o + 3NH_3 + H_2O$$

       Both aldehydes and ketones are also flammable and will undergo combustion.
       2. Benedict's and Fehling's tests use alkaline solutions of Cu^{2+} (blue) which forms a red, solid precipitate of Cu_2O when reduced in alkaline solutions.
   B. Reduction: Aldehydes are reduced to primary alcohols and ketones are reduced to the corresponding secondary alcohols using H_2 and a Ni or Pt catalyst.
   C. Hydration of Carbonyl Compounds
       1. The lighter aldehydes readily dissolve in water to form unstable *hydrates*.
       2. The hydrate of trichloroacetaldehyde (chloral hydrate) is a stable solid. It is a powerful sedative and in a drink is called a "Mickey Finn."
   D. Addition of Alcohols: Hemiacetals and Acetals
       1. Alcohols add to the carbonyl group of aldehydes (or ketones) to form *hemiacetals* (or *hemiketals*).

$$CH_3\text{-}\overset{O}{\overset{\|}{\underset{H\ (R)}{C}}} + H\text{-}O\text{-}CH_3 \longrightarrow CH_3\text{-}\overset{OH}{\overset{|}{\underset{H\ (R)}{C}}}\text{-}OCH_3$$

   aldehyde (ketone)   hemiacetal (hemiketal)

   Hemiacetals are normally rather unstable. Sugars are polyhydroxy aldehydes or ketones that form cyclic, intramolecular hemiacetals which are fairly stable.
       2. Hemiacetals (or hemiketals) can be made to react further by a dehydration reaction with a second alcohol molecule to form a stable *acetal* (or *ketal*).

$$R\text{-}\overset{OH}{\overset{|}{\underset{H}{C}}}\text{-}O\text{-}R' + H\text{-}O\text{-}R'' \longrightarrow R\text{-}\overset{O\text{-}R''}{\overset{|}{\underset{H}{C}}}\text{-}O\text{-}R' + H_2O$$

   Acetals are frequently used to protect aldehyde functional groups because acetals are resistant to oxidation whereas aldehydes are not.

E. The Hydrogen Shift: Tautomerism
   1. The alpha hydrogens near a carbonyl group are slightly acidic. A carbonyl compound with alpha hydrogens exists in equilibrium with an isomeric form that has the hydrogen shifted to the carbonyl oxygen atom, an enol. This is referred to as *keto-enol tautomerism*.
   2. *Aldol Condensation*: The alpha hydrogens of a carbonyl compound are sufficiently acidic to be pulled off by a strong base. This negatively charged carbanion will add to the carbonyl carbon of another carbonyl molecule in an aldol condensation reaction. The 3 carbon sugars of glyceraldehyde and dihydroxyacetone combine to form the 6 carbon sugar, fructose, by aldol condensation.

$$2\ \text{R-CH}_2\text{-}\overset{\overset{\displaystyle O}{||}}{\text{C}}\text{-H} \rightarrow \qquad \text{R-CH}_2\text{-}\overset{\overset{\displaystyle O\text{-H}}{|}}{\underset{\underset{\displaystyle H}{|}}{\text{C}}}\text{-}\overset{\underset{\displaystyle R}{|}}{\text{CH}}\text{-}\overset{\overset{\displaystyle O}{||}}{\text{C}}\text{-H}$$

(β-hydroxy product)

15.7 Some Common Carbonyl Compounds
   A. Formaldehyde   -- biological fixative (37% solution = formalin)
   B. Acetaldehyde   -- fermentation of sugars; oxidation of ethanol
   C. Acetone   -- solvent and one of the ketone bodies from lipid metabolism
   D. Benzaldehyde   -- oil of bitter almond
   E. Cinnamaldehyde   -- oil of cinnamon
   F. Others -- camphor, vanillin, muscone, progesterone, testosterone, etc.

DISCUSSION

   Tables 15.1 and 15.2 in Chapter 15 illustrate the nomenclature rules for aldehydes and ketones. You can use these tables to check your understanding of the common and IUPAC naming systems. If you have not already done so, answer the first twelve questions at the end of Chapter 15 for added practice.

   By far, the greater part of this chapter was devoted to chemical reactions involving aldehydes and ketones. The selection of reactions considered was based on their significance in living systems. We will soon encounter aldol condensations, keto-enol tautomerism, and acetal formation in our study of the chemistry of carbohydrates. Carbohydrates contain many functional groups and, on first encounter, strike one as very complex molecules. This is why we are taking the time now to look at reactions which we'll consider again later. By looking at simple molecules, we can concentrate on the general pattern of these reactions. That same pattern will be followed when the reacting molecules are more complex. The reactions of Chapter 15 are gathered below for easy reference.

Summary of Reactions of Aldehydes and Ketones

I. Oxidation - This is the reaction which most clearly distinguishes the aldehyde family from the ketone family.

   A. Aldehydes: $\text{R-C}\overset{\displaystyle O}{\underset{\displaystyle H}{}} \xrightarrow{\ [O]\ } \text{R-C}\overset{\displaystyle O}{\underset{\displaystyle OH}{}}$

   The usual oxidizing agents (like $K_2Cr_2O_7$) work, as do even weaker oxidizing agents (like Ag+ in the form of Tollens' reagent).

   B. Ketones: Under ordinary conditions, ketones give no reaction.

II. Addition reactions involving the carbonyl group -

   A. Addition of water (hydrate formation)

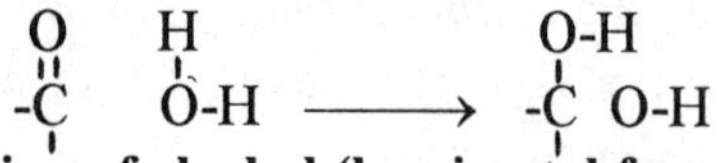

$$\overset{O}{\underset{|}{\overset{||}{-C}}} \quad \overset{H}{\underset{|}{O\text{-}H}} \longrightarrow \quad \overset{O\text{-}H}{\underset{|}{-C}}\, O\text{-}H$$

   B. Addition of alcohol (hemiacetal formation)

     1. Hemiacetal formation

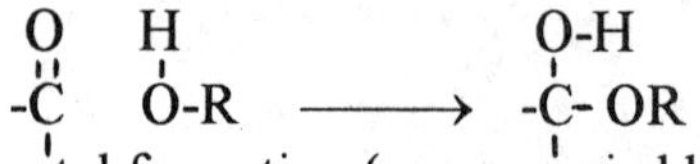

$$\overset{O}{\underset{|}{\overset{||}{-C}}} \quad \overset{H}{\underset{|}{O\text{-}R}} \longrightarrow \quad \overset{O\text{-}H}{\underset{|}{-C}}\text{-}OR$$

     2. Acetal formation (accompanied by elimination of water)

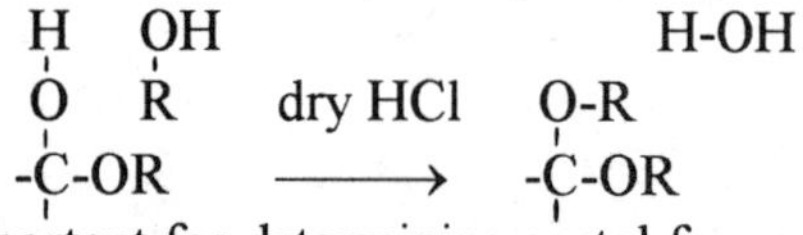

$$\overset{H \quad OH}{\underset{}{\overset{O \quad R}{-\underset{|}{C}\text{-}OR}}} \quad \overset{dry\ HCl}{\longrightarrow} \quad \overset{H\text{-}OH}{\overset{O\text{-}R}{-\underset{|}{C}\text{-}OR}}$$

     3. Shortcut for determining acetal formed from one carbonyl and two alcohol units.

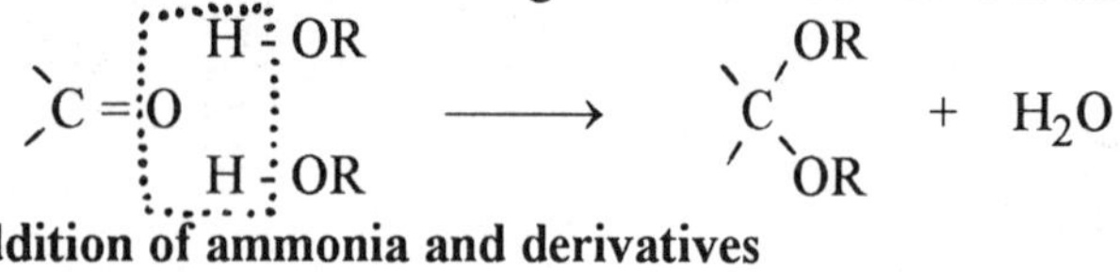

$$\overset{\diagdown}{\underset{\diagup}{C}}=O \quad \overset{H\vdots OR}{\underset{H\vdots OR}{}} \longrightarrow \quad \overset{\diagup OR}{\underset{\diagdown OR}{C}} \quad + \quad H_2O$$

   C. Addition of ammonia and derivatives

     1. Imine formation (accompanied by elimination of water)

$$\overset{O}{\underset{|}{\overset{||}{-C}}} \quad \overset{H}{\underset{H}{\overset{|}{N}\text{-}H}} \longrightarrow \quad [\,\overset{O\text{-}H}{-\underset{H}{\overset{|}{C}}\text{-}\underset{|}{N}\text{-}H\,] \longrightarrow \quad -C=N\text{-}H \quad + \quad H_2O$$

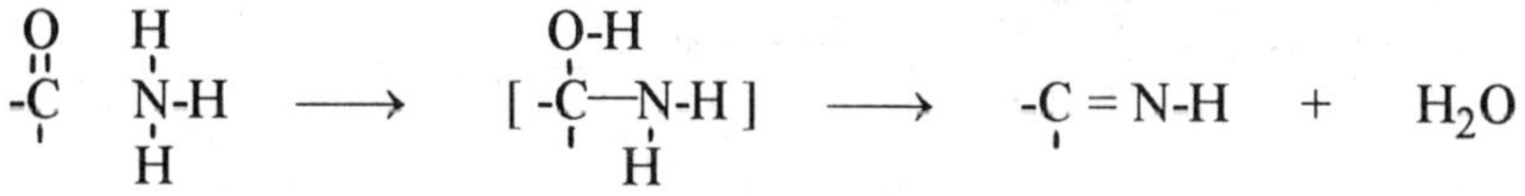

     2. Phenylhydrazone formation (accompanied by elimination of water)

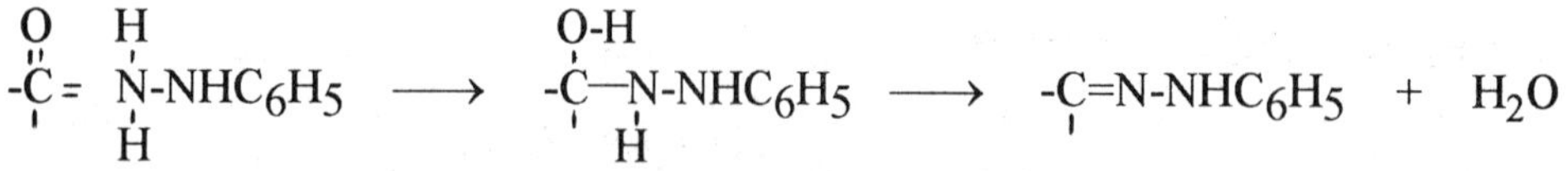

$$\overset{O}{\underset{|}{\overset{||}{-C}}}= \overset{H}{\underset{H}{\overset{|}{N}\text{-}NHC_6H_5}} \longrightarrow \overset{O\text{-}H}{-\underset{H}{\overset{|}{C}}\text{-}N\text{-}NHC_6H_5} \longrightarrow -\underset{|}{C}=N\text{-}NHC_6H_5 \quad + \quad H_2O$$

     3. Shortcut for determining product from ammonia or derivative

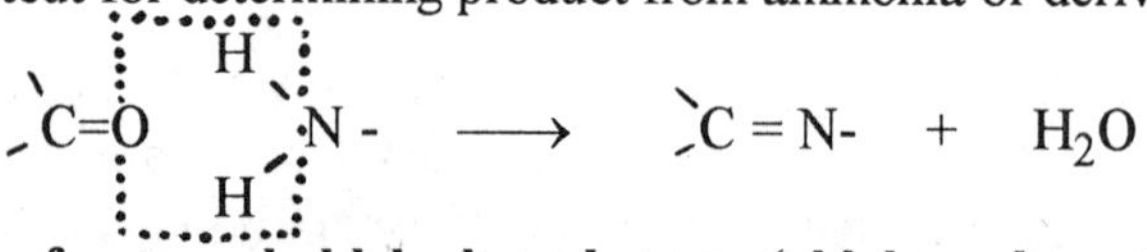

$$\overset{\diagdown}{\underset{\diagup}{C}}=O \quad \overset{H}{\underset{H}{N\text{-}}} \longrightarrow \quad \overset{\diagdown}{\underset{\diagup}{C}}=N\text{-} \quad + \quad H_2O$$

   D. Addition of a second aldehyde or ketone (aldol condensation)

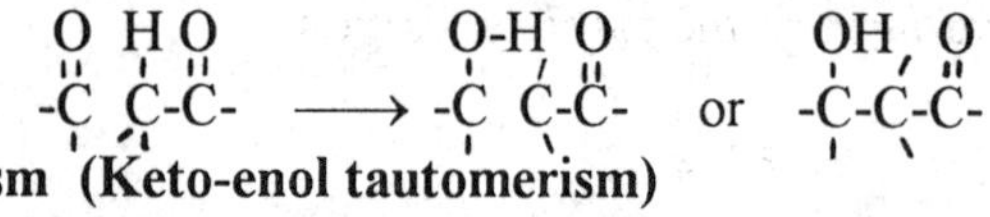

$$\overset{O}{\underset{|}{\overset{||}{-C}}}\ \overset{H}{\underset{|}{\overset{|}{C}}}\text{-}\overset{O}{\overset{||}{C}}\text{-} \longrightarrow -\underset{|}{\overset{O\text{-}H}{C}}\ \underset{|}{\overset{O}{\overset{||}{C}}}\text{-}C\text{-} \quad or \quad -\underset{}{\overset{OH}{C}}\text{-}C\text{-}\underset{}{\overset{O}{C}}\text{-}$$

III. Isomerism (Keto-enol tautomerism)

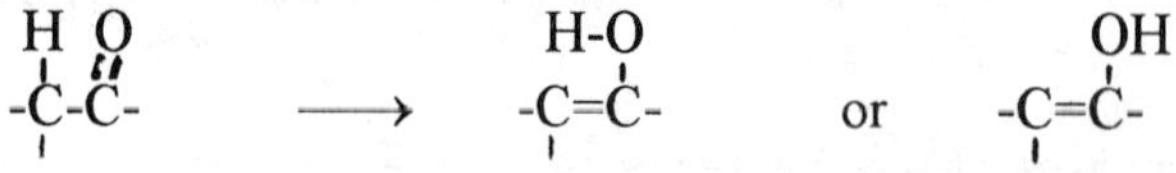

$$\overset{H}{\underset{|}{\overset{|}{C}}}\text{-}\overset{O}{\overset{||}{C}}\text{-} \longrightarrow -\underset{|}{C}=\underset{}{\overset{H\text{-}O}{C}}\text{-} \quad or \quad -C=\underset{|}{\overset{OH}{C}}\text{-}$$

Problems: Draw the products of the reactions shown below:

1. 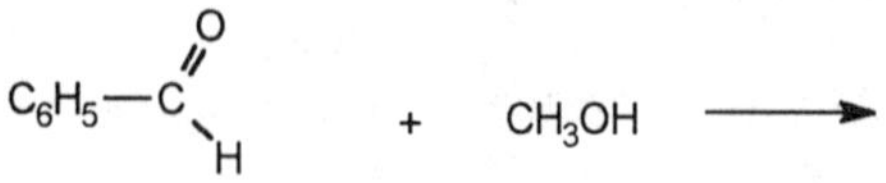
$$C_6H_5\text{---}\overset{O}{\overset{||}{C}}\diagdown_H \quad + \quad CH_3OH \longrightarrow$$

2. 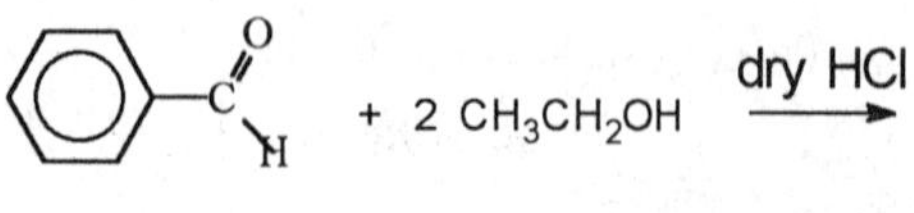
$$\bigcirc\!\!-\overset{O}{\overset{||}{C}}\diagdown_H \quad + \ 2\ CH_3CH_2OH \quad \overset{dry\ HCl}{\longrightarrow}$$

3.

   + 2 CH$_3$OH $\xrightarrow{\text{dry HCl}}$

4.

   $\longrightarrow$ a hemiacetal

5.

   $\xrightarrow{\text{K}_2\text{Cr}_2\text{O}_7 ,\ \text{H}^+}$

6.

   $\xrightarrow{\text{K}_2\text{Cr}_2\text{O}_7 ,\ \text{H}^+}$

7.

   + NH$_3$ $\longrightarrow$

8.

   + H$_2$N—NH— $\longrightarrow$

9.

2   $\longrightarrow$ aldol condensation

SELF TEST

1. Which structural feature is possessed by aldehydes but not ketones?
   a. an alpha hydrogen   b. a hydrogen on the carbonyl carbon
   c. a hydroxyl group on the carbonyl carbon
2. A group which both aldehydes and ketones have in common is:
   a. -COOH   b. -C=O   c. -C=O   d. -OH   e. -O-
                        |
                        H
3. The name of the functional group of aldehydes and ketones is:
          a. carbonyl group   b. carboxyl group   c. double bond   d. hydroxyl group
4. The precipitate that is produced in a positive Benedict's test is :
          a. Ag   b. AgCl   c. Cu   d. Cu$_2$O   e. CuO
5. The compound CH$_3$COCH$_3$ is:
          a. methyl alcohol   b. formic acid   c. formaldehyde   d. acetone   e. methanone
6. Benzaldehyde is:
          a. CH$_3$CH$_2$CH$_2$CH=O   b.   c.   d.

7. The name of $CH_3CH_2C\text{-}CH_3$ is:
  O

    a. methyl propyl ketone   b. 2-pentanone   c. 3-butanone   d. 2-butanone

8. $CH_3\text{-}C\text{-}CH_3$ is <u>not</u>:
  O

    a. acetone   b. dimethyl aldehyde   c. dimethyl ketone   d. propanone

9. The compound 3-chlorobutanal is also properly called:

    a. 3-chlorobutanol   b. 3-chlorobutyraldehyde   c. α-chlorobutanal

    d. α-chlorobutyraldehyde   e. β-chlorobutyraldehyde

10. An aqueous solution of formaldehyde is called:

    a. aldol   b. acetone   c. formalin   d. formic acid   e. methanal

11. In general, aldehydes and ketones exhibit lower water-solubility than:

    a. alcohols   b. alkenes   c. ethers

12. Which compound has the <u>lowest</u> boiling point?

    a. CH_3CH_2OH b. $CH_3CH{=}O$ c. $CH_3\text{-}O\text{-}CH_3$

13. Tollens' reagent will oxidize a(n):

    a. aldehyde   b. alcohol   c. ketone   d. carboxylic acid

14. When an aldehyde is oxidized, the product is a(n):

    a. alcohol   b. ketone   c. carboxylic acid   d. aldehyde

15. Which structure would give a positive Tollens' test?

    a. $CH_3CH{=}O$ b.   c.   d. CH_3COOH

16. An aldehyde can be distinguished from a ketone by means of:

    a. the Tollens' test

    b. reaction with phenylhydrazine

    c. Both contain carbonyl groups and cannot be distinguished by the above tests.

17. A ketone can be distinguished from an alcohol by means of:

    a. the Tollens' test

    b. reaction with phenylhydrazine

    c. Both contain oxygen and cannot be distinguished by the above tests.

18. Ketones are prepared by the oxidation of:

    a. primary alcohols   b. secondary alcohols   c. tertiary alcohol

    d. carboxylic acids   e. Ketones can not be prepared by oxidation reactions.

19. Which reaction does not involve addition to the aldehyde carbonyl oxygen?

    a. hydrate formation   b. hemiacetal formation   c. imine formation   d. oxidation

20. Both tautomerism and the aldol condensation depend on the relative acidity of the:

    a. hydrogen alpha to the carbonyl group   b. hydrogen on the carbonyl carbon atom

    c. carbon of the carbonyl group   d. oxygen of the carbonyl group

21. In general, which is the most stable type of compound?

    a. hydrate   b. hemiacetal   c. acetal

22. Which organic compound would be isolated from the reaction:

    a. CH_3CH_2COOH b. $CH_3\overset{COOH}{\underset{|}{CH}}CH_3$ c. $CH_3\overset{O}{\overset{||}{C}}CH_3$ d. $CH_3\overset{O}{\overset{||}{C}}COOH$.

23. What must be added to acetaldehyde to form $CH_3\text{-}\overset{\overset{\displaystyle H}{|}}{\underset{\underset{\displaystyle OCH_3}{|}}{C}}\text{-OH}$?

    a. CH_3CH_2OH b. $CH_3\text{-}\overset{\overset{\displaystyle O}{\|}}{C}\text{-H}$ c. CH_3OH d. $CH_2\text{=}O$

24. Which compound represents the tautomer of $CH_3\text{-}\overset{\overset{\displaystyle O}{\|}}{C}\text{-}CH_3$?

    a. $CH_3CH_2\overset{\overset{\displaystyle O}{\|}}{C}\text{-H}$ b. $CH_3CH\text{=}\overset{\overset{\displaystyle OH}{|}}{C}H$ c. $CH_3\overset{\overset{\displaystyle OH}{|}}{C}HCH_3$ d. $CH_2\text{=}\overset{\overset{\displaystyle OH}{|}}{C}\text{-}CH_3$

25. Which of the following reagents is required to accomplish each of the transformations shown below:

    a. H^+, H_2O b. dry HCl   c. NaOH   d. $K_2Cr_2O_7$, H^+ e. no additional reagent required

A. $CH_3\text{-}\overset{\overset{\displaystyle O}{\|}}{C}\text{-H}$ $\longrightarrow$ $CH_3\text{-}\overset{\overset{\displaystyle O}{\|}}{C}\text{-OH}$

B. $CH_3\text{-}\overset{\overset{\displaystyle O}{\|}}{C}\text{-H}$ $+$ $2\ CH_3OH$ $\longrightarrow$ $CH_3\text{-}\overset{\overset{\displaystyle O\text{-}CH_3}{|}}{\underset{\underset{\displaystyle H}{|}}{C}}\text{-O-}CH_3$

C. $CH_3\text{-}\overset{\overset{\displaystyle O}{\|}}{C}\text{-H}$ $+$ H_2O $\longrightarrow$ $CH_3\text{-}\overset{\overset{\displaystyle OH}{|}}{\underset{\underset{\displaystyle H}{|}}{C}}\text{-OH}$

D. $2\ CH_3\text{-}\overset{\overset{\displaystyle O}{\|}}{C}\text{-H}$ $\longrightarrow$ $CH_3\text{-}\overset{\overset{\displaystyle OH}{|}}{C}\text{-}CH_2\text{-}\overset{\overset{\displaystyle O}{\|}}{C}\text{-H}$

26. Oxidation of wood alcohol by liver enzymes produces the toxic substance:

    a. ethanol   b. formaldehyde   c. methanol   d. nicotine

27. Addition of ammonia to an aldehyde produces a(n) _____ and water.

    a. alcohol   b. ketal   c. hydrate   d. N-acetal   e. imine

28. Isopropanol could be made from the reduction of which compound?

    a. propionic acid   b. ethyl methyl ketone   c. acetone   d. acetaldehyde

29. A β-hydroxy product is formed when an aldehyde reacts with a(n) _____.

    a. alcohol   b. aldehyde   c. ketone   d. ammonia

30. Which of these compounds would be most soluble in water?

    a. $CH_3CH_2CH_2CH_2CH_3$ b. $CH_3CH_2CH_2\text{-O-}CH_3$

    c. $CH_3CH_2CH_2CH_2OH$ d. $CH_3CH_2CH_2\text{-}\overset{\underset{\underset{\displaystyle H}{|}}{}}{C}\text{=}O$

ANSWERS

Problems

1.

2.

3.

4.

5.

No reaction

6.

7.

8.

9.

Self-Test

1. b	6. d	11. a	16. a	21. c	26. b
2. c	7. d	12. c	17. b	22. c	27. e
3. a	8. b	13. a	18. b	23. c	28. c
4. d	9. e	14. c	19. d	24. d	29. b, c
5. d	10. c	15. a	20. a	25. A. d, B. b, C. e, D. c	30. c

CHAPTER 16: CARBOXYLIC ACIDS AND DERIVATIVES

KEY WORDS

carboxylic acid	*acetic acid*	*anhydrides*	*amides*	*carboxyl*
acetate	*esterification*	*anilides*	*hydrolysis*	*esters*
saponification	*carbonyl*	*hydroxyl*	*polyester*	*polyamides*

SUMMARY

16.1 Carboxylic Acids and Their Derivatives: The Functional Groups

    A. The *carbonyl* group is also found in carboxylic acids and their derivatives, but comprises only a part of the functional groups of these families. The *carboxyl* group is a combination of the *carbonyl* + *hydroxyl* groups. This new combination now has acidic properties.

    B. *Amides* and *esters* are derived from carboxylic acids by replacing the -OH group with either an amine (amide) or an alcohol (ester) and named accordingly.

$$\underset{carboxyl}{\overset{\overset{\textstyle O}{\|}}{-C}-OH \;(-COOH)} \qquad \underset{amide}{\overset{\overset{\textstyle O}{\|}}{-C}-NH-} \qquad \underset{ester}{\overset{\overset{\textstyle O}{\|}}{-C}-O-C-}$$

$$\underset{\text{acetic acid}}{CH_3-\overset{\overset{\textstyle O}{\|}}{C}-OH} \qquad \underset{\text{acetamide}}{CH_3-\overset{\overset{\textstyle O}{\|}}{C}-NH_2} \qquad \underset{\text{methyl acetate}}{CH_3-\overset{\overset{\textstyle O}{\|}}{C}-OCH_3}$$

16.2 Some Common Carboxylic Acids: Structures and Names

    A. Organic or *carboxylic acids* are weak acids, often having pungent odors. Many have very old histories and go by their common names, using Greek letters to indicate the positions of substituents.

$$-\underset{\gamma}{C}-\underset{\beta}{C}-\underset{\alpha}{C}-COOH$$

    B. The IUPAC rules for naming carboxylic acids use the name of the corresponding alkane, but drop the "-e" ending and add "-oic acid." Substitutents are numbered using the carboxyl carbon as carbon "1."

$$-\underset{4}{C}-\underset{3}{C}-\underset{2}{C}-\underset{1}{COOH}$$

    C. Common carboxylic acids, R-COOH:

HCOOH	formic acid (methanoic)	ant bites
CH$_3$COOH	*acetic acid* (ethanoic)	vinegar
CH$_3$-(CH$_2$)$_{14}$-COOH	palmitic acid	animal fat
CH$_3$-(CH$_2$)$_{16}$-COOH	stearic acid	animal fat

benzoic acid

16.3 Preparation of Carboxylic Acids

    A. Oxidation of primary alcohols: ethanol $—[O]→$ acetaldehyde $—[O]→$ acetic acid

    B. *Hydrolysis* of fats: triglycerides $—[H_2O, H^+]→$ glycerol + fatty acids

16.4. Physical Properties of Carboxylic Acids
  A. The carboxyl group is very polar and capable of acting as both a hydrogen bond donor and acceptor. This gives rise to strong intermolecular forces, and high boiling points. Methanoic (C1) through nonanoic (C9) are colorless liquids with foul odors.
  B. Hydrogen bonded dimers of carboxylic acids are found even in the vapor phase. Those carboxylic acids containing 4 Cs or less are completely miscible with water.

$$CH_3-C \overset{\displaystyle O \; ----- \; HO}{\underset{\displaystyle OH \; ----- \; O}{}} C-CH_3$$

   Acetic acid dimer

  C. Pure *acetic acid* freezes at 16.6 °C, just below room temperature, and frequently used to be observed to freeze on the laboratory shelf. The common name for pure acetic acid is "glacial acetic acid."

16.5 Chemical Properties of Carboxylic Acids: Neutralization
   $RCOOH + NaOH \longrightarrow RCOO^-Na^+ + H_2O$
  A. Carboxylic acids are weak acids that ionize slightly; (pK_a 3~5).
    $HCl, H_2SO_4, HNO_3 > H_3PO_4 > RCOOH > H_2CO_3 > ArOH > H_2O > ROH > RH$
    (strongest) ←←←←←←←←←←←←←←←←←←←←←←←←←← (weakest)
  B. Carboxylic acids turn blue litmus red and react with bases to form salts and water. The salts are named by naming the cation first, then naming the anion by changing the "-ic" ending to "-ate."
    CH_3COOH acetic acid
    $CH_3COO^-Na^+$ sodium *acetate*
  C. Propionate, benzoate and sorbate salts are frequently used as food preservatives.

16.6 An Ester by Any Other Name
  A. *Esters* are produced when a carboxylic acid reacts with an alcohol with loss of water. Many esters have very pleasant odors. *Polyesters* are important in biology and textiles.
  B. Esters are named much the same way that carboxylate salts are named except that the alkyl (or aryl) group from the alcohol is named first in place of the cation.

$$CH_3\overset{O}{\overset{\|}{C}}\underset{OH}{} + HOCH_3 \longrightarrow CH_3\overset{O}{\overset{\|}{C}}-O-CH_3 + H_2O$$

   acetic acid + methanol   methyl acetate

16.7 Physical Properties of Esters
  A. Many fragrances of fruits and flowers are esters.
  B. Esters are polar but pure esters are <u>not</u> capable of intramolecular hydrogen bonding because they are not hydrogen donors.
  C. Esters have lower boiling points and somewhat reduced solubility in water than the isomeric carboxylic acids. Ethyl acetate is a common organic solvent.

16.8 Preparation of Esters: *Esterification*
  A. Esters are prepared by heating the corresponding acid and alcohol in the presence of a mineral acid catalyst. To obtain high yields of the ester, it is usually necessary to supply one of the reactants in excess or remove one of the products as it forms.

$$R-COOH + HO-R' \longrightarrow R-\overset{O}{\overset{\|}{C}}-O-R' + H_2O$$

B. Esters are more commonly prepared in the laboratory by the reaction of acyl chlorides and alcohols.

$$R\text{-}\overset{\overset{\displaystyle O}{\|}}{C}\text{-Cl} + \text{HO-R'} \longrightarrow R\text{-}\overset{\overset{\displaystyle O}{\|}}{C}\text{-O-R'} + \text{HCl}$$

C. Acetate esters are usually prepared from acetic anhydride. (*Anhydrides* are prepared by removal of water from two acid molecules.)

$$CH_3\text{-}\overset{\overset{\displaystyle O}{\|}}{C}\text{-O-}\overset{\overset{\displaystyle O}{\|}}{C}\text{-}CH_3 + \text{HO-}CH_3 \longrightarrow CH_3\text{-}\overset{\overset{\displaystyle O}{\|}}{C}\text{-}OCH_3 + CH_3\text{-COOH}$$

D. *Polyesters* (Dacron) are polymers made from the condensation of diols with dicarboxylic acids.

HO—$CH_2CH_2CH_2CH_2CH_2CH_2$—OH + [structure] $\longrightarrow$

16.9 Chemical Properties of Esters: *Hydrolysis*

A. Esters are neutral compounds, neither acidic or basic.

B. Hydrolysis (splitting with water)

1. Acid hydrolysis is the reverse of esterification.

$$\text{ester} \xrightarrow{\ \ H^+\ \ } \text{carboxylic acid} + \text{alcohol}$$

2. Basic hydrolysis produces the salt of the acid and the corresponding alcohol. Alkaline hydrolysis of fats and oils is called *saponification* (to make soap).

$$R\text{-}\overset{\overset{\displaystyle O}{\|}}{C}\text{-O-R'} + \text{NaOH} \longrightarrow R\text{-}\overset{\overset{\displaystyle O}{\|}}{C}\text{-O}^-\text{Na}^+ + \text{HO-R'}$$

16.10 Esters of Phosphoric Acid

A. Esters can also be made from the reaction of inorganic acids and alcohols. Nitroglycerin is a powerful explosive (dynamite), but is also used to relieve chest pains by relaxing smooth heart muscles. Alfred Nobel (Nobel prizes) discovered dynamite in 1866.

B. Important esters of inorganic acids include the diphosphate, also called pyrophosphoric acid, which is found in adenosine diphosphate (ADP) and the triphosphate found in adenosine triphosphate (ATP). Phosphate esters of sugars such as glucose-6-phosphate are important in carbohydrate metabolism.

ATP

Glucose-6-phosphate

16.11 Amides: Structures and Names

A. *Amides* are prepared when a carboxylic acid reacts with ammonia or its derivatives (amines) with the loss of water.

B. Simple amides are named by dropping the "-ic" suffix and adding "- amide." Substituted amides are named by using an "N" to indicate that the substituent is on the nitrogen. Phenyl substituents are referred to as *anilides*.

Benzamide   Acetamide   N-methyl acetamide   Acetanilide

16.12 Physical Properties of Amides

   A. Most amides are solids at room temperature indicating the presence of strong intermolecular forces.

   B. The hydrogen bonds in polyamides are very important in determining the three dimensional structure of proteins.

16.13 Synthesis of Amides

   A. First step: Preparation of acyl chloride

$$R-\overset{\overset{\displaystyle O}{\|}}{C}-OH \; + \; SOCl_2 \; \longrightarrow \; R-\overset{\overset{\displaystyle O}{\|}}{C}-Cl \; + \; SO_2 \; + \; HCl$$

   B. Second step: Treatment of acyl chloride with ammonia (or amine)

$$R-\overset{\overset{\displaystyle O}{\|}}{C}-Cl + 2\,NH_3 \; \longrightarrow \; R-\overset{\overset{\displaystyle O}{\|}}{C}-NH_2 + NH_4Cl$$

   C. Nylon and proteins are examples of *polyamides*.

16.14 Chemical Properties of Amides: *Hydrolysis*

   A. Amides are neutral compounds. The lone pair of electrons of the basic ammonia have been delocalized in forming a partial double bond with the carbonyl C.

Planar amide gro

   B. Amides are fairly stable in water but hydrolyze in acidic and basic solutions. Hydrolysis of amides bonds occurs during the digestion of proteins.

DISCUSSION

     We have included here a summary of all the nomenclature rules and the chemical properties of carboxylic acids and their derivatives presented in Chapter 16.

Nomenclature of Carboxylic Acids and Derivatives			
Type of compound	Common	IUPAC	Structure
carboxylic acids	valeric acid	pentanoic acid	$CH_3CH_2CH_2CH_2\overset{\overset{\displaystyle O}{\|}}{C}OH$
salts of acids	sodium valerate	sodium pentanoate	$CH_3CH_2CH_2CH_2\overset{\overset{\displaystyle O}{\|}}{C}O^-Na^+$
esters	ethyl valerate	ethyl pentanoate	$CH_3CH_2CH_2CH_2\overset{\overset{\displaystyle O}{\|}}{C}OCH_2CH_3$
simple amide	valeramide	pentanamide	$CH_3CH_2CH_2CH_2\overset{\overset{\displaystyle O}{\|}}{C}NH_2$
substituted amide	N,N-dimethylvaleramide	N,N-dimethylpentanamide	$CH_3CH_2CH_2CH_2\overset{\overset{\displaystyle O}{\|}}{C}-N-CH_3$ with CH_3
anilides	valeranilide	pentananilide or N-phenylpentanamide	$CH_3CH_2CH_2CH_2\overset{\overset{\displaystyle O}{\|}}{C}-N-Ar$ with H

Reactions of Carboxylic Acids and Derivatives

Preparation of Acids (oxidation of primary alcohols or aldehydes)

$$RCH_2OH \xrightarrow{\quad K_2Cr_2O_7,\ H^+ \quad} RCH=O \longrightarrow RCHOOH$$

Salt formation

$$RCOOH + NaOH \longrightarrow RCOO^-Na^+ + H_2O$$

$$RCOOH + NaHCO_3 \longrightarrow RCOO^-Na^+ + H_2O + CO_2$$

$$2\ RCOOH + Na_2CO_3 \longrightarrow 2\ RCOO^-Na^+ + H_2O + CO_2$$

Ester formation

$$\overset{O}{\underset{\|}{RC}}\text{-OH} + HO \xrightarrow{\quad H^+ \quad} \overset{O}{\underset{\|}{R\text{-}C}}\text{-O-R'} + H_2O$$

$$\overset{O}{\underset{\|}{CH_3C}}\text{-O-}\overset{O}{\underset{\|}{CCH_3}} + HOR \longrightarrow \overset{O}{\underset{\|}{CH_3C}}\text{-O-R} + \overset{O}{\underset{\|}{CH_3C}}\text{-OH}$$
$$\qquad\qquad\qquad\qquad\qquad\qquad\qquad \text{ester} \qquad \text{acid byproduct}$$

Ester hydrolysis

Acid-catalyzed: $\quad \overset{O}{\underset{\|}{R\text{-}C}}\text{-O-R'} + H_2O \xrightarrow{\quad H^+ \quad} \overset{O}{\underset{\|}{R\text{-}C}}\text{-OH} + HOR'$

Base-catalyzed: $\quad \overset{O}{\underset{\|}{R\text{-}C}}\text{-O-R'} + H_2O \xrightarrow{\quad OH^- \quad} \overset{O}{\underset{\|}{R\text{-}C}}\text{-O}^- + HOR'$

Amide formation

Simple amide: $\quad \overset{O}{\underset{\|}{R\text{-}C}}\text{-OH} \xrightarrow{\quad SOCl_2 \quad} \overset{O}{\underset{\|}{R\text{-}C}}\text{-Cl} \xrightarrow{\quad NH_3 \quad} \overset{O}{\underset{\|}{R\text{-}C}}\text{-NH}_2$

Substituted amide: $\quad \overset{O}{\underset{\|}{R\text{-}C}}\text{-OH} \xrightarrow{\quad SOCl_2 \quad} \overset{O}{\underset{\|}{R\text{-}C}}\text{-Cl} \xrightarrow{\quad H_2N\text{-}R' \quad} \overset{O}{\underset{\|}{R\text{-}C}}\text{-}\underset{\overset{|}{H}}{N}\text{-R'}$

$$\overset{O}{\underset{\|}{R\text{-}C}}\text{-OH} \xrightarrow{\quad SOCl_2 \quad} \overset{O}{\underset{\|}{R\text{-}C}}\text{-Cl} \xrightarrow{\quad HNR'_2 \quad} \overset{O}{\underset{\|}{R\text{-}C}}\text{-}\underset{\overset{|}{R'}}{N}\text{-R'}$$

Amide hydrolysis

Acid-catalyzed: $\quad \overset{O}{\underset{\|}{R\text{-}C}}\text{-NH}_2 \xrightarrow{\quad H^+,\ H_2O \quad} \overset{O}{\underset{\|}{R\text{-}C}}\text{-OH} + NH_4^+$

Base-catalyzed: $\quad \overset{O}{\underset{\|}{R\text{-}C}}\text{-NH}_2 \xrightarrow{\quad OH^-,\ H_2O \quad} \overset{O}{\underset{\|}{R\text{-}C}}\text{-O}^- + NH_3$

(substituted amides give the corresponding substituted ammonia derivatives, e.g., RNH_2 or RNH_3^+)

Problems: The following problems will test your understanding of the chemistry of acids and acid derivatives. Remember -- no matter how complicated individual structures may appear, the chemistry is determined by the functional group and follows the patterns summarized previously. Identify the functional groups in each of the following compounds. There may be more than one functional group in a single compound. Also, the same functional group may appear in more than one compound.

Functional Groups	Compound	Functional Groups Present

Functional Groups

a. alcohol
b. aldehyde
c. amide
d. carboxylic acid
e. ester
f. ether
g. ketone
h. phenol

Compound

1.
$$OH \quad O$$
$$CH_3\text{-}CH\text{-}C\text{-}O\text{-}CH_3$$

2. $CH_3CH_2\text{-}O\text{-}CH_2CH_2OH$

3. $CH_3\text{-}O\text{-}CH_2C\text{-}OH$
   $$O$$

4. $CH_3\text{-}C\text{-}O\text{-}CH_2CH_2\text{-}OH$
   $$O$$

5. $CH_3\text{-}C\text{-}O\text{-}CH_2C\text{-}H$
   $$O \qquad O$$

6. $CH_3\text{-}O\text{-}C\text{-}CH_2\text{-}C\text{-}NH_2$
   $$O \qquad O$$

7. $HO\text{-}CH_2CH_2\text{-}C\text{-}OH$
   $$O$$

8.

9.

10.

Functional Groups Present

1. a b c d e f g h
2. a b c d e f g h
3. a b c d e f g h
4. a b c d e f g h
5. a b c d e f g h
6. a b c d e f g h
7. a b c d e f g h
8. a b c d e f g h
9. a b c d e f g h
10. a b c d e f g h

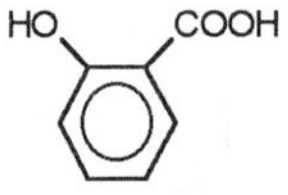

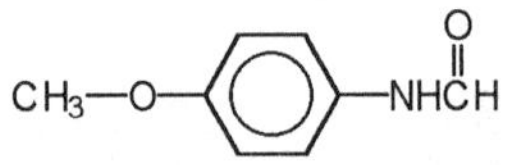

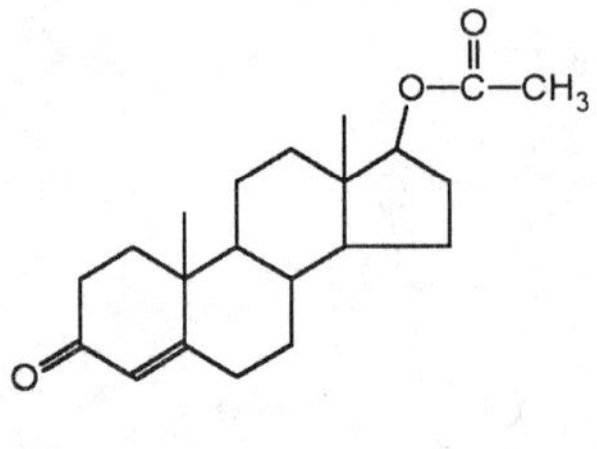

Reactions - Draw the principal organic products of the reactions.

1. [benzoic acid structure: C6H5-C(=O)-OH] + CH3—CH(OH)—CH3 $\xrightarrow{H^+}$

2. [acetic anhydride: H3C-C(=O)-O-C(=O)-CH3] + [phenol: C6H5-OH] $\longrightarrow$

3. [HO-C(=O)-CH2CH2-C(=O)-OH] + 2 CH3OH $\xrightarrow{H^+}$

4. CH3—C(=O)—Cl + [aniline: C6H5-NH2] $\longrightarrow$

5. [benzoyl chloride: C6H5-C(=O)-Cl] + NH3 $\longrightarrow$

6. CH3—CH(CH3)—C(=O)—Cl + CH3—NH—CH3 $\longrightarrow$

7. CH3CH2—C(=O)—OH + KOH $\longrightarrow$

8. [benzene with two COOH groups (ortho)] + Na2CO3 $\longrightarrow$

9. CH3CH2—C(=O)—OCH2CH3 + H2O $\xrightarrow{OH^-}$

10. CH3CH2—C(=O)—OCH2CH3 + H2O $\xrightarrow{H^+}$

11. HO—[benzene ring]—NH—C(=O)—CH3 + H2O $\xrightarrow{H^+}$

12. [pyridine ring with C(=O)—NH2] + H2O $\xrightarrow{OH^-}$

SELF-TEST

1. Which group bestows functional group properties of an amide?
    a. -CH=O   b. -NH$_2$ c. C$_6$H$_5$$^-$ d. -CH$_2$OH   e. -$\overset{\text{O}}{\underset{}{\text{C}}}$-NH$_2$ f. -$\overset{\text{O}}{\underset{}{\text{C}}}$-OH

2. The -COOH group is called a(n):
    a. carboxyl group   b. carbonyl group   c. aldehyde group   d. hydroxyl group

3. Which is not a mineral acid?
    a. HNO$_3$ b. HCl   c. HCOOH   d. H$_2$SO$_4$

4. Which is the acid found in vinegar?
    a. nitric acid   b. acetic acid   c. valeric acid   d. formic acid

5. The product of the reaction between an amine and an acid is known as a(n):
    a. acid anhydride   b. amide   c. ester   d. ether   e. salt

6. The correct name of the compound CH$_3$CH$_2$CH$_2$CH$_2$$\overset{\text{O}}{\underset{}{\text{C}}}$-OH is:

    a. pentanoic acid   b. caproic acid   c. succinic acid   d. butanonic acid

7.   CH$_3$ O
    CH$_3$CHCH$_2$-C-OH is:
    a. α-methylbutyric acid   b. β-methylbutyric acid
    c. 2-pentanoic acid   d. 1-methylbutanoic acid

8. Ammonium acetate is:
    a. CH$_3$$\overset{}{\underset{\text{O}}{\text{C}}}$-O- NH$_4$$^+$ b. CH$_3$$\overset{}{\underset{\text{O}}{\text{C}}}$-NH$_2$ c. CH$_3$$\overset{}{\underset{\text{O}}{\text{C}}}$-O$^-Na^+$ d. NH$_4$$^+Cl^-$

9. The name of H-$\overset{\text{O}}{\underset{}{\text{C}}}$-O$^-$ Na$^+$ is not:
    a. sodium carbonate   b. sodium formate   c. sodium methanoate

10. The correct name of CH$_3$CH$_2$O-$\overset{}{\underset{\text{O}}{\text{C}}}$-CH$_3$ is:

    a. ethyl acetate   b. ethyl formate   c. ethyl methyl ketone
    d. methyl acetate   e. ethyl methyl ester

11. Which acid is palmitic acid?
    a. CH$_3$(CH$_2$)$_{12}$COOH   b. CH$_3$(CH$_2$)$_{10}$COOH   c. CH$_3$(CH$_2$)$_{14}$COOH   d. CH$_3$(CH$_2$)$_{16}$COOH

12. Methyl acetate is:
    a. C$_2$H$_5$COOCH$_3$ b. CH$_3$COOC$_2$H$_5$ c. CH$_3$COOCH$_3$ d. C$_2$H$_5$COOC$_2$H$_5$

13. Butyramide is:
    a. CH$_3$CH$_2$CH$_2$$\overset{\text{O}}{\underset{}{\text{C}}}$-O-NH$_4$$^+$ b. $\overset{\text{NH}_2}{\underset{}{\text{CH}_2}}CH_2CH_2$$\overset{\text{O}}{\underset{}{\text{C}}}$-OH   c. CH$_3CH_2CH_2$$\overset{\text{O}}{\underset{}{\text{C}}}$-NH$_2$

14.   CH$_3$$\overset{}{\underset{\text{O}}{\text{C}}}$-NHCH$_3$ is:
    a. N-methylamide   b. methylformamide   c. N-methylethanamide   d. N-methylmethanamide

15. The compound is:

    a. methylbenzamide   b. N-methylethanamide   c. methananilide   d. acetanilide

16. Dacron is a synthetic fiber representative of which type of compound?
    a. amide   b. etherc. polyester   d. ester   e. polyamide

17. Proteins are representative of which type of compound?

      a. amide   b. ether   c. polyester   d. ester   e. polyamide

18. Glacial acetic acid is:
     a. a frozen solution of acetic acid
     b. a mixture of acetic acid and water
     c. pure acetic acid

19. Which compound is the weakest acid?
     a. CF_3COOH b.   c. $CH_3\overset{O}{\overset{\|}{C}}\text{-}OH$ d. H_2CO_3

                             ⬡—OH

20. Which compound is the strongest acid?
     a. CF_3COOH b.   c. $CH_3\overset{O}{\overset{\|}{C}}\text{-}OH$ d. H_2CO_3

                             ⬡—OH

21. Which compound is oxalic acid?
     a.   b. $HOOC\text{-}COOH$ c. $HOOC\text{-}CH_2COOH$ d.

22. For which pure compound is hydrogen bonding not possible?
     a. $CH_3\overset{O}{\overset{\|}{C}}\text{-}O\text{-}CH_3$ b. $CH_3\overset{O}{\overset{\|}{C}}\text{-}OH$ c. $CH_3\overset{O}{\overset{\|}{C}}\text{-}NHCH_3$ d. CH_3CH_2OH

23. Which compound(s) would produce a nearly neutral solution in water?
     a. amide   b. carboxylic acid   c. phenol   d. ester   e. amine

24. Which compound has the highest boiling point?

     a. $CH_3CH_2O\text{-}CH_2CH_3$ b. $CH_3\overset{O}{\overset{\|}{C}}\text{-}O\text{-}CH_3$ c. $CH_3\overset{O}{\overset{\|}{C}}CH_2CH_3$
     d. $CH_3CH_2CH_2CH_2OH$ e. $CH_3CH_2\underset{\underset{O}{\|}}{C}\text{-}OH$

25. Which compound has the lowest boiling point?

     a. $HO\text{-}CH_2CH_2CH_2OH$ b. $CH_3CH_2\overset{O}{\overset{\|}{C}}\text{-}OH$ c. $CH_3\overset{O}{\overset{\|}{C}}\text{-}O\text{-}CH_3$

26. The odors associated with the smaller members of this class of compounds are distinctly unpleasant.
     a. amides   b. alcohols   c. esters

27. The aromas associated with this class of compounds are regarded, in general, as pleasant.
     a. amides   b. carboxylic acids   c. esters

28. Alkaline hydrolysis of large, fatty esters is called _____.
     a. solvation   b. saponification   c. sublimation d. hydration

29. If $CH_3CH_2\underset{\underset{O}{\|}}{C}\text{-}O\text{-}CH_2CH_3$ is hydrolyzed in base, which set of products is formed?

     a. CH_3CH_2OH b. $CH_3CH_2O\text{-}Na^+$ c. CH_3CH_2OH d. $CH_3CH_2O^-Na^+$
        CH_3CH_2COOH CH_3CH_2COOH $CH_3CH_2COO^-Na^+$ $CH_3CH_2COO^-Na^+$

30. Esters can be synthesized from carboxylic acids and alcohols in the presence of mineral acids. Which alcohol is needed to synthesize this ester?
                       $CH_3CH_2CH_2CH_2O\text{-}\overset{O}{\overset{\|}{C}}CH_3$
     a. ethanol   b. propanol   c. methanol   d. pentanol   e. butanol

ANSWERS

Functional Groups

1. a,e	3. d,f	5. b,e	7. a,d	9. c,f
2. a,f	4. a,e	6. c,e	8. d,h	10. e,g

Reactions

1.

2.

3.

4.

5.

6.

7.

8.

9.

10.

11.

12.

Self-Test

1. e	7. b	13. c	19. b	25. c
2. a	8. a	14. c	20. a	26. a
3. c	9. a	15. d	21. b	27. c
4. b	10. a	16. c	22. a	28. b
5. b	11. c	17. e	23. a, d	29. c
6. a	12. c	18. c	24. e	30. e

Special Topic F: Drugs: Some Carboxylic Acids, Esters and Amides

KEY WORDS

analgesic	*agonists*	*opiates*	*hallucinogen*	*aspirin*
alkaloid	*antipyretic*	*antagonists*	*narcotic*	*salicylate*
lysergic acid	*THC*	*Ibuprofen*	*prostaglandins*	*endorphins*
enkephalins	*morphine*	*heroin*	*codeine*	*LSD*

SUMMARY

F.1 Aspirin and Other Salicylates

    A. "*Aspirin*" (acetylsalicylic acid) was introduced in 1899 as one of the first successful synthetic analgesics (pain relievers) and has become the largest selling drug in the world.

       1. Willow bark was a "home remedy" for reducing fever.

       2. Salicylic acid was isolated from willow bark in 1860. It was found to be a good *analgesic* (pain killer) and *antipyretic* (fever reducer) but is sour and irritating to take by mouth.

       3. Sodium *salicylate* (1875), phenyl salicylate (1866) and acetyl salicylate (1899) are chemical modifications of this natural drug introduced as having removed some of the undesirable effects of salicylic acid while retaining its desirable properties.

    B. *Aspirin* is synthesized in the laboratory by the treatment of salicylic acid with acetic anhydride to make the acetate ester. "Bufferin" is aspirin that contains antacids but it is not truly buffered. Ordinary aspirin contains ~325 mg/tablet while "extra strength" aspirin contains ~ 500 mg/tablet.

Salicylic acid   acetic anhydride   aspirin   acetic acid

    C. Aspirin relieves minor aches and suppresses inflammation. It is often used to treat arthritis. Aspirin acts by inhibiting the enzyme (Chapter 22) cyclomonooxygenase which is needed for the synthesis of *prostaglandins* which affect blood pressure and inflammation.

    D. Aspirin is also an anticoagulant. This property may help aspirin reduce the risk of a coronary heart attack or stroke. It can also cause bleeding in the stomach.

    E. Hazards: Some people are allergic to aspirin.

F.2 Aspirin Substitutes and Combination Pain Relievers

    A. Many aspirin substitutes include the amide **acetaminophen** (p-hydroxyacetanilide) or a combination of aspirin, acetaminophen, caffeine and buffers. (Excedrin = aspirin, acetaminophen, salicylamide, and caffeine.) Overuse of acetaminophen is linked to liver and kidney damage in those who drink a lot. Also, using aspirin to treat children with fevers has been associated with Reye's syndrome.

B. *Ibuprofen* is an anti-inflammatory drug in common use (Advil, Nuprin, Motrin).

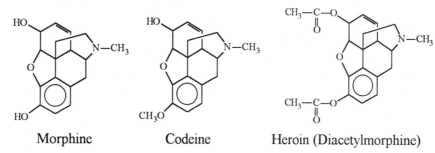

Acetaminophen   Ibuprofen   Caffeine

F.3 Opium Alkaloids

A. *Alkaloids* are physiologically active, N-containing compounds, such as nicotine and caffeine which are isolated from plants. *Opiates* are obtained from the "poppy" plant. *Morphine* is a narcotic producing sedation and analgesia, but is strongly addictive. It is a natural alkaloid from opium. Morphine was first isolated in 1805 and remains a standard for narcotic analgesics in medicine

B. *Codeine* is very similar to morphine, with -OCH_3 in place of the -OH group. It is less potent and less addictive than morphine.

C. *Heroin* is the common name of diacetylmorphine, introduced by Bayer Co. of Germany in 1874 as a synthetic analgesic and antidote for morphine addiction. Heroin produces a strong feeling of euphoria but is strongly addictive and illegal in the U.S.

Morphine   Codeine   Heroin (Diacetylmorphine)

F.4 Synthetic *Narcotics*: Analgesia and Addiction

A. Thousands of morphine analogs have been synthesized.
   1. Meperidine (Demerol)
   2. Methadone is also highly addictive but does not cause the sleepy stupor of heroin so that the addict can still hold a job and function to care for his or her self.

B. *Agonists* are molecules with drug-like action. *Antagonists* are drugs that block the action of other drugs.

F.5 A Natural High: The Brain's Own Opiates

A. The human brain receptors used by the opiates are designed for our bodies' natural pain killers, a family of peptides called *endorphins*. The two most characteristic of these compounds are pentapeptides called *enkephalins*: Leu-enkephalin (Tyr-Gly-Gly-Phe-Leu); Met-enkephalin (Tyr-Gly-Gly-Phe-Met).

B. Endorphins are released by extreme trauma, acupuncture, and strenuous physical activity (the "high" of the long distance runner).

F.6 LSD: A Hallucinogenic Drug

A. *LSD* (N,N-diethylamide of lysergic acid) was discovered by Hofmann in 1943. It is a *hallucinogenic* drug related to *lysergic acid* and other ergot alkaloids. As little as 10 μg of this powerful drug can bring on colorful hallucinations. It was the popular "acid" of the 1960's but its use has declined after reports that LSD damages chromosomes. It is an illegal drug in the U.S. and Great Britain.

B. Thalidomide was a popular tranquilizer in Germany during the 1950s and early 1960s. It was responsible for numerous birth defects and is now banned. It was never approved for use in the U.S.

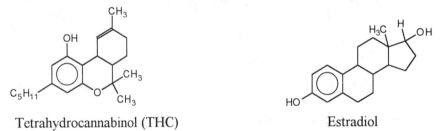

LSD   Thalidomide

F.7 Marijuana: Some Chemistry of *Cannabis*

A. The plant *Cannabis* has long been used to provide tough fibers for making rope and to supply drugs for ceremonies. Marijuana ("pot") refers to a preparation made by drying the leaves, flowers and seeds of *Cannabis*.

B. *THC* or tetrahydrocannabinol is the main active ingredient in marijuana and represents ~ 0.1 to 1% of the "pot." Hashish or hash can have a THC content of 5 to 12%.

C. Smoking "pot" impairs complex motor skills, distorts one's sense of time, may cause brain damage, and also is reported to have "feminizing" properties.

Tetrahydrocannabinol (THC)   Estradiol

DISCUSSION

In this unit we have introduced some compounds that look rather unusual or should we say "unnatural." That is because these compounds are drugs, compounds which are not normally found in the body. Note the unusual ring systems that are found in heroin and thalidomide. We will see in latter chapters on biochemistry that such compounds are not normal substrates for our bodies' metabolic machinery, thus such compounds can have unexpected and undesirable side effects.

Several derivatives of carboxylic acids have found use as drugs to relieve pain. Willow bark has been used as a "home remedy" for thousands of years. The following SELF-TEST will help you check your understanding of this material.

SELF-TEST

1. Aspirin is:
     a. diacetylmorphine   b. acetylsalicylic acid   c. acetaminophen
2. Which of the following are valid pharmacological classifications of aspirin?
     a. antipyretic   b. tranquilizer   c. analgesic   d. hallucinogen
3. Which compound is salicylic acid?
     a.   b.   c.   d.

4. Aspirin acts to inhibit the enzyme cyclomonooxygenase which is needed for the synthesis of _____.
     a. acetic anhydride   b. caffeine   c. prostaglandins   d. morphine
5. Molecules that mimic the action of a drug are called:
     a. agonists   b. opiates   c. caffeine   d. antagonists
6. Alkaloids are _____.
     a. Buffered aspirin products that dissolve with a bubbling action.
     b. N-containing drugs of all sorts.
     c. N-containing, physiologically active compounds obtained from plants.
     d. forms of THC (tetrahydrocannabinol)
7. Which of these compounds was introduced by Bayer Co. of Germany and was once thought to be an antidote for morphine addiction?
     a. acetominophen   b. salicylamide   c. heroin   d. thalidomide
8. Which of the following compounds has been used extensively as an aspirin substitute for those who are allergic to aspirin?
     a. acetominophen   b. LSD   c. thalidomide   d. morphine
9. Which of the following compounds was marketed as a safe tranquilizer but found to cause birth defects when taken by expectant mothers during the first trimester of pregnancy?
     a. acetominophen   b. LSD   c. thalidomide   d. morphine
10. Which compound is classified as an hallucinogen?
     a. acetominophen   b. N,N-diethyllysergamide   c. morphine   d. thalidomide
11. Which of the following common drugs is not an alkaloid?
     a. morphine   b. heroin   c. THC (pot)   d. LSD
12. Natural, small pentapeptides that mimic some of the actions of opiates are called _____.
     a. heroins   b. enkephalins c. endorphins   d. analgesics   e. thalidomides

ANSWERS:

1. b	4. c	7. c	10. b
2. a, c	5. a	8. a	11. c
3. b	6. c	9. c	12. b

CHAPTER 17: AMINES and DERIVATIVES

KEY WORDS

1⁰ amine	*2⁰ amine*	*3⁰ amine*	*quaternary*	*imidazole*
aniline	*ninhydrin*	*nitroso*	*amides*	*purine*
pyrimidine	*indole*	*pyridine*	*alkaloid*	*hetrocyclic*

SUMMARY

17.1 Structure and Classification of Amines

A. **Amines** are basic compounds ("the bases of life") related to ammonia where one or more hydrogens have been replaced by alkyl or aryl groups.

B. Amines are classified according to the number of C atoms directly bonded to the N atom.

1⁰ (primary)	*2⁰ (secondary)*	*3⁰ (tertiary)*	*Quaternary*
amine	*amine*	*amine*	*ammonium ion*

17.2 Naming Amines

A. Simple aliphatic amines are named by specifying the alkyl groups and adding the suffix "-amine."

B. The simplest aromatic amine is called **aniline**.

C. Substituted ammonium ions are named by regarding the alkyl groups as substituents on the parent species, the ammonium ion.

CH_3-NH_2 Cl—⟨ ⟩—NH_2 $(CH_3-)_4N^+$ ⟨ ⟩—$N\begin{smallmatrix}CH_3\\H\end{smallmatrix}$

methyl amine   p-chloroaniline   tetramethylammonium ion   N-methylaniline

D. Sometimes the amino group is named as a substituent. ($H_2N-CH_2-CH_2-OH$ = 2-aminoethanol)

17.3 Physical Properties of Amines

A. Amines are polar compounds. Pure 1⁰ and 2⁰ amines are capable of forming intermolecular hydrogen bonds. All three classes of amines can hydrogen bond to water and are soluble as long as the C/N ratio does not exceed 5:1.

B. Many amines smell, two diamines are particularly well known for this.

$$H_2N-CH_2-CH_2-CH_2-CH_2-NH_2 \qquad H_2N-CH_2-CH_2-CH_2-CH_2-CH_2-NH_2$$
putrescine   cadaverine

C. Many aromatic amines are toxic or are potential carcinogens.

17.4 Amines as Bases

A. Ammonia and amines both contain a nitrogen with an unshared pair of electrons that can accept a proton and thus both are weak bases.

$$CH_3\overset{..}{N}H_2 \; + \; H_2O \; \rightleftharpoons \; CH_3\overset{+}{N}H_3 \; + \; OH$$

Aromatic amines are much weaker bases than ammonia because of the electron withdrawing property of the aromatic ring.

B. An amine and its salt serve as a c.b.-c.a. pair and can be used as effective buffers. The pK_a for most substituted ammonium ions is in the range of 7 to 9 so these systems buffer in the alkaline pH range.

C. Most amines (even the very weak bases) can react with strong acids to form water soluble salts. These cations are named as substituted ammonium ions.

17.5 Other Chemical Properties of Amines

A. *Amide* formation: 1^0 or 2^0 amines react with acid chlorides or acid anhydrides to form substituted amides. Proteins are polyamides.

$$\underset{\underset{\text{R-C-Cl}}{}}{\overset{\overset{O}{\|}}{}} \quad + \quad \underset{\underset{H}{}}{\text{H-N-R'}} \quad \rightarrow \quad \underset{\underset{H}{}}{\overset{\overset{O}{\|}}{\text{R-C-N-R'}}} \quad + \quad H_2O$$

Amide formation is also important in the synthesis of plastics like *Nylon* (also proteins).

$$Cl-\overset{\overset{O}{\|}}{C}-CH_2-CH_2-CH_2-CH_2-\overset{\overset{O}{\|}}{C}-Cl \quad + \quad H-\overset{\overset{H}{|}}{N}-CH_2-CH_2-CH_2-CH_2-CH_2-CH_2-\overset{\overset{H}{|}}{N}-H$$

$$\longrightarrow \quad -\overset{\overset{O}{\|}}{C}-CH_2-CH_2-CH_2-CH_2-\overset{\overset{O}{\|}}{C}-\underset{\underset{H}{|}}{N}-CH_2-CH_2-CH_2-CH_2-CH_2-CH_2-\underset{\underset{H}{|}}{N}-$$

B. Nitrous acid reactions:

1. 1^0 amines react with nitrous acid to give a quantitative yield of nitrogen gas.

$$R-NH_2 \quad + \quad HNO_2 \quad \rightarrow \quad N_2(g) + \text{other products}$$

2. 2^0 amines react with nitrous acid to form oily, dangerous *N-nitroso* compounds.

$$\underset{\underset{R}{|}}{\text{R-N-H}} \quad + \quad HO-N=O \quad \rightarrow \quad \underset{\underset{R}{|}}{\text{R-N-N=O}} \quad + \quad H_2O$$

These compounds may be the cause of the high rates of stomach cancer associated with nitrites in food.

3. 3^0 amines react to form a salt.

C. *Ninhydrin* reaction: Many amines react with ninhydrin to form a purple product. Ninhydrin solution is commonly sprayed on paper chromatograms to identify the positions of the separated amino acids.

17.6 Heterocyclic Amines

A. Heterocyclic compounds are ring structures containing N, O, S or some other element in addition to carbon.

B. Several heterocyclic N-ring systems are important in biochemistry.

pyrrole   *imidazole*   *pyridine*   *pyrimidine*   *purine*   *indole*

C. *Alkaloids* are naturally occurring, N-containing, compounds with pharmacological activity. Many alkaloids are heterocyclic amines with striking physiological properties; morphine, LSD, etc.

DISCUSSION

Amines are organic nitrogen containing compounds related to ammonia. It is important to remember that amines are also weak bases, the "bases of life." The nomenclature rules for amines are few and are presented in Section 17.2. The chemistry of amines is summarized here for your convenience.

Summary: Chemistry of Amines

I. Synthesis of amines

    A. Chloride substitution: R-Cl   + NH_3 →   R-NH_2 +   HCl

    B. Reductive amination: R-$\overset{O}{\overset{||}{C}}$-R NH_3, H_2, Ni →   R-$\overset{NH_2}{\underset{|}{C}H}$-R

II. Reactions of amines

    A. Salt formation:

    All classes of amines (1°,2°, 3°) react with acids to produce salts.

     R-NH_2 $\xrightarrow{\;HCl\;}$ $RNH_3^+ Cl^-$

     R_2NH $\xrightarrow{\;HCl\;}$ $R_2NH_2^+ Cl^-$

     R_3N $\xrightarrow{\;HCl\;}$ $R_3NH^+ Cl$

    B. Amide formation: (1° and 2° amines only)

    1. From acid chlorides: RNH_2 + Cl-$\overset{O}{\overset{||}{C}}$-R' → R-NH-$\overset{O}{\overset{||}{C}}$-R'

       R_2NH + Cl-$\overset{O}{\overset{||}{C}}$-R' → R-$\underset{R}{N}$-$\overset{O}{\overset{||}{C}}$-R'

    2. From acid anhydrides: RNH_2 + $CH_3\overset{O}{\overset{||}{C}}$-O-$\overset{O}{\overset{||}{C}}CH_3$ → R-NH-$\overset{O}{\overset{||}{C}}$-$CH_3$

       R_2NH + $CH_3\overset{O}{\overset{||}{C}}$-O-$\overset{O}{\overset{||}{C}}CH_3$ → R-$\underset{R}{N}$-$\overset{O}{\overset{||}{C}}$-$CH_3$

    3. Unsubstituted amides are commercially prepared by heating the ammonium salts of carboxylic acids.

     R-$\overset{O}{\overset{||}{C}}$-OH + NH_3 → R-$\overset{O}{\overset{||}{C}}$-O-$NH_4^+$ $\xrightarrow{heat}$ R-$\overset{O}{\overset{||}{C}}$-$NH_2$

    C. Reaction with nitrous acid: Each class of amines reacts with nitrous acid in its own way.

    1. 1° amines yield nitrogen gas and a variety of organic products. It is the nitrogen gas which is measured in the Van Slyke method for the quantitative determination of primary amino groups.

    2. 2° amines produce N-nitroso compounds: HO-N=O R_2NH $\longrightarrow$ R_2N-N=O

    3. 3° amines may undergo a variety of reactions, but salt formation is most important.

The last section of the chapter presented heterocyclic amines. Included in this group are pyrrole, imidazole, indole, the purines and pyrimidines, and a heterogeneous class of naturally occurring plant heterocyclic amines called alkaloids. We will encounter the imidazole and indole ring systems again in our study of the amino acids histidine and tryptophan (Chapter 21); the purines and pyrimidines in our study of nucleic acids (Chapter 23); and we referred to the alkaloids with our study on drugs (Special Topic E).

The questions at the end of the chapter serve as a review for the chemistry and nomenclature of amines. The **SELF-TEST** will further check your understanding of this material.

SELF-TEST

1. Amines are compounds that would be classified as _____.
    a. neutral salts   b. weak acids   c. weak bases   d. strong bases   e. strong acids
2. The group that identifies a primary amine is represented by ____.
    a. R-NH-R   b. R=N-O   c. $R_4N^+Cl^-$ d. R-NH$_2$
3. Predict how many isomers are possible for amines with the molecular formula $C_4H_{11}N$.
    a. 5   b. 6   c. 7   d. 8   e. 9
4. An example of a secondary amine is:
    a. $C_2H_5NH_2$ b. $(C_2H_5)_2NH$ c. $(C_2H_5)_3N$ d. $(C_2H_5)_4N^+$
5. Which compound is aniline?
    a.   b.   c.   d.

6. Which compound contains a primary amine and a secondary alcohol group?

    a. $\overset{OH}{C}H_2\overset{NH_2}{C}H\text{-}CH_2CH_3$ b. $CH_2CH_2\overset{NHCH_3}{C}H\overset{OH}{C}H_3$ c. $CH_3\overset{OH}{C}H\text{-}\overset{NH_2}{C}H\text{-}CH_3$

7. $CH_3\text{-}\overset{NH_2}{C}H\text{-}\overset{}{C}\text{-}OH$ is a(n):
           $\underset{O}{\|}$

    a. amide   b. primary amine   c. secondary amine   d. tertiary amine

8. $CH_3\text{-}\overset{H}{N}\text{-}CH_2CH_3$ is:
    a. 2-aminopropane   b. ethylmethylamine
    c. isopropylamine   d. methyldimethylamine

9. The compound   is:

    a. pyrrole   b. imidazole   c. pyridine   d. pyrimidine   e. indole

10. The compound   is:

    a. pyrrole   b. imidazole   c. pyridine   d. pyrimidine   e. indole

11. The compound [structure] is:

    a. pyrrole   b. imidazole   c. pyridine   d. pyrimidine   e. indole

12. CH_3-$\overset{\overset{NH_2}{|}}{\underset{\underset{CH_3}{|}}{C}}$-$CH_2CH_3$ is:

    a. isopentylamine   b. ethyldimethylamine

    c. 2-aminoisopentane   d. 2-amino-2-methylbutane

13. [structure] is:

    a. o-chloroaniline   b. aniline hydrochloride   c. anilinium chloride

14. Aniline hydrobromide is:

    a.   b.   c.   d.

15. Which is a quaternary ammonium ion?

    a. $[CH_3\text{-}\overset{\overset{H}{|}}{\underset{\underset{H}{|}}{N}}\text{-}H]^+$ b. $[CH_3\text{-}\overset{\overset{H}{|}}{\underset{\underset{CH_3}{|}}{N}}\text{-}H]^+$ c. $[CH_3\text{-}\overset{\overset{H}{|}}{\underset{\underset{CH_3}{|}}{N}}\text{-}CH_3]^+$ d. $[CH_3\text{-}\overset{\overset{CH_3}{|}}{\underset{\underset{CH_3}{|}}{N}}\text{-}CH_3]^+$

16. [structure] N—CH₃ is a(n):

    a. aniline   b. primary amine   c. secondary amine   d. tertiary amine

17. [structure] is:

    a. benzene   b. purine   c. pyridine   d. pyrimidine

18. Alkaloids can best be generally classified with the:

    a. alcohols   b. acids   c. amines   c. amides   e. esters

19. Which of the following compounds when pure is <u>not</u> associated through hydrogen bonding?

    a. $CH_3CH_2\text{-}OH$ b. $CH_3\text{-}\underset{\underset{O}{||}}{C}\text{-}OH$ c. $CH_3\text{-}\underset{\underset{O}{||}}{C}\text{-}NH_2$ d. $CH_3\text{-}NH\text{-}CH_3$ e. $CH_3\text{-}\underset{\underset{CH_3}{|}}{N}\text{-}CH_3$

20. Which has the highest boiling point?

    a. $CH_3CH_2CH_2OH$ b. $CH_3CH_2CH_2NH_2$ c. $CH_3NH\text{-}CH_2CH_3$ d. $CH_3\overset{\overset{CH_3}{|}}{N}\text{-}CH_3$

21. Which of the compounds shown in question 20 has the lowest boiling point?

    a.   b.   c.   d.

22. Some drugs which contain amino groups are converted to their salts to increase their:

    a. acidity   b. basicity   c. solubility

23. Amines react with strong acids to form:

    a. salts   b. esters   c. amino acids   d. bases

24. Which compound does <u>not</u> exhibit the properties of a base?

a. $CH_3CH_2CH_2NH_2$ b. CH_3CHCH_3 c. CH_3CNH_2 d. CH_3NCH_3 e.

a and b: $\underset{NH_2}{}$ c. $\underset{O}{}$ d. $\underset{CH_3}{}$ e. 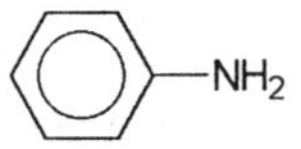 (ring)$-NH_2$

25. If a carboxylic acid and an amine react to form a salt, which of the following is the product?

a. $RCOO^-RNH_3^+$ b. $RCOO^+RNH_3^-$ c. $RCOOH^+RNH_2^-$ d. $RCOOH^+RNH_2^-$

26. The product of the reaction between isopropyl chloride and ammonia is:

a. $CH_3-\underset{NH_2}{\overset{Cl}{C}}-CH_3$ b. $CH_3-\overset{NH_2}{CH}-CH_3$ c. $CH_3-\overset{O}{C}-NH_2$

27. The reaction between acetic anhydride and aniline produces:

a. 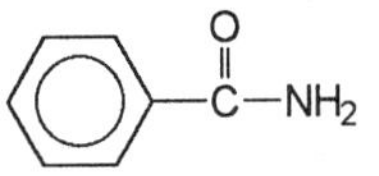 (ring)$-\overset{O}{C}-NH_2$ b. 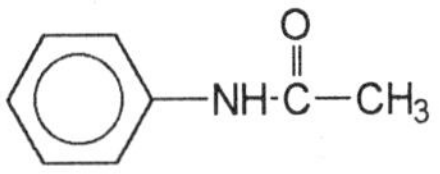 (ring)$-NH\cdot\overset{O}{C}-CH_3$ c. $CH_3-\overset{O}{C}-NH_2$ d. $CH_3-\overset{O}{C}-O^-NH_4^+$

28. What is the product of the following reaction: $CH_3\overset{O}{C}-CH_3$ $—H_2, NH_3, Ni \rightarrow$?

a. $CH_3-\overset{O}{C}-NH_2$ b. $CH_3-\overset{O}{C}-NH-CH_3$ c. $CH_3CH_2-\overset{O}{C}-NH_2$ d. $CH_3-\underset{NH_2}{CH}-CH_3$

29. Which compound would <u>not</u> react with an acid chloride to form an amide?

a. NH_3 b. CH_3NH_2 c. $CH_3-NH-CH_3$ d. $CH_3\underset{CH_3}{N}-CH_3$ e. 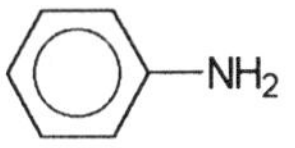 (ring)$-NH_2$

30. Which reaction is called reductive amination?

a. CH_3CH_2Cl $\xrightarrow{NH_3}$ $CH_3CH_2NH_2$

b. $CH_3\underset{O}{C}-CH_3$ $\xrightarrow{H_2, NH_3, Ni}$ $CH_3\underset{NH_2}{CH}-CH_3$

c. $CH_3-NH-CH_3$ $\xrightarrow{HNO_2}$ $CH_3-\underset{CH_3}{N}-N=O$

31. Which reagent is used to detect the presence of amino acids through a color reaction?

a. ninhydrin b. pyrimidine c. epinephrine

32. In the Van Slyke method, primary amino groups are detected by:

a. the development of a blue color

b. the change of litmus paper from red to blue

c. the evolution of nitrogen gas

33. Members of which class of compounds were not identified as carcinogens?

a. N-nitroso compounds b. aromatic amines c. amino acids

34. These amines react with nitrous acid to form dangerous N-nitroso compounds.

a. primary b. secondary c. tertiary d. quaternary

ANSWERS

1. c	7. b	13. a	19. e	25. a	31. a
2. d	8. b	14. d	20. a	26. b	32. c
3. d	9. b	15. d	21. d	27. b	33. c
4. b	10. a	16. d	22. c	28 d	34. b
5. c	11. e	17. d	23. d	29. d	
6. c	12. d	18. c	24. c	30. b	

Special Topic G: Brain Amines and Related Drugs

KEY WORDS

axon	*adrenaline*	*synapse*	*neurotransmitter*	*phenethylamines*
amphetamines	*stimulants*	*alkaloid*	*anesthetics*	*barbiturates*
tranquilizers	*dopamine*	*antihistamines*	*synergistic*	

SUMMARY

G.1 Some Chemistry of the Nervous System

    A. Nerve cells carry messages between the brain and other parts of the body. Although the *axons* of a nerve cell can be quite long, the nerve impulse must be transmitted across short gaps (*synapses*) via chemical messengers called *neurotransmitters*. Each type of neurotransmitter binds to a specific type of receptor site, completing the intended action.

    B. Many drugs (and poisons) act by either blocking or mimicking the action of these natural neurotransmitters.

    C. Since many neurotransmitters are amines, it is not surprising that many drugs also contain nitrogen.

G.2 Brain Amines

    A. The neurotransmitter norepinephrine is chemically related to the hormone *adrenaline* (epinephrine). It is synthesized from the amino acid tyrosine. High levels of norepinephrine are associated with a state of elation. Drugs that block its action cause depression while those that mimic its action act as stimulants.

norepinephrine   adrenaline (epinephrine)   tyrosine (an amino acid)

    B. Serotonin is a neurotransmitter that seems to play a role in mental illness. Serotonin is synthesized from the amino acid tryptophan. Serotonin agonists are used to treat depression and anxiety.

serotonin   tryptophan (an amino acid)

    C. Brain cells also make nitric oxide (NO), which serves as a chemical messenger.

G.3 Stimulant Drugs: Amphetamines

    A. The *phenethylamines* (*amphetamines*) form a group of synthetic *stimulants* that may act by mimicking the natural brain amine, norepinephrine.

Phenethylamine   Amphetamine   Methamphetamine
                            (Benzedrine)   (Methedrine)

    B. Amphetamine has been used for weight reduction. Methamphetamine is the "speed" of many drug users. Phenylpropanol amine is used as an appetite suppressant.

163

C. Designer drugs are synthetic analogs of compounds that have proven pharmacological activity. Angel Dust = PCP or phencyclidine; China White = α-methyl fentanyl (~ heroin); Ecstasy = MDMA or 3,4-methylene dioxymethamphetamine

G.4 Caffeine, Nicotine, and Cocaine

A. Caffeine is the most widely used stimulant. It is an *alkaloid* found in coffee, soft drinks, and available in "No-Doz" tablets. (~100 mg caffeine /tablet vs. ~ 200 mg/cup of strong coffee)

B. Nicotine is an alkaloid found in smoking tobacco. The lethal dose for humans is estimated at about 50 mg.

C. Cocaine was first isolated in 1860 from the leaves of the coca plant. Cocaine was once used as a local anesthetic, but is quite toxic. It is also a stimulant, increasing stamina and reducing fatigue by increasing the level of dopamines. It was the "sniff" of the jetset but is now widely used. The stimulant effects are short-lived, followed by depression. Overdoses may cause death.

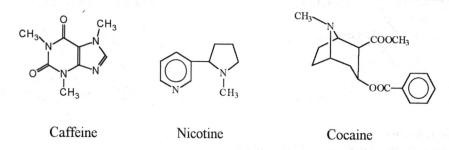

| Caffeine | Nicotine | Cocaine |

G.5 Local Anesthetics

A. Local anesthetics are drugs that block the nerve signals to the brain from the treated tissue. Many local *anesthetics* are ester derivatives of, or related to, p-aminobenzoic acid.

| p-aminobenzoic acid | Novocaine (Procaine·HCl) | Benzocaine |

B. Lidocaine or mepivicaine is often the local anesthetic of choice today.

C. A general anesthetic acts on the brain to produce unconsciousness. Two of the first general anesthetics used in surgical practice were diethylether (1846) and chloroform (1847). General anesthetics appear to act by dissolving fatty membranes of nerve cells.

G.6 Barbiturates: Sedation, Sleep, and Synergism

A. Barbituric acid was synthesized from urea and malonic acid in 1864 by von Baeyer. Since then thousands of *barbiturates* have been synthesized. They are generally sedatives (sleeping pills) but can be lethal in larger doses. Barbiturates are particularly dangerous when ingested with alcohol. The *synergistic* effect of these two depressants can enhance the effect of the barbiturate by factors up to 200-fold. Barbiturates are strongly addictive and withdrawal hazardous.

B. Barbiturates are cyclic amides that resemble pyrimidine and may act by substituting for pyrimidine bases (thymine) in nucleic acids (Chapter 23).

Barbital   Phenobarbital (Luminal)   Sodium Pentothal   Thymine

G.7 Dissociative Anesthetics: Ketamine and PCP

A. Ketamine is an anesthetic that also produces "near-death" type hallucinations.

B. PCP (phencyclidine) is also known as "angel dust" or "crystal." It is a dangerous drug but has found use as an animal *tranquilizer*. It also appears to depress the immune system.

Ketamine   Phencyclidine (PCP)

G.8 Antianxiety Agents

A. Ethanol is the most widely used tranquilizer.

B. Products such as Cope, Compoz and Vanquish contain aspirin plus an antihistamine. *Antihistamines* inhibit the release of histamine which in turn is responsible for redness, swelling and itching associated with allergies.

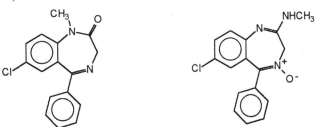

Histamine

C. The benzodiazephines contain a 7-membered heterocyclic ring system as found in Valium. After 20 years of use, Valium was found to be addictive.

Diazepam (Valium)   Chlordiazepoxide (Librium)

G.9 Antipsychotic Agents

A. Reserpine is the active alkaloid in the snake-root plant (*Rauwolfia serpentina*) used by people of India to treat fever, snakebite and maniacal forms of mental illness. It was found to reduce blood pressure and bring about sedation. By 1953, it replaced electroshock therapy for many psychotic patients.

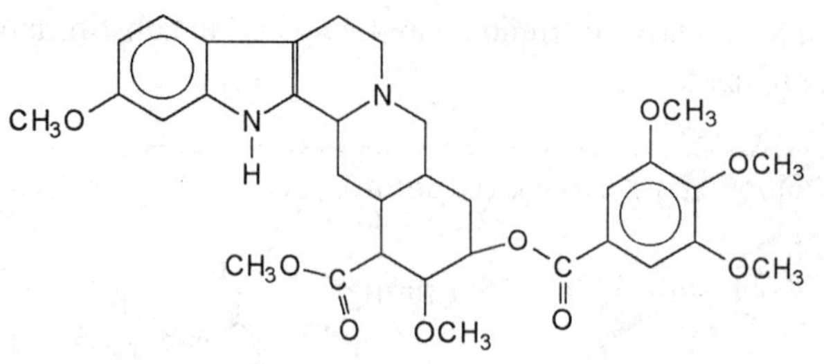
CH3O
N
H
N
OCH3
OCH3
OCH3
CH3O
O
OCH3
O
O

Reserpine

B. Slight structural changes can result in a profound change in properties. Promazine is a tranquilizer, imipramine (see below) is a psychic energizer. These are phenothiazines which act as dopamine antagonists to block the action of ***dopamine*** and to relieve the symptoms of schizophrenia. Today, more than 90% of all schizophrenics no longer need hospitalization.

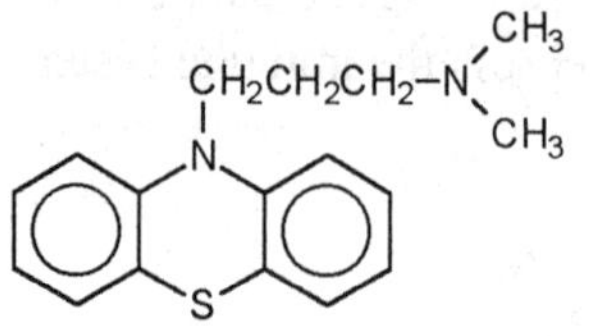
CH2CH2CH2–N
CH3
CH3
N
S

Promazine
(tranquilizer)

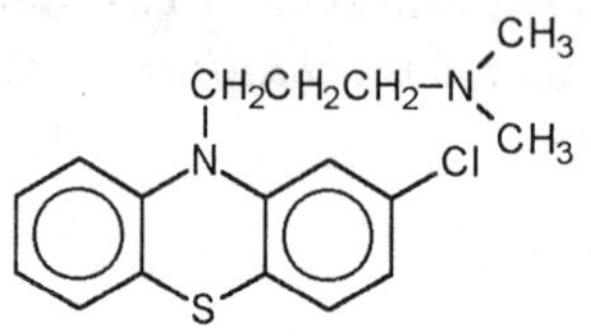
CH2CH2CH2–N
CH3
CH3
N
S
Cl

Chlorpromazine
(or Thorazine)

G.10 Antidepressants

A. Imipramine and Amitriptylene are closely related to Promazine but act as antidepressants instead of tranquilizers.

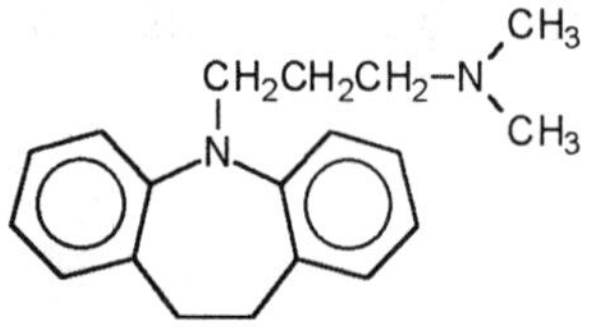
CH2CH2CH2–N
CH3
CH3
N

Imipramine
(Tofranil)

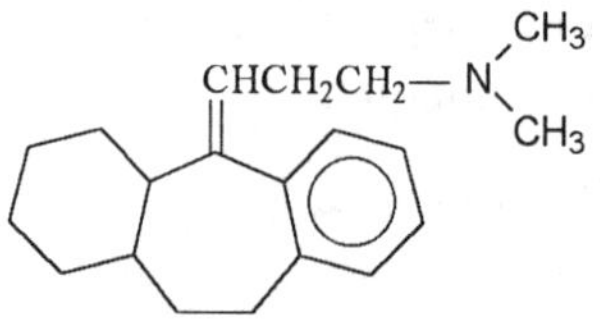
CHCH2CH2— N
CH3
CH3

Amitriptylene
(Elavil)

B. The most popular "new" antidepressant is fluoxetine (Prozac) with 1993 sales of over $3 billion. Prozac appears to block the reabsorption of serotonin, enhancing its effect. It has been prescribed to help people cope with obesity, fears and PMS.

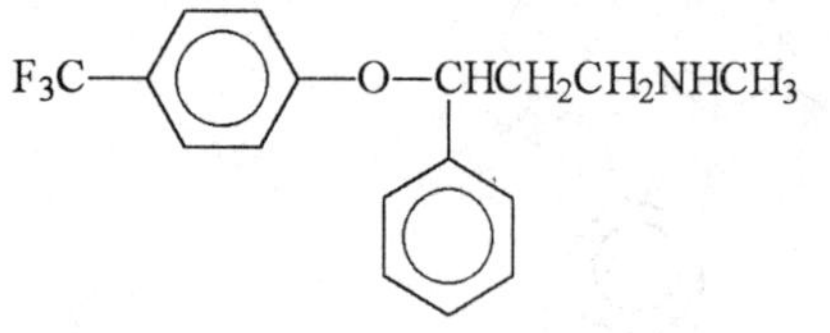
F3C
O–CHCH2CH2NHCH3

Fluoxetine (Prozac)

DISCUSSION

This special topic is devoted to physiologically important amines and drugs that affect our mental state. It is important that you realize that our moods, our sense of feeling "up" or "down", our sense of and tolerance to pain, etc., are all influenced by the presence or absence of chemical molecules that help regulate our body functions. We now know that many of the drugs that have been used and abused for centuries are capable of eliciting their effects because they somehow mimic a natural neurotransmitter or body regulator molecule. This usually involves some structural similarity that allows the drug molecule to bind to a receptor site intended for the normal body regulator molecule.

The listing below offers a brief summary of this material. The alkaloids are included here again but were first introduced in Special Topic F.

Physiologically Active Compounds

Compound	Common Structural Feature	Some Effects
Mood Hormones: epinephrine (adrenaline) norepinephrine serotonin	See section G.2	Balances between compounds produce states ranging from aggression to depression
Amphetamines amphetamine methamphetamine		Stimulants; can cause insomnia, tremors, hallucinations
Barbiturates barbital pentobarbital secobarbital phenobarbital amobarbital thiopental		Sedatives and soporifics are strongly addictive
Alkaloids Opium Alkaloids and Derivatives (morphine, codeine, heroin) coniine (from hemlock)	The alkaloids are nitrogen-containing heterocyclic compounds of varying degrees of complexity.	Narcotics; some are strongly addictive Nausea, paralysis and death
caffeine (from coffee, tea leaves, cola nuts)		Stimulant
nicotine (from tobacco) cocaine (from coca leaves)		Stimulant Powerful stimulant
Local Anesthetics benzocaine tetracaine procaine		Localized insensitivity to pain

Tranquilizers
    Carbamates
        ethyl carbamate
        meprobamate
    Benzodiazepines   see Section G.8
        diazepam
        chlordiazepoxide
    Promazines   see Section G.9
        promazine
        chlorpromazine
        thioridazine

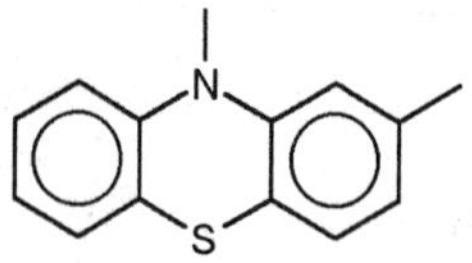

Calmatives and mild
    soporifics

The questions in the text serve as an excellent review of this material. The following SELF-TEST will further check your understanding of this material.

SELF-TEST

1. Adrenaline is structurally related to the amino acid _____.
    a. phenylalanine   b. alanine   c. tyrosine   d. methioine   e. tryptophan
2. Which compound is commonly referred to as adrenaline?
    a. serotonin   b. epinephrine   c. norepinephrine
3. The molecular theory of mental illness postulates an imbalance between two biochemicals. An excess
    of which compound produces mental depression?
    a. serotonin   b. epinephrine   c. norepinephrine
4. Which class of compounds are related to β-phenylethylamine?
    a. alkaloids   b. amphetamines   c. barbiturates   d. tranquilizers
5. Which compound is classified as a "downer"?
    a. amphetamine   b. barbital   c. cocaine
6. The amphetamines are structurally related to:
    a. the natural stimulants epinephrine and norepinephrine
    b. the alkaloids, cocaine and caffeine
    c. the tranquilizers Valium and Librium
7. Which molecular group is common to all barbiturates?
    a. 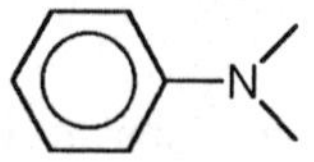   b. 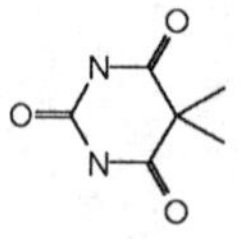   c. $-O-\overset{\overset{O}{\|}}{C}-N-$

8. Caffeine, nicotine and cocaine are all classified as:
    a. indole compounds   b. amphetamines   c. barbiturates   d. alkaloids
9. Esters of p-aminobenzoic acid are used widely as:
    a. "uppers"   b. "downers"   c. hallucinogens   d. local anesthetics

10. This compound was used by people of India to treat snakebite and is used today to reduce blood pressure and to bring about sedation.
    a. serotonin   b. adrenaline   c. nicotine   d. caffeine   e. reserpine

11. Valium and Librium are two common drugs that are widely used as:
    a. antianxiety drugs   b. anesthetics
    c. sleeping pills   d. major tranquilizers

12. Reserpine, lithium carbonate and the promazines are all used:
    a. in the treatment of mental illnesses
    b. as local anesthetics
    c. as general anesthetics

13. This popular antidepressant drug is thought to act by blocking the readsorption of serotonin.
    a. Valium   b. Promazine   c. Reserpine   d. Prozac   e. Novocaine

ANSWERS

1. c	3. a	5. b	7. b	9. d	11. a, c	13. d
2. b	4. b	6. a	8. d	10. e	12. a	

CHAPTER 18:   STEREOISOMERISM

KEY WORDS

polarized light	*levorotatory*	*stereoisomers*	*diastereomers*
optical activity	*chirality*	*enantiomers*	*meso compound*
specific rotation	*asymmetric carbon*	*nonsuperimposable*	*racemic mixture*
dextrorotatory	*geometric isomers*	*cis-, trans-*	*unpolarized light*

SUMMARY

Isomers are different compounds represented by the same molecular formula. There are two main categories of isomers: structural isomers and stereoisomers. Structural isomers include positional isomers (1-propanol vs. 2-propanol) and functional-group isomers (ethanol vs. dimethyl ether). In this chapter we are concerned with stereoisomers, or space isomerism, which can be distinguished by how the compounds interact with plane-polarized light.

18.1 Polarized Light and Optical Activity

A. Light is a wave with an oscillating electric vector. *Unpolarized light* can be pictured as a bundle of waves vibrating in all directions. *Polarized light* vibrates in only a single plane.

B. Certain substances can act on polarized light causing the plane of polarization to rotate. Such substances are said to be optically active. A polarimeter employs two polarizing lenses, one before and one after the solution being measured, to measure the degree of *optical activity*.

C. Optical activity is dependent on the substance, the concentration of the solution, the length of the tube, wavelength of the light, and the temperature of the solution. However, when these things are normalized, a *specific rotation* can be calculated which is a characteristic property of that substance.

   1. **Dextrorotatory**   (+)   - right or clockwise rotation of plane-polarized light

   2. **Levorotatory**   (-)   - left or counter clockwise rotation of plane-polarized light

18.2 Chiral Carbon Atoms

A. Optical activity arises from handedness or "*chirality*" made possible by the tetrahedral bonding by carbon atoms in the molecules. Organic compounds can be optically active if they have chiral carbon centers, carbons with four different groups attached. Chiral carbon centers are often referred to as *asymmetric carbons*.

mirror plane

B. Terms:

   1. **Stereoisomers** are isomers that differ only in the orientation of atoms in space. Stereoisomers not only have the same *molecular formula*, they have the same *structural formula*, but with a different configuration in space.

   2. **Enantiomers** are stereoisomers that are *nonsuperimposable* mirror images of each other. Fischer projection formulas assume that the vertical bonds lie behind the page and the horizontal bonds lie above the plane of the paper.

3. A *racemic mixture* is optically inactive because it contains equal amounts of both (+,−) enantiomers.

C. Enantiomers have identical physical properties except that they rotate plane polarized light in exactly opposite directions.

D. Enantiomers have the same chemical properties when reacting with molecules where handedness is not important. However, they can have drastically different chemical properties when reacting with a chiral molecule such as an enzyme or receptor site. Enantiomers may have different tastes and smells, or the one isomer might be physiologically active and the other not.

18.3 Multiple Chiral Centers

A. Molecules may have several chiral centers. If a molecule has **n** chiral centers, then there are 2^n possible stereoisomers of that compound (van't Hoff's rule; 1st Nobel prize in chemistry in 1901). For example, a molecule with three chiral carbons will have $2^3 = 8$ stereoisomers, or 4 sets of enantiomeric pairs. Those that are not enantiomers will be related as *diastereomers*. Diastereomers can have different physical and chemical properties.

B. A *meso compound* has at least two optically active chiral C atoms but contains an internal mirror plane which renders the molecule as a whole optically inactive. A meso compound is superimposable on its own mirror image.

18.4 Geometric Isomerism (Cis-Trans Isomerism)

A. *Geometric isomers* are compounds that have different configurations due to a restraint in the structure such as a cyclic ring structure or double bonds.

B. Nomenclature: Use *cis-* for compounds where the similar groups on the same side, and use *trans-* when the similar groups are on opposite sides of the ring or double bond.

Examples: cis-2-butene   trans-2-butene   trans-1,2-dichlorocyclopropane

18.5 Biochemical Significance

A. Chemical reactions in living organisms are catalyzed and controlled by protein molecules called *enzymes*. These are chiral molecules and usually will operate only on specific chiral substrates.

B. Food stuffs and medicines must have the proper "handedness" to be used by these enzymes and thus be beneficial. (Most natural sugars are "D"-sugars and most natural amino acids are "L"-amino acids.)

DISCUSSION

We have introduced the study of optical isomers and the problem of "handedness" in three dimensional molecules. Stereoisomers are molecules with the same structural formula but which differ in the way the bonds of the molecule are oriented in space. This is a very important distinction, however, because we will find that most biochemical processes are specific for only one "hand" of a given molecule. We will learn in Chapter 19 that carbohydrates found in nature are mostly D-sugars and in Chapter 21 that proteins are composed of L-amino acids. For now, we want you to be able to recognize chiral molecules, to master the terminology used to describe these isomers, and to work with the various ways of representing the formulas of such compounds. We have gathered some of the important terms of this Chapter here for easy reference.

Isomers - different compounds that have the same chemical formula or composition.

Stereoisomers - isomers that have the same structural formula but differ in the spatial arrangement of the atoms.

Chirality - a "handedness" property associated with organic compounds which have one or more carbon atoms with four different groups attached. If there are **n** chiral carbon centers, then there are 2^n stereoisomers possible.

Enantiomers - stereoisomers that are mirror images of each other, i.e., D-glucose and L-glucose.

Diastereomers - stereoisomers that are not mirror-images of one another, i.e ., glucose and galactose.

Racemic modification - an equal mixture of a pair of enantiomers. A racemic mixture is not optically active because it contains equal amounts of the (+) and (-) enantiomorphic forms.

Meso form - a molecule containing chiral carbon centers but which is not itself optically active because of an internal mirror plane.

The remaining problems at the end of the chapter and the **SELF-TEST** given here will help you check your understanding of these concepts.

SELF-TEST

1. How many chiral carbon centers are in the molecule shown?

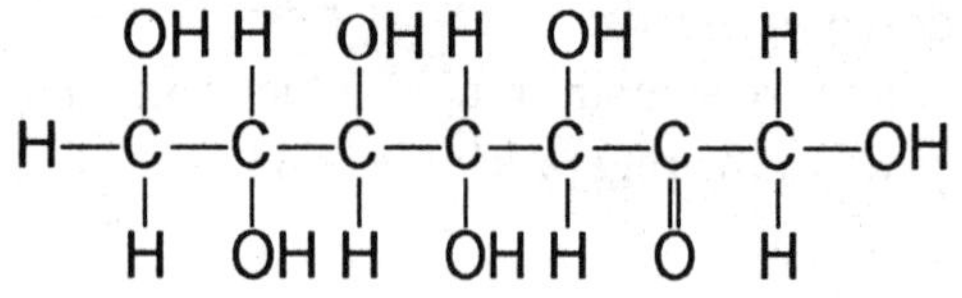

    a. 1   b. 2   c. 3   d. 4   e. 5

2. How many stereoisomers are possible for the compound shown in Question 1?
    a. 1 b. 2 c. 3 d. 4 e. 5 f. 8 g. 10 h. 16 i. 24 j. 32

3. Which of the following one-carbon compounds is <u>not</u> chiral?

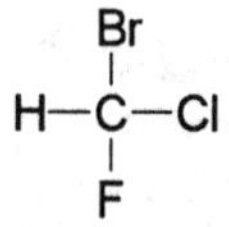

4. Which of the following properties would be different for each of two enantiomers?
    a. solubility in water
    b. density
    c. interaction with polarized light

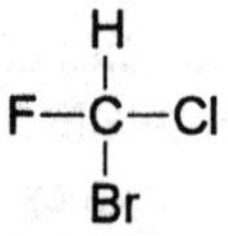

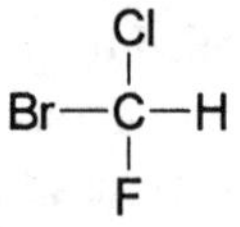

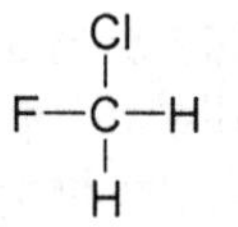

5. The extent of optical activity of a solution depends on which of the following?
    a. concentration of the solution
    b. temperature
    c. wavelength of light used in the experiment
    d. length of the polarimeter light path
    e. all of the above

6. Substances that rotate polarized light to the left or in a counterclockwise manner are said to be:
    a. dextrorotatory   b. levorotatory

7. Which compound would be expected to exist as a pair of mirror image isomers?

a.   b.   c.   d.

The remaining questions refer to the following compounds.

$$
\begin{array}{cccc}
\text{CH}_3 & \text{CH}_3 & \text{CH}_3 & \text{CH}_3 \\
\text{Br}-\text{C}-\text{H} & \text{H}-\text{C}-\text{Br} & \text{H}-\text{C}-\text{Br} & \text{Br}-\text{C}-\text{H} \\
\text{Br}-\text{C}-\text{H} & \text{H}-\text{C}-\text{Br} & \text{Br}-\text{C}-\text{H} & \text{H}-\text{C}-\text{Br} \\
\text{CH}_3 & \text{CH}_3 & \text{CH}_3 & \text{CH}_3 \\
\text{I} & \text{II} & \text{III} & \text{IV}
\end{array}
$$

8. Which of the above compounds represent enantiomers?
    I   II   III   IV

9. Which of the above compounds represent diastereomers?
    I   II   III   IV

10. Which of the above compounds represent a meso-form?
    I   II   III   IV

11. Which of the following solutions would rotate polarized light?
    a. 0.2 M of compound I
    b. 0.2 M II
    c. 0.2 M III
    d. 0.2 M IV
    e. 0.2 M III plus 0.2 M IV
    f. 0.2 M II plus 0.2 M III

ANSWERS

1. d	3. c	5. e	7. a	9. I and III, I and IV
2. h	4. c	6. b	8. III and IV	10. I or II (I = II)
				11. c, d, f

Special Topic H: Molecules to See and to Smell

KEY WORDS

rhodopsin   *cone cells*   *opsin*   *retinal*   *isomerization*   *olfactory*

SUMMARY

We perceive the world around us through our five senses: sight, sound, smell, taste and touch. Here we look at the molecules for seeing and smelling.

H.1 Vision: Cis-Trans Isomerism

A. The retina of the human eye contains two kinds of receptor cells, rods and cones. *Cone cells* in the eye contain *rhodopsin*, which consists of a protein (*opsin*) in complex with a small organic molecule derived from vitamin A (11-cis-*retinal*).

B. The "vision" cycle (photochemical isomerization)

1. Light is absorbed by 11-cis retinal which converts the molecule to its trans isomer, 11-trans-*retinal*. This *isomerization* is initiated in a few picoseconds.
2. The structural change from the bent cis-isomer to the more linear trans-isomer acts like a switch to trigger a nerve impulse in the optic nerve that is sent to the brain. Also, during this stage the rhodopsin complex splits into the protein opsin and free retinal.
3. Enzymes are used to reform the 11-cis isomer.
4. The cis isomer complexes with opsin to reform rhodopsin so the cycle can start again.

11-cis-retinal   11-trans-retinal

H.2 Odors: The shapes of the things we smell

A. The process of olfaction (smelling) involves the binding of an odorous molecule to a receptor cell of the *olfactory* system (nose).
B. The receptors in the nose have been divided into seven primary odor associated types (see Table H.1). Molecules that can bind to multiple receptor sites will send a "mixed" odor signal to the brain.
C. The theory of taste by the taste buds is very similar to that proposed here for smell, e.g. there may be small number of distinct taste receptors that are mixed and matched to produce a broad spectrum of different tastes.

SELF-TEST

1. The protein part of the visual receptor in cone cells is called _____.
      a. retina   b. opsin   c. rhodopsin   d. retinal   e. sightase
2. The pigment part of the visual receptor in cone cells is called _____.
      a. retina   b. opsin   c. rhodopsin   d. retinal   e. sightase
3. The adsorption of light causes a(n) _____ of the receptor molecules.
      a. oxidation   b. reduction   c. cis-trans isomerization   d. cleavage

ANSWERS   1. b   2. d   3. c

CHAPTER 19:   CARBOHYDRATES

KEY WORDS

sugar	*ketose*	*lactose*	*acetal*	*monosaccharide*
aldose	*sucrose*	*α-D-glucose*	*disaccharide*	*D-glucose*
maltose	*β-D-glucose*	*polysaccharide*	*mannose*	*starch*
amylopectin	*"reducing" sugar*	*galactose*	*glycogen*	*mutarotation*
hemiacetal	*fructose*	*amylose*	*cellulose*	*Tollens' reagent*
Fischer	*lactose intolerance*	*triose*	*pentose*	*hexose*
Haworth	*glycosidic linkage*	*invert sugar*		

SUMMARY

19.1 Carbohydrates: Definitions and Classifications
   A. Many carbohydrates have the molecular formula $(C \cdot H_2O)_n$ but they are not hydrates of carbon as
      their name implies. Carbohydrates are polyhydroxy aldehydes (aldoses) or ketones (ketoses).
   B. The terms carbohydrate, saccharide, and *sugar* are used interchangeably.
      1. **Monosaccharides**   - simple sugar molecules
      2. **Disaccharides**   - carbohydrates that can be hydrolyzed to two monosaccharides
      3. **Polysaccharides**   - carbohydrates made up of many monosaccharides
   C. **Sugars** are also classified as "**reducing**" or "**non-reducing**" sugars depending on whether the sugar
      will reduce **Tollens'** or related reagents that are mild oxidants.
   D. Most carbohydrates are crystalline solids at room temperature with high melting points.
   E. Carbohydrates readily form hydrogen bonds and are very soluble in water (e.g. 100 g glucose/100
      mL H_2O at 25°C).

19.2 Monosaccharides: General Terminology
   A. Monosaccharides (-ose ending) are classified according to whether the carbonyl is present as an
      aldehyde (*aldoses*) or ketone (*ketoses*).
   B. They are also classified by the number of C atoms
         (3, tri*ose*;   4, tetr*ose*;   5, pent*ose*;   6, hex*ose*).

19.3 Stereochemistry
   A. The simplest *sugars* are triose oxidation products of glycerol. There are 2 aldotrioses because the
      glyceraldehyde molecule has one chiral C center, but only one ketotriose since it has none. Usually
      carbohydrates found in nature are D-sugars. By convention, all D-type sugars are drawn with the "-
      OH" on the right at the asymmetric C atom furthest from the carbonyl carbon (usually the
      penultimate carbon) as shown in the *Fischer* projections below.

L-   D-
glyceraldehyde   dihydroxyacetone
   B. D- and L-glyceraldehyde are optical isomers and differ in the way they rotate plane polarized light.
      D(+) indicates that a D-sugar rotates plane polarized light in a clockwise (+) or dextrorotatory
      direction, and D(-) indicates a counterclockwise (-) or levorotatory direction.

C. Major monosaccharides in biochemistry
  1. *Trioses*: glyceraldehyde, dihydroxyacetone (above 19.3A)
  2. *Pentoses*: D-ribose is found in ribonucleic acids (RNAs) and 2-deoxyribose occurs in deoxyribonucleic acids (DNAs)

```
        CHO                    CHO
      H—C—OH               H—C—H
      H—C—OH               H—C—OH
      H—C—OH               H—C—OH
       CH₂OH                CH₂OH
```

$$\begin{array}{cc}
\text{CHO} & \text{CHO} \\
\text{H—C—OH} & \text{H—C—H} \\
\text{H—C—OH} & \text{H—C—OH} \\
\text{H—C—OH} & \text{H—C—OH} \\
\text{CH}_2\text{OH} & \text{CH}_2\text{OH}
\end{array}$$

D-ribose   2-deoxy-D-ribose

  3. *Hexoses*: Glucose is an aldohexose and the most abundant sugar occurring in nature.

$$\begin{array}{cccc}
\text{CHO} & \text{CHO} & \text{CHO} & \text{CH}_2\text{OH} \\
\text{H—C—OH} & \text{H—C—OH} & \text{HO—C—H} & \text{C=O} \\
\text{HO—C—H} & \text{HO—C—H} & \text{HO—C—H} & \text{HO—C—H} \\
\text{H—C—OH} & \text{HO—C—H} & \text{H—C—OH} & \text{H—C—OH} \\
\text{H—C—OH} & \text{H—C—OH} & \text{H—C—OH} & \text{H—C—OH} \\
\text{CH}_2\text{OH} & \text{CH}_2\text{OH} & \text{CH}_2\text{OH} & \text{CH}_2\text{OH}
\end{array}$$

D(+)-*glucose*   **D(+)-*galactose***   **D(+)-*mannose***   **D(-)-*fructose***

19.4 Hexoses

A. **D-Glucose** is the normal "blood sugar" and the sugar our cells use directly for the production of energy. D-glucose (or dextrose) is the monomer of *starch* and *cellulose,* and is also found in the familiar disaccharides *lactose* and *sucrose*.

B. D-Glucose has 4 asymmetric carbon centers, thus there are 2^4 or 16 possible stereoisomers of D-glucose. However, only 2 of the other aldohexoses are very common in nature.
  1. *Mannose* - differs from glucose only at the second C atom; a component of the polysaccharide mannan.
  2. *Galactose* - differs from glucose only at the fourth C atom; bound with glucose to form the disaccharide, lactose (milk sugar); component of galactans and glycolipids of nerve and brain tissue called cerebrosides and gangliosides.

C. **D-Fructose** (also called levulose) is a ketohexose. Fructose and glucose combine to make the common disaccharide, *sucrose*. It is found in honey and is the sweetest of all natural sugars.

D. Aspartame, saccharin and sodium cyclamate are popular artificial sweeteners, 100x-300x as sweet as fructose. Aspartame (Nutrasweet) is an ester of a dipeptide and breaks down into aspartic acid, phenylalanine, and methanol. Individuals sensitive to phenylalanine should regulate their consumption of Nutrasweet. Acesulfame K has recently been approved as an artificial sweetener. It is reported to be more heat-stable than Nutrasweet and can survive the cooking process.

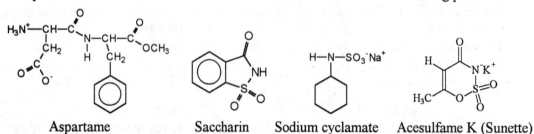

Aspartame   Saccharin   Sodium cyclamate   Acesulfame K (Sunette)

19.5 Monosaccharides: Cyclic Structures

A. Monosaccharides are polyhydroxy aldehydes or ketones. Aldehydes and ketones can react with alcohols to form hemiacetals or hemiketals. Pentoses and hexoses exist in solution as internal *hemiacetals*, forming stable 5- or 6-membered rings.

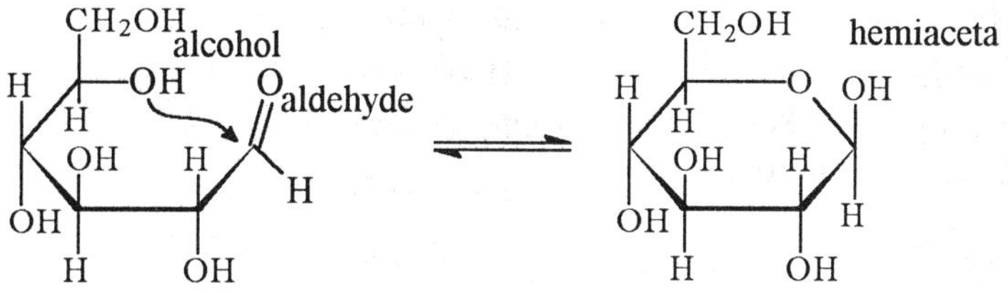

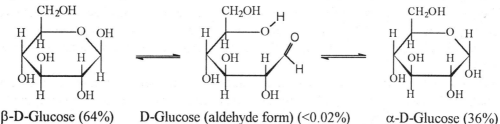

B. *α*- and *β*-*D-Glucose*: the internal hemiacetal reaction creates a new asymmetric carbon at the C-1 position of glucose. These two different forms of glucose are called *α-D-glucose* and *β-D-glucose*, shown here as *Haworth* formulas. The β form always has the new -OH group on the same side of the ring as the terminal -CH_2OH group. These compounds are not enantiomers and have slightly different physical properties as well as different chemical properties.

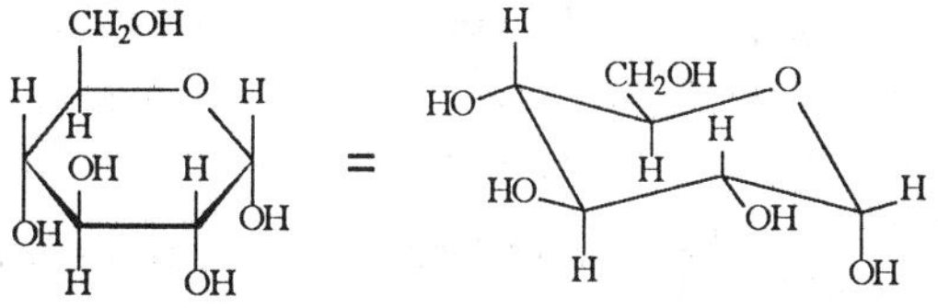

α-D-glucose (m.pt. 146 °C) 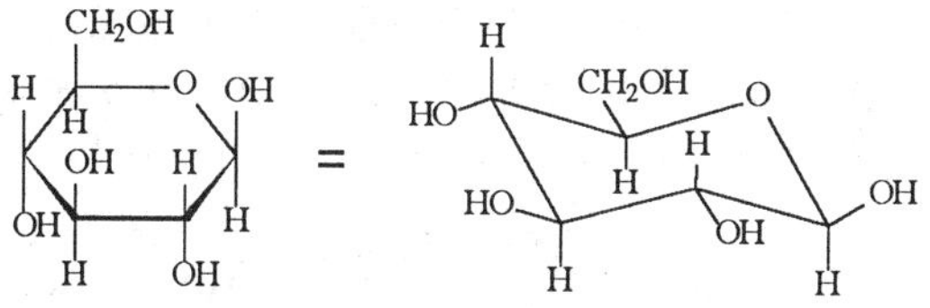 *β-D-glucose* (m.pt. 150 °C)

C. The β form of D-Glucose is more stable than the α form, but both forms are always in equilibrium with a very small amount of the free aldehyde. The interconversion of α- and β-isomers via the reopening and reclosing of the hemiacetal form is called *mutarotation*.

β-D-Glucose (64%)   D-Glucose (aldehyde form) (<0.02%)   α-D-Glucose (36%)

19.6 Properties of Some Monosaccharides

A. Most sugars are crystalline solids at room temperature and are water soluble.

B. Chemical properties

1. The -OH groups on sugars behave like typical alcohols, reacting to form esters and ethers.

2. Mild oxidation of the aldehyde by *Tollens'* (reduction of Ag^+), *Benedict's*, or *Fehling's* (reduction of Cu^{2+}) *reagents* is used for the detection of *reducing sugars*. Note: all monosaccharides are "reducing sugars" because even ketoses exhibit some aldehyde character in basic solution.

3. Hemiacetals react with alcohols to form *acetals*. This reaction is important in forming disaccharides and polysaccharides. Acetals are stable and will not undergo mutarotation or reduce Tollens' reagent.

19.7 Disaccharides
   A. Disaccharides are distinguished by their composition and linkage. The three major disaccharides
      are sucrose, maltose and lactose.
   B. *Sucrose* is the common table sugar, cane sugar, beet sugar or just *sugar*. It is composed of α-D-
      glucose and β-D-fructose with an α(1→2) *glycosidic linkage* from the C 1 carbon of glucose to the
      C 2 carbon of fructose. Sucrose is a nonreducing sugar since the latent carbonyl groups of both
      units are involved in the acetyl linkage. *Invert sugar* is a 1:1 mixture of glucose and fructose and
      has properties that differ from sucrose.

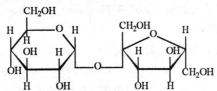

Sucrose

   C. *Maltose* is the disaccharide produced during the partial hydrolysis of starch. It is composed of two
      D-glucose units, connected "head to tail" by an α (1→4) glycosidic linkage. It is classified as a
      reducing sugar because it still also possesses a hemiacetal on one end.
   D. *Lactose* or milk sugar is composed of a β-D-galactose unit with a β(1→4) glycosidic *acetal* linkage
      to C 4 of D-glucose. Lactose is also a reducing sugar because of the presence of the hemiacetal
      group in the glucose ring. Most infants have a "lactase" enzyme and can digest lactose more readily
      than adults. Over 70% of the world's adult population suffers from *lactose intolerance*
      characterized by cramps and diarrhea when milk lactose is left undigested.

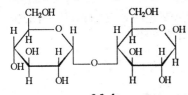

Maltose

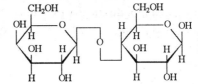

Lactose

19.8 Polysaccharides
   A. Polysaccharides are large polymers of sugars that are used as food/energy reserves (starch) or
      structural components (cellulose). Starch, glycogen and cellulose are all homopolymers comprised
      from just one sugar, D-glucose.
   B. *Starch* is a polymer of α-D-glucose. Plants make glucose from carbon dioxide by photosynthesis
      and then store it in the form of starch.   Starch can be separated into two fractions.
      1. *Amylose* (~20%): Unbranched chains of 60 to 300 glucose units with α (1→4) linkages; water
         soluble.

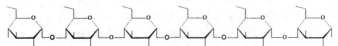

      2. *Amylopectin* (~80%): A branched chain polymer of 300 to 6000 glucose units; the chain
         segments have α (1→4) linkages as in amylose but also are connected by α (1→6) acetal linkages
         at the branch points; water insoluble.

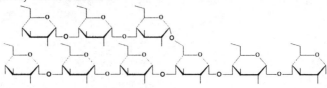

C. *Glycogen* is the equivalent of starch in animals. Glycogen is structurally a branched polymer of D-glucose similar to amylopectin but even more highly branched. Glucose reserves are stored as glycogen in liver and muscle tissues.

D. *Cellulose* is a linear polymer of D-glucose similar to amylose but with β acetal linkages. The β linkage is more stable and confers a different three-dimensional structure on cellulose than that found for starch. Man and most animals cannot digest cellulose but grazing animals and termites can because of the action of the enzymes in the bacteria of their digestive tracts. Although it has no nutritive value for man, cellulose makes up the greater part of dietary fiber. Cotton fibrils are nearly pure cellulose. Chemical modifications of the -OH groups of cellulose have produced a wide variety of synthetic polymers (Celluloid).

DISCUSSION

In Chapter 19 the terminology and molecular architecture associated with carbohydrates were presented. Our study of carbohydrates will continue in Chapters 24 and 25 when we trace the critical biochemical role of these compounds. To do that it is essential that you familiarize yourself now with carbohydrate structures. You should aim at being able to read carbohydrate structures as well as you now read the structures of simpler compounds. For example, when we say "the hydroxyl group of ethanol," with only the slightest pause you should think "CH_3-CH_2-OH." After studying the material in this chapter, you should also be able to look at a carbohydrate structure and, with a pause only a bit longer than before, locate the acetal linkage or determine whether the compound is glucose or fructose or mannose, or whether or not it is a reducing sugar.

Before we present the **SELF-TEST**, let's establish a way of drawing saccharides in abbreviated form. For the open-chain form, we'll adopt this shorthand notation:

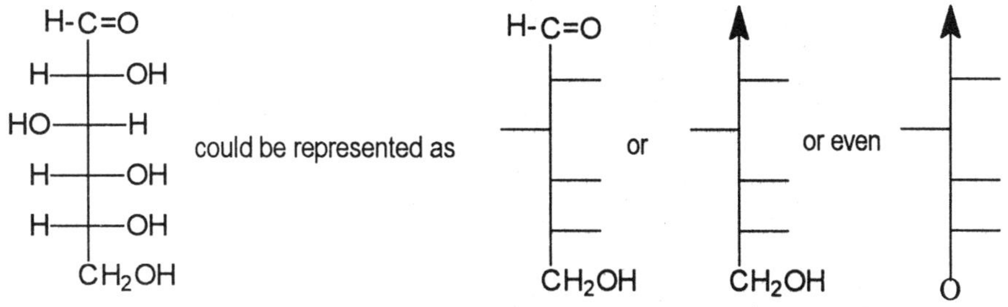

The branches on the stem of the abbreviated formula give the orientation of the secondary hydroxyl groups. The same simplification can be used for ring forms:

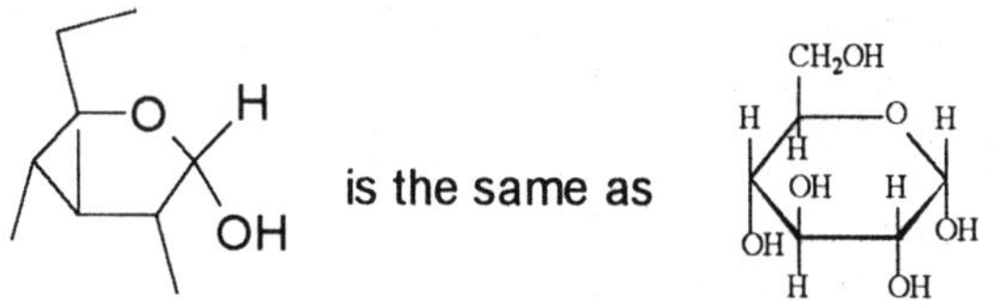

We'll use the simplified structures in the **SELF-TEST**. Be sure you're able to translate these forms to the more familiar ones before you proceed.

SELF-TEST

Refer to the following structures in answering questions 1 through 6.

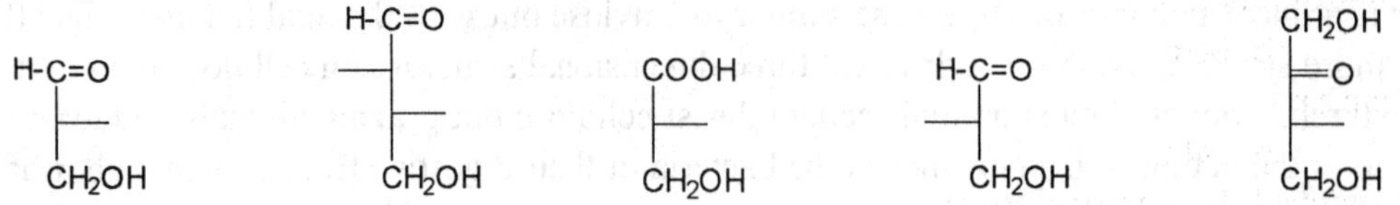

H-C=O   H-C=O   COOH   H-C=O   CH$_2$OH

CH$_2$OH   CH$_2$OH   CH$_2$OH   CH$_2$OH   =O ... CH$_2$OH

(a)   (b)   (c)   (d)   (e)

1. Which of the compounds is not a sugar?	a	b	c	d	e
2. Which is not a member of the D-family of sugars?	a	b	c	d	e
3. Which is D-glyceraldehyde?	a	b	c	d	e
4. Which is the product of oxidation of D-glyceraldehyde?	a	b	c	d	e
5. Which is a ketotetrose?	a	b	c	d	e
6. Which is(are) tetroses?	a	b	c	d	e

Refer to the following structures in answering questions 7 through 14.

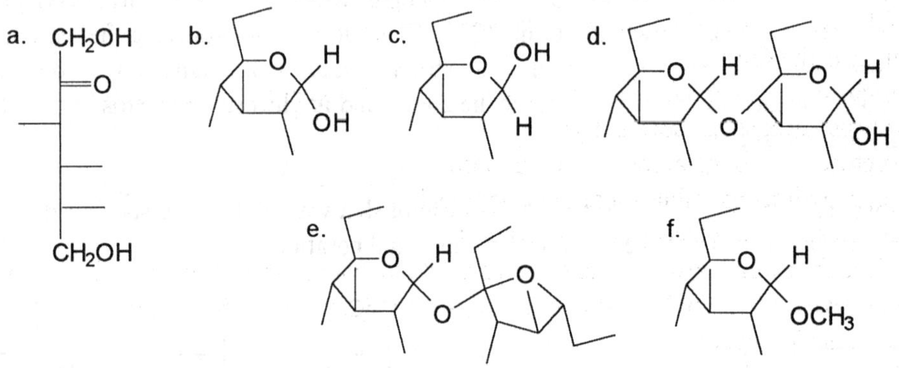

a. CH$_2$OH =O CH$_2$OH
b. ... OH
c. ... OH H
d. ...
e. ...
f. ... OCH$_3$

7. Which compound(s) is (are) not reducing sugars?	a	b	c	d	e	f
8. Which is D-fructose?	a	b	c	d	e	f
9. Which contains 2 acetal functions?	a	b	c	d	e	f
10. Which contain no hemiacetal function?	a	b	c	d	e	f
11. Which is the beta-form of D-glucose?	a	b	c	d	e	f
12. Which is an intermediate hydrolysis product of starch?	a	b	c	d	e	f
13. Which is sucrose?	a	b	c	d	e	f
14. Which can be classified as glycosides?	a	b	c	d	e	f

Refer to the following structure in answering questions 15 through 22.

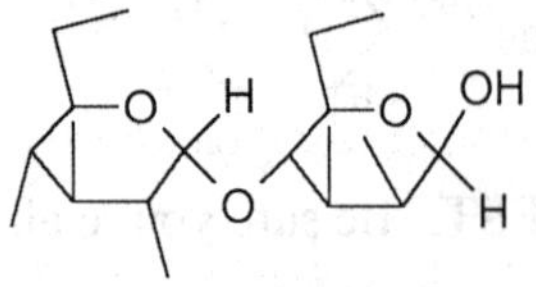

15. The monosaccharide unit on the right is:
    a. fructose   b. galactose   c. glucose   d. lactose   e. maltose
    f. mannose   g. sucrose   h. none of these

16. The monosaccharide unit on the left is:
    a. fructose   b. galactose   c. glucose   d. lactose   e. maltose
    f. mannose   g. sucrose   h. none of these

17. The disaccharide is:
     a. fructose   b. galactose   c. glucose   d. lactose   e. maltose
     f. mannose   g. sucrose   h. none of these

18. The hemiacetal group is:
     a. alpha   b. beta

19. The acetal group is:
     a. alpha   b. beta

20. The rings are attached through positions:
     a. 1,4   b. 1,6   c. ortho   d. meta   e. para

21. The compound is a:
     a. reducing sugar   b. nonreducing sugar

22. On hydrolysis, the compound yields:
     a. aldohexoses   b. aldopentoses   c. ketohexoses   d. ketopentoses

23. Which of the following yields a sugar other than glucose upon complete hydrolysis?
     a. amylopectin   b. cellulose   c. lactose   d. maltose   e. starch

24. Common table sugar is more formally described as:
     a. glucose   b. lactose   c. maltose   d. sucrose

25. Hydrolysis of which disaccharide gives glucose and fructose as products?
     a. cellulose   b. galactose   c. lactose   d. maltose   e. sucrose

26. Blood sugar is the same as:
     a. fructose   b. galactose   c. glucose   d. glycogen   e. lactose   f. sucrose

27. On hydrolysis, milk sugar does <u>not</u> yield:
     a. fructose   b. galactose   c. glucose

28. On complete hydrolysis, table sugar does <u>not</u> yield:
     a. galactose   b. glucose   c. fructose

29. Which of the following carbohydrates would <u>not</u> yield maltose if it were partially hydrolyzed?
     a. amylose   b. amylopectin   c. cellulose   d. glycogen   e. starch

30. Fructose is also known as:
     a. dextrose   b. milk sugar   c. levulose   d. table sugar

31. The mixture of monosaccharides produced by hydrolysis of sucrose is called:
     a. blood sugar   b. invert sugar   c. milk sugar   d. table sugar

32. Saccharin is a(n):
     a. hexose   b. aldose   c. reducing sugar   d. glycoside   e. none of these

33. Fructose is a(n):
     a. aldohexose   b. aldopentose   c. ketohexose   d. ketopentose   e. triose

34. 2-Deoxyribose is an isomer of:
     a. fructose   b. glyceraldehyde   c. ribose   d. none of these

35. Dihydroxyacetone is an isomer of:
     a. glyceraldehyde   b. glucose   c. ribose   d. saccharin   e. none of these

36. Ribose is a(n):
     a. aldopentose   b. ketohexose   c. ketotriose   d. aldotetrose   e. none of these

37. Cellulose is a(n):
     a. monosaccharide   b. disaccharide   c. polysaccharide   d. none of these

38. In which of the following are monosaccharide units <u>not</u> joined by alpha linkages?
     a. maltose   b. amylose   c. glycogen   d. cellulose

39. Which shorthand formula correctly shows the orientation of the secondary hydroxy groups in D-mannose?

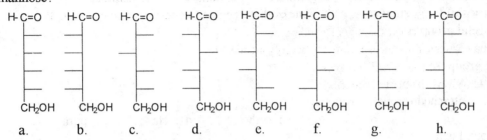

   a.   b.   c.   d.   e.   f.   g.   h.

40. Which compound contains a β-acetal linkage?
    a. amylose   b. glycogen   c. lactose   d. maltose   e. starch

41. Which compound does not show 1,6-branching?
    a. amylopectin   b. amylose   c. glycogen

42. Which compound contains α-acetal linkages and 1,6-branching?
    a. amylose   b. cellulose   c. glycogen   d. sucrose

43. Fructose is not a(n):
    a. alcohol   b. aldehyde   c. carbohydrate   d. sugar   e. saccharide

44. Which is not a reducing sugar?
    a. fructose   b. galactose   c. glucose   d. lactose
    e. maltose   f. sucrose

45. If a carbohydrate gives a positive Fehling's test, the carbohydrate:
    a. is a reducing sugar   b. is reduced   c. will give a negative Tollen's test

46. Which reagent will accomplish the reaction:

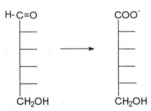

    a. Tollen's reagent   b. Fehling's reagent   c. Benedict's reagent
    d. All of these reagents will yield the product shown.
    e. None of these reagents will yield the product shown.

47. Which compound will not be oxidized by Fehling's reagent?

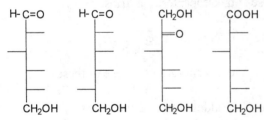

   a.   b.   c.   d.   e. All will be oxidized.

48. Is the following compound a reducing sugar?

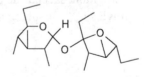

    a. yes   b. no

49. Which compound can <u>not</u> be metabolized by human beings?
     a. amylopectin   b. amylose   c. cellulose   d. maltose   e. starch

50. Which structural feature prevents the digestion of the compound described in question 49.
     a. the branches formed through 1,6-linkages
     b. the presence of galactose units in the polysaccharide
     c. the β form of the acetal linkages
     d. the length of the polysaccharide

ANSWERS

1. c	11. c	21. a	31. b	41. b
2. d	12. d	22. a	32. e	42. c
3. a	13. e	23. c	33. c	43. b
4. c	14. d, e, f	24. d	34. d	44. f
5. e	15. f	25. e	35. a	45. a
6. b, e	16. c	26. c	36. a	46. d
7. e, f	17. h	27. a	37. c	47. d
8. a	18. b	28. a	38. d	48. b
9. e	19. a	29. c	39. g	49. c
10. a, e, f	20. a	30. c	40. c	50. c

CHAPTER 20:   LIPIDS

KEY WORDS

lipids	*fats*	*"hard" water*	*glycolipids*	*fatty acids*
oils	*phosphatides*	*steroids*	*saturated*	*triglycerides*
lecithins	*cholesterol*	*unsaturated*	*saponification*	*cephalins*
polyunsaturated	*iodine number*	*soap*	*sphingolipids*	*membranes*
hydrogenation	*detergent*	*choline*	*ethanolamine*	*integral*
rancidity	*antioxidants*	*hydrophobic*	*hydrophilic*	*peripheral*
cerebrosides	*semipermeable*	*eutrophication*	*biodegradable*	*micelles*
facilitated diffusion	*active transport*	*bile salts*	*wax*	*fluid mosaic*
arteriosclerosis	*ganliocides*	*bilayers*	*gallstones*	*heart attack*
nonsaponifiable	*stroke*	*cis-double bond*		

SUMMARY

20.1 What is a Lipid?

A. **Lipids** are a diverse class of biomolecules defined on the basis of being more soluble in nonpolar solvents like diethylether than in water.

B. Lipids represent an important energy source, play a major role in membranes, and serve as vitamins and hormones.

C. Types of compounds included as lipids are:

   1. fatty acids   5. glycolipids
   2. triglycerides   6. steroids
   3. waxes   7. prostaglandins
   4. phospholipids   8. fat-soluble vitamins

20.2 Fatty Acids

A. **Fatty acids** are long-chain carboxylic acids. Most natural fatty acids contain an even number of carbon atoms and are components of fats and oils.

B. Fatty acids are divided into two subclasses:

   1. **Saturated**--the hydrocarbon "tail" of a saturated fatty acid is fairly straight, permitting close dispersion forces resulting in higher melting points; **fats**

   2. **Unsaturated**--most natural unsaturated fatty acids have **cis double bonds** which cause the hydrocarbon portion to bend, thus lessening the strength of intermolecular forces and resulting in lower melting points; **oils**

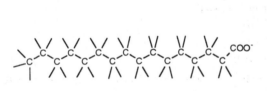

Saturated fatty acid

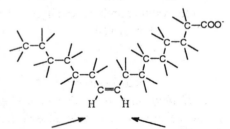

Unsaturated fatty acid (*cis* double bond)

C. Some common fatty acids: (Δ-9 refers to the position of a double bond after C9, etc.)

Saturated Fatty Acids			
	$CH_3(CH_2)_{12}COOH$	C_{14}	Myristic acid
	$CH_3(CH_2)_{14}COOH$	C_{16}	Palmitic acid
	$CH_3(CH_2)_{16}COOH$	C_{18}	Stearic acid

Unsaturated Fatty Acids			
	C_{18}	Δ 9	Oleic acid
	C_{18}	Δ 9, 12	Linoleic acid
	C_{18}	Δ 9, 12, 15	Linolenic acid
	C_{20}	Δ 5, 8, 11,14	Arachidonic acid

20.3 Fats and Oils

A. Most "*fats*" are fatty acid esters of glycerol called *triglycerides*. Animal fats are usually solids at room temperature because their triglycerides contain mostly saturated fatty acids. Fats can be broken down by basic hydrolysis (*saponification*) to yield glycerol and the salts of the fatty acids (*soaps*).

B. Oils are fats that are liquids at room temperature. Their lower melting points are due to a higher proportion of unsaturated fatty acid units. They are principally obtained from vegetable sources. Some polyunsaturated fatty acids are "essential" fatty acids that must be supplied in the diet for good health.

C. Saturated fats and cholesterol have been implicated in *arteriosclerosis* (hardening of the arteries).

20.4 Properties of Fats and Oils

A. Physical properties: Fats and oils are lighter than water ($0.8 g/cm^3$). Most are colorless, odorless, and tasteless.

B. Chemical properties

1. Hydrolysis - Basic hydrolysis = soap making = saponification

2. *Iodine Number*: The degree of unsaturation is measured in terms of the "iodine number" which is defined as the number of grams of iodine that will be consumed by 100 g of fat or oil. The larger the "iodine number," the higher the degree of unsaturation.

Fat or Oil	Iodine Number
Butter	25-40
Lard	47-70
Sunflower oil	130-140

3. *Hydrogenation* of oils can produce solids or semisolids. Margarine is a butter substitute consisting of vegetable oils that have been partially hydrogenated.

4. *Rancidity* (production of odorous breakdown products) of fats and oils occurs by hydrolysis of ester bonds and oxidation of unsaturated fatty acids. *Antioxidants* are added to increase shelf life of foods.

20.5 Soaps
  A. Natural *soaps* are made by the saponification (basic hydrolysis) of fats. The sodium or potassium salts of the released fatty acids have an ionic head group and a nonpolar or "oily" tail. The ionic end (*hydrophilic*) keeps it dissolved in water while the *hydrophobic* hydrocarbon tail helps disperse oils. The oil and water form an emulsion which cleans away the dirt and oil. Many liquid soaps and shampoos are potassium salts which produce a finer lather and are more soluble.
  B. Problems with natural soaps
    1. Acidic conditions--natural soaps are converted to insoluble fatty acids under acidic conditions that precipitate as "greasy scum."
    2. *"Hard" water*--"hard" water refers to the presence of calcium, magnesium, or iron ions that form insoluble salts with the fatty acid anions that precipitate as "bath tub ring."
  C. Synthetic *detergents* (syndets) have soluble calcium salts so that they are still effective in "hard" water. Today there is great emphasis on detergents that must also be *biodegradable* and not contribute to the *eutrophication* of our lakes and rivers.

20.6 Waxes
  A. A *wax* is an ester formed from a long-chain fatty acid and a long-chain monohydric alcohol.

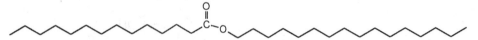

  B. Waxes serve as the protective coatings on fruits and are used in many cosmetics and ointments.
    1. Beeswax is a by-product of honey production.
    2. Spermaceti is obtained from the oil taken from the head of the sperm whale.
    3. Lanolin is a wax from sheep's wool. It is a mixture of esters and polyesters.

20.7 Phospholipids and Glycolipids
  A. *Phosphatides*: lipid esters of glycerol containing two fatty acid groups + one phosphoric acid residue + one amino alcohol. Phospholipids are a major component of cell *membranes*.
    1. *Cephalins* are phosphatides containing *ethanolamine*. They are found in brain and nerve tissue.
    2. *Lecithins* are phosphatides containing *choline*. Lecithins are found in brain and nerve tissue and are widely used in foods as emulsifying agents. Lecithin is plentiful in egg yolk and is a common emulsifying agent in foods.

cephalins   lecithins

  B. *Sphingolipids*: Sphingolipids are based on the unsaturated amino alcohol, sphingosine, rather than glycerol. The sphingosine molecule contributes one fatty acid-like group and binds a second in an amide linkage. Sphingomyelin is an important constituent of the myelin sheath that surrounds the axis of a nerve cell.

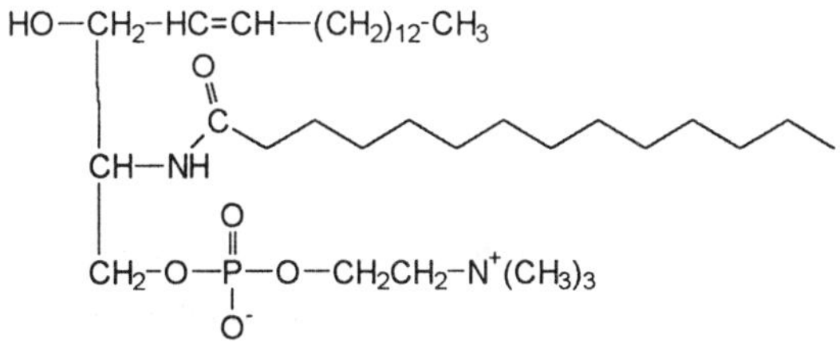

$$HO-CH_2-HC=CH-(CH_2)_{12}-CH_3$$

Sphingomyelin

C. Glycolipids

1. *Glycolipids* are distinguished by the presence of a sugar unit, but no phosphoric acid unit.

2. Glycolipids composed of galactose, a fatty acid, and sphingosine are called *cerebrosides*. They are important constituents of the membranes of nerve and brain cells. Gaucher's disease results from the substitution of glucose for galactose in these glycolipids.

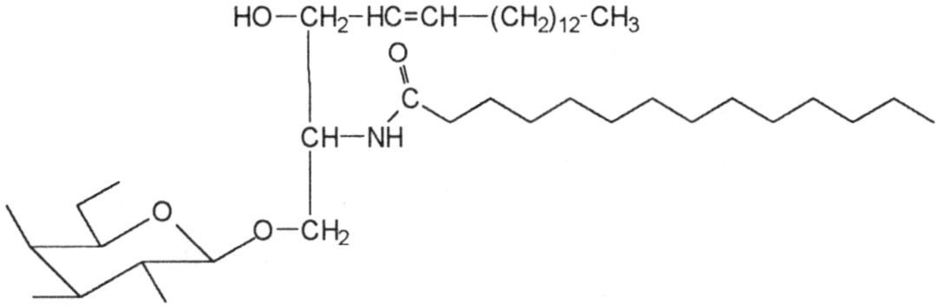

$$HO-CH_2-HC=CH-(CH_2)_{12}-CH_3$$

3. Gangliosides are similar to cerebrosides but contain more complex oligosaccharide in place of galactose.

20.8 Cell Membranes

A. Polar lipids form *micelles*, monolayers, and bilayers. The *bilayers* have the polar head groups interacting with the polar aqueous media and have the nonpolar hydrophobic tails of the fatty acids interacting with each other on the inside (see figure of membrane below).

B. Major lipid classes present in cell membranes are phospholipids, glycolipids and cholesterol.

C. Cell *membranes* are phospholipid bilayers but also contain several proteins. *Peripheral* proteins are associated with the inside or the outside of the lipid bilayer, while *integral* proteins completely penetrate the cell membrane. In the *"fluid mosaic"* model of cell membranes, the proteins are viewed as moving in a sea of lipid.

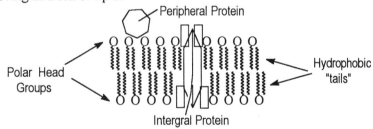

D. Cell membranes are *semipermeable*, allowing only certain materials to pass across the membranes. Many proteins in the membrane are receptors and involved in the active transport of materials into the cell.

1. If the direction of transport is dictated by a favorable concentration gradient, this is called *"facilitated diffusion."*

2. If the movement takes place against a concentration gradient, this requires energy and is called *"active transport."*

20.9 Steroids: Cholesterol and Bile Salts

A. *Steroids* are a group of *nonsaponifiable* lipids that include the bile salts, cholesterol and the sex hormones. All steroids share a common structural unit - four fused rings (three 6-membered + one 5-membered rings; see below).

B. *Cholesterol*, a steroidal alcohol, is the most abundant steroid. It is a common component of animal cell membranes and represents about 10% of the brain, but does not occur in plants. Cholesterol is the precursor of cholic acid and come hormones and vitamins.

cholesterol

C. *Bile salts* are emulsifying agents released from the gall bladder into the digestive tract to aid in the digestion of fats. They are derived from the steroid, cholic acid. About 500 mL of yellowish-green bile liquid is secreted each day by the gall bladder. *Gallstones* are solid, precipitates of cholesterol.

20.10 Cholesterol and Cardiovascular Disease

A. Animal food products (meat, eggs, cheese, etc.) are normally high in cholesterol. A single egg contains about 200 mg of cholesterol.

B. The liver will reduce its production of cholesterol if dietary cholesterol is high, but individuals with diets high in cholesterol tend to have elevated cholesterol levels in the blood. Lower cholesterol levels appear to reduce the risk of coronary heart disease.

C. Cholesterol and other lipids form complexes with water-soluble proteins and are transported as lipoproteins. Lipoproteins are classified according to their density and composition. High levels of LDLs (low density lipoproteins) which are rich in cholesterol have been associated with increased heart disease.

Lipoprotein	Density	% Protein	% Triglyceride	% Cholesterol (free)	(ester)	% Phospholipid
Chylomicrons	<0.94	1-2	85-95	1-3	2-4	3-6
VLDL	0.94-1.006	6-10	50-65	4-8	16-22	15-20
LDL	1.006-1.0063	18-22	4-8	6-8	45-50	18-24
HDL	1.0063-1.21	45-55	2-7	3-5	15-20	26-32

D. *Heart attacks* occur when a coronary artery is blocked. The cells deprived of nutrients soon die. A *stroke* occurs when a clot or a plaque deposit obstructs and artery supplying the brain.

DISCUSSION

The CHAPTER SUMMARY provides you with the structures of all the saponifiable lipids discussed in Chapter 20. The compounds have been drawn without hydrogens to emphasize similarities in the structures and to make it easier to compare the structures. You should be able to draw from memory a typical triglyceride structure. You should be able to recognize the others. That's not as hard as it sounds, particularly if you have a good grasp of the triglyceride structure. After all--if you know "glyco" comes from glycose, which means sugar, then identifying a glycolipid should be a snap because we've just spent some time looking at sugars in Chapter 19. Identifying a phospholipid should be even easier. Look for phosphorus. The same can be said of sphingosine-based lipids. If you know what the glycerol unit in a triglyceride looks like, then the sphingosine unit in sphingosine-based lipids is obviously different and identifiable.

Note that phospholipid is a more general term than phosphatide. All phosphatides are phospholipids, but not all phospholipids are phosphatides. The phosphatides are those compounds which contain both phosphorus and the glycerol unit. Names like lecithin and cerebroside give no hint of the corresponding structure (in contrast to designations like phospholipid or glycolipid). Therefore, associating these names with structural features involves some straight memorization. For example, if you want to be able to recognize a cerebroside, you'll have to mentally translate that to "a sphingosine-based glycolipid" and then look for a sphingosine unit and a sugar unit.

The nonsaponifiable steroids are very easy to recognize because of their characteristic fused-ring structure. Actually writing out the structure frequently impresses it much more firmly on one's mind, and we advise you to do this. Why all this talk about structure? Because as we begin discussing bigger and more complicated molecules, the very appearance of those molecules gets in our way. When such a structure appears on a page, a message seems to travel from eye to brain and says, "WARNING...COMPLICATED STRUCTURE...YOU'LL NEVER UNDERSTAND WHAT THEY'RE TALKING ABOUT!" By spending the time to familiarize ourselves with the structures we are shutting off (or at least turning down) that alarm system.

It isn't important that you be able to draw out perfectly the structure of a phospholipid. But you should be able to recognize a significant difference between the phospholipid and a triglyceride. One incorporates an ionized group, the other doesn't. Is that important? Well, one (the triglyceride) is actually stored in the body as droplets of fat within special cells (that's what adipose tissue or "fat" is). The other, because it has a polar end (the ionized group) and long, nonpolar hydrocarbon chains, can organize its molecules into bilayers and is the structural material of membranes. You can see what very different roles these molecules play in the body because of their structure. Be sure to go through the problems at the end of the chapter in the text before attempting the **SELF-TEST**.

SELF-TEST

1. Which of these compounds would <u>not</u> be classified as a lipid?
       a. prostaglandins   b. steroids   c. triglycerides   d. glycolipids   e. glycogen
2. Which is a <u>not</u> a major role of lipids?
       a. membranes   b. vitamins   c. enzymes   d. hormones   e. energy storage
3. Animal fats and vegetable oils are natural:
       a. polymers   b. soaps   c. esters   d. hydrocarbons   e. carboxylic acids
4. The body's principal energy reserves are in the form of:
       a. alcohol   b. carbohydrates   c. enzymes   d. fats   e. proteins
5. The double bond in an unsaturated fatty acid causes a bend in the hydrocarbon chain. Because of this, these compounds _____ compared to saturated fatty acids:
       a. experience weaker intermolecular attractive forces
       b. have higher melting points
       c. do not react with glycerol
6. Mixed triglycerides contain:
       a. at least two different fatty acid units
       b. a phosphate unit and fatty acid units
       c. choline and ethanolamine

7. Oils typically have a greater percentage of _____ fatty acids.
    a. saturated   b. unsaturated   c. steroidal

8. In general, a vegetable triglyceride would <u>not</u> be hydrogenated to produce:
    a. margarine   b. shortening   c. cooking oil

9. The iodine number of a sample of a butter is 27; the iodine number of three samples of margarine are 72-(I), 80-(II), and 92-(III). Which sample is the more highly unsaturated fat?
    a. butter   b. margarine I   c. margarine II   d. margarine III

10. Hydrogenation of arachidonic acid yields:
    a. lauric acid   b. linoleic acid   c. linolenic acid   d. stearic acid   e. none of these

11. When butter turns rancid, which chemical reaction is <u>not</u> involved?
    a. hydrogenation   b. hydrolysis   c. oxidation

12. Basic hydrolysis of a triglyceride is called:
    a. esterification   b. hydrogenation   c. polymerization   d. saponification

13. Sodium salts of long-chain fatty acids are called:
    a. lecithins   b. soaps   c. micelles   d. synthetic detergents

14. Complete saponification of a fat yields:
    a. salts of fatty acids and glycerol
    b. salts of fatty acids and a glyceride
    c. fatty acids and glycerol
    d. fatty acids and a glyceride

15. Modern synthetic detergents are <u>not</u>:
    a. biodegradable   b. soluble in hard water   c. soaps

16. Saponification refers to the reaction of lipids with:
    a. an enzyme   b. hydrogen   c. phosphate   d. sodium hydroxide

17. A wax is:
    a. a solid fat
    b. any solid lipid
    c. the ester of a long-chain fatty acid and a long-chain alcohol

18. Which is a wax according to the chemical definition of that term?
    a. carbowax   b. carnauba wax   c. paraffin wax

19. Spermaceti is a wax obtained from:
    a. honeycombs   b. palm leaves   c. whales

20. Which compound would <u>not</u> be expected to exhibit detergent action?
    a. $CH_3CH_2CH_2CH_2CH_2CH_2CH_2CH_2CH_2CH_2CH_2CH_2CH_2CH_2CH_2COO^-Na^+$
    b. $CH_3CH_2CH_2CH_2CH_2CH_2CH_2CH_2CH_2CH_2CH_2CH_2CH_2CH_2CH_2COOH$
    c. $CH_3CH_2CH_2CH_2CH_2CH_2CH_2CH_2CH_2CH_2CH_2CH_2CH_2CH_2CH_2OSO_3^-Na^+$

21. Which fatty acid salt is soluble in water solutions?
    a. $RCOO^-K^+$ b. $(RCOO^-)_2Mg^{2+}$ c. $(RCOO-)_2Ca^{2+}$ d. none are soluble

22. Phosphatides are <u>not</u>:
    a. amine-containing lipids   b. glycerol-based lipids   c. sphingosine-based lipids

23. Which of the lipids does <u>not</u> incorporate glycerol as part of its structure?
    a. cephalins   b. lecithins   c. sphingomyelins

24. One distinguishes between a cephalin and a lecithin on the basis of:
    a. the amino alcohol unit incorporated in the molecule
    b. the presence or absence of a phosphate group
    c. the presence or absence of a sugar unit

25. The amino alcohol incorporated in the compound below is called _____ .

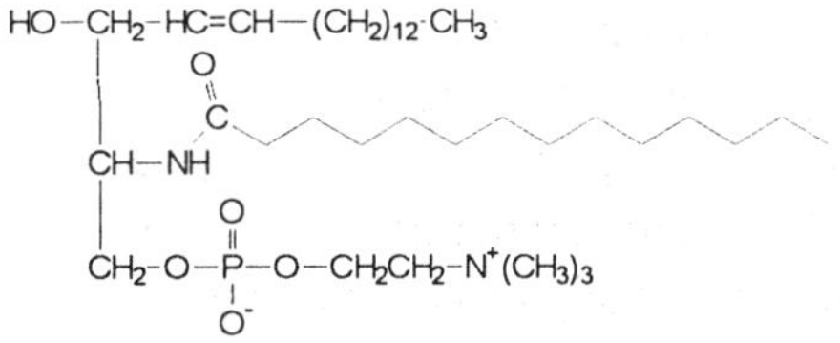

HO−CH$_2$−HC=CH−(CH$_2$)$_{12}$ CH$_3$
CH−NH
CH$_2$−O−P−O−CH$_2$CH$_2$−N$^+$(CH$_3$)$_3$

   a. lecithin   b. cephalin   c. cerebroside   d. sphingosine   e. cholesterol

26. Sphingomyelins are lipids based on sphingosine rather than glycerol. In all other respects sphingomyelins resemble:
   a. glycosides   b. phosphatides   c. triglycerides

27. The process by which materials are moved across cell membranes with an energy input is called:
   a. passive transport   b. active transport   c. facilitated diffusion

28. Proteins that span the lipid bilayer of the cell membrane are called _____.
   a. long proteins   b. integral proteins   c. peripheral proteins   d. conjugated proteins

29. A phospholipid that is abundant in egg yolk is _____.
   a. lecithin   b. cephalin   c. cerebroside   d. sphingosine   e. cholesterol

30. The bile salts are not:
   a. fatty acids   b. emulsifying agents   c. steroids

31. This compound is:

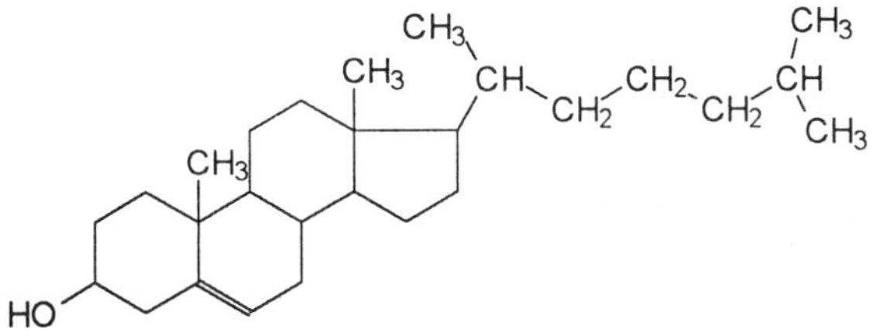

   a. cholesterol   b. prostaglandin   c. a steroid

32. Cholesterol is not:
   a. an alcohol   b. a lipid   c. saponifiable   d. a steroid

33. The prostaglandins are derivatives of:
   a. cholesterol   b. a saturated fatty acid   c. glycerol   d. arachidonic acid

34. In their physiological action, the prostaglandins resemble:
   a. carbohydrates   b. cholesterol   c. enzymes   d. hormones

35. Which special arrangement of polar lipids comes closest to the structure of cell membranes?
   a. bilayers   b. micelles   c. monolayers

   Answer questions 36 through 40 by referring to the following structure.

CH$_2$-O-C-CH$_2$CH$_2$CH$_2$CH$_2$CH$_2$CH$_2$CH$_2$CH$_2$CH$_2$CH$_2$CH$_2$CH$_2$CH$_2$CH$_2$CH$_2$CH$_3$
CH--O-C-CH$_2$CH$_2$CH$_2$CH$_2$CH$_2$CH$_2$CH$_2$CH=CHCH$_2$CH=CHCH$_2$CH=CHCH$_2$CH$_3$
CH$_2$-O-C-CH$_2$CH$_2$CH$_2$CH$_2$CH$_2$CH$_2$CH$_2$CH=CHCH$_2$CH=CHCH$_2$CH=CHCH$_2$CH$_3$

36. The compound is a:
   a. glyceride   b. phosphatide   c. sphingolipid   d. steroid

37. Hydrolysis of the compound would not yield:
   a. choline   b. glycerol   c. stearic acid

38. A high proportion of this type of lipid is found in:

a. animal fats   b. cell membranes   c. vegetable oils
39. Compared to a similar but saturated fat, this compound will turn rancid:
        a. more rapidly   b. less rapidly
40. If a galactose unit were substituted for the third fatty acid unit, the compound would be a:
        a. cephalin   b. cerebroside   c. glycolipid

ANSWERS

1.	e	11.	a	21.	a	31.	a
2.	c	12.	d	22.	c	32.	c
3.	c	13.	b	23.	c	33.	d
4.	d	14.	a	24.	a	34.	d
5.	a	15.	c	25.	d	35.	a
6.	a	16.	d	26.	b	36.	a
7.	b	17.	c	27.	b	37.	a
8.	c	18.	b	28.	b	38.	c
9.	d	19.	c	29.	a	39.	a
10.	e	20.	b	30.	a	40.	c

Special Topic I: Hormones

KEY WORDS

hormone	*pituitary*	*steroidal*	*ductless glands*	*endocrine*
receptor site	*androgen*	*aldosterone*	*hypothalamus*	*cortisone*
estrogen	*progesterone*	*inflammation*	*testosterone*	*estradiol*

SUMMARY

I.1   The Endocrine System

  A. ***Hormones*** are organic compounds that serve as chemical messengers. They are synthesized by the ***ductless glands*** of the ***endocrine*** system and are transported by the circulatory system to other parts of the body where they bring about marked physiological changes. Most hormones are either steroids or peptide-like compounds.

  B. The messenger system

  1. A nerve impulse signals the ***hypothalamus*** to secrete releasing factors.

  2. The releasing factors stimulate the ***pituitary*** to secrete pituitary hormones.

  3. The pituitary hormone travels to some target endocrine gland and causes it to secrete its hormones.

  4. The released hormones bind at receptor sites on their target tissue, and the tissue responds with altered metabolism. This whole messenger system is usually regulated by some sort of feedback or servo mechanism.

  C. Refer to Table I.1 in the text for a list of human hormones and their physiological effects.

I.2   Adrenocortical Hormone

  A. ***Aldosterone*** is called a ***mineralocorticoid*** and is involved in regulating the exchange of Na+, K+, and H+.

  B. ***Cortisone*** is a steroidal hormone involved in carbohydrate metabolism and is a ***glucocorticoid***. These hormones increase glucose production and mobilize fatty acids. Cortisone and cortisol were once used widely in medicine to reduce ***inflammation*** and to treat arthritis, but today they have been largely replaced by a synthetic analogue, prednisolone.

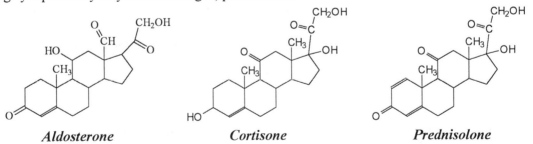

Aldosterone   *Cortisone*   *Prednisolone*

I.3   Sex Hormones and Anabolic Steroids

  A. The sex hormones are also ***steroidal*** hormones. They are responsible for stimulating and maintaining sexual characteristics.

  B. ***Androgens*** are male sex hormones, such as ***testosterone***, which are secreted by the testes.

  C. ***Estrogens*** are female sex hormones, such as ***estradiol***, secreted by the ovaries. ***Progesterone*** prepares the uterus for pregnancy and prevents the further release of eggs from the ovaries.

  D. Anabolic steroids are usually derivatives of testosterone. Dianabol will increase muscle bulk and strength, but there are serious health hazards with its use.

Testosterone   *Estradiol*   *Progesterone*

E. Progesterone serves as an effective birth control drug when injected. Oral birth control pills usually combine an estrogen with a progestin (a synthetic mimic of the hormone progesterone). The estrogen regulates the menstrual cycle while the progestin signals a state of false pregnancy so ovulation does not occur.

I.4 Conception and Contraceptives
   A. The menstrual cycle.
      1. FSH (follicle-stimulating hormone) is released by the pituitary.
      2. FSH causes the follicle to secrete estrogen hormones that prepares the uterus for the fertilized eggs.
      3. As levels of estrogen increase, the levels of FSH decrease. LH (luteinizing hormone) is now released by the pituitary and brings about ovulation.
      4. A third hormone (LTH or luteotrophic hormone) secreted by the pituitary, influences the development of tissue called the corpus lumen.
      5. If the egg is not fertilized the corpus lumen disintegrates and, with the blood vessels that rupture, forms the menstrual discharge.
   B. The "pill" is a mixture of two synthetic analogues of female hormones to deceive the body into thinking it is pregnant (false pregnancy).
   C. Mifepristone is a "morning after" pill that blocks the action of progesterone which is essential for maintenance of pregnancy.
   D. Danazol is a male contraceptive, but most male contraception is by a surgical procedure to block sperm emission - the vasectomy.

I.5 Estrogen Replacement Therapy
   A. Menopause usually occurs in the late forties as ovulation no longer occurs, estrogen levels drop, and menstrual cycles cease.
   B. Side effects of menopause such as irritability, "hot flashes" anxiety and fatigue can be overcome by daily doses of estrogens. Such therapy may also significantly reduce the risk of heart attacks and coronary disease.

I.6 Prostaglandins
   A. *Prostaglandins* are hormone-like substances synthesized from a 20-carbon, polyunsaturated fatty acid called arachidonic acid.

Prostaglandin E$_2$

B. The prostaglandin family of compounds are among the most potent body regulators. They all induce smooth muscle contraction, lower blood pressure, and contribute to the inflammatory response. Aspirin obstructs the synthesis of prostaglandins from arachidonic acid by inhibiting the enzyme cyclooxygenase which processes arachidonic acid.

C. One clinical use of prostaglandins has been to cause uterine contractions to induce abortion.

DISCUSSION

Hormones are like vitamins in that they are relatively small organic compounds that are needed in small amounts. However, unlike the vitamins, hormones can be synthesized in the body by the endocrine glands. Also, rather than functioning as enzyme "helpers" or coenzymes, the hormones are "chemical messengers" that help regulate our body's metabolism. The hormones also vary considerably in structure, but those listed in Table I.1 are either proteins, amino acid derivatives, or steroids. Perhaps the most notable feature of the sex hormones discussed in this unit is the extraordinary similarity of compounds that elicit such distinctive responses in our bodies.

SELF-TEST

1. Hormones function as:
   a. chemical messengers   b. coenzymes   c. provitamins
2. Hormones are synthesized by the _____.
   a. stomach   b. rod cells   c. cone cells   d. ductless glands of the endocrine system
3. Which gland is responsible for the production of releasing factors that trigger the pituitary gland?
   a. adrenal cortex   b. hypophysis   c. hypothalamus
4. Which of these hormones plays a major role in regulating the exchange of K^+?
   a. testosterone   b. estrogen   c. prostaglandin E2   d. progesterone   e. aldosterone
5. Which are male sex hormones?
   a. androgens   b. estrogens   c. progestins
6. Which component of the typical birth control pill is responsible for regulating the menstrual cycle?
   a. androgen   b. estrogen   c. progestin
7. Which compound is used in the synthesis of prostaglandins?
   a. cortisone   b. estrogen   c. arachidonic acid   d. aspirin
8. T F Cortisone is a vitamin that exhibits anti-inflammatory properties.
9. T F All hormones are steroids synthesized in trace amounts by the endocrine glands.
10. T F Hormones are secreted by endocrine glands located in the target organs.
11. T F Male sex hormones have been used to treat breast cancer in women.
12. T F The presence of estrogen in contraceptive pills is thought to be responsible for most of the undesirable side effects of these pills.

ANSWERS

1. a	4. e	7. c	10. F
2. d	5. a	8. F	11. T
3. c	6. b	9. F	12. T

CHAPTER 21: PROTEINS

KEY WORDS

L-α-amino acid	globular	protein	prosthetic group	zwitterion
isoelectric pH	primary structure	salt bridge	"R" group	polypeptide
electrophoresis	secondary structure	disulfide	side chain	peptide bond
α-helix	tertiary structure	hydrophobic	N-terminal	C-terminal
β-sheet	quarternary	a.a. sequence	denaturation	dipeptide
tripeptide	fibrous	silk	wool	collagen
residues	hydrogen bonds	gelatins	net charge	

SUMMARY

21.1 Amino Acids

A. **Proteins** are essential for all cells and function in body building and maintenance. Proteins are copolymers composed from about 20 different amino acids.

B. The common amino acids differ from one another only in the size and nature of the **"R" group** or amino acid **"side chain"** attached to the alpha carbon. NOTE: Some of the amino acids could fit more than one of the groups listed below. See Table 21.1 in the text for structures and abbreviations.

	"R" - type	**Amino acids**
	hydrogen	Gly
	hydrocarbon	Ala, Val, Leu, Ile, Pro
$H_2N-C^\alpha H-COOH$	alcohol containing	Ser, Thr
$\mid$	sulfur containing	Met, Cys
R	aromatic	Phe, Tyr, Trp
	basic	Lys, Arg, His
	acidic	Asp, Glu
	amide	Asn, Gln

C. Amino acids could also be classified by polarity (nonpolar, polar-neutral, polar-acidic, polar-basic) or size of the **R**-group.

D. The functional variety of the "R" groups permits various types of side chain interactions, such as hydrogen bonding, salt bridges, disulfide bond formation, and hydrophobic interactions.

21.2 General Properties of Amino Acids

A. Most of these monomers are **L-α-amino acids**, indicating that the carboxyl and amino groups are both on the same carbon and that they all have the same L-configuration about that carbon.

 1. Glycine is an exception, having two hydrogens on its α-carbon, so it does not have L- and D-forms.

 2. Proline is also unusual in that it is a secondary amine, whereas all of the others are primary amines.

B. Amino acids are solids at room temperature and form internal salts called **zwitterions**. This ionic species is also the dominant form in solution at neutral pH conditions.

$$H_3N^+-\overset{\overset{\displaystyle H}{|}}{\underset{\underset{\displaystyle R}{|}}{C}}*-\overset{\overset{\displaystyle O}{\diagup\!\!\!\diagup}}{\underset{\underset{\displaystyle O^-}{\diagdown}}{C}}$$

(*The central carbon attached "alpha" to the carboxylate group is called the alpha carbon or C^α).

21.3 Reactions of Amino Acids

A. Acid-Base Properties

1. Amino acids can act either as weak acids or weak bases and thus make good buffers in living systems.

2. Charge behavior - all amino acids have at least two titratable groups. Some have additional titratable groups in their side chains. At low pH (<2) when these groups are all in their conjugate acid forms, all amino acids are positively charged owing to the protonated amino group. At high pH (>12) all amino acids are negatively charged owing to the presence of the carboxylate ion. The net charge on any given amino acid varies with pH from (+) at low pH to (-) at high pH.

3. The *isoelectric* pH is that pH at which the *net charge* on the molecule is zero.

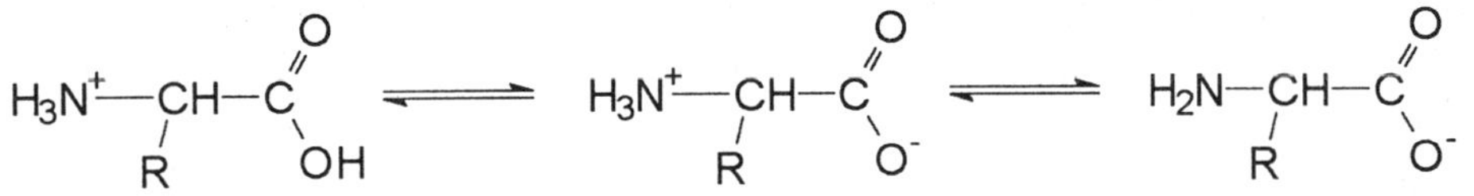

Low pH (+ charge)   pH = pI (no net charge)   High pH (− charge)

4. Amino acids and proteins can be separated on the basis of relative mobilities in an electric field. This process is called *electrophoresis*.

B. Amino acids also undergo other reactions typical of carboxylic acids and amines. The most important such reaction is the polymerization reaction through peptide bond formation.

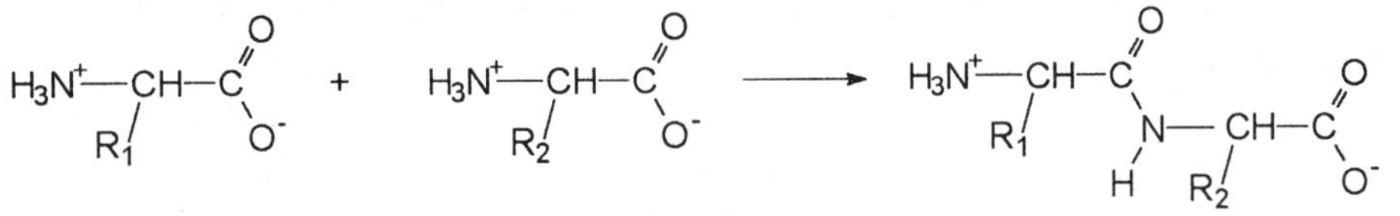

21.4 The Peptide Bond

A. The *peptide bond* is a special name given to the amide linkage joining amino acid *residues*.

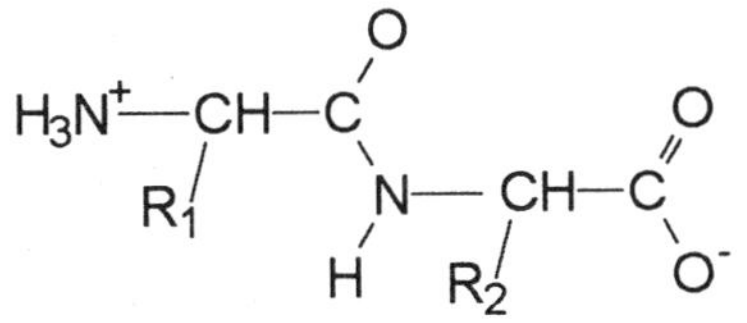

The nitrogen in the peptide bond is not basic owing to delocalization of its unshared pair of electrons. This gives the C-N bond partial double bond character and constrains the atoms of the peptide bond to be planar.

B. *Dipeptides* have two amino acid residues linked by one peptide bond; *tripeptides* have three amino acid residues, tetrapeptides have four, etc.

C. Peptides have an *N-terminal* (or free amino) end and a *C-terminal* (carboxyl) end and are named starting from the N-terminal end according to the sequence of amino acid residues present. Amino acid residues are named by dropping the "-ine" ending of the amino acid and adding "-yl."

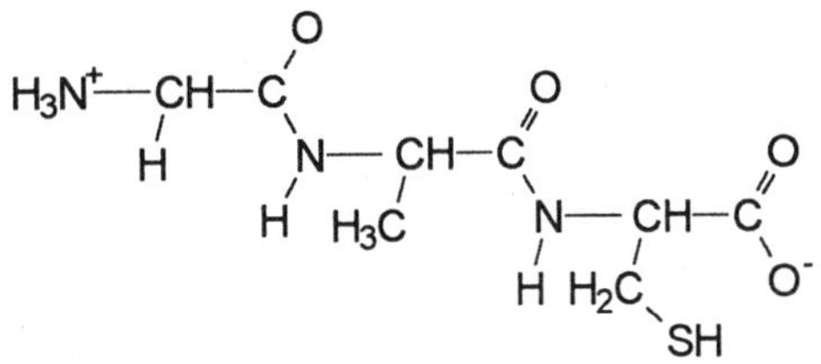

glycyl alanyl cysteine = **Gly-Ala-Cys** = **G-A-C** (one letter codes)

D. *Proteins* are linear polymers of hundreds of amino acids linked by peptide bonds, *polypeptides* are proteins.

21.5 The Sequence of Amino Acids

A. Each protein is a highly specific polymer with usually just one biological function. It is crucial that the amino acids of each protein be present in the proper order (*amino acid sequence* or *primary (1⁰) structure*) for the protein to function correctly. Often, a given protein, whether isolated from horse, human, or yeast, will have a very similar amino acid sequence.

B. By convention, amino acid sequences are read from the N-terminal end of the polypeptide. This is important because Gly-Ala-Asp (GAD) is just as different from Asp-Ala-Gly (DAG) as the word "dog" is from "god."

C. Living systems make (and need) from 10-100 thousand different proteins from the same small set of amino acid monomers. Each polypeptide or *protein* can be likened to a different "word" made from the same set of 20 "letters" in this alphabet. Because proteins are so vital to living systems, the amino acids have been called "the alphabet of life." (Note: Protein "words" are very long, often 100 to 500 amino acids)

H_3N^+- ACGGDKLVIMTWAEVLMLHALLSTAGCLHKHKPSLIVHLVAPRDVALIMCS-COO⁻
(1⁰ structure of a small protein consisting of 51 amino acid residues using the one letter codes for a.a.)

D. We will see later that the sequence of amino acids is dictated by the DNA sequence. By the spring of 1996, the entire yeast genome (~ 13,000,000 bases) had been sequenced.

21.6 Some Peptides of Interest

A. Amino acids play important physiological roles in addition to being the building blocks for proteins. Many small peptides are hormones (oxytocin) or neurotransmitters (γ-aminobutyric acid).

B. Some peptides of physiological importance follow:

1. Vasopressin and oxytocin are cyclic nonapeptide pituitary hormones. With only 2 out of 9 amino acids different, these two hormones produce some similar but yet other very different effects.

Phe-Tyr-Cys | S-S | Gln-Asn-Cys-Pro-Arg-Gly **Vasopressin**

Ile-Tyr-Cys | S-S | Gln-Asn-Cys-Pro-Leu-Gly **Oxytocin**

2. Bradykinin is a nonapeptide that has properties similar to the prostaglandins.

3. Angiotensin II is an octapeptide (Asp-Arg-Val-Tyr-Ile-His-Pro-Phe) produced in the kidneys. It is a powerful vasoconstrictor important to the control of hypertension.

4. Met-enkephalin (Tyr-Gly-Gly-Phe-Met), a pentapeptide produced by the brain, acts as a potent pain killer, a brain "opiate."

5. Glutathione (γ–glutamyl cysteinyl glycine) is a tripeptide that is involved in thiol/disulfide interchange in the cell.

21.7 Classification of Proteins

A. Proteins are unique polymers in that each type of protein molecule has a definite composition and amino acid sequence (1⁰ structure).

B. Proteins can be classified on the basis of solubility or function.

1. *Fibrous* proteins are insoluble in water. They usually perform structural, connective, or protective functions. Examples are collagen, myosin, and elastin.

2. *Globular* (~spherical) proteins are usually soluble in aqueous media. Examples are the albumins, globulins, and nearly all enzymes (Chapter 22).

21.8 Structure of Proteins
A. For a protein molecule to function properly, it must also have the correct three-dimensional structure.
B. The structures of proteins can be described in terms of 4 levels.
1. *Primary structure*   - linear sequence of amino acids linked by peptide bonds.
2. *Secondary structure*   - a local, fixed arrangement of the polypeptide chain usually stabilized by hydrogen bonds; *α-helix* and *β-sheet*.
3. *Tertiary structure*   - the three-dimensional structure of how a protein chain is folded in space.
4. *Quaternary structure* - the arrangement of subunits in a multisubunit protein.

Met-Ala-Arg-Val-

-Ile-Asn-His-Ala-

-Cys-Lys-Glu-

-Arg-Thr

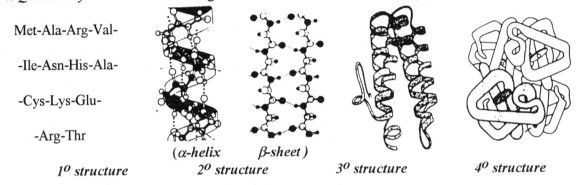

(*α-helix*   *β-sheet*)

1⁰ structure   *2⁰ structure*   *3⁰ structure*   *4⁰ structure*

21.9 Secondary Structure of Proteins
A. X-ray studies by Linus Pauling and others led to the discovery of the α-helix and β-sheet. These secondary structures are stabilized by intrachain hydrogen bonds.
B. The physical properties of wool and silk reflect their secondary structures.
1. *Wool* is a natural protein fiber. The structure of wool is that of a right-handed *α-helix*. Segments of this structure are also found in many globular proteins. There are 3.6 amino acid residues per turn of an α-helix. The helix coil is stabilized by intrasubunit hydrogen bonds from the carbonyl oxygen of one residue to the -N-H of another residue in the next turn. The helical structure permits wool to stretch like the coils of a spring.
2. *Silk* is a protein fiber (fibrion) produced by silkworms. It is composed mostly of glycine (45%), alanine (30%), serine (12%), and few other amino acids (13%). Over much of the amino acid sequence, every other amino acid residue is a glycine (-Gly-Ser-Gly-Ala-Gly-Ala-Gly- etc.). The structure of silk is found to be a *β-pleated sheet* arrangement, in which the polypeptide chains are nearly fully extended and hydrogen bonded to one another. This gives silk its great strength, flexibility, and resistance to stretching.

21.10 Tertiary Structure of Proteins
A. Many proteins have nearly spherical shapes with nonpolar (hydrophobic) residues on the inside and polar residues on the surface ("oil drop model").

B. Intramolecular forces stabilizing the tertiary structure of proteins:
    1. *Hydrogen bonds*   2. *Salt bridges*   3. *Disulfide linkages*   4. *Hydrophobic interactions*

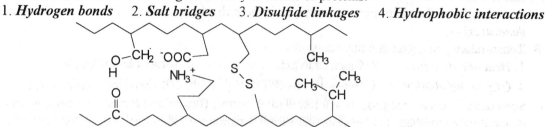

       (1)   (2)   (3)   (4)

C. Hydrogen bonds are highly directional, giving rise to ordered secondary and tertiary structures.
D. Disulfide bonds are strong, covalent bonds. Disulfide bonds are rare in intracellular proteins but more common in extracellular proteins (proteases, antibodies, etc.).
E. Hair is protein and the disulfide linkages in human hair can be broken (reduced) and reformed (oxidized) to produce a "permanent wave."

21.11 Quaternary Structure of Proteins
  A. Quarternary structure describes the arrangement of subunits and thus is only present in oligomeric proteins. Quarternary structure is stabilized by the same set of interactions that maintain tertiary structure.
  B. Myoglobin / Hemoglobin
    1. Globular proteins have nearly spherical three-dimensional structures, which makes them water soluble as colloidal dispersions.
    2. Myoglobin is a well-studied example of a globular protein. It is a heme protein that serves to store oxygen in muscle tissue. The heme group is called a *prosthetic group*. It has 153 amino acid residues that form eight helical segments, which pack together to produce a nearly spherical molecule. Hemoglobin consists of four globin chains ($\alpha_2\beta_2$), each with an iron containing heme group. John Kendrew and Max Perutz shared the Nobel Prize in 1962 for their studies that led to the elucidation of the three-dimensional structure of myoglobin and hemoglobin.
  C. Collagen: The Protein of Connective Tissues
    1. *Collagen* is the principal protein of connective tissue. As much as 60% of all mammalian protein is collagen, which is found in skin, bones, tendons, and teeth.
    2. Collagen is not readily digestible but can be converted to digestible *gelatins* by boiling in water.
    3. Collagen is rich in the amino acids glycine, proline, and hydroxyproline.
    4. Collagen consists of 3 protein chains wound in a triple helix with glycines packed on the inside of the helix. The chains are held by hydrogen bonds, dispersion forces, and covalent cross-links.

21.12 Electrochemical Properties of Proteins
  A. Polypeptide chains usually carry a variety of positive and negative charges resulting from the ionization properties of certain amino acid side chains.
  B. The charge will vary with pH, but at pH 6, the following R groups contribute to the overall charge.
    1. (+) charge: His, Lys, Arg ("basic" amino acids)
    2. (−) charge: Glu, Asp ("acidic" amino acids)
  C. All proteins (and amino acids) carry a positive (+) charge at very low pH and a negative (−) charge at very high pH. Most proteins are least soluble at their isoelectric pH where the net charge is zero. Bacteria produce lactic acid during the spoilage of milk, lowering the pH of milk from 6.6 to about 4.6, near the isoelectric pH of casein which proceeds to separate from milk as white curds.

21.13 Denaturation of Proteins

A. The tertiary structure of protein molecules is stabilized by a great many weak forces. It is possible to modify a protein molecule so it no longer folds or functions properly; this process is called ***denaturation***.

B. Denaturation can occur in many ways:

1. Heat
2. Changes in pH
3. Ultraviolet radiation
4. Organic solvents
5. Heavy metals (Pb^{2+}, Hg^{2+})
6. Alkaloid reagents (tanning)

C. Sometimes, a denatured protein will refold to its correct (functional) tertiary structure when the denaturant is removed. This implies that the information needed to form the correct tertiary structure is implicit in the amino acid sequence.

DISCUSSION

As in the preceding two chapters, Chapter 21 concentrates on structure. The proteins are more comparable in structure to the carbohydrates than to the lipids. Like the polysaccharides, they are polymers. Unlike most polysaccharides, the proteins are copolymers--incorporating more than twenty different monomers, and the monomers are amino acids, not sugars. It is this increased structural complexity that permits proteins to play so many different roles in the body. We'll point out now what will become obvious as you familiarize yourself with these compounds. Except for glycine, all the amino acids can be considered as variations on the alanine structure, that is, each has a functional group attached at the side-chain methyl group of alanine. This fact should make them a bit easier to memorize. You should learn the structures of several representative amino acids. We recommend the following:

Nonpolar Side Chains | **Polar Side Chains** | **Ionizable Side Chains** (*Acidic*, *Basic*)

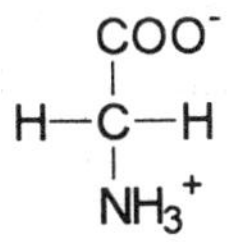

glycine

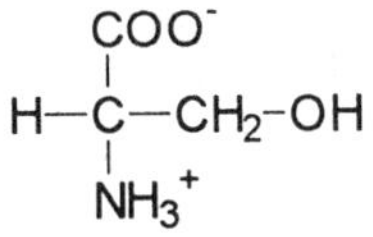

serine

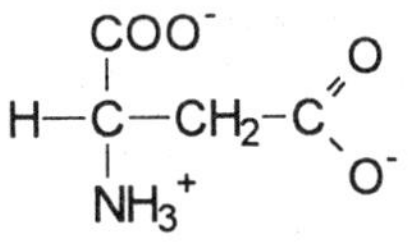

aspartic acid

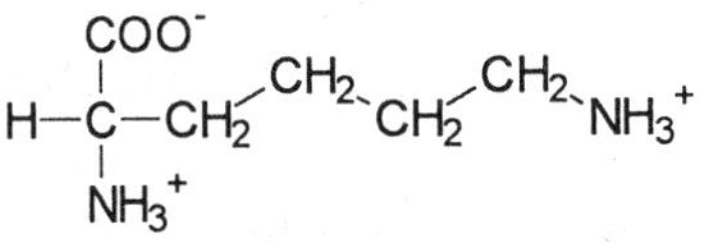

lysine

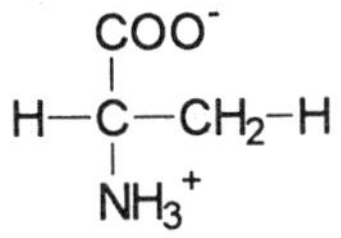

alanine

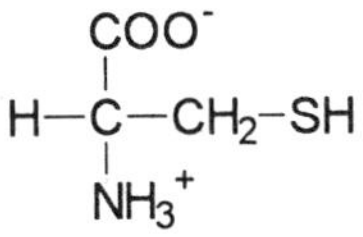

cysteine

(**cystine** is the disulfide formed from two cysteines)

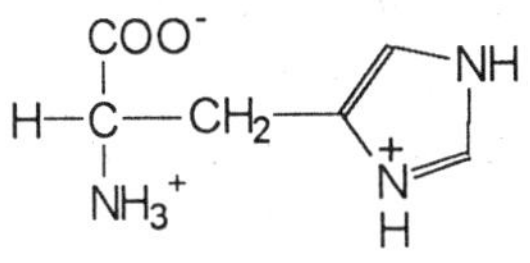

histidine

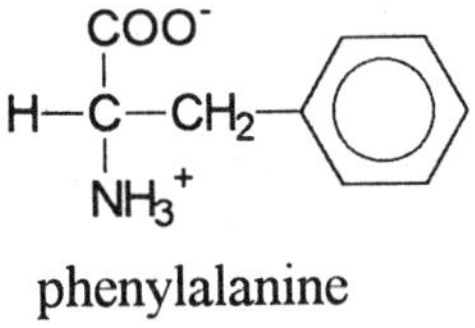

phenylalanine

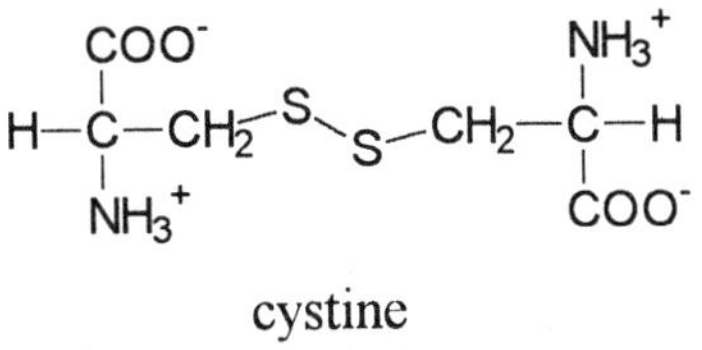

cystine

One aspect of the chemistry of amino acids and proteins that frequently causes confusion is the c.a. and c.b. forms of the compounds. In Section 21.4 in the text, the structures of a simple amino acid in acidic and basic solutions are given. Let's look at a slightly more complex situation in which the amino acid contains an acidic or basic side chain. Consider lysine and aspartic acid in a solution of low pH.

Remember-- low pH means acidic, and acidic means that lots of protons are around. If there are lots of protons available, then every group on the amino acid that can carry a proton does so.

Thus, at low pH aspartic acid and lysine look like this:

At low pH (< 2)	$CH_2\text{-}COOH$	$(CH_2)_4\text{-}N^+H_3$
	|	|
	$H_3N^+\text{-}CH\text{-}COOH$	$H_3N^+\text{-}CH\text{-}COOH$
Every ionizable group has a proton.	aspartic acid (+1)	lysine (+2)

At high pH the solution is basic and all available protons are plucked from the amino acids.

At high pH (> 12)	CH_2COO^-	$(CH_2)_4NH_2$
	|	|
	$H_2N\text{-}CH\text{-}COO^-$	$H_2N\text{-}CH\text{-}COO^-$
Every group has lost its proton.	aspartic acid (-2)	lysine (-1)

As the pH of a solution is changed from high to low, one after another of the ionizable groups picks up a proton. The strongest bases (those with amino groups) react first, then the carboxylate groups ($-COO^-$) react. In cases in which two similar groups are present, each picks up a proton at a characteristic pH. Without knowing the individual pK_a values, you would have no way of predicting which of the two similar groups reacts first, but we can show you the progressive change for our two model compounds, Asp and Lys.

Aspartic Acid

$$CH_2COOH \xrightarrow[H^+]{OH^-} CH_2COOH \xrightarrow[H^+]{OH^-} CH_2COO^- \xrightarrow[H^+]{OH^-} CH_2COO^-$$

CH_2COOH	CH_2COOH	CH_2COO^-	CH_2COO^-
|	|	|	|
$H_3N^+\text{-}CH\text{-}COOH$	$H_3N^+\text{-}CH\text{-}COO^-$	$H_3N^+\text{-}CH\text{-}COO^-$	$H_2N\text{-}CH\text{-}COO^-$
(+1)	(0)	(-1)	(-2)

Low pH   the zwitterion at the isoelectric point (pH 2.77)   *High pH*

Lysine

$(CH_2)_4N^+H_3$	$(CH_2)_4N^+H_3$	$(CH_2)_4N^+H_3$	$(CH_2)_4NH_2$
|	|	|	|
$H_3N^+CH\text{-}COOH$	$H_3N^+CH\text{-}COO^-$	$H_2N\text{-}CH\text{-}COO^-$	$H_2N\text{-}CH\text{-}COO^-$
(+2)	(+1)	(0)	(-1)

the zwitterion at the isoelectric point (pH 9.74)

The same principle applies to the chemistry of polypeptides and proteins.

PROBLEMS

The problems that follow are meant to supplement those in the text. They focus attention on the details of the molecular structure of simple peptides (and their constituent amino acids).

1. For the following structure pick out the peptide bond, a disulfide bond, and an ionizable side chain.

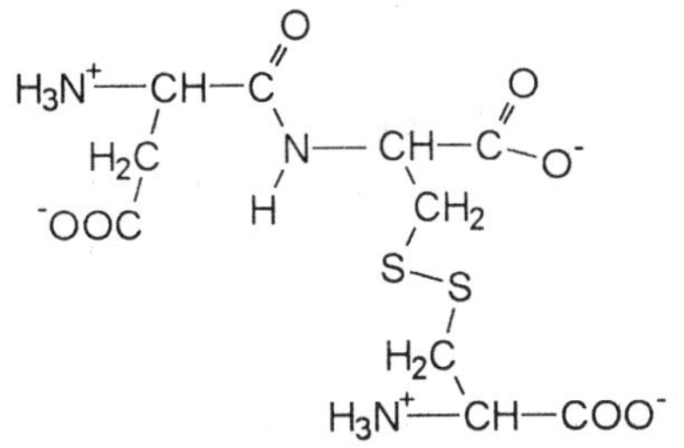

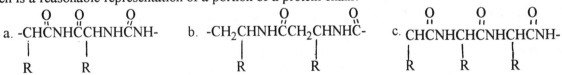

2. Draw the complete structural formulas of two different dipeptides that incorporate serine and cysteine.

3. Draw the products of complete hydrolysis of:

$$H_3N^+\text{-}CH\text{-}\overset{O}{\overset{\|}{C}}\text{-}NH\text{-}CH_2\text{-}\overset{O}{\overset{\|}{C}}\text{-}NH\text{-}CH\text{-}\overset{O}{\overset{\|}{C}}\text{-}O^-$$
$$\hspace{1.0cm}CH_3\hspace{3.0cm}CH_2OH$$

4. Draw the abbreviated formulas (e.g., Gly-Ala-Ser) for all tripeptides that incorporate one unit each of glycine, alanine, and serine.

5. How would the sets of products isolated from complete hydrolysis of each of the tripeptides of Problem 4 differ?

We emphasize again that you should complete the questions at the end of the chapter in the text before attempting the **SELF-TEST**.

SELF-TEST

1. Almost all proteins are composed from a set of about _____ amino acids.
   a. 4   b. 10   c. 20   d. 50   e. 100

2. Chemically, proteins are:
   a. nucleic acids   b. polyamides   c. polyesters   d. polysaccharides

3. The isomers of amino acids incorporated in peptides and proteins are members of the:
   a. D-family   b. L-family

4. Which is a reasonable representation of a portion of a protein chain?

   a. $-\overset{O}{\overset{\|}{C}}H\overset{O}{\overset{\|}{C}}NH\overset{O}{\overset{\|}{C}}CHNHC NH-$ b. $-CH_2CHNH\overset{O}{\overset{\|}{C}}CH_2CHNH\overset{O}{\overset{\|}{C}}-$ c. $CHCNHCH\overset{O}{\overset{\|}{C}}NHCH\overset{O}{\overset{\|}{C}}NH-$

   $\hspace{0.8cm}\overset{|}{R}\hspace{1.0cm}\overset{|}{R}\hspace{3.0cm}\overset{|}{R}\hspace{1.5cm}\overset{|}{R}\hspace{2.0cm}\overset{|}{R}\hspace{0.8cm}\overset{|}{R}\hspace{0.8cm}\overset{|}{R}$

5. Which compound is <u>not</u> an alpha amino acid?

   a. $HO\text{-}CH_2\overset{\overset{\displaystyle NH_2}{|}}{C}HCOOH$ b. $H_2N\text{-}\overset{\overset{\displaystyle COOH}{|}}{C}H\text{-}CH_3$ c. $H_2N\text{-}\overset{\overset{\displaystyle CH_3}{|}}{C}H\text{-}CH_2COOH$ d. $H\text{-}\overset{\overset{\displaystyle H}{|}}{\underset{\underset{\displaystyle COOH}{|}}{C}}\text{-}NH_2$

6. $H_3N^+\text{-}\overset{\overset{\displaystyle CH_3}{|}}{C}H\text{-}CONH\text{-}CH_2CONH\text{-}\overset{\overset{\displaystyle CH_2OH}{|}}{C}H\text{-}COO^-$ is a(n):
   a. amino acid   b. tripeptide   c. dipeptide   d. polypeptide   e. protein

7. Which is <u>not</u> considered evidence of the zwitterionic structure of amino acids?
    a. They show greater solubility in water than in nonpolar solvents.
    b. They have high decomposition points.
    c. They can polymerize to form proteins.

8. Amino acid side chains do <u>not</u> include:
    a. hydrocarbon groups   b. ionized groups   c. polar groups
    d. a disulfide bond   e. phosphate esters

9. Cysteine is:
    a. $^+NH_3$ b. $^+NH_3$ c. NH_3^+ d. SH NH_3^+
       CH_2COO^- CH_3CHCOO^- $CH_2CH_2COO^-$ CH_2-$CHCOO^-$

10. Which amino acid contains an hydroxyl group?
    a. cysteine   b. leucine   c. lysine   d. serine

11. Which amino acid has an imidizolium side chain group?
    a. Trp   b. His   c. Arg   d. Lys   e. Ile

12. Which amino acid's "R" group can form H-bonds?
    a. Ile   b. Gly   c. Val   d. Ser   e. Leu

13. γ-Aminobutyric acid is:
    a. an essential amino acid
    b. the principal amino acid incorporated in the protein of silk
    c. a chemical neurotransmitter found in the brain

14. To indicate the order of a segment of peptide is Lys-Gly-Ala-Cys is to describe its _____ structure.
    a. primary   b. secondary   c. tertiary   d. quaternary

15. If we say that a protein contains an alpha helix, we are describing its _____ structure.
    a. primary   b. secondary   c. tertiary   d. quaternary

16. Which amino acid side chain will participate primarily in hydrophobic interactions to maintain the tertiary structure of a protein?
    a. Asp   b. Lys   c. Trp   d. Ser   e. Glu

17. By describing the relative position of the four polypeptide chains of the hemoglobin molecule, we specify its structure.
    a. primary   b. secondary   c. tertiary   d. quaternary

18. The structure of collagen can be described as a(n):
    a. alpha helix   b. double helix   c. triple helix   d. pleated sheet

19. Which term is <u>not</u> used in describing protein structure?
    a. alpha helix   b. double helix   c. pleated sheet   d. triple helix

20. Which amino acid has an phenol functional group in its side chain?
    a. serine   b. valine   c. glutamine   d. tyrosine   e. proline

21. Which of the following terms cannot be used to describe the structure of alanine at its isoelectric point?
    a. dipolar ion   b. electrically neutral   c. inner salt   d. zwitterion   e. peptide

22. In a strongly acidic solution, which form of Ala will predominate?
         NH_2 $^+NH_3$ NH_2 $^+NH_3$
    a. CH_3-CH-$COOH$ b. CH_3-CH-COO^- c. CH_3-CH-COO^- d. CH_3-CH-$COOH$

23. In a solution of very high pH, aspartic acid molecules would exist as:
         CH_2COOH CH_2COO^- CH_2COOH
    a. H_2N-CH-$COOH$ b. H_2N-CH-COO^- c. H_3N^+-CH-COO^-

         CH_2COO^- CH_2COOH
    d. H_3N^+-CH-COO^- e. H_3N^+-CH-$COOH$

24. Which amino acid would be expected to form a salt bridge with glutamic acid?

     a. Asp   b. Ser   c. Lys   d. Leu   e. Trp

25. Which amino acid will form disulfide bonds?

     a. Cys   b. Ser   c. His   d. Pro   e. Leu

26. Which amino acid side chain would normally be expected to be positively charged at pH 4?

     a. Gly   b. Asp   c. Leu   d. Pro   e. His

27. At the isoelectric point of proteins:

     a. the proteins are least soluble

     b. the proteins contain no charged groups

     c. the proteins have a large excess of positive charge

     d. the pH of the solution is always 7

28. Oxytocin and vasopressin are polypeptide:

     a. enzymes   b. hormones   c. structural material

29. Which is <u>not</u> a globular protein?

     a. albumin   b. collagen   c. myoglobin

30. Which compound does <u>not</u> contain heme as a prosthetic group?

     a. albumin   b. hemoglobin   c. myoglobin

31. Which of the following processes is least likely to have occurred during the denaturation of a protein?

     a. disruption of hydrogen bonds b. hydrolysis of peptide bonds

     c. cleavage of disulfide bonds   d. disruption of salt bridges

32. Which is <u>not</u> a denaturing agent?

     a. heat   b. CH_3CH_2OH c. Hg^{2+} d. alkaloidal reagents   e. H_2O

33. Which type of protein is more easily denatured?

     a. fibrous   b. globular

34. T F An essential amino acid is one which must be incorporated in every protein.

35. T F The most abundant amino acid in silk protein is glycine.

36. T F Wool fibers are considerably more elastic than silk fibers because the secondary structure of wool protein is alpha helical.

37. T F The amino acid sequences of hemoglobins from man and insect show no variation with species.

38. T F The peptide bonds in proteins are identical to the bonds that link monomer units in the nylon polymer.

39. T F In the Van Slyke analysis, proteins are treated with ninhydrin and produce a purple color.

40. T F The hydrogen bonds formed between different peptide linkages play a major role in establishing both the pleated sheet and the alpha helix conformations in proteins.

ANSWERS

Problems

1.

2.
$$CH_2OH \quad CH_2SH$$
$$H_3N^+\text{-}CH\text{-}C\text{-}NH\text{-}CH\text{-}COO^- \text{ and}$$
$$\overset{\|}{O}$$
$$CH_2SH \quad CH_2OH$$
$$H_3N^+\text{-}CH\text{-}C\text{-}NH\text{-}CH\text{-}COO^-$$
$$\overset{\|}{O}$$

3.
$$H_3N^+\text{-}CH\text{-}COO^- \qquad H_3N^+\text{-}CH_2\text{-}COO^- \qquad H_3N^+\text{-}CH\text{-}COO^-$$
$$\overset{|}{CH_3} \qquad\qquad\qquad\qquad\qquad\qquad\qquad \overset{|}{CH_2OH}$$

4. Gly-Ala-Ser;   Gly-Ser-Ala;   Ala-Gly-Ser;
    Ala-Ser-Gly;   Ser-Gly-Ala;   Ser-Ala-Gly

5. There would be no difference. Hydrolysis of each tripeptide would yield a mixture of glycine, alanine, and serine.

Self-Test

1.	c	11.	b	21.	e	31.	b
2.	b	12.	d	22.	d	32.	e
3.	b	13.	c	23.	b	33.	b
4.	c	14.	a	24.	c	34.	F
5.	c	15.	b	25.	a	35.	T
6.	b	16.	c	26.	e	36.	T
7.	c	17.	d	27.	a	37.	F
8.	e	18.	c	28.	b	38.	T
9.	d	19.	b	29.	b	39.	F
10.	d	20.	d	30.	a	40.	T

CHAPTER 22:   ENZYMES

KEY WORDS

enzyme	*activation energy*	*enzyme activity*	*zymogens*
biocatalyst	*lock-and-key*	*pH optimum*	*apoenzyme*
enzyme assay	*induced fit*	*denatured*	*cofactor*
primary structure	*active site*	*allosteric effectors*	*coenzyme*
substrate	*transition state*	*feedback inhibition*	*holoenzyme*
specificity	*saturation*	*proenzymes*	*inhibitors*
enzyme-substrate complex	*competitive*	*noncompetitive*	*turnover number*
stereospecific	*antimetabolites*	*irreversible*	*neurotransmitters*
linkage specific	*group specific*	*optimal temperature*	*ribozymes*

SUMMARY

Structure-function: The amino acid sequence or primary structure of an enzyme reveals little about the mechanism of action of that enzyme. An enzyme only functions or is "active" when it has the proper tertiary structure. Knowledge of both primary and tertiary structures is needed to understand the mode of action of protein molecules. One of the most thoroughly studied classes of proteins are enzymes, the biocatalysts response for cellular reactions.

22.1 Classification and Naming of Enzymes
   A. *Enzymes* are proteins that serve as *biocatalysts*. There is usually a specific enzyme to catalyze each reaction in cellular metabolism. *Ribozymes* are RNA biocatalysts.
   B. The first enzymes discovered were given common names, which often reflected their source (pepsin) or substrate (maltase). A *substrate* is the reactant in an enzyme-catalyzed reaction. For example, the substrate cleaved by maltase is the disaccharide maltose.
   C. Enzymes are generally classified according to the type of reaction they catalyze. Most enzyme names end in "-ase."
      1. Oxidoreductases - redox reactions; dehydrogenases
      2. Transferases   - transfer of groups; transaminases, kinases
      3. Hydrolases   - hydrolysis reactions; proteases, lipases
      4. Lyases   - removal of groups; decarboxylases
      5. Isomerases   - isomeric conversions
      6. Ligases   - formation of new bonds; synthetases

22.2 Characteristics of Enzymes
   A. Many enzymes require the help of small, nonprotein molecules (*cofactors*) to be active with their substrates.
      1. *Apoenzyme*--protein part of the enzyme
      2. *Cofactor*--the nonprotein component needed for activity, usually a metal ion or a small organic molecule
      3. *Coenzyme*--an organic cofactor; many vitamins are related to coenzymes
      4. *Holoenzyme*--active enzyme cofactor complex
   B. *Proenzymes* (or *zymogens*) are proteins that can be converted to enzymes, usually by loss of a few amino acid residues. Examples are pepsinogen, trysinogen, procarboxypeptidase. Many enzymes that are secreted for activities outside the cell (e.g., enzymes used in digestion), are synthesized as proenzymes to protect the cell before they are secreted.

22.3 Mode of Enzyme Action
A. Enzymes act by providing an alternative pathway for a chemical reaction with a lower *activation energy* for the *transition state*. This involves formation of *enzyme-substrate complexes*, [ES].

$$E + S \rightleftharpoons [ES] \rightleftharpoons E + P$$

B. Models of enzyme action: *"lock-and-key"* with *"induced fit"*
  1. The substrate binds to a cleft on the surface of the enzyme called the *active site*. Part of the active will contribute substrate specificity and part will be responsible for catalysis. The active site will normally consist of amino acid side chains that are close together in space or in the tertiary structure of the enzyme but may be far apart in the *amino acid sequence* or *primary structure*.
  2. The topography of the active site ("lock") is usually complementary to the *transition state* of the substrate ("key") so a portion of the binding energy can be used to distort ("induced fit") the substrate toward product, thus providing a pathway of lower *activation energy*.
C. Enzymes, like all catalysts, do not alter the equilibrium constant for the reaction but merely speed up both forward and reverse reactions. The *turnover number* (the number of substrate molecules converted to product/minute/molecule) provides an indication of how rapidly the enzyme "turns over" substrate and varies from only a few to several million!

22.4 Specificity of Enzymes
A. Most enzymes are highly specific catalysts, acting on only one or a few related substrates.
  1. A few enzymes have *absolute specificity* - they have activity with only one substrate (urease).
  2. Many enzymes are *stereospecific* - specificity for one stereoisometric substrate form (L-LDH).
  3. Enzymes with *group specificity* act on molecules that have the same functional group.
    a. Trypsin - splits peptide bonds that are located on the carboxyl side of Lys or Arg.
    b. Urease - catalyzes a single reaction, the hydrolysis of urea.
  4. *Linkage specific* enzymes act on a particular type of bond (lipases).
B. Enzyme specificity is very important in overall regulation of cellular metabolism.

22.5 Factors That Influence *Enzyme Activity*
A. Concentration of Substrate: The rates of enzyme catalyzed reactions initially increase with increasing substrate concentration or [S], but then reach a "saturation" condition at which no further increase in enzyme activity occurs.
B. Concentration of Enzyme: When the concentration of substrate is in great excess, the rate of an enzyme catalyzed reaction will increase as the enzyme concentration increases. This is the basis for clinical and biochemical *enzyme assays*.
C. Temperature: Most reaction rates are influenced by temperature, and enzyme reactions also initially increase with increasing temperature. However, enzymes are proteins with delicate three-dimensional structures that can be *denatured* (unfolded) by high temperatures. Many enzymes have an *optimal temperature* for maximal activity. This is often near 37 °C - our body temperature.
D. pH: A change in pH can alter the charge distribution of an enzyme and render it inactive. Most enzymes have a *pH optimum* at which they are most active. This usually corresponds closely with the pH of the body in which the enzyme works.

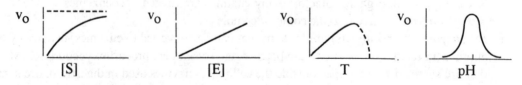

22.6 Enzyme Inhibition: Poisons

A. *Inhibitors* are molecules that bind to enzymes and make them less active, thus small concentrations of an inhibitor or poison can have big effects by decreasing catalytic activity.

1. *Competitive* inhibitors (C.I.) bear a close structural resemblance to the substrate, bind at the active site, and thus "compete" with the natural substrate for the enzyme's specificity pocket. Bacteria require p-aminobenzoic acid to synthesize THF (tetrahydrofolate). Sulfanilamide was one of the early sulfa drugs whose potency was due to its being able to serve as a competitive inhibitor of p-aminobenzoic acid and block the synthesis of THF (See 22.8).

2. *Noncompetitive* inhibitors (Nc.I.) bind at "other" sites on the enzyme and in binding alter the structure and activity of the enzyme.

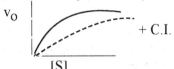 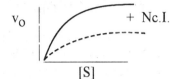

3. *Irreversible* inhibition usually involves covalent modification of the enzyme, often at its active site. Many heavy metal ions like those of mercury and lead will react with the sulfhydryl groups on an enzyme, rendering it inactive. This is an example of noncompetitive, irreversible inhibition.

B. Nerve poisons: nerve signals are propagated across the synapse by *neurotransmitters*, small molecules such as acetyl choline. Once the impulse has been relayed, it is important that the acetyl choline be hydrolyzed to acetate and choline so the receptors can ready themselves for the next impulse and not be in a continuously "on" state. Insecticides such as malathion are organic compounds of phosphorous that bind as competitive inhibitors to cholinesterase, thus making it unavailable to break down acetyl choline.

C. Enzyme Regulation and Allosterism

1. In addition to their active sites, many enzymes possess regulatory or allosteric sites for binding effectors or modulators of their activity. The binding of the effector to the enzyme alters its structure to either increase (activator, positive effector) or decrease (negative effector) its activity. Such enzymes are called allosteric enzymes.

low activity E   high activity E

2. Allosteric enzymes are usually found near the beginning of a multi-step sequence of reactions. The final product of the sequence is often a negative effector. Once its concentration builds to a sufficient level, the effector can bind to the allosteric enzyme and stop the whole sequence. This type of allosteric regulation is called "*feedback inhibition*."

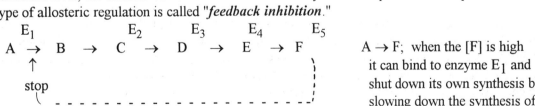

$A \to F$; when the [F] is high it can bind to enzyme E_1 and shut down its own synthesis by slowing down the synthesis of of the precursor compound, B.

22.7 Chemotherapy

A. ***Antimetabolites*** possess structures closely related to the normal metabolite (substrate). Sulfa drugs resemble p-aminobenzoic acid and thus are readily incorporated by bacteria into a "false" form of folic acid, which serves as a competitive inhibitor of folic acid.

p-aminobenzoic acid   sulfanilamide

B. Antibiotics are compounds produced by one microorganism that are toxic to another organism.

1. Penicillin is an inhibitor of the enzyme transpeptidase.

2. Other antibiotics or synthetic analogues include aureomycin, streptomcin, tetracyclines, and chloramphenicol.

Tetracycline

C. Enzymes are finding increased uses in industry (e.g., soaps, meat tenderizers) and in medicine. Clinical analysis of enzymes in body fluids or tissues is now a common diagnostic tool. Elevated levels of an enzyme (LDH) in the blood can point to a tissue that has been damaged (heart).

D. Advances in recombinant DNA technology will open a multitude of new applications for these efficient biocatalysts.

DISCUSSION

Enzymes are delicate protein structures with active sites for catalyzing chemical reactions. This enables cellular processes to occur under relatively mild conditions of pH and temperature. Many enzymes have sophisticated regulatory properties that allow their activity to be turned on or shut down.

In Section 22.1 we presented the classification of enzymes by the type of reaction they catalyzed. The best way to illustrate what we mean by "type of reaction" is to write a representative equation. Therefore, we present below an example for each of the six general types of enzymes. Remember that these examples are only illustrative. We could have written many others, some seemingly quite different. We chose to use as examples reactions that you have already or will soon encounter in this text.

Types of Enzymes with Examples

I. **Oxidases** (oxidoreductases) - example discussed in Section 24.6

$$CH_3\text{-}CH\text{-}COOH \ + \ NAD^+ \ \xrightleftharpoons[\text{dehydrogenase}]{\text{lactate}} \ CH_3\text{-}C\text{-}COOH \ + \ NADH \ + \ H^+$$

with OH on lactic acid and O (double bond) on pyruvic acid

lactic acid   pyruvic acid

II. **Transferases** - example discussed in Section 24.5

glucose + ATP $\xrightleftharpoons{\text{glucokinase}}$ glucose-6-phosphate + AD

glucose   glucose-6-phosphate

III. **Hydrolases** - example discussed in Section 22.6

$$(CH_3)_3N^+\text{-}CH_2CH_2\text{-}O\text{-}C\text{-}CH_3 \ + \ H_2O \ \xrightleftharpoons[\text{esterase}]{\text{acetylcholine-}} \ (CH_3)_3\overset{+}{\text{-}}N\text{-}CH_2CH_2\text{-}OH \ + \ HO\text{-}C\text{-}CH_3$$

acetylcholine   choline   acetic acid

IV. **Lyases** - example discussed in section 24.7

$$CH_3\text{-}C\text{-}COOH \ \xrightleftharpoons{\text{pyruvate decarboxylase}} \ CH_3\text{-}C\text{-}H \ + \ CO_2$$

pyruvic acid   acetaldehyde

V. **Isomerases** - example discussed in section 23.8

UDP-glucose $\xrightleftharpoons{\text{UDP-glucose epimerase}}$ UDP-galactose

UDP-glucose   UDP-galactose

VI. **Ligases** - example discussed in section 26.3

$$CoA\text{-}SH \ + \ HO\text{-}C\text{-}R \ + \ ATP \ \xrightleftharpoons{\text{acyl-CoA synthetase}} \ CoA\text{-}S\sim C\text{-}R \ + \ AMP \ + \ Pi$$

fatty   thio ester
acid   of fatty acid

SUMMARY

Answer the problems at the end of the chapter in the text, then complete the **SELF-TEST**.

SELF-TEST

1. A compound that catalyzes a chemical reaction in a living organism is called a(n):
       a. carbohydrate   b. enzyme   c. lipid   d. vitamin
2. Enzymes belong to which class of organic compounds?
       a. carbohydrates   b. esters   c. hydrocarbons   d. lipids   e. proteins
3. The compound that has a reaction catalyzed by an enzyme is called a(n):
       a. activator   b. coenzyme   c. cofactor   d. substrate
4. Which type of enzyme is classified as an oxidoreductase?
       a. dehydrogenase   b. lipase   c. pepsin   d. peptidase   e. protease
5. Kinases belong to which class of enzymes?
       a. hydrolases   b. isomerases   c. ligases
       d. lyases   e. oxidases   f. transferases
6. To which of the classes listed in question 5 does a synthetase belong?
       a   b   c   d   e   f
7. Which type of enzyme listed in question 5 would catalyze the conversion of L-alanine to D-alanine?
       a   b   c   d   e   f
8. The substrate pyruvate is a 3-C keto-acid that can be reduced to lactate by Lactate Dehydrogenase (LDH). What amino acid "R"-group in the enzyme might be expected to interact with the $-COO^-$ group of pyruvate?
       a. Glu   b. Leu   c. Asp   d. Ieu   e. Arg
9. An apoenzyme is always a(n):
       a. protein   b. nonprotein organic molecule   c. inorganic ion
10. Which is not found as a cofactor of an enzyme?
        a. a protein   b. a vitamin   c. an inorganic ion
11. A <u>non</u>covalently bonded vitamin derivative required for the functioning of an enzyme system is called a(n):
        a. activator   b. apoenzyme   c. coenzyme
12. When all of the active sites on enzyme molecules are saturated, an increase in _____ concentration will not increase the rate of the reaction.
        a. enzyme   b. substrate
13. An optimum pH of enzymes operating in the stomach is in the ___ range.
        a. acidic   b. neutral   c. basic
14. The optimum temperature for most enzymes operating in the human body is:
        a. 273 K   b. 37 $^{\circ}$C   c. 98.6 $^{\circ}$C   d. 120 $^{\circ}$C
15. The allosteric site on a regulatory enzyme binds the:
        a. effector   b. proenzyme   c. substrate
16. Which is <u>not</u> a proenzyme?
        a. pepsinogen   b. prothrombin   c. trypsinogen   d. all are proenzymes
17. Pepsin is a protease that acts in the:
        a. mouth   b. stomach   c. intestines
18. What will happen to the rate of an enzyme catalyzed reaction already at very high [S] when more substrate is added?
        a. increase   b. decrease   c. no change
19. What will happen to the rate of an enzyme catalyzed reaction at very high [S] when a competitive inhibitor is added?
        a. increase   b. decrease   c. no change
20. Which is <u>not</u> a poison that affects enzymes?
        a. CN^- b. Fe^{3+} c. Pb^{2+} d. AsO_4^{3-}

21. Which poison does <u>not</u> act by tying up sulfhydryl groups of an enzyme?
    a. CN^- b. AsO_4^{3-} c. Pb^{2+}
22. EDTA is an effective antidote for acute poisoning by:
    a. CN^- b. AsO_4^{3-} c. Pb^{2+}
23. The combination of the apoenzyme and its cofactor produce an active enzyme or _____.
    a. vitazyme   b. holoenzyme   c. ribozyme   d. coenzyme
24. Which protein has the larger polypeptide chain, insulin or pre-pro insulin?
    a. insulin   b. pre-pro insulin
25. Activation of an enzyme can occur through:
    a. conversion of a proenzyme to the enzyme
    b. combination of an apoenzyme with a cofactor
    c. release of an inhibitor from the allosteric site of a regulatory enzyme
    d. all of the above
26. Which compound is responsible for transmitting an impulse across a nerve synapse?
    a. choline   b. acetylcholine   c. cholinesterase
27. Which of the compounds listed in question 26 is the enzyme responsible for resetting the receptor to "off" after transmission of a signal across the synapse?
    a. choline   b. acetylcholine   c. cholinesterase
28. Phosphorus-containing compounds serve as:
    a. pesticides   b. nerve gases   c. intermediates in carbohydrate metabolism
    d. a and b   e. a, b, and c
29. When the [S] is low, what will happen to the rate of the enzyme catalyzed reaction when the [S] is doubled?
    a. no change   b. increase 10X   c. increase 2X   d. decrease 10X   e. decrease 2X
30. If one effector (Ef) activates one enzyme E-A, which in turn activates 100 molecules of enzyme E-B, each of which activates 100 molecules of enzyme E-C, and each molecule of enzyme E-C converts 1000 substrate molecules to product, what is the enhancement factor of the effector "Ef"?
    a. 100X   b. 10,000X   c. 100,000X   d. 1,000,000X   e. 10,000,000X
31. T F Enzymes are heat stable catalysts.
32. T F Factors that affect the activity of an enzyme include temperature, pH, enzyme concentration, and substrate concentration.
33. T F Saliva contains the enzyme pepsin.
34. T F The active site of an enzyme is the point at which an effector attaches.
35. T F The carbohydrase lysozyme was the first enzyme to have its three-dimensional structure determined by scientists.
36. T F A stereospecific enzyme would catalyze only reactions involving both members of a mirror image pair of isomers.
37. T F If an enzyme exhibits absolute specificity, it catalyzes a single reaction.
38. T F The formation of an activated enzyme-substrate complex is postulated to explain the catalytic effect of an enzyme.
39. T F Addition of an enzyme changes the speed and the equilibrium position of a reaction.
40. T F The induced-fit theory states that the substrate must fit precisely the active site of the enzyme for the catalyst to be most effective.
41. T F The amino acid side chains associated with the active site of an enzyme must be adjacent in the primary sequence of the protein.
42. T F The inhibitor of an allosteric enzyme is frequently the end product of the sequence of reactions controlled by the enzyme.
43. T F CPK and GOT are abbreviations for the enzymes used in detergent formulations and meat tenderizer.

44. T F The term "regulatory enzyme" is applied to any enzyme that catalyzes a chemical reaction.
45. T F Conversion of a proenzyme to the active enzyme frequently involves cleavage of a portion of the protein chain.

Match the enzymes listed in column A with their type of reactions illustrated in column B.

Column A	Column B
a. carbohydrase	___46. $\sim\overset{O}{\overset{\|}{C}}\text{-NH-CH}_2\sim\ +\ H_2O \rightleftharpoons \sim\overset{O}{\overset{\|}{C}}\text{-OH}\ +\ H_2N\text{-CH}_2\sim$
b. dehydrogenase	
c. isomerase	
d. peptidase	___47. $H_3{}^{+}N\text{-}\underset{H}{\overset{CH_3}{C}}\text{-COO-} \rightleftharpoons \text{-OOC-}\underset{H}{\overset{CH_3}{C}}\text{-N}^{+}H_3$
e. transferase	

___48. 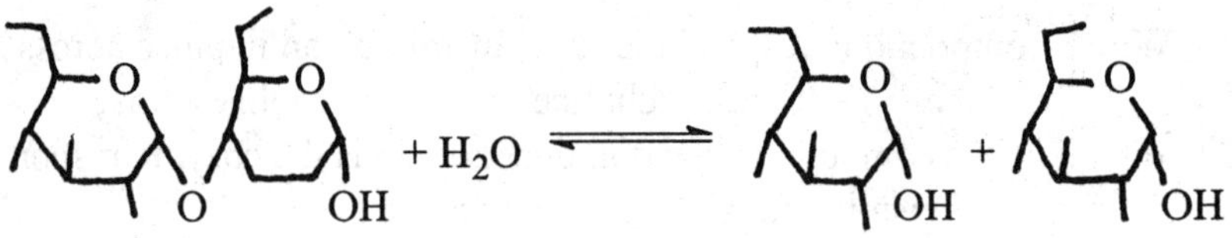

___49. $\overset{OH}{CH_3\text{-}CH_2} \rightleftharpoons CH_3\text{-}\overset{O}{\overset{\|}{C}}\text{-H}\ +\ 2\ H$

___50. $CH_3\text{-}\overset{O}{\overset{\|}{C}}\text{-OH}\ +\ ATP \rightleftharpoons CH_3\text{-}\overset{O}{\overset{\|}{C}}\text{-O-}\underset{O^-}{\overset{O}{\overset{\|}{P}}}\text{-O}^-\ +\ ADP$

ANSWERS

1. b	11. c	21. a	31. F	41. F
2. e	12. b	22. c	32. T	42. T
3. d	13. a	23. b	33. F	43. F
4. a	14. b	24. b	34. F	44. F
5. f	15. a	25. d	35. T	45. T
6. c	16. d	26. b	36. F	46. d
7. b	17. b	27. c	37. T	47. c
8. e	18. c	28. e	38. T	48. a
9. a	19. c	29. c	39. F	49. b
10. a	20. b	30. e	40. F	50. e

Special Topic J: Vitamins

KEY WORDS

vitamin	*deficiency*	*provitamin*	*thiamine*	*biotin*
disease	*calciferol*	*riboflavin*	*folic acid*	*scurvy*
rickets	*niacin*	*lipoic acid*	*beriberi*	*tocopherol*
pantothenic acid	*cobalamin*	*pellagra*	*B complex*	*pyridoxine*
ascorbic acid	*retinol*	*antioxidants*		

SUMMARY

J.1 What Are Vitamins?

    A. *Vitamins* are organic substances that our bodies need for good health but cannot synthesize; they must be included in one's diet.

    B. Some vitamins were discovered early because of vitamin-*deficiency diseases* such as *scurvy* (vitamin C deficiency), *beriberi* (thiamine or B1 deficiency), and *pellagra* (niacin). The first such compounds characterized were amines, hence the name "vitamin."

    C. Vitamins are divided into two broad categories.

        1. Fat-soluble vitamins: A, D, E, K

        2. Water-soluble vitamins: B complex and C

J.2 Vitamin A

    A. Vitamin A is an unsaturated alcohol called *retinol*. It was first isolated from fish oils but is also found in eggs and dairy products. Excess vitamin A is stored in the body and large excesses can be harmful. Carrots and certain other vegetables contain a carotenoid pigment, β-carotene, which is a *provitamin* that can be converted into vitamin A.

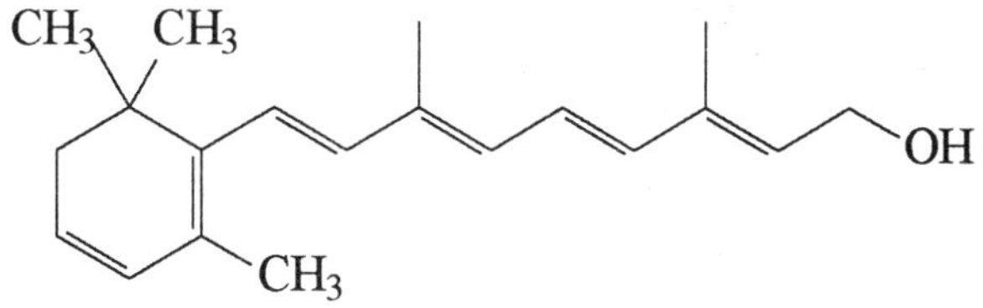

Vitamin A$_2$

    B. Signs of vitamin A deficiency are night blindness and mucous membranes that harden and crack.

    C. Vitamin A and the visual cycle

        1. Vitamin A is converted to 11-cis-retinal, which combines with opsin to form rhodopsin.

        2. When light strikes rhodopsin, 11-cis-retinal is converted to the trans isomer, triggering an electrical impulse (vision) and splitting rhodopsin to form opsin and the free aldehyde.

        3. The all-trans retinal is converted back to 11-cis-retinal and combined with opsin to complete the visual cycle (Refer to Special Topic G).

J.3 Vitamin D

A. Vitamin D is actually several related compounds. Vitamin D_2, or ergo*calciferol*, is formed by the action of sunlight on the steroid ergosterol.

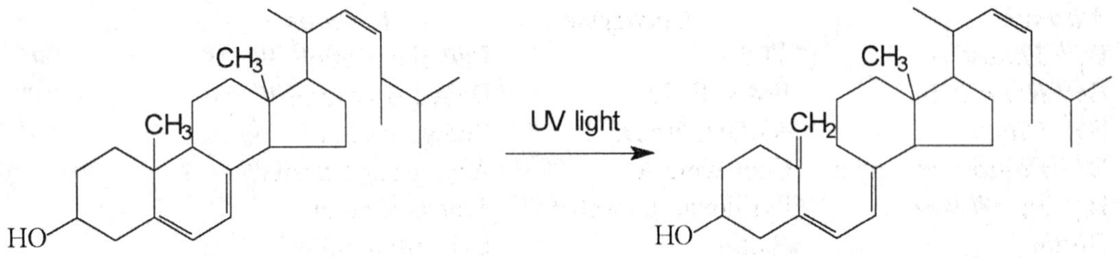

| Ergosterol | Vitamin D_2 (ergocalciferol) |

B. Vitamin D promotes the uptake of calcium and phosphorous. A deficiency of vitamin D results in abnormal bone formation, a condition known as *rickets*.

C. Vitamin D is the "sunshine vitamin." Sunlight can convert 7-dehydro-cholesterol in the skin to vitamin D. It is also found in milk and fish oils. Large excesses of vitamin D are dangerous.

J.4 Vitamin E

A. Vitamin E is a mixture of compounds called *α-tocopherols*. The tocopherols are phenols that are *antioxidants*. The loss of vitamin E's antioxidant effect is believed to be responsible for the symptoms of vitamin E deficiency. Vitamin E protects vitamin A, and vitamin E deficiency usually also leads to vitamin A deficiency.

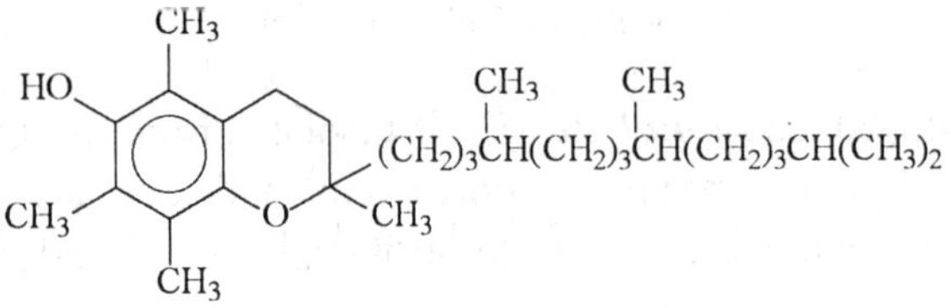

Vitamin E (α-tocopherol)

B. Vitamin E is also stored in the body but is not as toxic in excess as vitamins A and D. Good sources of vitamin E are wheat germ oil, vegetables, egg yolk, and meat.

J.5 Vitamin K

A. There are many compounds with vitamin K activity. Vitamin K has a fused ring structure related to naphthalene with one ring also being a quinone. Often the hydrocarbon "tail" is similar to that found in Vitamins A and E.

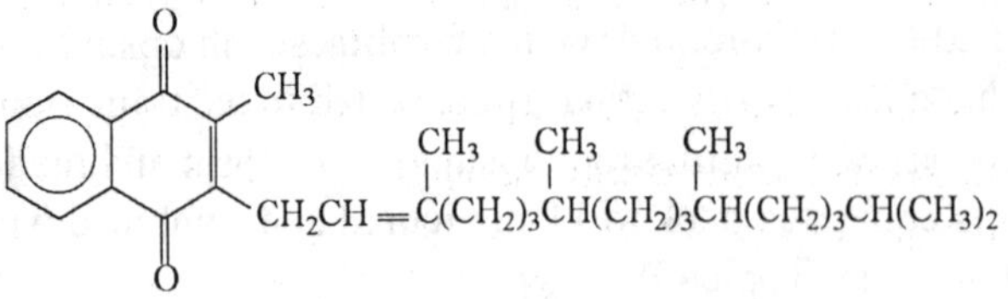

Vitamin K_1

B. Vitamin K is necessary for the function of *prothrombin*, an enzyme precursor involved in blood clotting. Symptoms of vitamin K deficiency are bleeding under the skin, which results in ugly "bruises" from minor blows.

C. Good sources of vitamin K are spinach and leafy green vegetables. Bacteria in the large intestine also produce the vitamin, and it can be absorbed from them.

J.6 The B Complex

A. Vitamin **B complex** refers to a group of water-soluble vitamins. Many coenzymes are vitamin B derivatives. Water soluble vitamins are not stored by the body. (Refer to Table J.1 in the text.)

B.

Vitamin	*Coenzyme*	*Reaction*
B_1 - *Thiamine*	TPP	Decarboxylation
B_2 - *Riboflavin*	FMN, FAD	Dehydrogenation
B_3 - *Niacin*	NADH, NADPH	Redox reactions
B_5 - *Pantothenic acid*	Coenzyme A	Acyl group transfer
B_6 - *Pyridoxine*	Pyridoxal phosphate	Transamination
Biotin	Biotin	CO_2 group transfer
Folic acid	Tetrahydrofolate	1 C transfer
B_{12}- Cyano*cobalamin*	dA cobalamin	Alkyl group transfer
Lipoic acid	Lipoamide	Acyl group transfer

C. Structures of some B vitamins.

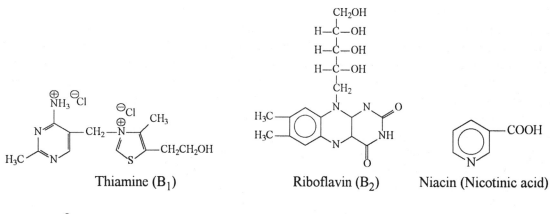

Thiamine (B_1)   Riboflavin (B_2)   Niacin (Nicotinic acid)

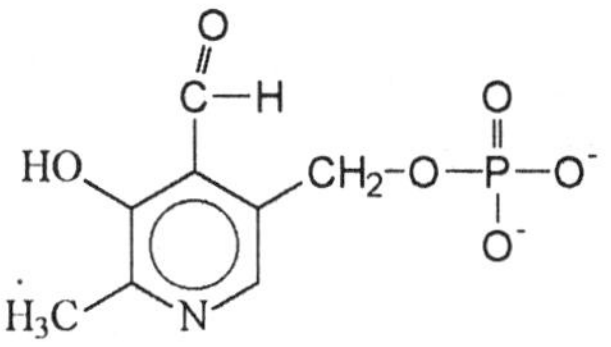

Pyridoxal-phosphate 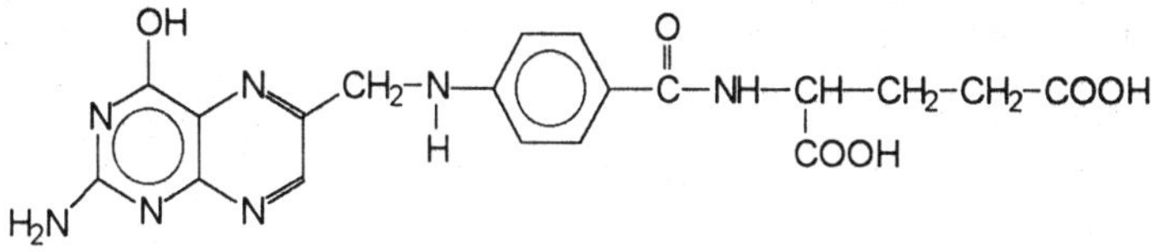   Folic acid

J.7 Vitamin C

A. Vitamin C is **ascorbic acid**. It is required for hydroxylation reactions important to the synthesis of collagen.

B. Vitamin C deficiency results in scurvy. Only 40 to 75 mg of ascorbic acid per day are necessary to prevent scurvy. Linus Pauling has advocated taking from 250 to 15,000 mg of vitamin C per day. Citrus fruits are rich in Vitamin C.

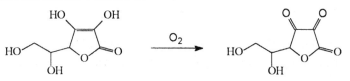

Ascorbic acid (Vitamin C)   Dehydroascorbic acid (oxidized Vit. C)

DISCUSSION

This unit, like the preceding ones, deals with complex molecules. However, there is no structural feature common to all vitamins. Proteins are polyamides, and it is possible to describe in a general way the structural features common to thousands of different protein molecules. The same can be said about carbohydrates and even about lipids, that is, they have general structural features. But vitamins cannot be so easily categorized by structure. Because vitamins have such complex structures, they frequently intimidate students (who, because of exams, worry a great deal about being able to draw a structure like vitamin B_{12}). Therefore, let us first comment that there is not one chemist in a hundred (or more) who can draw the structure of vitamin B_{12} from memory. So why did we bother to show the structures of all of these molecules? Because we want you to see that molecular architecture is more than a chemist's playground; it frequently determines the state of one's health. Consider the discussion of vitamin A in section J.2. This is a large, relatively nonpolar molecule. We've discussed polarity, hydrogen bonding, and solubility many times. Here you have a concrete example of the significance of this "chemistry." Vitamin A is nonpolar and soluble in nonpolar media like the fatty tissue of the body. It does not form hydrogen bonds with water in sufficient numbers to make it soluble in aqueous body fluids. That means that it is not rapidly excreted from the body with such fluids. Thus, individuals can build up a reserve and protect themselves against the effects of deprivation. It is also true that this same property of vitamin A permits one to overdose on the vitamin. In other words, you can store too much of it--the body doesn't automatically dump the excess over one's immediate needs.

In contrast, look at vitamin C (J.7). It's a relative of the carbohydrates--lots of hydroxyl groups, very polar, and very water-soluble. Now, perhaps, you can understand some of the controversy surrounding Linus Pauling's recommendation to take massive doses of vitamin C. What difference does it make, say some scientists, whether you ingest 250 or 15,000 mg of vitamin C when evidence suggests that the aqueous body fluids wash out all but 200 mg? With these facts in mind, spend some time just looking at (not memorizing) some of the vitamin structures. Notice that vitamins A, D, E, and K, the fat-soluble vitamins, are all lipid-like. They have lots of carbon and hydrogen and very little else. There's an occasional oxygen, but mostly there are long, nonpolar chains of carbon.

Now look at the B complex vitamins (Table J.1). All of them contain nitrogen. Even more important, however, is the fact that they all contain a relatively high proportion of groups that can interact through hydrogen bonding. The variation in structure among the B vitamins is great, but B_2 (riboflavin) is typical. Like most of the fat-soluble vitamins, it has a side chain. Now look closely at the riboflavin side chain. It carries 4 hydroxyl groups, and there are four nitrogens and two other oxygens in the molecule. Look at vitamin B_{12} (cyanocobalamin). The laboratory synthesis of this complex molecule was regarded as one of the outstanding achievements of organic chemistry in this century. What should you know about the structure? Certainly that it contains cobalt, which is somewhat unusual, but primarily that it is loaded with groups that confer water-solubility--amides and other nitrogen-containing functions, hydroxyl groups, and a phosphate group.

You should use the problems at the end of the chapter in the text to organize for yourself some pertinent data about each of the vitamins. Go through all of the problems in the text before taking the **SELF-TEST**.

SELF-TEST

1. Vitamins are:
   a. amines required by an organism for good health
   b. organic compounds produced in trace amounts by the endocrine glands
   c. organic molecules that an organism requires in trace amounts but cannot synthesize for itself
   d. steroids that act as sex hormones

2. Which is <u>not</u> a fat-soluble vitamin?
   a. vitamin A   b. vitamin C   c. vitamin D
   d. vitamin E   e. vitamin K

3. Which is <u>not</u> a water-soluble vitamin?
   a. cholecalciferol   b. cyanocobalamine   c. niacin   d. vitamin B_6

4. Which is <u>not</u> a member of the B complex?
   a. biotin   b. thiamine   c. folic acid   d. niacin
   e. pantothenic acid   f. riboflavin   g. retinol

5. The plant pigment named β-carotene is a:
   a. coenzyme   b. contraceptive   c. hormone   d. provitamin   e. vitamin

6. A critical event in the chemistry of vision involves the conversion of:
   a. a cis isomer to a trans isomer
   b. a D isomer to an L isomer
   c. an ortho isomer to a para isomer
   d. ergosterol to calciferol

7. Which is <u>not</u> true of rhodopsin?
   a. It is a complex of a protein and a derivative of vitamin A.
   b. It is the visual pigment found in some receptor cells of the retina.
   c. It is converted to vitamin A by the absorption of light.

8. Which is <u>not</u> true of vitamin D?
   a. It is formed from steroidal precursors by the absorption of ultraviolet light.
   b. It is called the "sunshine vitamin."
   c. A deficiency of this vitamin results in abnormal bone formation.
   d. No harmful effects have been documented for overdoses of this vitamin.

9. Vitamin E is:
   a. an antioxidant
   b. frequently missing from the diet of vegetarians
   c. approved by medical authorities for the prevention of aging

10. The vitamin associated with blood clotting is vitamin:
    a. A   b. B complex   c. C   d. D   e. E   f. K

11. The B complex vitamins are frequently incorporated in:
    a. coenzymes   b. provitamins   c. contraceptives   d. rhodopsin

12. The vitamin Thiamine is associated with the disease _____ .
    a. scurvy   b. rickets   c. beriberi   d. baldness   e. senility

13. The B complex vitamins can be stored in almost unlimited quantities in the:
    a. adipose tissue   b. bone marrow   c. liver
    d. retina   e. They are not stored in significant amounts in the body.

14. Vitamin C activity is exhibited by:
    a. several pigments isolated from various colored plants
    b. steroid-like compounds found in the skin of various animals
    c. a carbohydrate-like compound found in citrus fruit
15. The coenzymes NADH and NADPH are derived from the vitamin _____ .
    a. riboflavin   b. thiamine   c. ascorbic acid   d. niacin   e. Vitamin E

Matching: Match the names in column B with the vitamins in column A.

Column A	Column B
16. vitamin B_1	a. ascorbic acid
17. vitamin D	b. calciferol
18. vitamin B_2	c. cyanocobalamine
19. vitamin B_{12}	d. retinol
20. vitamin E	e. riboflavin
21. vitamin A	f. thiamine
22. vitamin C	g. α-tocopherol

Match the deficiency disease or symptom in column D with the relevant vitamin in column C.

Column C	Column D
23. ascorbic acid	a. scurvy
24. cyanocobalamine	b. hemorrhage
25. vitamin A	c. pellagra
26. thiamine	d. pernicious anemia
27. vitamin E	e. rickets
28. vitamin K	f. beriberi
29. vitamin D	g. sterility
30. niacin	h. night blindness

ANSWERS

1. c	11. a	21. d
2. b	12. c	22. a
3. a	13. e	23. a
4. g	14. c	24. d
5. d	15. d	25. h
6. a	16. f	26. f
7. c	17. b	27. g
8. d	18. e	28. b
9. a	19. c	29. e
10. f	20. g	30. c

CHAPTER 23: NUCLEIC ACIDS AND PROTEIN SYNTHESIS

KEY WORDS

purine	*nucleotide*	*replication*	*codons*	*pyrimidine*
phosphodiester	*semiconservative*	*translation*	*DNA, RNA*	*double helix*
discontinuous	*tRNA*	*deoxyribose*	*base pairing*	*transcription*
anticodons	*rRNA*	*differentiation*	*mRNA*	*recombinant DNA*
nucleoside	*restriction enzymes*	*genes*	*polymerase*	*operator*
exons	*introns*	*mutagen*	*ribose*	*ribosome*
cytosine	*thymine*	*uracil*	*adenine*	*guanine*
antiparallel	*template*	*DNA ligase*	*universal*	*degenerate*
plasmid	*DNA fingerprinting*	*sugar-phosphate*	*genetic disease*	*substitution*
insertion	*deletion*	*initiation*	*termination*	*"A", "P" sites*
RFLP	*PCR*			

SUMMARY

23.1 The Building Blocks: Sugars, Phosphates, and Bases
   A. Two kinds of nucleic acid polymers
      1. **DNA**s (**deoxyribonucleic** acids) are the genetic material generally found in the cell nucleus. DNAs consist of the bases A, G, T, or C linked to a **2'-deoxyribose** sugar and an inorganic phosphate.
      2. **RNA**s (**ribonucleic** acids) have many roles. RNAs consist of the bases A, G, U, or C linked to a **ribose** sugar and an inorganic phosphate.
   B. Nucleic acids are polymers of **nucleotides**. Each nucleotide consists of a **purine** or **pyrimidine** nitrogeneous base, a ribose sugar, and an inorganic phosphate.
      1. **Pyrimidines**

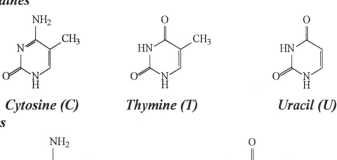

Cytosine (C)   *Thymine (T)*   *Uracil (U)*

      2. **Purines**

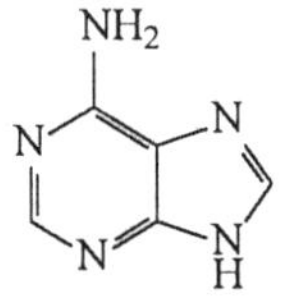

Adenine (A) 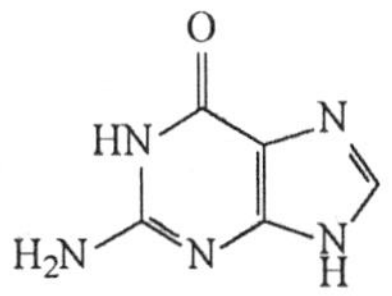   *Guanine (G)*

221

C. *Nucleosides*: A *nucleoside* is a purine or pyrimidine base linked to the C1' position of a ribose sugar.

1. ribonucleoside = ribose + (A, G, C, or U)

2. deoxyribonucleoside = 2'-deoxyribose + (A, G, C, or T)

Adenosine (nucleoside)

3. Nomenclature:

Base	Sugar	Nucleoside
Adenine	ribose	Adenosine
Guanine	ribose	Guanone
Uracil	ribose	Uridine
Thymine	deoxyribose	deoxythymidine
Cytosine	deoxyribose	deoxycytidine

D. *Nucleotides* (Sugar + Base + Phosphate): Nucleotides are C5' phosphoesters of nucleosides.

1. Adenosine the nucleoside becomes Adenosine monophosphate (AMP) the nucleotide.

Adenosine monophosphate or AMP (nucleotide)

2. Nomenclature
   i. Two systems
      a. drop "-ine" or "osine" ending and add "-ylic acid" ending: uridylic acid, adenylic acid
      b. as a nucleoside monophosphate: uridine monophosphate, UMP
   ii. Use "deoxy" or "d" for deoxyribose nucleotides AMP vs. dAMP

3. Roles of nucleotides
   i. Monomers for building DNAs: dAMP, dGMP, dCMP, dTMP
   ii. Monomers for building RNAs: AMP, GMP, CMP, UMP
   iii. Energy exchange: ATP, ADP, GTP, GDP
   iv. Coenzymes: NADH, FADH$_2$
   v. Secondary messenger: c-AMP
   vi. Allosteric effectors of regulatory enzymes

23.2 The Base Sequence: Primary Structure of Nucleic Acids

    A. Nucleic acids are linear polymers of nucleotides. DNAs are synthesized from dNTPs and RNAs are formed from NTPs, (N = nucleoside). The nucleotides are connected by *3', 5' phosphodiester* bonds. Each strand has one free 5' hydroxyl and one free 3' hydroxyl group.

    B. The primary structure of a nucleic acid is the sequence of the bases attached to the ribose. DNA sequences are always read in the 5' → 3' direction.

        For example: 5' - AGGTCTCAAGCTATAAGCCATCATC - 3'

    C. Nucleic acid sequences are determined by using gel electrophoresis of radio labeled nucleic acid fragments prepared with *restriction enzymes*. The human genome project seeks to determine the primary structure of human DNA estimated to consist of ~5.5 billion base pairs. In 1996 the sequence of the yeast genome of ~13 million base pairs was completed.

23.3 *Base Pairing* and the Double Helix: Secondary Structure of DNA

    A. Composition: Chargaff (1950) - %A = %T; %G = %C implying that the bases must be paired, A to T and G to C.

    B. *Double helix* of Watson and Crick (1953)

        1. DNA model of two *antiparallel* strands in a *double helix* with the *sugar-phosphate* backbone on the outside and complimentary *base pairs* on the inside. Single stranded RNAs can also fold back on themselves to create short double helical segments.

        2. Complimentary *base pairing* of A = T and G ≡ C arises due to the complimentary hydrogen bonds made between these purine-pyrimidine pairs.

        3. The double helix has ~10 bp/turn with a helical repeat of ~34Å or 3.4 nm (see Fig. 23.8).

        4. The antiparallel strands create "major" and "minor" groves which can bind various proteins to form nucleoprotein complexes.

        5. Human DNA consists of about 5,500,000,000 nucleotides arranged on 23 chromosomes.

    C. The double helix of DNA permits us to understand the processes of replication and protein synthesis.

23.4 DNA: Self-Replication
   A. Genes are the basic units of heredity. A *gene* is that portion (a section or a series of sections) of
     DNA in a chromosome that codes for the synthesis of a particular protein. Each amino acid in the
     protein is encoded by a three-base sequence. Cells in the human body have 26 chromosomes with
     enough DNA to form over 5 billion base pairs. In theory, each cell in the body is capable of
     producing all of the different proteins that the body needs. In practice, different cells become
     specialized during *differentiation* and use only a small portion of their genetic content.
   B. DNA *Replication*: Synthesis of DNA from a DNA template (see Fig. 23.12, 23.13)
     1. The double helix of DNA is unwound by unwinding proteins to yield a single stranded *template*.
     2. RNA and DNA *polymerase* enzymes then produce the growing complementary nucleic acid
       strands by using nucleotide triphosphates as a source of nucleotides and available energy.
     3. The process is *semiconservative* in that each double helix produced contains one new and one
       original strand of DNA.
     4. The synthesis proceeds in the 5' → 3' direction in a *discontinuous* fashion, i.e., short segments of
       DNA are synthesized as the DNA double helix is unwound. These are later linked together by a
       DNA ligase enzyme.
   C. *DNA fingerprinting* refers to the process of making cuts and then separating the resulting DNA
     fragments by size using gel electrophoresis. The sizes of the DNA fragments are unique to that
     individual and can be used as a "fingerprint" in criminal investigations or to screen for genetic
     diseases (*RFLPs* = Restriction Fragment Length Polymorphisms).

23.5 RNA: The Different Ribonucleic Acids
   A. DNA directs the synthesis of RNAs during *transcription*. In this process a DNA molecule is
     partially unwound, then a limited portion of 1 of the 2 DNA strands is used to direct the synthesis of
     a complementary RNA molecule (A ⇒ U; G ⇒ C; T ⇒ A; C ⇒ G).
   B. RNAs of three basic types of single-stranded nucleic acid.
     1. *Messenger RNA (mRNA)* contains the "*codons.*" Codons are 3-base triplets that code for the
       amino acid sequence of the protein to be synthesized (See Table 23.5 for the genetic code.)
     2. *Ribosomal RNA (rRNA)* is the most abundant type of RNA in the cell and represents a major
       component of the *ribosome* which is the site of protein synthesis.
     3. *Transfer RNAs (tRNA)* are low molecular weight nucleic acid molecules which can contain
       about 90 nucleotides and transport activated amino acids to the ribosome. The X-ray structures
       of several tRNAs have been determined. Most tRNAs are "L" shaped having the 3-base
       "anticodon" at one end and the attachment site for the amino acid at the other (3') end.

23.6 Protein Synthesis
   A. *Translation* - The decoding of the mRNA molecule and its use in directing the synthesis of a protein
     molecule.
     1. Protein biosynthesis takes place on ribosomes in the cytoplasm of the cell.
     2. The mRNA with its triplet *codons* travels from the nucleus to the cytoplasm.
     3. Each tRNA can transport only one kind of amino acid as specified by a 3-base sequence called its
       anticodon. The anticodon of a tRNA can form a complementary base pair with the
       corresponding codon in the mRNA bound to the ribosome.
     4. Protein biosynthesis is initiated as the mRNA, the first activated tRNA (f-met tRNA), and the
       ribosomal subunits bind together to form a complex.

5. The ribosome binds tRNAs to both the *"P"* (peptidyl) *site* and the *"A"* (aminoacyl) *site* with their anticodons paired with the codons on the mRNA. A peptide bond is formed when the "peptide" attached to the tRNA in the "P" site is transferred to make a new peptide bond to the free amino group of the amino acid attached to the other tRNA in the "A" site (See Figure 23.18).

6. During a translocation step, the ribosome moves "one codon" along the mRNA.

7. Another aminoacyl tRNA binds to the "A" site at the next codon and another peptide bond forms.

8. Steps 6 and 7 are repeated until protein biosynthesis is terminated by "stop" codons.

B. Genetic regulation
1. A human cell contains about 100,000 genes. Many of the genes in plants and animals are segmented with the parts that are expressed called *exons* and the parts that are not expressed referred to as *intervening* sequences or *introns*.
2. We now know that there are *operator* genes, promotor genes, regulatory genes, and repressor molecules that help regulate the expression of proteins. The majority of DNA in a human cell is <u>not</u> used to code for amino acids.

23.7 The Genetic Code
A. The genetic code shows how the codon triplets in an mRNA specifies the particular amino acid.
B. There are 4 N bases used in mRNA (A, U, G, C) or (4 x 4 x 4 = 64) possible triplets to specify the 20 common amino acids, e.g. UUU = phenylalanine, AUG = methionine, etc. (Table 23.3)
1. This code is essentially *universal*, and used by all plant, animal and bacterial cells.
2. The code is *degenerate* in that amino acids are specified by multiple codons.
3. AUG codes for Met and is also the *initiation codon*.
4. Three of the 64 triplets do not code for amino acids and are used as *termination codons*.
5. The 2nd base is most important (A/G $\Rightarrow$ polar; C/U $\Rightarrow$ nonpolar).

23.8 Mutations and Genetic Disease
A. Any chemical or physical change that alters the sequence of bases in a DNA is termed a *mutation* and the causative agent is called a *mutagen*. Mutants can involve *substitution*, *insertion*, or *deletion* of a base.
1. UV light - produce a thymine (T=T) dimer.
2. Hydroxylamine (NH_2OH) deaminates cytosine so that it base pairs with adenine (C'=A) instead of guanine (C$\equiv$G).
3. Nitrous acid (HNO_2) can convert cytosine to uracil.
B. Over 1200 *genetic diseases* in humans are caused by gene mutations. Many such diseases have been traced to a problem with one enzyme. (Table 23.6) The human genome project is helping to identify the locations of genes associated with many genetic diseases.
1. PKU (phenylketonuria) - phenylalanine hydroxylase
2. Sickle cell anemia - hemoglobin
3. Albinison - tyrosinase
4. Galactosemia - Galactose 1-P-uridyl transferase
5. Tay-Sachs disease - hexosaminidase A

23.9 Genetic Engineering: Biotechnology
A. *Recombinant DNA* refers to the splicing together of DNA from different species. It is possible using recombinant DNA technology to insert a gene (from a human or synthesized to order) into a *plasmid*, or circular piece of DNA, and then into a bacterium in such a way that the bacterial cell will now produce the corresponding protein of the new gene (see Fig. 23.23).

1. *Restriction enzymes* (endonucleases) are used to cut out the gene of interest and open up the plasmid. There are over 100 restriction enzymes available, each one is specific for cutting at a particular DNA sequence. The endonuclease EcoRI cuts double-stranded DNA at the sequence - GAATTC-.
2. The sticky ends of the foreign DNA are complementary to those of the nicked plasmid.
3. A DNA ligase seals the foreign DNA segment into the plasmid.
4. The modified plasmid can be inserted into treated *E. coli* cells.

B. Human insulin and other proteins can now be produced by bacteria. This technique holds great promise for producing large quantities of otherwise very rare proteins such as interferon and growth hormone.

C. Genetic screening (DNA fingerprinting) often involves a distinctive pattern from RFLPs. Small amounts of DNA can be amplified by use of Polymerase Chain Reaction (*PCR*) methodology.

DISCUSSION

In the **SELF-TEST**, we expect you to be able to recognize the distinguishing features of nucleic acids, nucleotides, and nucleosides. We'll also expect you to recognize which type of compound is being discussed from its name. Although you will not be asked to draw the complete structure of the various bases, you should recognize a purine (two fused heterocyclic rings) and a pyrimidine (one heterocyclic ring) when you see one. You should also know which bases are purines (adenine and guanine) and which are pyrimidines (cytosine, thymine, and uracil).

To give you a warm-up before the **SELF-TEST**, try the following problems, which review other points covered in the chapter. In each labeled drawing, there is an **error**. You are being asked to **spot the error**.

Problems

1. A typical nucleoside

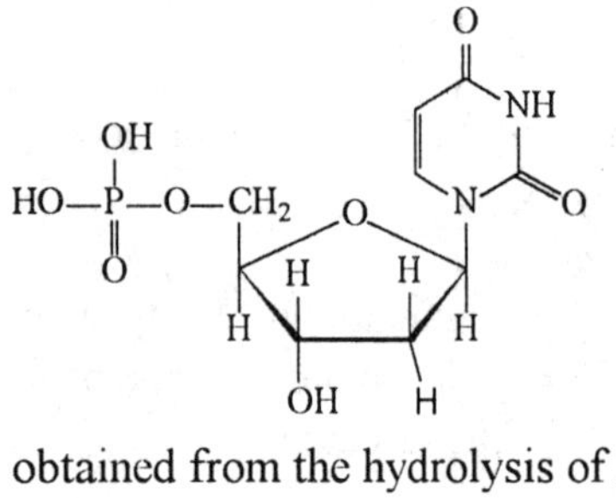

2. A nucleotide obtained from the hydrolysis of DNA

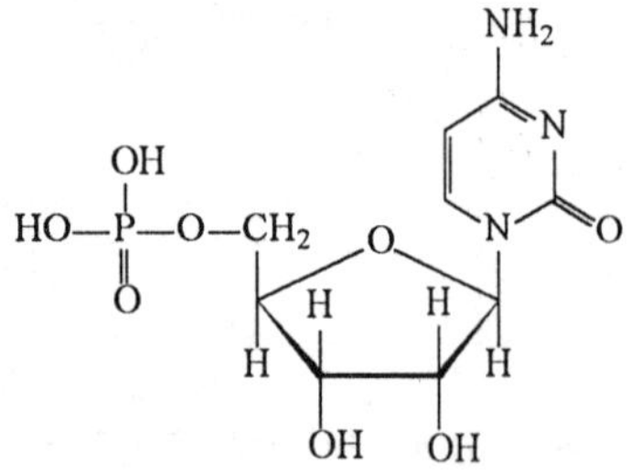

3. A typical base pair in a nucleic acid

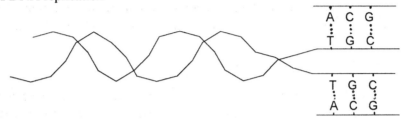

4. Beginning of DNA replication

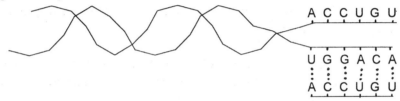

5. DNA serving as a template for the formation of an mRNA molecule.

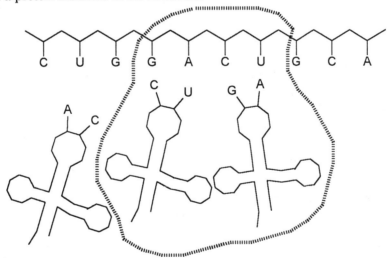

6. Formation of a protein molecule at the ribosome.

SELF-TEST

1. An individual unit of heredity is called a(n) _____ .
   a. nucleotide   b. nucleoside   c. gene   d. protein
2. DNA segments that interrupt a gene and are <u>not</u> involved in directing polypeptide synthesis are called

   _____ .
   a. genettes   b. gamma genes   c. exons   d. introns

3. Human DNA consists of approximately _____ base pairs.
   a. 13 million   b. 4 million   c. 200,000   d. 2 billion   e. 5 billion

4. If a nucleic acid is completely hydrolyzed, which type of compound is <u>not</u> one of the products?
   a. a purine   b. a pyrimidine   c. phosphoric acid
   d. an amino acid   e. a sugar

5. Which set of bases does <u>not</u> make up a base pair usually found in nucleic acids?
   a. adenine-thymine   b. cytosine-guanine   c. uracil-thymine   d. adenine-uracil

6. The t-RNA molecules incorporate _____ sugars.
   a. ribose   b. deoxyribose

7. Which group is <u>not</u> part of the backbone of a strand of nucleic acid?
   a. sugar unit   b. base unit   c. phosphoric acid unit

8. Base pairing is accomplished through the formation of:
   a. hydrogen bonds   b. phosphate linkages   c. hemiacetal linkages

9. The nucleus of a human body cell has _____ chromosomes.
   a. 2   b. 12   c. 23   d. 36   e. 46

10. Which base is <u>not</u> normally found in RNA?
    a. adenine   b. cytosine   c. guanine   d. thymine   e. uracil

11. Which molecule is a nucleoside?
    a. cytosine   b. cytidine   c. cytidine monophosphate
    d. deoxycytidine monophosphate

12. Which contains the codon?
    a. DNA   b. mRNA   c. tRNA   d. the protein molecule

13. Which molecule carries the anticodon?
    a. mRNA   b. tRNA   c. the ribosome   d. the protein molecule

14. There are about _____ base pairs per turn of the double helix.
    a. 2   b. 6   c. 10   d. 16   e. 20

15. If the triplet were 5'-U-G-C-3', the anticodon (5' → 3') would be _____ .
    a. ACG   b. GCA   c. AUG   d. AGC

16. Where does gene replication take place?
    a. in a cell nucleus   b. at a ribosome complex   c. at the cell membrane

17. Where does the transcription of information from DNA to mRNA take place?
    a. in a cell nucleus   b. at a ribosome complex   c. at the cell membrane

18. After replication, each daughter DNA molecule:
    a. contains only purines or pyrimidines, but not both
    b. contains one strand of the parent molecule
    c. is the mirror image isomer of the other daughter molecule

19. Which process occurs at the ribosome complex?
    a. replication of DNA   b. transcription of mRNA   c. translation to protein

20. When active protein synthesis is taking place in the cell, which material is <u>not</u> required at the ribosomes?
    a. DNA   b. mRNA   c. tRNA   d. growing protein chain

21. The compound below is:

    a. AMP   b. c-AMP   c. ADP   d. ATP

22. The strands of DNA run in a(n) _____ direction.

    a. parallel   b. antiparallel

23. About how many bases (minimum) are needed to code for a 240 amino acid protein?

    a. 80   b. 480   c. 720   d. 240   e. 120

Answer Questions 24 through 29 by referring to the following structure.

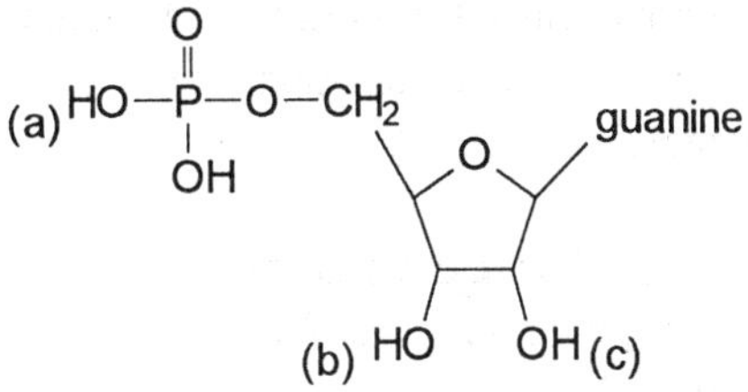

$$\text{(a)}\ HO-\underset{\underset{OH}{|}}{\overset{\overset{O}{\|}}{P}}-O-CH_2-\cdots O \cdots \text{guanine}$$

$$\text{(b) HO}\quad\quad\text{OH (c)}$$

24. The compound is a:

    a. nucleoside   b. nucleotide   c. nucleic acid

25. The compound is:

    a. guanine   b. guanine monophosphate   c. deoxyguanine

    d. guanosine monophosphate   e. deoxyguanosine monophosphate

26. The compound incorporates a:

    a. purine   b. pyrimidine

27. The compound could be incorporated in:

    a. DNA   b. RNA

28. Three of the -OH groups have been labeled a, b, and c. Which of these would <u>not</u> be used in formation of the nucleic acid polymer?

    a   b   c

29. If the compound were incorporated in a nucleic acid, which base would <u>not</u> appear in the same polymer?

    a. adenine   b. cytosine   c. guanine   d. thymine   e. uracil

30. T F The molecular weights of nucleic acids are generally greater than those of proteins.

31. T F In nucleoproteins the basic side chains of the protein form salt bridges with the base pairs of the nucleic acids.

32. T F Nucleotides are formed in the hydrolysis of nucleosides.

33. T F Adenylic acid is identical to adenosine monophosphate.

34. T F It is the presence of the ribose unit in the nucleic acid RNA that makes the compound an acid.

35. T F The pairing of a purine with a pyrimidine permits the strands of a double helix to maintain a constant spacing.

36. T F It is impossible for base pairing to occur in single-stranded RNA.

37. T F Transfer RNA contains both the anticodon and the amino acid called for by the codon.

38. T F The codons that do <u>not</u> call for a specific amino acid signal the termination of protein synthesis.

39. T F Thymine and uracil are both purines.

40. T F Some codons call for more than one kind of amino acid.

ANSWERS

Problems

1. A nucleoside would not have a phosphate group attached to the sugar ring.
2. The sugar unit is ribose. DNA would yield only deoxyribose.
3. Both bases are purines. A typical base pair would include a purine and a pyrimidine.
4. The bases on the complementary strands of the DNA molecule are not complementary. T was paired with T, G with G, etc. In DNA a strand carrying T and G and C would be matched with one carrying A and C and G.
5. Among the bases attached to the double-stranded DNA molecule is uracil. This base is only found in RNA.
6. The tRNAs are pairing with doublets rather than with the correct triplets.

Self-Test

1. c	11. b	21. c	31. F
2. d	12. b	22. b	32. F
3. e	13. b	23. c	33. T
4. d	14. c	24. b	34. F
5. c	15. b	25. d	35. T
6. a	16. a	26. a	36. F
7. b	17. a	27. b	37. T
8. a	18. b	28. c	38. T
9. e	19. c	29. d	39. F
10. d	20. a	30. T	40. F

Special Topic K: Viruses and Cancer

KEY TERMS

virus	*protein coat*	*RNA virus*	*DNA virus*	*retrovirus*
AZT	*carcinogen*	*benign*	*malignant*	*oncogenes*
Ames Test	*epidemiological*	*antimetabolites*	*reverse*	*transcriptase*
benzpyrene	*cisplatin*	*5-fluorouracil*	*methotrexate*	*BHT*

SUMMARY

K.1 The Nature of Viruses

    A. *Viruses* are infectious agents composed of a nucleic acid core and a *protein coat*. Infectious diseases of viral origin include the common cold, polio, rabies, hepatitis, chicken pox, measles, mumps, herpes, and AIDS.

    B. Viruses can be subdivided into two classes depending on the type of nucleic acid present.

        1. *DNA Viruses*: Viral DNA is replicated in the host cell and directs the production of coat protein(s) to assemble new viruses.

        2. *RNA Viruses*: RNA viruses called *retroviruses* synthesize DNA by a process that is the opposite of transcription using an enzyme called *reverse transcriptase*. The human immunodeficiency virus (HIV) that causes AIDS is an example of a *retrovirus*.

K.2 Antiviral Drugs

    A. Antiviral compounds can act in a variety of ways.

        1. Block cell membrane receptors.

        2. Prevent viral particles from releasing nucleic acid.

        3. Block replication of the viral nucleic acid.

    B. *AZT* (azidothymidine) and DDI (2',3'-dideoxyinosine) are two drugs approved by the FDA to treat AIDS.

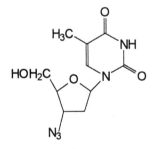

AZT = azidothymidine   DDI = 2',3'-dideoxyinosine

K.3 Cancer and Its Causes

    A. *Carcinogens* are cancer causing substances that promote the growth of tumors.

        1. *Benign* tumors grow slowly and do not invade neighboring tissues.

        2. *Malignant* tumors are "cancers" that invade and destroy neighboring tissue.

    B. Most cancers are caused by exposure to environmental factors. However, most of the carcinogens that we ingest are produced naturally in nature.

    C. The genes that are implicated in the process of turning normal cells into cancerous ones are called *oncogenes* and usually are genes that are involved in regulating cell growth and division.

K.4 Chemical Carcinogens
   A. Aromatic hydrocarbons
      1. 3,4-*benzpyrene* is formed from the incomplete combustion of organic materials (cigarette smoking, barbecue, etc.)
      2. β-naphthylamine and benzidine - dye industry
      3. 4-dimethylaminoazobenzene - amino azo dye
   B. Nonaromatics
      1. Dimetylnitrosoamine
      2. Vinyl chloride

K.5 Testing for Carcinogens
   A. Bacterial screening: the *Ames Test* is a simple and relatively cheap screening test, but it can also pick up carcinogens that are produced by metabolism.
   B. Animal Tests: Use of very large doses on laboratory animals.
   C. *Epidemiological* Methods: Use of statistical analysis of affected population and the probable common cause, e.g. cigarette smoking and lung cancer.

K.6 Chemicals Against Cancer
   A. Many of the compounds used in cancer chemotherapy are designed to inhibit DNA synthesis. Because cancer cells are undergoing rapid growth, they are generally affected to a greater extent than normal cells.
   B. Examples of *Antimetabolites*
      1. *Cisplatin* - a cis isomer of a platinum complex that binds to and blocks DNA replication.
      2. *5-fluorouracil* - incorporates into DNA and slows the rate of replication.
      3. 6-mercaptopurine - substitutes for adenine

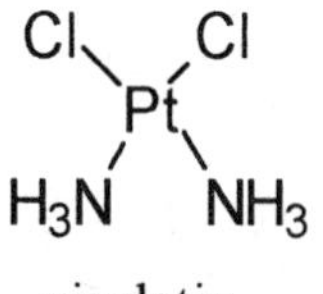

cisplatin 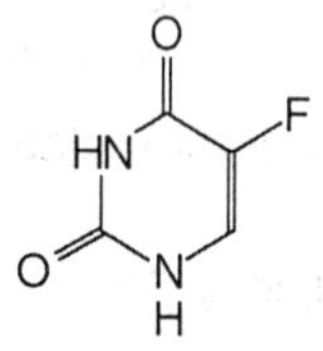   5- fluorouracil 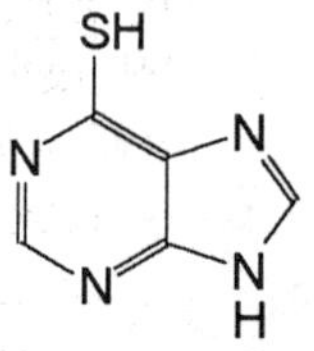   6-mercaptopurine

   4. *Methotrexate* - an analog of folic acid that prevents the enzyme from using good folic acid.

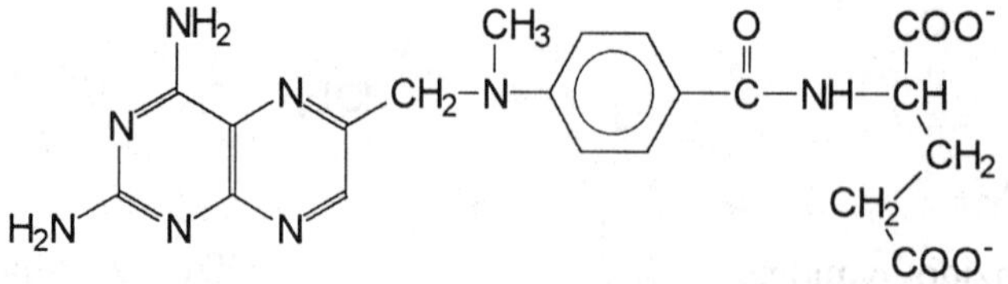

Methotrexate

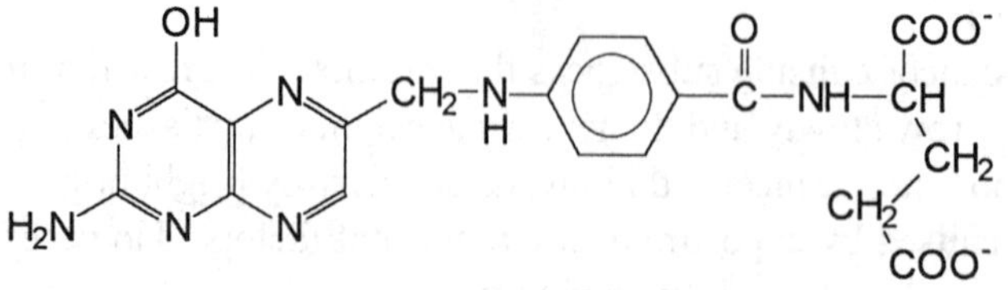

Folic Acid

K.7 Miscellaneous Anticancer Agents
   A. Actinomycin (molds), alkaloids (plants), sex hormones, the food preservative butylated hydroxytoluene (*BHT*), Vitamins A and C, broccoli and many other substances have all been correlated with some positive value in protecting against various forms of cancer.
   B. Surgical removal of tumors
   C. Radiation therapy to kill malignant cells.

SELF-TEST

1. Which of the following diseases is <u>not</u> caused by a virus?
      a. mumps   b. polio   c. AIDS   d. gonorrhea   e. measles   f. warts
2. AIDS is an example of a _____ virus.
      a. RNA   b. DNA   c. tRNA   d. mRNA   e. retrovirus
3. AZT, an anti-AIDS drug, is structurally similar to:
      a. an amino acid   b. purine   c. nucleoside   d. nucleotide
4. A cancer is often synonymous with _____.
      a. pollutants   b. carcinogen   c. benign tumor   d. malignant tumor
5. Genes that trigger the formation of cancerous cells are called:
      a. regulatory genes   b. oncogenes   c. Z genes   d. X genes
6. Which compound(s) among the following is(are) <u>not</u> an anticancer drug?
      a. methotrexate   b. fluoro unacil   c. cisplatin   d. cytidine
7. 3,4 benzpyrene is a known _____ .
      a. carcinogen   b. vitamin   c. amino acid   d. neurotransmitter   e. cofactor

Matching:

8. ___ Ames Test
9. ___ Actinomycin
10. ___ BHT
11. ___ antimetabolite
12. ___ AIDS

a. food additive, preservative
b. inhibits protein synthesis
c. methotrexate
d. bacterial screening for mutagens
e. retrovirus
f. carcinogen, barbecue
g. oncogenes

ANSWERS

| 1. d | 3. c | 5. b | 7. a | 9. b | 11. c |
| 2. a, e | 4. d | 6. d | 8. d | 10. a | 12. e |

CHAPTER 24: CARBOHYDRATE METABOLISM I

KEY WORDS

anabolism	*respiration*	*exergonic*	*endergonic*	*metabolism*
catabolism	*coupling*	*free energy*	*intermediates*	*metabolites*
digestion	*α-amylase*	*dextrins*	*passive transport*	*active transport*
hypoglycemia	*cortisone*	*cytoplasm*	*hyperglycemia*	*glycogen*
anaerobic	*insulin*	*creatine*	*fermentation*	*diabetes mellitus*
glycogenolysis	*glucose tolerance*	*phosphorylase*	*glucagon*	*Cori cycle*
epinephrine	*glycolysis*	*photosynthesis*	*blood sugar level*	*renal threshold*
substrate-level	*phosphorylation*	*gluconeogenesis*	*galactosemia*	*lactate*
pyruvate	*phosphofructokinase*	*adenyl cyclase*	*ATP, ADP, cAMP*	*sec. messenger*

SUMMARY

Life requires a continuous input of energy. Green plants use *photosynthesis* to capture the sun's energy. Animals rely on the stored chemical energy found in carbohydrates, fats, and proteins. The coordinated chemical reactions that sustain life are called *metabolism*.

1. *Catabolism* - reactions involved in breaking down foodstuffs
2. *Anabolism* - biosynthetic reactions

Most foodstuffs represent reduced forms of carbon which are ultimately oxidized to carbon dioxide and water. *Respiration* refers to all metabolic processes whereby gaseous oxygen is used to oxidize organic foodstuffs to CO_2, H_2O and energy. Energy is released when bonds are formed and energy is required to break bonds.

1. *Exergonic* reactions release energy; this is typical of catabolic pathways.
2. *Endergonic* reactions require energy input; this is typical of anabolic pathways.

24.1 ATP: Universal Energy Currency

A. *ATP* (adenosine triphosphate) and *ADP* (adenosine diphosphate) release large amounts of Gibbs' *free energy* upon hydrolysis. Such compounds are called "energy-rich" compounds and the pyrophosphate bond a "high-energy" bond ($\Delta G^{O'} \sim$ -7300 cal/mole or -7.3 kcal/m).

B. ATP is a "middle-weight" among energy-rich compounds, low enough to be produced when coupled with certain *catabolic* reactions but high enough to drive most *anabolic* reactions. ATP is often called the "energy currency" of the cell.

C. Coupled Reactions

1. Nearly all anabolic reactions within a living cell are *endergonic*, or nonspontaneous. However, these reactions can be carried out by "*coupling*" the unfavorable reaction to another reaction that is very favorable. The ΔG for the coupled reaction is the sum of the individual ΔG values.

2. Energy coupling of reactions requires that the two reactions share a common intermediate.

Glucose + fructose	$\rightarrow$	sucrose + H_2O	$\Delta G^{O'}$ = +7.0 (unfavorable)
H_2O + ATP	$\rightarrow$	ADP + P_i	$\Delta G^{O'}$ = -7.3 (favorable)
Glucose + fructose + ATP	$\rightarrow$	sucrose + ADP + P_i	$\Delta G^{O'}$ = -0.3 (also favorable)

D. The "burning" of foodstuffs to carbon dioxide via metabolic pathways proceeds by a series of small steps that produce many chemical *intermediates*, called *metabolites*. Some of the reactions involving these metabolic intermediates are sufficiently exergonic that they can be coupled to drive the formation of ATP.

phosphoenol pyruvate (PEP) $\rightarrow$ pyruvate $+$ P_i $\Delta G^{O'} = -12.8$ kcal/m   (favorable)

P_i $+$ ADP $\rightarrow$ ATP $\Delta G^{O'} = +7.3$ kcal/m   (not favorable)

PEP $+$ ADP $\rightarrow$ pyruvate $+$ ADP $\Delta G^{O'} = -5.5$ kcal/m   (favorable)

24.2 Digestion and Absorption of Carbohydrates

A. *Digestion* is the "hydrolytic process whereby food molecules are broken down into simpler chemical units that can be absorbed by the body." Our bodies contain a "tunnel" called the digestive tract (or alimentary canal) that begins at the mouth and ends at the anus. Foodstuffs that are digested during this passage can be absorbed and used by the body.

B. The digestion of starch (carbohydrate).

1. Mouth - saliva: food is lubricated with mucin; *α-amylase* (ptyalin) begins cleavage of glycosidic bonds.

2. Stomach: small amount of acid hydrolysis, but little carbohydrate digestion takes place here.

3. Small Intestine: a second amylase converts starch and *dextrins* to maltose.

4. Disaccharidases convert maltose and other disaccharides to primarily glucose, fructose, and galactose.

C. Uptake of monosaccharides requires energy.

1. Some substances can be absorbed by *"passive transport"* via simple diffusion or osmosis.

2. Simple sugars cross the small intestinal wall (*villi*) by an energy-requiring process, such processes are termed *"active transport."*

D. Absorbed glucose is carried by the blood stream to the liver where is can be stored as *glycogen* or converted to fat. The average person has sufficient glycogen stored to supply about 18 hours of her energy needs.

24.3 Blood Glucose

A. After sugars enter the bloodstream, they are carried to the liver where they are phosphorylated. The liver helps regulate the *blood sugar level*.

1. Normal: 80-100 mg of glucose per 100 mL of blood (or ~6g or 1 tsp. of total blood glucose in the body).

2. *Hypoglycemia* - low blood sugar levels; overdose of insulin.

3. *Hyperglycemia* - high blood sugar levels; lack of insulin, starvation.

B. The brain uses ~125g of glucose per day compared to ~ 200g for the remainder of the body when at rest.

C. The liver helps maintain glucose levels by releasing glucose to the blood or absorbing excess glucose and converting it into glycogen or fat.

D. The kidneys will excrete glucose into the urine when the blood glucose levels exceed the "*renal threshold*" of ~ 170 mg/100 mL. A *glucose tolerance test* is used to diagnose *diabetes mellitus*, a major cause of hypoglycemia.

24.4 Hormonal Regulation of Blood Sugar Level

A. Blood glucose is regulated primarily by hormones that control the synthesis or breakdown of glycogen in the liver.

B. Insulin, a protein hormone secreted by the pancreas, promotes anabolic processes and lowers blood sugar levels by increasing the uptake and utilization of glucose, enhancing glycogenesis and suppressing gluconeogenesis, synthesis of new glucose.

C. The hormones *glucagon* and *epinephrine* act to increase blood sugar levels by increasing the rate of glycogen breakdown into glucose. They are "primary messengers" that bind to their respective receptors, activating the enzyme *adenyl cyclase* to convert $ATP \rightarrow cAMP$. The cAMP serves as a "*secondary messenger*" inside the cell that initiates a "cascade" of events that leads to the breakdown of glycogen to form glucose-1-phosphate.

ATP   cAMP

   1. *Glucagon* is a polypeptide (29-mer) hormone also produced in the pancreas.
   2. *Epinephrine* (*adrenaline*) is the "fight or flight" hormone produced by the medulla of the adrenal glands.
D. *Cortisone* and cortisol from the adrenal cortex are steroidal hormones that stimulate the synthesis of glucose from amino acids.
E. The disease *diabetes mellitus* can result from faulty insulin production, its release, or lack of sufficient receptors.
   1. Type I or insulin-dependent diabetes is caused by a lack of insulin and is treated with daily insulin injections. Lack of insulin can lead to severe acidosis and diabetic coma.
   2. Type II (non-insulin-dependent) diabetes is the more common, occurring later in life and resulting from beta cells not secreting enough insulin. Oral drugs can be taken to stimulate insulin release or sensitivity.

Chlorpropamide (Diabinese)

24.5 Embden-Meyerhof Pathway

A. Glycogen and glucose can be oxidized to 3-carbon *pyruvate* in the absence of oxygen (*anaerobic*). This also results in the reduction of NAD^+ to NADH. In order to regenerate the NAD^+ and keep the pathway going, the pyruvate can be further converted to either *lactate* (glycolysis) or ethanol (fermentation).
   1. *Glycolysis* = "splitting of sugar." In glycolysis a 6C glucose is converted to two 3C lactates.
   2. *Fermentation* results in pyruvate $\rightarrow$ ethanol + CO_2
B. Breakdown (*glycogenolysis*)
   1. *Glycogen phosphorylase* catalyzes the splitting off of a glucose unit as glucose-1-phosphate.
   2. Epinephrine increases the breakdown of glycogen by causing the activation of glycogen phosphorylase.
C. Summary of key features of *anaerobic glycolysis* (refer to Fig 24.12)
   1. The splitting of glucose to lactate requires 11 steps involving 10 different enzymes. All steps take place in the *cytoplasm* of the cell.
   2. All common monosaccharides can ultimately be converted to fructose-6-phosphate.* The conversion of glucose to fructose 1,6-diphosphate (steps 1-3) requires the input of 2 "high energy" ATP molecules. ATP molecules are a kind of energy currency.

*Note: Infants with *galactosemia* cannot tolerate milk because they lack the enzyme necessary to convert galactose (produced from the hydrolysis of milk sugar lactose) into glucose.
   3. Step 3 is the crucial, **regulatory** step in the pathway. The allosteric enzyme, *phosphofructokinase*, is inhibited by high energy conditions such as high levels of ATP and citrate, and it is stimulated by low energy conditions such as high levels of ADP.
   4. Step 6 is the *substrate-level phosphorylation* of an aldehyde (G-3-P) to the phosphate ester of a carboxylic acid. One molecule of NADH is produced for each G-3-P at this step. The energy released during the oxidation is partially conserved in the new phosphate ester bond that is produced in 1,3-DPG.
   5. Step 7: Two ATPs are produced as the phosphate ester bonds are hydrolyzed in each 1,3 DPG $\rightarrow$ 3 PG
   6. Step 10: Two more ATPs are produced as the PEPs are converted to pyruvates. Thus a net yield of 2 ATP per glucose $\rightarrow$ 2 pyruvates is realized.

24.6 Glycolysis
   A. In anaerobic glycolysis, pyruvate is reduced to lactate (Step 11a) to regenerate the NAD^+ needed in Step 6.
   B. High lactate levels result muscle "fatigue." Most of the lactate produced diffuses out of the muscle and is transported by the blood back to the liver to be remade into new glucose (gluconeogenesis).
   C. The *Cori cycle* describes the storage and utilization of glucose to maintain blood sugar levels.

      — (muscle cells) —⌐   ⌐— (Liver cells) —

Glucose $\rightarrow$ Lactate $\leftarrow$ *(Blood)* $\rightarrow$ Lactate $\rightarrow$ Glucose
    └— *(glycolysis)* —┘   └—*(gluconeogenesis)*—┘

24.7 Fermentation
   A. The first 10 steps in the *fermentation* of sugar to alcohol is identical to glycolysis. However, pyruvate is decarboxylated to acetaldehyde (Step 11b), and the NAD^+ required for the pathway is regenerated when acetaldehyde is reduced to ethanol (Step 12). (See Figure 24.12)
   B. Limited amounts of alcohol can be "detoxified" by the liver. However, this will not protect the fetus of an alcoholic mother and excessive drinking can cause FAS (fetal alcohol syndrome) and mental retardation.
   C. More than 200,000 people die each year of alcoholism. Alcohol-impaired driving is the leading cause of death for those under 25 years of age.
   D. Chronic alcoholism can be treated with the drug disulfiram (Antabuse) which blocks the conversion of acetaldehyde to acetate. The increased levels of acetaldehyde bring on general discomfort with nausea, vomiting, blurred vision, etc. However, acetaldehyde is chemically very similar to formaldehyde and such treatment should only be administered by a physician.

$$CH_3CH_2 \diagdown \underset{CH_3CH_2 \diagup}{N} - \overset{\overset{S}{\|}}{C} - S - S - \overset{\overset{S}{\|}}{C} - \underset{\diagdown CH_2CH_3}{\overset{\diagup CH_2CH_3}{N}}$$

Disulfiram (Antabuse)

24.8 Reversal of Glycolysis and Fermentation
   A. Catabolic and anabolic pathways may seem to be similar or simply the reverse of one another, but they are usually separated and involve irreversible steps so that each pathway can be controlled or regulated.
   B. The synthesis of glucose from lactate (or ethanol) is not the simple reverse of glycolysis (or fermentation). Steps 1, 3, and 10 in glycolysis are not reversible and thus require other enzymes to be invoked to synthesize new glucose or *gluconeogenesis*. Steps 1 and 3 involve phosphatase

enzymes that remove the phosphate groups without ATP production. The conversion of pyruvate back to PEP involves several new steps as shown by the dashed arrows below.

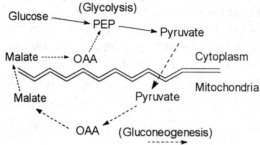

24.9 Bioenergetics of Glycolysis and Fermentation
    A. The energy balance sheet for anaerobic metabolism
        1. (Blood Glucose)   Glucose $\rightarrow$ 2 Lactates + 2 ATP
        2. (Muscle Glycogen)   Glucose-1-phosphate $\rightarrow$ 2 Lactates + 3 ATP
        3. (Fermentation in Yeast)   Glucose $\rightarrow$ 2 ethanols + 2 ATP + 2 CO_2
    B. Recall that the complete oxidation of 1 mol of glucose should release 686 kcal of free energy and that 1 mol of ATP conserves about 7.3 kcal, thus anaerobic metabolism taps only ~ 2 to 3 % of the total energy available from the combustion of the glucose molecule. This is the big advantage of going to aerobic metabolism (Chapter 25).

24.10 Storage of Chemical Energy
    A. ATP turnover is very high. There is insufficient ATP in resting muscle to sustain exercise for even a few seconds. A typical human will hydrolyze and resynthesize his own body weight in ATP each day.
    B. Creatine kinase catalyzes the reaction of creatine phosphate (stored in muscle tissue) with ADP to regenerate needed ATP until glycolysis can meet the demands. However, even the stored creatine phosphate can only provide energy for about 20 sec of strenuous muscle activity. For longer periods of work the body must rely on the metabolism of blood glucose or muscle glycogen.
    C. Glycogen is composed of chains of D-glucose joined with an α-(1-4) linkage with frequent branches joined by an α-(1-6) linkage. Its structure is similar to that of amylopectin in starch, but more highly branched. Glycogen is stored in the liver (~100 g) and muscle (~350 g) tissues. This does not represent very much stored energy. Additional carbohydrate in the diet is converted to fat, a more efficient form of fuel storage, and stored in adipose tissue.

DISCUSSION

    This chapter introduces the subject of metabolism and energy balance in living systems. Metabolism refers to the whole series of reactions needed to sustain life. We learned that our bodies are able to convert the foods we eat into useful forms of chemical energy. The rules that govern such energy conversions are found in the study of thermodynamics. We need concern ourselves with only two aspects of thermodynamics: (1) the relationship between free energy changes and "spontaneity," and (2) the coupling of a very exergonic reaction with an endergonic reaction so the net coupled reaction is still exergonic.

    What determines whether the reaction A $\rightarrow$ B is more favored than the reverse reaction, B $\rightarrow$ A? There are two factors that determine the "spontaneity" or favored direction of a chemical reaction. The first factor is the tendency to minimize energy (rocks roll down a hill, not up). The second factor is the tendency to maximize entropy, which is related to probability or what is often called "randomness." For example, we postulate that gas molecules will disperse to fill a large container, even when no energy changes take place, because it is simply more probable that the gas molecules would disperse throughout the container rather than order in one small part of the container. The Gibbs free energy change for a reaction measures the net effect of both of these factors.

$$\Delta G = \Delta H - T\Delta S$$

(where ΔG = **free energy** change, ΔH = **enthalpy** (energy) change, ΔS = **entropy** change)

It is not necessary for you to have a complete understanding of these quantities to appreciate the usefulness of the Gibbs free energy change, ΔG. The relationships between spontaneity and ΔG are summarized below:

ΔG	"spontaneity"	K_{eq}	
+ (endergonic)	nonspontaneous	<1	(unfavorable)
0	system at equilibrium	1	
- (exergonic)	spontaneous	>1	(favorable)

We have stated that catabolic pathways (the ones that degrade foodstuffs) are generally considered to be exergonic, that is, energetically favorable with a negative ΔG. For instance, recall that for the combustion of glucose: $C_6H_{12}O_6 + 6\ O_2\ \rightarrow\ 6\ CO_2 + 6\ H_2O$ $\Delta G^{0'} = -686$ **kcal/mol**

This is a very energetically favorable reaction. If we burn carbohydrates in air, we obtain CO_2, H_2O, and a lot of energy released as heat. Living cells metabolize ("burn") sugar slowly, employing several dozen metabolic steps in order to conserve some of the free energy released. The free energy cannot be deposited in a bank for later withdrawal, rather, it must be stored in the form of "high energy" bond formation. This is accomplished by coupling the exergonic step in the catabolic pathway with another reaction that requires an input of energy to proceed, such as the synthesis of ATP from ADP. Reaction coupling requires that both the exergonic and endergonic reactions must share a common chemical intermediate. For example, the formation of sucrose actually proceeds through an intermediate, glucose-1-phosphate.

glucose + ATP	$\rightarrow$	Glucose-1-phosphate + ADP
glucose-1-phosphate + fructose	$\rightarrow$	sucrose + P_i
glucose + fructose + ATP	$\rightarrow$	sucrose + ADP + P_i

The free energy changes for the hydrolysis of some common phosphates are:

Compound		Hydrolysis Products		$\Delta G^{0'}$ (Kcal/mol)
Phosphoenol pyruvate (PEP)	$\rightarrow$	pyruvate	+ P_i	−12.8
Creatine phosphate	$\rightarrow$	creatine	+ P_i	−10.5
ATP	$\rightarrow$	ADP	+ P_i	− 7.3
ADP	$\rightarrow$	AMP	+ P_i	− 6.5
Glucose-6-phosphate	$\rightarrow$	glucose	+ P_i	− 3.3
AMP	$\rightarrow$	adenosine	+ P_i	− 2.2

The reactions listed above ATP in this table could be used to drive the synthesize ATP, and the hydrolysis of ATP can in turn be coupled to drive the synthesis of the phosphate esters listed below ATP in the Table.

Now let's focus on the Embden-Meyerhof pathway (Figure 24.12). In essence, here's what happens: phosphate groups are added to sugar molecules, which split in two and pick up more phosphate until, finally, a high-energy phosphate (1,3-diphosphoglyceric acid) is formed. The beauty of this compound lies in its ability to transfer a phosphate group to ADP. That is its function. After the transfer, the remaining compound rearranges a bit to become another high-energy phosphate, phosphoenol pyruvate or PEP. PEP is also able to transfer phosphate to ADP. That leaves pyruvate, which can be reduced to lactate (the end product of the Embden-Meyerhof pathway) or fed into the Krebs cycle. In the Embden-Meyerhof pathway, a sugar derivative is oxidized at Step 6 and NAD^+ is reduced to NADH; but in Step 11, a sugar derivative is reduced and NADH is oxidized to NAD^+. Thus, there is **no net oxidation** or reduction in the Embden-Meyerhof pathway.

Below is a summary of the Embden-Meyerhof pathway showing only glucose and its products. See if the comments give you a sense of the direction of the reactions, a sense of a grand design in which everything is done for a purpose. Also, you might notice again how the sacrifice of two ATP molecules during the early "priming" stage prepares the way for the synthesis later of four ATP molecules. (These systems reflect an old rule of business--you must sometimes spend money to make money.)

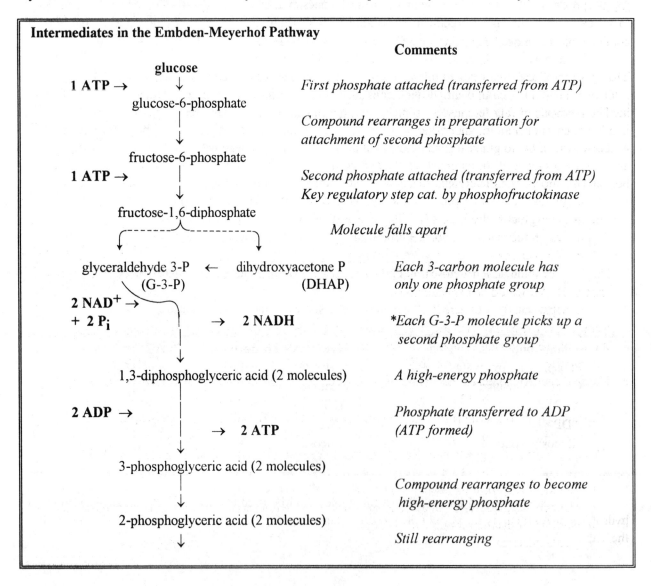

Intermediates in the Embden-Meyerhof Pathway

Comments

glucose

1 ATP →   *First phosphate attached (transferred from ATP)*

glucose-6-phosphate

Compound rearranges in preparation for attachment of second phosphate

fructose-6-phosphate

1 ATP →   *Second phosphate attached (transferred from ATP) Key regulatory step cat. by phosphofructokinase*

fructose-1,6-diphosphate

Molecule falls apart

glyceraldehyde 3-P ← dihydroxyacetone P   *Each 3-carbon molecule has*
(G-3-P)   (DHAP)   *only one phosphate group*

$2 NAD^+$ →
+ $2 P_i$ → 2 NADH   **Each G-3-P molecule picks up a second phosphate group*

1,3-diphosphoglyceric acid (2 molecules)   *A high-energy phosphate*

2 ADP →   *Phosphate transferred to ADP*
    → 2 ATP   *(ATP formed)*

3-phosphoglyceric acid (2 molecules)

Compound rearranges to become high-energy phosphate

2-phosphoglyceric acid (2 molecules)

Still rearranging

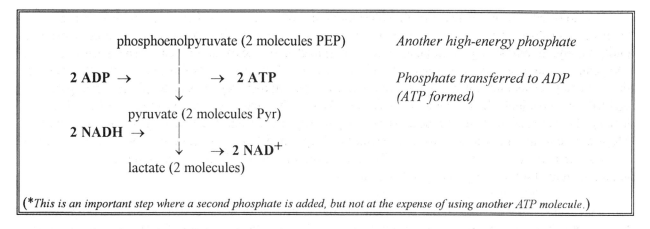

(*This is an important step where a second phosphate is added, but not at the expense of using another ATP molecule.)

Chapter 24 also considers the regulation of blood glucose levels. These topics are reviewed here in the **SELF-TEST** and in the end-of-the-chapter problems.

SELF-TEST

1. The molecule described as the "energy currency" of metabolism is:
    a. glucose   b. stearic acid   c. cAMP   d. Vitamin A   e. ATP
2. Digestion of carbohydrates begins with saliva in the mouth and the action of the enzyme _____ .
    a. insulin   b. α-amylase   c. kinase   d. mutase
3. The synthesis of fats for energy storage is an example of:
    a. catabolism   b. anabolism
4. Converting CO_2 to glucose is an example of a(n) _____ reaction.
    a. exergonic   b. metabolite   c. endergonic
5. The chemically significant feature of nucleotides like ATP and GTP is the _____ linkage.
    a. glycosidic   b. amide   c. pyrophosphate   d. peptide
6. The free energy of hydrolysis, $\Delta G^{O'}$, for ATP is about:
    a. 12.5 Kcal/mol   b. 7.3 Kcal/mol   c. 3.5 Kcal/mol
    d. -7.3 Kcal/mol   e. -3.5 Kcal/mol
7. The K_{eq} for the reaction A $\rightarrow$ B is 10. Under conditions such that the concentration of A is ten times that of B, ΔG would be expected to be:
    a. negative   b. zero   c. positive
   (Refer to the list of $\Delta G^{O'}$ values given in the **DISCUSSION** above to answer Questions 8-11.)
8. Which of the following compounds would not be considered a "high energy" compound?
    a. PEP   b. ATP   c. Glucose-6-phosphate   d. ADP
9. The free energy change for the synthesis of glucose-6-phosphate from glucose and ATP is:
    a. -11.1 b. $+11.1$ c. -7.3 d. $+4.0$ e. -4.0
10. Calculate $\Delta G^{O'}$ (Kcal/mol) for the synthesis of ATP from ADP and creatine phosphate.
    a. -5.5 b. -3.2 c. $+3.2$ d. -17.8 e. $+17.8$
11. What is the free energy change (Kcal) required to convert one mole of AMP to ATP via ADP?
    a. 13.8   b. -13.8 c. -2.2 d. $+2.2$ e. 16.0
12. The Embden-Meyerhof pathway is also known as:
    a. anaerobic glycolysis   b. glyconeogenesis   c. Krebs cycle   d. oxidative phosphorylation
13. An overdose of insulin produces a condition called:
    a. galactosemia   b. hyperglycemia   c. hypoglycemia

14. Which hormone triggers a decrease in blood sugar levels?
    a. cortisone   b. glucagon   c. insulin
    d. epinephrine   e. human growth hormone
15. Which is <u>not</u> a pancreatic hormone?
    a. adrenaline   b. glucagon   c. insulin
16. Which compound does glycogen most closely resemble?
    a. amylopectin   b. amylose   c. cellulose   d. glucose
17. The Cori cycle describes:
    a. the relationship between glycogenesis and glycogenolysis
    b. the conversion of acetic acid to carbon dioxide
    c. the interconversion of monosaccharides
18. Which compound serves as the intermediate through which all of the monosaccharides enter the Embden-Meyerhof pathway?
    a. galactose   b. fructose-6-phosphate   c. glucose-1-phosphate   d. pyruvate
19. Normal blood glucose levels are about _____ .
    a. 10 g/L   b. 100 g/L   c. 100 mg/100 mL   d. 240 mg/L   e. 100 mg/mL
20. The molecule described as the "secondary messenger" is _____ .
    a. ATP   b. adrenaline   c. glycogen   d. cAMP   e. glucagon
21. What is the end product of aerobic glycolysis?
    a. acetate   b. ethyl alcohol   c. glycogen   d. lactate   e. pyruvate
22. Which high-energy phosphate serves as the <u>direct</u> source of energy in muscle contraction?
    a. ATP   b. creatine phosphate   c. PEP
23. The key regulatory enzyme of the glycolyic pathway is the allosteric enzyme _____ .
    a. glycokinase   b. aldolase   c. LDH
    d. phosphofructokinase   e. glucomutase
24. In fermentation pyruvate is converted to _____ and then on to ethanol.
    a. acetaldehyde   b. lactate   c. acetate   d. fructose
25. For every mole of glucose degraded to pyruvate, _____ moles of ATP and _____ moles of NADH are produced.
    y. 2, 2   b. 2, 1   c. 2, 0   d. 5, 0   e. 4. 1
26. The biggest difference between glycolysis and gluconeogenesis is the step(s) that reform _____ .
    a. fructose-6-P   b. pyruvate   c. PEP   d. glucose-6-P   e. glyceraldehyde-3-P
27. The only oxidative step in glycolysis occurs with the oxidation of _____ .
    a. fructose-6-P   b. pyruvate   c. PEP   d. glucose-6-P   e. glyceraldehyde-3-P
28. T F Glucose is stored in the body in the form of glycogen.
29. T F The glucose tolerance test is used to diagnose galactosemia.
30. T F There are no redox reactions in the Embden-Meyerhof pathway.
31. T F In periods of normal (not strenuous) activity, energy is supplied to muscles through aerobic pathways.
32. T F While the Embden-Meyerhof pathway supplies the ATP required for muscular activity, the body incurs an oxygen debt.

ANSWERS

1. e	6. d	11. a	16. a	21. e	26. c	31. T
2. b	7. a	12. a	17. a	22. a	27. e	32. T
3. b	8. c	13. c	18. b	23. d	28. T	
4. c	9. e	14. c	19. c	24. a	29. F	
5. c	10. b	15. a	20. d	25. a	30. F	

CHAPTER 25: CARBOHYDRATE METABOLISM II

KEY WORDS

acetyl~SCoA	catabolic	thioesters	cytochromes	chemiosmotic
pyruvate	respiratory chain	oxaloacetate	citrate	coenzyme A
mitochondria	NADH, FADH$_2$	glycogenolysis	oxygen debt	citric acid cycle
anaerobic	electron carriers	electron transport	aerobic	Krebs cycle
ETS	oxidative	pyruvate dehydrogenase	lactic acid	TCA cycle
actin	phosphorylation	complex (PDC)	myosin	actomyosin

SUMMARY

In the aerobic oxidation of glucose, glucose is first converted to pyruvate as we saw in Chapter 24, but *pyruvate* is now converted to *acetyl~SCoA* and on to carbon dioxide and water. These processes release ~93% of the remaining free energy that was stored in glucose. The oxidation of pyruvate to CO$_2$ involves the *pyruvate dehydrogenase complex* and the *Krebs cycle* which produce several molecules of the reduced coenzymes *NADH* and *FADH$_2$*. The other product, water, is produced when these reduced coenzymes are reoxidized and their electrons flow through the *electron transport* system (*ETS*) to reduce oxygen to water. The term *"oxidative phosphorylation"* refers to the coupled synthesis of ATP to the flow of electrons through the ETS.

25.1 The Krebs Cycle
- A. In *aerobic* oxidation of glucose, glucose is converted to *pyruvate* which is then converted to *acetyl~SCoA (or Acetyl~CoA)*, a high-energy *thioester*. (Step 1, Fig 25.1)
  - 1. Using five vitamin-related cofactors this conversion is carried out by multiple copies of three different enzyme activities in one multi-enzyme complex, the *pyruvate dehydrogenase complex* (PDC).
  - 2. This step produces 1 molecule each of carbon dioxide and NADH in addition to the acetyl~SCoA.
  - 3. The PDC is allosterically regulated by the energy level of the cell. E$_1$ in the complex is turned off when a phosphate group is added by a kinase (regulation by covalent modification).
- B. *Acetyl~SCoA* is the thioester of *coenzyme A* with acetic acid. *Thioesters* are "high energy" compounds. The fate of acetyl~SCoA is described by the *Krebs cycle*, also known as the *TCA cycle* or *citric acid cycle*. (Refer to Fig. 25.1)
  - 1. The 10 steps of the Krebs cycle take place in the *mitochondria*.
  - 2. *Oxaloacetate (OAA)* initially condenses with acetyl~SCoA to form the 6C citrate. The citric acid will undergo several oxidative steps to regenerate the OAA just consumed, thus completing the cycle.
  - 3. During one turn of the cycle, the net effect is that a 2C acetyl group is lost and 2 molecules of carbon dioxide, 3 of NADH, 1 FADH, and 1 GTP are produced. The reduced coenzymes serve as *electron carriers* and will be regenerated when they donate their electrons to the *electron transport system*.
  - 4. Regulation of the pathway occurs primarily at Steps 2 and 4. Citrate synthetase is inhibited by ATP and NADH. At Step 4, isocitrate dehydrogenase is also inhibited by high energy conditions such as high levels of ATP and NADH, but also is turned on by high levels of ADP.
  - 5. The α-ketoglutarate dehydrogenase complex of Step 6 is very similar to the complex described for pyruvate in Step 1.

25.2 Respiratory Chain: Electron-Transport Chain
  A. Oxidation is the removal of electrons. When foodstuffs are oxidized, something must be reduced. The most common *electron carriers* of these reducing equivalents are the two coenzymes NADH and $FADH_2$.
    1. $NAD^+ + H^+ + 2 e^- \rightarrow NADH$ (nicotinamide adenine dinucleotide)
    2. $FAD + 2 H \rightarrow FADH_2$ (flavin adenine dinucleotide)
  B. The reactions of the Krebs cycle, electron transport, and oxidative phosphorylation take place within organelles called *mitochondria*. Mitochondria are called "the powerhouses" of the cell.
  C. The passage of electrons from NADH and $FADH_2$ to oxygen to produce water does not take place directly, but occurs stepwise as the electrons are passed through a series of electron carriers (including heme-containing proteins called *cytochromes*) that make up the "*respiratory chain*." Each intermediate in the respiratory chain is first reduced by the addition of electrons and then re-oxidized as it passes those electrons on to the next carrier. These *electron carriers* are found associated with the inner mitochondrial membrane and can be divided into different types:
    1. 2 electron carriers: NADH, $FADH_2$, and $CoQH_2$ dependent proteins.
    2. 1 electron carriers: Various cytochromes that contain a heme-like group with iron that can flip oxidation states from +3 to +2.
  D. The ETS is made up of four membrane associated complexes. Only Complex IV, containing cytochrome oxidase, has the ability to transfer electrons to molecular O_2 to produce water.
  E. Hydrogen cyanide and its salts release cyanide that can bind to and tie up the heme groups, thus inhibiting electron transfer and causing cell respiration to cease.
    1. Cyanide was used in the mass suicide at Jonestown, Guyana.
    2. Cyanide was also the lethal contaminant found in capsules of Tylenol.

25.3 Oxidative Phosphorylation
  A. *Catabolic* pathways utilize NAD^+ and FAD to oxidize the foodstuffs in our diets to carbon dioxide, thus producing large amounts of the reduced coenzymes NADH and $FADH_2$. These coenzymes must be reoxidized to NAD^+ and FAD to keep the catabolic pathways going.
  B. The hydrogens ($H^+ + e^-$) from NADH and $FADH_2$ are passed on to oxygen to form water. The energy released during this exergonic process is coupled to the synthesis of ATP by a process referred to as "*oxidative phosphorylation.*" It is possible to uncouple these processes and have electron transport without ATP synthesis. This strong evidence supporting the "*chemiosmotic*" hypothesis for ATP synthesis.
    1. Oxidation of each NADH in the mitochondria by oxygen is accompanied by the production of 3 molecules of ATP.
    2. Oxidation of each $FADH_2$ by oxygen leads to the production of 2 ATP.
    3. Energetics summary: 1 NADH   = 3 ATP;
                             1 $FADH_2$ = 2 ATP;
              thus   1 acetyl~SCoA = 12 ATP

25.4 Energy Yield of Carbohydrate Metabolism
  A. The conversion of glucose to CO_2 and water involved many oxidative steps and involved several pathways in different locations of the cell. These processes are summarized below:

Glycolysis	Glucose$\rightarrow$ 2 pyruvates+ 2 NADH + 2 ATP	= 6 ATP
PDC	2 pyruvates $\rightarrow$ 2 acetyl~SCoA + 2 NADH + 2 CO_2	= 6 ATP
Krebs cycle	2 acetyl~SCoA $\rightarrow$ 4 CO_2 + 6 NADH + 2 $FADH_2$ + 2 GTP	= 24 ATP
	Glucose $\rightarrow$ 6 CO_2 + 2 ATP + 10 NADH + 2 $FADH_2$ + 2 GTP	= 36 ATP

B. The efficiency of a metabolic pathway can be estimated by comparing the free energy value of all of the ATP molecules synthesized with the free energy released during the oxidation of the foodstuff.

$$C_6H_{12}O_6 + 6\ O_2 + 36\ ADP + 36\ P_i\ \rightarrow\ 6\ CO_2 + 36\ ATP + 42\ H_2O$$

For the oxidation of glucose, $\Delta G^{O'}$ = -686 kcal/mol in released free energy vs. −263 kcal conserved as new ATP (36 x −7.3 kcal/mole ATP) or 38% efficient. *Note: You will sometimes see this reported as 38 ATP. The variance arises from different assumptions as to how to treat the transport of the NADH equivalents produced during glycolysis into the mitochondria for ETS. It frequently is converted into $FADH_2$.

C. Different foods yield different amounts of energy per gram [Fats (~9 kcal/g); carbohydrates and proteins (~4 kcal/g)] because the carbon atoms in fats, for example, are in a more highly reduced state than the carbon atoms in carbohydrates or proteins. However, all catabolic pathways are ~40% efficient at storing the energy released as newly synthesized ATP; the rest is lost as heat, which helps keep our bodies warm.

25.5 Muscle Power

A. Muscle contains the proteins *actin* and *myosin* in a loose complex called *actomyosin*. When ATP is added to isolated actomyosin, the muscle fibers contract, which implies that ATP is the energy source for muscle contraction.

B. Muscle fibers are divided into two categories:

1. "Fast twitch" - Type IIB - white muscle; low in mitochondria and myoglobin; high in enzymes for *glycogenolysis*; designed for short bursts of vigorous work; sprinters have lots of white muscle.

2. "Slow twitch" - Type I - red muscle; high in mitochondria and myoglobin to supply the oxygen for aerobic respiration; designed for sustained, moderate levels of physical activity; long distance joggers have lots of red muscle; endurance training can increase the number of mitochondria in muscle fibers.

C. *Oxygen debt*: During strenuous exercise the energy demands can exceed the ability to supply oxygen to muscle tissue. Muscle metabolism shifts to anaerobic processes that convert pyruvate to lactate in order to regenerate the NAD^+ needed to keep glycolysis operable. This *lactic acid* buildup leads to a pH drop and deactivation of muscle enzymes, described as "muscle fatigue," and can cause lactic acid acidosis. The overworked muscles are incurring an oxygen debt that needs to be repaid after the strenuous exercise is over.

DISCUSSION

We've referred to metabolism, metabolites, and metabolic products frequently in past chapters. In this chapter, we are taking an extended look at metabolic processes in human beings. The single most noticeable feature of metabolic reactions is that transformations, which can be summarized in one equation, usually proceed by mechanisms that involve many steps. The very complexity of these processes makes life possible, but it also makes studying the processes difficult. Let's take another look at the Embden-Meyerhof pathway (Chapter 24) and compare it to the Krebs cycle, noting overall patterns that might make each of these metabolic pathways easier to comprehend. First, remember that both of these pathways are designed to produce energy, that is, to yield ATP molecules. Second, there is an obvious difference between the two series of reactions--one is cyclic (the Krebs cycle) and the other is not (the Embden-Meyerhof pathway). The latter starts with glucose and ends with lactic acid. The former starts and ends with oxaloacetate.

How about the reaction patterns of the Krebs cycle? The Krebs cycle is designed to oxidize acetate to two molecules of carbon dioxide. A chemist can do this in the laboratory by burning acetic acid, that is, by carrying out the combustion of acetic acid. Cells are far more subtle. The Krebs cycle (Figure 25.1) starts by taking the acetic acid (activated by attachment to coenzyme A) and bonding it to one of the intermediates of the cycle (oxaloacetic acid). The resulting product is "manipulated" to produce an organic molecule that is especially suited to being decarboxylated. By "manipulated" we mean that water is removed, then replaced in a different position, and then hydrogen is removed. The product does just what it is supposed to do--it decarboxylates. The product from that reaction decarboxylates again--producing the two carbon dioxide molecules. Now all that remains is manipulate the product succinate a bit to regenerate the starting molecule, OAA. To accomplish this hydrogen is removed (fumarate), water is added (malate), and more hydrogen is removed (oxaloacetate). And there's oxaloacetic acid again. What we want to see is the reasonableness of the process. If a cell cannot set fire to acetic acid to achieve its ends, then it simply builds molecules (enzymes) that use multiple steps to accomplish the same results.

Recall that no net oxidation or reduction took place in the Embden-Meyerhof pathway, but oxidation is recurring in the Krebs cycle. It occurs at four different points in the cycle (Steps 4, 6, 8, and 10). The oxidizing agents required for these steps are regenerated by the electron transport system, which operates in conjunction with oxidative phosphorylation. It is here that ATP is actually synthesized in reactions coupled to the transport of electrons to oxygen to form water (oxidative phosphorylation).

The other topic in Chapter 25 that often causes confusion is the role of electron carriers such as NADH and $FADH_2$ in the oxidation of foodstuffs to CO_2 and H_2O. As the fats, carbohydrates, and proteins in our diet are oxidized to CO_2, something else must be reduced. Ultimately, the final electron acceptor will be O_2 as it is reduced to water, H_2O. However, there are many intermediate electron carriers along the way. Most of these "reducing equivalents" are initially transferred to the coenzymes NAD^+ and FAD to produce NADH or $FADH_2$. These molecules then function as carriers of two electrons to deliver the electrons released during the oxidation of food- stuffs to CO_2 in the various pathways to the electron transport system (ETS) found in the mitochondria. As electrons pass along the ETS, the energy released is indirectly coupled to the synthesis of ATP by a process known as oxidative phosphorylation. These processes are summarized below

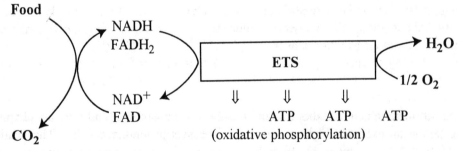

The rest of the material in Chapter 25 is reviewed in the **SELF-TEST**.

SELF-TEST

1. Which is <u>not</u> another name for the Krebs cycle?
     a. citric acid cycle   b. Cori cycle   c. tricarboxylic acid cycle
2. The reactions of the Krebs cycle take place in the _____ of the cell.
     a. mitochondria b. cytoplasm   c. nucleus   d. ribosomes
3. The conversion of pyruvate to acetyl~SCoA involves a multienzyme complex. Which of these vitamin related cofactors is <u>not</u> required for this process?
     a. NADH   b. Lipoic acid   c. FAD   d. ATP   e. Thymine PP

4. Through what intermediate do pyruvate and lactate enter the Krebs cycle?

    a. acetyl coenzyme A   b. ADP   c. fructose-6-phosphate   d. NAD^+

5. Which oxidizing agent is used in both anaerobic glycolysis and in the Krebs cycle?

    a. FAD   b. NAD^+ c. O_2

6. In which sequence of reactions is CO_2 produced?

    a. anaerobic glycolysis   b. Krebs cycle   c. oxidative phosphorylation

7. In which sequence of reactions is ATP not formed?

    a. anaerobic glycolysis   b. Krebs cycle   c. oxidative phosphorylation

8. Which is not one of the intermediates in the Krebs cycle?

    a. citric acid   b. isocitric acid   c. fumaric acid   d. lactic acid   e. succinic acid

9. Two molecules undergo decarboxylation in the Krebs cycle. Which does not?

    a. α-ketoglutaric acid   b. oxaloacetic acid   c. oxalosuccinic acid

10. Which molecule combines with acetyl~SCoA to form citrate in the TCA cycle?

    a. OAA   b. pyruvate   c. fumarate   d. lactate   e. succinate

11. What process does not occur in electron transport coupled with oxidative phosphorylation?

    a. conversion of oxygen to water

    b. synthesis of the oxidizing agents NAD^+ and FAD

    c. synthesis of ATP from ADP

    d. oxidation of lactic acid to pyruvic acid

    e. All of the above occur in oxidative phosphorylation.

12. Which is not true of the cytochromes?

    a. They are iron-containing proteins.

    b. They participate in the series of reactions called the respiratory chain.

    c. Their action is strongly inhibited by carbon dioxide.

    d. All of the above are true of the cytochromes.

13. Which of the following would be described as a 1 e- carrier?

    a. NADH   b. cytochromes   c. $FADH_2$

14. The reduced form of nicotinamide adenine dinucleotide is represented as:

    a. $FADH_2$ b. FADH   c. NAD^+ d. $NADH_2$ e. NADH

15. The oxidized form of flavin adenine dinucleotide is given as:

    a. $FADH_2$ b. FAD^+ c. FAD   d. NAD^+ e. NADH

16. The synthesis of ATP coupled with the passage of electrons to molecular O_2 to form water is called:

    a. respiratory chain   b. electron transport chain   c. Krebs cycle

    d. oxidative phosphorylation

17. Which of the following metabolic processes does not occur in the mitochondria?

    a. glycolysis   b. Krebs cycle   c. electron transport chain

    d. oxidative phosphorylation

18. The final electron acceptor in respiration is:

    a. H_2O b. FAD   c. NAD^+ d. O_2 e. cytochromes

19. An exergonic reaction has a K_{eq} that is:

    a. >1   b. 0   c. <1

20. The efficiency of most metabolic pathways is about:

    a. 10%   b. 20%   c. 40%   d. 80%   e. 100%

21. Cyanide is a lethal poison because it interferes with which of the following macromolecules?

    a. NADH   b. actomyosin   c. cytochromes   d. creatine kinase

22. Fats release more calories per gram than carbohydrates because the average oxidation number of C in fats is _____ than it is in carbohydrates.

    a. higher   b. lower

23. Each NADH that is reoxidized through the ETS produces the equivalent of _____ ATP.

      a. 1   b. 2   c. 3   d. 5   e. 8

24. Each acetyl unit converted to carbon dioxide and water produces the equivalent of _____ ATP.

      a. 1   b. 4   c. 8   d. 12   e. 20

25. Actomyosin is:

      a. the enzyme that catalyzes the transfer of phosphate from creatine phosphate to ADP

      b. the protein complex that constitutes the contractile tissue of muscle

      c. the drug used to counter the effects of an accumulated oxygen debt

26. T F The iron in cytochromes may be in the +2 or +3 oxidation state.

27. T F The ΔG for a two-step process is equal to the product of the ΔGs for the individual steps.

28. T F Carbon dioxide represents a highly oxidized, high energy form of carbon.

29. T F Creatine phosphate is stored in muscle tissue to help regenerate ATP for muscle contraction.

30. T F High levels of Type I muscle fibers are appropriate for aerobic oxidation.

31. T F Cytochromes are proteins involved in electron transport.

32. T F Cyanide compounds act as poisons by disrupting the Embden-Meyerhof pathway.

ANSWERS

1. b	9. b	17. a	25. b
2. a	10. a	18. d	26. T
3. d	11. d	19. a	27. F
4. a	12. c	20. c	28. F
5. b	13. b	21. c	29. T
6. b	14. e	22. b	30. T
7. b	15. c	23. c	31. T
8. d	16. d	24. d	32. F

CHAPTER 26: LIPID METABOLISM

KEY WORDS

lipoproteins	*fatty acid spiral*	*ketone bodies*	*adipose tissue*
ketosis	*obesity*	*β-oxidation*	*malonyl~SCoA*
acidosis	*lipid storage*	*acetyl~SCoA*	*bile*
DHAP	*disease*	*VLDL, LDL*	*triglycerides*
cholesterol	*lipases*	*acetone*	

SUMMARY

26.1 Fats as Fuels

    A. Energy is supplied by the oxidation of carbohydrates and lipids. Lipids are more highly reduced than carbohydrates (or proteins) and thus release more energy when oxidized to CO_2 and H_2O (~9.5 Kcal/g vs. 4.2 Kcal/g).

    B. Lipids can also be stored more efficiently with less water of hydration, thus lipids are the body's primary energy reserve.

        1. The average human carries a 20-30 day energy reserve as fat verses 1-2 day reserve as glycogen.

        2. A camel's hump is mostly fat (adipose tissue).

    C. The American Heart Association recommends that no more than 25% of the total calories in the diet be provided by lipids.

        1. Fatty acids in triacylglycerides can be saturated or unsaturated.

        2. The diet should contain 2-3 g of the "essential," polyunsaturated fatty acids like linoleic and linolenic acids.

26.2 Digestion and Absorption of Lipids

    A. Fats are emulsified by the **bile** salts, digested by **lipases**, absorbed into the lymph system, and finally enter the blood circulation. Being water insoluble, fats must be transported by **lipoproteins** in the blood.

    B. Blood **lipoproteins** are classified by their density.

        1. **VLDL**s (Very-low-density-lipoproteins) mainly transport triglycerides.

        2. **LDL**s (Low-density-lipoproteins) are the carriers of cholesterol.

        3. HDLs (High-density-lipoproteins) also carry cholesterol.

    C. The "Normal Fasting Levels" of lipids in blood plasma are given in Table 26.1. Abnormally high levels of **triglycerides** and **cholesterol** are associated with hardening of the arteries and increased potential for stroke or heart attack.

        1. Total cholesterol: 120-250mg/100mL

        2. Triglycerides: 25-260mg/100mL

        3. Total phospholipids: 150-250mg/100mL

        4. Total lipids: 400-700mg/100mL

26.3 Fat Depots

    A. Fat is stored throughout the body in a special kind of connective tissue called **adipose tissue**.

    B. Fats serve as a protective cushion around organs, help insulate against temperature changes, and are the body's most efficient form of energy storage. Phospholipids are important components of cell membranes.

C. *Triglycerides* are stored as fat droplets in adipose tissue. Excess dietary carbohydrates are first used to replenish liver and muscle glycogen and any remaining excess is then converted to fats for storage.

D. "Brown fat" contains specialized mitochondria that oxidize fat to produce heat instead of energy. This is important for hibernating animals and newborn infants.

26.4 Fatty Acid Oxidation

A. Activation of fatty acid metabolism involves a hormonal signal similar to that found for the breakdown of glycogen (glucagon, epinephrine, norepinephrine).

1. Hormonal signal → receptor binding → activation of adenyl cyclase to produce cAMP
2. cAMP activates a kinase that turns on lipases and promotes release of fatty acids from adipose tissue.
3. Lipases hydrolyze triglycerides, releasing free fatty acids.

B. Triglycerides → Free fatty acids + Glycerol

1. The glycerol is phosphorylated to glycerol phosphate and then converted to dihydroxyacetone phosphate which is a metabolite of the glycolytic pathway.
2. The free fatty acids react with ATP and then coenzyme A to form a fatty acyl~SCoA and AMP.

   i) Fatty acid + ATP → Fatty acyl adenylate + PP ($\to 2\ P_i$).

   ii) Fatty acyl adenylate + HSCoA → Fatty acyl~CoA + AMP

3. These processes take place in the cytoplasm.
4. The fatty acyl~SCoA can not cross the mitochonrial membrane. This requires a small carrier molecule, carnitine.

C. The *fatty acid spiral* (See Figure 26.3) or *β-oxidation* takes place within the mitochondria.

1. Dehydrogenation to produce a double bond and $FADH_2$
2. Hydration of the double bond to produce a β-hydroxy fatty acyl~SCoA
3. β-oxidation of the hydroxyl group to form a β-keto ester of CoA and 1 NADH
4. Attack of the β carbonyl C to cleave off a 2 C *acetyl~SCoA* unit and to form a new shortened molecule of fatty acyl~SCoA. If the resulting fatty acyl group has more than 4 Cs, go back to step 1.
5. During the final pass through the cycle, the cleavage of the 4C β-keto ester produces two molecules of acetyl~SCoA (See summary of catabolic pathways).
6. Note: Recall that acetyl~SCoA was also formed from glucose metabolism. It is important to note that excess carbohydrate is converted to fat, but that man **cannot** use fat to synthesize carbohydrates.

26.5 Bioenergetics of Fatty Acid Oxidation

A. The oxidation of fats produces approximately 9 kcal/g, twice as much per gram as the oxidation of carbohydrate or protein.

B. A 16 C palmitate fatty acyl~SCoA requires 7 turns of the *fatty acid spiral* to produce:

8 Acetyl~SCoA	x 12	=	96 ATP
7 NADH	x 3	=	21 ATP
7 $FADH_2$	x 2	=	14 ATP
			131 ATP
Activation Costs (ATP → AMP)			−2
			129 ATP Net yield

26.6 Glycerol metabolism
  A. Glycerol is transported to the liver where it is converted in 2 steps to dihydroxyacetone
     phosphate *(DHAP)*.
     Glycerol $\rightarrow$ 3-P-Glycerol $\rightarrow$ DHAP $\rightarrow$ Pyr. $\rightarrow$ Acetyl~SGA $\rightarrow$ CO_2
       (-1 ATP)   (+1 NADH = 2 ATP)   (+2ATP)   (+1 NADH = 3ATP)   (+12 ATP)
  B. DHAP follows the glycolytic pathway (DHAP $\rightarrow$ Pyr $\rightarrow$ PDC $\rightarrow$ TCA cycle).
  C. Summary: Glycerol to CO_2 (= 20 mol ATP)

26.7 Ketosis
  A. The *ketone bodies* are acetoacetic acid, β-hydroxybutyric acid, and *acetone*. Acetoacetic acid is
     synthesized in the liver from 2 molecules of acetyl~SCoA, and the other two ketone bodies are
     produced from acetoacetic acid.
  B. Low levels of the ketone bodies are normal components of the blood and are used as energy sources.
  C. High levels of ketone bodies (or *ketosis*) can occur during starvation or illnesses such as diabetes
     mellitus.
  D. Two of the ketone bodies are acids. Uncontrolled ketosis can lead to *acidosis* and death. Short
     oxygen supply and dehydration are symptoms of acidosis. Acidic blood cannot transport oxygen
     very well and the kidneys eliminate lots of fluids trying to remove the excess acids.

26.8 Obesity, Exercise, and Diets
  A. If you eat more food than you need, you gain weight. Obesity is an increasing problem in the
     developed nations. *Obesity* is the condition when excessive fat is stored in adipose tissue and the
     individual becomes overweight (20% > ideal weight). Foods (carbohydrate, fat, or protein) eaten in
     excess of immediate energy requirements are stored as fat. This puts an extra load on the heart and
     is a major factor in diseases of the heart and circulatory system.
  B. Crash diets are often deficient in essential nutrients and can be harmful. Reducing the caloric intake
     by just 100 cal/day can result in the loss of a pound of fat (3500 cal) in 35 days. A person who is
     moderately active needs ~15 Kcal/lb. (e.g. 160 lb = 2400 Kcal)
  C. Burning Calories with exercise:

Activity:	*Walking*	*Bicycling*	*Basketball*	*Swimming*	*Mowing*
Kcal/hr :	420	420	360-660	360-750	450

  D. "Set-Point theory" postulates that the hypothalamus senses when the level of fatty acids in the blood
     drops below some "set" level and that triggers the hunger response. Exercise may help lower this
     "set-point."
  E. The Body Mass Index (BMI) is between 20-25 for most adults.

$$BMI = 700 \times \frac{\text{Body wt. (lb)}}{(\text{Hgt, in.})^2}$$

Note: Optional Material - Some courses will include the biosynthesis of lipids presented below.

26.9 Biosynthesis of Fatty Acids
  A. The biosynthesis of fatty acids accomplishes the reverse of the oxidative steps employed during β-
     oxidation. However, fatty acid synthesis is catalyzed by a *fatty acid synthetase* complex in the
     cytoplasm.

B. Malonyl~SCoA and fatty acid synthesis
1. The carbon source for fatty acid synthesis is acetyl~SCoA, but only one molecule of acetyl~SCoA is used directly during the synthesis. The others are activated by a biotin-dependent carboxylation reaction that forms *malonyl~SCoA*.
2. Malonyl~SCoA condenses with the enzyme-bound acetyl~S-E to form acetoacetyl~S-E plus carbon dioxide. The carbon dioxide serves only to activate the alpha C position for the condensation reaction.
3. The β-keto acetoacetyl~S-E is then reduced to the β-hydroxy compound, dehydrated to give the double bond, and hydrogenated to produce a saturated hydrocarbon chain.
4. The growing fatty acyl~S-E is now ready for another cycle by undergoing condensation with another molecule of malonyl~SCoA.
5. Each repetition of the cycle adds two carbons to the length of the chain.

26.10 Biosynthesis of Fats
A. Fats are synthesized from fatty acids and glycerol. The acetyl~SCoA needed to synthesize fatty acids can come from the degradation of carbohydrates, proteins, or lipids. The same is true for glycerol, so an excess of any of the major foodstuffs can be converted to fat.
B. Synthesis of triglycerides
1. Two molecules of activated fatty acyl~SCoA react with glycerol phosphate to produce phosphatidic acid.
2. A phosphatase removes the phosphate to produce a diglyceride.
3. The diglyceride reacts with another molecule of fatty acyl~SCoA to complete the synthesis of the triglyceride.

26.11 Biosynthesis of Phospholipids
A. Phospholipids are synthesized from a diglyceride and an activated form of the organophosphate group.
B. In the biosynthesis of phosphoethanolamine, a cytidine nucleotide acts as the activator and carrier. CDP-ethanolamine reacts with the diacylglycerol to form the phosphatidylethanolamine.
C. The phosphoethanolamine can be methylated to form lecithin, or the ethanolamine can be exchanged with serine to form cephalin.

26.12 Cholesterol and Some Other Steroids
A. Cholesterol and other steroids are nonsaponifiable lipids.
B. Cholesterol is synthesized from acetyl~SCoA. Other steroids can be synthesized from cholesterol.

26.13 Lipid Storage Diseases
A. Glycolipids are important components of brain and nerve tissue. Abnormal accumulation of these compounds can produce mental disorders and neurological problems.
B. *Lipid storage diseases* are genetic diseases caused by defective enzymes. Tay-Sachs disease, Gaucher's disease, and Niemann-Pick disease are examples.

DISCUSSION

We emphasized in Chapter 26 that fat metabolism cannot be divorced from the metabolism of carbohydrates (Also see the summary figure in the next unit, p.260). What may not have been quite so obvious is the similarity between the chemistry of the fatty acid cycle and that of the Krebs cycle. Since metabolic pathways may strike students as endless collections of unrelated reactions, we emphasize patterns and relationships whenever we can.

Let's recall some significant features of the Krebs cycle. During the first half of the Krebs cycle, a molecule that will release two carbon dioxide units is synthesized. In the later part of the cycle, the remaining molecule is converted back to the original starting material. Here's a summary of these later reactions.

Krebs cycle (steps 8, 9, and 10, p.705 of the text)

$$\text{HOOC-CH}_2\text{-CH}_2\text{-}\overset{O}{\overset{\|}{C}}\text{-OH} \xrightarrow[\text{FAD} \quad \text{FADH}_2]{} \text{HOOC-CH=CH-}\overset{O}{\overset{\|}{C}}\text{-OH} \xrightarrow[\text{H}_2\text{O}]{} \text{HOOC-}\overset{OH}{\overset{|}{CH}}\text{-CH}_2\text{-}\overset{O}{\overset{\|}{C}}\text{-OH} \xrightarrow[\text{NAD}^+ \quad \text{NADH + H}^+]{} \text{HOOC-}\overset{O}{\overset{\|}{C}}\text{-CH}_2\text{-}\overset{O}{\overset{\|}{C}}\text{-OH}$$

Now look at the analogous reactions from the fatty acid cycle.

Fatty acid cycle (excluding final step)

$$\text{R-CH}_2\text{-CH}_2\text{-}\overset{O}{\overset{\|}{C}}\text{~SCoA} \xrightarrow[\text{FAD} \quad \text{FADH}_2]{} \text{R-CH=CH-}\overset{O}{\overset{\|}{C}}\text{~SCoA} \xrightarrow[\text{H}_2\text{O}]{} \text{R-}\overset{OH}{\overset{|}{CH}}\text{-CH}_2\text{-}\overset{O}{\overset{\|}{C}}\text{~SCoA} \xrightarrow[\text{NAD}^+ \quad \text{NADH + H}^+]{} \text{R-}\overset{O}{\overset{\|}{C}}\text{-CH}_2\text{-}\overset{O}{\overset{\|}{C}}\text{~SCoA}$$

Except that the fatty acid reacts in the form of its thioester, the reaction sequence is the same. Two saturated carbons are unsaturated, then the components of water are added, and finally the hydroxyl group is oxidized to a carbonyl group. In both cases, it is the carbonyl group that reacts in the next step. In the Krebs cycle, the carbonyl group adds acetyl coenzyme A. In the fatty acid cycle, the carbonyl group releases acetyl coenzyme A.

Krebs cycle: $\text{HOOC-}\overset{O}{\overset{\|}{C}}\text{-CH}_2\text{-}\overset{O}{\overset{\|}{C}}\text{-OH} + \text{H}_2\text{O} \longrightarrow \text{HOOC-}\overset{OH}{\overset{|}{C}}\text{-CH}_2\text{-}\overset{O}{\overset{\|}{C}}\text{-OH} + \text{CoASH}$

$+$

$\text{CH}_3\text{-}\overset{}{\underset{O}{C}}\text{~SCoA}$ $\overset{}{\underset{O}{CH_2}}\text{-C-OH}$

Fatty acid cycle: $\text{R-}\overset{O}{\overset{\|}{C}}\text{-CH}_2\text{-}\overset{O}{\overset{\|}{C}}\text{~SCoA} \longrightarrow \text{R-C}\overset{O}{\diagup}_{\diagdown \text{S-CoA}} + \text{CH}_3\text{-}\overset{O}{\overset{\|}{C}}\text{~SCoA}$

$+$

CoA-S-H

Just as the Krebs cycle yields reduced species (FADH$_2$ and NADH) for the respiratory chain, so also does the fatty acid cycle. Thus both of these processes generate ATP indirectly through oxidative phosphorylation. (Remember that the fatty acid cycle not only supplies FADH$_2$ and NADH formed in every turn of the cycle, but it also produces acetyl~coenzymeA. Acetyl~CoA then feeds into the Krebs cycle where it generates additional FADH$_2$ and NADH.)

Optional Material: The biosynthesis of fatty acids occurs through a near reversal of the fatty acid cycle. By "near" we mean that, except for the initial step in each turn of the reverse cycle, the sequence of reactions is essentially the same.

$$\underset{\text{start with carbonyl}}{\overset{O \quad\quad O}{\overset{\| \quad\quad \|}{\text{-C-CH}_2\text{-C-}}}} \longrightarrow \overset{HO \quad\quad O}{\overset{| \quad\quad \|}{\text{-CH-CH}_2\text{-C-}}} \longrightarrow \overset{O}{\overset{\|}{\text{-CH=CH-C-}}} \longrightarrow \underset{\text{end with saturated C}}{\overset{O}{\overset{\|}{\text{-CH}_2\text{-CH}_2\text{-C-}}}}$$

However, there are many differences in the way these reaction steps are carried out. Beta oxidation takes place in the mitochondria, while fatty acid biosynthesis occurs in the cytoplasm where the growing fatty acid molecule reacts as an enzyme complex (rather than as a coenzyme A~ester). Also, whereas each two-carbon would be added in the form of acetyl~coenzymeA in a direct reversal, it is malonyl~CoA that adds (with the loss of carbon dioxide) in the near reversal. In the near reversal the reducing agent is NADPH; whereas in a direct reversal, NADH and FADH$_2$ would be used. Finally, remember that phosphate (glycolysis) or coenzyme A, when attached to a molecule, serves to activate that molecule. In this sense, these groups play similar roles.

The rest of the material in Chapter 26 is reviewed in the problems at the end of the chapter and in the **SELF-TEST**.

SELF-TEST

1. The oxidation of 1 g of fat to carbon dioxide yields about:
    a. one calorie   b. four kilocalories   c. nine calories   d. nine kilocalories

2. The average percent body fat for an adult female is about _____ %.
    a. 5   b. 10   c. 15   d. 20   e. 25

3. Which is <u>not</u> true of fats?
    a. They supply more energy per gram than carbohydrates.
    b. They can be stored with less water than carbohydrates.
    c. They can be mobilized more quickly than carbohydrates.
    d. All of the above statements are true.

4. The lymphatic system transports fats:
    a. from the small intestine to the blood
    b. from the small intestine to the cells
    c. from the blood to the cells

5. Normal fasting level for total cholesterol in blood plasma is about _____ .
    a. 200 g/L   b. 10-20 mg/100 mL   c. 120 g/L   d. 120-250 mg/100 mL   e. 2 mg/100mL

6. How is fat stored in the adipose tissue?
    a. as droplets of fat within cells   b. as bilayers forming cell membranes
    c. complexed with protein molecules

7. Which energy reserve is used first?
    a. depot fat   b. fat stored in the liver   c. glycogen

8. The CoA~thioesters of fatty acids need the help of _____ to cross the mitochondrial membrane.
    a. NADH   b. ATP   c. glucose   d. insulin   e. carnitine

9. Fatty acids that enter the fatty acid cycle are first activated by their conversion to:
    a. coenzyme A thioesters   b. enzyme complexes   c. phosphate esters

10. Which is the product of β-oxidation?
    a. $\overset{O}{\overset{\|}{R-CH=CH-C-SCoA}}$ b. $\overset{OH\quad O}{\overset{\quad\ \ \|}{R-CH-CH_2-C-SCoA}}$ c. $\overset{O\quad\ \ O}{\overset{\|\qquad\|}{R-C-CH_2-C-SCoA}}$

11. Which oxidizing agent is employed in the fatty acid cycle?
    a. FADH$_2$ b. NAD$^+$ c. NADP$^+$ d. O$_2$

12. What is the end product obtained from the fatty acid in the fatty acid cycle?
    a. acetyl coenzyme A   b. dihydroxyacetone phosphate   c. malonyl coenzyme A

13. If 8 FADH$_2$ and 8 NADH molecules enter the respiratory chain, how many ATP molecules can be produced?
    a. 11   b. 22   c. 27   d. 32   e. 40

14. Which category of foodstuff can<u>not</u> supply acetyl~coenzyme A for the biosynthesis of fatty acids?
    a. carbohydrates   b. fats   c. proteins   d. All 3 types supply acetyl~SCoA.

15. Which is not a path entered by acetyl~coenzyme A?
    a. synthesis of steroids   b. Krebs cycle   c. fatty acid synthesis
    d. formation of ketone bodies   e. glycogen synthesis
    f. Acetyl~coenzyme A follows all of the above routes.

16. Before fat biosynthesis begins, glycerol must be activated in the form of:
    a. its phosphate ester   b. its coenzyme A thioester
    c. UDP-glycerol   d. CDP-glycerol

17. For fat biosynthesis, fatty acids are activated in the form of:
    a. their phosphate esters   b. their coenzyme A thioesters
    c. UDP-acid   d. CDP-acid

18. Fast walking burns about _____ Kcal/hr.
    a. 100   b. 200   c. 400   d. 800   e. 1000

19. In phospholipid biosynthesis, the cytidine nucleotide does which of the following?
    a. catalyzes the conversion of ethanolamine to choline
    b. acts as a carrier molecule or activator
    c. picks up a phosphate unit from ATP

20. The ketone bodies do not include:
    a. acetoacetic acid   b. acetone   c. β-hydroxybutyric acid   d. pyruvic acid

21. High concentrations of ketone bodies in the blood:
    a. cause diabetes mellitus   b. are a symptom of starvation
    c. increase the pH of the blood   d. All of the above are correct.

22. How many NADHs are produced during the β-oxidation of an 18-C fatty acid?
    a. 20   b. 10   c. 9   d. 8   e. 5

23. The initial activation of free fatty acids occurs in the _____ of the cell.
    a. mitochondria   b. cytoplasm   c. nucleus

24. The starting material for cholesterol biosynthesis is _____ .
    a. glucose   b. oxaloacetate   c. pyruvate   d. acetate   e. lactate

25. In a person suffering from diabetes mellitus, which of the following does not lead to an increase in the production of ketone bodies.
    a. conversion of body tissues to fat metabolism
    b. reliance on gluconeogenesis for glucose required by cells
    c. breakdown of insulin to fatty acids
    d. All of the above lead to increased production of ketone bodies.

26. T F Fats are transported in the blood primarily as lipoproteins.

27. T F Blood lipid levels are not affected by normal body processes and remain relatively constant under most conditions.

28. T F The glycerol obtained from the hydrolysis of fats is fed into the Embden-Meyerhof pathway as dihydroxyacetone phosphate.

29. T F Condensation of malonyl coenzyme A with a growing fatty acid chain produces fatty acids with an odd number of carbon atoms.

30. T F In phospholipid biosynthesis in humans, the cytidine nucleotide usually activates the diglyceride molecule.

31. T F Some ketone bodies are excreted in the urine of healthy individuals.

32. T F "Air hunger" accompanies acidosis because the ability of the blood to transport oxygen decreases with decreasing pH.

33. T F Most obesity is the result of glandular malfunction.

34. T F The lipid-storage diseases, such as Niemann-Pick disease, produce arteriosclerosis.

35. T F The oxidative step in β-oxidation is the formation of the β-alcohol.

ANSWERS

1.	d	11.	b	21.	b	31.	T
2.	e	12.	a	22.	d	32.	T
3.	c	13.	e	23.	b	33.	F
4.	a	14.	d	24.	d	34.	F
5.	d	15.	e	25.	c	35.	F
6.	a	16.	a	26.	T		
7.	c	17.	b	27.	F		
8.	e	18.	c	28.	T		
9.	a	19.	b	29.	F		
10.	c	20.	d	30.	F		

CHAPTER 27: PROTEIN METABOLISM

KEY WORDS

amino acid pool	*essential a.a.*	*decarboxylases*	*ornithine*
catabolism	*nonessential a.a.*	*gluconeogenesis*	*uric acid*
anabolism	*transamination*	*glutamate, α-KG*	*gout*
nitrogen balance	*oxidative deamination*	*urea cycle*	*kwashiorkor*
carbamyl phosphate	*glutamine*	*arginine*	*starvation*

SUMMARY

27.1 Digestion and Absorption of Proteins
   A. Intact proteins cannot be absorbed across intestinal membranes. Digestion of proteins into amino acids by proteases takes place primarily in the stomach (pepsin) and the small intestine (pancreatic enzymes such as trypsin, chymotrypsin, carboxypeptidase).
      1. Pepsin   - cleaves after Trp, Tyr, Phe, Met, Leu
      2. Trypsin   - cleaves after Lys, Arg
      3. Chymotrypsin - cleaves after Phe, Trp, Tyr
      4. Carboxypeptidase   - cleaves off C-terminus
   B. Amino acids are *actively transported* across the intestinal wall and carried to the liver. Ingested protein satisfies two needs.
      1. Replaces N eliminated as urea
      2. Supplies essential amino acids that we are unable to synthesize

27.2 Nitrogen Balance
   A. Protein molecules are constantly being broken down *(catabolism)* and resynthesized *(anabolism)* in the body. Liver proteins turn over every few days, while collagen molecules last for a few years.
   B. Protein synthesis is an ongoing need but is limited by the availability of the essential amino acids.
   C. *Nitrogen balance = N_{in} minus N_{out}*
      1. Positive nitrogen balance: Growth, pregnancy
      2. Negative nitrogen balance: Fasting, starvation, fever diet lacking essential amino acids

27.3 The Essential Amino Acids
   A. Higher plants and many micro organisms are capable of synthesizing all their amino acids from CO_2, H_2O and inorganic salts. Animals can synthesize only about half (the *nonessential*) amino acids.
      1. Ala: from transamination of pyruvate
      2. Glu: from transamination of α-ketoglutarate
      3. Asp: from transamination of oxaloacetate
      4. Ser: made from phosphoglycerate
      5. Gly: made from Serine
      6. Cys: made from Methionine
      7. Gln: made from Glutamate
      8. Asn: made from Aspartate
      9. Pro: made from Glutamate
      10. Tyr: from hydroxylation of Phenylalanine

B. *Essential* amino acids are those that cannot be synthesized and need to be supplied in the diet (Lys, His, Met, Arg, Thr, Leu, Val, Ile, Phe, Trp). We need well-balanced (complete) protein, not just protein in the diet.

27.4 The Chemistry of Starvation

A. A body totally deprived of food soon uses up its glycogen reserves and needs to convert to fat metabolism, thus bringing on ketosis. During starvation or uncontrolled diabetes mellitus, acetyl~SCoA concentration is high and oxaloacetate ketosis is followed by **acidosis**.

B. During *starvation*, the body will also break down its own proteins to try to meet its metabolic needs and to provide glucose to the brain via gluconeogenesis.

C. *Kwashiorkor* is a protein deficiency disease that produces emaciation, bloatedness, mental apathy, etc.

27.5 Amino Acid Metabolism

A. Proteins we eat are hydrolyzed to amino acids which become part of the amino acid pool. These amino acids can be used to synthesize new proteins. They can also be metabolized for energy production or stored as glycogen and fat.

B. Catabolism of amino acids

1. *Transamination:* The amino group removed is transferred to an α-keto acid (commonly this is α-ketoglutarate) to produce the corresponding amino acid (e.g., glutamate) and the new α-keto acid. The human body contains about 100g of free amino acids, with about half of that coming to from Glu and Gln.

Alanine	$+ \alpha$-*ketoglutarate*	$\rightarrow$	Pyruvate	$+$ *Glutamate*
Aspartate	$+ \alpha$-*ketoglutarate*	$\rightarrow$	Oxaloacetate	$+$ *Glutamate*
etc.				

2. *Oxidative deamination*: The glutamic acid formed during the transamination reactions can be converted back to α-ketoglutarate.

   Glutamate $\overset{[O]}{\rightarrow}$ α-*ketoglutarate* $+$ ammonia

3. Both transaminases and decarboxylases utilize pyridoxal phosphate (Vit. B_6) as a cofactor.

4. *Decarboxylases* remove CO_2 to convert primary amino acids into primary amines. Histamine, serotonin, tyramine, dopamine, GABA, and polyamines are produced in this way.

5. C skeletons: After the N is removed from amino acids via transamination, the ketoacid carbon skeleton that remains is catabolized by from one to many steps to a TCA cycle intermediate (see Fig. 27.6). The keto acid carbon skeletons make their way to intermediates of the Krebs cycle, pyruvate, or acetyl~SCoA. Each amino acid has its unique pathway involving from one to many steps.

C. Gluconeogenesis is the synthesis of new glucose from glycerol or from amino acid carbon skeletons. This process requires six high-energy phosphates per glucose molecule synthesized. Although expensive, this process helps keep the brain fueled with glucose.

27.6 Storage of Nitrogen

A. Carbohydrates can be stored in the body as glycogen and the fats as triglycerides in the fat depots. Proteins are not stored, but a limited supply of amino acids circulates in the bloodstream and is called the *amino acid pool.*

B. *Glutamine* is a high nitrogen compound used by many tissues and in the blood as a temporary storage of N.

C. The excess ammonium ion is converted to urea and excreted.

27.7 Excretion of Nitrogen
    A. Levels of NH_3 greater than 5mg/100mL of blood are toxic to humans. Ammonia levels are normally kept at 1-3mg/100mL blood. Excess N must be excreted.
        1. Vertebrates excrete excess N as urea.
        2. Birds, reptiles excrete excess N as uric acid.
        3. Marine organisms, fish excrete excess N as free ammonia.
    B. Over 80% of the N from protein catabolism is excreted by the kidneys into urea. Urea is made primarily in the liver. The ***urea cycle*** describes how N from amino acid ***catabolism*** is converted to urea. **(Optional material)**
        1. Excess nitrogen is transferred to α-ketoglutarate to produce glutamate or to oxaloacetate to produce aspartate.
        2. NH_3 is produced by the oxidative deamination of α-ketoglutarate.
        3. NH_3 is activated by ATP and CO_2 to produce ***carbamyl phosphate***.
        4. Carbamyl phosphate condenses with ***ornithine*** to form citrulline.
        5. Citrulline condenses with aspartate to form arginosuccinate, which splits off fumaric acid, leaving arginine.
        6. ***Arginine*** is hydrolyzed to ***urea*** and ***ornithine***.
    C. Nucleoprotein Metabolism
        1. Nucleic acids are hydrolyzed during digestion to nucleotides and then to nucleosides. The nucleosides are absorbed and then split by nucleosidases to form ribose sugars and the purine and pyrimidine bases.
        2. Purines (Adenine, Guanine) are metabolized to uric acid.
          a. Birds and reptiles excrete excess N as ***uric acid*** to conserve water, fish remove N as NH_3.
          b. ***Gout*** is a metabolic disorder caused by the deposition of ***uric acid*** salts in cartilage.
        3. Pyrimidines are metabolized to carbon dioxide, water, and urea. Cytosine and uracil form beta-alanine, while thymine goes through beta-aminoisobutyric acid.
        4. The purine and pyrimidine bases can be synthesized from amino acids and other metabolites and thus are not essential in the diet.

27.8 Relationships Among the Metabolic Pathways
    A. The metabolic pathways are interconnected (See summary on next page and Figure 27.8).
    B. Catabolism of all three types of major foodstuffs tends to converge to acetyl~SCoA and the Krebs cycle.
    C. Anabolism tends to diverge. Starting with a few key metabolites, the building blocks of biochemistry are synthesized and from them millions of different biomolecules (e.g., proteins) can be formed.

       The summary below shows the inter-relatedness of many aspects of the various metabolic pathways that were presented in Chapters 24 - 27. Although it appears to be a very complicated figure, take time to see how all of the separate pathways that were presented in the past four chapters are tied together in this one figure. Note that only 1 ATP is required to prime the glucose C skeleton for glycolysis when starting with glycogen instead of glucose and remember that the second stage of glycolysis takes place twice for each glucose that enters the pathway. An (*) denotes a key enzyme that helps regulate the flux through the pathway. Note that the activation of fatty acids also takes place in the cytoplasm of the cell, but that β-oxidation occurs inside the mitochondria. Also shown, but less obvious, are examples of how amino acids such as Ala, Asp, Gln and Glu are metabolized through the combination of transamination reactions to remove the nitrogen and oxidative deamination to produce ammonia for later removal as urea. The convergent nature of catabolism is evident as the metabolism of carbohydrates, fats, and proteins (amino acids) all converge to just a few common intermediates such as pyruvate, oxaloacetate, α-ketoglutarate and acetyl~SCoA.

SUMMARY OF CATABOLIC PATHWAYS

DISCUSSION

The study of the metabolism and biosynthesis of amino acids is both easier and more difficult than the study of comparable processes involving carbohydrates and fats. It is easier because most of the emphasis can be placed on two key reversible reactions, both of which involve the fate of the amine group-- transamination and oxidative deamination.

The fact that amino acid metabolism neatly blends into carbohydrate metabolism also makes the former a little easier to understand. Many of the ketoacids that result when amine groups are removed from amino acids are already quite familiar to you as intermediates of the glycolytic pathway or the citric acid cycle. What makes this topic more difficult than the analogous material covered in Chapters 24 through 26 is the fact that the variety of amino acids is considerably greater than the variety of monosaccharides or fatty acids. All monosaccharides isomerize to common intermediates and then use the same metabolic pathways. Different length fatty acids cycle through the same spiral pathways (e.g. β-oxidation), varying only the number of turns required. But there is no common intermediate or common metabolic pathway for the complete degradation of amino acids. As Figure 27.6 indicates, they do all ultimately end up in the citric acid cycle. However, the same figure also indicates that their points of entry are quite varied. We've gotten around this difficulty by simply acknowledging it and not bothering to specify all of the details. One metabolic pathway that we do not cover in detail is the urea cycle, which describes the fate of most of the nitrogen removed from amino acids. The amino acid arginine is cleaved by arginase into urea and another amino acid, ornithine. Ornithine is converted back into arginine by the steps of the urea cycle, thus ornithine serves a role similar to OAA in the other Krebs cycle.

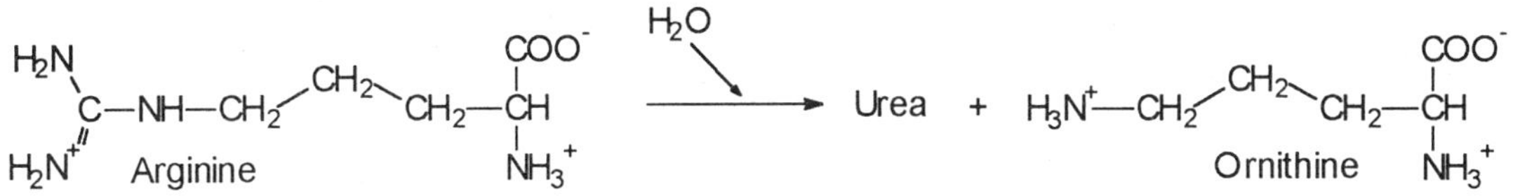

The following diagram summarizes the source of the atoms incorporated into the urea product.

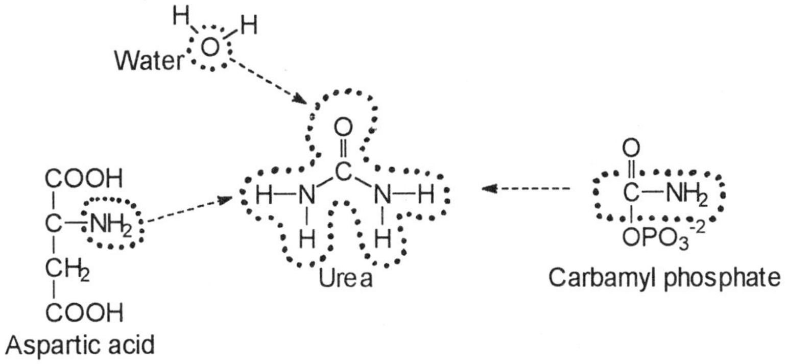

However, remember that the nitrogen supplied by aspartic acid may come from any of the amino acids by way of transamination reactions. Any amino acid can supply the nitrogen transferred from carbamyl phosphate, too, through a combination of transamination and oxidative deamination. As usual, much of the descriptive material in the chapter is reviewed in the problems at the end of the chapter.

SELF-TEST

1. The principal digestive component of gastric juice is
     a. amylase   b. pepsinogen   c. carboxypeptidase   d. phosphofructokinase
2. The principal organ responsible for the degradation and synthesis of amino acids is the _____ .
     a. brain   b. liver   c. stomach   d. pancreas   e. intestines
3. The biosynthesis of muscle protein from amino acids is classified as:
     a. anabolism   b. catabolism   c. digestion   d. transamination

4. The essential amino acids:
    a. can be synthesized in the body if nonessential amino acids are supplied in the diet
    b. are not present in the amino acid pool
    c. can be the limiting factor in determining the extent of protein biosynthesis
    d. All of the above are correct.

5. Amino acids are stored:
    a. with glycogen in liver and muscle
    b. in depots analogous to the fat storage areas
    c. in the nuclei of cells
    d. There are no storage facilities in the body for amino acids.

6. Which of the following amino acids is <u>not</u> an essential amino acid?
    a. Lys   b. Trp   c. Val   d. Glu   e. His

7. The amino acid pool can be supplied by:
    a. dietary amino acids
    b. the breakdown of tissue protein
    c. the biosynthesis of nonessential amino acids
    d. All of the above processes contribute to the population of the amino acid pool.

8. Protein biosynthesis:
    a. occurs only after prolonged starvation has severely depleted body protein
    b. is dictated by the genetic code
    c. occurs primarily in the small intestine
    d. All of the above are correct.

9. Growing children are in a state of:
    a. nitrogen balance   b. positive nitrogen balance   c. negative nitrogen balance

10. Proteins in the diet can be:
    a. used for the production of energy
    b. used in the replacement of tissue protein
    c. converted to carbohydrates
    d. converted to fats
    e All of the above are true.

11. A common protein deficiency disease is called _____ .
    a. diarrhea   b. kwashiorkor   c. beriberi   d. scurvey   e. rickets

12. Which amino acid is most often metabolized via oxidative deamination?
    a. glutamate   b. α-ketoglutarate   c. ornithine   d. aspartate

13. In amino acid metabolism, which compound most commonly serves as the amine group acceptor during transamination reactions?
    a. glutamate   b. α-ketoglutarate   c. ornithine   d. aspartate

14. Which amino acid is converted to oxaloacetic acid through transamination?
    a. glutamate   b. α-ketoglutarate   c. ornithine   d. aspartate

15. Transaminases use a cofactor related to the vitamin _____ .
    a. B_1 b. B_2 c. B_6 d. B_{12} e. niacin

16. Glutamate oxaloacetate transaminase (GOT) is the enzyme that catalyzes:
    a. the conversion of phenylalanine to tyrosine
    b. the conversion of phenylalanine to phenylpyruvic acid
    c. the transfer of phosphate from creatine phosphate to ADP
    d. the transfer of an amine group from glutamic acid to oxaloacetic acid

17. The term Krebs cycle is not applied to:
    a. the citric acid cycle   b. the urea cycle   c. the fatty acid cycle

18. Glutamic acid is converted to α-ketoglutarate and _____ by oxidative deamination.
    a. asparate   b. ammonia   c. citrate   d. oxaloacetate   e. alanine
19. The urea formed in the urea cycle does not incorporate atoms contributed by:
    a. aspartic acid   b. carbamyl phosphate   c. ornithine   d. water
20. In addition to urea, which compound is formed by the cleavage of arginine in the urea cycle?
    a. arginine   b. aspartic acid   c. citrulline   d. ornithine
21. Which product is used by birds to excrete excess nitrogen?
    a. urea   b. ammonia   c. uric acid   d. glutamate
22. Which compounds can be converted to uric acid?
    a. adenine and guanine   b. adenine and thymine
    c. guanine and cytosine   d. uracil and thymine
23. Glycine is not an essential amino acid because it can be produced from:
    a. phenylalanine   b. β-alanine   c. serine   d. glutamate
24. T F The amino acid pool is depleted to obtain material for the synthesis of nitrogen-containing compounds such as heme.
25. T F After proper chemical modification, all amino acids can contribute compounds to the tricarboxylic acid cycle.
26. T F It is possible for the composition of the amino acid pool to be adjusted to fit current needs of the body.
27. T F Infants suffering from PKU lack the normal pigmentation in skin, hair, and eyes.
28. T F In fish, nitrogen is excreted primarily as ammonia.
29. T F Nucleic acids are not required in the diet of human beings.
30. T F The precipitation of salts of uracil is characteristic of gout.

ANSWERS

1. b	11. b	21. c
2. b	12. a	22. a
3. a	13. b	23. c
4. c	14. d	24. T
5. d	15. c	25. T
6. d	16. d	26. T
7. d	17. c	27. F
8. b	18. b	28. T
9. b	19. c	29. T
10. e	20. d	30. F

CHAPTER 28: BODY FLUIDS

KEY WORDS

acidosis	alkalosis	blood pressure	osmotic pressure	systolic
diastolic	heparin	stroke	fibrin	sweat
lymphocytes	platelets	thrombocytes	osmosis	anemia
blood	fibrinogen	gamma globulins	kidneys	erythrocytes
thrombin	antigen	urine	leukocytes	immune
antibody	perspiration	Sickle cell	albumins	hemoglobin
tears	plasma	capillaries	bilirubin	milk
serum	edema	lymph	hematocrit	shock

SUMMARY

28.1 Blood: An Introduction
  A. **Blood** is the principal transport system in the human body. It moves through a ~100,000 km long network of **capillaries** and blood vessels. It carries:
    1. Oxygen from the lungs to tissues
    2. Carbon dioxide from the tissues to the lungs
    3. Nutrients from the intestines to tissues
    4. Metabolic wastes to excretory organs
    5. Hormones from endocrine glands to target tissue
    6. Blood cells
  B. A 150 lb. human has about 5L of blood, of which about 40% is formed elements and 60% **plasma** (refer to Table 28.1.)
    1. The formed elements include red blood cells or **erythrocytes** (~4,000,000/mm^3), white blood cells or **leukocytes** (~7000/mm^3), and **thrombocytes** or **platelets** (~250,000/mm^3).
    2. The fluid portion of blood is called **plasma**.
    3. Blood **serum** is the fluid remaining after blood clotting has occurred.

28.2 Electrolytes in Plasma and Erythrocytes
  A. Cations: Sodium ions are the main cations found in plasma. Potassium ions are found mainly in the **erythrocytes**. Calcium and magnesium ions are also found in blood plasma. (Na^+, K^+, Ca^{++}, Mg^{++})
  B. Anions: The major anion electrolyte in blood plasma is chloride. In addition, sulfate ions and the buffer ions of bicarbonate and hydrogen phosphate are present. (Cl^-, $SO_4^=$, HCO_3^-, $HPO_4^=$)
  C. The levels of many electrolytes are influenced by a number of disease states.

28.3 Proteins in the Plasma
  A. Protein level is about 7-8g/100mL of blood plasma; most of these are synthesized in the liver.
  B. Three major classes of plasma proteins
    1. **Albumins** - (~55%) transport and osmotic pressure
    2. **Globulins** - (~40%)
        i) α- and β-globulins (~ 2 g/100 mL) are involved in transport.
        ii) γ-globulin (~ 1 g/100 mL) antibody immune response
    3. **Fibrinogen** (~5%) and prothrombin - blood clotting proteins. Blood serum lacks fibrinogen and thus is unable to clot.

28.4 The Formed Elements
   A. *Erythrocytes* (red blood cells) are formed in red bone marrow.
      1. A drop of blood may contain as many as 500 million erythrocytes. A *hematocrit* value of 45 implies that 45% of the blood cell volume is red cells.
      2. *Anemia* refers to any condition that lowers the percentage of red blood cells or hemoglobin in blood.
      3. Erythrocytes do not have any aerobic metabolism and do not contain either mitochondria or a nucleus. They cannot reproduce, have no aerobic metabolism, and cannot synthesize fats or carbohydrates. They meet their energy needs from glucose metabolism via the glycolytic pathway and the pentose phosphate pathway.
      4. The major function of erythrocytes is to carry hemoglobin which transports oxygen from the lungs to the tissues.
      5. Human red cells have a life span of about 4 months. It has been estimated that about 3 million red blood cells are destroyed every second and have to be replaced.
      6. Blood type (A, B, AB or O) is determined by which short-chain polysaccharide type (A or B, both or neither) is bound to the glycoproteins of the membranes of erythrocytes.
   B. *Leukocytes* (white blood cells) are more like normal cells. Leukocytes constitute the body's primary defense against foreign elements.
      1. *Lymphocytes* - synthesis and storage of antibodies.
      2. Phagocytes (macrophages) - engulf and digest the invading organism.
      3. Normal levels: ~ 7000 leukocytes/mm^3 blood. Leukemia is a cancer characterized by the uncontrolled production of immature white blood cells that are unable to destroy invading pathogens.
   C. Thrombocytes *(platelets)* are instrumental in blood clotting. There are normally ~ 250,000 platelets/mm^3 blood.

28.5 The Immune Response
   A. The *gamma globulins* are produced by the body as part of the *immune* response. When a foreign body (*antigen*) invades the body, *antibody* proteins are produced to bind and incapacitate the antigen.
   B. A vaccine primes this defense mechanism by presenting the body with a weakened or dead form of the antigen to practice on. The body can thus gain an immunity to that particular antigen.
   C. Rejection of transplanted tissue is caused by the generation of antibodies, which attack the transplant.
   D. A variety of diseases are associated with immune system defects.
      1. Multiple sclerosis is an auto immune disease that destroys the myelin sheath of nerve cells.
      2. Some forms of arthritis are auto immune diseases that destroy connective tissue.
      3. In AIDS (Acquired Immune Deficiency Syndrome) the immune system is destroyed by the HIV virus, which leaves the victim without a defense system.

28.6 Osmotic Pressure
   A. *Osmosis* refers to diffusion of solvent from a dilute solution into a more concentrated solution. This requires *osmotic pressure* to prevent the reverse process (diffusion) from dominating.
      1. The pressure of blood plasma proteins produces an osmotic pressure differential of about 25 mm Hg.
      2. A pumping heart creates a "*blood pressure*" of about 32 mm Hg at the arterial end of the capillaries, thus nutrients are forced from the blood into the interstitial fluid.

B. Capillary diffusion

1. Blood moves from the high-pressure arterial end of the capillaries to the low-pressure venous end.

2. Interstitial fluid and blood plasma have similar electrolyte concentrations, but blood plasma also has proteins that cannot move through the capillary walls.

3. At the arterial end of the capillaries, the hydrostatic pressure forces fluids, which carry nutrients to the cells, from the capillaries into the interstitial space.

4. At the venous end of the capillaries, the hydrostatic pressure is low, so the high osmotic pressure of the blood causes fluid to diffuse back from the interstitial space into the blood.

C. If the plasma protein concentration drops, the osmotic pressure also drops, causing swelling (*edema*) as fluids flow into the interstitial space.

D. *Shock* is a physiological condition that results in a rapid decrease in blood volume and a dramatic drop in blood pressure.

28.7 Blood Pressure

A. *Blood pressure* is the force exterted by the blood in the arteries.

1. *Systolic* pressure is the maximum pressure achieved during contraction of the heart ventricles (~120 mm Hg).

2. *Diastolic* pressure is the lowest pressure that remains in the arteries before the next ventricular contraction (~80 mm Hg).

B. High blood pressure (hypertension) can be influenced by larger blood volume, sodium ion levels, blockage of arteries, etc.

28.8 Clotting of Blood

A. Blood clotting involves the formation of *fibrin* from fibrinogen by the action of a protease called *thrombin*.

1. The activation of thrombin from its proenzyme or zymogen form (prothrombin) involves Ca^{++} ions and an elaborate cascade of activating proteins that are released when a tissue is cut or injured.

2. Blood serum is blood plasma without the *fibrinogen*.

B. Anticoagulants

1. Plasmin is another protease that is activated later to dissolve the blood clot.

2. *Heparin* is a sulfate rich polysaccharide that appears to block the action of thrombin.

3. Vitamin K is needed as a coenzyme to help an enzyme make γ-carboxyglutamate residues that in turn are needed by prothrombin to bind Ca^{++} so that prothrombin can be converted to thrombin. Dicumarol is a drug antagonist of vitamin K that helps prevent blood clots from forming.

4. Hemophilia is an inherited disorder characterized by inadequate production of clotting factors.

C. Blood clots can become lodged and cause cells in nearby tissue to become starved for oxygen and die.

1. *Stroke* - tissue death occurs in the brain.

2. Myocardial infraction (coronary thrombosis) - tissue death occurs in the heart.

3. Aspirin may help prevent strokes and heart attacks by inhibiting thrombosis.

28.9 Hemoglobin: Oxygen and Carbon Dioxide Transport

A. The *hemoglobin* molecule:

1. Four protein chains (2 α and 2 β), each with a heme prosthetic group.

2. Each of the four chains has several helical coils, which fold to produce a roughly globular structure with a hydrophobic crevice that binds the heme group.

3. The heme group is a planar protophorphyrin ring containing an iron (Fe^{2+}) iron bound to 4 N's. A Histidine side chain donates another N to fill the 5th binding site on iron.

4. Oxygen binds to the 6th binding position on the heme iron. The binding of oxygen to hemoglobin is cooperative in that the binding of the 1st oxygen enhances the binding of the others. The release of oxygen at the tissues is also cooperative. The 15 g of Hb in 100 mL of blood combine with ~20 mL of oxygen (compared with only 0.3 mL of gaseous oxygen that could dissolve in 100 mL of saline solution).

5. Oxygen pressure in the lungs is about 90-100 mm Hg which is conducive to forming oxyHb. At respiring tissue, oxygen is about 25-40 mmHg, thus oxygen is released and deoxyHb is formed.

6. CO_2 concentrations are high in respiring tissue. CO_2 is removed as bicarbonate (HCO_3^-; 70%) or bound to Hb (~20%).

B. CO binds very tightly to Hb, interfering with O_2 transport. Nitrites can oxidize the heme iron from Fe^{2+} to Fe^{3+} to form methemoglobin.

C. Red blood cells last approximately 120 days. The globin protein is broken down and its amino acids recycled. The heme portion breaks down into *bilirubin* products with yellow-brown pigments (jaundice).

D. Many abnormal hemoglobins have been studied. Sickle cell Hb has a valine instead of a glutamic acid in the 6th amino acid position of the β chain. This small difference causes the red blood cells to sickle and be rapidly destroyed, which results in anemia. *Sickle cell anemia* is only one of many hereditary traits associated with metabolic or genetic diseases.

28.10 Blood Buffers

A. Blood pH must be maintained within a very narrow range, around pH 7.4. The four major buffer systems in blood plasma are:

1. Bicarbonate/carbonic acid system; $pK_a \sim 6.3$.
$$(H^+ + HCO_3^- \leftrightarrow H_2CO_3 \leftrightarrow H_2O + CO_2)$$

2. Monohydrogen phosphate/dihydrogen phosphate system; $pK_a \sim 7.2$
$$(H^+ + HPO_4^{-2} \leftrightarrow H_2PO_4^-)$$

3. Plasma proteins

4. Hemoglobin

B. Hemoglobin has both acidic and basic forms. The release of oxygen and the picking up of hydrogen ions from respiring tissue helps convert the carbonic acids of respiration to the bicarbonate ion. The addition of oxygen and the release of hydrogen ions at the lungs promotes the formation of carbonic acid, which is rapidly converted to carbon dioxide and exhaled.

C. Respiratory rate also affects blood pH.

1. Hypoventilation   = too slow   → *acidosis*

2. Hyperventilation   = too fast   → *alkalosis*

28.11 Lymph: A Secondary Transport System

A. The *lymph* system is composed of veins and capillaries, but no arteries. Interstitial fluid absorbed into the lymph capillaries moves into lymph veins, which empty into the veins of the blood circulatory system.

B. The lymph system also absorbs fat from the intestine and produces some forms of white blood cells.

28.12 Urine: Formation and Composition

A. The kidneys remove metabolic waste products from blood while helping to maintain a proper balance of water, electrolytes, and other components of body fluids.

1. Blood flows from an artery into the capillary network of the **kidneys** and back out, into the vein. Waste products, such as urea, uric acid, and excess salts, are passed into collecting tubules and are eventually excreted as **urine**. A healthy adult passes 1.1-1.5 L of urine each day.

2. About 170 L/day are filtered into the tubules. Many substances, such as glucose, are normally reabsorbed by the blood. However, most have a threshold level above which the excess is no longer absorbed. This happens with glucose and is often symptomatic of diabetes.

B. Some materials have very low solubilities in the urine and precipitate out as "kidney stones." These usually consist of calcium phosphate, magnesium ammonium phosphate, and calcium carbonate or calcium oxalate.

C. The "artificial kidney" dialysis machine was invented in the 1950s.
In the early 1990s, ~60,000 people were on dialysis at an annual cost of approximately $1,800,000,000.

28.13 Sweat

A. The skin is an organ of excretion. Through it passes **sweat**. Sweat is 99% water but also contains electrolytes, urea, lipids, creatine, lactic acid, and pyruvic acid.

B. Water loss via **perspiration**
1. Insensible perspiration   - ~700 mL/day via skin and respiration
2. Sensible perspiration   - 2.5 million sweat glands, output varies with activity

C. Evaporation of sweat carries off ~540 cal heat/g water lost. Heat stroke occurs when our heat regulation system fails.

28.14 Tears: The Chemistry of Crying

A. Tears keep the eyes moist and contain **lysozyme**, an enzyme that ruptures bacterial cell walls to help prevent eye infections.

B. **Tears** are multilayered: inner mucus layer, thin layer of lachrymal secretions, oily outer layer.

C. Tear gases such as α-chloroacetophenone are specially designed eye irritants to induce copious flow of tears.

α - Chloroacetophenone

28.15 The Chemistry of Mother's Milk

A. **Milk** is the secretion of the mammary glands. It contains fats, carbohydrates, proteins, minerals and vitamins.
1. Casein - precipitated milk protein
2. Lactose - milk sugar; a disaccharide of glucose and galactose

B. Mother's milk probably is more nutritional for infants than is cow's milk and it may also add to the infants immunological defenses against disease.

C. Some people are unable to drink milk because their bodies cannot metabolize galactose. This condition is known as galactosemia and can cause mental retardation in infants.

DISCUSSION

Chapter 28 represents a change of pace. For some time now we have been examining various classes of biochemically important molecules. Our survey of these important compounds is now complete, and we are embarking on an examination of how these materials function in the body. In this chapter we've begun that examination by considering the properties of many of the fluids in which biochemical reactions take place. So in this chapter there's very little that's new as far as molecules are concerned. Hemoglobin is the only compound structure considered in any detail, and we have encountered hemoglobin previously (Section 21.11).

Much of the material in the chapter, therefore, is descriptive. Many applications of chemical principles in living systems are provided. For the most part, this chapter does not require that you learn new scientific principles, but rather that you relate familiar chemistry to biological systems.

If you turn through the pages of Chapter 28, you'll notice that the only point at which we use chemical equations to any extent is in our discussion of the transportation of carbon dioxide by the blood. The transportation of CO_2 is thus more chemical than biological.

In Capillaries Serving Metabolically Active Tissue

Carbon dioxide produced as a metabolic product in tissue cells migrates into the erythrocytes where it combines with water.
$$CO_2 \;+\; H_2O \;\rightarrow\; H_2CO_3$$

The resulting carbonic acid protonates the conjugate base of the hemoglobin buffer in the erythrocyte.
$$H_2CO_3 \;+\; Hb^- \;\rightarrow\; HCO_3^- \;+\; HHb$$

The bicarbonate ion dissolves in the fluid within the erythrocyte and in the surrounding blood plasma. Any bicarbonate ion that migrates from the erythrocyte to the surrounding plasma is matched by the migration of a chloride ion from the surrounding plasma into the erythrocyte (chloride shift).

In Capillaries Serving the Lungs

The conjugate acid of the hemoglobin buffer picks up oxygen to become the conjugate acid of the oxyhemoglobin buffer.
$$HHb + O_2 \;\rightarrow\; HHbO_2$$

The conjugate acid of the oxyhemoglobin buffer protonates the bicarbonate ion.
$$HHbO_2 + HCO_3^- \;\rightarrow\; HbO_2^- \;+\; H_2CO_3$$

The resulting carbonic acid dissociates into water and carbon dioxide.
$$H_2CO_3 \;\rightarrow\; H_2O \;+\; CO_2$$
The carbon dioxide gas is exhausted to the atmosphere.

The only numerical problems associated with Chapter 28 deal with concentrations of electrolytes. Try the problems that follow.

Problems

1. Normal values for various electrolytes in urine collected over a 24-hour period are:

calcium (Ca^{2+}):	2.5 - 20 meq
chloride (Cl^-):	110 - 250 meq
magnesium (Mg^{2+}):	6.0 - 8.5 meq
potassium (K^+):	40 - 80 meq

sodium (Na^+):   80 - 180 meq

Analysis of a 24-hour urine sample detected the following amounts of electrolytes. Indicate for each ion whether the amount is normal or abnormal.

            calcium: 100 mg
            chloride: 3.55 g
            magnesium: 4.86 mg
            potassium: 1.955 g
            sodium: 6.9 g

2. Normal concentration ranges for various electrolytes in blood serum are:

            calcium: 4.5 - 5.3 meq/L
            chloride: 96 - 106 meq/L
            magnesium: 1.3 - 2.1 meq/L
            potassium: 3.5 - 5.0 meq/L
            sodium: 136 - 145 meq/L

The following concentrations were reported for a sample of serum. In each case indicate whether the value falls within the normal range.

            calcium: 4 mg%
            chloride: 355 mg%
            magnesium: 2.43 mg%
            potassium: 39.1 mg%
            sodium: 345 mg%

SELF-TEST

1. Which material does blood serum <u>not</u> include?
        a. electrolytes   b. fibrinogen   c. proteins
2. Which of the plasma proteins is associated with the immune response of the body?
        a. albumin   b. fibrinogen   c. globulins   d. prothrombin
3. Which of the plasma proteins contributes most to the osmotic pressure of blood?
        a. albumin   b. fibrinogen   c. globulin   d. prothrombin
4. Which of the cations is <u>not</u> one of the principal electrolytes in blood plasma?
        a. Na^+ b. K^+ c. Ca^{2+} d. Mg^{2+} e. Fe^{2+}
5. Which of the anions is <u>not</u> one of the principal electrolytes in blood plasma?
        a. Cl^- b. HCO_3^- c. CO_3^{2-} d. HPO_4^{2-} e. SO_4^{2-}
6. Material moves in and out of the capillaries primarily through the process of:
        a. diffusion   b. evaporation   c. filtration
7. A normal hematocrit value (% volume of packed erythrocytes) would be about ____.
        a. 5   b. 10   c. 20   d. 45   e. 65
8. Which ion is necessary for blood clotting?
        a. Cl^- b. HCO_3^- c. Ca^{2+} d. Fe^{2+}
9. Which ion is not part of the blood buffers?
        a. HCO_3^- b. HPO_4^{2-} c. HSO_4^-
10. A person of blood type _____ is a universal blood donor.
        a. A   b. B   c. AB   d. O   e. none is correct
11. Some doctors now recommend that older patients with histories of heart attack should take _____.
        a. Vitamin C   c. Vitamin E   c. Vitamin B_6 d. Aspirin   e. Iron
12. A principal anticoagulating agent is _____.

a. Thrombin   b. Zymogen   c. Heparin   d. Globulin   e. Fibrin

13. Colloid osmotic pressure refers to:

    a. the pressure imparted to the blood by the pumping action of the heart

    b. the osmotic pressure of the blood resulting from dissolved electrolytes

    c. the osmotic pressure of the blood resulting from proteins present in colloidal dispersion

14. The hydrostatic pressure of the blood is:

    a. higher at the venous end of a capillary

    b. higher at the arterial end of a capillary

    c. approximately the same at both ends of a capillary

15. Which describes the conditions at the arterial end of the capillaries?

    a. colloid osmotic pressure exceeds hydrostatic pressure and the net movement of fluid is into the interstitial space

    b. colloid osmotic pressure exceeds hydrostatic pressure and the net movement of fluid is into the capillary

    c. hydrostatic pressure exceeds colloid osmotic pressure and the net movement of fluid is into the interstitial space

    d. hydrostatic pressure exceeds colloid osmotic pressure and the net movement of fluid is into the capillary

16. In edema, there is a net flow of fluid into the interstitial space because:

    a. the colloid osmotic pressure of the blood increases

    b. the colloid osmotic pressure of the blood decreases

    c. the hydrostatic pressure of the blood decreases

17. An antibody is:

    a. a foreign macromolecule that triggers the body's immune response

    b. a protein formed by the body to attack specific foreign particles

    c. a pathogenic microorganism

18. A vaccine contains:

    a. a weakened antigen   b. a weakened antibody   c. gamma globulin

19. Carbon dioxide produced in metabolic reactions is carried to the lungs chiefly as:

    a. free CO_2 gas   b. dissolved CO_2 gas   c. HCO_3^- d. a prosthetic group of hemoglobin

20. Which reaction occurs in the capillaries of the lungs?

    a. $HHbO_2 \rightarrow HHb + O_2$

    b. $HHbO_2 + HCO_3^- \rightarrow HbO_2^- + H_2CO_3$

    c. $H_2CO_3 + Hb^- \rightarrow HHb + HCO_3^-$

21. To maintain electrical neutrality as the bicarbonate ions diffuse out of erythrocytes:

    a. potassium ions accompany the bicarbonate ions

    b. sodium ions accompany the bicarbonate ions

    c. chloride ions diffuse into the erythrocyte

22. Which is not true of a hemoglobin molecule?

    a. It is a conjugated protein.

    b. It incorporates iron in a +2 oxidation state.

    c. It contains four identical protein chains in a roughly tetrahedral arrangement.

    d. It incorporates four heme units, each of which can bind with an oxygen molecule.

23. Bilirubin is a product of:

    a. the breakdown of the prosthetic group of hemoglobin

    b. the breakdown of the alpha chain of hemoglobin

    c. the breakdown of the beta chain of hemoglobin

24. The abnormal hemoglobin that is characteristic of sickle cell anemia contains:
    a. iron in the +3 oxidation state
    b. a heme unit that has no iron ion
    c. peptide chains incorporating an incorrect amino acid
25. The constitution of the fluid within the lymphatic system is identical to:
    a. blood plasma   b. interstitial fluid   c. intracellular fluid
26. Lymph nodes are <u>not</u> involved in the manufacture of:
    a. antibodies   b. erythrocytes   c. leukocytes
27. Which type of nutrient is absorbed into the lymphatic system from the intestine?
    a. carbohydrate   b. fat   c. protein
28. Salts of which cation are <u>not</u> ordinarily found in kidney stones?
    a. Na^+ b. Ca^{2+} c. Mg^{2+}
29. Which substance is <u>not</u> filtered out of the blood at the glomerulus?
    a. erythrocytes   b. glucose   c. urea   d. water
30. Insensible perspiration is the water lost:
    a. through the respiratory tract   b. from the sweat glands c. from the lachrymal glands
31. Calcium oxalate is sometimes found in _____ .
    a. kidney stones   b. tears   c. milk   d. sweat
32. T F Heat is one of the major metabolic products carried off by perspiration.
33. T F Lysozyme is a type of bacteria occasionally found in lachrymal fluid.
34. T F Casein is the outer oily layer of tears.
35. T F Mammals living in cold climates produce milk with high fat content.
36. T F Anemia is a condition associated with abnormal concentrations of red blood cells.
37. T F Plasma can be isolated if an anticoagulant is first added to freshly drawn blood.
38. T F Sodium ions are found mainly in the plasma, and potassium ions are found mainly in the erythrocytes.
39. T F Metabolic disorders more commonly produce the condition known as alkalosis rather than acidosis.
40. T F The chloride shift refers to the loss of chloride ions to the urine when the chloride concentration threshold level is exceeded.

ANSWERS

Problems

1. calcium = 5 meq, normal
    chloride = 100 meq, slightly low
    magnesium = 0.4 meq, very low
    potassium = 50 meq, normal
    sodium = 300 meq, very high

2. calcium = 2 meq/L, low
    chloride = 100 meq/L, normal
    magnesium = 2 meq/L, normal
    potassium = 10 meq/L, high
    sodium = 150 meq/L, normal

Self-Test

1. b	11. d	21. c	31. a
2. c	12. c	22. c	32. T
3. a	13. c	23. a	33. F
4. e	14. b	24. c	34. F
5. c	15. c	25. b	35. T
6. a	16. b	26. b	36. T
7. d	17. b	27. b	37. T
8. c	18. a	28. a	38. T
9. c	19. c	29. a	39. F
10. d	20. b	30. a	40. F

SOLUTIONS TO
END OF CHAPTER EXERCISES

End-of-Chapter Solutions

REVIEW QUESTIONS

1. a. Chemistry: The study of matter and the changes it undergoes.
    b. Matter: The "stuff" of which all materials are made; matter has mass and occupies space.
    c. Mass: A measure of the quantity of matter.
    d. Weight: A measure of the force of attraction of the Earth for an object.
    e. Energy: The capacity for doing work.
    f. Calorie: The amount of heat required to raise the temperature of 1g of water 1 °C.
    g. Density: The amount of mass (or weight) per unit volume.
    h. Specific gravity: The ratio of the mass of a given volume of any substance to the mass of an equal volume of water (defined for a particular temperature).

2. A hypothesis is an educated guess at a solution to a problem. Hypotheses are tested by experimentation.

3. a, c, and d are all examples of matter.

4. Mass, a measure of the quantity of matter in an object, does not vary with location from place to place on the Earth (or within the universe) while weight, a measurement of force between two objects, depends on the gravitational pull of the Earth (or other body) upon an object.

5. Physical properties are characteristics which may be observed and described without reference to any other substance while chemical properties describe the reactivity of a substance with other substances. (Both chemical and physical properties are important in chemistry.)

6. A physical change is a change which does not result in a change in the composition of matter while a chemical change does result in a change in chemical composition.

7. Gases maintain neither a constant shape or volume; they take the shape of the vessel in which they are contained and they readily flow. Liquids maintain volume but not shape; they take the shape of the container in which they are held and readily flow. Solids maintain both shape and volume; they do not flow readily. Gases are compressible, liquids and solids are not.

8. Length: meter (m); volume: liter (L); mass: kilogram (kg).

9. Steam.

10. Substances have a definite composition while the proportion of the ingredients in a mixture can vary.

11. Substance.

12. An element is the fundamental substance from which all material is constructed. (As we shall see later, elements are defined by how many protons they contain.)

13. A chemical compound is a substance which is made up of more than one type of element in a defined proportion.

14. Kinetic energy is the energy involved when an object has motion while potential energy is the energy that an object has due to position or arrangement.

15.   a. They repel one another.
      b. They attract one another.

16. Length: meter (m); area: m^2; volume: m^3

PROBLEMS

SOME FUNDAMENTAL CONCEPTS

17. Yes. Since the gravitational pull on both objects is equal, the mass will be proportional to the weight.

18. No. The gravitational pull of the object on Earth is greater and it, therefore, would weigh more.

19. a. Physical change; b. Chemical change; c. Chemical change

20. a. Chemical change; b. Physical change; c. Physical change

ELEMENTS, COMPOUNDS AND MIXTURES

21. Elements: a and c. Their composition is made up of only one type of fundamental substance.

22. Element: b. Its composition is made up of only one type of fundamental substance.

23.   a. Substance; b. Mixture; c. Mixture

24. a. Mixture; b. Substance; c. Substance

25. a. homogeneous; b. homogeneous

26. a. heterogenous; b. homogeneous

27.   a. helium; b. nitrogen; c. fluorine; d. potassium; e. iron; f. copper

28. a. magnesium; b. silicon; c. sulfur; d. bromine; e. phosphorus; f. tin

29. a. H; b. C; c. O; d. Zn; e. I; f. Hg

30. a. Al; b. P; c. Na; d. Cl; e. Ca; f. Co

METRIC MEASUREMENT

31. a. 4.54 mg; b. 3.76 cm; c. 6.34 μg

32. a. 1.09 μL; b. 9.01 μL; c. 7.77 km

33. $1 \text{ m} \times \dfrac{1000 \text{ mm}}{1 \text{ m}} = 1000 \text{ mm}$

$1 \text{ m} \times \dfrac{100 \text{ cm}}{1 \text{ m}} = 100 \text{ cm}$

34. a. cm; b. kg; c. dL

35. a. L; b. equal in size

36. a. m; b. 1b; c. gal

37. a. $\dfrac{50 \text{ km}}{1} \times \dfrac{1000 \text{ m}}{1 \text{ km}} = 50{,}000 \text{ m}$

    b. $\dfrac{25 \text{ cm}}{1} \times \dfrac{1 \text{ m}}{100 \text{ cm}} = 0.25 \text{ m}$

38. a. $\dfrac{1.5 \text{ m}}{1} \times \dfrac{1000 \text{ mm}}{1 \text{ m}} = 1500 \text{ mm}$

    b. $\dfrac{16 \text{ cm}}{1} \times \dfrac{10 \text{ mm}}{1 \text{ cm}} = 160 \text{ mm}$

39. a. 10 dL; b. 0.2 dL

40. a. 2.056 L; b. 47,000 L

41. a. $\dfrac{15{,}000 \text{ mg}}{1} \times \dfrac{1 \text{ g}}{1000 \text{ mg}} = 15 \text{ g}$

    b. $\dfrac{0.086 \text{g}}{1} \times \dfrac{1000 \text{ mg}}{\text{g}} = 86 \text{mg}$

42. a. 149 mL
    b. 0.047 L

43. a. 1500 mL
    b. 0.018 L

44. a. 1 mL
    b. 15 mL

ENERGY: TEMPERATURE AND HEAT

45. The sprinter because of its greater speed.

46. The cannonball because of its larger mass.

47. The automobile.

48. They will have nearly the same kinetic energy.

49. The diver on the 10 m platform.

50. The elevator on the twentieth floor.

51. a. °C; b. Cal

52. 0 K (coldest), 0 °F, 0 °C

53. a. °F = 1.80 (°C) + 32
    °F = 1.80 (37 °C) + 32
    °F = 99°

    b. °F = 1.80 (°C) + 32
    °F = 1.80 (−100) + 32
    °F = −148°

    c. °F = 1.80 (°C) + 32
    °F = 1.80 (273 °C) + 32
    °F = 523°

54. 100 °C

55. a. °C = (°F − 32) 0.555
    °C = (98 − 32) 0.555
    °C = 37°

    b. °C = (°F − 32) 0.555
    °C = (5 − 32) 0.555
    °C = −15°

    c. °C = (°F − 32) 0.555
    °C = (−5 − 32) 0.555
    °C = −21°

56. a. $2.75 \text{ kcal} \times \dfrac{1000 \text{ cal}}{1 \text{ kcal}} = 2750 \text{ cal}$

    b. $0.74 \text{ Cal} \times \dfrac{1000 \text{ cal}}{1 \text{ Cal}} = 740 \text{ cal}$

57. Temperature change = 30 °C

    $\dfrac{1 \text{ cal}}{(1g)(1 \text{ °C})} \times \dfrac{30\text{°C}}{1} \times \dfrac{50 \text{ g}}{1} = 1500 \text{ cal}$

58. $\dfrac{1 \text{ cal}}{(1g)(1 \text{ °C})} \times \dfrac{80\text{°C}}{1} \times \dfrac{13 \text{ g}}{1} = 1040 \text{ cal} = 1000 \text{ cal}$ (significant figures)

59. $\dfrac{1 \text{ cal}}{(1\text{g})(1\ °\text{C})}$ x $\dfrac{1000 \text{ g}}{1 \text{ kg}}$ x $\dfrac{2.0 \text{ kg}}{1}$ x $\dfrac{70°\text{C}}{1}$ = 140,000 cal

60. $\dfrac{(1\text{g})(1\ °\text{C})}{1 \text{ cal}}$ x $\dfrac{800 \text{ cal}}{1}$ x $\dfrac{1}{30\ °\text{C}}$ = 27 g = 30 g (significant figures)

DENSITY

61. $\dfrac{78.0 \text{ g}}{25 \text{ mL}}$ = 3.1 g/mL

62. $\dfrac{57.0 \text{ g}}{50.0 \text{ mL}}$ = 1.14 g/cm^3

63. $\dfrac{1.32\text{g}}{\text{mL}}$ x $\dfrac{30.0 \text{ mL}}{1}$ = 39.6 g

64. $\dfrac{1.26 \text{ g}}{\text{mL}}$ x $\dfrac{1000 \text{ mL}}{1 \text{ L}}$ x $\dfrac{2.75 \text{ L}}{1}$ x $\dfrac{1 \text{ kg}}{1000 \text{ g}}$ = 3.47 kg

65. $\dfrac{1 \text{ cm}^3}{7.76 \text{ g}}$ x $\dfrac{1000\text{g}}{\text{kg}}$ x $\dfrac{898 \text{ kg}}{1}$ = 115721 cm3 = 116,000 cm3 (sig. figures)

66. $\dfrac{1 \text{ mL}}{2.90 \text{ g}}$ x $\dfrac{253 \text{ g}}{1}$ = 87.2 mL

67. 18.43 g – 1.21 g = 17.22 g

$\dfrac{17.22 \text{ g}}{3.29 \text{ cm}^3}$ = 5.23 g/cm^3

68. 54.51 g – 48.462 g = 6.048 g

$\dfrac{6.048 \text{ g}}{4.00 \text{ mL}}$ = 1.51 g/mL

69. 1.02

70. 1.1044 g/mL

ADDITIONAL PROBLEMS

71. $\dfrac{1 \text{ cm}^3}{19.3 \text{ g}}$ x $\dfrac{1 \text{ g}}{1000 \text{ mg}}$ x $\dfrac{5.79 \text{ mg}}{1}$ = 3.0 x 10^{-4} cm^3

$\dfrac{3.0 \text{ x } 10^{-4} \text{ cm}^3}{44.6 \text{ cm}^2}$ = 6.73 x 10^{-6} cm

72. $V = 0.80 \text{ m} \times 0.80 \text{ m} \times 1.20 \text{ m} = 0.768 \text{ m}^3$

$$\frac{3.2 \text{ kg}}{0.768 \text{ m}^3} \times \frac{1000 \text{g}}{1 \text{ kg}} \times \frac{1 \text{ m}^3}{1,000,000 \text{ cm}^3} = 0.0042 \text{ g/cm}^3$$

73. $\dfrac{100 \text{ lbs}}{1} \times \dfrac{1 \text{ kg}}{2.2 \text{ lb}} \times \dfrac{1000 \text{ g}}{1 \text{ kg}} = 45,000 \text{ g potatoes}$

$$\frac{15 \text{ gal}}{1} \times \frac{4 \text{ qt}}{1 \text{ gal}} \times \frac{1.0 \text{ L}}{1.1 \text{ qt}} \times \frac{1000 \text{ mL}}{1 \text{ L}} \times \frac{1 \text{ g}}{1 \text{ mL}} = 55,000 \text{ g water}$$

$$\frac{13.6 \text{ g}}{\text{mL}} \times \frac{1000 \text{ mL}}{1 \text{ L}} \times \frac{3.0 \text{ L}}{1} = 41,000 \text{ g mercury}$$

The water would be the heaviest object to lift into the truck.

74. $V = 5.625 \text{ cm}^3$

$\dfrac{28.12 \text{ g}}{5.625 \text{ cm}^3} = 5.00 \text{ g/cm}^3$ No, this couldn't be gold.

REVIEW QUESTIONS

1. A conversion factor is a pair of equivalent quantities written in fraction form for use in switching from one unit to another.

2. The numerator and denominator must be equivalent in value and describe the same quantity.

3. Switching all to meters:

1. 1.21 m

2. $\dfrac{75 \text{ in}}{1} \times \dfrac{2.54 \text{ cm}}{1 \text{ in}} \times \dfrac{1 \text{ m}}{100 \text{ cm}} = 1.91 \text{ m}$

3. 3 ft-5 in = $\dfrac{41 \text{ in}}{1} \times \dfrac{2.54 \text{ cm}}{1 \text{ in}} \times \dfrac{1 \text{ m}}{100 \text{ cm}} = 1.04 \text{ m}$

4. $\dfrac{36 \text{ in}}{1} \times \dfrac{2.54 \text{ cm}}{1 \text{ in}} \times \dfrac{1 \text{ m}}{100 \text{ cm}} = 0.91 \text{ m}$

$$4 \,(0.91 \text{ m}) < 3 \,(1.04 \text{ m}) < 1 \,(1.21 \text{ m}) < 2 \,(1.91 \text{ m})$$

4. Switching all to grams:

1. $\dfrac{5 \text{ lb}}{1} \times \dfrac{1 \text{ kg}}{2.2 \text{ lb}} \times \dfrac{1000 \text{ g}}{1 \text{ kg}} = 2273 \text{ g}$

2. $\dfrac{1.65 \text{ kg}}{1} \times \dfrac{1000 \text{ g}}{1 \text{ kg}} = 1650 \text{ g}$

3. 2500 g $2 \,(1650 \text{ g}) < 1 \,(2273 \text{ g}) < 3 \,(2500 \text{ g})$

5. $\dfrac{160 \text{ cm}}{1} \times \dfrac{1 \text{ in}}{2.54 \text{ cm}} = 63 \text{ in tall} = 5 \text{ ft-3 in}$ $\dfrac{94 \text{ kg}}{1} \times \dfrac{2.2 \text{ lb}}{1 \text{ kg}} = 207 \text{ lb}$

This young man is overweight.

6. $\dfrac{38.5 \text{ kg}}{1} \times \dfrac{2.2 \text{ lb}}{1 \text{ kg}} = 84.7 \text{ lb}$ Probably the gymnast (or else an incredibly skinny basketball center.)

7. a. $\dfrac{50 \text{ km}}{1} \times \dfrac{1000 \text{ m}}{1 \text{ km}} = 50{,}000 \text{ m}$ b. $\dfrac{546 \text{ mm}}{1} \times \dfrac{1 \text{ m}}{1000 \text{ mm}} = 0.546 \text{ m}$

c. $\dfrac{98.5 \text{ kg}}{1} \times \dfrac{1000 \text{ g}}{1 \text{ kg}} = 98{,}500 \text{ g}$ d. $\dfrac{47.9 \text{ mL}}{1} \times \dfrac{1 L}{1000 \text{ mL}} = 0.0479 \text{ L}$

e. $\dfrac{578 \text{ µg}}{1} \times \dfrac{1 \text{ mg}}{1000 \text{ µg}} = 0.578 \text{ mg}$ f. $\dfrac{237 \text{ mm}}{1} \times \dfrac{1 \text{ cm}}{10 \text{ mm}} = 23.7 \text{ cm}$

8. a. $\dfrac{87.6\ \mu g}{1} \quad x \quad \dfrac{1\ mg}{1000\ \mu g} \quad x \quad \dfrac{1\ g}{1000\ mg} \quad x \quad \dfrac{1\ kg}{1000\ g} \quad = 8.76 \times 10^{-8}\ kg$

   b. $\dfrac{1.00\ m}{1} \quad x \quad \dfrac{1000\ mm}{1\ m} \quad x \quad \dfrac{1000\ \mu m}{1\ mm} \quad = 1 \times 10^{6}\ \mu m$

   c. $\dfrac{0.0962\ km}{min} \quad x \quad \dfrac{1000\ m}{1\ km} \quad x \quad \dfrac{1\ min}{60\ sec} \quad = 1.60\ m/sec$

   d. $\dfrac{55\ mi}{1\ hr} \quad x \quad \dfrac{5280\ ft}{1\ mi} \quad x \quad \dfrac{12\ in}{1\ ft} \quad x \quad \dfrac{1\ m}{39\ in} \quad x \quad \dfrac{1\ km}{1000\ m} \quad x \quad \dfrac{1\ hr}{60\ min} \quad = 1.5\ km/min$

9. a. $\dfrac{413\ in}{1} \quad x \quad \dfrac{1\ yd}{36\ in} \quad = 11.5\ yd$ b. $\dfrac{8.08\ lb}{1} \quad x \quad \dfrac{16\ oz}{1\ lb} \quad = 129\ oz$

   c. $\dfrac{64.0\ fl\ oz}{1} \quad x \quad \dfrac{1\ cup}{8\ fl\ oz} \quad x \quad \dfrac{1\ qt.}{4\ cups} \quad = 2.00\ qt$ d. $\dfrac{12.6\ ft}{s} \quad x \quad \dfrac{1\ mi}{5280\ ft} \quad x \quad \dfrac{60\ s}{1\ min} \quad x \quad \dfrac{60\ min}{1\ hr} \quad = 8.59\ mi\ /hr$

10. a. $\dfrac{4.53\ ft}{1} \quad x \quad \dfrac{12\ in}{1\ ft} \quad = 54.4\ in$ b. $\dfrac{86.2\ oz}{1} \quad x \quad \dfrac{1\ lb}{16\ oz} \quad = 5.39\ lb$

    c. $\dfrac{6.13\ qt}{1} \quad x \quad \dfrac{4\ cups}{1\ qt} \quad x \quad \dfrac{8\ fl\ oz}{1\ cup} \quad = 196\ fl\ oz$

    d. $\dfrac{70.06\ mi}{hr} \quad x \quad \dfrac{5280\ ft}{1\ mi} \quad x \quad \dfrac{1\ hr}{60\ min} \quad x \quad \dfrac{1\ min}{60\ s} \quad = 102.8\ ft/s$

CONVERSIONS BETWEEN SYSTEMS

11. a. $\dfrac{16.4\ in}{1} \quad x \quad \dfrac{2.54\ cm}{1\ in} \quad = 41.7\ cm$ b. $\dfrac{4.17\ qt}{1} \quad x \quad \dfrac{0.946\ L}{1\ qt} \quad = 3.94\ L$

    c. $\dfrac{1.61\ kg}{1} \quad x \quad \dfrac{1\ lb}{0.454\ kg} \quad = 3.55\ lb$ d. $\dfrac{9.34\ g}{1} \quad x \quad \dfrac{1\ oz}{28.4\ g} \quad = 0.329\ oz$

12. a. $\dfrac{2.05\ fl\ oz}{1} \quad x \quad \dfrac{29.6\ mL}{1\ fl\ oz} \quad = 60.7\ mL$ b. $\dfrac{105\ lb}{1} \quad x \quad \dfrac{0.454\ kg}{1\ lb} \quad = 47.7\ kg$

    c. $\dfrac{143\ cm}{1} \quad x \quad \dfrac{1\ in}{2.54\ cm} \quad x \quad \dfrac{1\ ft}{12\ in} \quad = 4.69\ ft.$ d. $\dfrac{775\ mL}{1} \quad x \quad \dfrac{1\ L}{1000\ mL} \quad x \quad \dfrac{1\ qt}{0.946\ L} \quad = 0.819\ qt$

13. $\dfrac{320\ lb}{1} \quad x \quad \dfrac{0.454\ kg}{1\ lb} \quad = 145\ kg$

14. $\dfrac{7.3\ ft}{1} \quad x \quad \dfrac{12\ in}{1\ ft} \quad x \quad \dfrac{2.54\ cm}{1\ in} \quad = 222\ cm \qquad \dfrac{222\ cm}{1} \quad x \quad \dfrac{1\ m}{100\ cm} \quad = 2.2\ m$

15. $\dfrac{90 \text{ km}}{\text{hr}}$ x $\dfrac{1 \text{ mi}}{1.61 \text{ km}}$ = 56 mi/hr

16. $\dfrac{186,000 \text{ mi}}{\text{s}}$ x $\dfrac{1.61 \text{ km}}{1 \text{ mi}}$ x $\dfrac{1000 \text{ m}}{1 \text{ km}}$ = 2.99×10^8 m/s

17. $\dfrac{\$3.89}{\text{gal}}$ x $\dfrac{1 \text{ gal}}{4 \text{ qt}}$ x $\dfrac{1 \text{ qt}}{0.946 \text{ L}}$ = $1.03/L   The first price ($3.89/gal) is cheaper.

18. Example: The author of this study guide is 7 ft-6 in tall and weighs 423 lbs.

    7 ft-6 in = $\dfrac{90 \text{ in}}{1}$ x $\dfrac{2.54 \text{ cm}}{1 \text{ in}}$ = 229 cm $\dfrac{423 \text{ lb}}{1}$ x $\dfrac{0.454 \text{ kg}}{1 \text{ lb}}$ = 192 kg

DENSITY

19. $\dfrac{33.0 \text{ g}}{50.0 \text{ mL}}$ = 0.66 g/mL

20. $\dfrac{87.5 \text{ g}}{75.0 \text{ mL}}$ = 1.17 g/mL

21. $\dfrac{1.26 \text{ g}}{\text{mL}}$ x $\dfrac{30.0 \text{ mL}}{1}$ = 37.8 g

22. $\dfrac{0.0962 \text{ g}}{\text{mL}}$ x $\dfrac{125 \text{ mL}}{1}$ = 12.0 g

23. $\dfrac{475 \text{ g}}{1}$ x $\dfrac{\text{cm}^3}{8.94 \text{ g}}$ = 53.1 cm^3

24. $\dfrac{5.79 \text{ g}}{1}$ x $\dfrac{\text{cm}^3}{10.5 \text{ g}}$ = 0.551 cm^3

ADDITIONAL PROBLEMS

25. $\dfrac{250 \text{ cm}}{1}$ x $\dfrac{1 \text{ in}}{2.54 \text{ cm}}$ = 98 in *to* $\dfrac{350 \text{ cm}}{1}$ x $\dfrac{1 \text{ in}}{2.54 \text{ cm}}$ = 140 in

    $\dfrac{300 \text{ kg}}{1}$ x $\dfrac{1 \text{ lb}}{0.454 \text{ kg}}$ = 660 lb *to* $\dfrac{450 \text{ kg}}{1}$ x $\dfrac{1 \text{ lb}}{0.454 \text{ kg}}$ = 990 lb

26. 9 days, 3 min, 44 s = 216.06 h $\dfrac{25,102 \text{ mi}}{216.06 \text{ hr}}$ = 116.2 mi/h

27. $\dfrac{1 \text{ link}}{1}$ x $\dfrac{1 \text{ chain}}{100 \text{ links}}$ x $\dfrac{1 \text{ furlong}}{10 \text{ chains}}$ x $\dfrac{1 \text{ mi}}{8 \text{ furlongs}}$ x $\dfrac{5280 \text{ ft}}{1 \text{ mi}}$ x $\dfrac{12 \text{ in}}{1 \text{ ft}}$ = 7.92 in

28. $\dfrac{1 \text{ acre}}{1} \times \dfrac{1 \text{ mi}^2}{640 \text{ acre}} \times \dfrac{1.61 \text{ km}}{1 \text{ mi}} \times \dfrac{1.61 \text{ km}}{1 \text{ mi}} \times \dfrac{1000 \text{ m}}{1 \text{ km}} \times \dfrac{1000 \text{ m}}{1 \text{ km}} \times \dfrac{1 \text{ hm}}{100 \text{ m}} \times \dfrac{1 \text{ hm}}{100 \text{ m}} \times \dfrac{1 \text{ hectare}}{1 \text{ hm}^2} = 0.405$ hectare

An acre is smaller than a hectare.   Conversion factor: $\dfrac{1 \text{ acre}}{0.405 \text{ hectare}}$

29. $\dfrac{0.998 \text{ g}}{\text{cm}^3} \times \dfrac{1 \text{ lb}}{454 \text{ g}} \times \dfrac{(2.54 \text{ cm}^3)^3}{\text{in}^3} \times \dfrac{(12 \text{ in})^3}{\text{ft}^3} = 62.2 \text{ lb/ft}^3$

30. $\dfrac{1.762 \text{ g}}{1} \times \dfrac{1 \text{ cm}^3}{2.70 \text{ g}} = 0.653 \text{ cm}^3$ = volume

    V = 5.10 cm x 5.10 cm x thickness

    $0.653 \text{ cm}^3 = 26.01 \text{ cm}^2$ x thickness

    0.025 cm = thickness

REVIEW QUESTIONS

1. The atomistic view of matter supported the idea that there existed a smallest fundamental particle from which matter was constructed. The continuous view believed that matter was infinitely divisible and still retained the inherent properties of the whole.

2. Atomistic: a, b, e; continuous: c, d, f.

3. The main points of Dalton's atomic theory are:
    I. All elements are comprised of indivisible particles called atoms.
    II. Atoms of the same element are identical while atoms of different elements are dissimilar.
    III. Compounds are substances made of atoms of different elements.
    IV. Atoms are not changed in a chemical reaction; a chemical reaction is a recombination of atoms to form new compounds.

4. The phenomena of radioactivity demonstrated that atoms are capable, in certain situations, of being divided.

5. Proton: mass = 1 amu, charge = +1, location = nucleus
    Neutron: mass = 1 amu, charge = 0, location = nucleus
    Electron: mass = 0 amu, charge = −1, location = outside the nucleus

6. Attract

7. Neither, they should exert no electrical force.

8. The atomic nucleus is a dense region in the center of an atom where the protons and neutrons exist.

9. Electrons.

10. Dalton's model of the atom ended at the atom itself; all characteristics of the element would be explained by the properties of the atom. The nuclear model went further and defined the fundamental particles which comprise and dictate the nature of a particular atom.

11. a. 11; b. 12

12. Isotopes are forms of the same element (i.e. the same number of protons) which differ in the number of neutrons they contain. The mass number of an isotope is the total mass of that particular form of atom.

13. They represent the total mass (in atomic mass units) of a typical atom of that element. This is the total mass of the protons, neutrons and electrons of an atom.

14. Metals are usually malleable, usually ductile, have luster and are good conductors of heat and electricity. Metals are located to the left of the stepped, diagonal line originating between boron and aluminum on the periodic table. (Nonmetals are located to the right of this line.)

15. lithium-7

16. 10.8 u

17. Argon

18. Neon

19. Ground state is the state of an atom when all electrons are in their lowest possible energy levels. An excited state is when an atom has electrons in energy levels higher than ground state.

20. An electron moving from a higher energy orbital to a lower energy orbital releases energy in the form of light.

21. First energy level to the third.

22. a. 6; b. dumbbell-shaped; c. 3 orbitals

PROBLEMS

DALTON'S ATOMIC THEORY

23. Yes. Dalton said that all atoms of a given element are different. Since these two atoms have different masses, they must be different elements.

24. No. According to Dalton, since these two atoms have the same mass, they should be the same element. (This part of Dalton's theory is incorrect.)

25. No. According to Dalton, each atom of a single element should be identical. (This part of Dalton's theory is incorrect.)

26. No. According to Dalton, atoms are indivisible. (This part of Dalton's theory is incorrect.)

THE NUCLEAR ATOM

27. a. 20 each; b. 11 each; c. 9 each; d. 18 each

28. a. 4 each; b. 7 each; c. 26 each; d. 92 each

29.   a. 30 protons, 32 neutrons
       b. 94 protons, 147 neutrons
       c. 43 protons, 56 neutrons
       d. 42 protons, 57 neutrons

30.   a. 5 protons, 6 neutrons
       b. 62 protons, 92 neutrons
       c. 36 protons, 45 neutrons
       d. 52 protons, 69 neutrons

31. Isotope pairs: b

32.   a. $^{8}_{5}B$; b. $^{14}_{6}C$; c. $^{235}_{92}U$; d. $^{60}_{27}Co$

THE BOHR MODEL

33. 18

34. 12

35. a. 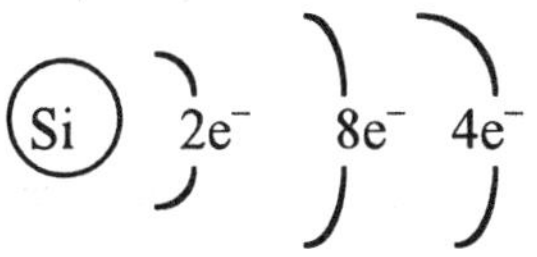 Si) $2e^-$) $8e^-$) $4e^-$ b. 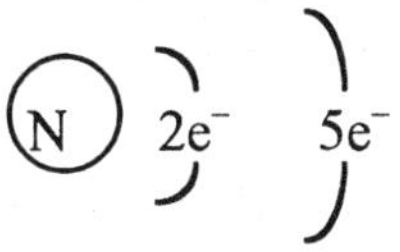 N) $2e^-$) $5e^-$

    c. 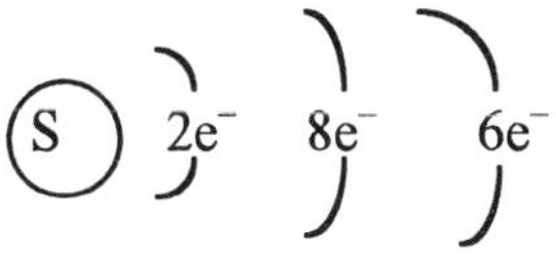 S) $2e^-$) $8e^-$) $6e^-$

36. a. 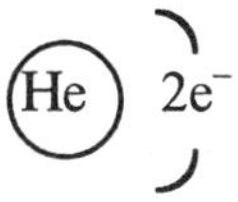 He) $2e^-$ b. 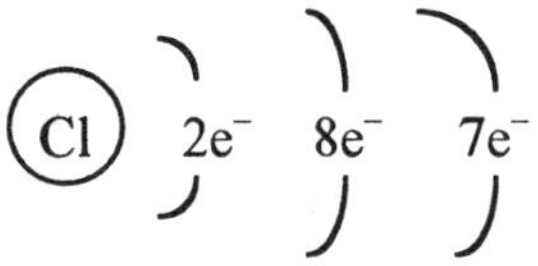 Cl) $2e^-$) $8e^-$) $7e^-$

    c. 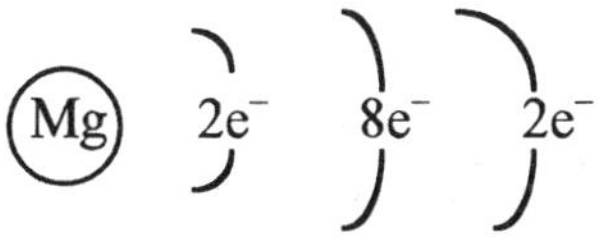 Mg) $2e^-$) $8e^-$) $2e^-$

37. Si: $1s^2 2s^2 2p^6 3s^2 3p^2$;   N: $1s^2 2s^2 2p^3$;   S: $1s^2 2s^2 2p^6 3s^2 3p^4$

38. a. Be; b. N; c. Al

39. a. 4; b. 7; c. 13

40. a. The 2p orbital needs to be filled before an electron enters the 3s orbital.
     b. The 2p orbital needs to contain 6 e^- to be filled.
     c. There is no such orbital as 2d.

41. a. Group: 4A, Period: 2, nonmetal
     b. Group: 2A, Period: 4, metal
     c. Group: 2B, Period: 5, metal
     d. Group: 7A, Period: 3, nonmetal
     e. Group: 3A, Period: 2, nonmetal
     f. Group: 2A, Period: 6, metal
     g. Group: 5A, Period: 6, metal
     h. Group: 7A, Period: 4, nonmetal

42.   a. Group: 6A, Period: 3, nonmetal
        b. Group: 4A, Period: 5, metal
        c. Group: Lanthanides, Period: 6, metal
        d. Group:2A, Period: 5, metal
        e. Group: 5B, Period: 6, metal
        f. Group: 7B, Period: 5, metal
        g. Group: 4B, Period: 4, metal
        h. Group: 3A, Period: 6, metal

43. a. Ga; b. Cu; c. I

44. a. C or Si; b. Tc; c. Li

45. b

46. a

47. b, d, e

48. a, c

49. Five electrons in a p orbital.

50. Two electrons in an s orbital.

ADDITIONAL PROBLEMS

51.

	Atomic No.	No. of Protons	No. of Electrons	No. of Neutrons	Mass No.
Pb	82	82	82	126	208
Sr	38	38	38	50	88
N	7	7	7	7	14
Cr	24	24	24	28	52
Ag	47	47	47	60	107
As	33	33	33	42	75

52. a. 1A; b. 1B – 8B; c. 7A d. 2A

53. a. Rb; b. Na; c. Zr

54. a. Cs; b. Sb; c. Ac

55. Oxygen has only 4 electrons in the 2p orbital while fluorine has 5.

56. Fluorine has an electron configuration of $1s^22s^22p^5$ while sulfur's electron configuration is $1s^22s^22p^63s^23p^4$

57. No

58. They both lack only one electron from completing a p orbital. The electron configuration of fluorine is $1s^2 2s^2 2p^5$ while that of chlorine is $1s^2 2s^2 2p^6 3s^2 3p^5$.

59. $1s^2 2s^2$

60. The number of electrons should total three. The correct diagram should be:

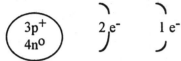

$3p^+$
$4n^o$
$2\ e^-$
$1\ e^-$

REVIEW QUESTIONS

1. a. Alpha particle: A particle identical to a helium nucleus which is emitted by some radioactive reactions. The particle consists of two protons and two neutrons and has a charge of +2.
   b. Artificial transmutation: A process by which one element is changed into another by artificial means.
   c. Rem: A unit of measurement of the relative biological damage of a particular dose of radiation (*r*oentgen *e*quivalent in *m*an).
   d. Electron capture: The process that occurs when a nucleus of an atom absorbs an electron from an inner shell. The movement of an electron from an outer shell to the unfilled inner shell results in the release of an X-ray.
   e. Roentgen(R): A unit of measurement of the effect of radiation on matter; measured as the ability of X-rays or gamma rays to ionize an air sample.
   f. Half-life: The period of time in which one-half the original number of atoms of a radioactive isotope undergoes radioactive decay.
   g. Ionizing radiation: Radiation that produces ions as it passes through matter.
   h. Radioisotope: Radioactive isotopes.
   i. Rad: A unit of measurement of the radiation absorbed by matter (*r*adiation *a*bsorbed *d*ose).

2. Gamma rays are of higher energy than X-rays. Both gamma rays and X-rays are forms of light energy (electromagnetic radiation).

3. a. beta particle; b. alpha particle

4. positron emission and electron capture

5. Mass number: no change
   Atomic number: no change

6. Mass number: minus 1 amu
   Atomic number: no change

7. a. Radioactive tracer: A radiation-releasing atom which, through its distribution throughout the body, indicates something about the cause of this distribution.
   b. Curie: A unit of measurement of the rate at which nuclear decay occurs in a radioactive isotope.

8. Nuclear fission results in two smaller nuclei from an original large nucleus while nuclear fusion combines two smaller nuclei to form a larger nucleus.

9. Rem is a better unit for measuring radiation dosage because it includes both a factor of exposure absorbed by the system *and* a factor for the potential for damage to human cells which a particular radiation might cause. Rad measures only the amount of exposure absorbed and doesn't take into consideration the type of radiation that is absorbed. (Some types of radiation do greater damage to human cells than others.)

10. In nuclear fusion, the product generated is helium and some neutrons. One does not generate radioactive material as a product which then needs to be properly disposed. This is a problem in nuclear fission.

11. The process of irradiating foods involves exposing the food to a radiation source (usually gamma rays coming from ^{60}Co or ^{137}Cs). The radiation kills microorganisms which would normally lead to spoiling. In essence, irradiation of food "pasteurizes" the food.

12. Neutrons

13. There is a tremendous repulsion of protons as they approach each other in nuclear fusion before they combine in a single nucleus. High temperatures are required to generate molecular speeds required to overcome this repulsion.

14. The two main dangers of nuclear fission are that tight control of fission is required to prevent a bomblike explosion and that the products of fission are themselves radioactive and, therefore, need to be adequately stored.

15.   a. Use shielding.
       b. Maintain a distance from the radioactive sample.
       c. Minimize the time of exposure.

16. The heavy alpha particles

17. Gamma

18. Alpha particles penetrate less, therefore spreading their energy over a smaller area. Beta particles, on the other hand, spread their damage over a larger area. Tissue is more susceptible to intense damage than diffuse radiation.

19. Radiation from radioisotopes is used to selectively kill cancerous cells while hopefully inflicting small damage to normal cells.

20. ^{131}I

21. A gamma-emitting radioisotope is ingested or injected, goes to the tissue or tissues of interest, and then the patient is scanned for radiation.

22. $^{99}_{43}\text{Tc}$ does not emit alpha or beta particles, it has a moderate half-life, and it produces gamma radiation of just the proper intensity for detection but which causes little damage to the body.

23. X-rays

24. Gamma rays

25. Nonionizing radiation does not cause the tissue damage that can be the result of ionizing radiation.

26. Ultrasonography and MRI

PROBLEMS

NUCLEAR SYMBOLS

27. a. helium-4; b. beta particle; c. neutron; d. deuterium

28. a. γ; b. $^{3}_{1}\text{H}$; c. β^{+}; d. $^{14}_{6}\text{C}$

NUCLEAR EQUATIONS

29. $^{209}_{82}Pb \longrightarrow ^{0}_{-1}e + ^{209}_{83}Bi$

30. $^{225}_{90}Th \longrightarrow ^{221}_{88}Ra + ^{4}_{2}He$

31. $^{31}_{16}S \longrightarrow ^{0}_{+1}e + ^{31}_{15}P$

32. $^{215}_{85}At$

33. $^{87}_{35}Br \longrightarrow ^{1}_{0}n + ^{86}_{35}Br$

34. $^{21}_{12}Mg \longrightarrow ^{1}_{1}H + ^{20}_{11}Na$

35. $^{24}_{12}Mg + ^{1}_{0}n \longrightarrow ^{1}_{1}H + ^{24}_{11}Na$

36. $^{14}_{7}N + ^{4}_{2}He \longrightarrow ^{17}_{8}O + ^{1}_{1}p$

37. a. $^{10}_{4}Be$; b. $^{1}_{1}H$; c. $^{4}_{2}He$

38. a. $^{153}_{62}Sm$; b. $^{133}_{55}Cs$; c. $5 \, ^{1}_{0}n$

39. a. $^{2}_{1}H + ^{2}_{1}H \longrightarrow ^{3}_{2}He + ^{1}_{0}n$

   b. $^{241}_{95}Am + ^{4}_{2}He \longrightarrow ^{243}_{97}Bk + 2 \, ^{1}_{0}n$

   c. $^{121}_{51}Sb + ^{4}_{2}He \longrightarrow ^{125}_{53}I + ^{1}_{0}n \longrightarrow ^{125}_{52}Te + \beta^{+}$

40. a. $\quad {}^{196}_{82}Pb \longrightarrow {}^{196}_{81}Tl \longrightarrow {}^{196}_{80}Hg$

   b. $\quad {}^{215}_{83}Bi \longrightarrow {}^{215}_{84}Po \longrightarrow {}^{215}_{85}At$

   c. $\quad {}^{231}_{91}Pa \longrightarrow {}^{4}_{2}He + {}^{227}_{89}Ac \longrightarrow {}^{4}_{2}He + {}^{223}_{87}Fr \longrightarrow {}^{4}_{2}He + {}^{219}_{85}At \longrightarrow {}^{4}_{2}He + {}^{215}_{83}Bi$

HALF-LIFE

41. One-eighth of its initial value means 3 half-lives. The length of time will be 24.12 days.

42. 24 hours represents four half-lives. The amount of material remaining will be 1/16th of the original or 8 mg.

43. 5 disintegrations per minute is 1/32nd of the original 160 disintegrations per minute. This represents 5 half-lives or 335 hrs.

44. 26 s

ADDITIONAL PROBLEMS

45. You would look to see if the element had changed. A γ emission does not change the atomic number of the atom and hence it should have all the characteristics of that element. An electron capture decreases the atomic number by one and hence the atom changes to a completely different element and thus has the properties of the new element.

46. $\quad {}^{99}_{43}Te + {}^{1}_{0}n \longrightarrow {}^{100}_{43}Te \longrightarrow {}^{100}_{44}Ru + \beta^{-}$

47. $\quad {}^{62}_{28}Ni + {}^{208}_{82}Pb \longrightarrow {}^{1}_{0}n + {}^{269}_{110}Z \xrightarrow{{}^{4}_{2}He} {}^{265}_{108}Y \xrightarrow{{}^{4}_{2}He} {}^{261}_{106}X \xrightarrow{{}^{4}_{2}He} {}^{257}_{104}W \xrightarrow{{}^{4}_{2}He} {}^{254}_{102}No$

48. α particles. The other two types of radiation are more penetrating and will not be affected by the thin paper.

49. Internal 10 mCi; external 500 Ci.

50. Treatment of malignancy: 150 mCi, imaging 15 μCi.

51. Compared to a lethal whole-body dose of about 500 rad, the diagnostic dose of 0.14 rad was about 0.028% of the lethal dose.

52. $^{218}_{84}Po$; $^{214}_{86}Pb$

53. $^{82}_{36}Kr$

54. After 4.5 s (one half-life), 1500 atoms of element 104 remain. After 9.0 s (two half-lives), 750 atoms of the element remain.

55. The "pros": far below surface, dry environment.
    The "cons": Can geological inactivity be extrapolated?

56. The discussions must include the impact of the following developments:
    a. Nuclear weapons
    b. Therapeutic and diagnostic radiation
    c. Nuclear fission and the potential for nuclear fusion

57. Cs^+ is chemically similar to Na^+ and K^+, which are body electrolytes. Therefore, Cs^+, radioactive or otherwise, can easily find its way into body fluids.

58. There are inherent dangers in transporting nuclear wastes into outer space and keeping them there. There are also some ethical questions on whether we should be treating outer space as a giant dump. On the other hand are the dangers involved in storing these wastes on Earth.

REVIEW QUESTIONS

1. Noble gases

2. A sodium atom contains 11 electrons while a sodium ion only contains 10 electrons. Sodium ions are much less chemically reactive than sodium atoms.

3. A sodium ion and a neon atom both contain 10 electrons, however, sodium has one more proton (and a couple more neutrons).

4. Chlorine atoms are single-nucleus entities with seventeen electrons; chlorine molecules are two chlorine atoms held together by a covalent band; and chloride ions are single-nucleus entities with eighteen electrons. Chlorine molecules and chloride ions are stable, chlorine atoms are reactive. Chlorine molecules and chlorine atoms are uncharged while chloride ions have a negative charge.

5. Hydrogen has one electron in its outer shell and needs only one electron to complete its outer shell. Because of this, hydrogen behaves both like an alkali metal (the group that has one electron in its outer shell) and the halogens (the group that needs one electron to complete its outer shell).

6. A chemical bond is a sharing of electrons by two atoms wishing to complete their outer electron shells. Neon has a filled outer electron shell and therefore has no need to match up with other atoms in a bond.

7. a. 1; b. 4; c. 2; d. 1; e. 3; f. 1

8. Molecules and atoms with an odd number of valence electrons (like NO and free radicals like a chlorine atom), some molecules containing group 3A elements (like BF_3), and some molecules containing third period elements and above (like PCl_5).

9. a. K^+ $2e^-$ $8e^-$ $8e^-$ b. S^{2-} $2e^-$ $8e^-$ $8e^-$

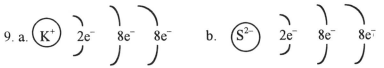

   c. F^- $2e^-$ $8e^-$ d. Al^{3+} $2e^-$ $8e^-$

10. a. Mg^{2+} $2e^-$ $8e^-$ b. Cl^- $2e^-$ $8e^-$ $8e^-$

   c. Li^+ $2e^-$ d. N^{3-} $2e^-$ $8e^-$

11. a. +2; b. −1

12. a. +1; b. −2

13. Ionic: a,c; polar covalent: b; nonpolar covalent: d

14. Ionic: b,c; polar covalent: a; nonpolar covalent: d

PROBLEMS

LEWIS STRUCTURES: ELEMENTS

15. a. Na• b. :Ö: c. :F̈• d. Al̈ •

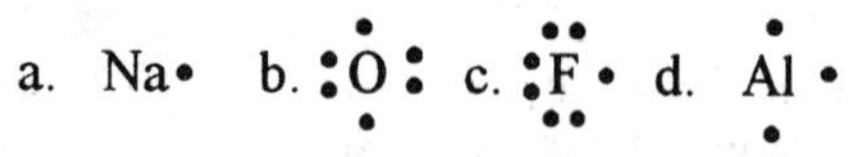

16. a. •C̈• b. K• c. Mg: d. :C̈l:

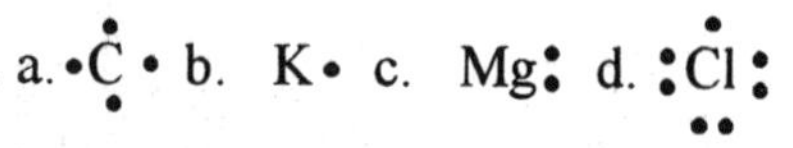

LEWIS STRUCTURES: IONS AND IONIC BONDING

17. a. Ba: $\longrightarrow$ $2e^-$ + Ba^{2+}

  b. :Br̈: + $1e^-$ $\longrightarrow$:Br̈: $^-$

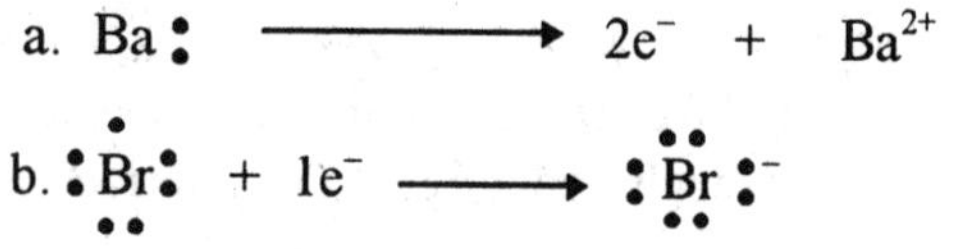

18. a. •Al̇ $\longrightarrow$ $3e^-$ + Al^{3+}

  b. :S̈ + $2e^-$ $\longrightarrow$:S̈: $^{2-}$

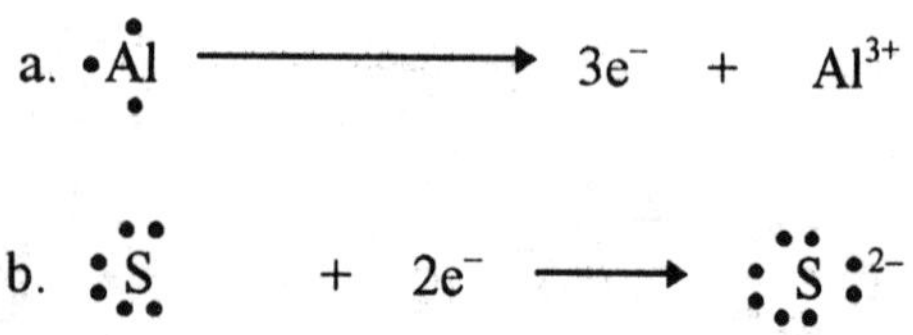

19. a. Ca: + :Br̈• + :Br̈• $\longrightarrow$ Ca^{2+} + :Br̈: $^-$ +:Br̈: $^-$

  b. Mg: + :S̈ $\longrightarrow$ Mg^{2+} + :S̈: $^{2-}$

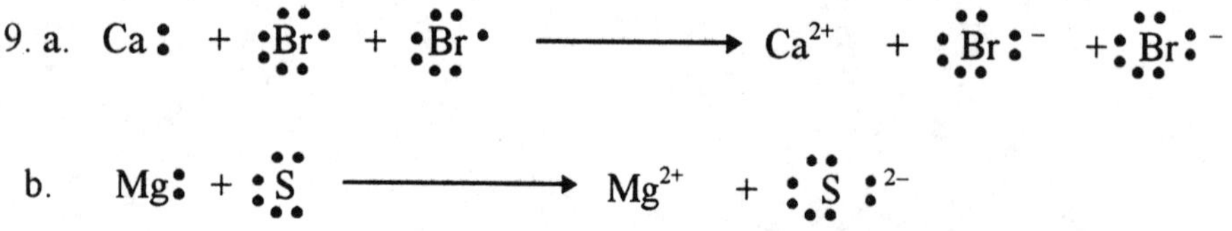

20. a. •Al̇ + •Al̇ + :S̈ + :S̈ + :S̈ $\longrightarrow$ 2 Al^{3+} + 3 :S̈: $^{2-}$

  b. Mg: + Mg: + Mg: + :P̈• + :P̈• $\longrightarrow$ 3 Mg^{2+} + 2 :P̈: $^{3-}$

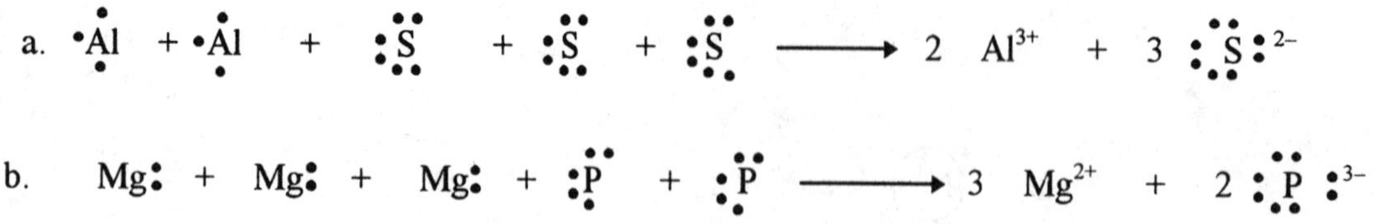

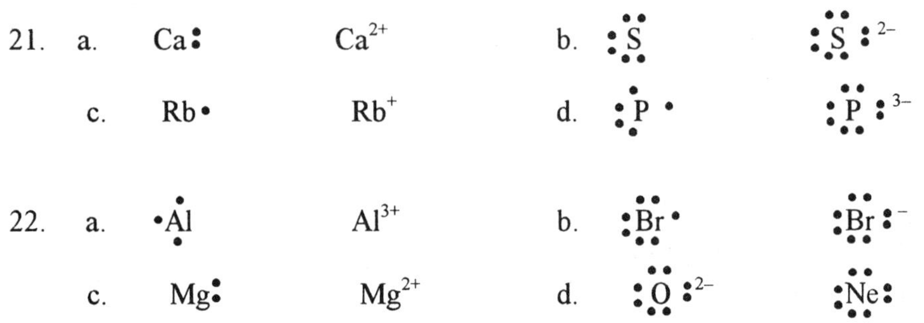

21. a. Ca: Ca^{2+} b. :S̈:   [:S̈:]$^{2-}$

    c. Rb· Rb^+ d. :P̈·   [:P̈:]$^{3-}$

22. a. ·Al̈ Al^{3+} b. :B̈r·   [:B̈r:]$^{-}$

    c. Mg: Mg^{2+} d. [:Ö:]$^{2-}$:N̈e:

LEWIS STRUCTURES: IONIC COMPOUNDS

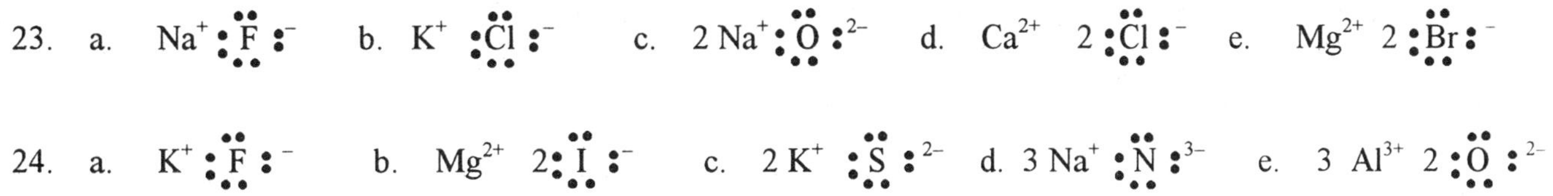

23. a. Na^+ [:F̈:]$^-$ b. K^+ [:C̈l:]$^-$ c. $2 Na^+$ [:Ö:]$^{2-}$ d. Ca^{2+} 2[:C̈l:]$^-$ e. Mg^{2+} 2[:B̈r:]$^-$

24. a. K^+ [:F̈:]$^-$ b. Mg^{2+} 2[:Ï:]$^-$ c. $2 K^+$ [:S̈:]$^{2-}$ d. $3 Na^+$ [:N̈:]$^{3-}$ e. $3 Al^{3+}$ 2[:Ö:]$^{2-}$

NAMING IONS AND IONIC COMPOUNDS

25.   a. sodium ion   d. chloride ion
      b. magnesium ion   e. oxide ion
      c. aluminum ion   f. nitride ion

26.   a. potassium ion   d. bromide ion
      b. calcium ion   e. lithium ion
      c. zinc ion   f. sulfide ion

27.   a. iron(III) ion (ferric)
      b. copper(II) ion (cupric)
      c. silver ion

28.   a. iron(II) ion (ferrous)
      b. copper(I) ion (cuprous)
      c. iodide ion

29. a. Br^-; b. Ca^{2+}; c. K^+; d. Fe^{2+}

30. a. Na^+; b. Al^{3+}; c. O^{2-}; d. Cu^{2+}

31. a. sodium bromide; b. calcium chloride; c. iron(II) chloride or ferrous chloride; d. lithium iodide;
      e. potassium sulfide; f. copper(I) bromide or cuprous bromide

32. a. potassium chloride; b. magnesium bromide; c. copper(II) iodide or cupric iodide; d. calcium sulfide;
      e. iron(III) chloride or ferric chloride; f. aluminum oxide

33. a. carbonate ion; b. monohydrogen phosphate ion; c. permanganate ion; d. hydroxide ion

34. a. nitrate ion; b. sulfate ion; c. dihydrogen phosphate ion; d. hydrogen carbonate (bicarbonate) ion

35. a. NH_4^+; b. HSO_4^-; c. CN^-; d. NO_2^-

36. a. PO_4^{3-}; b. HCO_3^-; c. $Cr_2O_7^{2-}$; d. $C_2O_4^{2-}$

37. a. $MgSO_4$; b. $NaHCO_3$; c. KNO_3; d. $CaHPO_4$

38. a. $CaCO_3$; b. KH_2PO_4; c. $Mg(CN)_2$; d. $LiHSO_4$

39. a. $Fe_3(PO_4)_2$; b. $K_2Cr_2O_7$; c. CuI; d. NH_4NO_2

40. a. $Fe_2(C_2O_4)_3$; b. $NaMnO_4$; c. $CuBr_2$; d. $ZnHPO_4$

LEWIS STRUCTURES: COVALENT BONDS AND MOLECULES

41. : represents bonding pair, : represents lone pair

42. : represents bonding pair, : represents lone pair

$\delta^+ \ldots\ldots \delta^-$

43. a.   b.

44. a.   b.

45. a.   b.   c.   d.

    e.   f.

46. a.   b. $H—C≡C—H$ c.   d.

    e.   f. $H—C≡N:$

NAMING COVALENT COMPOUNDS

47. a. N_2O; b. P_4S_3; c. PCl_5; d. SF_6

48. a. OF_2; b. N_2O_5; c. PBr_3; d. S_4N_4

49. a. carbon disulfide; b. dinitrogen tetrasulfide; c. phosphorus pentafluoride; d. disulfur decafluoride

50. a. carbon tetrabromide; b. dichlorine heptoxide; c. tetraphosphorous decasulfide; d. diiodine pentoxide

ELECTRONEGATIVITY

51. a. N; b. Cl; c. F

52. a. F; b. Br; c. Cl

53. a. B < N < F ; b. Ca < As < Br ; c. Ga < C < O

54. a. Rb < Sb < I ; b. Cs < Na < Li ; c. Sb < P < Cl

EXCEPTIONS TO THE OCTET RULE

55. a. 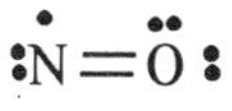 $:N=O:$ b. 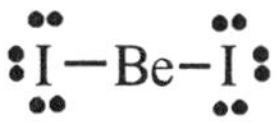 $:I-Be-I:$ c. 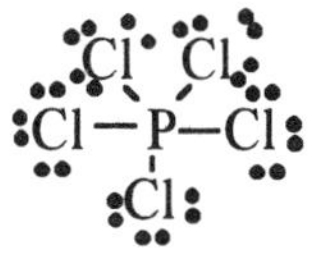 [Lewis structure of PCl_5]

56. a. 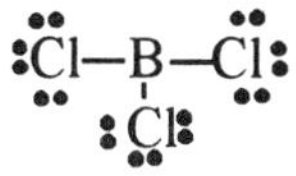 [Lewis structure of BCl_3] b. 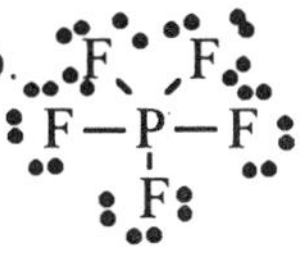 [Lewis structure of PF_5] c. 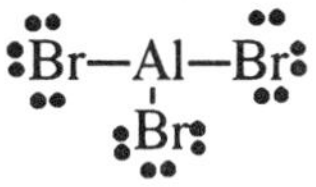 [Lewis structure of $AlBr_3$]

POLYATOMIC IONS AND THEIR COMPOUNDS

57. a. [Lewis structure ClO^-] b. 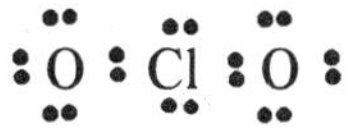 [Lewis structure ClO_2^-] c. 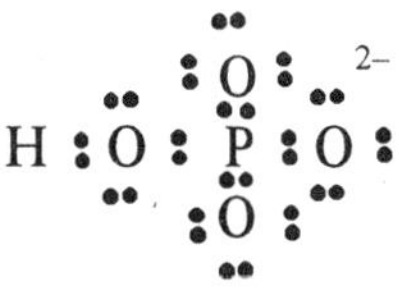 [Lewis structure HPO_4^{2-}] d. 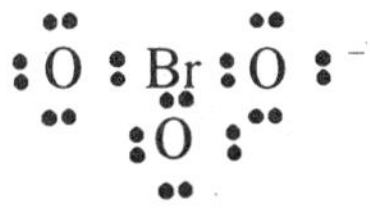 [Lewis structure BrO_2^-]

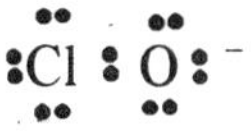

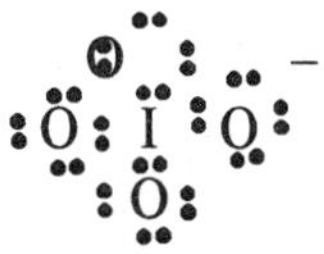

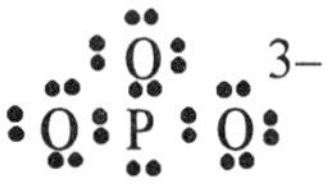

58. a. $:C:::N:^-$ b. [Lewis structure IO_3^-] c. [Lewis structure PO_4^{3-}] d. 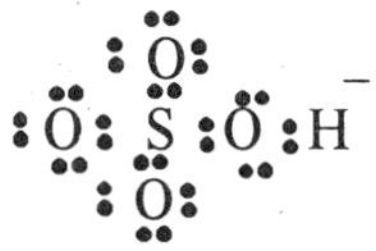 [Lewis structure HSO_4^-]

59. a. potassium nitrite; b. lithium cyanide; c. ammonium iodide; d. sodium nitrate; e. potassium permanganate; f. calcium sulfate

60. a. sodium hydrogen sulfate (or sodium bisulfate); b. aluminum hydroxide; c. sodium carbonate; d. potassium hydrogen carbonate (or potassium bicarbonate); e. ammonium nitrite; f. calcium hydrogen sulfate (or calcium bisulfate)

61. a. sodium monohydrogen phosphate; b. ammonium phosphate; c. aluminum nitrate; d. ammonium nitrate

62. a. lithium carbonate; b. sodium dichromate; c. calcium dihydrogen phosphate; d. ammonium oxalate

ADDITIONAL PROBLEMS

63.

	Element W	Element X	Element Y	Element Z
Group Number	7A	1A	2A	6A
Lewis Symbol	$:\ddot{W}:$	$X\cdot$	$\cdot Y\cdot$	$:\ddot{Z}\cdot$
Charge on Ion	1–	1+	2+	2–

64. a. X: Group 7; Y: Group 6; Z: Group 5

   b. 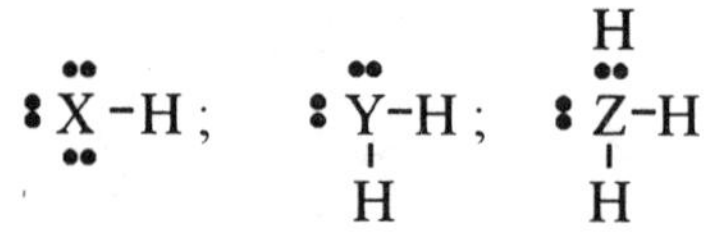 $:\ddot{X}-H$; $:\ddot{Y}-H$; $:\ddot{Z}-H$ with H above and H below

   c. 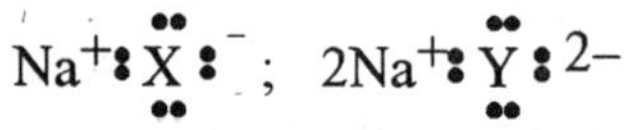 $Na^+:\ddot{X}:^-$; $2Na^+:\ddot{Y}:^{2-}$

65. I hope not! (Unless you'd like to do it for a *blast*!!) You would be taking the K^+ form as a salt of some compound.

66. NaCl is not a molecular compound. It is an ionic compound. In order to be a molecule, electrons must be shared.

67. 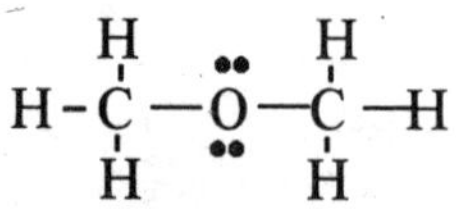 $H-\overset{H}{\underset{H}{C}}-\ddot{O}-\overset{H}{\underset{H}{C}}-H$ and $H-\overset{H}{\underset{H}{C}}-\overset{H}{\underset{H}{C}}-\ddot{O}-H$

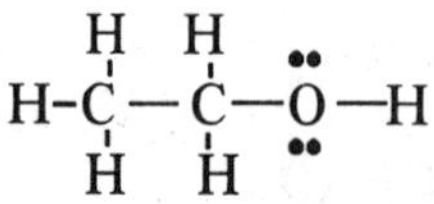

68. 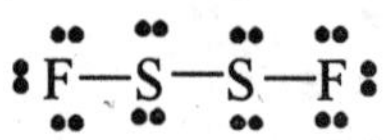 $:\ddot{F}-\ddot{S}-\ddot{S}-\ddot{F}:$ and $:\ddot{F}-\ddot{S}-S:$ with $:\ddot{F}:$ below

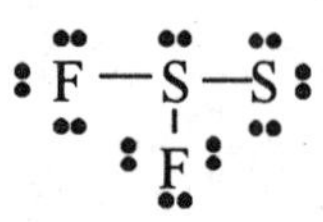

69. ClO_2

70. P_4S_3

71. AlP; Mg_3P_2

REVIEW QUESTIONS

1. The bond itself will connect two atoms in the shortest possible distance, i.e. a straight line. Since there are only two atoms in a diatomic molecule, the atoms and the bond must be linear.

2. Yes. If there are only two sets of bonds around the central atom(s), the molecule would be linear. (An example, using the octet rule, would be a central atom with a single and triple bond.)

3. In the term "molecular shape," we are describing the arrangement of the atoms around a central atom. In ammonia, the four pairs of electrons are arranged around the central nitrogen in a tetrahedron, but the arrangement of the three hydrogens in relation to the nitrogen (one lone pair is ignored) is pyrimidal.

4. Lone pairs (LP) of electrons will have the greatest repulsion for other pairs because their negative charge is only satisfied by the protons of one atom, not two.

5. Polar covalent.

6. a. $180°$; b. $120°$; c. $109.5°$

7. No.

8. VSEPR treats a multiple bond as a unit as one is spreading the electrons around a central atom.

9. Not every chemical bond would have a dipole moment. For example, neither atom in a N_2 molecule would have a stronger desire for the bonding pair of electrons than the other and hence there would be no dipole moment. Not every molecule would have a resultant dipole moment because a) not every molecule has a bond with a dipole moment and b) some molecules are symmetrical and therefore their dipole moments cancel out.

10. If a water molecule was linear, the dipole moment of the bonds between the oxygen and hydrogen atoms would cancel each other out, and the result would be a molecule of no polarity. The fact that water is polar means that the two dipole moments must result from bonds positioned in nonlinear directions.

PROBLEMS

VSEPR THEORY

11. a. linear; b. triangular

12. a. pyrimidal; b. tetrahedral

13. a. bent; b. tetrahedral

14. a. tetrahedral; b. bent

15. a. pyrimidal; b. bent

16. a. pyramidal; b. tetrahedral

POLAR AND NONPOLAR MOLECULES

17. a. polar; b. polar; b. nonpolar

18. a. polar; b. nonpolar; c. polar

19. a.   H — O   b. N — Cl
         δ⁺ δ⁻   δ⁺ δ⁻

20. a   Si — Cl   c. P — Cl
        δ⁺ δ⁻   δ⁺ δ⁻

21. Nonpolar. The dipole electric fields in the bonds between the Be and the F atoms are directed in opposite directions and thus cancel each other out.

22. Polar. SF_2 is a bent molecule. The dipole moments of the two S–F bonds are pointing in different directions and thus do not cancel each other out.

23. a. F — F, Cl — F, H — F ;   b. H — H, H — Br, H — F

24. a. H — H, H — C, H — N, H — O, H — F ;   b. C — C, C — I, C — Br, C — Cl, C — F

25. a. F — F, Cl — F, H — F ;   b. H — H, H — Br, H — F
          δ⁺ δ⁻ δ⁺ δ⁻   δ⁺ δ⁻ δ⁺ δ⁻

26. a. H — H, H — C, H — N, H — O, H — F ;   b. C — C, C — I, C — Br, C — Cl, C — F
        δ⁺ δ⁻ δ⁺ δ⁻ δ⁺ δ⁻ δ⁺ δ⁻   δ⁺ δ⁻ δ⁺ δ⁻ δ⁺ δ⁻ δ⁺ δ⁻

ADDITIONAL PROBLEMS

27. SO_2 is a bent molecule with the shape similar to H_2O. The dipole moments of the two sets of bonds between the sulfur and the oxygens are positioned in different directions and, therefore, a net dipole moment is seen. SO_3 is a symmetrical molecule with the oxygens positioned in a triangular shape around the sulfur. The individual dipole moments of the bonds between the oxygens and the sulfurs cancel each other out leaving no net dipole moment for the molecule.

28.   δ+   δ–
       H — F

29. a. not probable, if the atoms did line up, the dipole moments would cancel leading to a nonpolar molecule.
     b. probable
     c. not probable, there would be four sets of electrons located around the central P atom, this would create a pyramidal shape.

30. a. pyrimidal; b. tetrahedral; c. linear

31. a. tetrahedral; b. pyrimidal; c. triangular

32. One would guess in general that this would be true; the deviation to this rule occurs due to the canceling out of the individual bond dipole moments as they point in different directions from a central atom.

33. a. probable; b. not probable -- there would be only two sets of electrons around the central carbon. It would thus be a linear molecule.

REVIEW QUESTIONS

1. a. Endothermic: A reaction to which energy must be supplied in order to proceed.
    b. Exothermic: A reaction that releases heat.
    c. Energy of Activation: The minimum energy needed to initiate a reaction.
    d. Catalyst: A substance that increases the rate of a chemical reaction without itself being used up.
    e. Reversible Reaction: A reaction that can go in either direction.
    f. Equilibrium: A condition of a reversible reaction when the rates of the forward and reverse reactions become equal; the concentrations of both the reactants and products do not change once this condition is reached.

2. The atomic weight of nitrogen refers to the weight (mass) of one atom of nitrogen in amu units; the molecular weight of nitrogen (gas) refers to the weight (mass) of one molecule of N_2 (i.e. 2 atoms) in amu units. The atomic weight is read off the periodic table; the molecular weight is the atomic weight times two.

3. Avogadro's number is equal to 6.02×10^{23} objects. One mole of a substance is equal to Avogadro's number (i.e. 6.02×10^{23} of the substance's basic units).

4. Avogadro's hypothesis stated that equal volumes of all gases (at the same temperature and pressure) contain the same number of molecules. This accounting of the number of molecules in a given volume supported Gay-Lussac's claim that molecules react in defined proportions.

5. The molecular weight of CO_2 is equal to 44 amu's and the molar mass is equal to 44 g/mol. It is determined by summing up the weights of the various atoms (one carbon and two oxygen) in one unit of CO_2.

6. If, as Avogadro proposed, equal volumes implicate equal numbers of molecules; then the only way the reaction of hydrogen gas with nitrogen gas to make ammonia gas in a 3:1:2 ratio can take place is if H_2 and N_2 are diatomic.

7. 6.02×10^{23}; 12.04×10^{23}

8. $Ca^{2+} = 6.02 \times 10^{23}$; $Cl^- = 12.04 \times 10^{23}$

9. The law of conservation of matter states that matter cannot be destroyed during a chemical reaction. Therefore, the atoms which are part of the reactants must be accounted for as part of the products after the reaction is complete. This requires a <u>balanced</u> chemical equation, i.e., an equation where the number of each type of atom must be equal on each side of the arrow.

10. At the molecular level: One molecule of CH_4 will combine with two molecules of O_2 and rearrange bonds to produce one molecule of CO_2 and two molecules of H_2O. In terms of moles: One cannot see molecules and therefore larger numbers are needed. The proportions in moles are exactly the same as that of molecules since one mole equals a specific number (6.02×10^{23}). Thus, the reaction also can be interpreted as one mole of CH_4 will combine with two moles of O_2 and rearranging bonds to produce one mole of CO_2 and two moles of H_2O. In terms of mass: One mole of CH_4 or 16 g of CH_4 will react with two moles of O_2 or 64 g of O_2 to yield one mole of CO_2 or 44 g of CO_2 and 2 moles of H_2O or 36 g of H_2O. Notice that the law of conservation of mass holds true, i.e. 80 g of reactants produce 80 g of product.

11. a. Two moles (or molecules) of H_2 react with one mole (or molecule) of O_2 to produce two moles (or molecules) of water.

  b. Two moles (or molecules) of $KClO_3$ break down into two moles (or molecules) of KCl and three moles (or molecules) of oxygen.

  c. Two moles (or atoms) of Al react with six moles (or molecules) of HCl to form two moles (or molecules) of $AlCl_3$ and three moles (or molecules) of H_2.

12. a. C; b. B; c. A

13. Exothermic. The energy level of C is lower than that of the starting compound A. The difference in energy from going from A to C is released as heat.

14. Endothermic. The reverse reaction, i.e. C to A, requires going from a low energy compound to a high energy compound. Energy must be supplied to convert C molecules to A.

15. The rate will increase.

16. The rate will increase.

17. The rate will increase.

18. In order for a reaction to occur, the reactant molecules must collide. In most cases it is necessary that a particular spot on one reactant molecule collide with a particular location on a second reactant molecule. An effective collision (one that results in a reaction) requires that the reactant molecules be oriented correctly.

19. The mechanism of a reaction is a description of what events must occur with the reactant molecules (and any intermediates formed) in order to produce the product. It is the detailed explanation of exactly *how* the reactants come together to form the product.

20. A catalyst increases the rate of a reaction by lowering the activation energy. It does this by getting the reactants together in a more efficient collision.

PROBLEMS

MOLAR VOLUME

21. 22.4L for all three

22. a. 4g; b. 2.02g; c. 30g; (In each case it is the molar mass of the substance.)

MOLECULAR FORMULAS AND FORMULA UNITS

23. a. 4; b. 4; c. 8; d. 6

24. a. 9; b. 9

25. a. 12; b. 8

26. Al:2; C:12; H:18; O:12

BALANCING CHEMICAL EQUATIONS

27. balanced: a,d,e; not balanced: b,c

28. balanced: a,d,e; not balanced: b,c

29. a. $Cl_2O_5 + H_2O \longrightarrow 2HClO_3$
   b. $V_2O_5 + 2H_2 \longrightarrow V_2O_3 + 2H_2O$
   c. $4Al + 3O_2 \longrightarrow 2Al_2O_3$
   d. $Sn + 2NaOH \longrightarrow Na_2SnO_2 + H_2$
   e. $PCl_5 + 4H_2O \longrightarrow H_3PO_4 + 5HCl$

30. a. $TiCl_4 + 2H_2O \longrightarrow TiO_2 + 4HCl$
   b. $2C_4H_{10} + 13O_2 \longrightarrow 8CO_2 + 10H_2O$
   c. $WO_3 + 3H_2 \longrightarrow W + 3H_2O$
   d. $Al_4C_3 + 12H_2O \longrightarrow 4Al(OH)_3 + 3CH_4$
   e. $Al_2(SO_4)_3 + 6NaOH \longrightarrow 2Al(OH)_3 + 3Na_2SO_4$

31. a. $Na_3P + 3H_2O \longrightarrow 3NaOH + PH_3$
   b. $Cl_2O + H_2O \longrightarrow 2HClO$
   c. $2CH_3OH + 3O_2 \longrightarrow 2CO_2 + 4H_2O$
   d. $3Zn(OH)_2 + 2H_3PO_4 \longrightarrow Zn_3(PO_4)_2 + 6H_2O$
   e. $C_3H_8 + 5O_2 \longrightarrow 3CO_2 + 4H_2O$

32. a. $Ca_3P_2 + 6H_2O \longrightarrow 3Ca(OH)_2 + 2PH_3$
   b. $Cl_2O_7 + H_2O \longrightarrow 2HClO_4$
   c. $MnO_2 + 4HCl \longrightarrow MnCl_2 + Cl_2 + 2H_2O$
   d. $3Fe + 2O_2 \longrightarrow Fe_3O_4$
   e. $C_5H_{12} + 8O_2 \longrightarrow 5CO_2 + 6H_2O$

MOLECULAR WEIGHTS AND FORMULA WEIGHTS

33. a. (6 C x 12.0 g/mol) + (5 H x 1.0 g/mol) + (1 Br x 79.9 g/mol) = 156.9 g/mol
   b. (3 H x 1.0 g/mol) + (1 P x 31.0 g/mol) + (4 O x 16.0 g/mol) = 98.0 g/mol
   c. (2 K x 39.1 g/mol) + (2 Cr x 52.0 g/mol) + (7 O x 16.0 g/mol) = 294.2 g/mol

34. a. (2 C x 12 g/mol) + (5 H x 1.0 g/mol) + (1 N x 14.0 g/mol) + (2 O x 16.0 g/mol) = 75 g/mol
   b. (2 Na x 23.1 g/mol) + (2 S x 32.0 g/mol) + (3 O x 16.0 g/mol) = 158.2 g/mol
   c. 3 x [(1 N x 14g/mol) + 4 H x 1.0 g/mol)] + (1 P x 31.0 g/mol) + (4 O x 16.0 g/mol) = 149 g/mol

MOLAR MASSES

35. a. $\dfrac{0.00500 \text{ mol } MnO_2}{1} \times \dfrac{86.9 \text{ g}}{1 \text{ mol } MnO_2} = 0.435 \text{ g}$ b. $\dfrac{1.12 \text{ mol } CaH_2}{1} \times \dfrac{42.1 \text{ g}}{1 \text{ mol } CaH_2} = 47.2 \text{ g}$

   c. $\dfrac{0.250 \text{ mol } C_6H_{12}O_6}{1} \times \dfrac{180 \text{ g}}{1 \text{ mol } C_6H_{12}O_6} = 45.0 \text{ g}$

36. a. $\dfrac{4.61 \text{ g AlCl}_3}{1}$ x $\dfrac{133.5 \text{ g}}{1 \text{ mol AlCl}_3}$ =   615 g

    b. $\dfrac{0.615 \text{ mol Cr}_2\text{O}_3}{1}$ x $\dfrac{152 \text{ g}}{1 \text{ mol Cr}_2\text{O}_3}$ =   93.5 g

    c. $\dfrac{0.158 \text{ mol IF}_5}{1}$ x $\dfrac{221.9 \text{ g}}{1 \text{ mol IF}_5}$ =   35.1 g

37. a. $\dfrac{98.6 \text{ g HNO}_3}{1}$ x $\dfrac{1 \text{ mol HNO}_3}{63 \text{ g}}$ =   1.57 mol

    b. $\dfrac{9.45 \text{ g CBr}_4}{1}$ x $\dfrac{1 \text{ mol CBr}_4}{331.6 \text{ g}}$ =   0.0285 mol

    c. $\dfrac{9.11 \text{ g FeSO}_4}{1}$ x $\dfrac{1 \text{ mol FeSO}_4}{151.9 \text{ g}}$ =   0.0600 mol

    d. $\dfrac{11.8 \text{ g Pb(NO}_3)_2}{1}$ x $\dfrac{1 \text{ mol Pb(NO}_3)_2}{331.2 \text{ g}}$ =   0.0356 mol

38. a. $\dfrac{16.3 \text{ g SF}_6}{1}$ x $\dfrac{1 \text{ mol SF}_6}{146.1 \text{ g}}$ =   0.112 mol

    b. $\dfrac{25.4 \text{ g Pb(C}_2\text{H}_3\text{O}_2)_2}{1}$ x $\dfrac{1 \text{ mol Pb(C}_2\text{H}_3\text{O}_2)_2}{325.2 \text{ g}}$ =   0.0781 mol

    c. $\dfrac{35.6 \text{ g FeCl}_3}{1}$ x $\dfrac{1 \text{ mol FeCl}_3}{162.3 \text{ g}}$ =   0.219 mol

    d. $\dfrac{75.3 \text{ g Co(ClO}_3)_2}{1}$ x $\dfrac{1 \text{ mol Co(ClO}_3)_2}{225.9 \text{ g}}$ =   0.333 mol

VOLUME RELATIONSHIPS IN CHEMICAL EQUATIONS

39. a. $\dfrac{0.529 \text{ L C}_4\text{H}_{10}}{1}$ x $\dfrac{10 \text{ L H}_2\text{O produced}}{2 \text{ L C}_4\text{H}_{10} \text{ reacted}}$ =   2.65 L H_2O

    b. $\dfrac{16.1 \text{ L C}_4\text{H}_{10}}{1}$ x $\dfrac{13 \text{ L O}_2 \text{ needed}}{2\text{L C}_4\text{H}_{10} \text{ reacted}}$ =   104.7 L O_2

40. a. $\dfrac{2.93 \text{ L C}_2\text{H}_4}{1}$ x $\dfrac{2 \text{ L CO}_2 \text{ produced}}{1 \text{ mol L C}_2\text{H}_4}$ =   5.86 L CO_2

    b. $\dfrac{3.70 \text{ L CO}_2 \text{ needed}}{1}$ x $\dfrac{3 \text{ mol O}_2 \text{ required}}{2 \text{ mol CO}_2 \text{ produced}}$ =   5.55 mol O_2

MOLE RELATIONSHIPS IN CHEMICAL EQUATIONS

41. a. $\dfrac{2.09 \text{ mol } C_8H_{18}}{1} \times \dfrac{16 \text{ mol } CO_2}{2 \text{ mol } C_8H_{18}} = 16.7 \text{ mol } CO_2$

b. $\dfrac{4.47 \text{ mol } C_8H_{18}}{1} \times \dfrac{25 \text{ mol } O_2}{2 \text{ mol } C_8H_{18}} = 55.9 \text{ mol } O_2$

42. a. 25.3 mol; b. 2.60 mol

MASS RELATIONSHIPS IN CHEMICAL EQUATIONS

43. Balanced Equation: $N_2 + 3H_2 \longrightarrow 2NH_3$

$\dfrac{440 \text{ g } H_2}{1} \times \dfrac{1 \text{ mol } H_2}{2g \text{ } H_2} \times \dfrac{2 \text{ mol } NH_3}{3\text{mol } H_2} \times \dfrac{17 \text{ g } NH_3}{1\text{mol } NH_3} = 2490 \text{ g } NH_3$

44. $\dfrac{892 \text{ g } N_2}{1} \times \dfrac{1 \text{ mol } N_2}{28 \text{ g } N_2} \times \dfrac{3 \text{ mol } H_2}{1 \text{ mol } N_2} \times \dfrac{2 \text{ g } H_2}{1 \text{ mol } H_2} = 191\text{g } H_2$

45. 11.3 g O_2 (balanced equation: $2H_2O_2 \longrightarrow 2H_2O + O_2$)

46. 933 g HNO_3 (balanced equation: $C_7H_8 + 3HNO_3 \longrightarrow C_7H_5N_3O_6 + 1H_2O$)

47. 2050 g

48. $\dfrac{4.72 \times 10^9 \text{ g } CaCO_3}{1} \times \dfrac{1 \text{ mol}}{100 \text{ g } CaCO_3} \times \dfrac{1 \text{ mol } CaO}{1 \text{ mol } CaCO_3} \times \dfrac{56 \text{ g } CaO}{1 \text{ mol } CaO} \times \dfrac{1 \text{ kg}}{1000 \text{ g}} = 2.64 \times 10^9 \text{ g}$

49. 3600 g (balanced equation: $NH_3 + 2O_2 \longrightarrow HNO_3 + H_2O$)

50. 160 g O_2 (balanced equation: $2C_2H_2 + 5O_2 \longrightarrow 4CO_2 + 2H_2O$)

LE CHÂTELIER'S PRINCIPLE

51. a. Equilibrium shifts to the left.   b. Equilibrium shifts to the right.
    c. Equilibrium shifts to the right.

52. a. Equilibrium shifts to the left.   b. Equilibrium shifts to the right.
    c. Equilibrium shifts to the left.

ADDITIONAL PROBLEMS

53. Balanced Equation: $2 \text{ Al}(s) + 6 \text{ HCl}(g) \longrightarrow 2 \text{ AlCl}_3(s) + 3 \text{ H}_2(g)$

$\dfrac{35.1 \text{ g Al}}{1} \times \dfrac{1 \text{ mol Al}}{27.0 \text{ g}} \times \dfrac{2 \text{ mol AlCl}_3}{1 \text{ mol Al}} \times \dfrac{133.5 \text{ g}}{1 \text{ mol AlCl}_3} = 374 \text{ g AlCl}_3$

54. balanced: b; not balanced: a

55. Molecular: 1 molecule of C_3H_8 reacts with 5 molecules of O_2 to form 3 molecules of CO_2 and 4 molecules of H_2O. Molar: 1 mole of C_3H_8 reacts with 5 moles of O_2 to form 3 moles of CO_2 and 4 moles of H_2O. Mass: 44 g of C_3H_8 reacts with 160 grams of O_2 to form 132 g of CO_2 and 72 g of H_2O. (Note the total grams must add up!)

56. Molecular: 1 molecule of phosgene ($COCl_2$) reacts with 1 molecule of water (H_2O) to form 2 molecules of hydrogen chloride (HCl) and 1 molecule of CO_2. Molar: 1 mole of $COCl_2$ reacts with 1 mole of H_2O to form 2 moles of HCl and 1 mole of CO_2. Mass: 99 g of $COCl_2$ reacts with 18 g of H_2O to form 73 g of HCl and 44 g of CO_2.

57. Balanced equation: $2\ Ag_2O \longrightarrow 4\ Ag\ +\ O_2$

$$\frac{0.183\ g\ O_2}{1} \quad x \quad \frac{1\ mol\ O_2}{32\ g} \ = \ 0.0057\ mol\ O_2$$

$$\frac{0.0057\ mol\ O_2}{1} \quad x \quad \frac{2\ mol\ Ag_2O}{1\ mol\ O_2} \quad x \quad \frac{231\ g}{1\ mol\ Ag_2O} \quad = \quad 2.64\ g\ Ag_2O$$

$$\text{Mass \%} \ = \ \frac{2.64\ g\ Ag_2O}{2.95\ g\ Ag_2O} \quad x\ 100 \ = \ 89.6\ \%$$

58. Balanced Equation: $2\ Al(s)\ +\ 6\ HCl(g) \longrightarrow 2\ AlCl_3(s)\ +\ 3\ H_2(g)$

$$V = 12.3\ cm\ x\ 14.3\ cm\ x\ 0.22\ cm = 38.7\ cm^3$$

$$\frac{38.7\ cm^3}{1} \quad x \quad \frac{2.70\ g}{cm^3} \quad x \quad \frac{1\ mol\ Al}{27.0\ g} \quad x \quad \frac{3\ mol\ H_2}{2\ mol\ Al} \quad x\frac{2.0\ g}{1\ mol\ H_2} \ = \ 11.6\ g\ H_2$$

59. Balanced Equation: $C\ +\ O_2 \longrightarrow CO_2$

$$\frac{228\ trainloads}{1} \quad x \quad \frac{115\ cars}{trainload} \quad x \quad \frac{90.5\ metric\ tons}{car} \quad x \quad \frac{1000\ kg}{metric\ ton}\ x\ \frac{1000\ g}{kg} \ = 2.37\ x\ 10^{12}\ g\ C$$

$$\frac{2.37\ x\ 10^{12}\ g\ C}{1} \quad x \quad \frac{1\ mol\ C}{12\ g} \quad x \quad \frac{1\ mol\ CO_2}{1\ mol\ C} \quad x \quad \frac{44\ g\ CO_2}{1\ mol\ CO_2} \ = \ 8.70\ x\ 10^{12}\ g\ CO_2$$

$$\frac{8.70\ x\ 10^{12}\ g\ CO_2}{1} \quad x\ \frac{1\ kg}{1000\ g} \quad x \quad \frac{1\ metric\ ton}{1000\ kg} \ = \ 8.70\ x\ 10^6\ metric\ tons\ CO_2$$

60. $\dfrac{88.0\ mL\ CS_2}{1} \quad x \quad \dfrac{1.26\ g}{mL} \quad x \quad \dfrac{1\ mol\ CS_2}{76.2\ g} \ = \ 1.46\ mol\ CS_2$

$$\frac{1.46\ mol\ CS_2}{1} \quad x \quad \frac{2\ mol\ Na_2CS_3}{3\ mol\ CS_2} \quad x \quad \frac{154.3\ g}{1\ mol\ Na_2CS_3} \ = \ 150\ g\ Na_2CS_3$$

61. a. $40 \text{ g}/160 = 0.25$ g aspartame per can

b. $\dfrac{0.25 \text{ g aspartame}}{1 \text{ can}} \times \dfrac{1 \text{ mole aspartame}}{294\text{g aspartame}} \times \dfrac{1 \text{ mole methanol}}{1 \text{ mole aspartame}} \times \dfrac{16\text{g methanol}}{1 \text{ mole methanol}} = 0.014\text{g methanol/can}$

c. 1800 cans!

62.   Balanced Equation: $2 \text{ HgO} \longrightarrow 2 \text{ Hg} + \text{O}_2$

$\dfrac{10.8 \text{ g HgO}}{1} \times \dfrac{1 \text{ mol HgO}}{216.6 \text{ g HgO}} \times \dfrac{1 \text{ mol O}_2}{2 \text{ mol HgO}} \times \dfrac{32 \text{ g O}_2}{1 \text{ mol O}_2} = 0.800 \text{ g O}_2$

63. $\dfrac{8.80 \text{ g O}_2}{1} \times \dfrac{1 \text{ mol O}_2}{32 \text{ g O}_2} \times \dfrac{3 \text{ mol Fe}}{2 \text{ mole O}_2} \times \dfrac{55.8 \text{ g Fe}}{1 \text{ mol Fe}} = 23.0 \text{ g}$

64. $\dfrac{4.00 \text{ g NH}_4\text{NO}_3}{1} \times \dfrac{1 \text{ mole NH}_4\text{NO}_3}{80 \text{ g NH}_4\text{NO}_3} \times \dfrac{1 \text{ mol NO}_2}{1 \text{ mol NH}_4\text{NO}_3} \times \dfrac{46 \text{ g NO}_2}{1 \text{ mol NO}_2} = 2.30 \text{ g}$

66. $\dfrac{0.413 \text{ g Ca}}{1} \times \dfrac{1 \text{ mol Ca}}{40.1 \text{ g Ca}} \times \dfrac{1 \text{ mol H}_2}{1 \text{ mol Ca}} \times \dfrac{2.02 \text{ g H}_2}{1 \text{ mol H}_2} = 0.0208 \text{ g}$

67. $\dfrac{0.112 \text{ g XeF}_6}{1} \times \dfrac{1 \text{ mol XeF}_6}{245.3 \text{ g XeF}_6} \times \dfrac{3 \text{ mol F}_2}{1 \text{ mol XeF}_6} \times \dfrac{38.0 \text{ g F}_2}{1 \text{ mol F}_2} = 0.0521 \text{ g}$

68. $\dfrac{134 \text{ g PH}_3}{1} \times \dfrac{1 \text{ mol PH}_3}{34.0 \text{ g PH}_3} \times \dfrac{1 \text{ mol Mg}_3\text{P}_2}{2 \text{ mol PH}_3} \times \dfrac{134.9 \text{ g Mg}_3\text{P}_2}{1 \text{ mol Mg}_3\text{P}_2} = 266 \text{ g}$

REVIEW QUESTIONS

1. Oxygen atoms gained by a molecule represent oxidation; oxygen atoms lost represent reduction. An example of oxidation would be the burning of a carbon fuel like coal: $C + O_2 \longrightarrow CO_2$

2. Hydrogen atoms gained by a molecule represent reduction; hydrogen atoms lost represent oxidation. An example of reduction would be the addition of hydrogen to acetylene to make ethane:
$C_2H_2 + 2H_2 \longrightarrow C_2H_6$

3. Electrons gained by a molecule or atoms represent reduction; electrons lost represent oxidation. An example would be the oxidation of zinc metal with acid: $Zn + 2H^+ \longrightarrow Zn^{2+} + H_2$

4. Movement of the oxidation state of an atom to a more positive value is an oxidation; movement towards a more negative number is a reduction. An example of oxidation would be the chromium in $Cr_2O_3 \longrightarrow CrO_3$.

5. Oxygen (O_2); dichromate ($Cr_2O_7{}^{2-}$); hydrogen peroxide (H_2O_2); permanganate ($MnO_4{}^-$); halogens (Cl_2, Br_2, I_2).

6. Elemental carbon (C); hydrogen (H_2); hydroquinone [$C_6H_4(OH)_2$]

7. Antiseptics: Hydrogen peroxide (H_2O_2), sodium hypochlorite (NaOCl); benzoyl peroxide [$(C_6H_5COO)_2$]
Disinfectants: Calcium hypochlorite [$Ca(OCl)_2$]; chlorine (Cl_2)

8. Plants make usable fuels such as glucose by reducing carbon dioxide in the process of photosynthesis.

$$6CO_2 + 6H_2O + \text{light energy} \longrightarrow C_6H_{12}O_6 + 6O_2$$

These reduced chemicals (again, like glucose) can then be reoxidized to carbon dioxide by plants and animals to provide energy for many types of cellular activities (such as a heartbeat).

9. NaOCl: in normal laundry bleach; $Ca(OCl)_2$: in bleaching paper; H_2O_2: in bleaching paper and hair

10. Hydrogen: +1; Oxygen: +2. Exceptions: Hydrogen: as a hydride such as CaH_2; Oxygen: in H_2O_2.

11. When the element is oxidized, the oxidative state becomes more positive in value or less negative in value. When it is reduced, it becomes less positive in value or more negative in value.

12. No. Electrons are particles which follow the law of conservation of mass. They can not be created or destroyed. Therefore, something always must be giving electrons (oxidation) for every acceptance of electrons (reduction).

PROBLEMS

REACTIONS OF OXYGEN

13. a. $C + O_2 \longrightarrow CO_2$ b. $CH_4 + 2O_2 \longrightarrow CO_2 + 2H_2O$
c. $N_2 + O_2 \longrightarrow 2NO$ d. $C_3H_8 + 5O_2 \longrightarrow 3CO_2 + 4H_2O$

14. a. $S + O_2 \longrightarrow SO_2$ b. $CS_2 + 3O_2 \longrightarrow CO_2 + 2SO_2$
    c. $2H_2 + O_2 \longrightarrow 2H_2O$ d. $C_6H_{12}O_6 + 6O_2 \longrightarrow 6CO_2 + 6H_2O$

OXIDATION STATES

15. a. 0; b. +4; c. –2; d. +6

16. a. +4; b. –1; c. –3; d. +2

RECOGNIZING REDOX REACTIONS

17. a. oxidation (Cl: +4 to +5); b. oxidation (Mn: +2 to +4); c. reduction (Br: +1 to 0) ; d. oxidation (Sb: –3 to 0)

18. a. reduction (V: +5 to 0); b. oxidation (P: 0 to +5); c. neither (Cr stays at +6); d. oxidation (C: –2 to +4)

19. Some of the sulfurs in the H_2SO_4 are being reduced to form SO_2 (+6 to +4).

20. Yes, the oxygen in H_2O_2 is being oxidized (–1 to 0) and the Mn in MnO_4^- is being reduced (+7 to +2).

OXIDIZING AGENTS AND REDUCING AGENTS

21. a. $\underline{4\,Al} + 3\,\boxed{O_2} \longrightarrow 2Al_2O_3$

    b. $\underline{2SO_2} + \boxed{O_2} \longrightarrow 2SO_3$

22. a. $\boxed{Cl_2} + \underline{2\,KBr} \longrightarrow 2\,KCl + Br_2$

    b. $\boxed{C_2H_4} + \underline{H_2} \longrightarrow C_2H_6$

23. a. $\underline{Fe} + 2\,\boxed{HCl} \longrightarrow FeCl_2 + H_2$

    b. $\underline{CS_2} + 3\,\boxed{O_2} \longrightarrow CO_2 + SO_2$

24. a. $2\,\boxed{AgNO_3} + \underline{Cu} \longrightarrow Cu(NO_3)_2 + 2\,Ag$

    b. $\boxed{CuCl_2} + \underline{Fe} \longrightarrow FeCl_2 + Cu$

25. a. S is oxidized; N is reduced.
    b. I is oxidized; Cr is reduced.

26. a. H_2CO is oxidized, H_2O_2 is the oxidizing agent·
    b. C_2H_6O is oxidized; MnO_4^- is the oxidizing agent.

27. I^- is oxidized; Cl_2 is reduced.

28. MoO_3 is reduced; H_2 is the reducing agent.

29. Reduced.

30. Indoxyl is oxidized; O_2 is the oxidizing agent.

31. Acetylene is reduced; it is gaining hydrogens. (H_2 is being oxidized to the +1 state.)

32. Reduced; the addition of hydrogens (via H_2) to compound is a reduction.

33. NO_2^- is reduced; ascorbic acid is a reducing agent.

34. Oxidized.

ADDITIONAL PROBLEMS

35. Zr was oxidized; water was the oxidizing agent.

36. Per general rules, sulfur should have an oxidative state of +7. With two oxygens in the −1 state, oxygen "brings" a total charge of −14 to this molecule, sodium a +2, and therefore each sulfur will be in an oxidative state of +6.

37. − 1/2

38. The phosphorus in P_4 will have a O.S. of 0, in PH_3 it will have an O.S. of −3, and in H_3PO_4 it will have an O.S. of +5. Disproportionation is the process where an element in one oxidation state undergoes a reaction where some of the atoms are reduced while others are oxidized.

39. First reaction: Oxidizing agent: Cl_2, Reducing agent: NaCN. Second reaction: oxidizing agent: Cl_2, reducing agent: NaOCN.

40. Incineration is a way to get rid of many organic toxic chemicals so that people will not be exposed to them. However, the disadvantages are that it wastes energy, it produces HCl, and, if not carried out correctly will spew unburned toxic compounds into the atmosphere.

REVIEW QUESTIONS

1. troposhere; stratosphere.

2. N_2: 78%, O_2: 21%, Ar: 1%

3. The relative humidity is the percent of water vapor in the air vs the maximum amount the air could hold at that temperature.

4. a. Combined gas law: A combination of Boyle's, Charles', and Gay-Lussac's laws which relates the change in pressure, volume, or temperature of a gaseous system when the changes in two of the aforementioned parameters are known.
    b. Henry's law: A law which states that the solubility of a gas in a liquid (at a constant temperature) is directly proportional to the pressure exerted by that gas at the liquid-gas interface.
    c. mmHg: A unit of pressure representing the height of mercury that will balance the pressure onto it.
    d. Tidal volume: the amount of air that is moved in and out of the lungs with a normal breath.
    e. Vital capacity: The maximum amount of air that can be forced from the lungs by an individual (a volume ranging from 3-7 L).
    f. Vapor pressure: The partial pressure exerted by the molecules of a substance that are in the gas phase above the liquid phase of the substance.
    g. Diffusion: The movement of molecules form a region of high concentration to a region of low concentration.

5. The air is thinner (less per unit volume) at the top of a mountain (as compared to sea level) and thus the force exerted by the collisions of these molecules is less; i.e., less atmospheric pressure.

6. A gas is a phase of a substance in which the molecules have little affinity for one another for the given amount of movement (i.e. temperature) they experience. The molecules of a gas are, therefore, spread out greatly from one another.

7. Due to their constant collisions with one another, molecules of a gas are constantly moving in all random directions. This spreads them out in all directions and prevents them from settling in one confined area.

8. Gas pressure is the amount of force exerted on the walls of a container by the striking of molecules held within the container into the walls.

9. The mercury barometer measures the pressure of a system. It is constructed of a long glass tube (sealed at one end) inverted into a dish of mercury. The pressure of the atmosphere (or any system in which it is used) presses down on the mercury in the dish and drives mercury up into the tube. The greater the pressure, the greater the height of the mercury in the column. The average atmospheric pressure at sea level supplies force to support a mercury column 760mm in height.

10. Mercury is an ideal fluid to use for measuring atmospheric pressure due to its high density. Compared to other, less dense fluids like water, a lower volume of mercury is required to "counterbalance" the pressure exerted by the atmosphere. This means that a column of an appropriate length (~ 76 cm) can be used for the apparatus. A barometer with water would be more than ten times longer.

11. Boyle's law states that at a constant temperature, the volume of a gas varies inversely with the pressure. The mathematical relationship is shown by the equation: $V_1P_1 = V_2P_2$

12. This law says that if one decreases the volume of a system, the molecules will more frequently collide with the walls of the system (i.e the pressure will increase).

13. The high pressure compresses the gas into a very small volume. Thus, a greater amount of the gas can be stored in the given volume of a gas tank.

14. Charles' law: states that at a constant pressure, the volume of a gas is directly proportional to its temperature (in K). The mathematical equation is: $\dfrac{V_1}{T_1} = \dfrac{V_2}{T_2}$

15. This law says that if one decreases the temperature of the system, the movement of the molecules becomes slower, and the volume of the system must decrease in order to maintain the same frequency of collisions on the walls of the system (i.e. a constant pressure).

16. The proportional nature of volume in relation to temperature only occurs when one uses the Kelvin scale with absolute zero as the starting point rather than the Celsius scale with the freezing point of water as the starting point.

17. The size of the unit (one degree) is the same, but the Kelvin scale starts at absolure zero while the Celsius scale has its zero point at the freezing point of water.

18. a. decrease in volume; b. decrease in volume; c. increase in volume

19. a. increase in pressure; b. increase in pressure; c. increase in pressure

20. a. the temperature is decreasing; b. the pressure would decrease

21. Assuming the temperature in both containers is the same, the pressure is the same.

22. a. container A would have a greater density; b. the densities of A and B would be the same (just of different size); c. container B has a greater density.

23. Temperature: 0 °C (273 K); Pressure: 1 atm. Often, one would like to talk about the mass, moles, or volume of a gas without having to deal with their changes due to temperature and pressure. STP gives a consistent set of parameters that approximate typical room conditions that can be used for these discussions.

24. Molar volume is the volume occupied by one mole of a gas under specified conditions. At STP, the volume of a gas is 22.4 L.

25. The ideal gas law is the combined relationship between pressure, volume, moles, and temperature of a gaseous system. The mathematical equation for this relationship is $PV = nRT$.

26. Dalton's law of partial pressures says that the total pressure exerted by a mixture of gases is equal to the sum of the partial pressures of the individual gases in the mixture. Its equation is $P_{total} = P_1 + P_2 + P_3 + \ldots$

27. When gases are collected over water, the total pressure is the sum of those of the individual gases plus that exerted by the water vapor pressure.

28. Temperature is the measure of the average kinetic energy of molecules and reflects the speed of their motion.

29. The pressure exerted by the CO_2 in the headspace above the soda is greater than the atmospheric pressure. The removal of the cap allows molecules to move from an area of higher pressure to a region of lower pressure.

30. Not unless you like dead fish. The solubility of gases in water decreases with temperature. Boiling water will drive out nearly all the dissolved oxygen, oxygen needed by the fish to live.

31. Expand. Decreased. During exhalation, the chest cavity contracts creating a high pressure region. Air rushes from this high pressure region through your mouth to the outside (a low pressure region).

32. approx. 50 mmHg

33. Oxygen travels from lungs to cells. Carbon dioxide travels from cells to lungs.

34. The partial pressure of O_2 in the alveoli is greater than in the pulmonary capillaries, therefore, net movement to the capillaries occurs. Carbon dioxide travels in the reverse direction since the partial pressure of CO_2 in the capillaries is greater than in the neighboring alveoli.

PROBLEMS

PRESSURE

35. a. $\dfrac{0.985 \text{ atm}}{1} \quad \text{x} \quad \dfrac{760 \text{ mm Hg}}{1 \text{ atm}} \quad = \quad 749 \text{ mm Hg}$

  b. $\dfrac{849 \text{ mm Hg}}{1} \quad \text{x} \quad \dfrac{1 \text{ atm}}{760 \text{ mm Hg}} \quad = \quad 1.12 \text{ atm}$

  c. $\dfrac{721 \text{ mm Hg}}{1} \quad \text{x} \quad \dfrac{1 \text{ atm}}{760 \text{ mm Hg}} \quad = \quad 0.949 \text{ atm}$

36. a. $\dfrac{4.00 \text{ atm}}{1} \quad \text{x} \quad \dfrac{760 \text{ mm Hg}}{1 \text{ atm}} \quad = \quad 3040 \text{ mm Hg}$

  b. $\dfrac{642 \text{ mm Hg}}{1} \quad \text{x} \quad \dfrac{1 \text{ atm}}{760 \text{ mm Hg}} \quad \text{x} \quad \dfrac{1 \text{ Pa}}{1.01 \times 10^{-5} \text{ atm}} \quad \text{x} \quad \dfrac{1 \text{ kPa}}{1000 \text{ Pa}} \quad = 83.6 \text{ kPa}$

  c. $\dfrac{105.7 \text{ kPa}}{1} \quad \text{x} \quad \dfrac{1000 \text{ Pa}}{1 \text{ kPa}} \quad \text{x} \quad \dfrac{1.01 \times 10^{-5} \text{ atm}}{\text{Pa}} \quad \text{x} \quad \dfrac{760 \text{ mm Hg}}{\text{atm}} = 811.4 \text{ mm Hg}$

37. $\dfrac{213 \text{ mm}}{1} \quad \text{x} \quad \dfrac{1 \text{ in}}{25.4 \text{ mm}} \quad = \quad 8.39 \text{ in}$

38. $\dfrac{4.36 \text{ atm}}{1} \quad \text{x} \quad \dfrac{760 \text{ mm Hg}}{1 \text{ atm}} \quad \text{x} \quad \dfrac{1 \text{ in}}{25.4 \text{ mm}} \quad = \quad 130. \text{ in}$

BOYLE'S LAW

39. a. $P_1V_1 = P_2V_2$ (1572 mm Hg) (521 mL) = (752 mm Hg) (V_2) $V_2 = 1090$ mL

    b. $P_1V_1 = P_2V_2$ (1572 mm Hg) (521 mL) = (P_2)(315 mL) $P_2 = 2600$ mm Hg

40. a. $P_1V_1 = P_2V_2$ (4.50 atm)(10.3 mm³) = (1.00 atm) (V_2) $V_2 = 46.4$ m³

41. a. $\dfrac{750.0 \text{ mm Hg}}{1}$ x $\dfrac{1 \text{ atm}}{760 \text{ mm Hg}}$ = 0.987 atm

     $P_1V_1 = P_2V_2$ (150 atm)(60.0L) = (P_2)(0.987 atm) $P_2 = 9120$ L

    b. $\dfrac{9120 \text{ L}}{1}$ x $\dfrac{1 \text{ min}}{8 \text{ L}}$ = 1140 min = 19 hr

42. $P_1V_1 = P_2V_2$ (1.10 atm)(2.25L) = (P_2)(7.05L) $P_2 = 0.351$ atm

CHARLES'S LAW

43. 100 °C = 373 K,   10 °C = 283 K

$\dfrac{V_1}{T_1} = \dfrac{V_2}{T_2}$ $\dfrac{154 \text{ mL}}{373 \text{ K}} = \dfrac{V_2}{283 \text{ K}}$ $V_2 = 117$ mL

44. 26 °C = 299 K,   −78 °C = 195 K

$\dfrac{V_1}{T_1} = \dfrac{V_2}{T_2}$ $\dfrac{5.90 \text{ L}}{299 \text{ K}} = \dfrac{V_2}{195 \text{ K}}$ $V_2 = 3.85$ L

45. 305 °C = 578 K

$\dfrac{V_1}{T_1} = \dfrac{V_2}{T_2}$ $\dfrac{567 \text{ mL}}{578 \text{ K}} = \dfrac{425 \text{ mL}}{T_2}$ $T_2 = 433$ K = 160 °C

46. The temperature will triple. 273 K x 3 = 819 K

AVOGADRO'S LAW AND MOLAR VOLUME

47. a. $\dfrac{5.0 \text{ g } H_2}{1}$ x $\dfrac{1 \text{ mol } H_2}{2 \text{ g}}$ = 2.5 mol H_2 b. $\dfrac{50 \text{ L } SF_6}{1}$ x $\dfrac{1 \text{ mol}}{22.4 \text{ L}}$ = 2.23 mol SF_6

    c. $\dfrac{1.0 \times 10^{24} \text{ molecules } CO_2}{1}$ x $\dfrac{1 \text{ mol } CO_2}{6.02 \times 10^{23} \text{ molecules}}$ = 1.66 mol CO_2

    5.0 g H_2 has the greatest number of molecules.

48. $\dfrac{475 \text{ mL } CO_2}{1}$ x $\dfrac{1 \text{ L}}{1000 \text{ mL}}$ x $\dfrac{1 \text{ mol } CO_2}{22.4 \text{ L}}$ x $\dfrac{6.02 \times 10^{23} \text{ molecules}}{\text{mol}}$ = 1.28×10^{22} molecules

49. $\dfrac{0.837 \text{ g Xe}}{1}$ x $\dfrac{\text{mol}}{131 \text{ g Xe}}$ x $\dfrac{22.4 \text{ L}}{\text{mol}}$ = 0.143 L = 143 mL

50. $\dfrac{498 \text{ L}}{1}$ x $\dfrac{1 \text{ mol}}{22.4 \text{ L}}$ x $\dfrac{20.2 \text{ g Ne}}{1 \text{ mol}}$ = 449 g Ne

THE COMBINED GAS LAW

51. 25 °C = 298 K, 755 °C = 1028 K

$\dfrac{P_1V_1}{T_1}$ = $\dfrac{P_2V_2}{T_2}$ $\qquad$ $\dfrac{721 \text{ mm Hg}}{298 \text{ K}}$ = $\dfrac{P_2}{1028 \text{ K}}$ $\quad$ P_2 = 2490 mm Hg

52. 26 °C = 299 K

$\dfrac{P_1V_1}{T_1}$ = $\dfrac{P_2V_2}{T_2}$ $\quad$ $\dfrac{(775 \text{ mm Hg})(1.05 \text{L})}{299 \text{ K}}$ = $\dfrac{(725 \text{ mm Hg})(1.05 \text{L})}{T_2}$ $\quad$ T_2 = 280 K = 7.0 °C

53. –15 °C = 258 K, 25 °C = 298 K

$\dfrac{P_1V_1}{T_1}$ = $\dfrac{P_2V_2}{T_2}$ $\quad$ $\dfrac{(191 \text{ mm Hg})(2.53 \text{ m}^3)}{258 \text{ K}}$ = $\dfrac{(1142 \text{ mm Hg})(V_2)}{298 \text{ K}}$ $\quad$ V_2 = 0.49 m^3

54. 23 °C = 296 K

$\dfrac{P_1V_1}{T_1}$ = $\dfrac{P_2V_2}{T_2}$ $\quad$ $\dfrac{(725 \text{ mm Hg})(575 \text{ mL})}{296 \text{ K}}$ = $\dfrac{(760 \text{ mm Hg})(V_2)}{273 \text{ K}}$ $\quad$ V_2 = 506 mL

55. 15 °C = 288 K

$\dfrac{P_1V_1}{T_1}$ = $\dfrac{P_2V_2}{T_2}$ $\quad$ $\dfrac{(760 \text{ mm Hg})(4.65 \text{ L})}{273 \text{ K}}$ = $\dfrac{(756 \text{ mm Hg})(V_2)}{288 \text{ K}}$ $\quad$ V_2 = 4.93 L

56. 27 °C = 300 K

$\dfrac{P_1V_1}{T_1}$ = $\dfrac{P_2V_2}{T_2}$ $\quad$ $\dfrac{(722 \text{ mm Hg})(498 \text{ mL})}{300 \text{ K}}$ = $\dfrac{(760 \text{ mm Hg})(V_2)}{273 \text{ K}}$ $\quad$ V_2 = 431 mL

THE IDEAL GAS LAW

57. 62 °C = 335 K
$PV = nRT$ $\quad$ (1.38 atm)(V) = (1.12 mol H$_2$S)(0.082 L-atm-mol^{-1}-K^{-1})(335 K)
$\qquad$ V = 22.3 L

58. 31 °C = 304 K, 661 mm Hg = 0.870 atm
$PV = nRT$ $\quad$ (0.870 atm)(V) = (0.00600 mol)(0.082 L-atm-mol^{-1}-K^{-1})(304 K)
$\qquad$ V = 0.172 L = 172 mL

59. $29\,^\circ C = 302$ K

   $PV = nRT$ $(P)(3.96\ L) = (4.64\ mol\ CO)\ (0.082\ L\text{-atm-mol}^{-1}\text{-K}^{-1})(302\ K)$
   $P = 29.0$ atm

60. $37\,^\circ C = 310$ K

   $PV = nRT$ $(P)(0.265L) = (0.0108\ mol\ CH_4)\ (0.082\ L\text{-atm-mol}^{-1}\text{-K}^{-1})(310\ K)$
   $P = 1.04$ atm $= 787$ mm Hg

61. $45\,^\circ C = 318$ K, 698 mm Hg $= 0.918$ atm

   $PV = nRT$ $(0.918\ atm)(2.22\ L) = (n)\ (0.082\ L\text{-atm-mol}^{-1}\text{-K}^{-1})(318\ K)$
   $n = 0.078\ mol\ Kr$

62. $36\,^\circ C = 309$ K, 784 mm Hg $= 1.032$ atm

   $PV = nRT$ $(1.032\ atm)(0.745\ L) = (n)\ (0.082\ L\text{-atm-mol}^{-1}\text{-K}^{-1})(309\ K)$
   $n = 0.030\ mol\ CO$

   $$\frac{0.0303\ mol\ CO}{1} \quad x \quad \frac{28\ g}{mol\ CO} \quad = \quad 0.85\ g\ CO$$

GAS DENSITIES

63.   a. 1 mol CO $= 28.0$ g CO $\dfrac{28\ g\ CO}{22.4\ L}$ $= 1.25$ g/L CO

   b. 1 mol $AsH_3 = 77.9$ g AsH_3 $\dfrac{77.9\ g\ AsH_3}{22.4\ L}$ $= 3.48$ g/L

   c. 1 mol Ar $= 39.9$ g Ar $\dfrac{39.9\ g\ Ar}{22.4\ L}$ $= 1.78$ g/L

   d. 1 mol $N_2 = 28.0$ g N_2 $\dfrac{28.0\ g\ N_2}{22.4\ L}$ $= 1.25$ g/L

64. $\dfrac{2.57g}{L}$ x $\dfrac{22.4\ L}{1}$ $=$ 57.6 g which at STP will be equivalent to one mole and hence the molar mass.

DALTON'S LAW OF PARTIAL PRESSURES

65. From the table in the chapter, water has a partial pressure of 32 mm Hg at 30 $^\circ$C.

   $P_{total} = P_{O_2} + P_{H_2O}$
   742 mm Hg $= P_{O_2} + 32$ mm Hg
   $P_{O_2} = 710$ mm Hg

66. 0.95 atm (the sum of the 3 partial pressures)

67. 250 mmHg

68. 0. 97 atm

69. $\dfrac{5.7\ atm}{6.0\ atm}$ x 100 $= 95\%$

ADDITIONAL PROBLEMS

70. $PV = nRT$ $(1.02 \text{ atm})(1.70 \times 10^{10}) = (n)(0.082 \text{ L-atm-mol}^{-1}\text{-K}^{-1})(291 \text{ K})$
$$n = 7.3 \times 10^8 \text{ mol}$$

71. $\dfrac{P_1V_1}{T_1} = \dfrac{P_2V_2}{T_2}$ $\dfrac{(151 \text{ atm})(V_1)}{(298 \text{ K})} = \dfrac{(3.00 \text{ atm})(4.20 \times 10^3 \text{ L})}{(290 \text{ K})}$ $V_1 = 85.7 \text{ L}$

72. $P_1V_1 = P_2V_2$ $(760 \text{ mmHg})(2.0 \text{ L}) = (P_2)(1.7 \text{ L})$ $P_2 = 894 \text{ mmHg}$

The pressure is about 134 mmHg above normal external pressure.

73. $21 \,^{\circ}\text{C} = 294 \text{ L}$, $743 \text{ mm Hg} = 0.978 \text{ atm}$

$PV = nRT$ $(0.978 \text{ atm})(0.122 \text{ mL}) = (n)(0.082 \text{ L-atm-mol}^{-1}\text{-K}^{-1})(294 \text{ K})$
$$n = 0.0049 \text{ mol O}_2$$

$$\dfrac{0.0049 \text{ mol O}_2}{1} \times \dfrac{32 \text{ g}}{1 \text{ mol O}_2} = 0.16 \text{ g O}_2$$

$$\dfrac{0.0049 \text{ mol O}_2}{1} \times \dfrac{1 \text{ mol C}_6\text{H}_{12}\text{O}_6}{6 \text{ mol O}_2} \times \dfrac{180 \text{ g}}{1 \text{ mol C}_6\text{H}_{12}\text{O}_6} = 0.15 \text{ g C}_6\text{H}_{12}\text{O}_6$$

74. At the same temperature and pressure, the 100.0 mL volume should contain the same number of moles of each gas:

$$\dfrac{0.0080 \text{ g H}_2}{1} \times \dfrac{1 \text{ mol}}{2 \text{ g H}_2} = 0.0040 \text{ mol H}_2$$

$$\dfrac{0.1112 \text{ g N}_2}{1} \times \dfrac{1 \text{ mol}}{28 \text{ g N}_2} = 0.00397 \text{ mol N}_2$$

$$\dfrac{0.1281 \text{ g O}_2}{1} \times \dfrac{1 \text{ mol}}{32 \text{ g O}_2} = 0.0040 \text{ mol H}_2$$

$$\dfrac{0.1770 \text{ g CO}_2}{1} \times \dfrac{1 \text{ mol}}{44 \text{ g CO}_2} = 0.0040 \text{ mol CO}_2$$

$$\dfrac{0.2320 \text{ g C}_4\text{H}_{10}}{1} \times \dfrac{1 \text{ mol}}{58 \text{ g C}_4\text{H}_{10}} = 0.0040 \text{ mol C}_4\text{H}_{10}$$

$$\dfrac{0.4824 \text{ g CCl}_2\text{F}_2}{1} \times \dfrac{1 \text{ mol}}{121 \text{ g CCl}_2\text{F}_2} = 0.0040 \text{ mol CCl}_2\text{F}_2$$

These results are consistent with Avogadro's hypothesis. The moles for each are equivalent.

75. $P_1V_1 = P_2V_2$ $\quad$ $(14.7 \text{ psi})(V_1) = (1070 \text{ psi})(19{,}000{,}000 \text{ ft}^3)$
$$V_1 = 1{,}380{,}000{,}000 \text{ ft}^3$$

76. $PV = nRT$ $\quad$ $(P)(2.50 \text{ L}) = (1.00 \text{ mol})(0.082 \text{ L-atm-mol}^{-1}\text{-K}^{-1})(298 \text{ K})$
$$P = 9.77 \text{ atm}$$

77. $PV = nRT$ $\quad$ $(0.37 \text{ atm})(68 \text{ L}) = (0.78 \text{ mol O}_2)(0.082 \text{ L-atm-mol}^{-1}\text{-K}^{-1})(T)$
$$T = 393 \text{ K} = 120 \text{ °C}$$

78. Find the percentage of each to 820 mm Hg. $\quad$ CO_2: 360 mmHg; H_2: 310 mmHg; N_2: 140 mmHg; O_2: 10 mmHg; CH_4: 0.02 mmHg

79. 67% (The maximum P_{H_2O} at 20 °C is 18 mm Hg.)

80. $\quad$ a. Oxygen will flow from flask A to flask B.
$\quad\quad$ b. Nitrogen will flow from flask B to flask A.

81. $\dfrac{22.4 \text{ L}}{1}$ $\quad$ x $\quad$ $\dfrac{1 \text{ sec}}{0.080 \text{ L}}$ $\quad$ = $\quad$ 280 s

REVIEW QUESTIONS

1. a. Surface tension: The force on the surface of a liquid or solid that resists being penetrated.
    b. Condensation: The reverse of vaporization; the change from the gaseous state to the liquid state.
    c. Ionic crystal: A solid where ions (both positive and negative) hold lattice points in a crystal.
    d. Metallic solid: A solid where positive ions of metal atoms hold lattice points. Electrons are free to move throughout this lattice.
    e. Covalent network solid: A solid which has atoms at the lattice points of a crystal.
    f. Hydrogen bond: The dipole interaction between a hydrogen atom bonded to F, O or N in a donor molecule and an F, O, or N atom in a receptor molecule.
    g. Melting point: The temperature at which a solid changes to the liquid state.
    h. Molecular solid: A molecular solid where molecules are holding lattice points in a crystal.
    i. Molar heat of fusion: The amount of heat required to convert 1 mole of a solid to a liquid at the melting point.
    j. Molar heat of vaporization: The amount of heat involved in the evaporation (or condensation) of 1 mole of a material.

2. Gases are easily compressed while liquids and solids are not. Gases have great distances between individual molecules while liquids and solids have a tighter packing. Gases exhibit little intermolecular forces while these forces in liquid and solids may be great.

3. Both liquids and solids may have intermolecular forces; they are not easily compressed and they have relatively high densities (compared to gases). Solids are different from liquids in that they have a well-defined packing of atoms/molecules and that the forces that hold these atoms/molecules are sufficiently great to prevent movement of the atoms/molecules relative to one another.

4. Ionic bonds, dipole interactions, hydrogen bonds, dispersion forces.

5. An *intra*molecular force is a force of attraction within a particular molecule while an *inter*molecular force is a force of attraction between two or more molecules.

6. At low enough temperatures, the vibration of O_2 molecules are sufficiently reduced so that the weakest of bonds, dispersion forces, can take place. These temporary bonds hold molecules near each other creating a liquid state.

7. a. dispersion forces; b. dipolar forces; c. hydrogen bonds

8. High boiling temperature, high heat of vaporization, high specific heat, the solid form is less dense than the liquid form.

9. Liquids, compared to gases, have lower kinetic energy due to more intermolecular forces. These forces are weak enough to be occasionally broken, thereby leading to a fluid state. Solids have even less kinetic energy due to even more intermolecular forces. These forces are sufficiently strong to hold all molecules tightly in place, thereby resulting in a rigid, immovable structure.

10. Vaporization is a general term for the conversion of a liquid changing to a gas; boiling is a phenomenon which involves a transition of a liquid to a gas when the vapor pressure is equal to atmospheric pressure.

11. The boiling point of a liquid is the temperature at which the vapor pressure becomes equal to the external pressure while the normal boiling point is the temperature when the air pressure on the liquid surface is 1 atm.

12. In order for an object to penetrate a surface, the intermolecular forces of the solution must be broken. Therefore, solutions with greater intermolecular forces will have greater surface tension.

13. A viscous liquid is one which is relatively thick and difficult to pour.

14. By creating a partially pressurized system (the initial vapors given off upon heating are contained in the cooker), the boiling point of the fluid is raised. Therefore, higher temperature can be achieved thus decreasing the cooking time.

15. The heat of vaporization is the amount of heat required to vaporize a certain quantity of liquid. If there are great intermolecular forces holding the molecules in a liquid together, then it will take more heat to break these bonds in order to disperse the molecules into a gaseous state. Therefore, the greater the intermolecular forces, the greater the heat of vaporization.

16. The vapor pressure of liquids increases with temperature. As one increases the temperature of a liquid, the movement of the molecules becomes more rapid. This disrupts intermolecular forces and allows more molecules to enter the gaseous (i.e. isolated molecule) phase. A greater number of molecules in the gaseous phase is an increased vapor pressure.

17. An increase in temperature causes greater vibrations which, in turn, disrupt the intermolecular forces that hold the molecular "network." A less tightly held structure will have a decreased viscosity (resistance to flow).

18. An instantaneous dipole is one which forms on its own, by a chance occurrence when the electrons of a nonpolar molecule shift to one side of the molecule or the other. An induced dipole is a dipole caused when a nonpolar molecule moves near a polar molecule; this causes its electron cloud to be "pulled" or "pushed" so that the molecule has a temporary dipole.

19. A dispersion force is a momentary, usually weak, attractive force between molecules.

20. A polar molecule is a molecule with a permanent dipole moment while the term polarizability reflects the ability of a molecule to gain some polar nature by the effects of an induced dipole.

21. A polar liquid, i.e. a liquid made up of polar molecules, contains molecules that can form relatively strong $\delta+ \cdots \delta-$ attachments between molecules. These attachments cause the molecules *not* to want to become isolated and go into the gaseous phase. Hence, it will take a higher temperature to vibrate the molecules sufficiently to separate them. Nonpolar liquids lack these attachments and the molecules are more free, at a lower temperature, to escape to the gaseous phase.

22. CH_4 is a molecule with no dipole moment. There are few forces of attraction between the molecules to hold them together in a solid or liquid phase. They separate from one another and become a gas. H_2O is a molecule with a strong dipole nature. There are great force of attraction between the molecules which hold them close to one another in a liquid phase.

23. CH_3CH_3 is the gas at STP. The other two substances have a higher molecular mass (BF_3) and/or a dipole moment (NI_3) which will cause them to be liquids.

24. A larger ionic charge and a smaller size cause the melting point to increase.

25. A crystal lattice is a network of positively charged ions (cations) and negatively charged ions (anions) laid down in a three dimensional, periodic arrangement where each cation is surrounded by anions and each anion is surrounded by cations.

26. Boiling an egg will take longer at higher altitudes because the temperature of the boiling water is lower (due to the decreased atmospheric pressure). Since the heat transfer (i.e. specific heat) will not change much with altitude, frying an egg will take about the same time.

27. Because it has a lower density than water.

28. Steam, because of the large amount of heat generated during condensation, will release more heat than liquid water.

29. Ethane. Ethane has a higher molecular weight and therefore stronger dispersion forces.

30. Methanol. Methanol has stronger intermolecular forces due to its ability to hydrogen bond. The strong intermolecular forces lead to a greater tendency to stay in the condensed state.

31. Xe. Xe has a large molecular weight and therefore stronger dispersion forces.

32. a. melting; b. vaporization

33.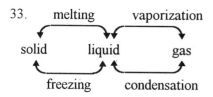

34. 760 mm Hg

PROBLEMS

HEAT OF VAPORIZATION

35. $\dfrac{45\ cal}{g}$ x $\dfrac{159.8\ g}{1\ mol\ Br_2}$ = 7200 cal/mol

36. $\dfrac{327\ cal}{g}$ x $\dfrac{17.0\ g}{1\ mol\ NH_3}$ = 5560 cal/mol

37. $\dfrac{5.81\ kcal}{mol}$ x $\dfrac{1000\ cal}{1\ kcal}$ x $\dfrac{1\ mol\ C_2H_4O_2}{60\ g}$ x $\dfrac{1.0\ g}{1}$ = 96.8 cal

38. $\dfrac{7.23\ kcal}{mol}$ x $\dfrac{1000\ cal}{1\ kcal}$ x $\dfrac{1\ mol\ C_3H_6O}{58\ g}$ x $\dfrac{5.80\ g}{1}$ = 723 cal

39. $\dfrac{1.00\text{ cal}}{g \cdot {}^\circ C}$ x $\dfrac{1\text{ kcal}}{1000\text{ cal}}$ x $\dfrac{25.0\text{ g }H_2O}{1}$ x $\dfrac{42\,{}^\circ C}{1}$ = 1.05 kcal

40. $\dfrac{0.60\text{ cal}}{g \cdot {}^\circ C}$ x $\dfrac{1\text{ kcal}}{1000\text{ cal}}$ x $\dfrac{42.4\text{ g }CH_3OH}{1}$ x $\dfrac{39.5\,{}^\circ C}{1}$ = 1.00 kcal

HEAT OF FUSION

41. $\dfrac{2.58\text{ kcal}}{\text{mol}}$ x $\dfrac{1\text{ mol }C_3H_6O}{60\text{ g}}$ x $\dfrac{7.75\text{ g}}{1}$ = 0.33 kcal

42. $\dfrac{25\text{ cal}}{g}$ x $\dfrac{107.9\text{ g}}{\text{mol Ag}}$ = 2700 cal/mol

43. $\dfrac{355\text{ g }H_2O(s)}{1}$ x $\dfrac{80\text{ cal}}{g}$ x $\dfrac{1\text{ kcal}}{1000\text{ cal}}$ = 28.4 kcal

44. $\dfrac{275\text{ mL }H_2O}{1}$ x $\dfrac{1\text{ g}}{1\text{ mL}}$ x $\dfrac{80\text{ cal}}{g}$ x $\dfrac{1\text{ kcal}}{1000\text{ cal}}$ = 22.0 kcal

INTERMOLECULAR FORCES

45. CS_2; neither has much of a dipole moment, but CCl_4, a larger molecule, has much greater dispersion forces and hence will have a greater desire to stay in the liquid state.

46. PH_3; neither of the two molecules have a very strong dipole moment. AsH_3 is a larger molecule and would have greater dispersion forces to hold the molecules together in a liquid form.

47. C_2H_5OH; C_2H_5OH molecules have the ability to hydrogen bond to one another. This creates a network of molecules held by intermolecular forces that would tend to stay in the liquid phase at a higher temperature.

48. H_2O; water molecules can hydrogen bond. These intermolecular forces will tend to hold the molecules in a liquid form at a higher temperature.

49. H_2S (lowest), H_2Se, H_2Te (highest); they are all relatively nonpolar molecules, the dispersion forces for the higher molecular weight compounds (H_2Se and H_2Te) would be greater.

50. CH_4 (lowest), HCl, H_2O (highest); CH_4 is a nonpolar molecule with few intermolecular forces, HCl has dipolar forces holding the molecules together, and H_2O has the stronger hydrogen bonds holding the molecules together in the liquid state.

ADDITIONAL PROBLEMS

51. Simple cubic: the basic cell is the arrangement of the atoms or ions or molecules at the corners of a cube.
    Body-centered cubic: the basic cell is a simple cubic pattern with an additional atom/ion/molecule located in the center of the cube.
    Face-centered cubic: the basic cell is a simple cubic pattern with an additional six atoms/ions/molecules located in the centers of each face of the cube.

52. $\dfrac{10.0\ g}{1}$ x $\dfrac{1\ mol\ CCl_4}{154\ g}$ x $\dfrac{0.78\ kcal}{mol}$ = 0.051 kcal

53. b,d (Molecule f can hydrogen bond with molecules like H_2O but can not hydrogen bond with molecules of its own type.)

54. 21 x 353 K = 7413 cal/mol (calc) vs 7300 cal/mol (actual)

55. Assuming equal masses, the gold will be hotter. (Gold takes less calories to raise a gram 1°C.)

56. Ethanol. (It takes more calories to vaporize a mole of ethanol than it does a mole of ethyl acetate.)

57. Heat required to raise temperature of ice from -5° to 0 °C:

$\dfrac{100\ g}{1}$ x $\dfrac{5\ °C}{1}$ x $\dfrac{0.5\ cal}{g\ •°C}$ = 250 cal

Heat required to melt ice (at 0 °C):

$\dfrac{100\ g}{1}$ x $\dfrac{80\ cal}{1\ g}$ = 8000 cal

Heat required to raise temperature of water from 0 ° to 100°C:

$\dfrac{100\ g}{1}$ x $\dfrac{1\ cal}{1\ g\ •1°C}$ x $\dfrac{100°C}{1}$ = 10,000 cal

Heat required to vaporize water (at 100°C):

$\dfrac{100\ g}{1}$ x $\dfrac{540\ cal}{g}$ = 54,000 cal

Total heat required = 250 cal + 8000 cal + 10,000 cal + 54,000 cal = 72250 cal

58. Heat required to raise temperature of ice from -12° to 0 °C:

$\dfrac{10\ g}{1}$ x $\dfrac{12\ °C}{1}$ x $\dfrac{0.5\ cal}{g\ •°C}$ = 60 cal

Heat required to melt ice (at 0 °C):

$\dfrac{10\ g}{1}$ x $\dfrac{80\ cal}{1\ g}$ = 800 cal

Heat required to raise temperature of water from 0 ° to 100°C:

$\dfrac{10\ g}{1}$ x $\dfrac{1\ cal}{1\ g\ •1\ °C}$ x $\dfrac{100\ °C}{1}$ = 1000 cal

Heat required to vaporize water (at 100 °C):

$\dfrac{10\ g}{1}$ x $\dfrac{540\ cal}{g}$ = 5400 cal

Heat require to raise temperature of water from 100 °C to 130 °C:

$\dfrac{10\ g}{1}$ x $\dfrac{0.47\ cal}{1g\ •\ 1\ °C}$ x $\dfrac{30\ °C}{1}$ = 141 cal

Total heat required = 60 cal + 800 cal + 1000 cal + 5400 cal + 141 cal = 7401 cal

59. $(\dfrac{5\ g}{1}$ x $\dfrac{80\ cal}{g})$ + $(\dfrac{5\ g}{1}$ x $\dfrac{1\ cal}{1g\ •\ 1\ °C}$ x $\dfrac{40\ °C}{1})$ = 600 cal = 0.6 kcal

60. $(\dfrac{1500\ g}{1}$ x $\dfrac{0.5\ cal}{1g\ •\ 1\ °C}$ x $\dfrac{10\ °C}{1})$ + $(\dfrac{1500\ g}{1}$ x $\dfrac{80\ g}{1g\ •\ 1\ °C})$ + $(\dfrac{1500\ g}{1}$ x $\dfrac{1\ cal}{1g\ •\ 1\ °C}$ x $\dfrac{37\ °C}{1})$ = 183,000 cal = 183 kcal

REVIEW QUESTIONS

1. a. Solution: A homogeneous mixture of two or more substances.
    b. Solvent: The substance that dissolves another substance (solute) to form a solution; usually present in a larger amount than the solute.
    c. Solute: The substance that is dissolved in another substance (solvent) to form a solution; usually present in a smaller amount than the solvent.
    d. Dilute solution: A relative term which describes a solution in which there is little solute dissolved in much solvent.
    e. Concentrated solution: A relative term describing a solution where much solute is dissolved in a small amount of solvent.

2. a. Aqueous: A solution with water as the solvent.
    b. Soluble: When an appreciable amount of a substance can dissolve into a solvent.
    c. Insoluble: When little of a substance can dissolve into a solvent.
    d. Miscible: When two liquids can be mixed to form a homogeneous solution.
    e. Precipitate: An insoluble or nearly insoluble solid.

3. a. Percent by Mass: The percentage of the mass of the solute to the total mass of the solution.
    b. Percent by Volume: The percentage of the volume of a solute to the total volume of the solution.
    c. Molarity: The number of moles of solute divided by the number of liters of solution.
    d. Mass/Volume Percent: The percentage of mass (in grams) per the total volume (in mL).

4. a. Unsaturated solution: A solution which contains less than the maximum amount of solute it possibly can.
    b. Saturated solution: A solution which contains all the solute it can at a given temperature.
    c. Supersaturated solution: An unstable state where a solution contains more solute than it possibly can at a given temperature.

5. a. Colligative Property: A property that depends on the number of particles in a solution.
    b. Semipermeable membrane: A porous material capable of allowing some substances through, but not all.
    c. Osmosis: The movement of water across a semipermeable membrane from a region of low solute concentration to a region of high solute concentration.
    d. Osmotic Pressure: The pressure needed to prevent the net flow of solvent from dilute to concentrated solutions.
    e. Isotonic Solution: A solution of the same osmotic pressure as the fluid inside a cell.
    f. Hypotonic Solution: A solution of lower osmolarity (particularly in regards to the osmolarity of a cell).
    g. Hypertonic Solution: A solution of higher osmolarity (particularly in regards to the osmolarity of a cell).
    h. Osmolarity: The moles of solute particles per liter of solution.

6. a. Suspension: The temporary dispersion of solute in solution.
    b. Colloid: Solute particles that are intermediate in size between solution solute and suspended particles.
    c. Tyndall Effect: The scattering of a beam of light as it passes through a colloid.
    d. Dialysis: The separation of small molecules from large molecules through use of a semipermeable membrane.
    e. Emulsifying Agent: A substance that stabilizes colloidal dispersions in water.

7.   a. Crenation: The shriveling of a cell due to water rushing from the cell to a hypertonic solution outside its membrane.
     b. Plasmolysis: The rupture of a cell by a hypotonic solution.
     c. Hemolysis: The plasmolysis of a red blood cell.

8.   a. Anhydrous: A compound without bound water.
     b. Hydrate: Compounds that have water bound to them in a crystalline state.
     c. Efflorescent: A hydrated compound that can lose its bound water to the atmosphere.
     d. Hygroscopic: A compound capable of picking water up from the atmosphere.
     e. Deliquescent: A hygroscopic compound that is so potent at removing water from the atmosphere that it will eventually dissolve in the water accumulated.

9. The process of the dissolving of the material is equal in rate to the process of the material precipitating out of solution.

10. Saturated. The amount of material that will precipitate out of solution will be exactly that amount by which the solution is over-saturated.

11. 1 ppt < 1ppb < 1ppm < 1mg/dL < 1%

12. No. To dissolve NaCl, the individual sodium and chloride ions must be broken apart and stabilized by other forces. Since there are no polar attractions between the NaCl ions and benzene, the NaCl ions will remain ionically bonded together and dissolution will not occur.

13. In water - no. In benzene - yes. Motor oil can not form bonds with water and thus can not break into the strongly held water network. Benzene molecules are loosely held together. Entropy (randomness) will be a sufficient force to allow the molecules of motor oil to disperse themselves throughout the benzene network.

14. The carbon dioxide in soda (uncorked) is relatively high due to the pressure over the solution in the headspace of the bottle. When the cap is removed, the pressure is lowered and the CO_2 solubility is lowered. CO_2 comes out of solution as a result.

15. Fish need oxygen to live. Since the solubility of oxygen in cold water is greater than in warm water, cold water can support more aquatic life than warm. Hence, the major fisheries are located in cold waters.

16. a. True solutions have solute particles of sizes of less than 0.25nm in diameter, colloids contain larger particles.
     b. In true solutions, the solute and solvent particles are randomly mixed; the same with a colloid.
     c. True solutions may be colored and they must be clear; colloids may be colored but will scatter light.
     d. The Tyndall effect is not observed in true solutions; it is observed for colloids.

17. Colloidal dispersions are larger particles distributed fairly evenly throughout a solution. Unlike true solutions, these solutions scatter light. Suspensions are temporary non-homogeneous mixtures of ever larger sized particles. The particles will settle out with time or they can be filtered with filter paper.

18. No. For a colloidal dispersion, you need to have one substance that does not dissolve in another. Gases, because they are isolated molecules, will also exist with the gas molecules randomly mixed with one another.

19. Osmotic membranes pass only solvent molecules while dialysis membranes may pass all molecules and ions under a certain size.

20. In both cases a more random situation results. In the gas example, gas molecules spread from the highly-concentrated, high pressure area throughout the system. In the liquid example, the terms "lower and higher concentration" refers to the solute. A low concentration of solute means a high concentration of *water* in the solution and, conversely, a high solute concentration means a low concentration of water. Therefore, the movement of water molecules in osmosis is from a high water concentration to a low water concentration; a more random distribution of water molecules.

21. Reverse osmosis is a process of driving water molecules across a semipermeable membrane *from* a solution into pure water, i.e. in the reverse direction than normal osmosis generally takes. This is done by exerting a pressure onto the salt water solution that exceeds the osmotic pressure. This process is used on ships and in the Middle East to turn salt water into drinkable water.

22. The osmotic pressure that determines whether a solution is hypotonic, isotonic, or hypertonic is based on the concentration of the total number of solute particles. Since NaCl ionizes into two particles, Na^+ and Cl^-, a 0.16 M solution of NaCl has an osmolarity of 0.32 M. Glucose stays as a single unit, and thus its osmolarity would be 0.31 M, approximately the same.

23. a. A 5.5% NaCl solution is a hypertonic solution. Water will move from the inside of the cells to the solution and the cells will shrivel. b. A 0.92% solution is hypotonic; water will move into the cell and cell will burst.

24. The forces that hold NaCl in its crystalline form, i.e. the ionic bonds between the Na^+ and Cl^-, are not as strong as the forces that are obtained by dissolving the individual Na^+ and Cl^- ions in water (i.e. hydration of the ions and entropy). Thus, NaCl dissolves.

25. If the temperature of a system containing undissolved solid solute is raised, the increased motion of the particles causes more particles to leave the solid and less to recrystallize back from the solution to form the solid. Hence, more solute is dissolved at higher temperatures in the solvent. The amount of gaseous solutes in a solution is dependent on how rapidly they can escape from the solution at the surface. Therefore, a higher temperature means more rapid motion which, in turn, leads to faster gaseous solute escape to the atmosphere. Thus, gases have a lower solubility at higher temperatures.

26. Ethyl alcohol, because of its -OH group, can hydrogen bond with water while ethyl chloride can not. Solubility in a solvent requires that the solute fits into the solvent network. In water, this requires breaking some of the water-to-water hydrogen bonds; a process not favorable *unless* other bonds are made in exchange. Ethyl alcohol can make these bonds, ethyl chloride can not.

27. . a. Soluble; both alkali and halides (outside "edges" of the periodic table) are generally soluble.
    b. Soluble; all nitrates are soluble.
    c. Insoluble; most carbonates are insoluble (except for alkali and ammonium salts).
    d. Insoluble; most phosphates are insoluble.

28. a. Soluble; all ammonium compounds are soluble.
    b. Soluble; halides are generally soluble.
    c. Soluble; most sulfates are soluble. (As it turns out $PbSO_4$ is <u>insoluble</u>!)
    d. Soluble; alkali are soluble.

PROBLEMS

MOLARITY

29. a. $\dfrac{6.0 \text{ mol HCl}}{2.50 \text{ L}}$ = 2.4 M   b. $\dfrac{0.00700 \text{ mol Li}_2\text{CO}_3}{10.0 \text{ mL}}$ x $\dfrac{1000 \text{ mL}}{1\text{L}}$ = 0.700 M

30. a. $\dfrac{2.50 \text{ mol H}_2\text{SO}_4}{5.00 \text{ L}}$ = 0.500 M   b. $\dfrac{0.200 \text{ mol C}_2\text{H}_5\text{OH}}{18.4 \text{ mL}}$ x $\dfrac{1000 \text{ mL}}{1\text{L}}$ = 10.9 M

31. a. $\dfrac{8.90 \text{ g H}_2\text{SO}_4}{100.0 \text{ mL}}$ x $\dfrac{1 \text{ mol H}_2\text{SO}_4}{98.1 \text{ g}}$ x $\dfrac{1000 \text{ mL}}{\text{L}}$ = 0.907 M

   b. $\dfrac{439 \text{ g C}_6\text{H}_{12}\text{O}_6}{1.25 \text{ M}}$ x $\dfrac{1 \text{ mol C}_6\text{H}_{12}\text{O}_6}{180 \text{ g}}$ = 1.95 M

32. a. $\dfrac{44.3 \text{ g KOH}}{125 \text{ mL}}$ x $\dfrac{1 \text{ mol KOH}}{56.1 \text{ g}}$ x $\dfrac{1000 \text{ mL}}{1\text{L}}$ = 6.32 M

   b. $\dfrac{2.46 \text{ g H}_2\text{C}_2\text{O}_4}{750.0 \text{ mL}}$ x $\dfrac{1 \text{ mol H}_2\text{C}_2\text{O}_4}{90 \text{ g}}$ x $\dfrac{1000 \text{ mL}}{1\text{L}}$ = 0.0364 M

33. a. $\dfrac{1.00 \text{ mol NaOH}}{1\text{L}}$ x $\dfrac{40 \text{ g}}{1 \text{ mol NaOH}}$ x $\dfrac{2.0 \text{ L}}{1}$ = 80 g NaOH

   b. $\dfrac{4.25 \text{ mol C}_6\text{H}_{12}\text{O}_6}{1\text{L}}$ x $\dfrac{180 \text{ g}}{1 \text{ mol C}_6\text{H}_{12}\text{O}_6}$ x $\dfrac{1\text{L}}{1000 \text{ mL}}$ x $\dfrac{10.0 \text{ mL}}{1}$ = 7.65 g C$_6$H$_{12}$O$_6$

34. a. $\dfrac{2.50 \text{ mol K}_2\text{Cr}_2\text{O}_7}{1\text{L}}$ x $\dfrac{242.2 \text{ g}}{1 \text{ mol K}_2\text{Cr}_2\text{O}_7}$ x $\dfrac{1\text{L}}{1000 \text{ mL}}$ x $\dfrac{250 \text{ mL}}{1}$ = 151 g K$_2$Cr$_2$O$_7$

   b. $\dfrac{0.0100 \text{ M KMnO}_4}{1\text{L}}$ x $\dfrac{158 \text{ g}}{1 \text{ mol KMnO}_4}$ x $\dfrac{1\text{L}}{1000 \text{ mL}}$ x $\dfrac{20.0 \text{ mL}}{1}$ = 0.0316 g KMnO$_4$

35. $\dfrac{1.25 \text{ mol NaOH}}{1}$ x $\dfrac{1\text{L}}{6 \text{ mol NaOH}}$ = 0.208 L

36. $\dfrac{1.05 \text{ mol}}{1}$ x $\dfrac{1\text{L}}{2.5 \text{ mol NaOH}}$ = 0.420 L

37. $\dfrac{8.10 \text{ g KMnO}_4}{1}$ x $\dfrac{1 \text{ mol KMnO}_4}{158 \text{ g}}$ x $\dfrac{1\text{L}}{0.025 \text{ mol KMnO}_4}$ = 2.05 L

38. $\dfrac{205 \text{ g C}_6\text{H}_{12}\text{O}_6}{1}$ x $\dfrac{1 \text{ mol C}_6\text{H}_{12}\text{O}_6}{180 \text{ g}}$ x $\dfrac{1\text{L}}{4.25 \text{ mol C}_6\text{H}_{12}\text{O}_6}$ = 0.268 L

PERCENT CONCENTRATION

39. a. $\dfrac{35 \text{ mL water}}{725 \text{ mL solution}}$ x 100 = 4.83%   b. $\dfrac{78.9 \text{ mL acetone}}{1550 \text{ mL solution}}$ x 100 = 5.09%

40. a. $\dfrac{58.0 \text{ mL water}}{625 \text{ mL solution}}$ x 100 = 9.28%   b. $\dfrac{79.1 \text{ mL methanol}}{755 \text{ mL solution}}$ x 100 = 10.5%

41. a. $\dfrac{4.12 \text{ g NaOH}}{104.12 \text{ g total}}$ x 100 = 3.96%   b. mass of ethanol = 5.00 mL x 0.789 g/mL = 3.945 g

    $\dfrac{3.945 \text{ g ethanol}}{53.95 \text{ g total}}$ x 100 = 7.32%

42. a. $\dfrac{175 \text{ mg NaCl}}{1 \text{ g}}$ x $\dfrac{1 \text{ g NaCl}}{1000 \text{ mg}}$ x 100 = 17.5%   b. 275 mL methanol x 0.791 g/mL = 217 g methanol

    $\dfrac{217 \text{ g methanol}}{1217 \text{ g total}}$ x 100 = 17.9%

43. 10.0% of 775 g = 77.5 g NaCl
    You would take 77.5 g NaCl and add it to 697.5 g of water.

44. 5.50% of 125 g = 6.88 g KOH
    You would take 6.88 g KOH and add it to 118 g of water.

45. 2.00% of 2.00 L = 0.0400 L acetic acid
    You would take 0.0400 L (40.0 mL) of acetic acid and add it to 1.96 L of water.

46. 30.0% of 500 mL = 150 mL isopropyl alcohol
    You would take 150 mL of isopropyl alcohol and add it to 350 mL of water.

47. 1.5% $MgSO_4$ = $\dfrac{1.5 \text{ g MgSO}_4}{100 \text{ mL solution}}$ x $\dfrac{250.0 \text{ mL}}{1}$ = 3.75 g of $MgSO_4$ dissolved in 250 mL of solution

48. 2.15 % $AlCl_3$ = $\dfrac{2.15 \text{ g AlCl}_3}{100 \text{ mL solution}}$ x $\dfrac{1000 \text{ mL}}{1 \text{L}}$ x $\dfrac{2.00 \text{ L}}{1}$ = 43.0 g $AlCl_3$ dissolved in 2.00 L of solution

49. 0.1% = 0.1 g/100 mL
    = 100 mg/100 mL
    = 100 mg/dL

50. $\dfrac{1 \text{ L}}{1}$ x $\dfrac{1000 \text{ mL}}{1\text{L}}$ x $\dfrac{1.01 \text{ g}}{\text{mL}}$ x $\dfrac{5.88 \text{ g}}{100 \text{ g solution}}$ = 59.4 g acetic acid

SATURATED, UNSATURATED, AND SUPERSATURATED SOLUTIONS

51. a. unsaturated; b. 38 °C

52. a. saturation = 18 g/100 g H_2O = $\dfrac{18\ g}{118\ g\ total}$ = 15 %

b. Assuming a density of the solution = 1.0 g/mL

$$\dfrac{3\ g\ Ce_2(SO_4)_3}{103\ g\ solution} \quad \text{x} \quad \dfrac{1\ mol\ Ce_2(SO_4)_3}{568.5\ g} \text{ x } \dfrac{1\ g}{1\ mL} \text{ x } \dfrac{1000\ mL}{1\ L} = \quad 0.051\ M\ Ce_2(SO_4)_3$$

OSMOLARITY AND COLLIGATIVE PROPERTIES

53. Solute Particles: a. two; b. one; c. three. Osmol per one mole: a. two; b. one; c. three.

54. Solute Particles: a. three; b. two; c. four. Osmol per one mole: a. three; b. two; c. four.

55. a. 0.1 M $NaHCO_3$; b. 1 M NaCl

56. a. 1 M $CaCl_2$; b. 3 M glucose

57. a. 0.5 mol; b. 1.0 mol; c. 0.33 mol

58. a. 0.33 mol; b. 0.5 mol; c. 0.25 mol

59. a. same; b. 2 osmol/L glucose ($C_6H_{12}O_6$)

60. a. 1.0 osmol/L $NaHCO_3$; 2.0 osmol/L CH_3OH

ADDITIONAL PROBLEMS

61. Let some of the water evaporate out.

62. Yes, many supersaturated solutions require a seed crystal to start crystallization. This state is not stable but it will exist as long as the seed crystal is lacking.

63. $\dfrac{4.43\ mg\ O_2}{100g\ H_2O}$ x $\dfrac{1\ g}{1\ mL}$ x $\dfrac{1\ g}{1000\ mg}$ x $\dfrac{1\ mol\ O_2}{32\ g}$ x $\dfrac{1000\ mL}{1L}$ = 0.00138 M

64. The most: $Al_2(SO_4)_3$; the least: CH_3OH and CH_3COOH. $Al_2(SO_4)_3$ produces the most solute particles per mole (5) while CH_3OH and CH_3COOH produce only one each.

65. The salt solution has the higher osmotic pressure. Since the pickle shrivels up, water must be moving from it to the salt solution. This indicates that the salt solution must have the higher solute concentration.

66. Changing both to M: Solution A: $\dfrac{3.00\ g\ glucose}{100\ mL\ solution}$ x $\dfrac{1\ mol\ glucose}{180\ g}$ x $\dfrac{1000\ ml}{1\ L}$ = 0.17 M

Since Solution A has a greater glucose concentration than Solution B, water will flow from B to A.

67. The charge on the aluminum ions is +3. This will be much more effective at precipitating out particles than the +1 charge of sodium ions.

68. $\text{Volume \%} = \dfrac{11.3 \text{ mL}}{73.5 \text{ mL}} \times 100 = 15.4\%$

$\text{Mass–Volume \%} = \dfrac{11.3 \text{ mL CH}_3\text{OH}}{73.5 \text{ mL}} \times \dfrac{0.793 \text{ g}}{\text{mL}} \times 100 = 12.2\%$

69. a. $\dfrac{6.0 \text{ moles}}{\text{L}} \times 1.0 \text{ L} = 6.0 \text{ moles}$

b. $\dfrac{6.0 \text{ moles}}{\text{L}} \times \dfrac{1 \text{ L}}{1000 \text{ mL}} \times 100 \text{ mL} = 0.60 \text{ moles}$

c. $\dfrac{6.0 \text{ moles}}{\text{L}} \times \dfrac{1 \text{ L}}{1000 \text{ mL}} \times 1.0 \text{ mL} = 0.0060 \text{ moles}$

70. $\dfrac{0.10 \text{ g glucose}}{100 \text{ g blood}} \times \dfrac{1000 \text{ g}}{\text{kg}} \times \dfrac{1 \text{ kg}}{1} = 1.0 \text{ gram}$

71. a. $\dfrac{1 \text{ lb NaCN}}{2000 \text{ lb water}} \times 100 = 0.05\% \text{ by mass}$ 　b. $\dfrac{1 \text{ lb NaCN}}{2000 \text{ lb water}} \times 1{,}000{,}000 = 500 \text{ ppm}$

c. $\dfrac{1 \text{ lb NaCN}}{2000 \text{ lb water}} \times \dfrac{454 \text{ g NaCN}}{1 \text{ lb}} \times \dfrac{1 \text{ lb}}{0.454 \text{ kg water}} = 0.5 \text{ g/kg}$

d. $\dfrac{1 \text{ lb NaCN}}{2000 \text{ lb water}} \times \dfrac{454 \text{ g NaCN}}{1 \text{ lb}} \times \dfrac{1 \text{ mol NaCN}}{49 \text{ g}} \times \dfrac{1 \text{ lb water}}{454 \text{ g}} \times \dfrac{1 \text{ g water}}{1 \text{ mL}} \times \dfrac{1000 \text{ mL}}{1 \text{ L}} = 0.01 \text{ M}$

72.

Conc. of Solute (g/L)	Molarity (mol/L)	Molecular Weight of Solute (g/mol)
98	1.0	98
32	0.5	64
0.74	0.01	74
2.6	0.1	26
2.0	0.025	80
120	3	40
17	0.25	68

REVIEW QUESTIONS

1. Turns blue litmus paper to red; reacts with active metals like zinc and iron to produce H_2 gas; has a sour taste, produces a stinging feeling on your skin, and reacts with bases to form water and a salt.

2. Turns red litmus paper to blue, feels slippery to the touch; tastes bitter, and reacts with acids to form water and a salt.

3. Hydrogen. No, to be an acid the hydrogen must be able to come off the compound as an ion. The hydrogens of many compounds are too covalently linked to be released, and thus aren't acids.

4. Turns blue litmus paper to red; reacts with active metals like zinc and iron to produce H_2 gas; has a sour taste, produces a stinging feeling on your skin, and reacts with bases to form water and a salt.

5. Turns red litmus paper to blue, feels slippery to the touch; tastes bitter, and reacts with acids to form water and a salt.

6. Hydronium ion (H_3O^+)

7. Hydroxide ion (OH^-)

8. None. The taste becomes salty; the solution is relatively unreactive, and litmus doesn't change in either direction.

9. Use blue and red litmus paper and see if it turns either one to the opposite color. There are also many other acid/base indicators which one could use. One could also use a pH meter. (More about this in the next chapter.)

10. No. Atoms that are typically present in a Bronsted-Lowry base are oxygens and nitrogens.

11. Monoprotic: HCl, HNO_3; Diprotic: H_2SO_4; Triprotic: H_3PO_4

12. A polyprotic acid is a compound that can release more than one H^+ to the solution. CH_4 is not a polyprotic acid (nor is it an acid at all) because all the hydrogens are so strongly attached to the carbon, they never release into the solution.

13. An acid anhydride is a substance that reacts with water to produce an acid. Nonmetal oxides are examples of this class. SO_3 is the acid anhydride of H_2SO_4.

14. A basic anhydride is a substance that reacts with water to produce a base. Metal oxides are examples of this class. BaO is the base anhydride of $Ba(OH)_2$.

15. By their NH_3 concentrations and by the addition of other ingredients such as detergents, scents, etc.

16. $H_2CO_3 \longrightarrow H_2O + CO_2$

17. $NaHCO_3$, $CaCO_3$, $Al(OH)_3$, $Mg(OH)_2$, $MgCO_3$, $AlNa(OH)_2CO_3$

18. A solution of ammonia (NH_3) dissolved in water. Many of the NH_3 molecules have reacted with water to form NH_4^+ (ammonium) and OH^- (hydroxide).

19. H_2SO_4

20. Strong acids react with cotton, silk, wool and synthetic cloths, breaking them down and creating holes in the process.

21. They both produce chemical burns.

22. They break down and inactivate proteins which are vital for cellular function. The donation or removal of hydrogen ions to or from cellular protein causes them to denature and lose their function. The cells die as a result.

23. Milk of magnesia; the Na^+ in baking soda is dangerous for people with hypertension.

24. The poor absorption of Mg^{2+} ions causes a net movement of water molecules into the colon (via osmosis) which results in the laxative effect. Yes.

PROBLEMS

STRONG AND WEAK ACIDS AND BASES

25. Strong: b; Weak: c, d; Neither: a

26. Strong: c, d; Weak: a; Neither: b

27. a. salt; b. strong base; c. salt; d. weak acid

28. a. strong acid; b. weak base; c. salt; d. strong base

29. strong base

30. strong acid

31. weak acid

32. weak base

33. an acid, weak

34. a base; weak

NAMES OF ACIDS AND BASES

35. a. HCl; b. H_2SO_4; c. H_2CO_3; d. LiOH; e. $Mg(OH)_2$; f. KOH

36. a. HNO_3; b. H_2SO_3; c. H_3PO_4; d. H_2S; e. $Ca(OH)_2$

37. a. sodium hydroxide; b. phosphoric acid; c. nitric acid; d. sulfurous acid; e. calcium hydroxide; f. hydrosulfuric acid.

38. a. hydrochloric acid; b. sulfuric acid; c. lithium hydroxide; d. carbonic acid; e. magnesium hydroxide

39. Bromide ion; Hydrobromic acid

40. Hydroselenic acid

41. Nitrite ion; Nitrous acid

42. Phosphite ion; Phosphorous acid.

43. Oxalic acid

44. Benzoic acid.

IONIZATION OF ACIDS AND BASES

45. a. $HI + H_2O \longrightarrow H_3O^+ + I^-$
     b. $CH_3CH_2COOH + H_2O \rightleftharpoons CH_3CH_2COO^- + H_3O^+$
     c. $HNO_2 + H_2O \rightleftharpoons NO_2^- + H_3O^+$
     d. $H_2PO_4^- + H_2O \rightleftharpoons HPO_4^{2-} + H_3O^+$

46. a. $HOClO + H_2O \rightleftharpoons OClO^- + H_3O^+$
     b. $CH_3CH_2COOH + H_2O \rightleftharpoons CH_3CH_2COO^- + H_3O^+$
     c. $HCN + H_2O \rightleftharpoons CN^- + H_3O^+$
     d. $C_6H_5COOH + H_2O \rightleftharpoons C_6H_5COO^- + H_3O^+$

47. a. $HNO_3 + H_2O \rightleftharpoons NO_3^- + H_3O^+$
     b. $KOH \longrightarrow K^+ + OH^-$
     c. $HCOOH + H_2O \rightleftharpoons HCOO^- + H_3O^+$
     d. $CH_3NH_2 + H_2O \rightleftharpoons CH_3NH_3^+ + OH^-$

48. a. $HC_2O_4^- + H_2O \rightleftharpoons HC_2O_4H + OH^-$
     b. $Ba(OH)_2 \longrightarrow Ba^{2+} + 2 OH^-$
     c. $HClO_2 + H_2O \rightleftharpoons ClO_2^- + H_3O^+$
     d. $C_6H_5NH_2 + H_2O \rightleftharpoons C_6H_5NH_3^+ + OH^-$

ACIDIC AND BASIC ANHYDRIDES

49. H_2SO_4; an acid

50. $Mg(OH)_2$; a base

51. KOH; a base

52. H_2CO_3; an acid

ACID-BASE REACTIONS

53. a. base; b. acid; c. acid

54. a. acid; b. base; c. acid

55. $NaOH + HCl \longrightarrow NaCl + H_2O$

56. $LiOH + HNO_3 \longrightarrow LiNO_3 + H_2O$

57. $Ca(OH)_2 + 2HCl \longrightarrow CaCl_2 + 2H_2O$

58. $H_2SO_4 + 2KOH \longrightarrow K_2SO_4 + 2H_2O$

59. $H_3PO_4 + 3NaOH \longrightarrow Na_3PO_4 + 3H_2O$

60. $NaHCO_3 + H_3O^+ \longrightarrow 2H_2O + CO_2 + Na^+$

61. $Na_2CO_3 + 2H_3O^+ \longrightarrow 3H_2O + CO_2 + 2Na^+$

62. $CaCO_3 + 2H_3O^+ \longrightarrow Ca^{2+} + 3H_2O + CO_2$

ADDITIONAL PROBLEMS

63. Yes. Arrhenius described bases as compounds that gave OH^- to solution.

64. $HPO_4^{2-} + H_2O \rightleftharpoons H^+ + PO_4^{3-}$
    $HPO_4^{2-} + H_2O \rightleftharpoons H_2PO_4^- + OH^-$

65. $Ca(OH)_2 + 2H^+ \longrightarrow Ca^{2+} + 2H_2O$

66. $2CH_3COOH + CaCO_3 \longrightarrow Ca^{2+} + 2CH_3COO^- + H_2CO_3$

67. $HCOOH + NaHCO_3 \longrightarrow HCOO^- Na^+ + H_2CO_3$

68. $0.10\ M\ H_2SO_4$

69. H_2SiO_3; $NaHSiO_3$

70. HBO_2; $NaBO_2$

REVIEW QUESTIONS

1. a. Equivalence Point: The stage in an acid-base titration when a base is neutralized completely by an acid or an acid by a base. In an actual titration this point is often determined as the point when one drop of acid or base reagent causes a color change in the indicator.
    b. Kw: The ion product of water. A constant which reflects water's equilibrium to produce H_3O^+ and OH^-.
    c. pH: The negative log of the hydronium ion concentration.
    d. pOH: The negative log of the hydroxide ion concentration.
    e. Titration: A procedure for determining the acidity or basicity of a solution by systematically adding known concentrations of either an acid or base to it and monitoring the pH (often by an indicator color change).
    f. Indicator: A dye whose color depends on the acidity of the solution.
    g. pH meter: An instrument which measures H_3O^+ concentration and thus can determine pH.
    h. Buffer: A weak acid/base system that reacts with added acid or base to keep the pH of a solution fairly constant.
    i. Acidosis: Condition that results when the pH of the blood falls below 7.35 and oxygen transport is subsequently hindered.
    j. Alkalosis: Condition that results when the pH of the blood raises above 7.45 and life-threatening events may occur.

2. a. basic; b. acidic; c. neutral; d. acidic

3. $CH_3COOH + H_2O \rightleftharpoons CH_3COO^- + H_3O^+$

The system above is an equilibrium system. When acid is added, the reaction shifts to the left neutralizing the acid added. When base is added, the reaction shifts to the right producing H_3O^+ which will neutralize the OH^- added.

4. $NH_3 + H_2O \rightleftharpoons NH_4^+ + OH^-$ (The NH_4Cl will breakdown to yield NH_4^+ and Cl^- ions.)
   Addition of acid: Reaction shifts right.
   Addition of base: Reaction shifts left.

5. Bicarbonate/carbonic acid buffer, phosphate buffer, and proteins.

6. $-COO^-$ and $-NH_3^+$ groups

7. decrease

8. Too high

9. a. no; b. yes

10. a. no; b. yes

11. Basic. The final drop of strong base would generate a basic solution.

12. Acidic. The final drop of strong acid would generate an acidic solution.

13. *Concentrated* acid or base means they produce a large number of H^+ or OH^- respectively. The term indicates that the acid or base has not been diluted much with water and is at or near maximum strength.

14. Yes, it is decreased. No, the number of moles is simply spread over a larger volume.

15. You would measure out accurately a volume of the acid and add a few drops of indicator to it. Then you would titrate the base of known concentration carefully into this solution until one drop makes the indicator change permanently. The volume of base can then be used to calculate how many moles of base it took to neutralize the acid. This is, in turn, equivalent to the number of moles of acid. From the number of moles of acid and the acid solution's volume, a molarity can be calculated.

16. a. less; b. greater; c. less; d. greater.

17. K_2CO_3

18. $HCl < CH_3COOH < CH_3COONa < KOH$

PROBLEMS

DILUTION OF SOLUTION

19. $M_{conc} \times V_{conc} = M_{dil} \times V_{dil}$
$(12.0 \text{ M}) (V_{conc}) = (1.00 \text{ M}) (2.00 \text{ L})$
$V_{conc} = 0.167 \text{ L}$

20. $M_{conc} \times V_{conc} = M_{dil} \times V_{dil}$
$(8.89 \text{ M}) (V_{conc}) = (1.00 \text{ M}) (2.00 \text{ L})$
$V_{conc} = 0.225 \text{ L}$

21. $M_{conc} \times V_{conc} = M_{dil} \times V_{dil}$
$(1.04 \text{ M}) (V_{conc}) = (1.00 \text{ M}) (0.500 \text{ L})$
$V_{conc} = 0.481 \text{ L}$

22. $M_{conc} \times V_{conc} = M_{dil} \times V_{dil}$
$(19.1 \text{ M}) (V_{conc}) = (6.00 \text{ M}) (2.00 \text{ L})$
$V_{conc} = 0.628 \text{ L}$

23. a. $M_{conc} \times V_{conc} = M_{dil} \times V_{dil}$
$(18.0 \text{ M}) (V_{conc}) = (6.00 \text{ M}) (1.25 \text{ L})$
$V_{conc} = 0.417 \text{ L}$

    b. $M_{conc} \times V_{conc} = M_{dil} \times V_{dil}$
$(18.0 \text{ M}) (V_{conc}) = (0.100 \text{ M}) (0.575 \text{ L})$
$V_{conc} = 0.00319 \text{ L}$

24. a. $M_{conc} \times V_{conc} = M_{dil} \times V_{dil}$
$(12.0 \text{ M}) (V_{conc}) = (1.25 \text{ M}) (0.125 \text{ L})$
$V_{conc} = 0.0130 \text{ L}$ --- Take 13.0 mL of the 12.0 M solution and fill to 125 mL

    b. $M_{conc} \times V_{conc} = M_{dil} \times V_{dil}$
$(12.0 \text{ M}) (V_{conc}) = (6.00 \text{ M}) (5.00 \text{ L})$
$V_{conc} = 2.50 \text{ L}$ --- Take 2.50 L of the 12.0 M solution and fill to 5.00 L

c. $M_{conc} \times V_{conc} = M_{dil} \times V_{dil}$
(12.0 M) (V_{conc}) = (1.00 M) (1.50 L)
   V_{conc} = 0.125 L   --- Take 125 mL of the 12.0 M solution and fill to 1.50 L.

ACID-BASE TITRATIONS

25. $\dfrac{33.2 \text{ mL}}{1}$ $\times$ $\dfrac{1 \text{L}}{1000 \text{ mL}}$ $\times$ $\dfrac{0.150 \text{ mol NaOH}}{\text{L}}$ = 0.00498 mol NaOH = 0.00498 mol HCl

$\dfrac{0.00498 \text{ mol HCl}}{0.020 \text{L}}$ = 0.249 M HCl

26. $\dfrac{18.3 \text{ mL}}{1}$ $\times$ $\dfrac{1 \text{L}}{1000 \text{ mL}}$ $\times$ $\dfrac{0.104 \text{ mol KOH}}{\text{L}}$ = 0.00190 mol KOH = 0.00190 mol HNO_3

$\dfrac{0.00190 \text{ mol } HNO_3}{0.0300 \text{ L}}$ = 0.0634 M HNO_3

27. $\dfrac{28.2 \text{ mL}}{1}$ $\times$ $\dfrac{1 \text{L}}{1000 \text{ mL}}$ $\times$ $\dfrac{0.0302 \text{ mol HCl}}{\text{L}}$ = 0.0008516 mol HCl

0.0008516 mol HCl $\times$ $\dfrac{1 \text{ mol Ca(OH)}_2}{2 \text{ mol HCl}}$ = 0.000426 mol $Ca(OH)_2$

$\dfrac{0.000426 \text{ mol Ca(OH)}_2}{0.0185 \text{ L}}$ = 0.0230 M $Ca(OH)_2$

28. $\dfrac{25.7 \text{ mL}}{1}$ $\times$ $\dfrac{1 \text{L}}{1000 \text{ mL}}$ $\times$ $\dfrac{0.0995 \text{ mol NaOH}}{\text{L}}$ = 0.00256 mol NaOH

0.00256 mol NaOH $\times$ $\dfrac{1 \text{ mol H}_2\text{C}_2\text{O}_4}{2 \text{ mol NaOH}}$ = 0.00128 mol $H_2C_2O_4$

$\dfrac{0.00128 \text{ mol H}_2\text{C}_2\text{O}_4}{0.0125 \text{ L}}$ = 0.102 M $H_2C_2O_4$

29. $\dfrac{0.10 \text{ mol NaOH}}{\text{L}}$ $\times$ $\dfrac{1 \text{ L}}{1000 \text{mL}}$ $\times$ $\dfrac{25 \text{ mL}}{1}$ = 0.0025 mol NaOH = 0.0025 mol HCl

$\dfrac{.0025 \text{ mol HCl}}{0.020 \text{ L}}$ = 0.125 M HCl

30. $\dfrac{0.0023 \text{ mol HCl}}{0.030 \text{ L}}$ = 0.077 M $\dfrac{0.0023 \text{ mol HCl}}{0.060 \text{ L}}$ = 0.038 M   Range = 0.038–0.077 M

31. $\dfrac{10.3 \text{ mL NaHCO}_3}{1}$ $\times$ $\dfrac{1 \text{L}}{1000 \text{ mL}}$ $\times$ $\dfrac{0.404 \text{ mol NaHCO}_3}{\text{L}}$ $\times$ $\dfrac{1 \text{ mol H}_2\text{SO}_4}{2 \text{ mol NaHCO}_3}$ = 0.00208 mole H_2SO_4

$$\frac{0.00208 \text{ mol } H_2SO_4}{1} \times \frac{1L}{0.100 \text{ mol } H_2SO_4} = 0.0208 \text{ L } H_2SO_4 = 20.8 \text{ mL } H_2SO_4$$

32. $\frac{30.0 \text{ mL } Ba(OH)_2}{1} \times \frac{1L}{1000 \text{ mL}} \times \frac{0.0887 \text{ mol } Ba(OH)_2}{L} \times \frac{1 \text{ mol } H_2SO_4}{1 \text{ mol } Ba(OH)_2} = 0.00266 \text{ mole } H_2SO_4$

$$\frac{0.00266 \text{ mol } H_2SO_4}{1} \times \frac{1L}{0.110 \text{ mole } H_2SO_4} = 0.0242 \text{ L } H_2SO_4 = 24.2 \text{ mL } H_2SO_4$$

33. a. $\frac{25.00 \text{ mL KOH}}{1} \times \frac{1 L}{1000 \text{ mL}} \times \frac{0.0365 \text{ mol KOH}}{L} \times \frac{1 \text{ mol HCl}}{1 \text{ mol KOH}} = 0.000913 \text{ mol HCl}$

$$\frac{0.000913 \text{ mol HCl}}{1} \times \frac{1L}{0.0195 \text{ mol HCl}} = 0.0468 \text{ L HCl} = 46.8 \text{ mL HCl}$$

b. $\frac{10.00 \text{ mL Ca(OH)}_2}{1} \times \frac{1 L}{1000 \text{ mL}} \times \frac{0.0213 \text{ mol Ca(OH)}_2}{L} \times \frac{2 \text{ mol HCl}}{1 \text{ mol Ca(OH)}_2} = 0.000426 \text{ mol HCl}$

$$\frac{0.000426 \text{ mol HCl}}{1} \times \frac{1L}{0.0195 \text{ mol HCl}} = 0.0218 \text{ L HCl} = 21.8 \text{ mL HCl}$$

c. $\frac{20.00 \text{ mL NH}_3}{1} \times \frac{1 L}{1000 \text{ mL}} \times \frac{0.0225 \text{ mol NH}_3}{L} \times \frac{1 \text{ mol HCl}}{1 \text{ mol NH}_3} = 0.000450 \text{ mol HCl}$

$$\frac{0.000450 \text{ mol HCl}}{1} \times \frac{1L}{0.0195 \text{ mol HCl}} = 0.0231 \text{ L HCl} = 23.1 \text{ mL HCl}$$

34. a. $\frac{20.00 \text{ mL } H_2SO_4}{1} \times \frac{1 L}{1000 \text{ mL}} \times \frac{0.0265 \text{ mol } H_2SO_4}{L} \times \frac{1 \text{ mol } Ba(OH)_2}{1 \text{ mol } H_2SO_4} = 0.000530 \text{ mol } Ba(OH)_2$

$$\frac{0.000530 \text{ mol } Ba(OH)_2}{1} \times \frac{1L}{0.0108 \text{ mol } Ba(OH)_2} = 0.0491 \text{ L } Ba(OH)_2 = 49.1 \text{ mL } Ba(OH)_2$$

b. $\frac{25.00 \text{ mL HCl}}{1} \times \frac{1 L}{1000 \text{ mL}} \times \frac{0.0213 \text{ mol HCl}}{L} \times \frac{1 \text{ mol } Ba(OH)_2}{2 \text{ mol HCl}} = 0.000266 \text{ mol } Ba(OH)_2$

$$\frac{0.000266 \text{ mol } Ba(OH)_2}{1} \times \frac{1L}{0.0108 \text{ mol } Ba(OH)_2} = 0.0247 \text{ L } Ba(OH)_2 = 24.7 \text{ mL } Ba(OH)_2$$

c. $\frac{10.00 \text{ mL CH}_3COOH}{1} \times \frac{1 L}{1000 \text{ mL}} \times \frac{0.0868 \text{ mol CH}_3COOH}{L} \times \frac{1 \text{ mol } Ba(OH)_2}{2 \text{ mol CH}_3COOH} = 0.000434 \text{ mol } Ba(OH)_2$

$$\frac{0.000434 \text{ mol } Ba(OH)_2}{1} \times \frac{1L}{0.0108 \text{ mol } Ba(OH)_2} = 0.0402 \text{ L } Ba(OH)_2 = 40.2 \text{ mL } Ba(OH)_2$$

pH AND pOH

35. a. $pH = -\log [H_3O^+]$
    $pH = -\log (1.0 \times 10^{-2})$
    $pH = 2$

    b. $pH = -\log [H_3O^+]$
    $pH = -\log (1.0 \times 10^{-4})$
    $pH = 4$

36. a. $pH = -\log [H_3O^+]$
    $pH = -\log (0.00010 \text{ M})$
    $pH = 4.0$

    b. $pH = -\log [H_3O^+]$
    $pH = -\log (0.00010 \text{ M})$
    $pH = 4.0$

    c. $pH = -\log [H_3O^+]$
    $pH = -\log (0.10 \text{ M})$
    $pH = 1.0$

37. a. $pOH = -\log [OH^-]$
    $pOH = -\log (1.0 \times 10^{-2})$
    $pOH = 2$

    b. $pOH = -\log [OH^-]$
    $pOH = -\log (1.0 \times 10^{-3})$
    $pOH = 3$

38. a. $pOH = -\log [OH^-]$
    $pOH = -\log (0.0010)$
    $pOH = 3.0$

    b. $pOH = -\log [OH^-]$
    $pOH = -\log (0.010)$
    $pOH = 2.0$

39. $pH + pOH = 14$ a. $pOH = 10.0$; b. $pOH = 10.0$; c. $pOH = 13.0$

40. $pH + pOH = 14$ a. $pH = 11.0$; b. $pH = 12.0$

41. a. $pH = -\log [H_3O^+]$
    $pH = -\log (3.3 \times 10^{-3} \text{ M})$
    $pH = 2.48$

    b. $pH = -\log [H_3O^+]$
    $pH = -\log (5.7 \times 10^{-5} \text{ M})$
    $pH = 4.24$

    c. $pH = -\log [H_3O^+]$
    $pH = -\log (8.1 \times 10^{-4} \text{ M})$
    $pH = 3.09$

42. a. $pH = -\log [H_3O^+]$
    $pH = -\log (3.6 \times 10^{-2})$
    $pH = 1.44$

    b. $pH = -\log [H_3O^+]$
    $pH = -\log (8.8 \times 10^{-4})$
    $pH = 3.06$

43. $pH = -\log [H_3O^+]$
    $pH = -\log (4.6 \times 10^{-8})$
    $pH = 7.34$

44. $pH = -\log [H_3O^+]$
    $pH = -\log (2.3 \times 10^{-6})$
    $pH = 5.64$

45. $pH = -\log [H_3O^+]$
    $pH = -\log (2.0 \times 10^{-12})$
    $pH = 11.7$

46. $pH = -\log [H_3O^+]$
    $pH = -\log (0.12)$
    $pH = 0.92$

47. $pH = -\log [H_3O^+]$
    $5.10 = -\log [H_3O^+]$
    $7.9 \times 10^{-6} \text{ M} = [H_3O^+]$

48. pH = – log [H$^+$]

    2.31 = – log [H$^+$]

    4.9 x 10^{-3} M = [H$^+$]

SALT SOLUTIONS: ACIDIC, BASIC, OR NEUTRAL?

49. $CH_3COO^- + H_2O \longleftrightarrow CH_3COOH + OH^-$

50. $NH_4^+ + H_2O \longleftrightarrow NH_3 + H_3O^+$

51. a. neutral; b. basic; c. unable to say

52. a. basic; b. acidic; c. neutral

ADDITIONAL PROBLEMS

53. $CH_3COOH + KOH \longleftrightarrow CH_3COO^- K^+ + H_2O$

$$\frac{31.45 \text{ mL KOH}}{1} \text{ x } \frac{1 \text{L}}{1000 \text{ mL}} \text{ x } \frac{0.2560 \text{ mol KOH}}{\text{L}} \text{ x } \frac{1 \text{ mol CH}_3\text{COOH}}{1 \text{ mol KOH}} = 0.008051 \text{ mol CH}_3\text{COOH}$$

$$\frac{0.008051 \text{ mol CH}_3\text{COOH}}{0.010 \text{ L}} = 0.8051 \text{ M CH}_3\text{COOH}$$

54. $NH_3 + HCl \longleftrightarrow NH_4^+ Cl^- + H_2O$

$$\frac{39.95 \text{ mL HCl}}{1} \text{ x } \frac{1 \text{L}}{1000 \text{ mL}} \text{ x } \frac{1.008 \text{ mol HCl}}{\text{L}} \text{ x } \frac{1 \text{ mol NH}_3}{1 \text{ mol HCl}} = 0.04027 \text{ mol NH}_3$$

$$\frac{0.04027 \text{ mol CH}_3\text{COOH}}{0.010 \text{ L}} = 4.027 \text{ M CH}_3\text{COOH}$$

55. $\frac{148 \text{ g Na}_2\text{CO}_3}{1} \text{ x } \frac{1 \text{ mol Na}_2\text{CO}_3}{106 \text{ g}} \text{ x } \frac{1 \text{ mol CO}_2}{1 \text{ mol Na}_2\text{CO}_3} \text{ x } \frac{22.4 \text{ L}}{1 \text{ mol CO}_2} = 31.3 \text{ L CO}_2$

56. $\frac{212 \text{ g Na}_2\text{SO}_3}{1} \text{ x } \frac{1 \text{ mol Na}_2\text{SO}_3}{126 \text{ g}} \text{ x } \frac{1 \text{ mol SO}_2}{1 \text{ mol Na}_2\text{SO}_3} = 1.68 \text{ mol SO}_2$

         PV = nRT   P = $\frac{764 \text{ mm Hg}}{760 \text{ mm Hg/atm}}$ = 1.005 atm

(1.005 atm)(V) = $\frac{(1.683 \text{ mol})(0.082 \text{ atm L})(299 \text{ K})}{\text{mol K}}$

         V = 41.1 L   T = 26 ^{o}C + 273 = 299 K

57. H_2SO_4 would have the highest [H$_3$O$^+$]. It and HI are the only strong acids of the group; H_2SO_4 would liberate more hydronium ions than HI because it is a diprotic acid.

58. $H_2SO_4 + Na_2CO_3 \overset{\longrightarrow}{\longleftarrow} Na_2SO_4 + CO_2 + H_2O$

$$\frac{1.5 \times 10^3 \text{ kg}}{1} \times \frac{1000 \text{ g}}{1 \text{ kg}} \times \frac{0.932}{1} \times \frac{1 \text{ mol } H_2SO_4}{98 \text{ g}} = 14{,}265 \text{ mol } H_2SO_4 = 14{,}265 \text{ mol } Na_2CO_3 \text{ needed}$$

$$\frac{14{,}265 \text{ mol } Na_2CO_3}{1} \times \frac{106 \text{ g}}{1 \text{ mol } Na_2CO_3} = 1{,}512{,}000 \text{ g } Na_2CO_3 = 1{,}512 \text{ kg } Na_2CO_3$$

59. $$\frac{31.08 \text{ mL HCl}}{1} \times \frac{1 \text{ L}}{1000 \text{ mL}} \times \frac{0.9928 \text{ mol HCl}}{L} \times \frac{1 \text{ mol } NH_3}{1 \text{ mol HCl}} = 0.03086 \text{ mol } NH_3$$

$$\frac{0.03086 \text{ mol } CH_3COOH}{0.00500 \text{ L}} = 6.171 \text{ M } CH_3COOH$$

REVIEW QUESTIONS

1. The common ion effect says that when an ion *common* (i.e. the same) to one in an equilibrium solution is added, the degree of ionization of that ion is decreased. This is seen with buffers since they are ionization reactions. When an ion (either H^+ or the ion form of the acid or base) is added to a buffer system, the equilibrium shifts to produce more of the un-ionized form of the acid or base.

2. $(HCOO)_2Ca$. These will release some formate ions ($HCOO^-$) which will then combine with H^+ in solution to decrease the amount of ionization of formic acid.

3. a. $HBO_2 \longrightarrow H_3O^+ + BO_2^-$

    b. $HClO_2 \longrightarrow H_3O^+ + ClO_2^-$

    c. $HC_9H_7O_4 \longrightarrow H_3O^+ + C_9H_7O_4^-$

    d. $H_2Se \longrightarrow H_3O^+ + HSe^-$

4. a. $C_4H_9NH_2 + H_2O \longrightarrow C_4H_9NH_3^+ + OH^-$

    b. $C_{11}H_{12}O_4N + H_2O \longrightarrow C_{11}H_{12}O_4NH^+ + OH^-$

    c. $C_3H_5N + H_2O \longrightarrow C_3H_5NH^+ + OH^-$

PROBLEMS

EQUILIBRIUM CONSTANT EXPRESSIONS

5. a. $K_a = \dfrac{[H^+][OCl^-]}{[HOCl]}$ b. $K_a = \dfrac{[H^+][C_6H_7O_6^-]}{[HC_6H_7O_6]}$ c. $K_a = \dfrac{[H^+][HCO_2^-]}{[HCO_2H]}$

6. a. $K_b = \dfrac{[OH^-][C_5H_5NH^+]}{[C_5H_5N]}$ b. $K_b = \dfrac{[OH^-][C_2H_5NH_3^+]}{[C_2H_5NH_2]}$ c. $K_b = \dfrac{[OH^-][H_2PO_4^-]}{[HPO_4^{2-}]}$

7. $K_a = \dfrac{[H^+][Z^-]}{[HZ]}$ $[H^+] = [Z^-] = .0002\ M$ $[HZ] = 0.100 - .0002\ M = .0998\ M$

    $K_a = \dfrac{(.0002)(.0002)}{(.0998)} = 4.00 \times 10^{-7}\ M$

8. $K_b = \dfrac{[Q+][OH^-]}{[QOH]}$ $[Q+] = [OH^-] = 0.0004\ M$ $[QOH] = .0200 - .0004\ M = .0196\ M$

    $K_b = \dfrac{(.0004)(.0004)}{(.0196)} = 8.16 \times 10^{-6}\ M$

EQUILIBRIA IN SOLUTIONS OF WEAK ACIDS AND WEAK BASES

9. $K_a = \dfrac{[H^+][CH_3COO^-]}{[CH_3COOH]} = 1.8 \times 10^{-5}$

$\dfrac{(X)(X)}{(.01-X)} = 1.8 \times 10^{-5}$ Assume $X \ll 0.01$, then:

$\dfrac{X^2}{0.01} = 1.8 \times 10^{-5}$ $X^2 = 1.8 \times 10^{-7}$

$X = 4.2 \times 10^{-4} M = [H^+]$

b. $K_a = \dfrac{[H^+][C_6H_5COO^-]}{[C_6H_5COOH]} = 6.3 \times 10^{-5}$

$\dfrac{(X)(X)}{(0.2-X)} = 6.3 \times 10^{-5}$ Assume $X \ll .2$, then:

$\dfrac{X^2}{0.2} = 6.3 \times 10^{-5}$ $X^2 = 1.26 \times 10^{-5}$

$X = 3.5 \times 10^{-3} M = [H^+]$

c. $K_a = \dfrac{[H^+][CN^-]}{[HCN]} = 6.2 \times 10^{-10}$

$\dfrac{(X)(X)}{(0.50-X)} = 6.2 \times 10^{-10}$ Assume $X \ll 0.50$, then:

$\dfrac{X^2}{0.50} = 6.2 \times 10^{-10}$ $X^2 = 3.10 \times 10^{-10}$

$X = 1.76 \times 10^{-5} M = [H^+]$

10.   a. $K_a = \dfrac{[H^+][HCOO^-]}{[HCOOH]} = 1.8 \times 10^{-4}$

$\dfrac{(X)(X)}{(0.10-X)} = 1.8 \times 10^{-4}$ Assume $X \ll 0.10$, then:

$\dfrac{X^2}{0.10} = 1.8 \times 10^{-4}$ $X^2 = 1.8 \times 10^{-5}$

$X = 4.2 \times 10^{-3} M = [H^+]$

b. $K_a = \dfrac{[H^+][F^-]}{[HF]} = 6.6 \times 10^{-4}$

$\dfrac{(X)(X)}{(0.15 - X)} = 6.6 \times 10^{-4}$ Assume X << 0.15, then:

$\dfrac{X^2}{0.15} = 6.6 \times 10^{-4}$ $X^2 = 9.90 \times 10^{-5}$

$X = 9.9 \times 10^{-3} M = [H^+]$

c. $K_a = \dfrac{[H^+][NO_2^-]}{[HNO_2]} = 7.2 \times 10^{-4}$

$\dfrac{(X)(X)}{(0.05 - X)} = 7.2 \times 10^{-4}$ Assume X << 0.050, then:

$\dfrac{X^2}{0.050} = 7.2 \times 10^{-4}$ $X^2 = 3.60 \times 10^{-5}$

$X = 6.0 \times 10^{-3} M = [H^+]$

11. $K_w = [H^+][OH^-]$
$1 \times 10^{-14} = [H^+][OH^-]$
   a. $[OH^-] = 2.38 \times 10^{-11}$ M
   b. $[OH^-] = 2.9 \times 10^{-12}$ M
   c. $[OH^-] = 5.7 \times 10^{-10}$ M

12. $K_w = [H^+][OH^-]$
$1 \times 10^{-14} = [H^+][OH^-]$
   a. $[OH^-] = 2.4 \times 10^{-12}$ M
   b. $[OH^-] = 1.0 \times 10^{-12}$ M
   c. $[OH^-] = 1.7 \times 10^{-12}$ M

13. a. $K_b = \dfrac{[OH^-][NH_4^+]}{[NH_3]} = 1.8 \times 10^{-5}$

$\dfrac{(X)(X)}{(0.025 - X)} = 1.8 \times 10^{-5}$ Assume X << 0.025, then:

$\dfrac{X^2}{0.025} = 1.8 \times 10^{-5}$ $X^2 = 4.50 \times 10^{-7}$ $X = 6.71 \times 10^{-4} M = [OH^-]$

b. $K_b = \dfrac{[OH^-][CH_3NH_3^+]}{[CH_3NH_2]} = 4.2 \times 10^{-4}$

$\dfrac{(X)(X)}{(0.10 - X)} = 4.2 \times 10^{-4}$ Assume X << 0.10, then:

$\dfrac{X^2}{0.10} = 4.2 \times 10^{-4}$ $X^2 = 4.20 \times 10^{-5}$ $X = 6.48 \times 10^{-3} M = [OH^-]$

c. $K_b = \dfrac{[OH^-][C_6H_5NH_3^+]}{[C_6H_5NH_2]} = 7.4 \times 10^{-10}$

$\dfrac{(X)(X)}{(0.10-X)} = 7.4 \times 10^{-10}$ Assume X $\ll$ 0.10, then:

$\dfrac{X^2}{0.10} = 7.4 \times 10^{-10}$ $X^2 = 7.4 \times 10^{-11}$ $X = 8.60 \times 10^{-6} M = [OH^-]$

14. a. $K_b = \dfrac{[OH^-][(CH_3)_2NH_2^+]}{[(CH_3)_2NH]} = 5.9 \times 10^{-4}$

$\dfrac{(X)(X)}{(0.010-X)} = 5.9 \times 10^{-4}$ Assume X $\ll$ 0.010, then:

$\dfrac{X^2}{0.010} = 5.9 \times 10^{-4}$ $X^2 = 5.9 \times 10^{-6}$ $X = 2.4 \times 10^{-3} M = [OH^-]$

b. $K_b = \dfrac{[OH^-][H_2NNH_3^+]}{[H_2NNH_2]} = 8.5 \times 10^{-7}$

$\dfrac{(X)(X)}{(0.15-X)} = 8.5 \times 10^{-7}$ Assume X $\ll$ 0.15, then:

$\dfrac{X^2}{0.15} = 8.5 \times 10^{-7}$ $X^2 = 1.28 \times 10^{-7}$ $X = 3.6 \times 10^{-4} M = [OH^-]$

c. $K_b = \dfrac{[OH^-][HONH_3^+]}{[HONH_2]} = 9.1 \times 10^{-9}$

$\dfrac{(X)(X)}{(0.030-X)} = 9.1 \times 10^{-9}$ Assume X $\ll$ 0.03, then:

$\dfrac{X^2}{0.030} = 9.1 \times 10^{-9}$ $X^2 = 2.73 \times 10^{-10}$ $X = 1.7 \times 10^{-5} M = [OH^-]$

15. $K_w = [H^+][OH^-]$
    $1 \times 10^{-14} = [H^+][OH^-]$ a. $[H^+] = 1.49 \times 10^{-11}$ M
                b. $[H^+] = 1.54 \times 10^{-12}$ M
                c. $[H^+] = 1.16 \times 10^{-9}$ M

16. $K_w = [H^+][OH^-]$
    $1 \times 10^{-14} = [H^+][OH^-]$ a. $[H^+] = 4.2 \times 10^{-12}$ M
                b. $[H^+] = 2.8 \times 10^{-11}$ M
                c. $[H^+] = 5.9 \times 10^{-10}$ M

BUFFER SOLUTIONS

17. a. $K_a = \dfrac{[H^+][CN^-]}{[HCN]} = 6.2 \times 10^{-10}$

$6.2 \times 10^{-10} = \dfrac{(X)(.25)}{(.25)}$ $\qquad 6.2 \times 10^{-10}\ M = X = [H^+]$

b. $K_a = \dfrac{[H^+][F^-]}{[HF]} = 6.6 \times 10^{-4}$

$6.6 \times 10^{-4} = \dfrac{(X)(.20)}{(.50)}$ $\qquad 1.65 \times 10^{-3}\ M = X = [H^+]$

c. $K_a = \dfrac{[H^+][C_6H_5COO^-]}{[C_6H_5COOH]} = 6.3 \times 10^{-5}$

$6.3 \times 10^{-5} = \dfrac{(X)(.045)}{(.033)}$ $\qquad 4.62 \times 10^{-5}\ M = X = [H^+]$

18. a. $K_a = \dfrac{[H^+][CN^-]}{[HCN]} = 6.2 \times 10^{-10}$

$6.2 \times 10^{-10} = \dfrac{(X)(.20)}{(.20)}$ $\qquad 6.2 \times 10^{-10}\ M = X = [H^+]$

b. $K_a = \dfrac{[H^+][F^-]}{[HF]} = 6.6 \times 10^{-4}$

$6.6 \times 10^{-4} = \dfrac{(X)(.20)}{(.50)}$ $\qquad 1.7 \times 10^{-3}\ M = X = [H^+]$

c. $K_a = \dfrac{[H^+][C_6H_5COO^-]}{[C_6H_5COOH]} = 6.3 \times 10^{-5}$

$6.3 \times 10^{-5} = \dfrac{(X)(.20)}{(.40)}$ $\qquad 1.3 \times 10^{-4}\ M = X = [H^+]$

19. $K_b = \dfrac{[OH^-][NH_4^+]}{[NH_3]} = 1.8 \times 10^{-5}$

$1.8 \times 10^{-5}\ M = \dfrac{(X)(0.040\ M)}{(0.40\ M)}$ $\qquad 1.8 \times 10^{-4}\ M = X = [OH^-]$

20. . $K_b = \dfrac{[OH^-][NH_4^+]}{[NH_3]} = 1.8 \times 10^{-5}$

$1.8 \times 10^{-5}\ M = \dfrac{(X)(0.020\ M)}{(0.040\ M)}$ $\qquad 3.6 \times 10^{-5}\ M = X = [OH^-]$

THE HENDERSON-HASSELBALCH EQUATION

21. $pH = pK_a + \log \dfrac{[A^-]}{[HA]}$ $pK_a = -\log K_a$ $pK_a = -\log(6.2 \times 10^{-10})$ $pK_a = 9.21$

    $pH = 9.21 + \log \dfrac{(0.040\ M)}{(0.040\ M)}$ $pH = 9.21 + 0 = 9.21$

22. $pH = pK_a + \log \dfrac{[A^-]}{[HA]}$ $pK_a = -\log K_a$ $pK_a = -\log(1.8 \times 10^{-4})$ $pK_a = 3.74$

    $pH = 3.74 + \log \dfrac{(0.20\ M)}{(0.20\ M)}$ $pH = 3.74 + 0 = 3.74$

23. $pH = pK_a + \log \dfrac{[A^-]}{[HA]}$ $pK_a = -\log K_a$ $pK_a = -\log(6.3 \times 10^{-5})$ $pK_a = 4.20$

    $pH = 4.20 + \log \dfrac{(0.15\ M)}{(0.15\ M)}$ $pH = 4.20 + 0 = 4.20$

24. $pH = pK_a + \log \dfrac{[A^-]}{[HA]}$ $pK_a = -\log K_a$ $pK_a = -\log(6.6 \times 10^{-4})$ $pK_a = 3.18$

    $pH = 3.18 + \log \dfrac{(0.50\ M)}{(0.20\ M)}$ $pH = 3.18 + 0.40 = 3.58$

25. $pH = pK_a + \log \dfrac{[A^-]}{[HA]}$ $pK_a = -\log K_a$ $pK_a = -\log(1.8 \times 10^{-4})$ $pK_a = 3.74$

    $pH = 3.74 + \log \dfrac{(0.60\ M)}{(0.15\ M)}$ $pH = 3.74 + 0.60 = 4.34$

26. $pH = pK_a + \log \dfrac{[A^-]}{[HA]}$ $pK_a = -\log K_a$ $pK_a = -\log(6.3 \times 10^{-5})$ $pK_a = 4.20$

    $pH = 4.20 + \log \dfrac{(0.96\ M)}{(0.11\ M)}$ $pH = 4.20 + 0.94 = 5.14$

27. $pH = pK_a + \log \dfrac{[A^-]}{[HA]}$ $pK_a = -\log K_a$ $pK_a = -\log(1.3 \times 10^{-5})$ $pK_a = 4.89$

    $pH = 4.89 + \log \dfrac{(0.0786\ M)}{(0.350\ M)}$ $pH = 4.89 + (-0.65) = 4.24$

28. $K_b = \dfrac{[OH^-][(CH_3\,CH_2)_2NH_2^+]}{[(CH_3\,CH_2)_2NH]} = 6.9 \times 10^{-4}$ $\dfrac{[OH^-](0.145\ M)}{(0.132\ M)} = 6.9 \times 10^{-4}$

    $[OH^-] = 6.28 \times 10^{-4}\ M$ $1.0 \times 10^{-14} = [OH-][H+]$ $[H+] = 1.59 \times 10^{-11}\ M$

                       $pH = 10.8$

29. $pH = pK_a + \log \dfrac{[A^-]}{[HA]}$ $pK_a = -\log K_a$ $pK_a = -\log (1.0 \times 10^{-10})$ $pK_a = 10.0$

$pH = 10.0 + \log \dfrac{(0.10 \text{ M})}{(0.10 \text{ M})}$ $pH = 10.0 + 0 = 10.0$

30. $pH = pK_a + \log \dfrac{[A^-]}{[HA]}$ $pK_a = -\log K_a$ $pK_a = -\log (1.0 \times 10^{-8})$ $pK_a = 8.0$

$pH = 8.0 + \log \dfrac{(0.05 \text{ M})}{(0.05 \text{ M})}$ $pH = 8.0 + 0 = 8.0$

ADDITIONAL PROBLEMS

31. a. No. In order to be a satisfactory buffer, both the un–ionized acid form and the ionized base form of the chemical must be present in solution. When placed together, HCl and NaOH will react completely with each other to form H_2O and NaCl. The NaCl that results can not act a buffer because it can neither release or take up H^+ ions. (NaCl is a salt.) b. Acetic acid can be considered a buffer because it has an acid form (CH_3COOH) and a corresponding base form (CH_3COO^-). This combination of an acid/base pair can pick up and release H^+ ions to solution upon addition of a second acid or base.

32. $K_a = \dfrac{[H^+][HCOO^-]}{[HCOOH]} = 1.8 \times 10^{-4}$

$\dfrac{(X)(X)}{(1.50 - X)} = 1.8 \times 10^{-4}$ Assume $X \ll 1.50$, then:

$\dfrac{X^2}{1.50} = 1.8 \times 10^{-4}$ $X^2 = 2.7 \times 10^{-4}$

$X = 1.6 \times 10^{-2} M = [H^+]$ $pH = -\log [H^+]$ $pH = -\log [1.6 \times 10^{-2} \text{ M}]$
$pH = 1.78$

33. $\dfrac{1.25 \text{ g } C_5H_5N}{0.125 \text{ L}} \times \dfrac{1 \text{ mol}}{79 \text{ g } C_5H_5N} = 0.127 \text{ M } C_5H_5N$

$K_b = \dfrac{[OH^-][C_5H_5NH^+]}{[C_5H_5N]} = 1.5 \times 10^{-9}$

$\dfrac{(X)(X)}{(0.127 - X)} = 1.5 \times 10^{-9}$ Assume $X \ll 0.127$, then:

$\dfrac{X^2}{0.127} = 1.5 \times 10^{-9}$ $X^2 = 1.91 \times 10^{-10}$ $X = 1.38 \times 10^{-5} M = [OH^-]$

$1 \times 10^{-14} = [H^+][OH^-]$
$1 \times 10^{-14} = [H^+](1.38 \times 10^{-5} M)$
$7.24 \times 10^{-10} M = [H^+]$
$pH = -\log [H^+]$
$pH = 9.14$

34. $pH = -\log[H_3O^+]$

        $3.10 = -\log[H_3O^+]$

        $7.94 \times 10^{-4}\ M = [H_3O^+] = [N_3^-]$

$$Ka = \frac{[H_3O^+][N_3^-]}{[HN_3]}$$

$$1.9 \times 10^{-5} = \frac{(7.94 \times 10^{-4})(7.94 \times 10^{-4})}{X}$$

$$1.9 \times 10^{-5}\ X = (7.94 \times 10^{-4})(7.94 \times 10^{-4})$$

$$[HN_3] = X = 0.033\ M$$

REVIEW QUESTIONS

1. a. Cathode: An electrode that bears a negative charge.
    b. Anode: An electrode that bears a positive charge.
    c. Cation: A positively charged ion.
    d. Anion: A negatively charged ion.
    e. Electrolysis: The process of splitting a compound by means of electricity.
    f. Strong electrolyte: A compound which completely ionizes in water, thus making the solution a good conductor.
    g. Weak electrolyte: A compound which only partially ionizes in water, thus making the solution a weak conductor.
    h. Nonelectrolyte: A compound which fails to ionize in water, generating no electrical conduction.
    i. Ionization: The formation of ions from a compound when it dissolves in water.
    j. Ion Dissociation: The separation of ions of an ionic compound when it dissolves in water.
    k. Activity Series: A listing of metals in order of decreasing reactivity.
    l. Solubility Product Constant: An equilibrium constant reflecting the solubility of a compound in water.

2. Each mole of NaCl produces 2 moles of ions. Each ion or undissociated compound reduces the freezing point by an equal amount. The depression for the salt solution is not quite twice that for the sugar solution because of the interaction between ions when in a concentrated solution.

3. HCl ionizes in water by the following reaction:

$$HCl + H_2O \longrightarrow H_3O^+ + Cl^-$$

4. $HI + H_2O \longrightarrow H_3O^+ + I^-$

5. Lead chromate is an insoluble compound which does not liberate ions into solution.

6. The main ideas are:
    1. An electrolyte is a compound which produces ions upon dissolving in water.
    2. The net sum of all the positive and negative charges is zero.
    3. All dissolved species (either ions or undissociated) have the same effect on boiling point, freezing point, and osmotic pressure when compared on a number (mole) basis.
    4. Weak electrolytes produce only relatively small amounts of ions in solution.
    5. Nonelectrolytes produce, for all practical purposes, no ions in solution.

7. The reaction of iron to make rust is:

$$4Fe + 3O_2 + 6H_2O \longrightarrow 4Fe(OH)_3$$

    As can be seen by the reaction, O_2 and water are required. An electrolyte is also required to couple the oxidation and reduction reactions.

8. Aluminum upon initial exposure to air forms a dense oxidized coating which discourages further oxidation. (Oxygen can not penetrate through this layer.)

9. Metallic silver oxidizes in air to form Ag^+ which then may react with hydrogen sulfide to form blackish Ag_2S. The tarnish can be removed by using aluminum metal to reduce the Ag^+ ions back to silver metal.

10. An electrolytic cell uses electricity to produce a chemical reaction while an electrochemical cell uses chemical reactions to produce electricity.

11. In molten NaCl, the ions can move towards the appropriate electrode -- a process needed for electrical current. In crystalline, solid NaCl, the ion positions are fixed and thus electricity is not conducted.

12. Covalent.

13. Cathode. The cathode is the negatively charged electrode. You want to attract the positive charged, "plating" metal ions to this electrode so that these ions can then be reduced to form the metallic coating.

14. Goiter is a deficiency of iodine. It is prevented by ingestion of iodine, available in seafoods and iodized salt.

15. Anemia is a condition where O_2 is insufficiently carried to tissues. Some forms of anemia are the result of iron deficiency. They are prevented by increasing iron intake.

16. Calcium and phosphorus are the components of the inorganic structure (calcium phosphate) of bones and teeth. Young children require these elements (in the forms of Ca^{+2} and PO_4^{3-}) for proper development of these structures.

17. Hypertension is high blood pressure.

18. A diuretic is a compound which induces fluid loss through urination.

19. Tooth decay is caused by the formation of mucin on the surface of teeth which can form plaque. The metabolic reactions that subsequently occur in the plaque cause the pH on the surface of teeth to decrease which then allows the phosphate in the structure of the tooth to dissolve.

20. Bulimia is a condition where an individual attempts to lose weight by inducing vomiting. The HCl of stomach acid may react with teeth to dissolve phosphate from the structure of the tooth.

21. Chromic acidosis (long-term, acidic blood) results in less PO_4^{3-} being incorporated into bone structure, thus causing poor bone formation.

22. The salivary glands bathe the teeth in a calcium and phosphate-rich solution which discourages the calcium and phosphate in teeth from dissolving. Loss of function of the salivary glands results in mouth fluids which are low in Ca^{2+} and PO_4^{3-}. This shifts the equilibrium of the calcium phosphate in teeth towards dissolution and teeth erode.

PROBLEMS

STRONG ELECTROLYTES, WEAK ELECTROLYTES, AND NONELECTROLYTES

23. Strong: a,b,d,e; Weak: c

24. Strong: b,c; Weak: e; Nonelectrolyte: a,c

ACTIVITY SERIES

25. a. $Ca + 2HCl \longrightarrow H_2 + CaCl_2$
     b. $Ni + 2HCl \longrightarrow H_2 + NiCl_2$
     c. $Mg + 2HNO_3 \longrightarrow H_2 + Mg(NO_3)_2$

26. a. $Zn + H_2SO_4 \longrightarrow H_2 + ZnSO_4$
     b. $2Al + 3H_2SO_4 \longrightarrow 3H_2 + Al_2(SO_4)_3$
     c. $Pb + 2HNO_3 \longrightarrow H_2 + Pb(NO_3)_2$

27. a. $2Na + 2H_2O \longrightarrow H_2 + 2NaOH$
     b. $Ba + 2H_2O \longrightarrow H_2 + Ba(OH)_2$

28. a. $Ca + 2H_2O \longrightarrow H_2 + Ca(OH)_2$
     b. $2K + 2H_2O \longrightarrow H_2 + 2KOH$

29. a. $Mg + Cu^{2+} \longrightarrow Mg^{2+} + Cu$
     b. $Ag + Pb^{2+} \longrightarrow$ no reaction
     c. $Fe + Zn^{2+} \longrightarrow$ no reaction
     d. $2Al + 3Ni^{2+} \longrightarrow 2Al^{3+} + 3Ni$

30. a. $Cr + Na^+ \longrightarrow$ no reaction
     b. $Au + Ag^+ \longrightarrow$ no reaction
     c. $Sn + K^+ \longrightarrow$ no reaction
     d. $3Ca + 2Al^{3+} \longrightarrow 3Ca^{2+} + 2Al$

SOLUBILITY PRODUCT AND PRECIPITATION CRITERIA

31. $[Mg^{2+}] = .001M$, $[CO_3^{-2}] = .001M$
    $(.001M)(.001M) = 1 \times 10^{-6}$

Since 1×10^{-6} is greater than 2.0×10^{-8} (the solubility constant of $MgCO_3$), precipitation will occur.

32. $[Ag^+] = 0.001M$, $[Cl^-] = .0001M$
    $(.001M)(.0001M) = 1 \times 10^{-7}$

Since 1×10^{-7} is greater than 1.2×10^{-12} (the solubility constant of $AgCl$), precipitation will occur.

33. $[Pb^{2+}] = 1 \times 10^{-6} M$, $[CrO_4^{-2}] = 1 \times 10^{-5} M$
    $(1 \times 10^{-6} M)(1 \times 10^{-5} M) = 1 \times 10^{-11}$

Since 1×10^{-11} is greater than 2.0×10^{-14} (the solubility constant of $PbCrO_4$), precipitation will occur.

34. $NaC_2H_3O_2 + AgNO_3 \longrightarrow AgC_2H_3O_{2(s)} + NaNO_3$

$AgC_2H_3O_{2(s)} + HNO_3 \longrightarrow C_2H_3O_2H + AgNO_3$

ADDITIONAL PROBLEMS

35. a. K and Br_2; b. Li and Cl_2; c. Al and O_2

36. $CaCO_3 + 2HCl \longrightarrow H_2CO_3 + CaCl_2$

    $(H_2CO_3 \longrightarrow H_2O + CO_2)$

37. a. base: $Ca(OH)_2 \longrightarrow Ca^{2+} + 2OH^-$
     b. acid: $HBr + H_2O \longrightarrow H_3O^+ + Br^-$
     c. salt: $Sr(NO_3)_2 \longrightarrow Sr^{2+} + 2NO_3^-$

38. $Ba(OH)_2 + H_2SO_4 \longrightarrow BaSO_{4(s)} + 2H_2O$

    The products of the reaction, insoluble $BaSO_4$ and water, are both nonelectrolytes.

39. $Ksp = [Pb^{2+}][SO_4^{2-}]$
    $1.1 \times 10^{-8} = [Pb^{2+}][.014M]$
    $[Pb^{2+}] = 7.9 \times 10^{-7}$ M would stay in solution

40. $7t = 14,000$ lbs $= 6364$ Kg $= 6.364 \times 10^6$ g $= 66989$ moles PO_4^{3-}

    This requires 33494 moles $Fe_2(SO_4)_3$, which $= 1.34 \times 10^7$ g $=$ 13400 kg $= 29,480$ lbs $= 15t$

41. $[F^-] = \dfrac{1 g}{10^3 L} \times \dfrac{mol}{19 g} = 5.26 \times 10^{-5}$ M

    $[Ca^{2+}][F^-] = (2 \times 10^{-4})(5.26 \times 10^{-5})^2 = 5.5 \times 10^{-13}$

    This is less than the K_{sp} and, therefore, CaF_2 will not precipitate.

REVIEW QUESTIONS

1. a. Inorganic chemistry: The chemistry of all elements excluding carbon.
    b. Noble gas: Relatively unreactive gases that occupy the column at the far right side of the periodic table.
    c. Halogen: An element in Group 7A of the periodic table.
    d. Alkali metal: An element in Group 1A of the periodic table.
    e. Alkaline Earth metal: An element in Group 2A of the periodic table.
    f. Transition element: Metallic elements situated in the center portion of the periodic table in the B groups.

2. They are unreactive. They contain a filled outermost shell which neither wants to gain nor lose electrons.

3. Helium is unreactive while hydrogen is combustible.

4. Argon decreases the tendency of the tungsten filament to vaporize. This increases bulb filament lifetime.

5. When electrical current is passed through a neon atmosphere, the neon atoms emit a light.

6. They are soft metals with low melting points and they are easily oxidized by oxygen in the atmosphere. They all have a single electron in their outermost shell which they give up readily.

7. As metals, they are all relatively soft and reactive. They all have two electrons in their outer shell; they give up these electrons readily.

8. Be; it does not react with water and it exists in metal form without the rapid oxidation observed of the other alkaline earth metals.

9. One use given below; there may be others.
    a. Chlorine: Used to kill bacteria.
    b. Iodine: An antiseptic.
    c. NaF: A source of fluoride ion for toothpaste and fluoridation of drinking water.
    d. AgBr: Used in photographic film.
    e. NaOCl: Ingredient in household bleaches.
    f. KCl: A nutrient supplying both K^+ and Cl^- needed for life.

10. NaF inhibits the growth of bacteria on the surface of teeth which prevents plaque buildup (see previous chapter) and enamel erosion.

11. Basic oxides are oxides of metals. They react with water to liberate OH^- ions.

$$CaO + H_2O \longrightarrow Ca^{2+} + 2OH^-$$

12. Acidic oxides are oxides of nonmetals. They react with water to liberate H_3O^+ ions.

$$SO_3 + H_2O \longrightarrow H_2SO_4 + 2H_2O \longrightarrow 2H_3O^+ + SO_4^{2-}$$

13. Li

14. Al

15. Industrial smog is a pollution made up of smoke, fog, soot, sulfur oxides, and H_2SO_4. It is formed by foggy conditions and the burning of sulfur-containing coal (see previous question). The latter leads to the smoke, soot, and sulfur oxides.

16. The sunshine in L.A. leads to the photochemical reactions necessary for nitric oxide formation in photochemical smog while high coal burning and wet conditions favor industrial smog.

17. The greenhouse effect is a phenomenon in which carbon dioxide and other gases lead to a situation where the heat radiating from the Earth is trapped in the atmosphere.

18. The vital force theory postulated that some special forces were contained by life forms in order to make biological compounds. F. Wohler demonstrated that urea, a biological compound, could be synthesized in the laboratory.

19. It is formed by elements within the Earth.

20. Some of them are reactive (namely krypton and xenon).

21. Halogens are Group 7A elements. They received their group title from Greek words meaning "salt formers." (They form salts readily with reactive metals.)

22. Nitrogen fixation is the transformation of N_2 in the atmosphere to a more readily useable form for plants and bacteria.

23. Low oxygen (O_2) availability.

24. Carbon monoxide binds tightly to hemoglobin preventing it from carrying O_2 to tissues.

25. Na^+ and K^+

26. Chlorophyll

27. As a component in bones, for muscle contraction (including heart action), and for clotting of blood.

28. Water with relatively high levels of Ca^{2+}, Mg^{2+}, or Fe^{2+}. These ions bind soap molecules and precipitate them forming what we know as soap scum. This prevents the soap molecules from performing their cleansing action.

29. They conduct electricity, they have a characteristic luster, they are malleable.

30. Fe (functioning of hemoglobin and cytochromes), Co (a component of Vitamin B_{12}), Cu (a component of cytochromes), Zn (a component of several enzymes). Others: Mn, V, Cr, Mo

31. It is considerably lighter and corrodes less rapidly than iron.

32. Photochemical smog is a type of air pollution caused by the reaction of sunlight on nitrogen oxides. Nitrogen dioxide (NO_2).

33. Synergism means that the product or effect is greater than the sum of the two (or more) ingredients.

34. Allotropes are different forms of the same element in the same state. Carbon (graphite and diamond) and oxygen (dioxygen and ozone).

PROBLEMS

LEWIS SYMBOLS

35. a. Ne or $:\overset{..}{\underset{..}{Ne}}:$;　b. $:\overset{..}{O}\cdot$;　c. $:\overset{..}{F}\cdot$

36. a. $K\cdot$;　b. $\cdot Ba\cdot$;　c. $:\overset{\cdot}{\underset{\cdot}{N}}\cdot$

37. a. $:\overset{..}{\underset{..}{F}}:^{-}$　b. $:\overset{..}{\underset{..}{I}}:^{-}$　c. $:\overset{..}{\underset{..}{O}}:^{2-}$

38. a. $:\overset{..}{\underset{..}{S}}:^{2-}$　b. K^{+}　c. Sr^{2+}

CHEMICAL EQUATIONS

39. a. $4Li + O_2 \longrightarrow 2Li_2O$
    d. $CaO + H_2O \longrightarrow Ca(OH)_2$
    c. $S + O_2 \longrightarrow SO_2$

40. b. $2Ca + O_2 \longrightarrow 2CaO$
    e. $SO_2 + H_2O \longrightarrow H_2SO_3$
    f. $Ca + S \longrightarrow CaS$

ADDITIONAL PROBLEMS

41. $\cdot\overset{\cdot}{\underset{\cdot}{Ga}}$, Ga^{3+}

42. Oxygen atoms – very reactive, wants to lose two electrons. Oxygen molecules = O_2, two oxygen atoms linked by a double covalent bond, react with metals to form oxide ions. Ozone = O_3; three oxygen atoms linked by covalent bonds; very unstable, breaks down into O_2.

43. The sulfur in coal burns to form SO_2 which can further oxidize to SO_3. Sulfur trioxide can react with moisture in air to form H_2SO_4, an acid.
    $$2 SO_2 + O_2 \longrightarrow 2 SO_3$$
    $$2 SO_3 + H_2O \longrightarrow H_2SO_4$$

44. $$N_2 + O_2 \longrightarrow 2NO$$
    $$2NO + O_2 \longrightarrow 2 NO_2$$
    $$3NO_2 + H_2O \longrightarrow 2HNO_3 + NO$$

45. Ozone in the stratosphere reacts with ultraviolet light, preventing a large portion of it from reaching the earth's surface. This protects us from the harmful effects of ultraviolet light, i.e. a higher rate of mutation in cells including, in humans, a greater incidence of skin cancer. Ozone in the troposphere can cause many different types of problems; two important ones are the respiratory problems in animals and the growth retardation in plants.

46. a. $N_2 + O_2 \longrightarrow 2\,NO$

   b. $NO_2 + \text{sunlight} \longrightarrow NO + O$

● **REVIEW QUESTIONS**

1. Lower melting points, flammable, nonconducting (See Table 13.1 for other differences.)

2.   a. Hydrocarbon: An organic compound that contains only carbon and hydrogen.
    b. Alkane: A hydrocarbon containing no double or triple bonds.
    c. Paraffin: An alkane, a saturated hydrocarbon.
    d. Saturated hydrocarbon: A hydrocarbon with only single bonds.
    e. Unsaturated hydrocarbon: A hydrocarbon with double or triple bonds.
    f. Substituent: A group that can substitute for a hydrogen in a hydrocarbon.
    g. Alkene: A hydrocarbon containing one or more double bonds.
    h. Alkyne: A hydrocarbon containing one or more triple bonds.
    i. Alkyl group: A saturated hydrocarbon group that is attached to a second organic compound.
    j. Isomers: Compounds that have the same molecular formula but different structural formulas and properties.
    k. Polymer: A molecule, with a large molecular mass, which is made up of repeating smaller units.
    l. Aromatic compound: Any organic compound that contains a benzene ring.
    m. Aliphatic compound: A nonaromatic hydrocarbon.
    n. Phenyl group: A benzene ring as a substituent.
    o. Alkyl halides: Alkanes which contain one or more halogen atoms.
    p. Chlorofluorocarbons: A carbon compound that contains chlorine and fluorine.
    q. Homologous Series: A series of organic compounds which varies in an orderly progression, usually by addition of -CH_2- groups.
    r. Carcinogen: A chemical which causes a cancerous growth of cells in an organism.

3. a. 2; b. 7; c. 4; d. 9

4. ethane, methane

5.   a. alkyl group: CH_3CH_2–   alkane: CH_3CH_3

    b. alkyl anion: CH_3–   aryl group:

    c. common name: isopentane   IUPAC name: 2-methylbutane

    d. propyl group $CH_3CH_2CH_2$-   isopropyl group CH_3-$\overset{\displaystyle CH_3}{\underset{\displaystyle H}{\mid}}$C-

    e. straight chain: $CH_3CH_2CH_2CH_3$ branched chain: $CH_3\overset{\displaystyle CH_3}{\overset{\mid}{C}}HCH_3$

6.   a. Natural gas is composed of 80 % methane, 10 % ethane, and 10 % mixture of higher alkanes; it has a density of 0.65 g/L. Bottled gas is composed chiefly of propane; it has a density of 1.6 g/L.
    b. Physical properties can be described without reference to any other specific chemical substance: density, melting point, boiling point, etc. Chemical properties describe the reactions of a substance with other chemicals, e.g., halogenation, hydrogenation, oxidation.
    c. Exothermic reaction is one in which heat is liberated. Endothermic reaction is one in which heat is used up.

7. Saturated: c,d; unsaturated: a,b

8. a. C_6H_{10}; b. C_7H_{12}; c. C_4H_8; d. C_7H_8

9. aromatic: a,d; aliphatic: b,c

10. a. para; b. ortho; c. meta

11. In the lungs, alkanes dissolve fatlike molecules causing the alveoli to secrete fluids. This creates a situation similar to viral or bacterial pneumonia.

12. The lighter chain alkanes dissolve body oils while the heavier chain alkanes (like mineral oils) act as skin softeners.

13. They are carcinogenic.

14. Benzene is a proven carcinogen and can cause nausea, respiratory or heart failure, and aplastic anemia.

15. They are both anesthetics.

16. plastic bags, bottles, toys, electrical insulation

17. Addition polymerization is a polmerization reaction where the monomers add to one another in a fashion so that the final polymer contains all the monomers. An example is polyethylene formation.

18. Quite often they contain a double bond.

PROBLEMS

ORGANIC VERSUS INORGANIC

19. Organic: a, c; Inorganic: b

20. Organic: a; Inorganic: b, c

21. a. NaOH; b. KCl

22. a. $C_{40}H_{82}$; b. LiH

ISOMERS

23. a. same; b. same; c. isomers

24. a. isomers; b. same

25. a. isomers; b. same; c. isomers

26. a. same; b. same

ALKANES: STRUCTURES AND NAMES

27. a. $CH_3CH_2CH_2CH_2CH_2CH_2CH_3$

b. $CH_3CH_2\overset{\displaystyle |}{\underset{\displaystyle CH_3}{C}}HCH_2CH_3$

c. $CH_3\overset{\displaystyle CH_3}{\underset{\displaystyle CH_3}{\overset{\displaystyle |}{\underset{\displaystyle |}{C}}}}CH_2CH_2\overset{\displaystyle |}{\underset{\displaystyle CH_3}{C}}HCH_3$

d. $CH_3CH_2\overset{\displaystyle CH_3}{\overset{\displaystyle |}{C}}H\overset{\displaystyle |}{\underset{\displaystyle CH_2CH_3}{C}}HCH_2CH_2CH_2CH_3$

28.

a. $CH_3\overset{\displaystyle |}{\underset{\displaystyle CH_3}{C}}HCH_2CH_2CH_3$

b. $CH_3\overset{\displaystyle |}{\underset{\displaystyle CH_3}{C}}HCH_2\overset{\displaystyle |}{\underset{\displaystyle CH_2CH_3}{C}}HCH_2CH_3$

c. $CH_3\overset{\displaystyle CH_3}{\underset{\displaystyle CH_3}{\overset{\displaystyle |}{\underset{\displaystyle |}{C}}}} - \overset{\displaystyle CH_3}{\underset{\displaystyle CH_3}{\overset{\displaystyle |}{\underset{\displaystyle |}{C}}}}CH_3$

d. $CH_3CH_2\overset{\displaystyle CH_2CH_3}{\overset{\displaystyle |}{C}}H\overset{\displaystyle |}{\underset{\displaystyle \underset{\displaystyle CH_3}{\overset{\displaystyle |}{CH\text{-}CH_3}}}{C}}HCH_2CH_2CH_2CH_3$

29. a. 3-methylpentane; b. 2,3-dimethylbutane

30. a. 3-methylpentane; b. 2,2,4,4-tetramethylhexane

31. a. CH_3CH_2-; b. $CH_3\overset{\displaystyle |}{\underset{\displaystyle CH_3}{C}}H-$

32. a. CH_3- ;   b. $CH_3\ CH_2\ CH_2-$

33.

```
  H H H H         H  H  H
  | | | |         |  |  |
H-C-C-C-C-H     H-C–C–C-H
  | | | |         |  |  |
  H H H H         H  |  H
                  H-C-H
                     |
                     H
 Butane        isobutane or
               methylpropane
```

365

34. CH$_3$CH$_2$CH$_2$CH$_2$CH$_2$CH$_3$ CH$_3$CHCH$_2$CH$_2$CH$_3$ CH$_3$CH$_2$CHCH$_2$CH$_3$

       hexane   CH$_3$ CH$_3$

                             2-methylpentane   3-methylpentane

                                    CH$_3$

       CH$_3$CH– CHCH$_3$ CH$_3$CCH$_2$CH$_3$

            CH$_3$ CH$_3$ CH$_3$

        2,3-dimethylbutane   2,2-dimethylbutane

CYCLIC HYDROCARBONS

35. a. methylcyclopropane; b. 1,2-diethyl-4-methylcyclopentane; c. cyclobutene; d. 3-ethylcyclohexene

36. a. cycloheptane; b. cyclohexene; c. 1,2-dichlorocyclohexane; d. 1-bromo-2-methylcyclopentene;
     e. methylcyclopentane

37. a. 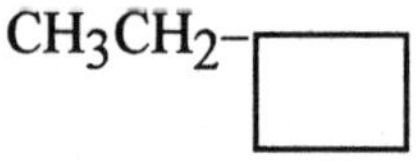 CH$_3$CH$_2$–▢   b. 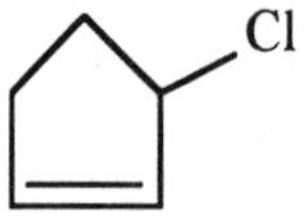 Cl

38. a. 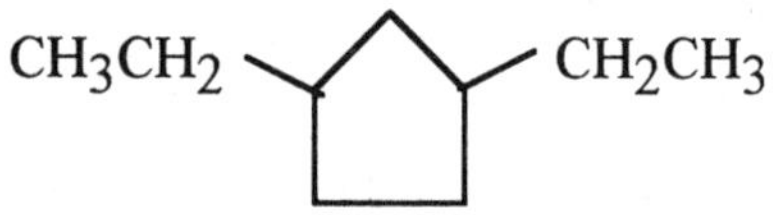
    CH$_3$CH$_2$ ⌅ CH$_2$CH$_3$ b. 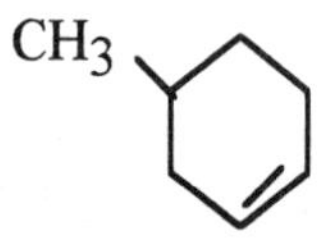   CH$_3$ ⬡

HALOGENATED HYDROCARBONS

39. a. CH$_3$Cl;   b. CHCl$_3$

40. a. CH$_3$CH$_2$Br;   b. CCl$_4$

41. CH$_3$CHCH$_3$ BrCH$_2$CH$_2$CH$_3$

      Br

   isopropyl bromide   propyl bromide

    2-bromopropane   1-bromopropane

42.
                                                 Br

   BrCH$_2$CH$_2$CH$_2$CH$_3$ CH$_3$CHCH$_2$CH$_3$ CH$_3$CCH$_3$ CH$_3$-CH-CH$_2$Br

                         Br   CH$_3$ CH$_3$

    1-bromobutane   2-bromobutane   2-bromomethylpropane   1-bromomethylpropane

ALKENES AND ALKYNES

43. a. $HC \equiv CH$;   b.   c. $HC \equiv CHCHCH_2CH_2CH_3$ with $CH-CH_3$ and CH_3 branches   d. $CH_3C = CCH_3$ with CH_3 CH_3 branches

44. a. CH_3—[square]—CH_3 b. $CH_3CH=CCH_2CH_3$ with CH_2CH_3 branch   c.   d. $CH_3CH=CHCHCH_2CH_3$ with CH_3 branch

45. a. $CH_3C=CH_2CH_2CH_3$ with CH_3 branch   b. $CH_2=CHCH_2CH_2CHCH_3$ with CH_3 branch

46. a. $CH_2=CCH_2CH_3$ with $CH_2 CH_3$ branch   b. $CH_3C=CHCHCH_2CCH_3$ with CH_3, CH_3 and CH_3, CH_3 branches

47. a. 2-methyl-1-pentene; b. 2-methyl-2-pentene; c. 2,5-dimethyl-2-hexene

48. a. 2-methyl-2-butene; b. 1,1,6-trichloro-3-heptene; c. 2,2,4-trimethyl-3-hexene

AROMATIC COMPOUNDS

49. . a. CH_3 [benzene ring]   b. CH_2CH_3 [benzene ring]—CH_2CH_3 c. CH_3 [benzene ring with] NO_2 NO_2

50. a. Cl [benzene ring] Cl b.   f. CH_3 [benzene ring]—CH_3, CH_3

51. a. ethylbenzene; b. isopropylbenzene; c. 2-nitrotoluene; d. 3,5-dichlorotoluene

52. a. propylbenzene; b. 2,4-dichloro-1-ethylbenzene; c. 1,3,5-trinitrobenzene; d. 3-nitrotoluene

PHYSICAL PROPERTIES

53. a. pentane; b. $CH_3(CH_2)_4CH_3$; c. cyclohexane; d. $CH_3(CH_2)_7CH_3$

54. a. pentane; b. pentane; c. cyclohexane; d. $CH_3(CH_2)_7CH_3$

CHEMICAL REACTIONS

55. a. $(CH_3)_2CBrCH_2Br$; b. $CH_3CH(CH_3)CH_2CH_3$; c.

56. a. $CH_3CH_2CH_2CH_3$; b. $(CH_3)_2C(OH)CH(CH_3)_2$; c.

57. a. H_2, Ni; b. H_2O, H^+

58. a. H_2O, H^+; b. Cl_2

59. a.   b.

60. a. $CH_2=CH_2$; b. $CH_2=CHCH_3$;

ADDITIONAL PROBLEMS

61.
$X = CH_3\overset{\underset{\displaystyle CH_3}{|}}{C}=CHCH_3$ $Y = CH_3\overset{\underset{\displaystyle CH_3}{|}}{C}HCH=CH_2$ $Z = CH_2=\overset{\underset{\displaystyle CH_3}{|}}{C}CH_2CH_3$

62. Add a few drops of a dilute potassium permanganate solution to each sample. Pentane does not react, the purple color remains. 1-Pentane reacts with $KMnO_4$ and we observe a color change from purple to brown. A second test is to add a few drops of bromine to each sample. With pentane there is no reaction, and the red-brown color of the bromine remains. Pentene reacts with the bromine, and the color disappears.

63.   a. Should be 2,2-dimethylpropane (identify each group with a number).
 b. Should be 2,2,3-trimethylbutane (lowest numbers)
 c. Should be 3,5-dimethylheptane (use longest chain)
 d. Should be 3,4,5-trimethyloctane (use longest chain)

64. a. Should be 6-methyl-3-heptene (use lowest number for double bond).
     b. Should be 5-methyl-3-heptene (use longest chain)
     c. Should be 4,4-dimethyl-2-pentene (use lowest number for double bond); should be pentene
     d. Should be 3-bromocyclobutene 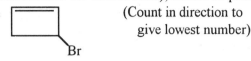 (Count in direction to give lowest number)

65. Organic

66. a. $CH_4 + 2 O_2 \longrightarrow CO_2 + 2 H_2O$

    b. $2 C_8H_{18} + 25 O_2 \longrightarrow 16 CO_2 + 18 H_2O$

67. $2 C_6H_6 + 15 O_2 \longrightarrow 12 CO_2 + 6 H_2O$

    39g benzene = 0.5 moles benzene; this will produce 6 times as many moles of CO_2 = 3.0 moles = 132g CO_2

68. $2 C_8H_{18} + 25 O_2 \longrightarrow 16 CO_2 + 18 H_2O$
    1 gal = 4 qt = 3.8L
    mass of 3.78L of gasoline = (0.69)(3780) = 2608g
    2608 g of octane = 26008/114 moles of octane = 22.3 moles of octane
    22.3 moles of octane will yield 178 moles of CO_2 and 201 moles of H_2O
    mass of CO_2 produced = (178)(44) = 7830 g
    mass of H_2O produced = (201)(18) = 3620 g

REVIEW QUESTIONS

1. Hydrocarbons make up the bulk of petroleum. These include compounds in the groups of natural gas, gasoline, kerosene, heating oil, lubricating oil, and heavier hydrocarbon residues.

2. Straight run gasoline is the gasoline fraction after refining. It has not yet been adulterated with all the additives oil companies add to gasoline to improve its performance in automobilies.

3. Create branched-chain alkanes by isomerization with H_2SO_4 and $AlCl_3$; perform catalytic reforming to generate some high octane aromatic compounds; add octane boosters like tetraethyllead and methyl *tert*-butyl ether

4. Methane, ethane, and some other small alkanes.

5. Alkanes are converted to aromatic compounds.

6. Plastics, drugs, fertilizers, detergents, dyes

7. Natural gas is the product of microorganism breakdown of plants and marine organisms.

8. It burns relatively cleanly without sulfur emissions typical of other petroleum products.

REVIEW QUESTIONS

1. A functional group is a group of atoms that confers characteristic properties on a family of organic compounds.

2. . a. R=R, double bond; b. R–OH, hydroxyl group; c. R–O–R, alkoxy group

3.   a. Absolute alcohol: 100% alcohol
    b. General anesthetic: Any substance that causes unconsciousness or insensitivity to pain.
    c. Antiseptic: Any substance that kills bacteria and other microorganisms, intended for use on living tissue.
    d. Disinfectant: Substance that kills microorganisms, intended for use on nonliving articles.
    e. 86 Proof: 43% alcohol by volume
    f. LD_{50}: The dose of a toxic substance that is fatal to 50% of the individuals ingesting the drug.
    g. Azeotrope: A constant boiling point mixture of two components (in a fixed composition).
    h. Gasohol: Gasoline to which alcohol (either ethanol or methanol) has been added.

4. Denatured alcohol is ethanol which has been treated with certain additives, making it unfit to drink. Alcohol for consumption is heavily taxed. In order to insure that ethanol for uses other than ingestion is employed only for those purposes (and not for consumption) toxic additives are added.

5. Methanol is rapidly converted to formaldehyde - a toxic compound!

6. Because we transform ethylene glycol (via enzyme reactions) to oxalic acid - a compound that crystallizes with Ca^{2+} in the kidney causing renal damage. Propylene glycol is converted to pyruvic acid - a normal metabolite in our body.

7. Ethanol. It ties up the liver enzymes which convert methanol and ethylene glycol to their toxic compounds (formaldehyde and oxalic acid, respectively).

8. All other alkenes upon hydration would position the added -OH group at a preferred (see Markovnikov's rule) 2° or 3° carbon.

9. It is a rule useful in predicting the isomeric product of a hydration of an alkene. It states that an added H^+ (across a double bond) will prefer to go to the carbon with the most hydrogens.

10. Because if the temperature climbs up to the 180 °C range, you will get ethylene as a product (by a dehydration reaction).

11. That it might be safe for humans to drink methanol.

12. hydroxyl, ether

13. A polyhydric alcohol is an organic compound with more than one -OH group.

14. A glycol is an organic compound with two -OH groups.

15. Diethyl ether is highly flammable and, when mixed with air, is explosive. Caution should be taken to avoid flames and sparks when working with this substance.

16. They have relatively high vapor pressures. Thus, they evaporate readily, and the evaporation removes heat from the skin and serves to lower body temperature.

PROBLEMS

ALCOHOLS: NAMES AND STRUCTURAL FORMULAS

17. a. 1-hexanol; b. 2-hexanol

18. a. 2,2-dimethyl-3-pentanol; b. isobutyl alcohol or 2-methyl-1-propanol

19. a. 4,4-dichloro-2-butanol; b. 3,3-dibromo-2-methyl-2-butanol.

20. a. 1-methylcyclohexanol; b. 3-ethyl-3-hexanol

21. a. $CH_3CH_2CHOHCH_2CH_2CH_3$; b. $CH_3CHOHC(CH_3)_2CH_3$

22. a.  OH

b. $CH_3CHOHCH_2CH(CH_3)CH_2CH_3$

23. a. $CH_3CH_2CHOHCH(CH_3)CH(CH_3)CH_2CH_3$ b. 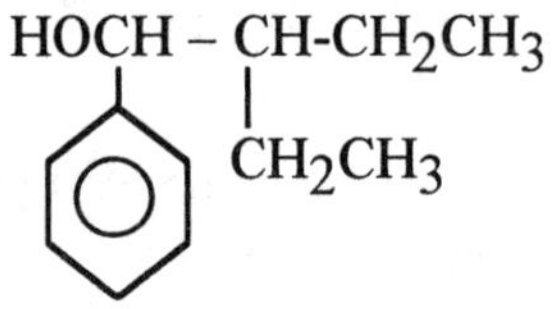 $HOCH - CH-CH_2CH_3$ with CH_2CH_3

c. $CH_3CHOHCH_2OH$

24. a. 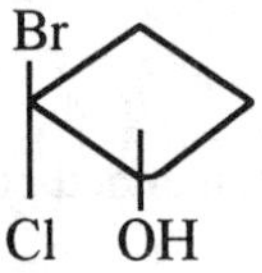 Br   Cl   OH

b. 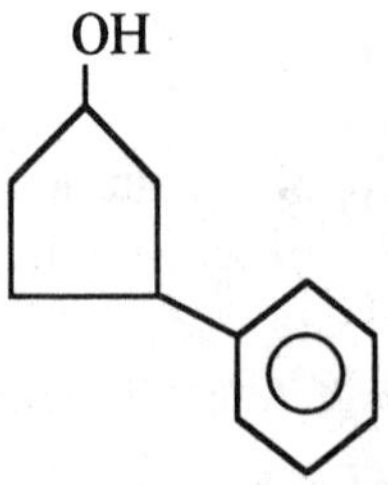 OH

c. $CH_2OHCHOHCH_2OH$

ETHERS: NAMES AND STRUCTURAL FORMULAS

25. a. dipropyl ether; b. diphenyl ether

26. a. ethyl isopropyl ether; b. methyl phenyl ether

27. a. $CH_3CH_2OCH_3$ c. 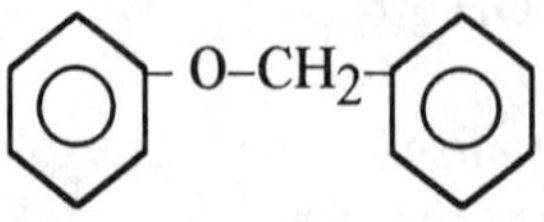 ⬡ $- O-CH_2-$ ⬡

28. a. CH_3CH-O-$CHCH_3$ b. -O-$CH_2CH_2CH_3$

         | |
        CH_3 CH_3

PHENOLS: NAMES AND STRUCTURAL FORMULAS

29. a. 2-nitrophenol; b. 4-bromophenol

30. a. 3-chlorophenol; b. *o*-isopropylphenol

31. a.   b.

32. a.   b.

CHEMICAL REACTIONS

33. a. oxidation; b. dehydration; c. hydration

34. a. oxidation; b. hydration; c. dehydration

35.

$$CH_3CH_2CH_2CH_2OH \rightarrow CH_3CH_2CH_2\overset{\overset{\displaystyle O}{\|}}{C}OH$$

$$CH_3CH_2CHOHCH_3 \rightarrow CH_3CH_2\overset{\overset{\displaystyle O}{\|}}{C}CH_3$$

$$(CH_3)_2CHCH_2OH \rightarrow (CH_3)_2CH\overset{\overset{\displaystyle O}{\|}}{C}OH$$

$$(CH_3)_3COH \quad \rightarrow \quad \text{no reaction}$$

36. a.

$$CH_3CHOHCH_3 \xrightarrow[180\ °C]{conc.\ H_2SO_4} CH_3CH=CH_2 + H_2O$$

b.

$$CH_3CHOHCH_3 + ROH \xrightarrow[140\ °C]{conc.\ H_2SO_4} \underset{\underset{CH_3}{|}}{CH_3CH}\text{-O-R} + H_2O$$

37.

38.

39. a. $CH_3CHOHCH_2CH_3$ b.

40. a. $CH_3\overset{\overset{O}{||}}{C}CH_3$ b.

41. a. H^+, H_2O; b. $K_2Cr_2O_7$, H^+; c. conc. H_2SO_4, 140 °C, excess alcohol

42. a. H^+, H_2O; b. H_2SO_4, 180 °C; c. $K_2Cr_2O_7$, H^+

43. a. $CH_3CH=CH_2$ b.

   c. $\underset{\underset{CH_3}{|}}{CH_3C}=CH_2$

44. a. $CH_2=CH_2$ b.

   c. $CH_2=CHCH_2CH_3$ or $CH_3CH=CHCH_3$

45. a.

$$\text{C}_6\text{H}_5\text{OH} + \text{NaOH} \longrightarrow \text{C}_6\text{H}_5\text{O}^-\text{Na}^+ + \text{H}_2\text{O}$$

b. No reaction.

46.

$$\text{C}_6\text{H}_5\text{OH} + \text{H}_2\text{O} \longrightarrow \text{C}_6\text{H}_5\text{O}^- + \text{H}_3\text{O}^+$$

PHYSICAL PROPERTIES

47. methanol, ethanol, 1-propanol

48. butane, 1-propanol, ethylene glycol

49. methanol, 1-butanol, 1-octanol

50. pentane, diethyl ether, propylene glycol

ADDITIONAL PROBLEMS

51. a. ethanol; b. methanol; c. 2-propanol; d. phenol

52. diethyl ether, 1-butanol, propylene glycol

53. 1-propanol: $HOCH_2CH_2CH_3$
   isobutyl alcohol: $(CH_3)_2CHCH_2OH$
   3-methyl-1-butanol: $HOCH_2CH_2CH(CH_3)_2$
   2-methyl-1-butanol: $HOCH_2CH(CH_3)CH_2CH_3$

54. a. methanol or methyl alcohol: solvent
   b. ethanol or ethyl alcohol: alcoholic beverage
   c. isopropyl alcohol or 2-propanol: rubbing alcohol
   d. ethylene glycol or 1,2-ethanediol: radiator antifreeze
   e. glycerol or 1,2,3-propanetriol: lubricant
   f. phenol: germicide

55.   a. 1-pentanol, $CH_3CH_2CH_2CH_2CH_2OH$

      b. 2-pentanol, $CH_3CH_2CH_2\underset{\underset{OH}{|}}{C}HCH_3$

      c. 3-pentanol, $CH_3CH_2\underset{\underset{OH}{|}}{C}HCH_2CH_3$

      d. 3-methyl-1-butanol, $CH_3\underset{\underset{CH_3}{|}}{C}HCH_2CH_2OH$

      e. 3-methyl-2-butanol, $CH_3\underset{\underset{CH_3}{|}}{C}H\!-\!\underset{\underset{OH}{|}}{C}HCH_3$

      f. 2-methyl-2-butanol, $CH_3CH_2\overset{\overset{OH}{|}}{\underset{\underset{CH_3}{|}}{C}}CH_3$

      g. 2-methyl-1-butanol, $CH_3CH_2\underset{\underset{CH_3}{|}}{C}HCH_2OH$

      h. Dimethylpropanol, $CH_3\overset{\overset{CH_3}{|}}{\underset{\underset{CH_3}{|}}{C}}\!-\!CH_2OH$

56. Primary: a,d,g,h   Secondary: b,c,e   Tertiary: f

57. $CH_3CH_2CH_2CH_2OCH_3$ - butyl methyl ether
     $CH_3CH(CH_3)CH_2OCH_3$ - isobutyl methyl ether
     $CH_3CH_2CH(CH_3)OCH_3$ - sec-butyl methyl ether
     $CH_3C(CH_3)_2OCH_3$ - tert-butyl methyl ether
     $CH_3CH_2CH_2OCH_2CH_3$ - ethyl propyl ether
     $CH_3CH(CH_3)OCH_2CH_3$ - ethyl isopropyl ether

58.   a. Menthol: 2-isopropyl-5-methylcyclohexanol
      b. Thymol: 2-isopropyl-5-methylphenol or
                3-hydroxy-4-isopropyltoluene

59.

        benzyl alcohol   4-methylphenol (p-cresol)

      a. Approximately equally insoluble.
      b. In NaOH, the 4-methylphenol will lose a H^+ making it charged and much more soluble.

60. $CH_2 = CH_2 + H_2O \longrightarrow CH_3CH_2OH$

$$\frac{14\ kg}{1} \ \times \ \frac{1000\ g}{1\ kg} \ \times \ \frac{1\ mol}{28g\ CH_2 = CH_2} \ \times \ \frac{1\ mol\ CH_3CH_2OH}{1\ mol\ CH_2 = CH_2} \ \times \ \frac{46\ g\ CH_3CH_2OH}{1\ mol} \ \times \ \frac{1\ kg}{1000\ g} \ = 23\ kg$$

61. a. 70 Cal – [(0.2g x 4 Cal/g) + (5.77g x 4 Cal/g)] = 46 Cal due to alcohol; = 65.7%
    b. 46 Cal ÷ 7 Cal/g = 6.6 g
    c. 6.6 g ÷ 0.789 g/mL = 8.4 mL. This equals 8.4 % by volume.

REVIEW QUESTIONS

1. Benzaldehyde, cinnamaldehyde, biacetyl (see Figure 16.1 for others).

2. The aldehydes that are formed by the oxidation of primary alcohols are themselves easily oxidized further to carboxylic acids and therefore some aldehyde is lost through this process. Ketones formed from the oxidation of secondary alcohols cannot be further oxidized.

3. aldehyde, alcohol, ether

4. alkene, alcohol, ketone

PROBLEMS

NAMES AND STRUCTURAL FORMULAS

5. a. benzaldehyde ; b. 3-hydroxypropanal; c. 4,4-dimethylpentanal; d. 2-chlorobenzaldehyde

6. a. butanal; b. 2,2,3-trichlorobutanal; c. 2-ethylbutanal; d. 2,2-dimethyl-3-phenylpropanal

7. a. 5-methyl-3-hexanone; b. cyclopentanone; c. 2-pentanone; d. 4-bromo-2,2-dimethyl-3-pentanone

8. a. 1,1-dichloro-3-methyl-2-butanone; b. 3-methyl-2-pentanone; c. 1-methyl-1-phenyl-2-propanone; d. 2-iodo-4-methylcyclohexanone

9. a. $CH_3CH_2CH_2\overset{\overset{\text{O}}{\|}}{C}H$ b. $CH_3CH_2CH_2CH_2CH(CH_3)CH_2\overset{\overset{\text{O}}{\|}}{C}H$ c.

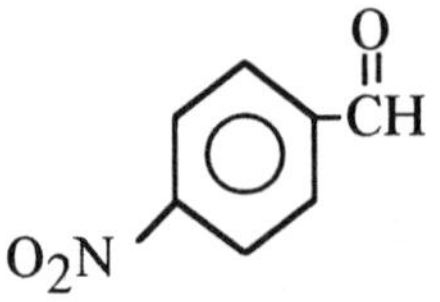

10. a. $CH_3CH_2CH_2CH_2CH(C_2H_5)CH_2CH_2\overset{\overset{\text{O}}{\|}}{C}H$ b. $CH_3\underset{\underset{\text{Cl}}{|}}{C}H\text{-}\overset{\overset{\text{O}}{\|}}{C}H$

c. $CH_3CH(CH_3)CH_2CH_2CH(CH_3)\overset{\overset{\text{O}}{\|}}{C}H$

11. a. $CH_3\overset{\overset{\text{O}}{\|}}{C}CH_2CH_2CH_2CH_3$ b. $CH_3\overset{\overset{\text{O}}{\|}}{C}CHBrCH_2CH_2CH_2CH_3$ c.

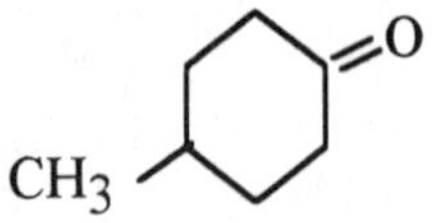

12. a. 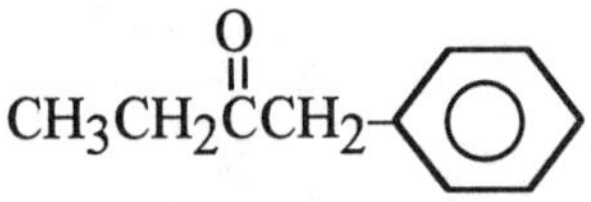 $CH_3CH_2\overset{\overset{\text{O}}{\|}}{C}CH_2\text{-}$

b. $CH_3\underset{\underset{\text{CH}_3}{|}}{\overset{\overset{\text{I}}{|}}{C}}CH_2\overset{\overset{\text{O}}{\|}}{C}CH_2CH_2CH_2CH_3$

c. $CH_3\underset{\underset{\text{OH}}{|}}{C}H\overset{\overset{\text{O}}{\|}}{C}CH_2CH_3$

PHYSICAL PROPERTIES

13. 2-propanol

14. 1-butanol

15. acetaldehyde

16. acetone

PREPARATION OF ALDEHYDES AND KETONES

17.

a.

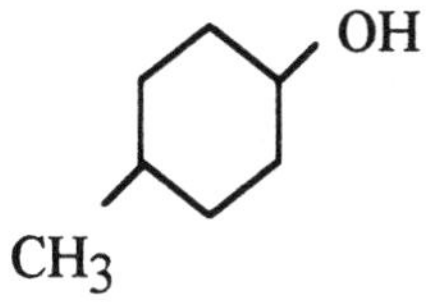

b. $(CH_3)_3CCH_2OH$ c. $HOCH_2CH_2CHBrCH_2CH_3$

18. a. $CH_3CHOHCH_2CH_2CH_3$;   b.

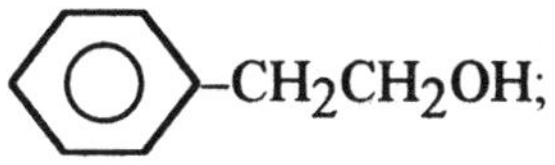

$-CH_2CH_2OH$;   c.

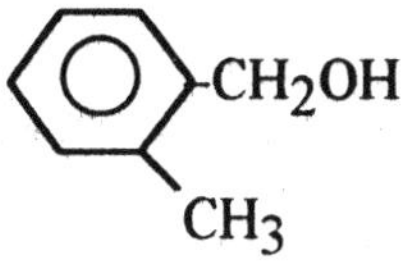

$-CH_2OH$

CHEMICAL REACTIONS

19. a. $CH_3\overset{O}{\overset{\|}{C}}H + CH_3OH \longrightarrow CH_3\overset{OH}{\underset{H}{\overset{|}{C}}}-O-CH_3$

b. $CH_3\overset{O}{\overset{\|}{C}}H + 2CH_3OH \xrightarrow{H^+} CH_3-\overset{O-CH_3}{\underset{H}{\overset{|}{C}}}-O-CH_3$

c. $CH_3\overset{O}{\overset{\|}{C}}H + HOCH_2CH_2OH \xrightarrow{H^+} CH_3\overset{O-CH_2}{\underset{H}{\overset{|}{C}}}-O-CH_2$

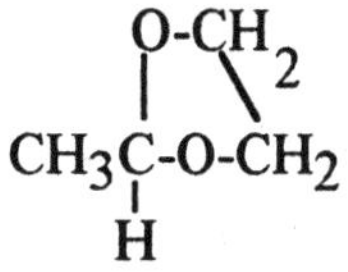

20. a. $CH_3\overset{O}{\overset{\|}{C}}H + 2Cu^{2+} \xrightarrow{OH^-} CH_3\overset{O}{\overset{\|}{C}}-O^- + Cu_2O + 3H_2O$

b. $CH_3\overset{O}{\overset{\|}{C}}H \xrightarrow{K_2Cr_2O_7, H^+} CH_3\overset{O}{\overset{\|}{C}}OH$

c. $CH_3\overset{O}{\overset{\|}{C}}H + H_2 \xrightarrow{Ni} CH_3CH_2OH$

21. a.

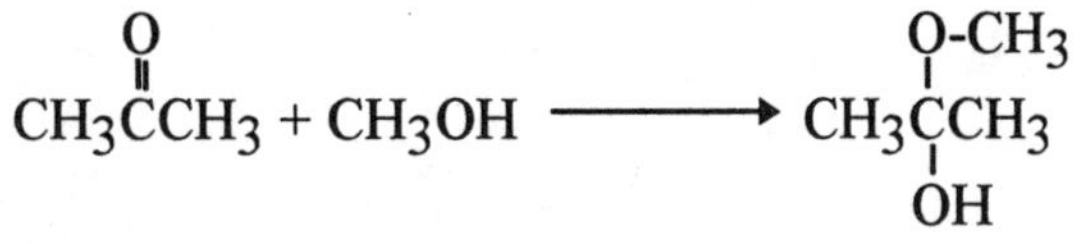

$$CH_3\overset{O}{\overset{\|}{C}}CH_3 + CH_3OH \longrightarrow CH_3\overset{O-CH_3}{\underset{OH}{\overset{|}{C}}}CH_3$$

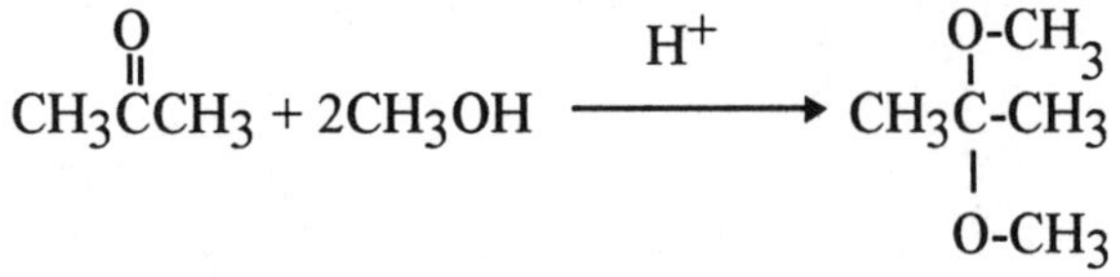

b.

$$CH_3\overset{O}{\overset{\|}{C}}CH_3 + 2CH_3OH \xrightarrow{H^+} CH_3\overset{O-CH_3}{\underset{O-CH_3}{\overset{|}{C}}}CH_3$$

c.

$$CH_3\overset{O}{\overset{\|}{C}}CH_3 + HOCH_2CH_2OH \longrightarrow$$

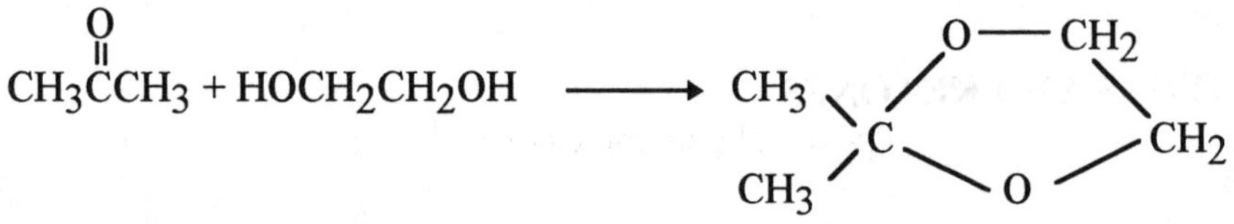

22. a. no reaction

   b. no reaction

   c.

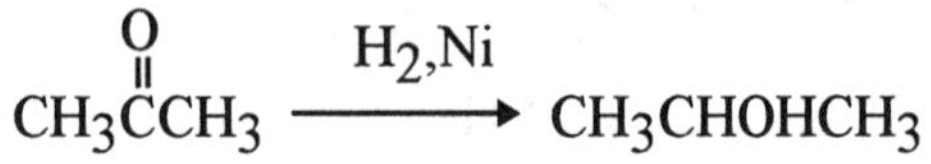

$$CH_3\overset{O}{\overset{\|}{C}}CH_3 \xrightarrow{H_2,Ni} CH_3CHOHCH_3$$

23. a. Yes; only pentanal would test positive.
    b. No.
    c. Yes, only pentanal would test positive.
    d. Yes, only pentanal would test positive.
    e. No

24. a. No
    b. Yes, 2-pentanol would test positive.
    c. Yes, pentanal would test positive.
    d. Yes, pentanal would test positive.
    e. No

25. Phenylhydrazine gives an orange precipitate with 2-pentanone.

26. Tollens' reagent. Pentanal would test positive (resulting in a silver mirror formation) while 2-pentanone would not react.

27. a. Ag^+, NH_3; b. CrO_3, HCl, pyridine, CH_2Cl_2; c. $2CH_3OH$, H^+

28. a. $K_2Cr_2O_7$, $4H_2SO_4$; b. H_2O; c. H_2, Ni

HYDRATES, HEMIACETALS, AND ACETALS

29. a,d

30. b,f

31. c,e

32.

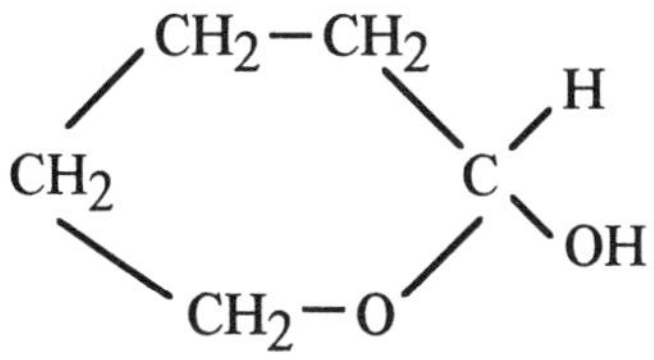

$$CH_2-CH_2$$
$$CH_2 \qquad C-H$$
$$CH_2-O \qquad OH$$

ADDITIONAL PROBLEMS

33.
$$\overset{O}{\overset{\|}{CH_3CH_2CH_2CH_2CH}}$$

pentanal (valeraldehyde)

$$\overset{O}{\overset{\|}{(CH_3)_2CHCH_2CH}}$$

3-methylbutanal
(β-methylbutyraldehyde)

$$\overset{O}{\overset{\|}{CH_3CH_2CH(CH_3)CH}}$$

2-methylbutanal
(α- methylbutyraldehyde)

$$\overset{O}{\overset{\|}{(CH_3)_3CCH}}$$

dimethylpropanal
(dimethylpropionaldehyde)

34.
$$\overset{O}{\overset{\|}{CH_3CCH_2CH_2CH_3}}$$

2-pentanone (methyl propyl ketone)

$$\overset{O}{\overset{\|}{CH_3CH_2CCH_2CH_3}}$$

3-pentanone (diethyl ketone)

$$\overset{O}{\overset{\|}{CH_3CCH(CH_3)_2}}$$

methyl butanone (methyl isopropyl ketone)

35.
$$\overset{O}{\overset{\|}{HOCH_2CHCH}} \text{ and } \overset{O}{\overset{\|}{HOCH_2CCH_2OH}}$$
$$\underset{OH}{|}$$

36.
$$\overset{O}{\overset{\|}{HCCH_2CH_2CH_2CH}}\overset{O}{\overset{\|}{}}$$

37.
$$\overset{OH}{\underset{|}{CCl_3CH-OCH_3}}$$

38. a. Cu^{2+}; b. Cu^{2+}, c. Ag^+

39. Benzaldehyde, cinnamaldehyde, vanillin, cis-3-hexenal, trans-2-cis-6-nonadienal

REVIEW QUESTIONS

1. a. $\overset{\overset{\displaystyle O}{\|}}{R\text{-}CH}$ b. $\overset{\overset{\displaystyle O}{\|}}{R\text{-}C\text{-}R}$ c. $\overset{\overset{\displaystyle O}{\|}}{R\text{-}COH}$ d. $\overset{\overset{\displaystyle O}{\|}}{R\text{-}C\text{-}O\text{-}R}$ e. $R\text{-}O\text{-}R$ f. $\overset{\overset{\displaystyle O}{\|}}{R\text{-}C\text{-}N\text{-}}$

2. a. formic; b. acetic; c. propionic; d. butyric

3. short chain carboxylic acids; esters

4. a. The reaction of an acid and a base to produce salt and water.

Example: $CH_3\overset{\overset{\displaystyle O}{\|}}{C}OH + NaOH \longrightarrow CH_3\overset{\overset{\displaystyle O}{\|}}{C}\text{-}O^- Na^+ + H_2O$

   b. The reaction of an acid and an alcohol to form an ester.

Example: $CH_3\overset{\overset{\displaystyle O}{\|}}{C}\text{-}OH + CH_3OH \xrightarrow{\ H^+\ } CH_3\overset{\overset{\displaystyle O}{\|}}{C}\text{-}O\text{-}CH_3 + H_2O$

   c. The splitting apart of a compound by adding water across a bond and using acid as a catalyst.

Example: $CH_3\overset{\overset{\displaystyle O}{\|}}{C}\text{-}O\text{-}CH_3 \xrightarrow{\ H^+, H_2O\ } CH_3\overset{\overset{\displaystyle O}{\|}}{C}\text{-}OH + HOCH_3$

   d. The hydrolysis of an ester using base to produce a salt and an alcohol.

Example: $CH_3\overset{\overset{\displaystyle O}{\|}}{C}\text{-}O\text{-}CH_3 \xrightarrow{\ NaOH\ } CH_3\overset{\overset{\displaystyle O}{\|}}{C}\text{-}O^- Na^+ + HOCH_3$

PROBLEMS

CARBOXYLIC ACIDS: NAMES AND STRUCTURAL FORMULAS

5. a. $CH_3CH_2CH_2CH_2CH_2CH_2\overset{\overset{\displaystyle O}{\|}}{C}OH$ b. $(CH_3)_2CHCH_2\overset{\overset{\displaystyle O}{\|}}{C}OH$

  c.   d.

6. a.

$$\text{(benzene ring with } \overset{\overset{\displaystyle O}{\|}}{C}\text{-OH and } NO_2 \text{ substituent)}$$

b.

$$Cl\text{-(benzene ring)-}\overset{\overset{\displaystyle O}{\|}}{C}\text{-OH}$$

c. $CH_3CH_2CHClCH_2\overset{\overset{\displaystyle O}{\|}}{C}OH$

d. $\text{(benzene ring)-}CH_2CH_2\overset{\overset{\displaystyle O}{\|}}{C}OH$

7. a. $HO\overset{\overset{\displaystyle O}{\|}}{C}-\overset{\overset{\displaystyle O}{\|}}{C}OH$

b. $CH_3\overset{\overset{\displaystyle OH}{|}}{C}HCH_2\overset{\overset{\displaystyle O}{\|}}{C}OH$

8. a. $CH_3\overset{\overset{\displaystyle Cl}{|}}{C}H-\overset{\overset{\displaystyle O}{\|}}{C}OH$

b. $\text{(benzene ring)-}CH_2\overset{\overset{\displaystyle O}{\|}}{C}OH$

9. a. 3-methylbutanoic acid;   b. 3,4,4-trimethylpentanoic acid;   c. 4-hydroxybutanoic acid;
    d. 2,4-dimethylpentanoic acid

10. a. decanoic acid; b. 4,4-dichloro-5-methylhexanoic acid; c. 3-ethyl-4-hydroxy-2-iodopentanoic acid
    d. 4-bromobenzoic acid

SALTS: NAMES AND STRUCTURAL FORMULAS

11. a. $CH_3\overset{\overset{\displaystyle O}{\|}}{C}O^- K^+$

b. $(CH_3CH_2\overset{\overset{\displaystyle O}{\|}}{C}O^-)_2Ca^{+2}$

12. a. lithium benzoate   b. ammonium butanoate

ESTERS: NAMES AND STRUCTURAL FORMULAS

13. a. $CH_3\overset{\overset{\displaystyle O}{\|}}{C}\text{-O-}CH_3$

b. $CH_3\overset{\overset{\displaystyle O}{\|}}{C}\text{-O-(benzene ring)}$

14. a. $CH_3CH_2CH_2CH_2\overset{\overset{\displaystyle O}{\|}}{C}\text{-O-}CH_2CH_3$ b. $CH_3CH_2CH_2CH(CH_3)CH_2\overset{\overset{\displaystyle O}{\|}}{C}\text{-O-}CH_2CH_3$

15. a. 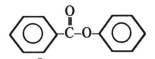 $\text{(benzene ring)-}\overset{\overset{\displaystyle O}{\|}}{C}\text{-O-}CH_2CH_3$

b. $\text{(benzene ring)-}\overset{\overset{\displaystyle O}{\|}}{C}\text{-O-(benzene ring)}$

16. a. $CH_3CH_2CH_2\overset{\overset{\displaystyle O}{\|}}{C}\text{-O-}CH_2CH_3$ b. $CH_3CH_2\overset{\overset{\displaystyle O}{\|}}{C}\text{-O-}CH(CH_3)_2$

17. a. methyl benzoate; b. methyl formate (or methyl methanoate);   c. ethyl propionate (or ethyl propanoate)

18. a. propyl acetate (or propyl ethanoate); b. propyl propionate (or propyl propanoate); c. phenyl butanoate

AMIDES: NAMES AND STRUCTURAL FORMULAS

19. a. $CH_3CH_2CH_2\overset{\displaystyle O}{\overset{\|}{C}}-NH_2$
    b. $CH_3CH_2CH_2CH_2CH_2\overset{\displaystyle O}{\overset{\|}{C}}-NH_2$
    c. $CH_3\overset{\displaystyle O}{\overset{\|}{C}}-NH-CH_3$

20. a. $H\overset{\displaystyle O}{\overset{\|}{C}}-NH_2$
    b. $CH_3CH_2\overset{\displaystyle O}{\overset{\|}{C}}-NH_2$
    c.

21. a. benzamide; b. 2-methylbutanamide; c. acetamide

22. a. N,N-dimethylpropionamide; b. *p*-chlorobenzamide; c. N-phenylbutanamide

PHYSICAL PROPERTIES

23. II; Butanoic acid has the ability to form dimers which are hydrogen bonded to one another; the ether can't hydrogen bond.

24. II; Butanoic acid has the ability to form dimers which are hydrogen bonded to one another; pentanol can hydrogen bond but won't have as high a boiling point as the acid.

25. I; The amide can hydrogen bond while the ester can't.

26. I; The acid can hydrogen bond while the ester can't.

27. I; The acid can both hydrogen bond with water and ionize slightly in water. This helps its solubility. The alkane is completely insoluble in water due to its lack of polarity.

28. II; The amide can hydrogen bond with water and is thus more soluble.

29. I; The longer hydrocarbon chain of II will make it less able to mix with the polar water.

30. II; Ions are always more soluble than nonionic compounds. Thus II will be more soluble.

CHEMICAL REACTIONS

31. a. $CH_3CH_2CH_2\overset{\displaystyle O}{\overset{\|}{C}}OH + NaOH \longrightarrow CH_3CH_2CH_2\overset{\displaystyle O}{\overset{\|}{C}}\text{-}O^-Na^+ + H_2O$

    b. $CH_3CH_2CH_2\overset{\displaystyle O}{\overset{\|}{C}}OH + NaHCO_3 \longrightarrow CH_3CH_2CH_2\overset{\displaystyle O}{\overset{\|}{C}}\text{-}O^-Na^+ + CO_2 + H_2O$

32. a.

    b.

33. $CH_3\overset{O}{\overset{\|}{C}}O\text{-}CH_2CH_3 + H_2O \xrightarrow{H^+} CH_3\overset{O}{\overset{\|}{C}}OH + HOCH_2CH_3$

34. $CH_3\overset{O}{\overset{\|}{C}}\text{-}O\text{-}CH_2CH_3 + NaOH \longrightarrow CH_3\overset{O}{\overset{\|}{C}}\text{-}O^- Na^+ + HOCH_2CH_3$

35. $\text{-}\overset{O}{\overset{\|}{C}}\text{-}NH_2 + H_2O \xrightarrow{H^+}$ $\text{-}\overset{O}{\overset{\|}{C}}OH + NH_4^+$

36. $\text{-}\overset{O}{\overset{\|}{C}}\text{-}NH_2 + NaOH \longrightarrow$ $\text{-}\overset{O}{\overset{\|}{C}}\text{-}O^- Na^+ + NH_3$

37. a. $CH_3CH_2\overset{O}{\overset{\|}{C}}\text{-}O^- Na^+ + H_2O$ b. $\begin{array}{l}COO^- Na^+ \\ COO^- Na^+ \end{array} + 2H_2O + 2CO_2$

38. a. $Na^+ {}^-OOC\text{-}COO^- Na^+ + 2H_2O$ b. $COO^- K^+ + H_2O$

39. a. $\text{-}\overset{O}{\overset{\|}{C}}\text{-}O^- Na^+ + HOCH_2CH_2CH_3$ b. $\text{-}O\text{-}\overset{O}{\overset{\|}{C}}CH_3 + H_2O$

40. a. $\text{-}CH_2\text{-}O\text{-}\overset{O}{\overset{\|}{C}}CH_3$ b. $CH_3\overset{O}{\overset{\|}{C}}\text{-}O^- K^+ + HOCH(CH_3)_2$

41. a. $CH_3\overset{O}{\overset{\|}{C}}\text{-}O\text{-}CH_2CH_2CH_3 + H_2O$ b. $CH_3\text{-}O\text{-}\overset{O}{\overset{\|}{C}}CH_2\overset{O}{\overset{\|}{C}}\text{-}O\text{-}CH_3 + 2H_2O$

42. a. $CH_3CH_2CH_2OH + HO\overset{O}{\overset{\|}{C}}\text{-}$ b. $(CH_3)_2CH\overset{O}{\overset{\|}{C}}OH + HOCH_2CH_3$

43. a. $CH_3\overset{O}{\overset{\|}{C}}\text{-}OH + NH_4Cl$ b. $\text{-}\overset{O}{\overset{\|}{C}}\text{-}O^- Na^+ + HN(CH_3)_2$

44. a. $CH_3CH_2\overset{O}{\overset{\|}{C}}\text{-}O^- K^+ + NH_3$ b. $\text{-}\overset{O}{\overset{\|}{C}}\text{-}OH + NH_3CH_3^+ Cl^-$

45. a. $K_2Cr_2O_7, H^+$; b. $K_2Cr_2O_7, H^+$; c. NaOH

46. a. NH_3; b. $HOCH_3, H^+$

385

47. a. $CH_3\overset{\displaystyle O}{\overset{\|}{C}}OH$, H^+;   b. LiOH

48. a. H_2O, HBr;   b. KOH, H_2O

PHOSPHORUS COMPOUNDS

49. a. $CH_3CH_2O-\overset{\displaystyle O}{\underset{\displaystyle OH}{\overset{\|}{P}}}-OCH_2CH_3$ b. $CH_3O-\overset{\displaystyle O}{\underset{\displaystyle OH}{\overset{\|}{P}}}-OH$

    c. $HO-\overset{\displaystyle O}{\underset{\displaystyle OH}{\overset{\|}{P}}}-O-\overset{\displaystyle O}{\underset{\displaystyle OH}{\overset{\|}{P}}}-O-\overset{\displaystyle O}{\underset{\displaystyle OH}{\overset{\|}{P}}}-OH$

50. a. pyrophosphoric acid   b. ethyl dihydrogen phosphate

ADDITIONAL PROBLEMS

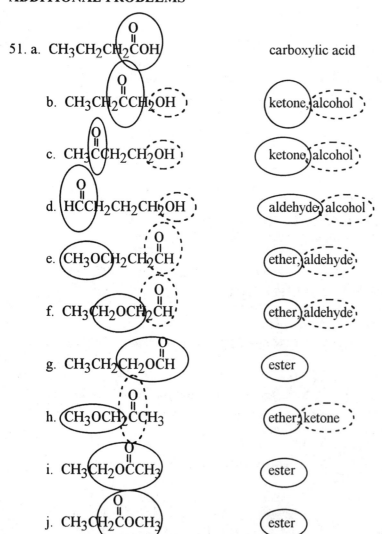

51. a. $CH_3CH_2CH_2COH$ carboxylic acid

    b. $CH_3CH_2CCH_2OH$ ketone, alcohol

    c. $CH_3CCH_2CH_2OH$ ketone, alcohol

    d. $HCCH_2CH_2CH_2OH$ aldehyde, alcohol

    e. $CH_3OCH_2CH_2CH$ ether, aldehyde

    f. $CH_3CH_2OCH_2CH$ ether, aldehyde

    g. $CH_3CH_2CH_2OCH$ ester

    h. $CH_3OCH_2CCH_3$ ether, ketone

    i. $CH_3CH_2OCCH_3$ ester

    j. $CH_3CH_2COCH_3$ ester

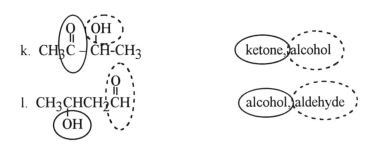

k. CH₃C–CH-CH₃ ⬭ketone, alcohol

l. CH₃CHCH₂CH ⬭alcohol, aldehyde

52. toluene < benzyl alcohol < phenol < benzoic acid

53. pentane < methyl acetate < butyl alcohol < propionic acid

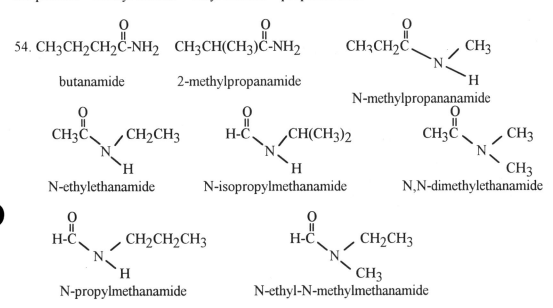

54. CH₃CH₂CH₂C-NH₂   CH₃CH(CH₃)C-NH₂

butanamide   2-methylpropanamide   N-methylpropananamide

N-ethylethanamide   N-isopropylmethanamide   N,N-dimethylethanamide

N-propylmethanamide   N-ethyl-N-methylmethanamide

55. The insoluble benzoic acid would become soluble (a white powder would dissolve).

56. a. Ethyl acetate does not have a hydrogen atom directly bonded to an oxygen atom and therefore cannot participate in intermolecular hydrogen bonding. There is considerable intermolecular hydrogen bonding in methyl alcohol and in formic acid.

b. Salts are ionic compounds, and water molecules readily surround the individual cations and anions. Hydrogen bonding between the carboxyl group of benzoic acid and water is not sufficient to dissolve benzoic acid molecules.

c. The alkaline hydrolysis of an ester yields an alcohol and a salt. These products cannot react to reform the ester. The acid hydrolysis of esters yields alcohols and acids, which can react to reform the ester.

d. The hydrolysis of an amide either produces a salt of the carboxylic acid (base hydrolysis) or of the amine (acid hydrolysis). These cannot react to reform the amide.

57. a. CH₃CH₂CH₂OH;   b. HOCH₂CH₂OH;   c. CH₃OH;   d. (CH₃)₂CHCH₂CH₂OH

58. a. HOCH₂CH₂COH   b. HOCH₂CH₂CH₂CO⁻ Na⁺

59. a. $\underset{\quad\quad\quad\quad\quad\overset{\displaystyle O}{\overset{\|}{\quad}}}{H_2N\text{-}CH_2CH_2C\text{-}O^-\ Na^+}$ b. $\underset{\quad\quad\quad\quad\quad\quad\overset{\displaystyle O}{\overset{\|}{\quad}}}{{}^+H_3N\text{-}CH_2CH_2CH_2C\text{-}OH}$

60. $\underset{\quad\quad\quad\overset{\displaystyle O}{\overset{\|}{\quad}}}{CH_3CH_2C\text{-}OCH_2CH_2CH_3}$

61. $RCOOH + NaOH \longrightarrow RCOO^- Na^+ + HOH$
    moles of NaOH = (0.4)(0.125) = 0.0500 = moles of acid
    molecular weight of acid = $\dfrac{5.1}{0.050}$ = 102 g/mol

    Empirical formula of acid, $C_5H_{10}O_2$: possible structural formulas are

$CH_3CH_2CH_2CH_2COOH$ $CH_3CH_2CH(CH_3)COOH$ $(CH_3)_2CHCH_2COOH$ $(CH_3)_3CCOOH$

62. $\underset{\quad\quad\overset{\displaystyle O}{\overset{\|}{\quad}}}{CH_3COH}$ + CH_3OH $\underset{\quad\quad\quad\overset{\displaystyle O}{\overset{\|}{\quad}}}{CH_3COCH_3}$ + HOH

    moles of acetic acid - $\dfrac{3.0}{60}$ = 0.050

    moles of methyl acetate formed = 0.050
    grams of methyl acetate = (0.050)(molecular weight of methyl acetate)
                            = (0.050)(74) = 3.7 g

63. $2 \underset{\overset{\displaystyle |}{Cl}}{\overset{\overset{\displaystyle Cl}{|}}{HC}}\overset{\overset{\displaystyle O}{\|}}{C}\text{-}OH + Ba(OH)_2 \longrightarrow 2 \underset{\overset{\displaystyle |}{Cl}}{\overset{\overset{\displaystyle Cl}{|}}{HC}}\overset{\overset{\displaystyle O}{\|}}{C}\text{ - }O^- + Ba^{2+} + 2\ HOH$

    moles of dichloroacetic acid = $\dfrac{0.5\ g}{129\ g}$ = 4 x 10^{-3} mol

    moles of $Ba(OH)_2$ required to neutralize the acid = 2 x 10^{-3} mol

    volume of $Ba(OH)_2$ required = $\dfrac{2\ x\ 10^{-3}}{0.100\ M}$ = 0.020L = 20.0 mL

REVIEW QUESTIONS

1. a. Drug: Any chemical substance that affects an individual in such a way as to bring about physiological, emotional, or behavioral change.
   b. Analgesic: A pain-relieving compound.
   c. Antipyretic: A fever-reducing substance.
   d. Pyrogen: Fever-producing compounds that are produced by and released from leukocytes and other circulating cells.
   e. Reye's Syndrome: A disease brought on by use of aspirin following certain flus or chickenpox.
   f. Narcotic: A chemical that induces sleep or causes a state of stupor.
   g. Opium: The crude extract from the poppy plant (*Papaver somniferum*).
   h. Agonist: A substance that mimics the action of a particular drug or natural compound.
   i. Antagonist: A substance that blocks the action of a particular drug or natural compound.
   j. Endorphins: Natural peptides which work to reduce pain in our bodies.
   k. Enkephalin: An endorphin containing five amino acids.

2. Heroin has a pair of acetyl groups esterified to the free -OH groups of morphine. The acetylation causes heroin to be more nonpolar; thus, it can more easily cross the blood-brain barrier and be more of a euphoriant.

3. a. 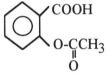   Acetylsalicylic acid

   b. Different doses; different additives (such as buffering agents, acetaminophen, caffeine).

   c. All must contain acetylsalicylic acid.

4. An alkaloid is any nitrogen-containing, plant derived compound that causes physiological effects. Examples: morphine, codeine, nicotine, cocaine.

5. An hallucinogenic drug (like LSD) is a drug that produces visions and sensations that are not part of reality.

6. Methadone blocks the euphoria normally caused by heroin but prevents the withdrawal symptoms from occurring.

7. a. Acupuncture causes the body to release endorphins to block the pain caused by the needles. The release of these endorphins causes a sensation similar to when morphine is taken.

   b. A soldier has released sufficient endorphins to cope with the pain.

8. It has been difficult to assess both the long-term toxic effects of LSD and its potential for causing chromosomal damage.

9. It is disputed whether marijuana causes brain damage and long-term psychoses.

10. Chemists have synthesized the active component of marijuana and have designed procedures for accurately monitoring levels of these compounds in the blood.

11. It is proposed that THC works at estradiol receptors which activate the feminization processes.

12. It is relatively fat soluble and held in fat tissue for extended periods of time.

13. Movement control centers. Marijuana causes a loss of coordination which is tied to the inactivation of these movement control receptors.

14. 3

PROBLEMS

15. Carboxylic acid

16. Isobutyl. "Ibu" *Isobu*tyl; "Pro" *pro*panoic acid; "fen" *phen*yl group.

17. a. $HOCH_3$, H^+ b. $NaOH$

18. a. NH_3, heat; b. acetic acid

PROJECTS

19. ——

20. ——

REVIEW QUESTIONS

1. Amides, with the exception of formamide, are all solids. Most are colorless and odorless. The lower members are soluble in both water and alcohol, water solubility decreasing as the carbon chain increases. Amides are neutral compounds with abnormally high boiling points and melting points.

   Amines exist as gases, liquids, or solids. All have pronounced odors and are basic. The lower members are soluble in water; water solubility decreases with increasing length of carbon chain.

2. Lemon juice donates H^+ ions to the amines to generate the ionized form. The ionized (protonated) forms of amines are much less volatile, thus reducing the "fishy" odors.

3. acidic: c; basic: a; neutral: b,d

4. They stink! The smells range from ammonia-like for the simplest to putrid for the slightly longer amines.

5. Nitrites can react with stomach acid (HCl) to form nitrosamines, compounds shown to be carcinogenic.

6. A heterocyclic compound is a cyclic compound in which one or more atoms in the ring are not carbon.

PROBLEMS

CLASSIFICATION OF COMPOUNDS

7. a. amide; b. neither; c. both

8. a. neither; b. amide; c. amine

9. a. alcohol (1°); b. amine (1°); c. alcohol (2°); d. amine (1°); e. ether; f. phenol

10. a. amine (2°); b. ether; c. amine (3°); d. alcohol (3°); e. amine (2°); f. amine (1°)

AMINES: STRUCTURES AND NAMES

11. a. CH_3NHCH_3 b. $CH_3CH_2N\text{-}CH_2CH_3$ with CH_3 below the N   c. square ring with OH and NH_2 d. $HOCH_2CH_2NH_2$

12. a. $CH_3CH_2\overset{NH_2}{\underset{|}{C}}HCH_2CH_3$ b. $H_2NCH_2CH_2CH_2CH_2CH_2CH_2NH_2$

    c. cyclohexane with NH_2 d. CH_3CH_2NH–(benzene ring)

13. a. benzene ring with NH_2 b. Br benzene ring with NH_2 c. pyrimidine ring with two N   d. benzene ring with $NHCH_2CH_3$

391

14. a.

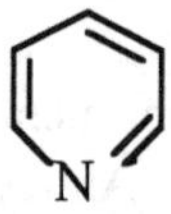

b.

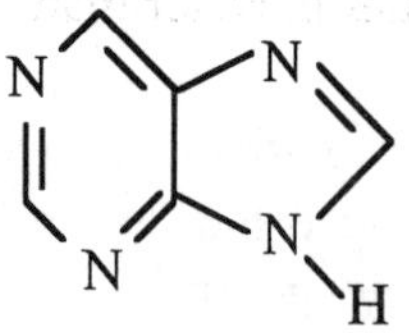

c.

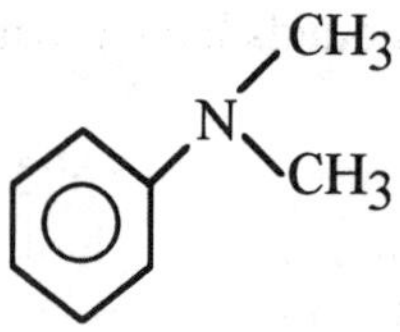

d.

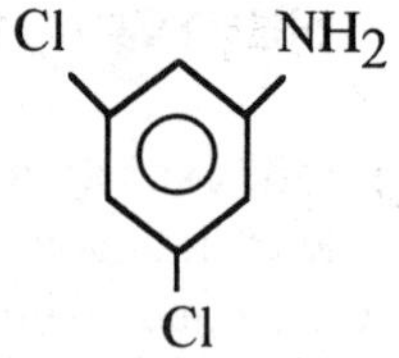

15. a. propylamine; b. methylisopropylamine; c. triethylamine; d. 2-aminopentane

16. a. *p*-nitroaniline; b. ethylphenylamine or N–ethylaniline

NAMES AND FORMULAS OF AMINE SALTS

17. a. 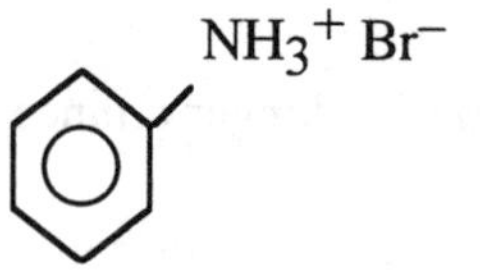 $NH_3^+ Br^-$

b. 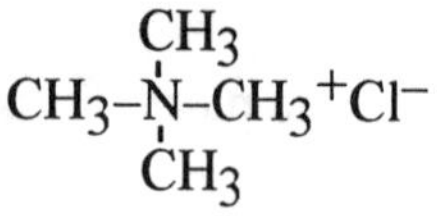 $CH_3–\overset{\underset{|}{CH_3}}{\underset{|}{N}}–CH_3^+Cl^-$

18. a. $CH_3CH_2–\overset{}{\underset{\underset{CH_3}{|}}{NH_2}} {}^+Cl^-$

b. 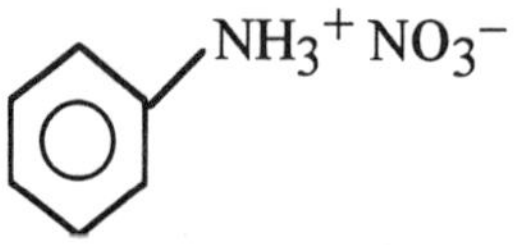 $NH_3^+ NO_3^-$

19. a. diethylammonium bromide   b. tetraethylammonium iodide

20. a. anilinium chloride   b. tetramethylammonium nitrate

PHYSICAL PROPERTIES

21. Butylamine. It can hydrogen bond (while pentane cannot) causing a more tightly held liquid structure.

22. Butyl alcohol. Alcohols form hydrogen bonds with each other which are stronger than the hydrogen bonds in amines.

23. Propylamine. Tertiary amines have no hydrogen bonded to the nitrogen; therefore they do not undergo hydrogen bonding.

24. $CH_3CH_2CH_2CH_2CH_2NH_2$ would have the higher boiling point. All else being the same, molecules of higher molecular size have greater London forces which causes an increase in the boiling temperature.

25. $CH_3CH_2NH_2$. It has the ability to hydrogen bond with water.

26. $CH_3CH_2CH_2NH_2$. Long hydrocarbon chains decrease the solubility of compounds in water. (The chains do not have the capability to hydrogen bond with water.)

27. $CH_2CH_2\overset{\underset{|}{NH_2}}{CH}CH_2\overset{\underset{|}{NH_2}}{CH}CH_3$ The more hydrogen bonding groups placed on a compound, the more its solubility in water.

28. 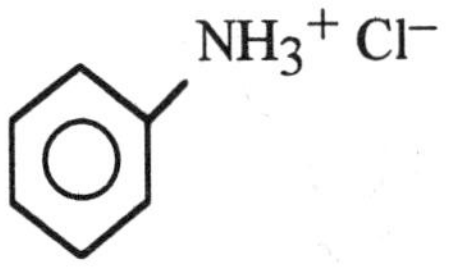 $NH_3^+ Cl^-$ Ionic compounds have greater solubilities in water than nonionic compounds.

CHEMICAL REACTIONS

29. $CH_3NH_3^+Br^-$

30. 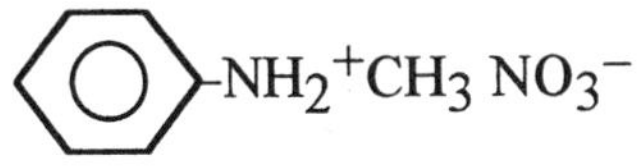 $-NH_2^+CH_3\ NO_3^-$

31. $[(CH_3)_3NH^+]_2SO_4^{-2}$

32. 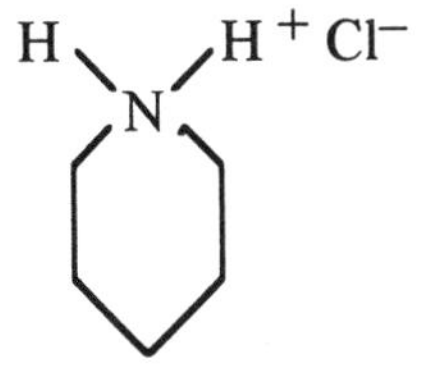 $H\diagdown_N\diagup^{H\ +}\ Cl^-$

33. $CH_3(CH_2)_4\overset{\overset{\displaystyle O}{\|}}{C}-NH(CH_2)_3CH_3$

34. $CH_3CH_2\overset{\overset{\displaystyle O}{\|}}{C}-N\diagup^{CH_3}_{\diagdown CH_3}$

35. 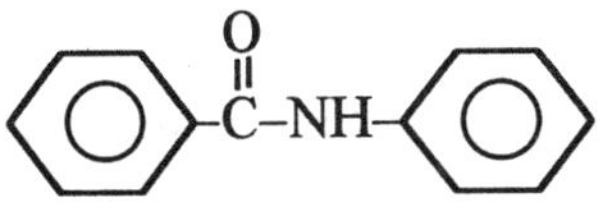 $\overset{\overset{\displaystyle O}{\|}}{C}-NH-$

36. no reaction

37. $CH_3CH_2NHCH_3$ and $HO\overset{\overset{\displaystyle O}{\|}}{C}CH_2CH_3$

38. 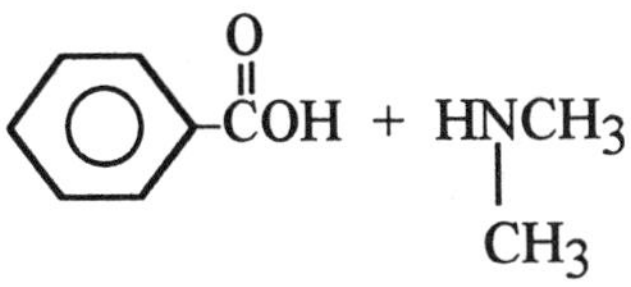 $-\overset{\overset{\displaystyle O}{\|}}{C}OH\ +\ HNCH_3$ CH_3

39. 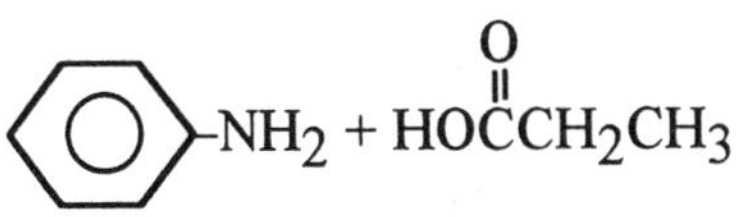 $-NH_2 + HO\overset{\overset{\displaystyle O}{\|}}{C}CH_2CH_3$

40. 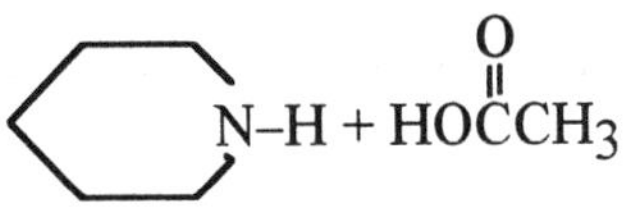 $N-H + HO\overset{\overset{\displaystyle O}{\|}}{C}CH_3$

41.

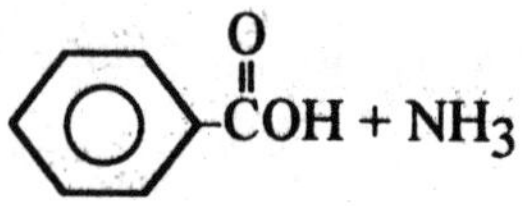

42.

43. a. HCl   b. HNO_3

44. a. HNO_2 b. HCl

ADDITIONAL PROBLEMS

45. The protonation of amine X results in the formation of the ion X^+ which greatly improves solubility.

46. $CH_3CH_2CH_2CH_2NH_2$
  butylamine (1°)

  $CH_3CH_2CH_2NHCH_3$
  methylpropylamine (2°)

  $CH_3CHCH_2NH_2$
  |
  CH_3
  isobutylamine (1°)

  $CH_3CH_2CHNH_2$
  |
  CH_3
  sec-butylamine (1°)

  $CH_3CHNHCH_3$
  |
  CH_3
  isopropylmethylamine (2°)

  CH_3C-NH_2 with CH_3 above and CH_3 below
  tert-butylamine (1°)

  $CH_3CH_2NHCH_2CH_3$
  diethylamine (2°)

  $CH_3N-CH_2CH_3$ with CH_3 above
  dimethylethylamine (3°)

47.

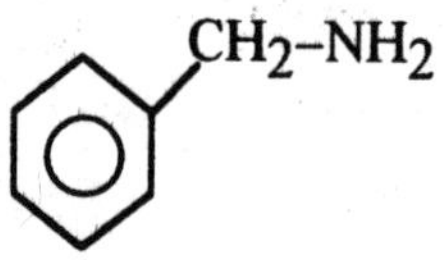

benzylamine (1°) 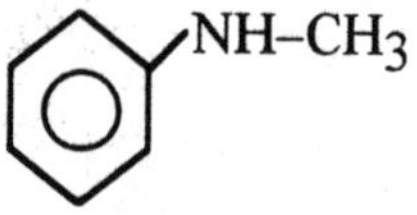   methylphenylamine (2°)

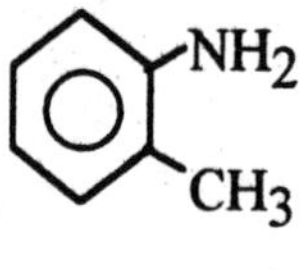

2-methylaniline (1°) 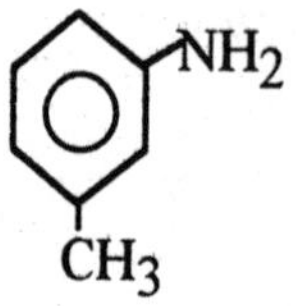   3-methylaniline (1°) 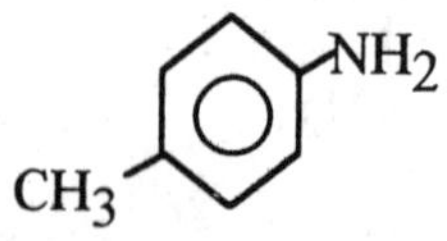   4-methylaniline (1°)

394

48. H₂N–CH₂$\overset{\overset{\displaystyle O}{\|}}{C}$OH + H₂N–CH₂–$\overset{\overset{\displaystyle O}{\|}}{C}$OH

49. a.

b.

c.

d.

50. 0.25g CH₃CH₂NHCH₂CH₃ = .0034 moles; which requires 0.0034 moles HCl. This is equivalent to 23 mL of 0.15 M HCl.

REVIEW QUESTIONS

1. a. Neurons: nerve cells.
    b. Synapse: A small gap between a neuron and a second cell (perhaps a second neuron).
    c. Neurotransmitter: Chemical released by a neuron into a synapse to signal the next cell.

2. Norepinephrine: Regulates mood from depression (low levels) to mania (high level) and
   Serotonin: Involved in sleep, sensory perception and mood.

3. a. Tryptophan (precursor of serotonin) and tyrosine (precursor of norepinephrine and dopamine).
    b. It has been proposed that ingestion of these amino acids (as part of protein foods) will directly affect the level of neurotransmitter into which they may be transformed. (Ingestion of glucose has also been tied to increased serotonin levels.)

4. They mimic natural amines (particularly dopamine) in our brains which are responsible for stimulatory effects.

5. Cocaine prevents re-uptake of dopamine by neurons, thus prolonging dopamine's stimulatory effects.

6. A local anesthetic is a compound that blocks neural transmission when applied directly onto the nerve. It works by prohibiting a nerve impulse from traveling down a nerve.

7. A general anesthetic is a depressant that acts on the brain to produce unconsciousness as well as insensitivity to pain.

8. Ketamine and phencyclidine. They work on associated pathways before they innervate the brainstem to produce a "removed from body" anesthetic effect.

9. a. Amphetamines cause stimulation or bring an individual "up."
    b. Barbiturates cause central nervous system depression or bring an individual "down."

10. Synergism is when the effect of a combination of actions is greater then the sum of the effects of the individual actions.

11. Mania is thought to be due to high levels of biological amines in certain areas of the brain. Blockage of norepinephrine release will result in less of this neurotransmittor in the synapse and, thus, less of the mania-type state.

12. Depression

PROBLEMS

STRUCTURAL FORMULAS AND FUNCTIONAL GROUPS

13. a. Barbiturates all contain a six-membered barbituric acid ring structure.
    b. Groups are added to a carbon located between a pair of carbonyl groups to alter the drug's properties such as effectiveness and length of duration.

14.

   a. Ether groups: circled
   b. Amine groups: boxed
   c. Ester groups: marked with an arrow

15. Amide, ketone, phenol, alcohol, amine

16.

TOXICITIES

17. Cocaine.

18. 350 mg. No; but it is quite often the best evidence we have for forecasting a drug's toxicity prior to human trials.

ADDITIONAL PROBLEMS

19. Cocaine hydrochloride is readily absorbed through the mucous membrane of the nose where it then passes into the blood. In order to vaporize cocaine for smoking, cocaine hydrochloride must be converted to the free base (unionized) form. This greatly reduces the boiling point of the cocaine.

20. Fluoride, ketone, amine, alcohol, chloride

REVIEW QUESTIONS

1. a. Chiral center: A carbon that is attached to four different groups.
    b. Enantiomers: Stereoisomers that are nonsuperimposable mirror images.
    c. Polarimeter: An instrument that detects and measures the effects of various substances on plane-polarized light.
    d. Optically active: Any substance that rotates plane-polarized light.
    e. Specific rotation: The amount of rotation caused by 1g of an optically active substance per cubic centimeter in a 1dm sample tube.
    f. Geometric isomers: Compounds that have different configurations because of the presence of a rigid structure in the molecule.
    g. Polarized light: Light vibrating in a single plane.
    h. Diastereomers: Stereoisomers which are not enantiomers.
    i. Stereoisomer: An isomer that has the same structural formula as another, but the two molecules differ in the arrangement of their atoms.
    j. Meso compund: A compound which contains at least two chiral centers but which, because of an internal symmetry, is not chiral.
    k. Racemic mixture: A mixture containing equal amounts of two members of a pair of enantiomers.
    l. Levorotatory: Rotates plane-polarized light in a counter-clockwise direction.
    m. Dextrorotatory: Rotates plane-polarized light in a clockwise direction.
    n. Pheromone: A chemical scent released by insects and other animals to attract members of the opposite sex.

2. Yes, yes

3. Yes, no

4. a. identical; b. identical; c. identical in magnitude, different in sign (+,−); d. identical;
    e. identical; f. may react at different rates.

5. (+)-Menthol melts at 43 °C, boils at 212 °C, has a density of 0.89g/cm^3 and a specific rotation of +50°.

6. a. yes; b. no; c. no

7. a. No; b. No; c. Yes. The attacking HCl could come equally from each side (top or bottom) of the double bond thus creating a racemic mixture of the + and − forms.

8. a. $CH_3CH_2CH_2CH_3$ and $CH_3CH(CH_3)_2$ b. CH_3CH_2OH and $CH_3\text{-}O\text{-}CH_3$

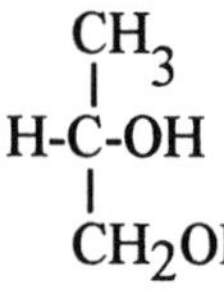

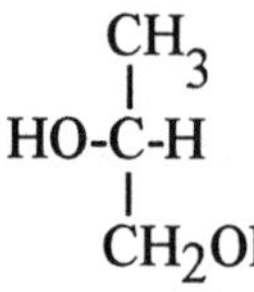

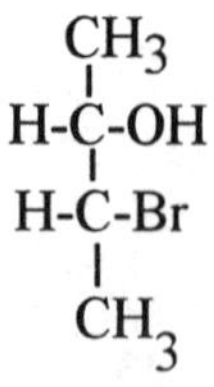

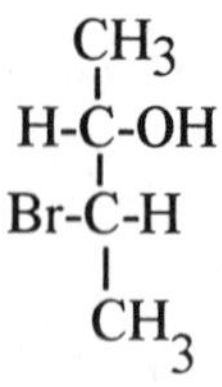

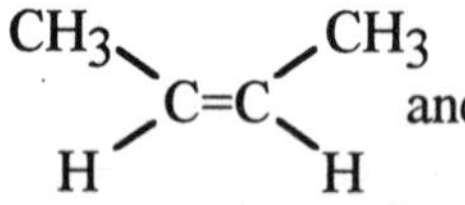

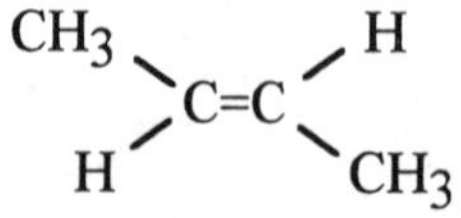

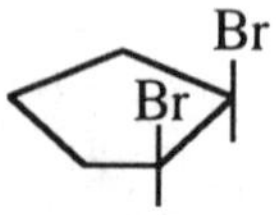

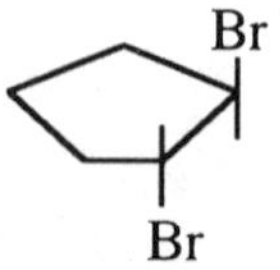

9. Enantiomers have the same physical and chemical properties. They rotate plane-polarized light the same number of degrees but differ in the direction (counterclockwise vs clockwise) the light is rotated.

10. A meso compound is one single compound which, because of an internal plane of symmetry, is not chiral. A racemic mixture is a mixture which contains an equal amount of + and – forms and thus shows no net optical activity.

PROBLEMS

CHIRALITY

11. a. the carbon of the –CH– group; b. none

12. a.

    b.

13 a.   b.

   c.   d.

   e.   f.

14. a.   b.

15. a. yes; b. no, c. yes; d. no

16. a. no; b. no (meso); c. yes; d. yes

ENANTIOMERS

17. a.

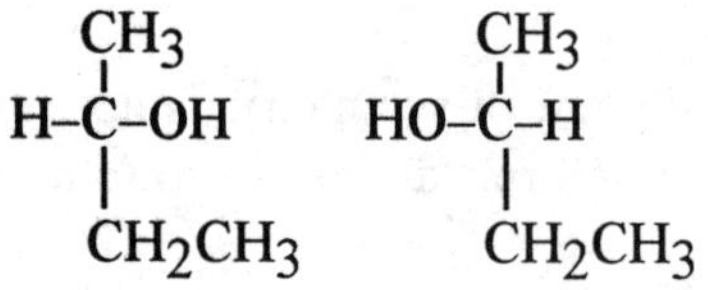

$$\begin{array}{cc}
CH_3 & CH_3 \\
| & | \\
H-C-OH & HO-C-H \\
| & | \\
CH_2CH_3 & CH_2CH_3
\end{array}$$

   b.

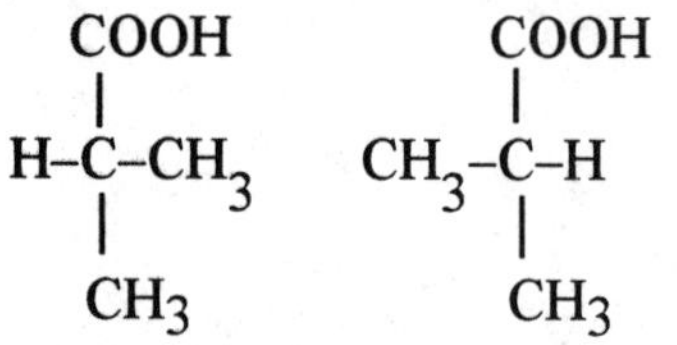

$$\begin{array}{cc}
COOH & COOH \\
| & | \\
H-C-CH_3 & CH_3-C-H \\
| & | \\
CH_3 & CH_3
\end{array}$$

18. a.

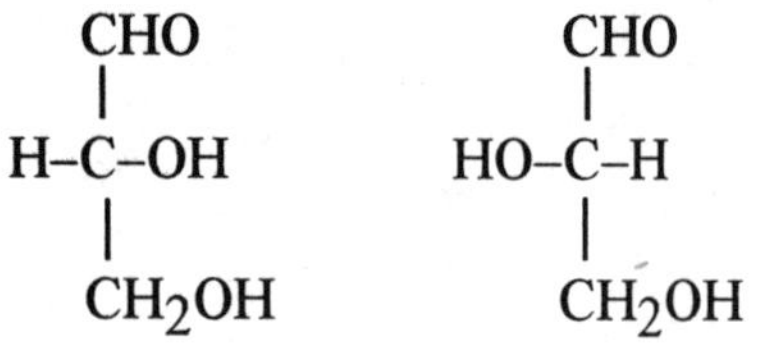

$$\begin{array}{cc}
CHO & CHO \\
| & | \\
H-C-OH & HO-C-H \\
| & | \\
CH_2OH & CH_2OH
\end{array}$$

   b.

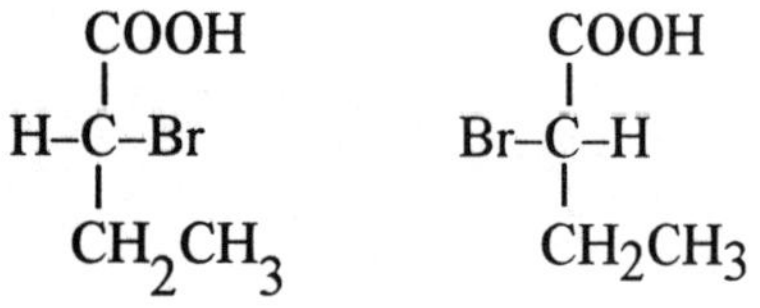

$$\begin{array}{cc}
COOH & COOH \\
| & | \\
H-C-Br & Br-C-H \\
| & | \\
CH_2CH_3 & CH_2CH_3
\end{array}$$

19.

$$\begin{array}{cccc}
CHO & CHO & CHO & CHO \\
| & | & | & | \\
H-C-Cl & Cl-C-H & H-C-Cl & Cl-C-H \\
| & | & | & | \\
Cl-C-H & H-C-Cl & H-C-Cl & Cl-C-H \\
| & | & | & | \\
CH_3 & CH_3 & CH_3 & CH_3
\end{array}$$

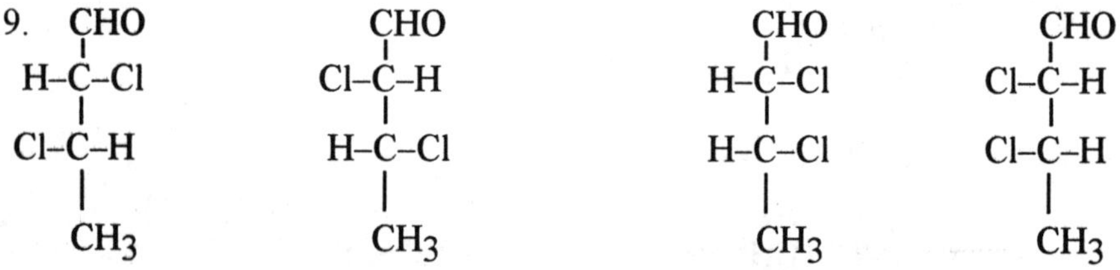

      enantiomers   enantiomers

20.

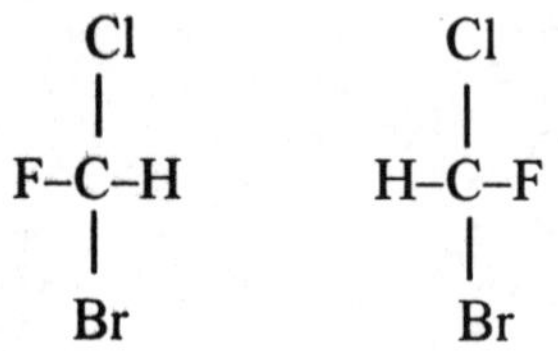

$$\begin{array}{cc}
Cl & Cl \\
| & | \\
F-C-H & H-C-F \\
| & | \\
Br & Br
\end{array}$$

MULTIPLE CHIRAL CENTERS

21. a,d

22. a,c

VAN'T HOFF'S RULE

23. a. 4; b. 8

400

24. 8

GEOMETRIC (CIS-TRANS) ISOMERS

25. a.

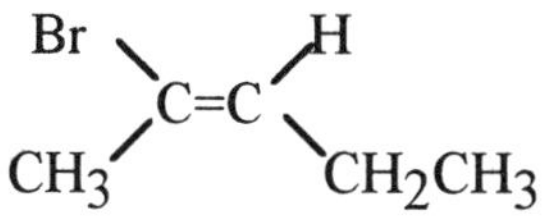

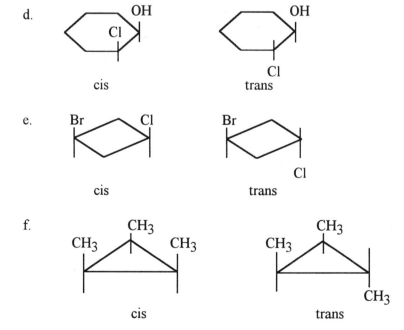

Br   H
  C=C
CH₃   CH₂CH₃
      cis

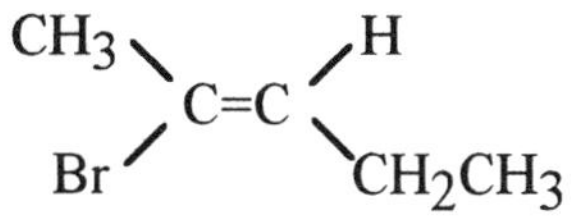

CH₃   H
  C=C
Br   CH₂CH₃
      trans

b.

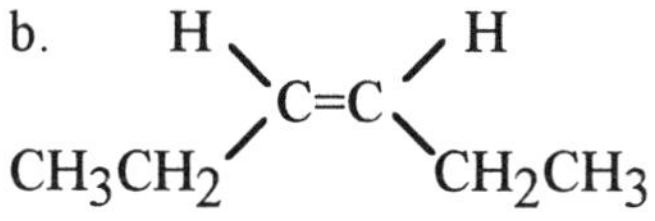

H   H
  C=C
CH₃CH₂   CH₂CH₃
      cis

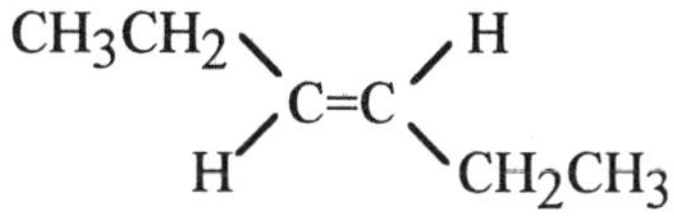

CH₃CH₂   H
  C=C
H   CH₂CH₃
      trans

c. None

d. None

e.

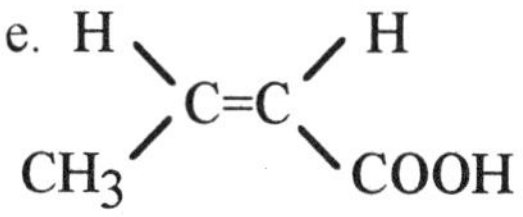

H   H
  C=C
CH₃   COOH
      cis

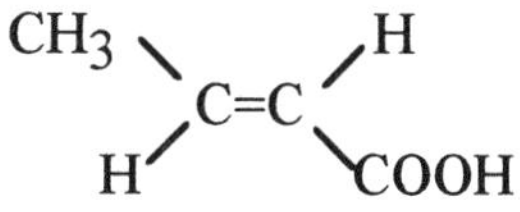

CH₃   H
  C=C
H   COOH
      trans

f.

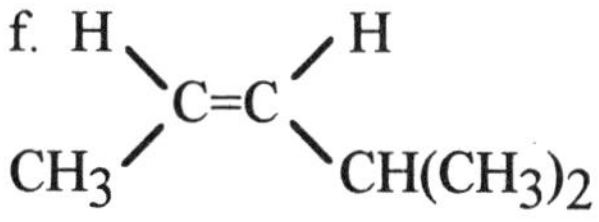

H   H
  C=C
CH₃   CH(CH₃)₂
      cis

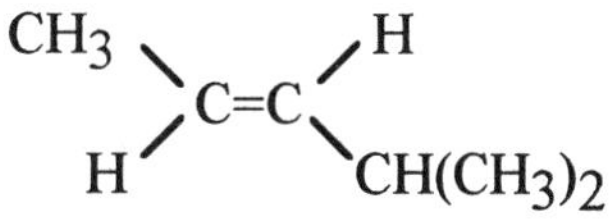

CH₃   H
  C=C
H   CH(CH₃)₂
      trans

26.   a. None; b. None; c. None

d.

OH / Cl cis   OH / Cl trans

e.

Br / Cl cis   Br / Cl trans

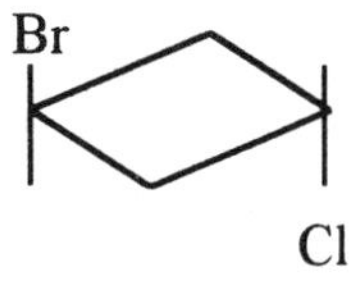

f.

CH₃ CH₃ CH₃ cis   CH₃ CH₃ / CH₃ trans

ADDITIONAL PROBLEMS

27.
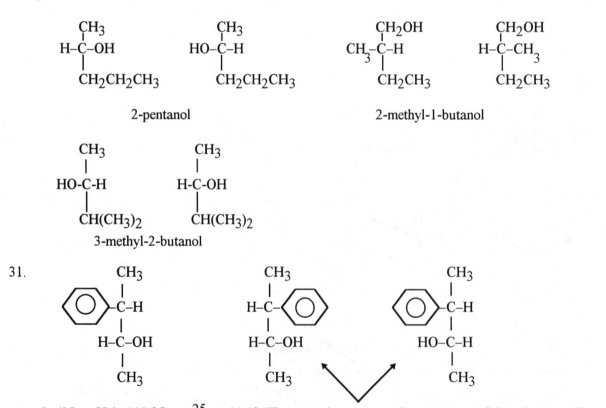

$$\begin{array}{cccc}
\text{CHO} & \text{CHO} & \text{CHO} & \text{CHO} \\
\text{H–C–Cl} & \text{Cl–C–H} & \text{H–C–Cl} & \text{Cl–C–H} \\
\text{Cl–C–H} & \text{H–C–Cl} & \text{H–C–Cl} & \text{Cl–C–H} \\
\text{CH}_3 & \text{CH}_3 & \text{CH}_3 & \text{CH}_3
\end{array}$$

        enantiomers   enantiomers

28. ⬡–CH₂–C(NH₂)(CH₃)H   ⬡–CH₂–C(H)(CH₃)NH₂

29.
$$\begin{array}{ccc}
\text{CH}_3 & \text{CH}_3 & \text{CH}_3 \\
\text{H–C–OH} & \text{HO–C–H} & \text{H–C–OH} \\
\text{HO–C–H} & \text{H–C–OH} & \text{H–C–OH} \\
\text{CH}_3 & \text{CH}_3 & \text{CH}_3 \\
\text{+ or –} & \text{+ or –} & \text{Meso}
\end{array}$$

One can not tell which is – and which is +.

30. 2-pentanol, 2-methyl-1-butanol, and 3-methyl-2-butanol

$$\begin{array}{cccc}
\text{CH}_3 & \text{CH}_3 & \text{CH}_2\text{OH} & \text{CH}_2\text{OH} \\
\text{H–C–OH} & \text{HO–C–H} & \text{CH}_3\text{–C–H} & \text{H–C–CH}_3 \\
\text{CH}_2\text{CH}_2\text{CH}_3 & \text{CH}_2\text{CH}_2\text{CH}_3 & \text{CH}_2\text{CH}_3 & \text{CH}_2\text{CH}_3
\end{array}$$

             2-pentanol   2-methyl-1-butanol

$$\begin{array}{cc}
\text{CH}_3 & \text{CH}_3 \\
\text{HO-C-H} & \text{H-C-OH} \\
\text{CH(CH}_3)_2 & \text{CH(CH}_3)_2
\end{array}$$

        3-methyl-2-butanol

31.
$$\begin{array}{ccc}
\text{CH}_3 & \text{CH}_3 & \text{CH}_3 \\
\text{⬡–C–H} & \text{H–C–⬡} & \text{⬡–C–H} \\
\text{H–C–OH} & \text{H–C–OH} & \text{HO–C–H} \\
\text{CH}_3 & \text{CH}_3 & \text{CH}_3
\end{array}$$

bp(25mmHg)=118 °C $[\alpha]_D^{25}$ = –30.9° These two isomers are diastereomers of the other two. Hence, they will have different boiling points and different specific rotations.

32.

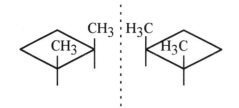 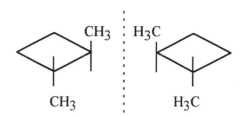

mirror
cis-1,2-Dimethylcyclobutane is achiral.
The mirror images are identical.

mirror
trans-1,2-Dimethylcyclobutane is chiral.
The mirror images are not identical.

cis- and *trans*-1,2-Dimethylcyclobutanes are diastereomers.

33.

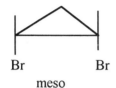 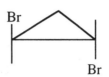

meso

enantiomers

34. a.

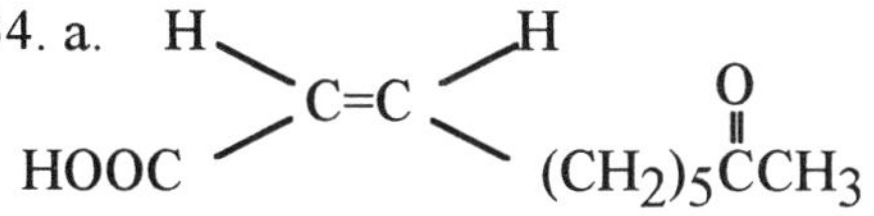

H   H
  C=C
HOOC   (CH₂)₅CCH₃
                   ‖
                   O

9-oxo-*cis*-2-decenoic acid

b.

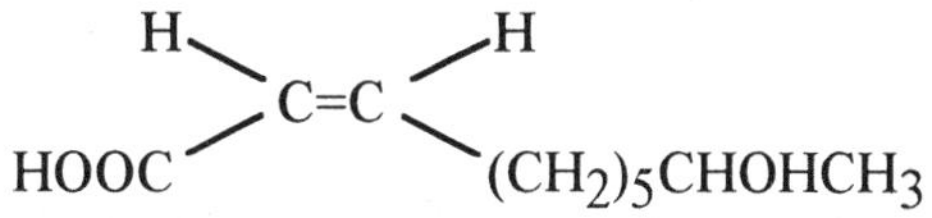

H   H
  C=C
HOOC   (CH₂)₅CHOHCH₃

9-hydroxy-*cis*-2-decenoic acid

c.

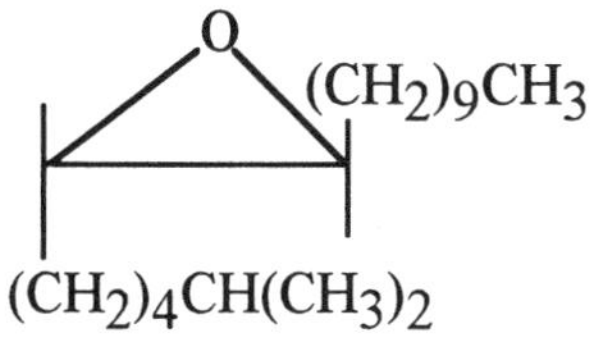

        O
           (CH₂)₉CH₃

(CH₂)₄CH(CH₃)₂

trans-7,8-epoxy-2-
methyloctadecane

d.

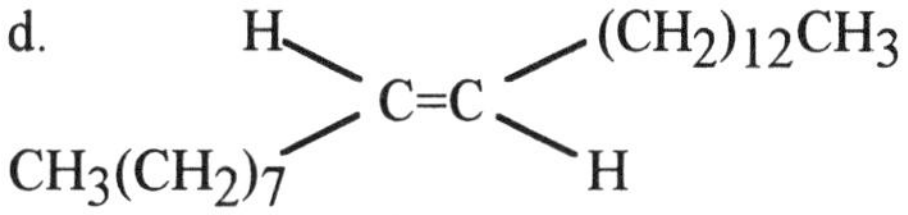

H   (CH₂)₁₂CH₃
  C=C
CH₃(CH₂)₇   H

trans-9-tricosene

e.

CH₃   H
   C = C
H   C=C   (CH₂)₆CH₂OH
            H   H

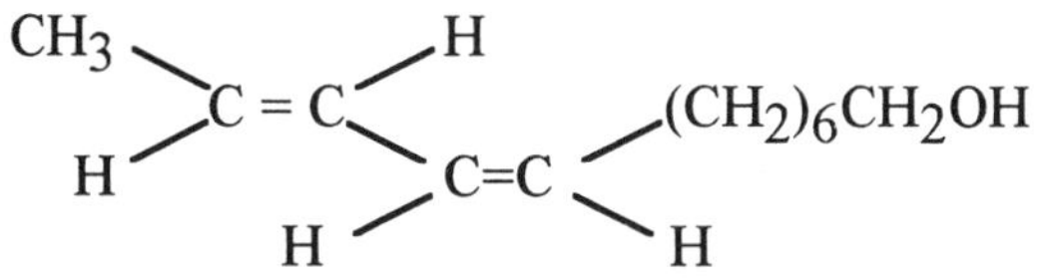

cis-8-*trans*-10-dodecadien-1-ol

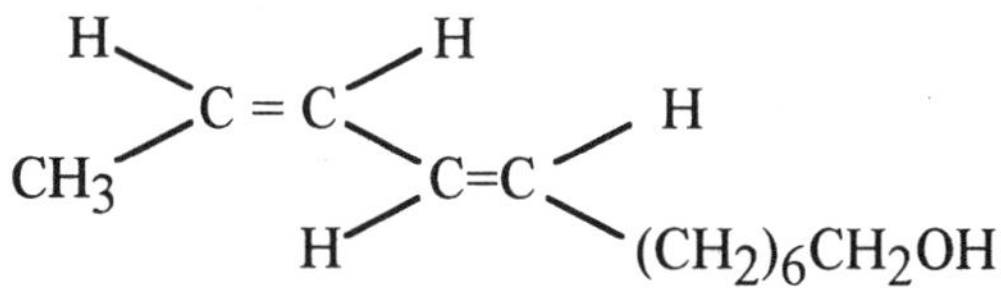

H   H
   C = C
CH₃   C=C   H
            H   (CH₂)₆CH₂OH

trans-8-*cis*-10-dodecadien-1-ol

H   H
   C=C
CH₃   C=C   (CH₂)₆CH₂OH
            H   H

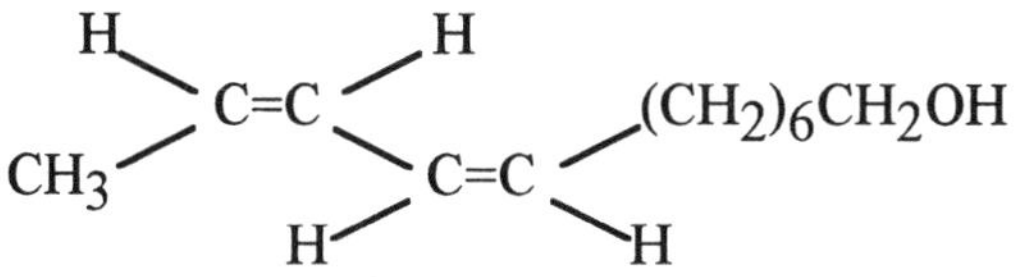

cis-8-*cis*-10-dodecadien-1-ol

f.

$$CH_3(CH_2)_2 \underset{H}{\overset{}{>}}C=C\underset{}{\overset{H}{<}}C=C\underset{(CH_2)_8CH_2OH}{\overset{H}{<}}$$

cis-10-*cis*-12-hexadecadien-1-ol

$$CH_3(CH_2)_2 \overset{H}{>}C=C\overset{(CH_2)_8CH_2OH}{<}\,C=C\,H$$

trans-10-*trans*-12-hexadecadien-1-ol

$$CH_3(CH_2)_2 \overset{H}{>}C=C\overset{H}{<}\,C=C\,(CH_2)_8CH_2OH$$

cis-10-*trans*-12-hexadecadien-1-ol

35.

OH OH ─(CH$_2$)$_7$─ C=C ─ CH$_2$ ─ C=C ─ CH$_2$CH$_2$CH$_3$

OH OH ─(CH$_2$)$_7$─ C=C ─ CH$_2$ ─ C=C ─ CH$_2$CH$_2$CH$_3$

OH OH ─(CH$_2$)$_7$─ C=C ─ CH$_2$ ─ C=C ─ CH$_2$CH$_2$CH$_3$

OH OH ─(CH$_2$)$_7$─ C=C ─ CH$_2$ ─ C=C ─ CH$_2$CH$_2$CH$_3$

36. Two:

$$\underset{H}{\overset{Br}{>}}C\underset{H}{\overset{Cl}{<}} \qquad \underset{H}{\overset{Br}{>}}C\underset{Cl}{\overset{H}{<}}$$

37.

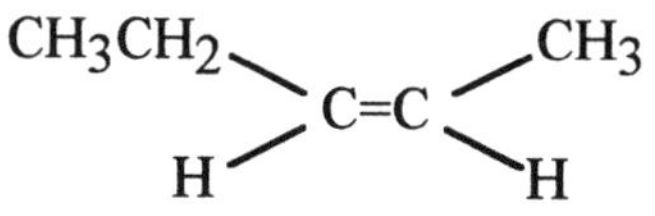

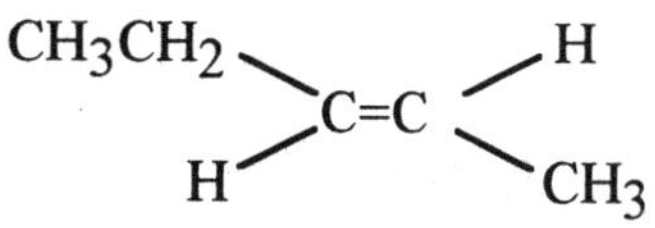

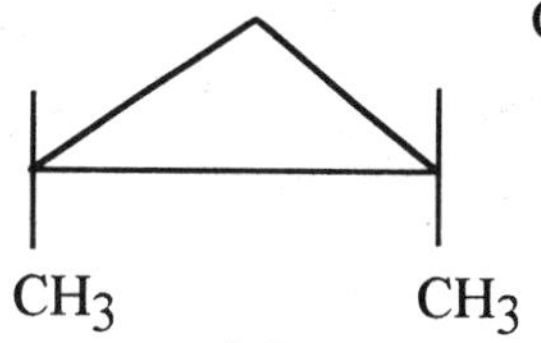

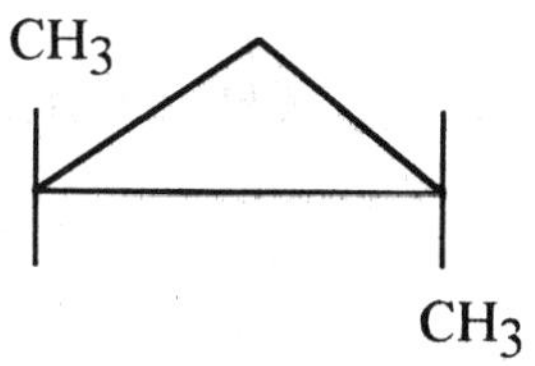

cis-2-pentene   *trans*-2-pentene

cis-1,2-
dimethylcyclopropane

*trans-*1,2-
dimethylcyclopropane

38. $CH_3CH_2CH(CH_3)CHO$

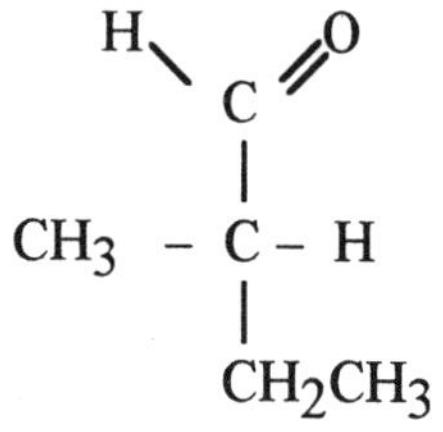

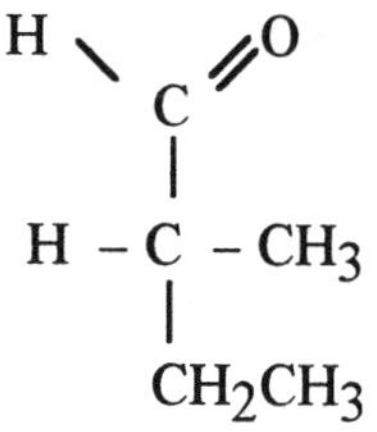

39. C_7H_{16}: $CH_3CH_2CH_2-\overset{\overset{\displaystyle CH_3}{|}}{\underset{\underset{\displaystyle H}{|}}{C}}-CH_2CH_3$ or $(CH_3)_2CH-\overset{\overset{\displaystyle CH_3}{|}}{\underset{\underset{\displaystyle H}{|}}{C}}-CH_2CH_3$

40.   a. $CH_3CH_2CH_2CH_2OH$ $CH_3CH_2CHOHCH_3$ $(CH_3)_2CHCH_2OH$ $(CH_3)_3COH$

b. $CH_3CH_2CHOHCH_3$

41.

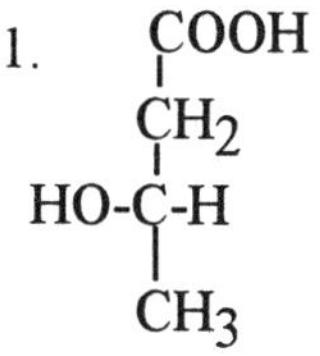

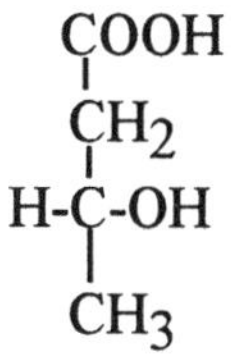

42.

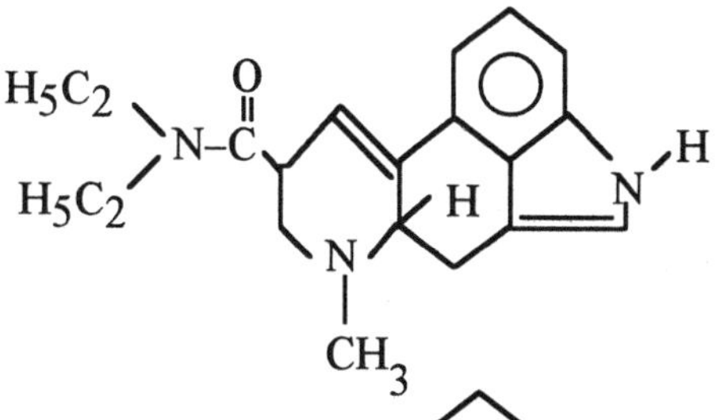

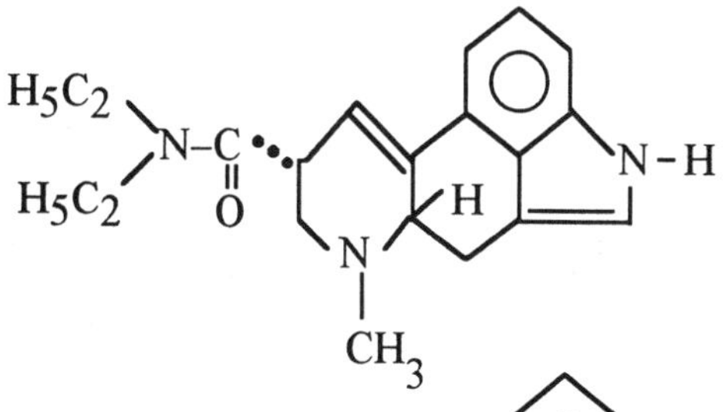

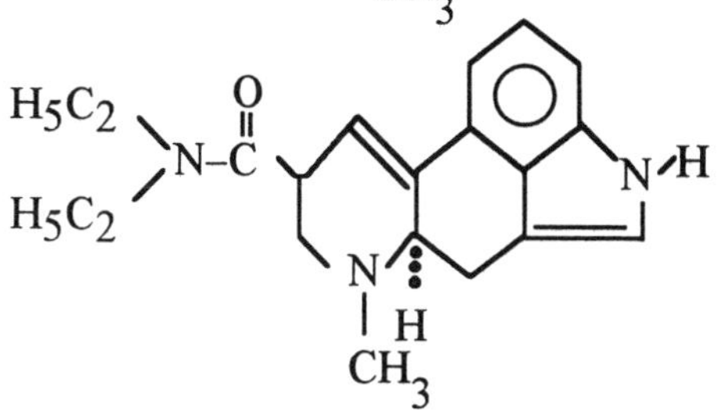

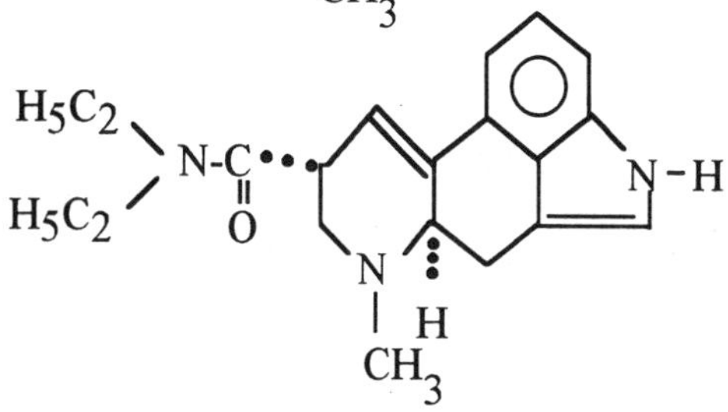

REVIEW QUESTIONS

1. The transformation is a photoisomerization, a reaction where a double bond in the molecule retinal is switched from the *cis* isomer to the *trans* isomer upon being hit by photons of light.

2. Vitamin A is the reduced form of retinal, the molecule involved in the visual reaction. It can be converted to retinal by enzyme reactions and subsequently used in the visual process.

3. The olfactory system is comprised of a number of different receptor cells. When a chemical or part of a chemical of a particular shape and charge fits into this receptor, it stimulates a nerve to the brain and an odor is perceived. Each odor is recognizable by the combination of the odor receptors it stimulates.

REVIEW QUESTIONS

1. a. Triose: a three carbon sugar
    b. Aldose: an aldehyde-containing sugar
    c. Hexose: a six carbon sugar
    d. Disaccharide: two monosaccharides connected by a glycosidic linkage
    e. Polysaccharide: high molecular weight polymers of monosaccharides joined by glycosidic linkages
    f. Aldopentose: a five carbon, aldehyde-containing sugar
    g. Ketotetrose: a four carbon, ketone-containing sugar
    h. Invert sugar: the products, fructose and glucose, of the hydrolysis of sucrose
    i. Mutarotation: the interconversion of alpha and beta forms of sugars
    j. Glycosidic linkage: acetal linkage between two sugars

2.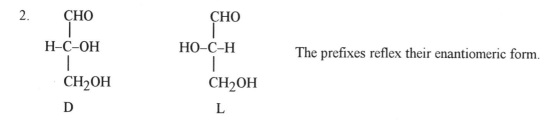

The prefixes reflex their enantiomeric form.

3. A latent carbonyl group is a functional group such as an acetal or hemiacetal that can be converted by some means to a carbonyl group.

4. A reducing sugar is any sugar capable of reducing certain agents (Cu^{+2}, Ag^+) and thus being oxidized itself.

5. Yes. They are small molecules with plenty of hydrogen-bonding –OH groups.

6. The rotation of plane polarized light (thus the +,– designation) is not tied to the L, D designation.

7. If one measures the specific rotation of the solution with polarimetry, one will find that the values will change from +112° to +52.7 (for an equilibrium mixture of alpha and beta forms).

8. Ribose has an –OH group on carbon #2 while deoxyribose has only hydrogens on this carbon.

9. Starch serves as fuel for the plant, particularly for the seedling. Cellulose is the structural support of the plant. It is what makes up the bulk of the stems, leaves, and trunk.

10. Glycogen serves as a fuel source for muscles and as a source of surplus glucose molecules for the liver.

11. a. glucose; b. lactose; c. glucose; d. fructose; e. sucrose; f. maltose

12. Amylopectin contains an occasional α-1,6-glycosidic linkage while amylose does not. They both have α-1,4- glycosidic linkages between glucose as their primary polymeric linkage.

13. Amylose contains α-1,4-glycosidic linkages while the linkage in cellulose is β-1,4. They both are polymers of glucose.

14. Glycogen has more frequent 1,6-glycosidic linkages than amylopectin.

PROBLEMS

CLASSIFICATION

15. a. D; b. L

16. a. L; b. L

17. Aldoses: a, b, c; Ketoses: d

18. Aldoses: a, c, d; Ketoses: b

19. a. hexose; b. pentose

20. a. hexose; b. triose

STRUCTURAL FORMULAS

21. 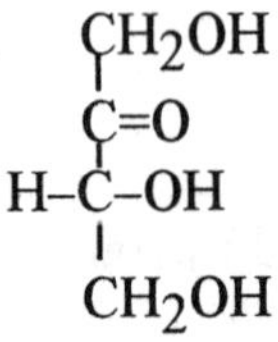
```
     CH2OH
     |
     C=O
     |
  H–C–OH
     |
     CH2OH
```

22. 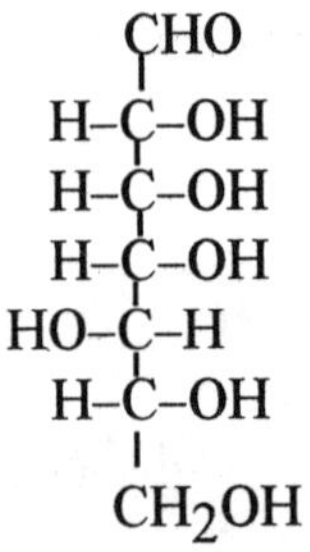
```
        CHO
        |
     H–C–OH
        |
     H–C–OH
        |
     H–C–OH
        |
    HO–C–H
        |
     H–C–OH
        |
       CH2OH
```

23. 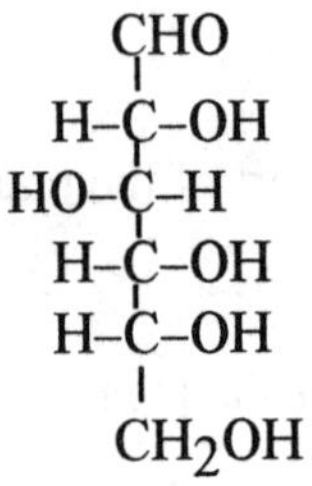
```
        CHO                        CHO
        |                          |
     H–C–OH                    HO–C–H
        |                          |
    HO–C–H                     HO–C–H
        |         D-Glucose        |          D-Mannose
     H–C–OH                     H–C–OH
        |                          |
     H–C–OH                     H–C–OH
        |                          |
       CH2OH                      CH2OH
```

24. 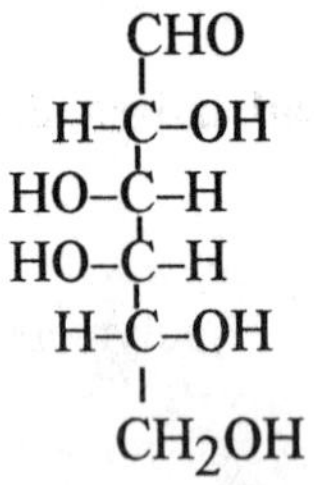
```
        CHO              CH2OH
        |                |
     H–C–OH              C=O
        |                |
    HO–C–H           HO–C–H
        |                |
    HO–C–H            H–C–OH
        |                |
     H–C–OH            H–C–OH
        |                |
       CH2OH            CH2OH

     D-Galactose       D-Fructose
```

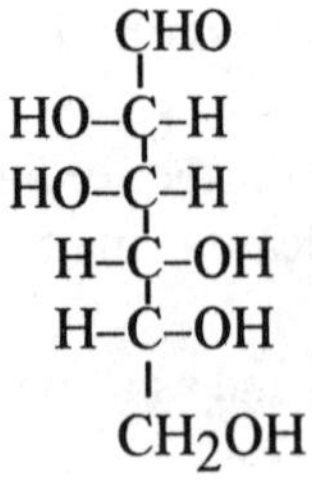

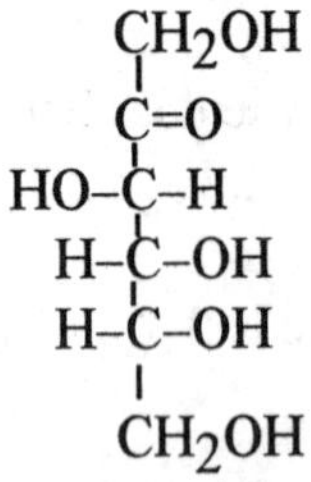

25.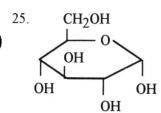

26.

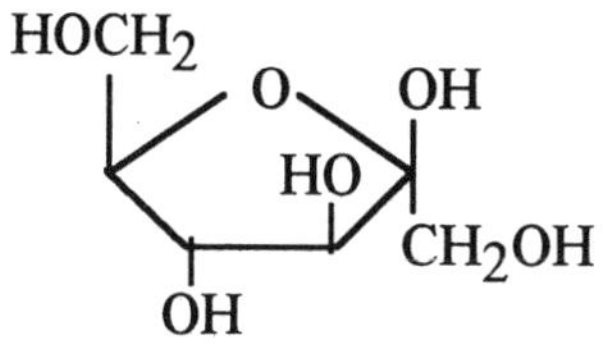

27.

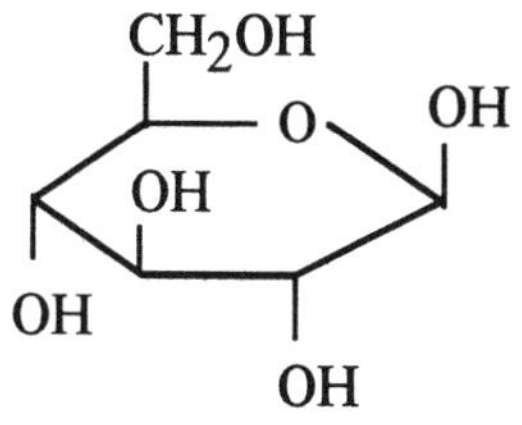

28.

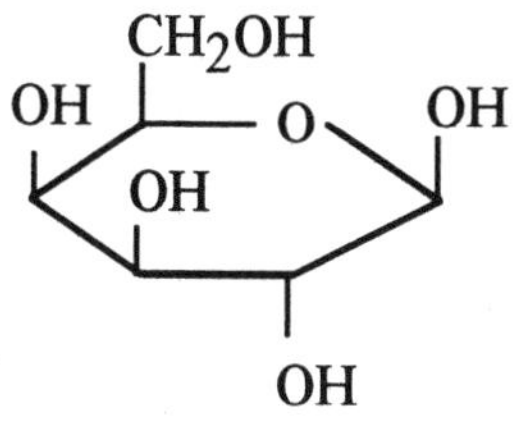

GLYCOSIDES

29. a. beta; b. alpha

30. a. beta; b. alpha

31. a. alpha; b. beta; both are reducing sugars

32. a. beta; b is *not* a reducing sugar

33. a. beta; b. no; c. no

34. galactose, glucose; alpha linkage; Yes, it is a reducing sugar. The hemiacetal carbon is the final carbon all the way to the right. It is in the alpha configuration.

35.

36.

CHEMICAL REACTIONS

37. a, b, c, and d will give positive tests

38. a, b, c, and f will give positive tests

39. a. glucose; b. glucose; c. glucose

40. a. glucose and fructose; b. glucose; c. glucose and galactose

41. a. $Ag(NH_3)_2^+$ b. CH_3OH, HCl

42. a. H^+ or maltase

ADDITIONAL PROBLEMS

43.

44. It needs to have one free hemiacetal carbon not involved in a glycosidic linkage.

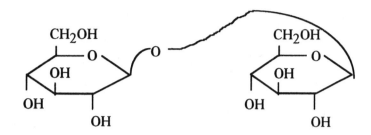

CH2OH
O
OH
O
OH
OH
CH2OH
O
OH
OH
OH

45.

CH2OH
OH
O
OH
OH
O
CH2
O
OH
OH
OH
HOCH2
O
O
HO
CH2OH
OH

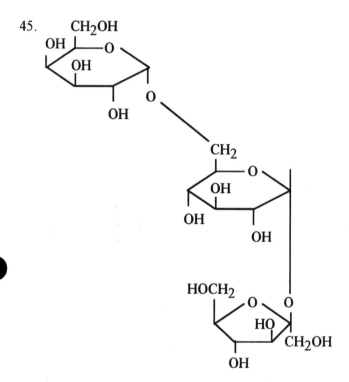

46. Glycogen

47. The L form of a ketopentose.

48. The L form of a ketotetrose.

49.

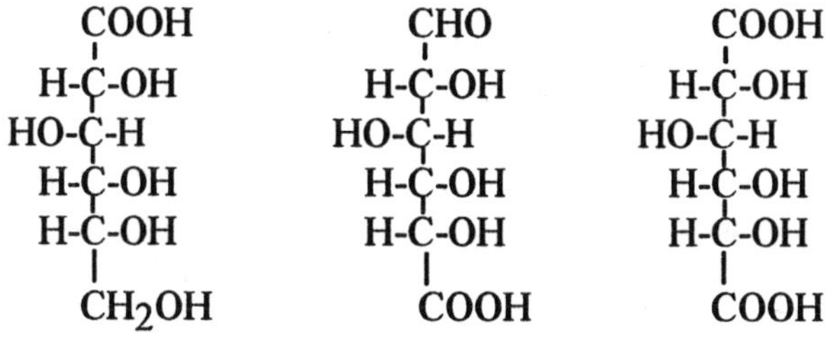

COOH
H-C-OH
HO-C-H
H-C-OH
H-C-OH
CH2OH
CHO
H-C-OH
HO-C-H
H-C-OH
H-C-OH
COOH
COOH
H-C-OH
HO-C-H
H-C-OH
H-C-OH
COOH

D-Gluconic Acid

D-Glucuronic Acid

D-Glucaric Acid

50. Galactose and fructose

REVIEW QUESTIONS

1. a. Triglyceride: An ester composed of three fatty acids joined to glycerol.
   b. Phosphatide: Esters of glycerol in which there are two fatty acids and one phosphate group.
   c. Iodine number: A measure of the degree of unsaturation of a fat or oil.
   d. Antioxidant: A compound that is added to foods, in very small amounts, to suppress randicity.
   e. Micelle: Aggregation of molecules that contain both polar and nonpolar groups.
   f. Semipermeable: A membrane or other boundary permeable to some solutes but not others.
   g. Steroid: Any compound that contains the perhydrocyclopentanophenanthrene structure.

2. a. A fat is a lipid that is a solid at room temperature (20 °C), whereas an oil is a liquid at the same temperature.
   b. A fat is a lipid comprised of three fatty acids esterified to glycerol, whereas a wax is a lipid comprised of a fatty acid esterified to a long-chain alcohol.
   c. A saponifiable lipid can be hydrolyzed under alkaline conditions, whereas a nonsaponifiable lipid cannot undergo hydrolysis because there are no ester linkages in the molecule.
   d. The H atoms lie on the same side of the double bond in the *cis*-configuration. In the *trans*-configuration, the H atoms lie on opposite sides of the double bond.
   e. In a simple triglyceride, the lipid molecule contains three identical fatty acids, whereas a mixed triglyceride is composed of two or three different fatty acid components.
   f. Butter is an animal fat that contains a relatively high percentage of low molecular weight fatty acids, whereas margarine is a butter-like substance obtained from the partial hydrogenation of vegetable oil.
   g. Oxidative rancidity arises from a complex process in which oxygen reacts with triglycerides that are rich in polyunsaturated fatty acids. Bond cleavage results in the production of short-chain carboxylic acids that are responsible for the disagreeable odor. Hydrolytic rancidity occurs under moist, warm conditions whereby microorganisms secrete lipases that catalyze the hydrolysis of the ester linkages present in lipid molecules. The eventual release of low molecular weight acids accounts for the offensive odor associated with rancidity.
   h. Hydrophobic generally refers to a substance that lacks an affinity for water, whereas hydrophilic substances are soluble in water.
   i. Saponification is the alkaline hydrolysis of an ester, whereas emulsification is the conversion of a large, water-insoluble lipid glob into a suspension of small lipid globules.
   j. A monolayer is a single layer of polar lipids one molecule thick while a bilayer is an arrangement of polar lipids two molecules thick with the inside of the arrangement being hydrophobic.
   k. Hard water contains certain metal ions such as calcium and magnesium. These ions form complexes with the carboxylate ions of soaps and form insoluble precipitates. Soft water lacks the metal ions that form such precipitates.
   l. Hard soaps are sodium salts of long-chain carboxylic acids (fatty acids), whereas soft soaps are potassium salts of long-chain carboxylic acids.
   m. Soaps are salts of fatty acids. They tend to form precipitates in hard water. Syndets are synthetic detergents that do not form precipitates in hard water.
   n. LDLs are lipid and protein-containing micelles which carry cholesterol whereas HDLs (also being lipid and protein-containing micelles) carry less cholesterol. LDLs are associated with laying down cholesterol onto arteries while HDLs have been associated with removal (or at least a less rapid laying down) of cholesterol onto arteries.

o. Phosphatides are glycerol esters which contain 2 fatty acids and a phosphate group while sphingolipids are phospholipids consisting of a sphingosine backbone (long-chain unsaturated amino alcohol), fatty acids, phosphate, and a polar alcohol component. Phospholipids are the main structural component of cell membranes.

p. Lecithin (phosphatidyl choline) is a phosphoglyceride comprised of the quaternary ammonium salt choline esterified to the phosphoric acid portion of a phosphatidic acid parent compound. The cephalins are phosphoglycerides comprised of either ethanolamine or serine compound. The cephalins are phosphoglycerides comprised of either ethanolamine or serine esterified to the phosphate group of the parent compound.

q. Bile is synthesized in the liver and concentrated within the gallbladder. It consists of water, cholesterol, and a variety of bile salts, acids, and pigments. The most important components of bile are the bile salts. They are derived from cholesterol and aid in the emulsification and absorption of dietary lipids.

3. Fats are the body's primary energy reserve. In addition, they perform a number of vital functions in the body including maintenance of body temperature and insulation of organs and tissues against mechanical and electrical shocks and are integral components of biological membranes.

4. All fats are solids. Saturated fatty acids are solids, but unsaturated fatty acids are liquids. Both fats and fatty acids are insoluble in water. Fats and oils are soluble in nonpolar organic solvents, e.g., benzene, carbon tetrachloride.

5. Unsaturated fatty acids have low melting points due to the stereochemical nature of their double bonds. In unsaturated fatty acids, the *cis* configuration of the double bonds causes severe kinks or bends in the long hydrocarbon tail of the molecule. This prevents molecules from packing tightly together and thus weakens the hydrophobic interactions that exist between adjacent fatty acids.

6. Triolein

7. Corn oil. The more double bonds in a compound, the lower the melting point and the greater the tendency for being an oil at room temperature. More double bonds means a higher iodine number.

8. Double bond

9. Liquid margarine. Liquid or liquid-like fats have more double bonds and thus a higher iodine number.

10. Tristearin. Tristearin.

11. a. fatty acids and glycerol
    b. salts of fatty acids and glycerol

12. a. butyric acid
    b. the hydrolysis of the ester linkages
    c. storing the butter covered in a refrigerator will protect the butter from water vapor in the air and the cold temperature will inhibit the growth of microorganisms that produce hydrolytic enzymes.

13. Yes, waxes can be converted into soaps. Waxes are esters of fatty acids and long-chain alcohols. Therefore, they may undergo alkaline hydrolysis (saponification) to yield salts of fatty acids (soaps) and alcohols.

14. a. Carnauba wax (myricyl cerotate): plant wax - used as a floor and automobile wax and as a coating on carbon paper and mimeograph stencils.
   b. Spermaceti wax (cetyl palmitate): animal wax - used in the manufacture of candles, cosmetics, and ointments.
   c. Lanolin (fatty acid esters of lanosterol and agnosterol): animal wax - used as a base for creams, ointments, and salves.
   d. Beeswax (myricyl palmitate): insect wax - used in the production of candles, wax paper, cosmetics, and medicinals.

15. The cleansing action of soap is largely dependent upon the dual nature of the fatty acid salts. The hydrophilic carboxylate group of the soap molecule is attracted to water, whereas the hydrophobic hydrocarbon tail is repelled from the aqueous surface. When in contact with grease, the hydrophobic groups dissolve in the lipid and the hydrophilic groups remain oriented toward the aqueous phase. Mechanical agitation serves to emulsify the grease into many water-soluble micelles that are easily washed away.

16. a. A detergent must have both a hydrophobic portion and a hydrophilic portion within the same molecule.
   b. The advantage of synthetic detergents is that they do not precipitate out of hard water.
   c. The disadvantage of detergents is that they may contribute to the eutrophication of lakes and streams.

17. Phospholipids are referred to as polar lipids because the phospholipid molecule contains both the nonpolar fatty acids as well as a polar component. An oxygen of the phosphate group is negatively charged, and the nitrogen (of the nitrogenous component) is positively charged.

18. They all are comprised of a polar, ionic "head" and long nonpolar tails.

19. c,d

20. Cholesterol is the compound that gets laid down by LDLs thus initiating the atherosclerosis process. Saturated fats somehow encourages this process by a mechanism little understood. There is evidence that fish oils lower cholesterol and triglyceride levels in the blood, thus decreasing the tendency for atherosclerosis to occur.

21. An integral protein is a protein that extends either partially or fully into the lipid bilayer. They may act as receptors, transport proteins, enzymes, or may have a structural function.

22. A peripheral protein is a protein that has a loose association with the lipid bilayer. They are found on both surfaces in contact with the polar head groups of the polar lipids.

PROBLEMS

CLASSIFICATION

23. Saturated: a,c; Unsaturated: b

24. Saturated: a,c; Unsaturated: b

25. b

26. c

27. Glycerol: a; Sphingosine: b; neither c

28. Glycerol: a and b; neither: c

STRUCTURES AND NAMES

29.　　a. $CH_3(CH_2)_{14}COOH$; b. $CH_3(CH_2CH=CH)_3(CH_2)_7COOH$

$$
\begin{array}{l}
\quad\quad\quad\quad\quad\quad\overset{\displaystyle O}{\overset{\|}{}} \\
c.\quad CH_2\!-\!O\!-\!\overset{\|}{C}(CH_2)_7CH\!=\!CH(CH_2)_7CH_3 \\
\quad\quad |\quad\quad\overset{\displaystyle O}{\overset{\|}{}} \\
\quad\quad CH\!-\!O\!-\!\overset{\|}{C}(CH_2)_7CH\!=\!CH(CH_2)_7CH_3 \\
\quad\quad |\quad\quad\overset{\displaystyle O}{\overset{\|}{}} \\
\quad\quad CH_2\!-\!O\!-\!\overset{\|}{C}(CH_2)_7CH\!=\!CH(CH_2)_7CH_3
\end{array}
$$

30. a.
$$
\begin{array}{l}
C_{15}H_{31}\overset{O}{\overset{\|}{C}}\!-\!O\!-\!CH_2 \\
\quad\quad\overset{O}{\overset{\|}{}} \quad | \\
C_{15}H_{31}\overset{\|}{C}\!-\!O\!-\!CH \\
\quad\quad\overset{O}{\overset{\|}{}} \quad | \\
C_{15}H_{31}\overset{\|}{C}\!-\!O\!-\!CH_2
\end{array}
$$
b. $C_{17}H_{35}\overset{O}{\overset{\|}{C}}\!-\!OC_{16}H_{33}$
c.
$$
\begin{array}{l}
C_{17}H_{33}\overset{O}{\overset{\|}{C}}\!-\!O\!-\!CH_2 \\
\quad\quad\overset{O}{\overset{\|}{}} \quad | \\
C_{17}H_{31}\overset{\|}{C}\!-\!O\!-\!CH \\
\quad\quad\overset{O}{\overset{\|}{}} \quad | \\
C_{17}H_{33}\overset{\|}{C}\!-\!O\!-\!CH_2
\end{array}
$$

31.　　a.
$$
\begin{array}{l}
C_{17}H_{29}\overset{O}{\overset{\|}{C}}\!-\!O\!-\!CH_2 \\
\quad\quad\overset{O}{\overset{\|}{}} \quad | \\
C_{17}H_{29}\overset{\|}{C}\!-\!O\!-\!CH \\
\quad\quad\overset{O}{\overset{\|}{}} \quad | \\
C_{17}H_{29}\overset{\|}{C}\!-\!O\!-\!CH_2
\end{array}
$$
b. $C_{17}H_{33}COO^-Na^+$
c. $(C_{13}H_{27}COO^-)_2Ca^{+2}$

32.

33.
$$
\begin{array}{ll}
CH_2OH & Na^+\ ^-OOC(CH_2)_6CH_3 \\
| & \\
CHOH \quad + & Na^+\ ^-OOC(CH_2)_4CH_3 \\
| & \\
CH_2OH & Na^+\ ^-OOC(CH_2)_8CH_3
\end{array}
$$

34.

$$\begin{matrix} CH_2-O-\overset{O}{\overset{\|}{C}}-(CH_2)_{10}CH_3 \\ | \quad\quad O \\ CH-O-\overset{\|}{C}-(CH_2)_{10}CH_3 \\ | \quad\quad O \\ CH_2-O-\overset{\|}{C}-(CH_2)_{10}CH_3 \end{matrix} \quad \xrightarrow{\text{3NaOH}} \quad \begin{matrix} CH_2OH \\ | \\ CH-OH \\ | \\ CH_2OH \end{matrix} \quad + \quad 3\ Na^+\ {}^-OOC(CH_2)_{10}CH_3$$

ADDITIONAL PROBLEMS

35. The fatty acids initially attached to the glycerol would be oleic acids and the result of the saponification would be glycerol and three sodium oleates.

36.

$$\begin{matrix} C_{15}H_{31}C-O-CH_2 \\ \quad O \\ C_{17}H_{33}C-O-CH \\ \quad\quad\quad\quad | \quad\quad O \\ \quad\quad\quad\quad H_2C-O-\overset{\|}{P}-O-CH_2CH_2\overset{+}{N}(CH_3)_3 \\ \quad\quad\quad\quad\quad | \\ \quad\quad\quad\quad\quad O^- \end{matrix}$$

37. an amide linkage; an acetal linkage

38.

$$\begin{matrix} OH \quad\quad OH \\ | \quad\quad | \\ \quad OH \\ | \quad\quad\quad\quad\quad\quad\quad -O-\overset{O}{\overset{\|}{P}}-O-CH_2 \\ OH \quad\quad\quad\quad\quad\quad\quad | \quad\quad O \\ \quad OH \quad\quad\quad\quad\quad\quad O^- \quad CH-O-\overset{\|}{C}-R \\ \quad\quad\quad\quad\quad\quad\quad\quad\quad\quad | \quad\quad O \\ \quad\quad\quad\quad\quad\quad\quad\quad\quad CH_2-O-\overset{\|}{C}-R \end{matrix}$$

39.

40. a. The melting point of elaidic acid ($C_{17}H_{33}COOH$) is lower than the melting point of the 18-carbon stearic acid (saturated), yet higher than the melting point of its *cis*-isomer, oleic acid. Although oleic acid and elaidic acid are both 18-carbon fatty acids containing one double bond, the H atoms in elaidic acid are oriented on opposite sides of the double bond (*trans*-configuration). The *trans*-configuration does not distort the linearity of the hydrocarbon tail and thus adjacent molecules experience strong intermolecular attractions. The tight packing of the molecules accounts for the elevated melting point of elaidic acid as opposed to its *cis*-isomer (oleic acid). b. The m.p. of *trans*-hexadecenoic acid would be lower than the m.p. of elaidic acid. The former has a lower molecular weight (fewer carbon and hydrogen atoms), and hence weaker van der Waals forces of attraction between molecules.

41. 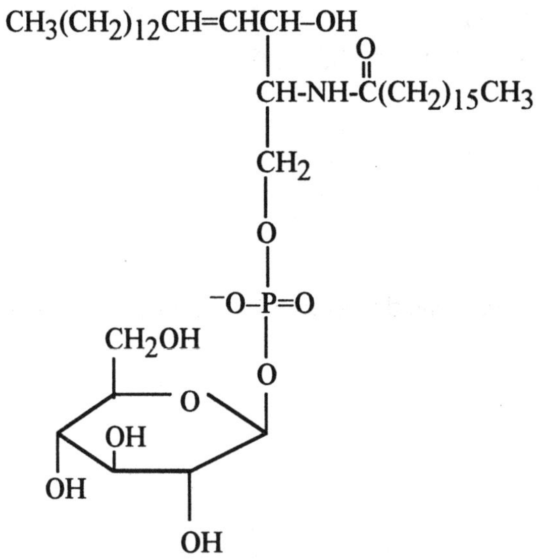 $CH_3(CH_2)_{12}CH=CHCH-OH$

   $CH-NH-\overset{\overset{O}{\|}}{C}(CH_2)_{15}CH_3$

   CH_2

   O

   $^-O-P=O$

   CH_2OH O

   O

   OH

   OH

   OH

42. Four -- one with three stearic acids, one with three oleic acids, one with two stearic acids and an oleic acid, and one with two oleic acids and a stearic acid.

43. $CH_3(CH_2)_{15}\overset{\overset{O}{\|}}{C}-O-CH_2(CH_2)_{14}CH_3$

44. glycerol, stearic acid, oleic acid, phosphate group; choline

45. 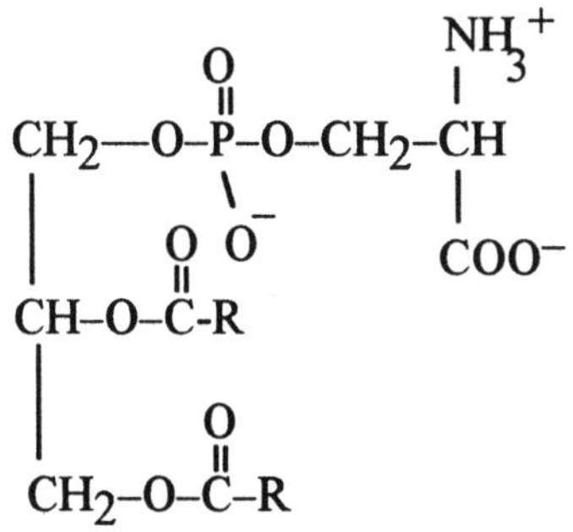 $CH_2-O-\overset{\overset{O}{\|}}{P}-O-CH_2-\overset{\overset{NH_3^+}{|}}{CH}$

   $\overset{\overset{|}{O} \overset{|}{O^-}}{}$ COO^-

   $CH-O-\overset{\overset{O}{\|}}{C}-R$

   $CH_2-O-\overset{\overset{O}{\|}}{C}-R$

PROJECTS

46. ——

47. ——

REVIEW QUESTIONS

1. Steps: 1) Hormone is synthesized in the endocrine gland. 2) Stimulation of gland by hormonal or neural stimulation causes release of hormone. 3) The hormone travels to the target tissue by the circulatory system. 4) The target tissue is affected in some manner by the hormone.

2. a. Hormone: A chemical messenger that is secreted into the blood by an endocrine gland. Example: insulin
   b. Androgen: A male sex hormone. Example: testosterone
   c. Estrogen: A female sex hormone. Example: estradiol;
   d. Progestin: A synthetic progesterone. Example: norethynodrel

3. a. 2; b. 3; c. 1; d. 4

4. Hypothalamus

5. Pituitary

6. Steps: 1) Neuron secretes neurotransmitter into synapse. 2) Neurotransmitter binds onto endocrine gland cell and stimulates it into releasing its hormone. 3) Hormone enters circulatory system and affects target tissue.

7. Steroids

8. The female sex hormone analogs used in oral contraceptives cause the body to shut down FSH and LH release at an inappropriate time for egg development. Thus the egg fails to develop correctly and the fertilization and growth process is halted.

9. The ethynyl group

10. The mineralocorticoids serve to regulate the exchange of sodium, potassium, and hydrogen ions across biological membranes. The glucocorticoids regulate many biological activities including the production of glucose, the mobilization of fatty acids and amino acids, and the inhibition of the inflammatory response.

11. Arachidonic acid serves as the precursor for the synthesis of the prostaglandins.

12. Potential therapeutic uses of the prostaglandins include the regulation of blood pressure, inhibition of gastric secretions, and relief of asthma and nasal congestion.

REVIEW QUESTIONS

1.
   a. Peptide bond: The amide linkage that joins two adjacent amino acids.
   b. Tripeptide: Three amino acids linked by peptide bonds.
   c. Disulfide Linkage: A sulfur-sulfur covalent bond formed between two cysteine R groups.
   d. Salt Linkage: An ionic bond between a positively-charged group (for example, a $-NH_3^+$ group) and a negatively charged group (for example, a $-COO^-$ group).
   e. Hydrophobic Interaction: The association of nonpolar groups as they attempt to get away from water in an aqueous environment.
   f. Primary Structure: The actual number and sequence of amino acids in a polypeptide chain.
   g. Secondary Structure: The description of the fixed conformation of a polypeptide backbone.
   h. Tertiary Structure: The unique three-dimensional conformation produced by folding and bending the polypeptide backbone.
   i. Quaternary Structure: A description of the association of polypeptide chains to one another in a multisubunit protein.
   j. Zwitterion: The dipolar ion form of an amino acid (electrically neutral).
   k. Isoelectric pH: The pH at which an amino acid exists in a zwitterion form (maintains a net charge = 0).
   l. Diuretic: A substance that increases the body's output of urine.
   m. Globular Protein: A protein that takes a roundish (as opposed to an extended) shape.
   n. Fibrous Protein: A protein that takes an extended shape.
   o. Electrophoresis: A process used to separate and identify charged compounds from a complex mixture of charged compounds by subjecting them to an electric field.
   p. Denaturation: Any change that alters the three-dimensional conformation of a protein without disrupting the integrity of the primary structure.

2. $NH_2-CH-COOH$
         |
         R

3. a. asparagine; b. glycine; c. hydroxyproline;

4. The L-family

5. A protein is the name given to a polypeptide of high molecular weight (generally greater than 10,000).

6. Amide bond

7. Globular

8. Globular

9. Heat, pH (acidic or basic conditions); disulfide reducing agents; organic compounds, heavy metal ions, hydrogen and salt bond-breaking agents.

10. Secondary, tertiary, and quaternary

11. Not usually.

12. a. An N-terminal amino acid is the amino acid at the end of the peptide chain that has a free amino group, whereas the C-terminal amino acid is at the opposite end of the chain and has a free carboxyl group.

   b. Oxytocin is a peptide hormone that controls lactation and promotes smooth muscle contraction. Vasopressin is a peptide hormone that induces a rise in blood pressure and serves to increase the retention of fluids by the kidney.

   c. The α-helical conformation of a polypeptide is a secondary structure maintained by intramolecular hydrogen bonding between the amide hydrogen of one peptide bond and a carbonyl oxygen of another peptide bond further along the chain. The β-pleated sheet is a secondary structure maintained by intermolecular hydrogen bonds between adjacent polypeptide chains.

   d. Primary structure is the actual number and sequence of amino acids in a polypeptide chain, whereas secondary structure describes the fixed conformation of a polypeptide backbone.

   e. Tertiary structure is a unique three-dimensional conformation produced by the folding and bending of a polypeptide backbone. Quaternary structure describes the conformation of proteins that consist of two or more polypeptide chains.

   f. Interchain H-bonds occur between components of two individual polypeptide chains, whereas intrachain H-bonds exist between components of a single polypeptide chain.

   g. Hemoglobin is a conjugated protein that consists of four polypeptide chains. (Each chain contains the prosthetic group heme.) Myoglobin is a conjugated protein that consists of a single polypeptide chain complexed to a heme group.

13. Bacteria in the milk produce lactic acid, which lowers the pH of the milk, causing the protein casein to precipitate out in the form of white curds.

14. a. The heat acts as a denaturing agent, disrupting the hydrogen bonds and hydrophobic interactions that stabilize the proteins present in the egg. This process results in the coagulation of the denatured proteins.

   b. Ultraviolet light and heat that are utilized as sterilization agents serve to disrupt the integrity of bacterial enzymes by denaturing the proteins that constitute those enzymes.

   c. The silver nitrate acts as an antiseptic in that it denatures bacterial enzymes and thus serves to prevent infection in the eyes of newborn infants.

15. A 100% alcohol solution only coagulates the proteins at the surface of the bacteria without killing them. A 70% solution is able to pass into the bacteria and denature enzymes vital to the survival of the bacteria.

16. Egg white is administered as an antidote for heavy metal poisoning because the proteins present within the egg white readily react with the heavy metal ions to form insoluble precipitates. The insoluble precipitate is then removed from the stomach in order to prevent the release of the poisonous ions upon digestion of the coagulated protein.

PROBLEMS

AMINO ACIDS: STRUCTURES AND NAMES

17.   —CH₂ ⟍
                  CH₂   b. –(CH₂)₄NH₂   c. –CH₂–⟨◯⟩–OH
       —CH₂ ⟋

18. a. $-CH_2COOH$ b. $-CH_2SH$ c. 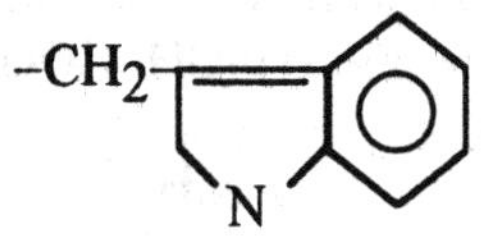 $-CH_2-$

19. a. NH_2-CH_2-COOH b. $NH_2-CH-COOH$
                                       |
                                      CH_3

c. $NH_2-CH-COOH$
         |
        CH
       / \
    CH_3 CH_3

20. a. $NH_2-CH-COOH$ b. 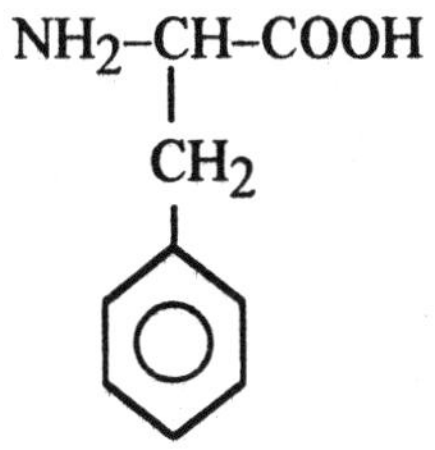 $NH_2-CH-COOH$ c. $NH_2-CH-COOH$
           | | |
         CH_2OH CH_2 $CH-CH_3$
                                                                |
                                                               CH_2
                                                                |
                                                               CH_3

21. $NH_3^+-CH-COO^-$
          |
         CH_2 Aspartic Acid (also Glutamic acid is an acidic amino acid)
          |
         $COOH$

22. $NH_3^+-CH-COO^-$
          |
        $(CH_2)_4$ Lysine (also arginine and histidine are basic amino acids)
          |
         NH_2

23. a. proline; b. histidine, tryptophan; c. phenylalanine, tyrosine, tryptophan; d. citrulline, ornithine, dihydroxyphenylalanine, thyroxine, homocysteine, homoserine, ß-alanine, γ-aminobutyric acid

24. a. arginine; b. cysteine; c. tyrosine; d. valine, leucine, isoleucine

PEPTIDES

25.
$$NH_3^+-CH_2-\overset{\overset{O}{\|}}{C}-NH-CH-COO^-$$
                                    |
                                   CH_3

b. $NH_3^+-CH-\overset{\overset{O}{\|}}{C}-NH-CH_2-COO^-$
          |
        CH_3

26.

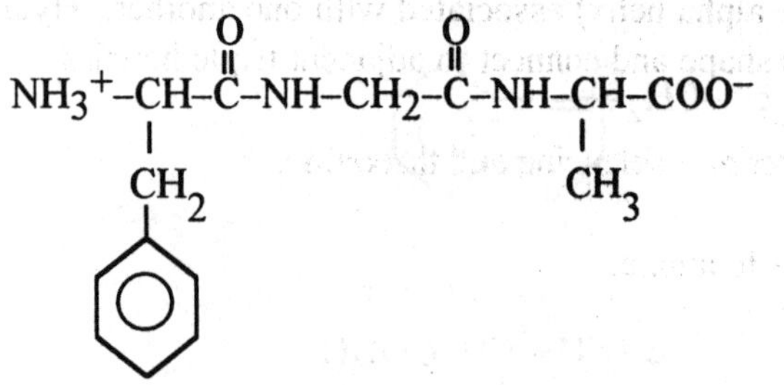

$$NH_3^+-CH-\overset{\overset{\displaystyle O}{\|}}{C}-NH-CH_2-\overset{\overset{\displaystyle O}{\|}}{C}-NH-CH-COO^-$$

with CH_2 branch (bearing a phenyl ring) on the first CH, and CH_3 branch on the last CH.

27. $NH_3^+-CH-\overset{\overset{\displaystyle O}{\|}}{C}-NH-CH-\overset{\overset{\displaystyle O}{\|}}{C}-NH-CH_2-COO^-$

with CH_2OH branch on the first CH and CH_3 branch on the second CH.

28. Ala–Ser–Cys–Phe

ACID–BASE REACTIONS

29. $H_2N-CH_2-COO^-\ Na^+$

30. $H_3N^+-CH_2-COOH$

31. a. low pH; b. high pH; c. isoelectric pH

32. At the isoelectric pH, the numbers of positive and negative charges on the protein are equal. The protein will not migrate in an electric field, will be least stable, and will most readily precipitate out of solution.

STRUCTURE OF PROTEINS

33. Silk has an arrangement of polypeptide chains in a manner where they run parallel to one another in a zigzag pattern. The chains are held together by hydrogen bonds. This secondary structure is called a ß-pleated sheet.

34. Wool has an arrangement of polypeptide chains where the polypeptide backbone coils on itself in a helical manner. Hydrogen bonds form between adjacent groups vertically in the helix. Wool is elastic because these hydrogen bonds can be stretched (elongated) and compressed (shortened) without disrupting its structure. This arrangement is called an alpha helix.

35. Salt linkages, hydrogen bonds, disulfide linkages, and hydrophobic interactions.

36. a. Salt linkages; b. hydrophobic bonding; c. hydrogen bonding; d. disulfide linkages

37. Globular: a; Fibrous: b,c

38. Globular: a,c; Fibrous: b

ADDITIONAL PROBLEMS

39. Collagen is made up of three helicies (different from the alpha helix) associated with one another. Hydrogen bonds and covalent bonds hold the triple helix in this shape and connect to adjacent triple helicies.

40. Two amino acids that contain more than one chiral center are isoleucine and threonine.

41. Alanine--stationary; histidine--to cathode; aspartic acid--to anode.

42. Lysine, alanine, phenylalanine, and glutamic acid.

43.
$$NH_3^+-CH-(CH_2)_2-\overset{\overset{O}{\|}}{C}-NH-CH-\overset{\overset{O}{\|}}{C}-NH-CH_2-COO^-$$
$$\underset{COO^-}{|} \qquad\qquad \underset{CH_2SH}{|}$$

44. The secondary structure of a protein is stabilized by hydrogen bonds between amino hydrogens and carbonyl oxygens (of the polypeptide backbone) either within the same molecule or between separate polypeptide chains. The hydrogen bonding that serves to stabilize the tertiary structure of proteins takes place between the amino acid side chains that project from the polypeptide backbone.

45. The acidic and basic groups in the side chains of the protein will react with bases and acids, respectively. This removes any excess acid or base, and thus the pH is maintained nearly constant.

46. a. +; b. +; c. −

47.
$$COO^-$$
$$|$$
$$H-C-NH_3^+$$
$$|$$
$$CH_3$$

48.
$$\overset{D}{\underset{|}{}}$$
$$NH_3^+-\overset{|}{C}-COO^-$$
$$\underset{H_2C-F}{|}$$

49.
$$NH_3^+-CH-CH_2-S-S-CH_2-CH-NH_3^+$$
$$\underset{COO^-}{|} \qquad\qquad\qquad \underset{COO^-}{|}$$

50. $NH_3^+-CH_2CH_2CH_2COO^-$; No; a neurotransmitter.

51. a

52.
$$NH_3^+-\underset{\underset{CH_3}{|}}{CH}-COO^- + H_3O^+ \longrightarrow NH_3^+-\underset{\underset{CH_3}{|}}{CH}-COOH + H_2O$$

$$NH_3^+-\underset{\underset{CH_3}{|}}{CH}-COO^- + OH^- \longrightarrow NH_2-\underset{\underset{CH_3}{|}}{CH}-COO^- + H_2O$$

53. Hemoglobin from different species has slightly different primary structures (although much of the sequence is identical).

54. Alanine

55. Inside: a, e   Outside: b, c, d, f

56. Since sugars are hydrophilic, water-soluble compounds, their incorporation as part of proteins improves the protein's overall solubility.

57.
$$NH_3^+-CH-\overset{\overset{O}{\|}}{C}-NH-CH-\overset{\overset{O}{\|}}{C}-O-CH_3$$

with CH_2 and COO^- substituents, and a CH_2–phenyl substituent.

REVIEW QUESTIONS

1. a. Enzyme: A complex organic catalyst produced by living cells.
    b. Substrate: The substance upon which an enzyme acts.
    c. Holoenzyme: An apoenzyme that is combined with a coenzyme to produce an active catalyst.
    d. Proenzyme: An enzyme that is synthesized in an inactive form and subsequently activated by covalent modification.
    e. Active site: The portion of an enzyme that binds to the substrate and at which transformation from substrate to product occurs.
    f. Chemotherapy: The use of chemicals (drugs) to destroy infectious microorganisms or cancer cells without damaging the cells of the host.
    g. Cofactor: An enzyme activator.
    h. Enzyme specificity: The concept that an enzyme will catalyze only a reaction involving a specific substrate or only a certain type of reaction.
    i. Irreversible inhibition: The permanent inactivation of an enzyme due to the covalent attachment of a molecule (the inhibitor).
    j. Sulfa drug: Derivative of sulfanilamide; an antibacterial agent.

2. a. Experiments performed *in vitro* are conducted in a test tube, whereas *in vivo* reactions take place within a living organisms.
    b. Intracellular enzymes are synthesized in cells and carry out their catalytic activities within those cells. Extracellular enzymes are synthesized within cells, then secreted to catalyze reactions outside the cell.
    c. Sucrose is the substrate molecule (disaccharide) that is hydrolyzed by the enzyme sucrase into its constituent monosaccharides (glucose and fructose).
    d. Trypsin is a proteolytic enzyme that catalyzes the hydrolysis of peptides in the small intestine. Trypsinogen is the inactive precursor form (zymogen) of the enzyme trypsin.
    e. The induced-fit theory depicts the active site of an enzyme as a flexible, dynamic structure. The contact groups are a cluster of amino acids responsible for the proper orientation of the substrate within the active site, whereas the catalytic groups are those amino acids that directly participate in the transformation of the substrate into product.
    f. Enzymes that exhibit absolute specificity catalyze a particular reaction for one particular substrate and do not react with structurally similar substrates. Those enzymes that exhibit stereochemical specificity react only with a particular stereoisomeric form of a particular substrate molecule (e.g., an enzyme that reacts with the D-form of a particular sugar but not with the L-form of that sugar).
    g. Group specificity refers to the enzymes that react with structurally similar molecules that have the same functional group. Enzymes that exhibit linkage specificity react with a particular type of chemical bond regardless of the structural features surrounding that linkage; they are the least specific of all the enzyme classes.
    h. Optimum temperature is the temperature at which a given enzyme exhibits maximum catalytic activity, whereas optimum pH is the pH value at which an enzyme exhibits maximum activity.
    i. A competitive inhibitor is a compound that is structurally similar to an enzyme's natural substrate and competes with that substrate for occupation of the same active site. A noncompetitive inhibitor is a compound that is structurally dissimilar from an enzyme's normal substrate and can combine with either the free enzyme or the enzyme-substrate complex.
    j. An antimetabolite is a compound that structurally resembles an enzyme's normal substrate and acts to competitively inhibit a significant metabolic reaction. An antibiotic is a substance that is produced by one microorganism (or synthesized in the laboratory) that functions to inhibit the growth of another microorganism.

3. a. Maltose; b. cellulose; c. proteins (peptides); d. lipids

4. Enzymes and ordinary catalysts both increase the rates of chemical reactions. Enzymes are much more specific than ordinary catalysts. Although an enzyme-catalyzed reaction's equilibrium is reached more quickly, the enzyme does not alter the position of equilibrium in a reversible reaction.

5. Because of the unique amino acid R-groups present at the active site and the unique geometric conformation of the active site.

6. Animals lack the enzymes necessary for the hydrolysis of the β-1,4-glucosidic linkage found in cellulose. Animals do possess the enzymes needed to hydrolyze the α-1,4 and α-1,6-glucosidic linkages that characterize the starch polymer.

7. Intracellular enzymes: lactic acid dehydrogenase, fumarase, succinic acid dehydrogenase. Extracellular enzymes: ptyalin, pepsin, trypsin.

8. Urease

9. The turnover number is the number of substrate molecules (in moles) that an enzyme can act upon per unit time (usually one minute).

10. Mercury ions have a strong affinity for carboxylate and sulfhydryl groups; groups that may be critical for catalytic activity or proper conformation. Irreversible.

11. Acetylcholine is a neurotransmitter released by cholinergic neurons. The cycle of its action is:
    1) Acetycholine is synthesized in the neuron from choline and acetyl CoA and stored in synaptic vesicles.
    2) Upon a neural stimulation, acetylcholine is released into the synapse. It binds to receptors on the target tissue (perhaps a second neuron) and stimulates that tissue.
    3) Acetylcholinesterase breaks the acetylcholine in the synapse down into acetate and choline. These are taken back into the presynaptic neuron and are resynthesized into acetylcholine.

12. Organic phosphorus compounds act as irreversible inhibitors of acetylcholinesterase. Thus, acetylcholine in the synapse remains there and continuously stimulates the target tissue. This overstimulation causes convulsions and death.

13. Sulfa drugs act as competitive inhibitors for bacterial enzymes which use a metabolite called p-aminobenzoic acid. We (humans) do not have this enzyme, therefore, sulfa drugs do not affect our cells.

14. Penicillin binds irreversibly to an enzyme called transpeptidase. Transpeptidase is an important enzyme responsible for a step in bacterial cell wall synthesis. Inhibition of this enzyme by penicillin prohibits proper formation of the cell wall and, thus, bacterial death.

15. They produce an enzyme, penicillinase, which breaks down penicillin before it can cause harm to the transpeptidase.

16. An inhibitor is any factor that suppresses the catalytic activity of an enzyme.

17. Enzymes function by first combining with a substrate molecule to form an intermediate compound referred to as an enzyme-substrate complex. (This intermediate is more reactive than the substrate alone.) In a subsequent step this intermediate reacts further (usually with another reactant) to form products and to regenerate the enzyme. Thus, the enzyme can run a reaction over and over again.

18. The lock and key theory is a static model. The substrate must have the correct conformation and the complementary groups to match the conformation and groups at the active site of the enzyme. Only those molecules that can bind to the active site will undergo reaction. The induced-fit theory, on the other hand, proposes that several different molecules can bind to the active site, but only those in which there is proper alignment of the catalytic groups will undergo further reaction.

19. Although two amino acids are far apart in the primary structure of a protein chain, they may be brought within proximity at the active site during the unique folding and bending that characterizes the three-dimensional globular nature of enzyme molecules (tertiary structure).

20. The other amino acids help hold the active site in a specific conformation required for catalysis.

PROBLEMS

CLASSIFICATION

21. a. Lyases; b. peptidases; c. transferases;

22. a. oxidoreductases; b. transferases; c. hydrolases

ENZYME ACTION

23. So that trypsin will not be active in the pancreas (where it's synthesized) and, thus, degrade important proteins in that tissue.

24. A hexapeptide is cleaved from trypsinogen to form active trypsin. This cleavage occurs in response to the presence of food in the intestine.

25. It doubles.

26. a. the rate decreases; b. the rate decreases

27. Less active in both cases.

28. a. Above the optimum temperature, excessive heat causes the denaturation of the enzyme. Heat, as a denaturing agent, disrupts those interactions responsible for maintaining the unique conformation of the enzyme. Below the optimum temperature, chemical reactions occur much more slowly because of a decrease in the kinetic energy of the molecules. Slow-moving molecules collide less frequently and therefore the probability of a favorable reaction (product formation) decreases.
    b. Above and below the optimum pH, the enzyme will become denatured.

29. It increases the rate. (More enzymes working at a given time on substrate)

30. a. hydrogen bonding groups; b. positively charged groups (salt linkages); c. hydrogen bonding groups;

d. negatively charged groups (salt linkages); e. hydrogen bonding groups; f. sulfhydryl groups (disulfide linkages); g. nonpolar groups (hydrophobic interactions); h. nonpolar groups (hydrophobic interactions)

CLASSIFICATION AND NAMING

31. a. ethanol; b. Zn^{+2}; c. protein molecule without the Zn^{+2} ion

32. No. Coenzymes are organic.

33. Yes. Yes.

34. Prothrombin

35. Lactase. Hydrolases.

36. An isomerase

37. Penicillin-like compounds can be synthesized which resist cleavage by penicillase; a penicillase inhibitor (like clauvulinic acid) can be combined with the penicillin to prevent its (the penicillin) degradation.

ADDITIONAL PROBLEMS

38. The R group of aspartic acid needs to be in the deprotonated, ionized form (i.e. $-CH_2COO^-$) in order for the catalysis to occur. This form is not present in acidic media but occurs in increasing concentatrations as the pH is raised.

39. Ethanol, at relatively high concentration, would out-compete methanol for the active site. This results in less action of alcohol dehydrogenase on methanol and less formation of the toxic product of methanol (formaldehyde).

40. A competitive inhibitor is a compound that structurally resembles the substrate and competes with the substrate for the active site of an enzyme. The inhibitory effect is reversible by increasing substrate concentration. A noncompetitive inhibitor is a compound that forms strong bonds with either the free enzyme or the enzyme-substrate complex. It bonds to the enzyme at a site remote from the active site, but in so doing, alters the conformation of the active site.

41. Yes; it is a competitive inhibitor.

42. Because they are both effective inhibitors of a wide variety of enzymes that are essential to the growth of microorganisms.

REVIEW QUESTIONS

1. a. Vitamin: Organic compound that cannot be synthesized by an organism, but which is essential.
    b. Provitamin: A precursor compound which will be converted into a vitamin form.
    c. Coenzyme: An organic cofactor for an enzyme.

2. a. Minerals are inorganic while vitamins are organic.
    b. Both minerals and vitamins are essential in our diets.
    c. Neither minerals nor vitamins are needed in large amounts in our bodies.

3. Fat-soluble is more dangerous. We generally excrete excess water-soluble vitamins readily in the urine. Fat-soluble vitamins build up in fatty tissues (including the brain). Large excesses can cause a variety of toxic effects.

4. No. We eliminate vitamins daily via the urine and feces. Without daily ingestion of vitamins the level of vitamins in the body would fall dangerously low.

5. The water soluble vitamins (vitamin C excluded) are transformed into coenzymes we need for normal metabolism.

6. The water-soluble vitamins would tend to leach out of the plant tissue, into the cooking water, and therefore be lost. The fat-soluble vitamins would be lost less readily.

7. Liver, red meat, and eggs. (Also green vegetables for many)

8. Because we can make Vitamin D in our skin by a reaction requiring sunlight and 7-dehydrocholesterol.

9. Polyunsaturated fatty acids (in cell membranes) and Vitamin A.

10. "B-complex" is a group of water soluble vitamins found in many foods.

11. Niacin

12. Riboflavin

13. Pantothenic acid

14. Water-soluble vitamins have polar groups attached which make them soluble while fat-soluble vitamins are comprised primarily of carbons and hydrogens.

PROBLEMS

NAMES AND CLASSIFICATION

15. Ascorbic acid – Vitamin C; Ergocalciferol – Vitamin D; Cyanocobalamin – Vitamin B_{12}; Retinol – Vitamin A; Tocopherol – Vitamin E.

16. a,c,d,e,f

17. Scurvy = vitamin C deficiency; Rickets = vitamin D deficiency; night blindness = vitamin A deficiency

18. Vitamin B_1 (thiamine): beriberi; Niacin: pellagra; Vitamin B_{12} (cyanocobalamin): pernicious anemia

SOLUBILITY

19. Water soluble: B_6, B_{12}, C; fat soluble: A, K

20. Water soluble: b,c; fat soluble: a,c

21. a. water soluble; b. fat soluble

22. Despite being of high molecular weight, vitamin B_{12} has many polar groups (particularly amide groups) that can hydrogen bond with water and, thus, make it soluble.

ADDITIONAL PROBLEMS

23.   a. Vitamin A: involved in photoreception, night blindness
      b. Vitamin D: involved in proper bone metabolism, rickets
      c. Vitamin E: works as an antioxidant, sterility in rats
      d. Vitamin C: works as an antioxidant to help proper collagen formation, scurvy

24. a. Niacin and riboflavin; b. Biotin; c. Thiamine; d. Pyridoxine; e. Folic acid; f. Cyanocobalamin

25. No, ascorbic acid is a chemical which is the same whether it is made naturally or synthetically. Vitamin C tablets can contain all sorts of other ingredients along with the ascorbic acid. Perhaps some of these help in preventing the vitamin C from deteriorating with time or in helping absorption or action of the vitamin C once in the body.

REVIEW QUESTIONS

1. a. Ribosome: A cellular substructure that serves as the site for protein synthesis.
    b. Template Replication: During replication, each strand of DNA serves as a pattern for the biosynthesis of its complementary strand.
    c. Multiplicity: The term applied to the situation in which several tRNAs can bind to and transfer the same amino acid.
    d. Complementary bases: The stable base pairs held together by hydrogen bonds in the double-stranded helix of DNA. Adenine pairs with thymine, and guanine pairs with cytosine.
    e. Genetic Code: The concept that the sequence of bases in DNA serves to direct the synthesis of proteins within the cell. 61 of the 64 possible three-base sequences signify a particular amino acid.
    f. Translocation: The movement of the ribosome along the mRNA strand a distance of 1 codon in the $5' \longrightarrow 3'$ direction.
    g. Code degeneracy: The concept that more than one nucleotide triplet (codon) can code for the same amino acid.
    h. Mutagens: Chemical or physical agents that can alter the base sequence of DNA.
    i. Genetic diseases: Diseases that arise from nonlethal mutations in the DNA of the germ cells.
    j. PKU: A genetic disease in which the afflicted individual is unable to convert phenylalanine to tyrosine; instead phenylalanine is converted to phenylpyruvate.
    k. Amniocentesis: A diagnostic assay of amniotic fluid.
    l. Recombinant DNA: A DNA molecule that is formed by splicing a segment of DNA from one organism into the DNA of a second organism.
    m. Plasmid: Small, closed loops of DNA, found in *E. coli*, that are used as the vectors in recombinant DNA research.
    n. Restriction enzyme: Enzymes that cleave phosphodiester bonds at sites along a DNA molecule containing a particular nucleotide sequence.

2. a. The pyrimidine bases are derivatives of pyrimidine; purine bases are derivatives of purine (a pyrimidine ring fused to an imidazole ring).
    b. The major bases are adenine, guanine, thymine, cytosine, and uracil. The minor bases are modified derivatives of the major bases.
    c. Ribose is the pentose sugar found in RNA. It has an OH group on carbon-2. Deoxyribose is the pentose found in DNA, and it has an H instead of OH on carbon-2.
    d. A nucleoside consists of a purine or pyrimidine base joined to either ribose or deoxyribose. A nucleotide is a nucleoside bonded to a phosphate group.
    e. Nucleic acids are polymers of nucleotides.
    f. DNA polymerase is the enzyme that catalyzes the biosynthesis of DNA by linking nucleotides together according to the pattern established by a DNA template. DNA ligase is an enzyme that catalyzes the linkage of short fragments of DNA during replication and repairs broken strands.
    g. The codon is the specific three-base sequence of nucleotides on the mRNA strand that codes for a particular amino acid. The anticodon is a complementary three-base sequence on the tRNA.
    h. Chromosomes are composed of DNA molecules. A gene is a segment of the DNA molecule that codes for the synthesis of a particular polypeptide.
    i. Transcription is the process of synthesizing a mRNA molecule from one strand of DNA that serves as the template. Translation is the synthesis of a polypeptide at the ribosome from the information encoded in the mRNA.

j. A mutation is any chemical or physical change that alters the sequence of bases in the DNA. If the alteration in the base sequence occurs at just one nucleotide in the DNA polymer, then it is called a point mutation.

3. a. ribonucleic acid (RNA) and deoxyribonucleic acid (DNA); b. DNA

4. DNA is usually found in a double helical form while RNA may exist in several forms dependent on the type of RNA (i.e. its primary sequence).

5. a. adenine, guanine, thymine, cytosine, deoxyribose, phosphoric acid
   b. adenine, guanine, uracil, cytosine, ribose, phosphoric acid

6. Thymine differs from uracil only in having a methyl group in place of a hydrogen on carbon number 5. This portion of the molecule does not participate in hydrogen bonding.

7. Phosphoric acid is a major structural component of the backbone of nucleic acid molecules. At physiological pH, the hydrogens of the acid are dissociated, and the phosphate group is negatively charged.

8. The backbone of the DNA strand is comprised of deoxyribose and phosphate groups. Adjacent nucleotides are linked by a 3',5'-phosphodiester bond that characterizes the sugar-phosphate backbone.

9. AMP contains a single phosphate group hooked onto a ribose sugar; ADP contains two phosphate groups; ATP contains three phosphate groups.

10. The sequence of nucleotides.

11. A purine-pyrimidine pair fits well with the diameter of the helix.

12. Hydrogen bonding

13. DNA replication is the process of making two DNA double helices when there is initially only one. The general process involves the splitting of the two strands of the parent DNA and then adding one nucleotide at a time to build new "daughter" strands. The synthesis of the new strands is in the direction 5' ⟶ 3'. The result of replication is two identical DNA double helices, each with a parent strand and a daughter strand.

14. mRNA is the "information" molecule carrying to the ribosome the instructions for the sequence of amino acids in a protein.

15. tRNA molecules are involved in transporting amino acids to the ribosome in an order dictated by mRNA. These amino acids then become incorporated into a growing protein chain.

16. DNA, RNA

17. mRNA, tRNA and rRNA

18. a. mRNA; b. tRNA

19. a. three b. Because this dictates which tRNA and, hence, which amino acid gets brought into the ribosome for incorporation into a growing peptide chain.

20. DNA is a long molecule which is our inheritable material and which holds the instructions for cellular metabolism. Genes are segments of the DNA which holds one particular piece of instruction (i.e. peptide sequence information). Chromosomes are individual pieces of DNA associated with proteins. There are many, many genes on a given chromosome.

21. The basic process of recombinant DNA involves the following steps:
    1. Isolating the gene you wish to clone.
    2. Isolating a suitable carrier or "vector" for transporting the gene into a target cell. A small circular DNA piece called a plasmid is often used.
    3. Treatment of both the gene and the vector with an enzyme of the class termed restriction enzymes produces "sticky ends" so that the two pieces can meld together. DNA ligase then produces the final linkage.
    4. The plasmids are then placed in a broth of bacterial cells and a few are able to cross the membrane. (This process is aided by $CaCl_2$). The gene is now cloned into a bacterial cell.
    5. The bacterial cells are allowed to divide to increase their population. When many cells are available, they are encouraged to make the product of the incorporated gene. This product is then harvested by normal biochemical isolation techniques.

22. Production of hormones or other blood proteins for use in individuals deficient in these compounds; production of nucleic acids and proteins for use in scientific research; production of enzymes for use in synthesis of organic compounds.

23. Physical mutagens: ultraviolet and gamma radiation
    Chemical mutagens: 5-bromouracil, 2-aminopurine, hydroxylamine, nitrous acid

24. Phenylketonuria - phenylalanine hydroxylase; histidinemia - histidase; goiter - iodotyrosine dehalogenase

PROBLEMS

BUILDING BLOCKS

25. ribose

26. deoxyribose

27. adenines, cytosines, guanines, and thymines

28. adenines, cytosines, guanines and uracils.

29. a. neither; b. nucleoside; c. nucleotide

30. a. neither; b. neither; c. nucleoside

31. Ribose: a,b   Deoxyribose: c

32. Ribose: b   Deoxyribose: a,c

STRUCTURES AND NAMES

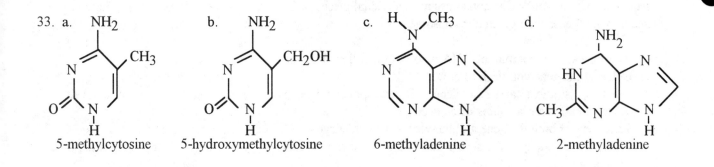

33. a. 5-methylcytosine   b. 5-hydroxymethylcytosine   c. 6-methyladenine   d. 2-methyladenine

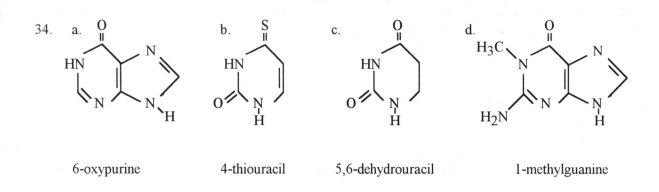

34. a. 6-oxypurine   b. 4-thiouracil   c. 5,6-dehydrouracil   d. 1-methylguanine

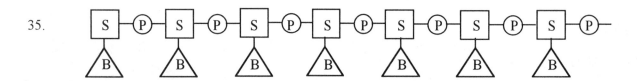

35.

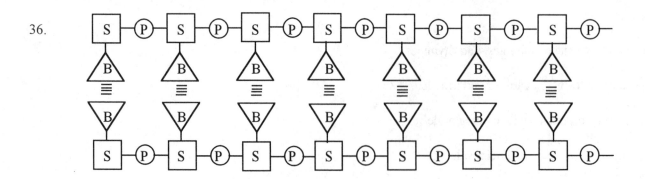

36.

BASE PAIRING

37. a. guanine; b. thymine; c. cytosine; d. adenine

38. a. uracil; b. cytosine; c. adenine; d. guanine

39. ...TAAGC...

40. ...UAAGC...

41. a. AAA; b. GUA; c. UCG; d. GGC

42. a. AAC; b. CUU; c. AGG; d. GUG

THE GENETIC CODE

43. a. Phe; b. His; c. Ser; d. Pro

44. a. Asn; b. Leu; c. Arg; d. Val

45. a. Leu–Pro–Gly
     b. Ala–Ser
     c. Pro–Pro–Pro

46. Asn–Glu–Ser (The codons on mRNA would be A–A–U–G–A–G–A–G–U)

ADDITIONAL PROBLEMS

47. Each is paired with a daughter strand.

48. DNA dictates the rate of transcription of mRNA molecules which will consequently be read to make proteins. Therefore, by controlling mRNA production, the DNA exerts control over which proteins are present in a cell at any given time.

49. ...AGGCTA...

50.

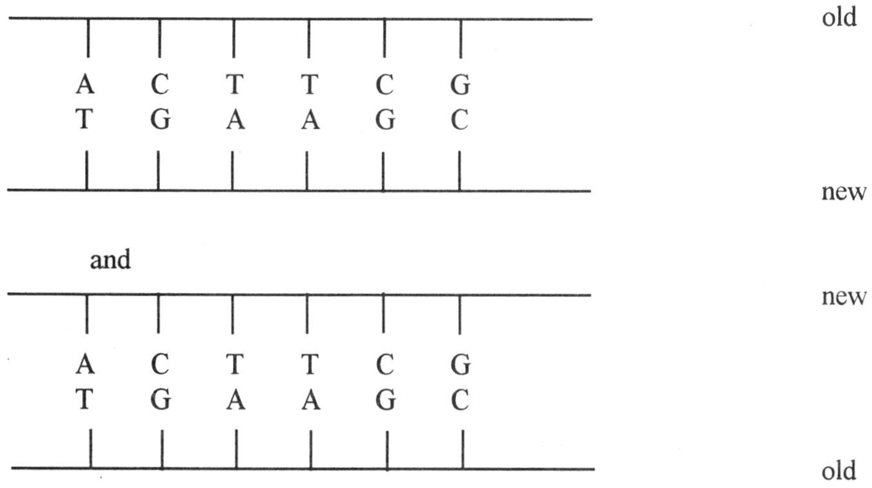

```
                                                old
    ┬   ┬   ┬   ┬   ┬   ┬
    A   C   T   T   C   G
    T   G   A   A   G   C
    ┴   ┴   ┴   ┴   ┴   ┴
                                                new

    and
                                                new

    ┬   ┬   ┬   ┬   ┬   ┬
    A   C   T   T   C   G
    T   G   A   A   G   C
    ┴   ┴   ┴   ┴   ┴   ┴
                                                old
```

51.

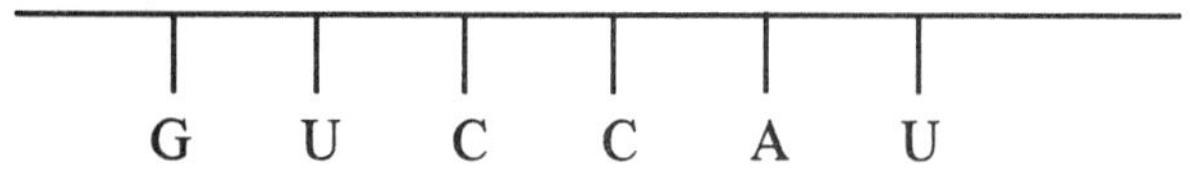

```
    ┬   ┬   ┬   ┬   ┬   ┬
    G   U   C   C   A   U
```

52. The site to which the amino acid binds (3'-position of the terminal adenosine nucleoside) and the three nucleotide residues that constitute the anticodon.

53. a. 60,000/120 = 500 amino acids present in the protein
    b. 500 codons specifying amino acid sequence and 1 termination codon.
    c. 500 codons = 1,500 nucleotide bases; termination codon = 3 nucleotide bases; sum = 1503 nucleotide bases

54. Met–Tyr–His–Gly–Thr–Arg–Val–Leu–Leu–Ala–Asp–Gly (termination)

55. Met–Leu–Arg–Ser–Tyr–Glu–Gly–Phe–His–Lys–Thr–Met (termination)

56. a. AUGGCUGGUUGUAAAAAUUUUUCUGGAAGACUUUUACCAGUUGCUAG
    b. TACCGACCAACATTTTTAAAAAAGACCTTCTGAAAATGGTCAACGATC

57. Chemical breakage of the DNA promotes a faster rate of mutation and recombination of the DNA. While we often think of these DNA manipulations as being detrimental, they are needed in order to occasionally produce beneficial results, thus driving the evolution process.

58. a. Thr, b. Gln, c. Ala

59. Codons for valine are GUU, GUC, GUA, and GUG; codons for glutamic acid are GAA and GAG. Therefore a single base substitution in the mRNA - GUA instead of GAA and/or GUG instead of GAG - could cause the incorporation of valine instead of glutamic acid. This would result from a base sequence of CAT instead of CTT and/or CAC instead of CTC in the DNA molecule.

60.

Type	Codon for Normal	Codon for Mutant
J	GCU, GCC	GAU, GAC
I	AAA, AAG	GAA, GAG
M	CAU, CAC	UAU, UAC
D	GAA, GAG	CAA, CAG
K	GGU, GGC	GAU, GAC

61. a. UGCAAUCGGGGUCGA   b. Cys–Asn–Arg–Gly–Arg
    c. (i) Cys–Asn–Trp–Gly–Arg; (ii) Cys–Asn–Gln–Gly–Ser; (iii) Cys–Asn–Gly–Val

62. a. The point mutation would result in a new codon (UUG instead of CUG), yet the amino acid at position 2 of the polypeptide would remain unchanged since both of those codons encode the incorporation of leucine.

    b. The mutation would result in a new codon for the amino acid at position 4 (UGA instead of UGU). Thus a termination codon replaces the codon for cysteine and a very much shortened, incomplete polypeptide is released. No functional enzyme is produced.

63. b (it is a more radical change)

REVIEW QUESTIONS

1. Nucleic acid (DNA or RNA) surrounded by a protein coat.

2. A DNA virus contains DNA as its genetic material while an RNA virus contains RNA.

3. Viruses can be of any shape and size (within limits). Because of their simplicity, they are often produced by relatively simple biomolecules packed into an ordered arrangement. This periodic arrangement of the units explains their frequent symmetry.

4. Bacteria are much larger than viruses (approximately 10 times larger).

5. A DNA virus attaches to a cell and injects its DNA into the cell. The DNA becomes incorporated into the cell's genome. This incorporated DNA then directs the cell to make viral protein and more viral DNA needed for reproduction.

6. An RNA virus attaches to a cell and injects its RNA into the cell. (In order to incorporate the nucleic acid into the genome, some RNA viruses undergo a reverse transcription process where the RNA piece is used to generate a double stranded DNA segment. This process is catalyzed by reverse transcriptase.) The nucleic acid induces viral protein and nucleic acid synthesis to yield many copies of the virus.

7. Viral origin: AIDS, chicken pox, hepatitis, influenza, polio. Bacterial origin: Cholera, diphtheria, syphilis, tetanus, tuberculosis (See Table K.1 for others).

8. Acyclovir, AZT, DDI. None are absolute cures.

9. A tumor is an abnormal growth of new tissue.

10. Benign tumors do not invade neighboring tissues while malignant tumors can spread and infect other tissues.

11. Smoking

12. Safrole, aflatoxins, compounds in mushrooms, pepper, citrus oils; there are many.

13. Oncogenes are genes we (and other animals) carry in our genomes which, through mutation, become converted to genes that cause cell proliferation.

14. Suppressor genes are genes whose products inhibit cell proliferation and encourage cell differentiation. Mutations in these genes cause a loss of control of cell growth and, thus, a cancerous state.

15. Antimetabolites, vinca alkaloids, sex hormones

16. A mutagen is a compound or physical agent that causes a mutation in the DNA (i.e. a change in the 1° sequence of the DNA).

PROBLEMS

CARCINOGENS

17. Charcoal-grilled meats, cigarette smoke, automobile exhausts, coffee, burnt sugar.

18. β-Naphthylamine; Benzidine

19. Dimethylnitrosamine, vinyl chloride

ANTICANCER DRUGS

20. Cisplatin binds to DNA and prohibits replication.

21. It is attached to sugar and phosphate groups and subsequently inhibits an enzyme involved in the formation of thymine nucleotides.

22. It inhibits the synthesis of adenine and guanine nucleotides.

23. Folic acid. It is a competitive inhibitor of an enzyme needed to transform folic acid into its active form. Without the active form of folic acid, thymine can not be synthesized and replication of the cell cannot occur.

REVIEW QUESTIONS

1. a. Metabolite: A metabolite is any compound that is involved in a metabolic reaction.
    b. Villi: Villi are small, finger-like appendages that extend from the intestinal epithelial cells into the lumen of the digestive tract. They function to increase the surface area for the absorption of dietary food-stuffs.
    c. Blood sugar level: The blood-sugar level is the concentration of glucose in the blood.
    d. Renal threshold: The renal threshold is 160-170 mg of glucose/100mL of blood. When the blood-sugar level exceeds this value, glucose passes into the kidneys and is excreted in the urine.
    e. Gluconeogenesis: Gluconeogenesis is the formation of glucose from a noncarbohydrate source.
    f. Glucose tolerance test: Glucose tolerance test is a diagnostic test for diabetes mellitus.
    g. Cyclic AMP: Cyclic AMP is an important intercellular messenger molecule that transmits messages received at the cell membrane to enzymes within the cell.
    h. Adenyl cyclase: Adenyl cyclase is the enzyme that catalyzes the formation of cyclic adenosine 3',5'-monophosphate (cAMP) from ATP.
    i. P : P is the symbol for the phosphite group, PO_3^{2-}.
    j. Metabolic pathway: A metabolic pathway is a sequence of metabolic reactions (steps) requiring the formation of several intermediates before the overall reaction is completed.
    k. Oxygen debt: Oxygen debt is a condition where the respiratory and circulatory systems cannot meet the body's oxygen demand for metabolic activities. As a result, muscle cells are forced to degrade glucose via the anaerobic pathway (glycolysis).
    l. Kinase: Kinase is an enzyme that catalyzes phosphorylation-dephosphorylation reactions involving ATP.
    m. FAS (Fetal alcohol syndrome): Fetal alcohol syndrome is a disorder that results when a pregnant woman regularly consumes alcohol. Alcohol that crosses the placental barrier builds up in the fetus whose liver is incapable of detoxifying the alcohol. FAS consists of facial deformities, growth deficiency, and mental retardation.
    n. Cori cycle: Cori cycle is the anaerobic catabolism of glucose to lactic acid in the muscle cells and the subsequent reconversion of that lactic acid to glucose in the liver.
    o. Carbohydrate loading: Carbohydrate loading is a method used by athletes to boost performance by eating a high carbohydrate diet in order to maximize their storage of glycogen.
    p. Antabuse: Antabuse is a drug (Disulfiram) used in the treatment of alcoholism. It inhibits the second step of alcohol metabolism in the liver by competing with the intermediate acetaldehyde for the active site of acetaldehyde dehydrogenase. The resulting accumulation of acetaldehyde produces severe discomfort in the patient.

2. a. Anabolism is the biosynthesis of large molecules from smaller molecules. Catabolism is the degradation of large molecules into smaller molecules.
    b. Photosynthesis describes the series of reactions by which glucose is formed from CO_2, H_2O, and energy from the sun. Respiration is the process whereby oxygen combines with food molecules (chiefly carbohydrates) to form CO_2 and H_2O and release energy.
    c. Digestion is the hydrolytic process whereby food molecules are broken down into smaller molecules so they can be absorbed. Metabolism describes the processes whereby the absorbed molecules from food are utilized by an organism to provide energy, growth, maintenance, and repair.
    d. Passive transport is the passage of a substance across an inert membrane by osmosis or diffusion. Active transport requires that energy be expended in order for a substance to pass across a selective cell membrane.
    e. Hypoglycemia is a condition resulting from a lower than normal concentration of sugar in the blood. Hyperglycemia results from a higher than normal blood sugar level.

f. Glycogenesis is the formation of glycogen from glucose. Glycogenolysis is the hydrolytic breakdown of glycogen to glucose.

g. Anaerobic reactions are those that do not require the presence of oxygen. Aerobic reactions are those that do require the presence of oxygen.

h. In glycolysis, muscle cells and other animal cells respiring anaerobically convert pyruvic acid into lactic acid. Under similar conditions, the enzymes in yeast convert the pyruvic acid into ethyl alcohol and CO_2 (fermentation).

i. A mutase catalyzes the intramolecular transfer of a particular group (e.g., phosphate group in glycolysis). An isomerase catalyzes the interconversion of one form of a molecule into another form (e.g., glucose 6-phosphate to fructose 6-phosphate).

j. A phosphatase is an enzyme that catalyzes the transfer of a phosphate group from one molecule to another. A phosphorylase is an enzyme that catalyzes the phosphorolytic cleavage of a molecule by a reaction that is analogous to a hydrolytic cleavage.

k. Facultative anaerobes may function with or without oxygen. Strict anaerobes cannot function in the presence of oxygen.

3. Hydrolysis

4. Mucin is a glycoprotein which attaches onto food particles. This lubricates them for easier swallowing.

5. Monosaccharides

6. Small intestine

7. Saliva amylase is breaking the starch down into glucoses which have a sweet taste.

8. No. Renal disease may also result in high glucose level in the urine.

9. Glycogen

10. Liver, muscle

11. Galactose is enzymatically converted to glucose.

12. Two

PROBLEMS

ATP: HIGH-ENERGY PHOSPHATES

13. AMP contains a single phosphate group attached to the ribose sugar, ADP has two phosphate groups hooked together onto the ribose sugar, ATP contains three phosphate groups.

14. Because its energy of hydrolysis is used by many enzymes and other biomolecules to drive unfavorable reactions.

15. a,c

16. a (b is somewhat high energy).

● **DIGESTIVE ENZYMES**

17. | Location | Function |
|---|---|
| a. mouth | –breaks down starch |
| b. intestine | –cleaves lactose to galactose and glucose |
| c. intestine | –cleaves sucrose to fructose and glucose |

18. | Location | Function |
|---|---|
| a. intestine | –breaks down starch |
| b. intestine | –cleaves maltose to two glucoses |

BLOOD SUGAR LEVELS

19. The synthesis and breakdown of glycogen in liver.

20. Insulin can bind to liver, muscle, and adipose cells and activate them to take up glucose from the blood.

21. Both epinephrine and glucagon work on the liver to cause glycogenolysis, i.e., the breakdown of glycogen to glucose. The glucose produced enters the blood and, thus, raises blood glucose levels.

22. It will be hydrolyzed by acid and protease actions in the stomach and intestine.

● 23. Insulin is a protein while the oral antidiabetic drugs are small molecules, all with a para arrangement of the sulfonyl group to another substitutent. The oral antidiabetic drugs don't work like insulin; they stimulate release of insulin from the islet cells of the pancreas.

24. Type I: Juvenile-onset diabetes is characterized by the inability of the pancreas to produce sufficient amounts of insulin. Patients suffering from Type I diabetes mellitus must be treated with daily injections of insulin. Type II: Adult-onset diabetes is characterized by the pancreatic production of insulin but there is a failure of that gland to secrete sufficient amounts of the vital hormone or there is a lack of insulin receptors on the target cells. This form of diabetes mellitus can be controlled with a combination of diet and exercise therapy.

CYCLIC AMP

25. On the outside of the cell membrane.

26. The binding of a hormone onto a transmembrane receptor causes a conformational change in the receptor which, in turn, causes a conformation change in adenylate cyclase. This latter conformation change activates this enzyme to make cAMP from ATP.

BIOCHEMICAL REACTIONS

27. a.
$$
\begin{array}{c}
H-C=O \\
H-C-OH \\
H-C-OH \\
CH_2O-\textcircled{P}
\end{array}
\quad + \quad
\begin{array}{c}
CH_2O-\textcircled{P} \\
C=O \\
CH_2OH
\end{array}
$$

b.
$$
\begin{array}{c}
H-C=O \\
H-C-OH \\
CH_2OH
\end{array}
\quad + \quad
\begin{array}{c}
CH_2O-\textcircled{P} \\
C=O \\
CH_2OH
\end{array}
$$

28. a. both   b. both in CO_2, neither in ethanol

29.   a. Step 6, glyceraldehyde 3-phosphate to 1,3-bisphosphoglyceric acid
      b. NAD^+

30.   a. In yeast cells, NADH is reoxidized by reacting with acetaldehyde to form ethanol.
      b. In muscle cells, NADH is reoxidized by reacting with pyruvic acid to form lactic acid (anaerobic conditions).

31. 70-80% of the lactic acid diffuses out of the muscle into the bloodstream and is transported to the liver. There it may be oxidized to pyruvic acid and hence to CO_2 and H_2O (via the Krebs cycle) or it may be converted back into glucose (gluconeogenesis). The remaining 20-30% remains in the muscle cells where it can be reoxidized to pyruvic acid, which then enters the Krebs cycle and is further oxidized to CO_2 and H_2O (assuming the availability of oxygen in the muscle cells).

32.   a. $C_6H_{12}O_6 \longrightarrow 2\ CH_3COCOOH + 4H^+ + 4e^-$

      b. $4e^- + 4H^+, + 2\ CH_3COCOOH \longrightarrow 2\ CH_3CHOHCOOH$

      c. $4e^- + 4H^+ + 2\ CH_3COCOOH \longrightarrow 2\ C_2H_5OH + 2\ CO_2$

33. a. acetaldehyde;   b. dihydroxyacetone phosphate + glyceraldehyde 3-phosphate; c. enolase; d. glucose 6-phosphate; e. glucose 1-phosphate; f. triose phosphate isomerase; g. glucose 6-phosphate; h. pyruvic acid

34. a. phosphofructokinase; b. glucose 6-phosphate; c. 1,3-bisphosphoglyceric acid; d. phosphoglycerokinase; e. 2-phosphoglyceric acid; f. pyruvic acid decarboxylase; g. phosphoenolpyruvic acid; h. glucose 6-phosphate

35. a. 33g, 34a;   b. 34d, 34g;   c. 33f, 34b;   d. 34c

36. a. 33a, 33h;   b. 33c;   c. 34f

ADDITIONAL PROBLEMS

37. Lactic acid, pyruvic acid, acetaldehyde, and ethanol are the only nonphosphorylated metabolites of glycolysis and fermentation. All the other metabolites are phosphorylated.

38. A "second generation" drug implies a new group of similarly-acting drugs (i.e. similar to the "first generation") which have added benefits or advantages. Glyburide increases the sensitivity of cell receptors to insulin, a characteristic not shown by the earlier oral anti-diabetics.

39. They both are involved in substrate phosphorylation reactions of ADP being transformed to ATP. Both molecules act as the phosphate donor.

40.

This is not surprising. Here is an example of an enzyme that exhibits stereochemical specificity but not absolute specificity.

41. The major role of the glycogen stores in the muscle cells is to provide energy for muscle contraction. In those cells glucose 6-phosphate is immediately converted to fructose 6-phosphate. The glycogen that is stored in the liver serves as a reservoir for glucose molecules that may be transported by the blood to other cells. Glucose 6-phosphate in the liver is converted to glucose by glucose 6-phosphatase. The dephosphorylated glucose molecules are then free to enter the circulation. Muscle cells lack the enzyme glucose 6-phosphatase and thus cannot export glucose into the bloodstream.

42.

$$HOCH_2 \text{—(fructose ring)—} CH_2OH \xrightarrow[\text{fructokinase}]{ATP \quad ADP} HOCH_2 \text{—(fructose ring)—} CH_2O\text{-}\textcircled{P}$$

$$HOCH_2 \text{—(fructose ring)—} CH_2O\text{-}\textcircled{P} \xrightarrow{\text{aldolase}} \begin{array}{c} H\text{—}C{=}O \\ | \\ H\text{—}C\text{—}OH \\ | \\ CH_2OH \end{array} + \begin{array}{c} CH_2O\text{-}\textcircled{P} \\ | \\ C{=}O \\ | \\ CH_2OH \end{array}$$

$$\begin{array}{c} H\text{—}C{=}O \\ | \\ H\text{—}C\text{—}OH \\ | \\ CH_2OH \end{array} \xrightarrow[\substack{\text{glyceraldehyde} \\ \text{kinase}}]{ATP \quad ADP} \begin{array}{c} H\text{—}C{=}O \\ | \\ H\text{—}C\text{—}OH \\ | \\ CH_2O\text{-}\textcircled{P} \end{array}$$

43. $CH_3CH_2OH \xrightarrow[\text{dehydrogenase}]{\text{alcohol}} CH_3\text{-}\overset{\overset{\textstyle O}{\|}}{C}\text{-}H \xrightarrow[\text{dehydrogenase}]{\text{acetaldehyde}} CH_3\text{-}\overset{\overset{\textstyle O}{\|}}{C}\text{-}OH \xrightarrow[\text{synthetase}]{\text{acetyl-CoA}} CH_3\text{-}\overset{\overset{\textstyle O}{\|}}{C}\text{-}S\text{-}CoA$

    a. acetaldehyde dehydrogenase

    b. The detoxification of alcohol in the liver results in the production of acetic acid. The acetic acid is released from the liver and transported by the blood to cells where it is converted into acetyl-CoA. Acetyl-CoA may be further oxidized via the Krebs cycle to produce energy for cellular activities.

44. The glycolytic pathway results in the production of 4 ATP when 1 mole of glucose is converted to lactic acid. The pathway requires the expenditure of 2 moles of ATP in converting a free glucose molecule to fructose 1,6-diphosphate [net 2 ATP]. The cleavage of a terminal glucose residue from a glycogen molecule by a phosphorylase does not require the expenditure of phosphate bond energy (ATP). The conversion of the resultant glucose 1-phosphate into fructose 1,6-diphosphate requires the expenditure of a single molecule of ATP [net 3 ATP]. Therefore, it is more efficient for anaerobic cells to utilize glycogen as a source of energy since it requires less energy to initiate the glycolytic pathway.

45.

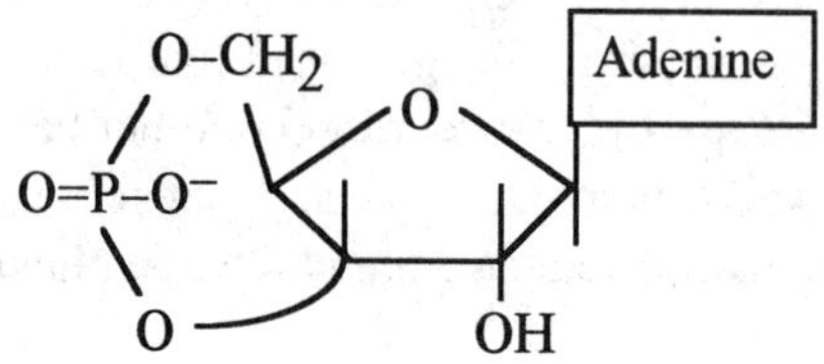

O–CH$_2$

Adenine

O=P–O$^-$

O

O

OH

46.   H–N–(P)

C=NH

N–CH$_3$

CH$_2$COO$^-$

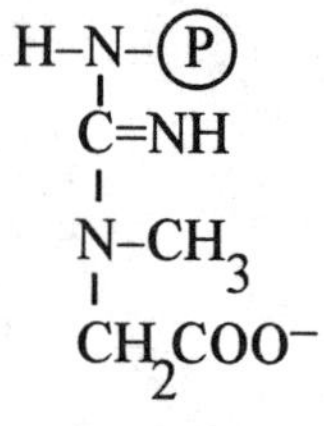

It serves as the storage form of high energy phosphate groups in nerve tissue and in muscle cells of vertebrates. It easily transfers its phosphate group to ADP to form ATP when the cell requires ATP for energy-demanding processes.

REVIEW QUESTIONS

1. a. Krebs cycle: The Krebs cycle is a cyclic series of reactions that represent the aerobic continuation of the degradation of glucose (and other metabolites) to CO_2 and H_2O.
    b. Oxidative decarboxylation: Oxidative decarboxylation is an oxidation-reduction reaction accompanied by the removal of CO_2 from the substrate molecule.
    c. Mitochondria: Mitochondria are cell organelles that are termed the "power plants" of the cell because they carry out reactions that generate energy for the cell.
    d. Respiratory Chain: The respiratory chain is also called the electron transport chain; the sequence of reactions whereby the reduced forms of the coenzymes are reoxidized and energy is released.
    e. Cytochromes: Cytochromes are heme-containing proteins found in mitochondria important in electron transport.
    f. Coenzyme Q_{10}: A critical election acceptor/donor in the respiratory chain.

2. The Krebs cycle aerobically metabolizes carbohydrates and other biomolecules to produce compounds (NADH, $FADH_2$) which can subsequently be "cashed" in to produce ATPs.

3. Guanosine triphosphate. It is a nucleotide equivalent in energy to an ATP.

4. The formation of ATP molecules by use of a high-energy phosphorylated compound.

5. The formation of ATP by use of O_2 as an electron acceptor.

6. Nicotinamide, adenine, ribose, phosphate. Nicotinamide is the vitamin.

7. The nicotinamide and flavin groups.

8. By way of the electron transport chain. The reoxidation of reduced coenzymes generates energy that is harnessed to drive the phosphorylation of ADP to ATP. ATP is the high-energy molecule that is utilized by the cell to supply energy for a variety of cellular processes.

9. The glycerol phosphate shuttle and the malic acid-aspartic acid shuttle.

10. a. Carbohydrates are the chief fuels of biological systems - they provide energy. b. Carbohydrate metabolism and the burning of table sugar are similar in that both processes release energy. When sugar is burned, all the energy given off is released into the environment as heat. c. When carbohydrates are metabolized, 38-40% of the energy released is conserved in the form of chemical energy (ATP).

PROBLEMS

KREBS CYCLE

11. CO_2

12. NAD^+, FAD

RESPIRATORY CHAIN

13. 3

14. 2

15. O_2, H_2O

16. To pass electrons down the chain, eventually to O_2.

BIOCHEMICAL REACTIONS

17. a. citric acid b. oxaloacetic acid + acetyl CoA
     c. L-malic acid d. isocitric acid dehydrogenase
     e. α-ketoglutaric acid dehydrogenase complex

18. a. oxaloacetic acid b. GTP + ADP
     c. pyruvic acid dehydrogenase complex
     d. succinic acid e. fumaric acid

19. a. 17a; b. 17a,17b,17c,18d; c. 17a

20. a. 17d,17e,18a,18c,18e; b. 17d,17e,18c; c. 18b

21.
$$CH_3\overset{O}{\overset{\|}{C}}COH + CoASH \longrightarrow CH_3\overset{O}{\overset{\|}{C}}SCoA + CO_2 + 2H^+ + 2e^-$$

$$HOOCCH_2CH(COOH)CHOHCOOH \longrightarrow HOOCCH_2CH(COOH)\overset{O}{\overset{\|}{C}}COOH + 2H^+ + 2e^-$$

$$HOOCCH_2CH_2\overset{O}{\overset{\|}{C}}COOH + CoASH \longrightarrow HOOCCH_2CH_2\overset{O}{\overset{\|}{C}}SCoA + CO_2 + 2H^+ + 2e^-$$

$$HOOCCH_2CH_2COOH \longrightarrow HOOCCH=CHCOOH + 2H^+ + 2e^-$$

$$HOOCCH_2CHOHCOOH \longrightarrow HOOCCH_2\overset{O}{\overset{\|}{C}}COOH + 2H^+ + 2e^-$$

22. $NAD^+ + 2H^+ + 2e^- \rightleftharpoons NADH + H^+$
     $FMN + 2H^+ + 2e^- \rightleftharpoons FMNH_2$
     $2Fe(III){\cdot}S + 2e^- \rightleftharpoons 2Fe(II){\cdot}S$
     $CoQ_{10} + 2H^+ + 2e^- \rightleftharpoons CoQ_{10}H_2$
     $2Cyt\ b{-}Fe(III) + 2e^- \rightleftharpoons 2Cyt\ b{-}Fe(II)$
     $2Fe(III){\cdot}S + 2e^- \rightleftharpoons 2Fe(II){\cdot}S$
     $2Cyt\ c_1{-}Fe(III) + 2e^- \rightleftharpoons 2Cyt\ c_1{-}Fe(II)$
     $2Cyt\ c{-}Fe(III) + 2e^- \rightleftharpoons 2Cyt\ c{-}Fe(II)$
     $2Cyt\ aa_3{-}Fe(III) + 2e^- \rightleftharpoons 2Cyt\ aa_3{-}Fe(II)$
     $\frac{1}{2}O_2 + 2H^+ + 2e^- \rightleftharpoons H_2O$

23. 1,3-bisphosphoglyceric acid $\longrightarrow$ 3-phosphoglyceric acid
     phosphoenolpyruvic acid $\longrightarrow$ pyruvic acid
     succinyl CoA $\longrightarrow$ succinic acid

24. $C_6H_{12}O_6 + 6\ O_2 + 36\ ADP + 36\ P_i \longrightarrow 6\ CO_2 + 42\ H_2O + 36\ ATP + 423{,}000\ cal$

MUSCLE METABOLISM

25. To carry out oxidative phosphorylation and, thus, produce ATPs.

26. Actomysin is the structural protein of muscle. It is able to hydrolyze ATP and couple this energy to drive the contraction process.

27. Carbohydrates

28. Fats

29. Anaerobic

30. Aerobic

31. Type I: Slow twitch, suited to aerobic oxidation; Type IIB: Fast twitch, suited to anaerobic glycolysis

32. Myoglobin is a storage form for O_2 to be used in aerobic metabolism upon demand. Mitochondria carry out aerobic metabolism and, thus, are found in high quantities in those tissues which work aerobically.

33. The high catalytic activity of actomyosin in Type IIB fibers suggests that the tissue can hydrolyze ATP at high rates and, thus, is important for bursts of vigorous physical activity.

34. The anaerobic process does not produce a relatively high amount of ATP per glucose (as compared to aerobic metabolism). Thus, fuel sources are rapidly depleted to generate the ATP needed for the intense physical activity. The muscle, therefore, fatigues ("runs out of gas") quickly.

35. Type I (slow twitch). Endurance training increases the size and number of mitochondria in Type I muscle fibers, therefore aiding the individual in performing aerobic work.

36. Pheasants: Type IIB (fast twitch); Herons: Type I (slow twitch)

ADDITIONAL PROBLEMS

37. The labeled carbon atom would be the α-carbon ($-CH_2$) in the molecule of oxaloacetic acid that results after one turn of the Krebs cycle.

38. a. One mole of acetyl CoA metabolized via the Krebs cycle will result in the production of 12 moles of ATP.
    (12)(7.30) = 87.6 kcal

    b. Efficiency = (87,600/200,000) 100% = 43.8%

39. Each mole of lactic acid is converted to one mole of pyruvic acid. This occurs in the cytoplasm of muscle cells and one mole of NADH is formed. The NADH enters the mitochondria via the glycerol phosphate shuttle and two moles of ATP are obtained by oxidative phosphorylation (and the respiratory chain). Each mole of pyruvic acid that enters the Krebs cycle is oxidized to produce 15 moles of ATP. Therefore, a total of 17 moles of ATP is obtained from each mole of lactic acid.

40. a. The oxidizing agent for this reaction is FAD, which is reduced to $FADH_2$. When $FADH_2$ is reoxidized by means of the electron transport chain, only two ATPs are formed.

    b. The oxidation of glyceraldehyde 3-phosphate to 1,3-diphosphoglyceric acid occurs in the cytosol. Under aerobic conditions, the NADH must be reoxidized by a mechanism that involves the passage of some metabolite into the mitochondria. The process in muscle and nerve cells utilizes the glycerol phosphate shuttle, and as a result of this shuttle a molecule of $FADH_2$ is reoxidized by the electron transport chain. Hence, only two ATPs are produced.

41. a. 38 ATPs (recall the malic acid-aspartic acid shuttle)
    b. $[(38)(7300)/686,000]\ 100\% = 40.4\%$

REVIEW QUESTIONS

1.   a. Essential fatty acid: An essential fatty acid is a fatty acid that cannot be synthesized by an organism and therefore must be supplied in the diet.
   b. Eczema: Eczema is an inflammatory skin disease characterized by the development of scales and crusts. It can often be relieved by the dietary intake of essential fatty acids.
   c. Bile salts: Bile salts are important components of bile that aid in lipid digestion by emulsifying the lipids.
   d. Lipases: Lipase is the general name for a class of enzymes that catalyze the hydrolysis of lipids.
   e. Chylomicrons: Chylomicrons are a class of lipoproteins (density of less than 0.94 g/mL) that are produced in the intestine.
   f. Lymph: Lymph is tissue fluid (water and dissolved substances) that has entered a lymphatic capillary.
   g. Fat deposits: Fat deposits are specialized cells (adipose tissue) that can store a high percentage of lipids within their cytoplasm.
   h. Obesity: Obesity is the condition in which an excessive amount of fat is deposited in adipose tissue.
   i. Lipolysis: Lipolysis is the hydrolysis of triacylglycerols.
   j. Mobilization: Mobilization is the release of fatty acids from adipose tissue.
   k. Adipose tissue: Specialized tissue where fat is stored for future energy use.
   l. β-Oxidation: β-oxidation is a sequence of reactions whereby the carbon atom beta to the carboxyl group of a fatty acid undergoes successive oxidations.
   m. Ketonemia: Ketonemia is the accumulation of excess ketone bodies in the blood at concentrations greater than 3 mg/100mL.
   n. Ketonuria: Ketonuria is the accumulation of ketone bodies in the urine.

2. The oxidation of 1.0 g of carbohydrate liberates about 4200 cal. The oxidation of 1.0 g of lipid liberates about 9500 cal.

3. Because of the presence of many hydroxyl groups, glycogen is extremely hydrated. Therefore, 1g of glycogen contains a higher percentage of water and a lower percentage of fuel mass than 1g of fat.

4. The essential fatty acids are those that contain more than one double bond.

5. When lipids reach the duodenum, the duodenum releases a hormone that stimulates the gallbladder to flow bile into this intestinal region.

6. Bile salts are polar lipids which can form micelles. These bile micelles serve as a location for the ingested fats to get away from the aqueous environment. Thus, the larger fat particles are broken down into smaller units, upon which digestive lipases can act more readily.

7. Monoglycerides, fatty acids, and free cholesterol.

8. To protect vital organs from mechanical injury, to insulate the organism against loss of temperature, to store reserve energy.

9. Epinephrine binds to receptor proteins in the membranes of adipose tissue. This binding prompts the stimulation of the enzyme adenyl cyclase, which converts ATP to cyclic AMP. cAMP stimulates the hydrolysis of lipids within the adipose cells and the subsequent release of fatty acids (mobilization) from those cells. Insulin, on the other hand, enhances the synthesis of triacylglycerols and the storage of fats in adipose tissue.

10. α and β Globulins transport lipids in the blood. Globulins are insoluble in water but are soluble in dilute salt solutions. Albumins transport fatty acids and while they are likewise soluble in dilute salt solutions, they are also soluble in water.

11. a. glucose b. fatty acids c. fatty acids d. glucose and fatty acids e. fatty acids f. glucose g. fatty acids h. ketone bodies

12. Energy intake exceeding energy output.

13. Both can yield much energy in the form of ATP. Triglycerides in adipose tissue is a more efficient storage form of energy. However, glycogen is more quickly metabolized and is the only one of the two that can directly yield glucose for the blood.

14. Skinfold calipers: not too accurate.
    Dunk tanks: Fat percent value is dependent on air in the lungs; not very convenient.

15. Vitamin and mineral deficiencies, insufficient protein intake, acidosis due to ketosis.

16. 3500 kcal

17. Excess body fat causes the heart to work harder to pump O_2 to move a larger object. It also increases the rate of atherosclerosis which makes the heart pump even harder.

18. The set-point theory states that each of us has a particular level of hunger which determines our homeostatic body-fat level.

19. Muscle loses glycogen and associated water (3 pounds of water for every 1 pound of glycogen) during the early portions of a fast.

20. Some quick weight loss diets contain a diuretic which causes water loss via the urine. Other diets are low in carbohydrates, thereby causing the rapid loss of glycogen and associated water. The weight in both cases is regained quickly when the individual rehydrates and starts eating carbohydrates.

21. The amount of glucose that can be stored as glycogen is limited. Therefore, ingestion of excess carbohydrates results in the formation of excess acetyl-CoA. The excess acetyl CoA molecules are utilized for the production of fats, which are then stored in adipose tissue.

22. Acetyl-CoA is the molecule that links carbohydrate and lipid metabolism.

23. A deficiency of carbohydrates leads to an increase in β-oxidation and, thus, an increase in acetyl CoA. Since Kreb cycle intermediates are low because of a funneling off of these molecules to make glucose, the level of acetyl CoA increases even further. Reactions of acetyl CoA then generate the three main ketone bodies.

24. Glycogen in the liver.

25. Fat reserves

26. Two of the three ketones produced during ketosis are acids; the pH of the blood will drop causing acidosis.

27. Starvation and fasting lead to increased ketosis which subsequently leads to acidosis.

28. Lack of insulin means poor glucose utilization (i.e. uptake) by the cells. This results in higher ketone body levels in the blood (the cells shift to fat breakdown for energy) and, thus, acidosis.

PROBLEMS

FATS AS FUELS

29. 2 hours

30. 200 kcal/day = 73,000 kcal/yr = 9.5 kg of fat

31. 0.1 hr

32. 5 kg fat = 38,500 kcal/100 kcal/yr = 385 km

DIGESTION AND ABSORPTION OF LIPIDS

33.

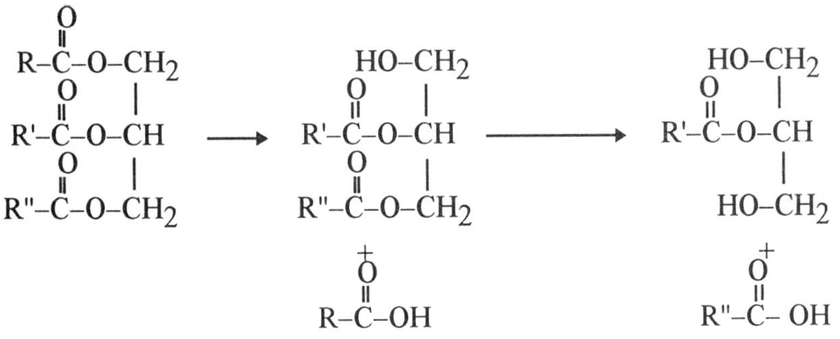

$$
\begin{array}{ccc}
\underset{\substack{O \\ \parallel}}{R-C-O-CH_2} & HO-CH_2 & HO-CH_2 \\
\underset{\substack{O \\ \parallel}}{R'-C-O-CH} & \underset{\substack{O \\ \parallel}}{R'-C-O-CH} & \underset{\substack{O \\ \parallel}}{R'-C-O-CH} \\
\underset{\substack{O \\ \parallel}}{R''-C-O-CH_2} & \underset{\substack{O \\ \parallel}}{R''-C-O-CH_2} & HO-CH_2 \\
& \overset{+}{\underset{\substack{\parallel \\ R-C-OH}}{O}} & \overset{+}{\underset{\substack{\parallel \\ R''-C-OH}}{O}}
\end{array}
$$

34. $C_{15}H_{31}COOH$ $C_{17}H_{35}COOH$ $C_{17}H_{33}COOH$ $C_{17}H_{31}COOH$
    palmitic acid   stearic acid   oleic acid   linoleic acid

35. After the products of lipid digestion cross the intestinal wall, they are immediately resynthesized into triglycerides, phospholipids, or cholesterol esters. These are then conjugated to proteins and transported to the blood via the lymphatic system.

36.   a. The triglycerides are transported in the blood as complexes with specialized proteins (lipoproteins).

     b. Some of the triglycerides are transported to the liver where they are utilized to produce energy. The remainder of the lipids either are deposited within fat storage cells (adipose tissue) or continue to circulate within the blood bound to proteins.

FATTY ACID OXIDATION

37.   a. Each turn of the spiral produces a fatty acyl CoA containing two fewer carbon atoms rather than reproducing the identical fatty acyl CoA.
     b. The carbon atom beta to the carboxyl group of the fatty acid undergoes successive oxidations.

38. Acetyl CoA molecules

39. Dehydrogenation, hydration, thiolation

40. Eight

41. Carbon 2 would appear in acetyl CoA. Carbons 4 and 6 would appear in the molecule of butyryl CoA.

42. a. 6 turns b. 7 turns c. 12 turns

43. Fatty acid biosynthesis proceeds by the addition of two carbon units at a time to the growing hydrocarbon chain. Hence, most fatty acids are even numbered.

44. The segment in which the acetyl CoA, produced from β-oxidation of fatty acids, is metabolized via the Krebs cycle.

45. In the mitochondria during oxidative phosphorylation.

46. 7 cycles of β-oxidation = 7 NADH
    Oxidation of 8 acetyl CoAs = 8 x 3 per Kreb cycle revolution = 24 NADH } 31 NADH

47. NADH produced = 31 x 3 ATPs/NADH = 93 ATPs
    $FADH_2$ produced = 15 x 2 ATPs/$FADH_2$ = 30 ATPs
    GTPs produced = 8 x 1 ATP/1GTP = 8 ATPs
    131 ATPs

    Since it costs 2 ATPs for initial fatty acid activation the net yield is 129 ATPs.

48. 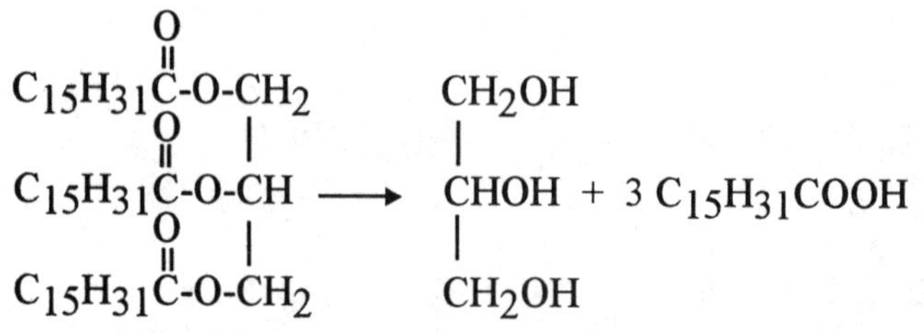
$$C_{15}H_{31}\overset{O}{\overset{\|}{C}}\text{-O-CH}_2 \qquad CH_2OH$$
$$C_{15}H_{31}\overset{O}{\overset{\|}{C}}\text{-O-CH} \longrightarrow CHOH + 3\ C_{15}H_{31}COOH$$
$$C_{15}H_{31}\overset{O}{\overset{\|}{C}}\text{-O-CH}_2 \qquad CH_2OH$$

Each mole of palmitic acid yields 129 moles of ATPs.
One mole of glycerol (enters at dihydroxyacetone phosphate set in glycolysis) yields 22 moles of ATP (takes one ATP to activate glycerol and then 1 $NAD^+ \longrightarrow$ 1 NADH to form dihydroxyacetone phosphate).

Total sum = 3(129 ATPs) + 22 moles ATPs
  = 409 moles of ATP

ADDITIONAL PROBLEMS

49. cholesterol esters > phospholipids > triglycerides

50. 85, 000 g/ 80,000 mL = 1.06 g/mL; lean

51.

$$\underset{\text{glycerol}}{\begin{matrix} CH_2OH \\ | \\ CHOH \\ | \\ CH_2OH \end{matrix}} \xrightarrow[\text{kinase}]{ATP \quad ADP} \underset{\substack{\text{glycerol} \\ \text{phosphate}}}{\begin{matrix} CH_2OH \\ | \\ CHOH \\ | \\ CH_2O \; \text{P} \end{matrix}} \xrightarrow[\text{dehydrogenase}]{NAD^+ \quad NADH+H^+} \underset{\substack{\text{dihydroxyacetone} \\ \text{phosphate}}}{\begin{matrix} CH_2OH \\ | \\ C=O \\ | \\ CH_2O \; \text{P} \end{matrix}}$$

Dihydroxyacetone phosphate can be degraded to produce energy by being incorporated into the glycolytic pathway.

52.

$$\underset{\beta\text{-hydroxybutyric acid}}{\overset{OH}{HOOCCH_2\overset{|}{C}HCH_3}} \xleftarrow[\quad]{NAD^+ \quad NADH \quad H^++} \underset{\text{Acetoacetic Acid}}{HOOCCH_2\overset{O}{\overset{||}{C}}CH_3} \xrightarrow{CO_2} \underset{\text{Acetone}}{CH_3\overset{O}{\overset{||}{C}}CH_3}$$

53. $R(CH_2)_5\overset{O}{\overset{||}{C}}-SCoA + H_3C-\overset{CH_3}{\overset{|}{{}^+N}}-CH_2-\overset{H}{\underset{OH}{\overset{|}{C}}}-CH_2-\overset{O}{\overset{||}{C}}-OH \xrightarrow{\text{acyl transferase}}$

fatty acyl-CoA   carnitine

$$H_3C-\overset{CH_3}{\overset{|}{{}^+N}}-CH_2-\overset{H}{\underset{\substack{O \\ | \\ C=O \\ | \\ (CH_2)_5 \\ | \\ R}}{\overset{|}{C}}}-CH_2-\overset{O}{\overset{||}{C}}-OH \;\; + \;\; CoA-SH$$

acyl carnitine

REVIEW QUESTIONS

1.   a. Peptidase: Peptidase is an enzyme that catalyzes the hydrolysis of proteins.
    b. Autocatalysis: Autocatalysis is the catalysis of a reaction by one of the products of the reaction.
    c. Protein turnover: Protein turnover is a measure that is a function of the rate at which body proteins are synthesized and degraded.
    d. Nitrogen balance: Nitrogen balance is the state in which an individual's intake of dietary nitrogen is equal to the amount of nitrogen in the excrement.
    e. Kwashiorkor: Kwashiorkor is an emaciating disease that results from protein deficiency.
    f. Starvation: When the human body is totally deprived of food.
    g. GABA: GABA (γ-aminobutyric acid) is an inhibitory neurotransmitter that is formed from the decarboxylation of glutamic acid.
    h. Parkinson's disease: Parkinson's disease is a disease in which there is a deficiency of the neurotransmitter dopamine in brain cells. It involves both a progressive paralytic rigidity and tremors of the extremities.
    i. L-Dopa: L-Dopa is a drug administered to patients with Parkinson's disease. It is converted to dopamine in brain cells.
    j. Hyperammonemia: Hyperammonemia is the presence of excess ammonia in the blood.
    k. Gout: Gout is a form of arthritis that is characterized by inflammation of the joints.
    l. Urea: Urea is the metabolic end-product of amino acids and other nitrogenous compounds.

2.   a. Pepsin is the active form of the proteolytic enzyme that functions in the stomach. Pepsinogen is the inactive precursor form (proenzyme) of pepsin.
    b. Chymotrypsin is an endopeptidase that preferentially cleaves peptide bonds involving the carboxyl groups of phenylalanine, tryptophan, and tyrosine. Trypsin is an endopeptidase that cleaves peptide bonds involving the carboxyl groups of lysine and arginine.
    c. An endopeptidase catalyzes the hydrolysis of peptide bonds at the interior of the protein molecule (e.g. pepsin). An exopeptidase hydrolyzes the peptide bonds at the terminal ends of the protein molecule (e.g., carboxypeptidase).
    d. Positive nitrogen balance occurs when the intake of nitrogen exceeds its excretion (e.g. growth); negative nitrogen balance occurs when the excretion of nitrogen exceeds intake (e.g. fasting).
    e. An essential amino acid cannot be synthesized by an organism, or at least not at a rate rapid enough to meet the needs of the organism (e.g. lysine). A nonessential amino acid can readily be synthesized by an organism (e.g. glycine).
    f. A complete protein contains an adequate amount of the essential amino acids. An incomplete protein is deficient in one or more of the essential amino acids.
    g. In transamination, the amino group is transferred from an amino acid to an α-keto acid and a new amino acid and a new α-keto acid are formed. In oxidative deamination, a hydrogen and an amino group are replaced by oxygen; an amino acid is converted to an α-keto acid.
    h. GPT and GOT are initials for specific transaminase enzymes. GPT is glutamic-pyruvic transaminase, and it is abundant in the liver. GOT is glutamic-oxaloacetic transaminase and it is abundant in heart muscle.
    i. A glucogenic amino acid can be converted into any one of the metabolites of carbohydrate metabolism (e.g. alanine). A ketogenic amino acid can be converted into a ketone body (e.g. leucine).
    j. Histamine results from the decarboxylation of histidine. It functions to dilate the blood vessels. Antihistamines are compounds that block the action of histamine.

3. The proteolytic enzymes are secreted in an inactive form. They are not activated until food is present in the digestive tract.

4. Since insulin is a protein, it would be digested (hydrolyzed) into its respective amino acids if it were taken orally. When injected directly into the blood, it is not subject to any hydrolytic attack.

5. Amino acids

6. The mixture of amino acids, derived either from the diet or from the degradation of tissue protein, that is contained within each cell.

7. Digestion of proteins, degradation of protein in our body, and synthesis of amino acids.

8. Protein synthesis, hormone production, breakdown of amino acids as an energy source.

9. It moves toward a negative nitrogen balance.

10. It moves toward a negative balance.

11. It shifts back toward a neutral nitrogen balance.

12. The turnover rate of enzymes is much more rapid than that of muscle proteins. Muscle proteins have half-lives of approximately 180-1000 days. The half-lives of enzymes may vary from approximately 10 min to 6 h depending on their metabolic importance and the cell in which they function.

13.   a. The essential amino acids contain carbon chains, or aromatic rings, that are not present as intermediates of carbohydrate or lipid metabolism. The inability to synthesize these amino acids results from the animal's inability to manufacture the correct carbon skeleton.
  b. Since all the amino acids required for the construction of a particular protein must be present at the time of its synthesis, a deficiency in one or more essential amino acids will prevent protein synthesis from proceeding.

14.   1) Protein synthesis
  2) Amino acids play an essential role in the metabolism of all nitrogenous compounds.
  3) Amino acids can be converted to carbohydrates and fats or oxidized to produce energy.

15. The reversibility of transamination reactions serves to link protein metabolism with the metabolism of carbohydrates and lipids. Transamination reactions convert certain amino acids into key metabolic intermediates that may be used to synthesize carbohydrates and lipids or may be oxidized to produce energy.

16. The loss of an amine group as ammonia from an amino acid combined with an oxidation of this product to a keto acid.

17. Uric Acid

18.   a. The liver is the organ responsible for the synthesis of urea in mammals.
  b. The kidney is the organ responsible for the excretion of urea in the urine.

PROBLEMS

PROTEIN DIGESTION

	Location	Function
19.	a. stomach	breaks down proteins
	b. intestine	breaks down proteins
	c. intestine	breaks down proteins
	d. intestine	breaks down proteins
	e. intestine	breaks down di- and tripeptides
	f. intestine	converts trypsinogen to trypsin

20.   a. alanine, phenylalanine, tyrosine --complete hydrolysis
     b. isoleucine, tyrosine, serine   --complete hydrolysis
     c. phenylalanine, arginine, leucine --complete hydrolysis
     d. threonine–glutamic acid–lysine   --no hydrolysis

21.   peptide linkage at the N-terminal end

22.   peptide linkage at the C-terminal end

AMINO ACID METABOLISM

23. $CH_3CH_2CH(CH_3)\overset{O}{\underset{\|}{C}}\text{–}\overset{O}{\underset{\|}{C}}OH$ $+$ $R\text{–}\overset{H}{\underset{NH_2}{\underset{|}{C}}}\text{–}COOH$ $\xrightarrow{\text{transaminase}}$

$$CH_3CH_2CH(CH_3)\overset{H}{\underset{\underset{NH_2}{|}}{\underset{|}{C}}}\text{–}\overset{O}{\underset{\|}{C}}\text{–}OH \;+\; R\text{–}\overset{O}{\underset{\|}{C}}\text{–}COOH$$

Isoleucine

24. 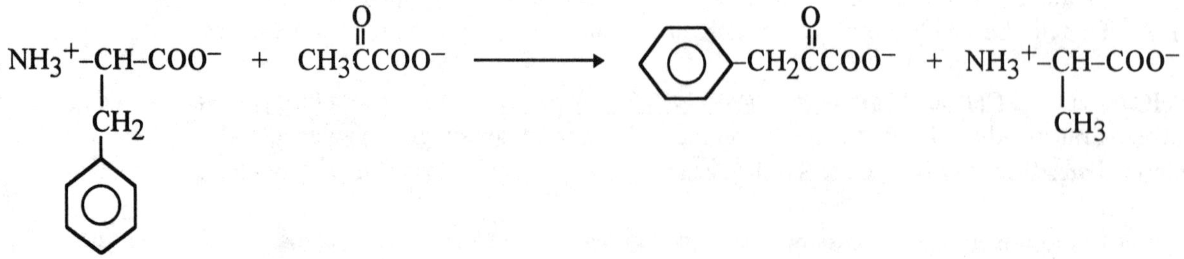 $NH_3^+\text{–}\underset{\underset{CH_2}{|}}{CH}\text{–}COO^-$ $+$ $CH_3\overset{O}{\underset{\|}{C}}COO^-$ $\longrightarrow$ $\langle O \rangle\text{–}CH_2\overset{O}{\underset{\|}{C}}COO^-$ $+$ $NH_3^+\text{–}\underset{\underset{CH_3}{|}}{CH}\text{–}COO^-$

25. The transfer of an amine group from aspartic acid to α-ketoglutarate.

26. The transfer of an amine group from alanine to α-ketoglutarate.

27. Pyruvic acid

28. α-ketoglutarate

29. a.

$$CH_3\overset{\overset{\displaystyle NH_2}{|}}{C}HCOOH \xrightarrow{\text{alanine oxidase}} CH_3\overset{\overset{\displaystyle O}{||}}{C}COOH + NH_3$$

    alanine   pyruvic acid

b. (imidazole ring)–$CH_2CHCOOH$ with NH_2 $\xrightarrow{\text{histidine decarboxylase}}$ (imidazole ring)CH_2CH_2 with NH_2 + CO_2

    histidine   histamine

c.

$$HOOCCH_2CH_2\overset{\overset{\displaystyle NH_2}{|}}{C}HCOOH \xrightarrow{\text{oxidase}} HOOCCH_2CH_2\overset{\overset{\displaystyle O}{||}}{C}COOH + NH_3$$

    glutamic acid α–ketoglutaric acid

d.

$$HOOCCH_2CH_2\overset{\overset{\displaystyle NH_2}{|}}{C}HCOOH + NH_3 \overset{\text{ATP} \quad \text{ADP}}{\underset{\text{synthetase}}{\xrightarrow{\hspace{2cm}}}} H_2N-\overset{\overset{\displaystyle O}{||}}{C}CH_2CH_2\overset{\overset{\displaystyle NH_2}{|}}{C}HCOOH + H_2O + Pi$$

    glutamic acid   glutamine

30. a.

$$H_2N-(CH_2)_4\overset{\overset{\displaystyle NH_2}{|}}{C}HCOOH \xrightarrow{\text{decarboxylase}} H_2N-(CH_2)_4CH_2NH_2 + CO_2$$

    lysine   cadaverine

b.

$$HOOCCH_2\overset{\overset{\displaystyle NH_2}{|}}{C}HCOOH \xrightarrow{\text{oxidase}} HOOCCH_2\overset{\overset{\displaystyle O}{||}}{C}COOH + NH_3$$

    aspartic acid   oxaloacetic acid

c. $HO-$(benzene ring)$-CH_2-\overset{\overset{\displaystyle }{|}}{C}H-COOH$ with NH_2 $\longrightarrow$ $HO-$(benzene ring)$-CH_2-CH_2-NH_2 + CO_2$

    Tyrosine   Tyramine

d. HO,$HO-$(benzene ring)$-CH_2-CHCOOH$ with NH_2 $\xrightarrow{\text{dopa decarboxylase}}$ HO,$HO-$(benzene ring)$-CH_2CH_2$ with NH_2 + CO_2

    3,4-dihydroxyphenylalanine   dopamine

31. a. leucine   b. α-ketoglutaric acid   c. α-ketoglutaric acid

32. a. 5-hydroxytryptophan   b. glutamic acid   c. glutamine

ADDITIONAL PROBLEMS

33. 100g

34. Through digestion, the plant proteins are degraded to the individual amino acids. The animal then uses these amino acids for the biosynthesis of the proteins it requires.

35. a. Most plant proteins are deficient in one or more essential amino acids. Therefore, vegetarians should consume a wide variety of vegetables in order to ensure their intake of the proper quantities of essential amino acids.
    b. The best source of essential amino acids is animal proteins.

36. 15 moles of ATP can be produced from the complete oxidation of 1 mole of pyruvic acid.

37. a. Ammonia (NH_3) and hydrogen peroxide (H_2O_2) are the toxic compounds formed in oxidative deamination reactions.
    b. Ammonia is converted to urea in the liver and excreted in the urine. Hydrogen peroxide is detoxified by the enzyme catalase which converts H_2O_2 into O_2 and H_2O.

38. $(CH_3)_2CH\text{-}CH_2\text{-}\overset{\overset{\displaystyle O}{\|}}{C}COO^-$

39. a. Benadryl is an antihistamine that exerts its effect by binding to H_1 receptors and thus inhibits the binding of histamine, a molecule which normally serves to initiate a hypersensitivity response.
    b. H_1 receptors are histamine receptors found in the walls of capillaries and in the smooth muscles of the respiratory tract. When bound to histamine, they affect vascular dilation and muscular constriction associated with hypersensitivity. H_2 receptors are found in the wall of the stomach and function to increase HCl secretions when activated.

REVIEW QUESTIONS

1. a. Lymph: Lymph is the extracellular fluid that is circulating through the lymphatic system.
    b. Formed elements: Formed elements are the blood cells.
    c. Hematocrit Value: Hematocrit value is the volume (in percent) of red blood cells in a sample that has been centrifuged under standard conditions.
    d. Leukemia: Leukemia is a cancerous condition where the leukocytes in the blood divide uncontrollably.
    e. Vaccine: A non-pathogen form of an antigen injected into the body to help build up the immune response.
    f. Osmosis: Osmosis is the diffusion of water from a dilute solution (low solute concentration) through a semipermeable membrane into a more concentrated solution (high solute concentration).
    g. Edema: Edema is the accumulation of fluids in a tissue causing swelling.
    h. Hypertension: Hypertension is high blood pressure.
    i. Hemophilia: Hemophilia is a sex-linked hereditary disease in which one of the protein factors involved in the formation of thrombin is lacking or is inactive.
    j. Anticoagulant: Anticoagulant is a substance that inhibits the clotting of blood.
    k. Thrombosis: Thrombosis is the formation of a clot within a blood vessel.
    l. Embolism: Embolism is a blood clot that has broken away from its site of origin and is carried away by the blood to be lodged in a small blood vessel elsewhere.
    m. Methemoglobinemia is the presence of a greater than normal concentration of methemoglobin in the blood.
    n. Jaundice: Jaundice is a yellow pigmentation that develops in the skin from the inappropriate deposition of bile pigments (bilirubin).

2. a. Aplastic anemia results form the decreased production of erythrocytes. Hemolytic anemia results from the increased destruction of erythrocytes.
    b. Anemia is a condition that is characterized by an abnormally low percentage of erythrocytes in the plasma. Conversely, polycythemia is the condition arising from an abnormally high percentage of red blood cells in the plasma.
    c. The lymphocytes (B- and T-cells) are a class of leukocytes that comprise the humoral and cell-mediated systems of immunity. The phagocytes are a special class of leukocytes whose function is the engulfing and digestion of foreign matter.
    d. Antibodies are proteins produced by sensitized B-cells which specifically bind to the antigen that stimulated their production. Antigens are molecules that stimulate antibody production in the body.
    e. Osmotic pressure is the pressure required to prevent the occurrence of osmosis. Blood pressure is the pressure of the blood that results from the pumping action of the heart.
    f. Systolic pressure is the maximum pressure achieved during contraction of the heart ventricles. Diastolic pressure is the lowest pressure that remains in the arteries before the next ventricular contraction.
    g. Vasodilation is an increase in the diameter of the blood vessels, whereas vasoconstriction is a decrease in the diameter of the blood vessels.
    h. Plasma is the fluid portion of the blood. Serum is the portion of the blood plasma remaining after the protein fibrinogen has been removed.
    i. Stroke is the condition that results from the death of tissue in the brain. Coronary thrombosis is the condition that results from the death of heart muscle tissue.
    j. Hypoventilation is a lower than normal rate of breathing, whereas hyperventilation is a higher than normal rate of breathing.

3. The three circulating fluids in the animal organism are blood, interstitial fluid, and lymph.

4.   1) To help maintain osmotic relationships between the tissues.
      2) To transport oxygen and nutritive materials to the cells and waste products to the excretory organs.
      3) To regulate the body temperature.
      4) To control the pH of the body.
      5) To protect the organism against infection.

5. Sweat. The evaporation of a liquid to a gas is an endothermic reaction. Therefore, during sweating, heat is "removed" from the body and the body cools.

6. An immune response is initiated when free antigen or antigen-bearing cells stimulate the phagocytes and lymphocytes that are routinely patrolling the body in search of such foreign molecules. The sensitization of T-cells elicits a maturation of their killer functions in that certain T-cells bind specifically to the antigen-bearing cells and release toxic factors that are lethal to the invaders (cellular immunity). Other sensitized T-cells stimulate B-cells to produce the highly specific antibodies that bind and agglutinate antigen-bearing cells (humoral immunity). The antigen-antibody complexes cue the destruction of foreign cells by phagocytes that engulf and degrade the invaders.

7.   a. At the arterial end of the capillary, the blood pressure exceeds the osmotic pressure. There is a flow of material (nutrients, oxygen, etc.) from the capillaries into the interstitial fluid.
      b. At the venous end of the capillary, the osmotic pressure is greater than the blood pressure. There is a flow of material (metabolic waste products) from the interstitial fluid into the capillary.

8. Osmotic pressure is directly related to the concentration of proteins (particularly albumins) in the plasma.

9. Blood pressure measurements are reported as a ratio of systolic pressure to diastolic pressure in units of mmHg (e.g., 120/80).

10.   1) Administer diuretics and/or reduce the sodium ion intake.
      2) Negate the stimulating effects of epinephrine binding sites.
      3) Administer vasodilators in order to promote the relaxation of the smooth muscles in the arterial walls.

11. hemoglobin, cytochromes, catalase

12. Biliverdin and bilirubin

13.   1) Infectious hepatitis where the liver is malfunctioning and cannot remove sufficient bilirubin from the blood.
      2) The obstruction of bile ducts by gallstones.
      3) An acceleration of erythrocyte destruction in the spleen.

14.   a. Arterial blood contains dissolved nutrients, oxygen, hormones, and vitamins. Venous blood contains metabolic waste products and has a lower oxygen content.
      b. Arterial blood, crimson; venous blood, dark red.

15. The normal pH range of the blood is 7.35-7.45.

16. Interstitial fluid: The fluid that fills the space around the cells.

17. Shock is a condition resulting from a loss of blood and the consequent decrease in O_2 and nutrient-transporting capabilities.

18. 1) Transportation of interstial fluid materials to the circulatory system.
    2) Transport of fats from intestine to liver.
    3) Production of some forms of white blood cells.

19. No. It is lacking in Fe^{+2}, Cu^{+2}, and vitamins C and D. Yes.

20. Mother's milk appears to contain gamma globulins which can improve the infant's immunological defenses.

PROBLEMS

BLOOD

21. Carbohydrates, lipids, amino acids, hormones (nonprotein), vitamins, inorganic ions.

22. Na^+, K^+, Ca^{2+}, Mg^{2+}, HCO_3^-, Cl^-, HPO_4^{2-}, SO_4^{2-}

23. a. Albumins maintain the osmotic balance and transport fatty acids.
    b. Globulins (alpha and beta) form complexes with lipids and transport them to all parts of the body.
    c. Fibrinogen functions in blood clotting.
    —They are all synthesized in the liver.

24. They function to combat infectious microorganisms, cancer cells, and chemical toxins present in the body. They are synthesized by B-lymphocytes.

25. Erythrocytes affect transportation of oxygen to the cells. Leukocytes destroy invading bacteria and other foreign substances. Thrombocytes liberate substances that are involved in blood clotting.

26. a. Red blood cells are similar to other cells in that they are bound by a phospholipid bilayer and are able to produce energy via substrate level phosphorylation in the Embden-Meyerhof pathway. Red blood cells differ in that they do not contain a nucleus or mitochondria. They cannot reproduce or respire aerobically, and are unable to synthesize carbohydrates, proteins, or lipids.
    b. Red blood cells are derived from stem cells in the bone marrow.
    c. Red blood cells are eliminated by special tissues in the liver and the spleen.

27. a. Prothrombin is a globulin plasma protein produced by the liver. It is a zymogen that when activated by autoprothrombin C, catalyzes the conversion of fibrinogen into fibrin.
    b. Thrombin is the actual clotting enzyme that catalyzes the activation of fibrinogen.
    c. Fibrinogen is the soluble plasma protein that is converted by thrombin into the insoluble protein fibrin.
    d. Thromboplastin is a group of compounds released by blood platelets and damaged tissue.
    e. Calcium ions are necessary for the catalytic activity associated with both thromboplastin and autoprothrombin C.
    f. Fibrin is the insoluble protein endproduct of the blood-clotting cascade. Fibrin monomers polymerize, resulting in the formation of needle-like threads that enmesh to seal off the area where a blood vessel has been damaged.

28. a. Vitamin K is a coenzyme involved in the activation of the zymogen prothrombin.
   b.Heparin blocks the catalytic activity of both thromboplastin and thrombin.
   c. Dicumarol, a metabolic antagonist of vitamin K, either represses prothrombin formation or inhibits the enzyme for which vitamin K is a coenzyme.
   d. These anions have a strong affinity for calcium ions. They tie up the calcium ions, and therefore free calcium ions are not present to help effect the conversion of prothrombin to thrombin.

   ```
          COOH
          |
   e. H2N-C-H
          |
          CH2
          |
        H-C-COOH
          |
          COOH
   ```

HEMOGLOBIN

29. Hemoglobin is a conjugated protein with a molecular weight of about 68,000 daltons. Upon hydrolysis it yields a simple protein, globin, and four heme groups. The heme groups account for about 4% of the total molecular weight.

30. a. Heme is the prosthetic group of the conjugated protein hemoglobin.
   b. Myoglobin is a protein consisting of 153 amino acid units arranged in a single polypeptide chain; hemoglobin contains four polypeptide chains - two identical α-chains and two identical ß-chains.
   c-e. Oxyhemoglobin is a hemoglobin bound to oxygen. CO-hemoglobin is a hemoglobin bound to carbon monoxide. Methemoglobin contains iron in the +3 oxidation state.
   f. Sickle cell hemoglobin has a Val in amino acid position #6 of the beta chains where normal hemoglobin has a Glu.

31. a. +2 b. +2 c. +3 d. +2

32. a. The ferrous ions have a much greater affinity for CO (carbon monoxide) than for O_2. Therefore, CO molecules occupy the sites of oxygen binding, and much less oxygen is transported to the cells by the blood. The brain cells, in particular, require a continuous supply of oxygen.
   b. By greatly increasing the oxygen concentration in the blood either by artificial respiration or by breathing pure oxygen from an oxygen tank.

BLOOD BUFFERS

33. The bicarbonate pair, H_2CO_3/HCO_3^-, and the phosphate pair, $H_2PO_4^-/HPO_4^{2-}$. The proper buffer ratio is maintained by the decomposition of any excess carbonic acid to water and carbon dioxide. The carbon dioxide is removed from the equilibrium condition by its elimination at the lungs.

34. When acids enter the blood they are neutralized by bicarbonate ions to produce carbonic acid.

$$H^+ + HCO_3^- \rightleftharpoons H_2CO_3$$

When a base enters the blood, it reacts with carbonic acid to produce bicarbonate ions.

$$OH^- + H_2CO_3 \longrightarrow HOH + HCO_3^-$$

URINE

35. In the kidneys, the glomerulus filters most components (except proteins and formed elements) into the kidney tubules. As this fluid passes through the tubules there is a selective re-uptake into the blood of important constituents that the body wishes to save. Waste products not desirable to the body are not reabsorbed and are excreted as urine.

36. Liquid uptake, amount of perspiration, presence of fever, presence of diarrhea.

SWEAT AND TEARS

37. Insensible perspiration is water lost through the skin or respiratory tract while sensible perspiration is water lost via sweat glands.

38. Inorganic: Na^+, Cl^-, Ca^{+2}
    Organic: Urea, lipids, creatinine

39. An inner layer of mucus, then a layer of lacrimal secretions, and then, on the outside, an oily film.

40. An anti-bacterial action; lysozyme cleaves cell walls of bacteria.

ADDITIONAL PROBLEMS

41. Urea, uric acid, excess salts

42. When acidosis occurs, the pH of the organism decreases. Since hemoglobin is a protein, it is denatured by changes in pH. This denaturation interferes with its oxygen-carrying capacity, among other things.

43. Assuming a weight of 150 pounds, $(0.08)(150) = 12$ lb, 1 lb = 454 g

    $$\text{volume of blood} = \frac{(454)(12)}{1.06} = 5140 \text{ mL} = 5.1 \text{ L}$$

44. Diffusion

45. a. Respiratory acidosis is brought about by hypoventilation. When the rate of breathing is too slow, carbon dioxide is not expelled from the lungs at a fast enough rate. The equilibrium is shifted to the left, increasing the concentration of hydrogen ions in the blood. The pH of the blood decreases.
    b. Respiratory alkalosis results from hyperventilation. When the rate of breathing is too rapid, there is an increased loss of carbon dioxide from the lungs. The equilibrium is shifted to the right, decreasing the concentration of hydrogen ions in the blood. The pH of the blood increases.

46. More fluid

47. Lower

48. The bicarbonate buffer system in your blood acts by the following reaction:
$$CO_2 + H_2O \rightleftharpoons H_2CO_3 \rightleftharpoons H^+ + HCO_3^-$$
Loss of HCO_3^- causes this equilibrium to shift to the right, generating more H^+ ions and thus acidosis.